THE OXFORD HAN

MW00788903

GENOCIDE
STUDIES

Donald Bloxham is Professor of Modern History at Edinburgh University.

A. Dirk Moses is the Chair in Global and Colonial History at the European University Institute, Florence.

THE OXFORD HANDBOOK OF

GENOCIDE STUDIES

Edited by

DONALD BLOXHAM

AND

A. DIRK MOSES

OXFORD
UNIVERSITY PRESS

OXFORD
UNIVERSITY PRESS

Great Clarendon Street, Oxford, OX2 6DP,
United Kingdom

Oxford University Press is a department of the University of Oxford.
It furthers the University's objective of excellence in research, scholarship,
and education by publishing worldwide. Oxford is a registered trade mark of
Oxford University Press in the UK and in certain other countries

First Edition published in 2010
First published in paperback 2013

Published in the United States of America by Oxford University Press
198 Madison Avenue, New York, NY 10016, United States of America

British Library Cataloguing in Publication Data
Data available

Library of Congress Control Number: 2010920519

ISBN 978-0-19-967791-7

Contents

PART V: THE CONTEMPORARY WORLD: RULES AND RESPONSES

LIST OF CONTRIBUTORS

Alex J. Bellamy is Professor of International Relations and Executive Director of the Asia-Pacific Centre for the Responsibility to Protect at the University of Queensland, Australia. His most recent book is *Responsibility to Protect: The Global Effort to End Mass Atrocities* (2009).

Donald Bloxham is Professor of Modern History at the University of Edinburgh. He is author of *The Great Game of Genocide: Imperialism, Nationalism, and the Destruction of the Ottoman Armenians* (2005), winner of the Raphael Lemkin Award for 2007; *The Final Solution: A Genocide* (2009); and *Genocide on Trial: War Crimes Trials and the Formation of Holocaust History and Memory* (2001). He is editor, with Mark Levene, of the Oxford University Press monograph series *Zones of Violence*.

Christopher R. Browning is the Frank Porter Graham Professor of History at the University of North Carolina at Chapel Hill. His publications include *Ordinary Men: Reserve Police Battalion 101 and the Final Solution in Poland* (1992) and *The Origins of the Final Solution: The Evolution of Nazi Jewish Policy, September 1939– March 1942* (2004).

Uradyn E. Bulag is reader in social anthropology at the University of Cambridge. Author of *Nationalism and Hybridity in Mongolia* (Clarendon Press, 1998), and *The Mongols at China's Edge: History and the Politics of National Unity* (Rowman and Littlefield, 2002), his interests broadly span East Asia and Inner Asia, especially China and Mongolia.

Cathie Carmichael is a Senior Lecturer in European History at the University of East Anglia. She is author of *Ethnic Cleansing in the Balkans* (2002) and *Genocide before the Holocaust* (2009), co-editor of *Language and Nationalism in Europe* (2000) with the late Stephen Barbour, and co-author of *Slovenia and the Slovenes* (2000) with James Gow.

Robert Cribb is Professor of Indonesian History at the Australian National University. His publications include *The Indonesian Killings of 1965–1966: Studies from Java and Bali* (1990), *Gangsters and Revolutionaries: The Jakarta People's Militia and the Indonesian Revolution 1945–1949* (1991), and (with Li Narangoa) *Imperial Japan and National Identities in Asia, 1895–1945* (2003).

Daniel Feierstein directs the Genocide Chair at the University of Buenos Aires. He is Researcher at the Consejo Nacional de Investigaciones Cientificas y Tecnicas and Director of the Center of Genocide Studies at the Universidad Nacional de Tres de Febrero. He is author of *Genocidio como práctica social* (2007). His publications also include *State Violence and Genocide in Latin America: The Cold War Years* (co-authored with Marcia Esparza and Henry Huttenbach, 2009).

James E. Fraser is Senior Lecturer in Early Scottish History and Culture at the University of Edinburgh. His publications include *The Battle of Dunnichen 685* (2002) and *From Caledonia to Pictland: Scotland to 795* (2009).

Gerd Hankel is Senior Research Fellow and Lecturer in International Public and International Criminal Law at the Hamburg Institute for Social Research. His publications include contributions to Antonio Cassese (ed.), *The Oxford Companion to International Criminal Justice* (2009), and 'Rwanda. A Small Nation in Africa', in Madelon de Keizer and Ismee Tames (eds), *Small Nations: Crisis and Confrontation in the Twentieth Century* (2008).

Elisa von Joeden-Forgey teaches History at the University of Pennsylvania. She is the author of articles and book chapters on race and colonialism in German history and is currently writing a book on gender and genocide, entitled *Killing God: The Family Drama of Genocide.*

Hilmar Kaiser received his PhD from the European University Institute, Florence, Italy. He specializes in Ottoman social and economic history with a special emphasis on the Armenian Genocide. Currently he works and lives in Ankara, Turkey.

Mark Levene is Reader in Comparative History at Southampton University. He is involved in a four-volume project on *Genocide in the Age of the Nation-State*, vols. 1 and 2 of which were published in 2005. Much of his current work is about the relationship between rapid anthropogenic climate change and violence. See Crisis Forum, http://www.crisis-forum.org.uk, and the Rescue!History network, http://rescue-history-from-climate-change.org/indexClassic.php, of which he is founder.

Benjamin Lieberman is Professor of History at Fitchburg State College. He is the author of *Terrible Fate: Ethnic Cleansing and the Making of Modern Europe* (2006), and 'Ethnic Cleansing in the Greek-Turkish Conflicts from the Balkan Wars through the Treaty of Lausanne: Identifying and Defining Ethnic Cleansing', in Steven Bela Vardy and T. Hunt Tooley (eds), *Ethnic Cleansing in Twentieth-Century Europe* (2003).

Omar McDoom is a lecturer in comparative politics at the London School of Economics and Political Science. He has previously held research fellowships at Harvard's Kennedy School and Oxford University. He is currently writing a book on the Rwandan genocide entitled *Why They Killed: Security, Authority, and Opportunity in Rwanda's Genocide.*

A. Dirk Moses is Associate Professor in History at the University of Sydney. He is the author of *German Intellectuals and the Nazi Past* (2007), and editor of *Genocide and Settler Society: Frontier Violence and Stolen Indigenous Children in Australian History* (2004), *Colonialism and Genocide* (2007, with Dan Stone), and *Empire, Colony, Genocide: Conquest, Occupation and Subaltern Resistance in World History* (2008). He an associate editor of the *Journal of Genocide Research.*

Devin O. Pendas is Associate Professor of History at Boston College. He is the author of *The Frankfurt Auschwitz Trial, 1963–1965: Genocide, History, and the Limits of the Law* (2006), as well as numerous articles and chapters concerning the history of Holocaust trials, transitional justice, and the history of international law.

Kevin Lewis O'Neill is an assistant professor in the Department and Centre for the Study of Religion at the University of Toronto. He is the author of *City of God: Christian Citizenship in Postwar Guatemala City* (2009).

Nicholas A. Robins is a Lecturer in the Department of History at North Carolina State University. His publications include *Priest-Indian Conflict in Upper Peru: The Generation of Rebellion* (2007), *Native Insurgencies and the Genocidal Impulse in the Americas* (2005), *Genocide and Millennialism in Upper Peru: The Great Rebellion of 1780–1782* (2002), and *The Culture of Conflict in Modern Cuba* (2003).

Geoffrey Robinson is Professor of History at UCLA, where he teaches and writes about Southeast Asia, political violence, and human rights. His works include: *The Dark Side of Paradise: Political Violence in Bali* (Cornell University Press, 1995); and *"If You Leave Us Here, We Will Die": How Genocide Was Stopped in East Timor* (Princeton University Press, 2010).

Paul A. Roth is Professor of Philosophy at the University of California-Santa Cruz. His publications include *Meaning and Method in the Social Sciences* (1987) as well as numerous articles on topics ranging from naturalism in epistemology to explanation in history. He is a member of the editorial board of the *Journal of the Philosophy of History.*

Len Scales teaches medieval European history at Durham University. He has a particular interest in the pre-modern history of ethnicity and nationhood. His publications include (ed., with Oliver Zimmer) *Power and the Nation in European History* (2005).

William A. Schabas is Professor of Human Rights Law at the National University of Ireland, Galway, where he directs the Irish Centre for Human Rights. He is the author of *Genocide in International Law, The Crime of Crimes* (2nd edn, 2009) and *Introduction to the International Criminal Court* (3rd edn, 2007).

Dominik J. Schaller is a lecturer and researcher at the Ruprecht-Karls-Universität Heidelberg. He is co-editor of *The Armenian Genocide and the Shoah* (ed., 2002), *Late Ottoman Genocides: The Dissolution of the Ottoman Empire and Young Turkish Population and Extermination Policies* (2009), and *The Origins of Genocide: Raphael Lemkin as a Historian of Mass Violence* (2009).

Martin Shaw is Research Professor of International Relations at the University of Sussex. As a sociologist who writes on global politics, war, and genocide, his recent books include *War and Genocide* (2003) and *What is Genocide?* (2007). He writes a regular column on genocide and war for http://www.opendemocracy.net

Martin Shuster is a PhD candidate at the Humanities Center of the Johns Hopkins University. He is interested in Kant, post-Kantian philosophy, and Jewish thought and philosophy.

Greg D. Smithers is a lecturer in the Department of History at the University of Aberdeen. He is the author of *Science, Sexuality, and Race in the United States and Australia, 1780s–1890s* (2008) and, with Clarence E. Walker, *The Preacher and the Politician: Jeremiah Wright, Barack Obama, and Race in American History* (2009).

Dan Stone is Professor of Modern History at Royal Holloway, University of London. His books include *Breeding Superman: Nietzsche, Race and Eugenics in Edwardian and Interwar Britain* (2002), *Constructing the Holocaust: A Study in Historiography* (2003), *Responses to Nazism in Britain, 1933–1939* (2003) and, as editor, *The Historiography of the Holocaust* (2004) and *The Historiography of Genocide* (2008).

Scott Straus is Associate Professor of Political Science and International Studies at the University of Wisconsin at Madison. He is author of *The Order of Genocide: Race, Power, and War in Rwanda* (2006), winner of the 2006 Award for Excellence in Political Science and Government from the Professional and Scholarly Publishing Division of the Association of American Publishers, and of *Rwanda, Intimate Enemy* (2006).

Alex de Waal is programme director at the Social Science Research Council (New York), Senior Fellow at the Harvard Humanitarian Initiative, and co-director of Justice Africa. He has written and edited several books related to war, famine, and genocide, including *Famine Crimes: Politics and the Disaster Relief Industry in Africa* (1997), *Islamism and Its Enemies in the Horn of Africa* (2004), and *War in Darfur and the Search for Peace* (2007).

Hans van Wees is Professor of Ancient History at University College London. He is the author of *Status Warriors: War, Violence and Society in Homer and History* (1992), and *Greek Warfare: Myths and Realities* (2004), as well as numerous articles on aspects of war and peace in the ancient world. He has edited, among other things, a volume on *War and Violence on Ancient Greece* (2000) and the *Cambridge History of Greek and Roman Warfare* (2007).

Anton Weiss-Wendt is Head of the Research Department at the Center for the Study of the Holocaust and Religious Minorities in Oslo, Norway. His publications include *Murder without Hatred: Estonians and the Holocaust* (2009); 'Problems in Comparative Genocide Scholarship', in Dan Stone (ed.), *The Historiography of Genocide* (2008); and 'Extermination of the Gypsies in Estonia during World War II', *Holocaust and Genocide Studies* 17:1 (2003).

Nicolas Werth is a research director at the Centre National de la Recherche Scientifique in France. He lived in Moscow from 1975 until 1993, and was one of the first Western historians to access Soviet Archives. He is the co-author of *The Black Book of Communism* (1999).

EDITORS' INTRODUCTION

CHANGING THEMES IN THE STUDY OF GENOCIDE

DONALD BLOXHAM

A. DIRK MOSES

THE STATE OF GENOCIDE STUDIES

AN *Oxford Handbook of Genocide Studies* is easily justified. 'Genocide' is unfortunately ubiquitous, all too often literally in the attempted destruction of human groups, but also rhetorically in the form of a word that is at once universally known and widely invoked—perhaps because it is frequently misunderstood. From its introduction to the international public sphere with the United Nations General Assembly resolution on genocide in 1946, the term was seized upon by all sides to name the criminality of their persecution. Indians and Pakistanis made representations to the UN, accusing the other of genocide during the partition while, soon thereafter, Baltic states likewise accused the Soviet Union, and African Americans the United States for lynchings and discrimination. Later, during the Vietnam War, leftist intellectuals assembled an unofficial court to indict the United States for a genocidal campaign. In the late 1960s and early 1970s, secessionist peoples,

such as the Ibo of Nigeria and the East Bengalis of East Pakistan, accused the state
of genocide in their ruthless suppressions. Now the Sudanese government stands
accused of committing genocide against its citizens in the Darfur region. This new
vocabulary of atrocity and destruction, coined by Raphael Lemkin only in 1943, is
unlikely to disappear. Now a discipline exists to study it scientifically.

The rise of academic genocide studies is illustrated by the emergence of new
scholarly journals since the 1990s: the *Journal of Genocide Research* and *Genocide
Studies and Prevention*, and the German *Zeitschrift für Genozidforschung*, which
complement the more Holocaust-centred journal *Holocaust and Genocide Studies*.
Encyclopaedias of genocide (printed and electronic), Internet discussion groups,
and a proliferation of comparative works and collections of case studies now make
scholarship increasingly accessible.[1] Universities everywhere are expanding existing
Holocaust programmes or specialist research centres to include genocide, although
usually maintaining the distinction between the Holocaust and genocide. At the
level of public policy, ad hoc international and 'hybrid' criminal tribunals sit in
judgement of genocide and crimes against humanity in Africa, Europe, and Asia;
an International Criminal Court (ICC) seeks to do the same on a more permanent
and universal basis; the UN now has special advisors on the crime; and the USA has
established a task force with a view to creating a dedicated machinery to help
forestall imminent genocides or intercede in ongoing cases. These responses to
genocide have in turn fostered an extensive literature in case law, jurisprudence,
and international relations. The field has come a long way since Raphael Lemkin's
struggles to gain acceptance for his neologism 'geno-cide' in the mid-1940s and, a
decade later, to publish his history of genocide.[2]

The comparative scholarship of genocide began with Raphael Lemkin himself
and was continued by a small group of dedicated scholars through the later Cold
War period.[3] It increased exponentially in the 1990s when the Rwandan slaughter
hammered home to Western scholars that genocide was not a thing of the past,
while the implosion of Yugoslavia showed that the West could still host the crime.
A raft of books that dealt with these and other cases in an episodic manner
appeared; i.e., each chapter was devoted to a particular instance of genocide,
unrelated to each other except as examples of a generic definition or to highlight
the author's thesis about the role of racism, democratization, modernization, and
so forth.[4]

[1] E.g. *Online Enyclopedia of Mass Violence*: http://www.massviolence.org
[2] Lemkin's papers in the New York Public Library contain numerous letters from publishing houses
declining his manuscript, which was never completed or published.
[3] Helen Fein, *Accounting For Genocide: National Responses and Jewish Victimization during the
Holocaust* (New York: Free Press, 1979); Leo Kuper, *Genocide: Its Political Use in the Twentieth Century*
(New Haven: Yale University Press, 1982).
[4] George J. Andreopolous (ed.), *Genocide: Conceptual and Historical Dimensions* (Philadelphia:
University of Pennsylvania Press, 1994); Norman Naimark, *Fires of Hatred: Ethnic Cleansing in*

Another strand of scholarship pointed in a different direction. If one term captured the political and therefore historical imagination after the end of the bipolar Cold War, it was 'globalization'. The idea of an increasingly interconnected world centred on a Western political-economic core sent some students of genocide in search of historical precursors and antecedents in the expansion of the West before the twentieth century. Rather than simply compare discrete events, they proposed a more contextual approach that places those events in relation to one another. Above all, they wanted to tie discrete events and national histories to transnational and international processes.[5] A contemporary interest in the connections between genocide in the European colonies and the Holocaust at Europe's core may be understood within this framework.[6]

Given these heady developments, it is easy to forget that genocide studies began as a marginal field, part offspring of, part uneasy junior partner to, the longer standing discipline Holocaust studies, itself a child of the 1970s. The relationship between study of the Holocaust and study of genocide warrants reflection, because it has been both negative and positive, characterized variously by synergies, processes of self-definition by mutual exclusion, and occasional resentment. On one

Twentieth-Century Europe (Cambridge, MA: Harvard University Press, 2001); Robert Gellately and Ben Kiernan (eds), *The Specter of Genocide: Mass Murder in Historical Perspective* (New York: Cambridge University Press, 2003); Eric D. Weitz, *A Century of Genocide: Utopias of Race and Nation* (Princeton, NJ: Princeton University Press, 2003); Samuel Totten, William S. Parsons, and Israel W. Charny (eds), *A Century of Genocide: Critical Essays and Eyewitness Accounts*, 2nd edn (New York: Routledge, 2004). This tendency of the literature is analyzed in various works over the past two decades by Mark Levene, culminating in his *Genocide in the Age of the Nation-State*, 2 vols. (London: Tauris, 2005). It is critiqued from a theoretical perspective in A. Dirk Moses, 'Toward a Theory of Critical Genocide Studies', *Online Encyclopedia of Mass Violence*, 18 April 2008: http://www. massviolence.org/Toward-a-Theory-of-Critical-Genocide-Studies. It is critiqued via a case study in Donald Bloxham, 'Three Imperialisms and a Turkish Nationalism: International Stresses, Imperial Disintegration and the Armenian Genocide', *Patterns of Prejudice* 36:4 (2002), 37–58 and Bloxham's subsequent *The Great Game of Genocide: Imperialism, Nationalism and the Destruction of the Ottoman Armenians* (Oxford: Oxford University Press, 2005).

[5] Mark Levene, 'Why Is the Twentieth Century the Century of Genocide?', *Journal of World History* 11:2 (2000), 305–36; A. Dirk Moses, 'Conceptual Blockages and Definitional Dilemmas in the "Racial Century": Genocide of Indigenous Peoples and the Holocaust', *Patterns of Prejudice* 36:4 (2002), 7–36; Bloxham, 'Three Imperialisms'; Bloxham, *The Great Game*.

[6] Early initiatives in this direction, though rarely cited in the comparative genocide literature, were Woodruff D. Smith, *The German Colonial Empire* (Chapel Hill, NC: University of North Carolina Press, 1978); idem, *The Ideological Origins of Nazi Imperialism* (New York: Oxford University Press, 1989). For the first post Cold War study, Sven Lindqvist, *'Exterminate All the Brutes'* (London: Granta, 1992). For more up-to-date work, see A. Dirk Moses and Dan Stone (eds), *Colonialism and Genocide* (London: Routledge, 2007); A. Dirk Moses (ed), *Empire, Colony, Genocide: Conquest, Occupation and Subaltern Resistance in World History* (New York: Berghahn Books, 2008); Jürgen Zimmerer and Joachim Zeller (eds), *Genocide In German South-West Africa: The Colonial War (1904–1908) in Namibia and Its Aftermath* (London: Merlin Press, 2008). For a different perspective, see Robert Gerwarth and Stephan Malinowski, 'Der Holocaust als kolonialer Genozid? Europäische Kolonialgewalt und nationalsozialistischer Vernichtungskrieg', *Geschichte and Gesellschaft* 33 (2007), 439–66.

side of the ledger, the notion of the Holocaust's 'uniqueness', based usually on the totality of the Nazis' murderous intent towards Jews, has worked to distinguish it from the rest of the field—with a number of distorting effects.[7] If the Holocaust is taken as an 'ideal type' genocide, scholars and advocates of particular cases often seek to fit theirs within a 'Holocaust paradigm' at the expense of careful context-ualization.[8] There are political consequences of this implicit hierarchy. The histo-rian Peter Novick was one of many commentators to note this function of Holocaust memory in the reluctance of Western policymakers to intervene in the former Yugoslavia in the 1990s because its civil war did not resemble the Holo-caust.[9] Then there is the tendency in university syllabi, textbooks, and the mantras of public commemoration of genocide to focus upon a few instances of genocide that, for a variety of reasons, have qualified for the canon of general acceptance: alongside the Holocaust, Armenia, Cambodia, Rwanda, and the former Yugoslavia, and now Darfur tend to be included, but virtually no other cases.

A related consequence of the influence of the Holocaust model has been to overemphasize the role of narrow political ideology in genocide. This tendency is manifested by placing the Holocaust (along, perhaps, with one or two of the other aforementioned select genocides) in a special class of 'ideological genocides', neatly distinguished from more supposedly utilitarian genocides, such as those com-mitted in the course of European imperial expansion, civil wars, and campaigns of resource appropriation.[10] Such a taxonomy ignores both the concessions that the Nazis did make to practicality in their murder campaigns and, more impor-tantly, the obviously ideological considerations that ultimately permitted, say, Europeans to murder, say, native Americans as if they were simply practical obstacles to be removed. This sort of specious dichotomy of motivation leads to the implicit but nevertheless tangible sense that Holocaust and genocide studies scholars exhibit the same Eurocentric insensitivities that have long characterized Western attitudes towards the indigenous peoples crushed beneath the wheels of occidental 'progress'.[11]

---

[7] Some scholars, such as Yehuda Bauer and Raimond Gaita, have at times sought to distinguish Holocaust from genocide, the former connoting the intention of total destruction, the latter something less absolute. See Bauer, 'Comparison of Genocides', in Levon Chorbajian and George Shirinian (eds), *Studies in Comparative Genocide* (Basingstoke: Palgrave MacMillan, 1999), 31–43; Gaita, 'Refocusing Genocide: A Philosophical Responsibility', in John K. Roth (ed.), *Genocide and Human Rights: A Philosophical Guide* (London: Palgrave MacMillan, 2005), 153–66.

[8] David Moshman, 'Conceptual Constraints on Thinking about Genocide', *Journal of Genocide Research* 3 (2001), 432.

[9] Peter Novick, *The Holocaust in American Life* (Boston: Houghton Mifflin, 1999), 245–55.

[10] E.g. Saul Friedländer, 'The Historical Significance of the Holocaust', in Yehuda Bauer and Nathan Rotenstreich (eds), *The Holocaust as Historical Experience* (London and New York: Holmes and Meier, 1981), 4.

[11] For a critique of this implicit theodicy, see Moses, 'Conceptual Blockages and Definitional Dilemmas in the "Racial Century" '; Donald Bloxham, 'Britain's Holocaust Memorial Days: Reshaping the Past in the Service of the Present', *Immigrants and Minorities* 21 (2003), 41–62.

On the equally important other side of the ledger, initial interest in the Holocaust has often provided a springboard from which many students of genocide, who were often Jewish, leapt to examine other cases in the 1980s, especially the Armenian one.[12] Moreover, the more advanced Holocaust historiography could provide ready-made analytical questions for application in the different circumstances of other genocidal situations.[13]

An obvious function that a volume such as this can perform is to provide one of the periodic updates that any field of enquiry needs. We seek to expand upon, summarize, and help to analytically hone the mass of scholarship now being conducted in the field across a variety of disciplines, and at the frontier interface between the academic and the activist spheres—a ground that a number of our authors occupy to the benefit of both sides. The diverse abundance of research and reflection on genocide is a cause for satisfaction, but there is also the need to ask what it all amounts to, and where it might be heading. If the present volume does not presume to prescribe one future direction, it does seek to promote what its editors see as some of the most fruitful avenues of analytic enquiry. Our interpretation of what qualifies as fruitful is, inevitably, conditioned by our own disciplinary presumptions, and this point brings us to a significant justification for the volume.

HISTORICIZATION AND CAUSATION

For us as editors it is important that this handbook is published within Oxford University Press's history list. The 'historicization' of genocide is one of the central goals of the volume. We argue for the importance of a historically based, interdisciplinary method that embeds critical theories more firmly in empirical data. In this way, we believe that the concept of genocide will become more useful to both historians and social theorists, and more relevant to scholars in other fields who do not currently regard the genocide concept as valuable for their particular area.

Our comments are categorically not a criticism of the existing collections of essays on genocide. Indeed, a major section of this volume (part II) is devoted to elucidating the ways in which the approaches of non-historians have illuminated and in some cases pioneered the investigation of the subject. Lawyers, for instance,

---

[12] This tendency culminated in Robert Melson, *Revolution and Genocide: On the Origins of the Armenian Genocide and the Holocaust* (Chicago: University of Chicago Press, 1992).

[13] Now, though, we are seeing how the quality of research among second and third generation genocide scholars can begin to shed light back onto the Holocaust. Scott Straus, 'Second Generation Comparative Research on Genocide', *World Politics* 59:3 (2007), 476–501.

have been at least as adept as historically oriented scholars in devising increasingly sophisticated conceptualizations of intent, which remains the key concept in establishing the case for genocide. Besides, other disciplines can illuminate important dimensions of genocide better than history as a result of their methodology: for instance, social psychologists contribute comparative insights from cross-cultural analysis of human behaviour in specific contexts, and anthropologists provide insights into cultural particularities in ways that have influenced historians much more than vice versa.[14] Our intention is, as much as anything, to call for more historians to bring their skills to bear in tandem with other traditions of scholarship: genocide studies should be an interdisciplinary exercise par excellence.

Where historians can make a particular contribution to the interdisciplinary exercise and where, therefore, the greater weight of analysis in this volume falls is in the consideration of temporality, contingency, and particularly the matter of causation. We understand causation not just in the terms of the immediate lead-up to the crime, or the deeper background causes that are often referred to as contexts, but in terms of the proposition that genocides are the outcome of processes rather than 'punctual' events: they, and the people who enact them, are constantly evolving phenomena, subject to a multiplicity of external influences as well as internal volition. Structure and agency are inextricably intertwined.

Leaving aside the scholarship on the 'final solution of the Jewish question', which has primarily been the preserve of historians, we find that, until recently, historians have contributed relatively little to the study of genocide. More precisely, while some historians have been involved in elucidating case studies, the shape and assumptions of the field have been governed by disciplines more at ease with making comparisons and contrasts across large tracts of time and space, and with dealing with contemporary affairs. Even those historians who have written wide-ranging studies on genocide and related matters have had perforce to write in the style not of the idiographic, cultural tradition of history, which is concerned with specificity and difference, but of the more nomothetic or law-creating tradition associated with the interface between history and the social sciences.[15] Both approaches have the obvious costs and benefits involved in the trade-off between detailed knowledge of particularities and general knowledge of broader applicability; and, in the event, every piece of historically oriented scholarship will inevitably combine aspects of both. This volume seeks to establish a somewhat different balance of the two than evinced in the existing scholarship. It attempts to blur the sharp division that comparable collections, such as the excellent, recent ones edited by Dan Stone and Ben Kiernan and Robert Gellately, still tend to exhibit between

---

[14] E.g., Alexander Laban Hinton (ed.), *Annihilation Difference: The Anthropology of Genocide* (Berkeley: University of California Press, 2002).

[15] Moses, 'Towards a Theory of Critical Genocide Studies'.

one-genocide-per-chapter empirical studies and broad thematic/conceptual studies, as mentioned above.[16]

The extant collections of commissioned essays are of varying coverage and approach, but some commonalities are apparent. As noted above, as with single-authored comparative works by the likes of Leo Kuper and Helen Fein, and latterly Eric D. Weitz, Norman Naimark, and Ben Kiernan, the collections edited by Israel Charny, Frank Chalk and Kurt Jonassohn, George J. Andreopoulos, Samuel Totten, and William S. Parson, have similar approaches to their subject matter.[17] They have either focused on a few ostensibly comparable cases to try to establish general similarities or patterns, and/or they have sought to categorize cases according to broad typologies. Such homogenizing or taxonomic approaches reflect the disciplinary grounding of most of the first genocide scholars in the social sciences, above all, political science and sociology. As a result of this approach, relatively little of the pioneering scholarship that established the sub-discipline of genocide studies was based on original, empirical research. Unsurprisingly, given the youth of the field that they were so important in shaping, these books also relied upon limited acquaintance with the lesser known cases studies with which they deal. Where specialists on these obscure instances were included, their enlistment nevertheless tended not to result in sufficient space being allocated for the particularity of the history to be fully revealed.

At the same time as being schematic in its approach, the earlier scholarship was also too exclusive in its frame of reference. It created a conceptual trap for itself because of a preoccupation with the definition and applicability of the term genocide. This phenomenological approach provided an interesting replication of the tired 'uniqueness' battle in Holocaust scholarship, in that it has served to exclude issues from debate rather than stimulating constructive reflection on the parameters of the subject. The approach has ramifications for historical understanding, with instances of outright genocide being accorded more attention than other related phenomena.

The problem of 'definitionalism' has not left us, and it is unlikely to, given the centrality of legal conceptualization at the 'hard' political end of genocide studies, and the political capital that groups and states invest in claiming or denying the applicability of the term to cases of particular concern to them. The inflated use of the term genocide is the other side of the coin to overly restricted usage. The question of definition inevitably recurs throughout this volume, but not to the end

---

[16] Dan Stone (ed.), *The Historiography of Genocide* (London: Palgrave, 2008); Gellately and Kiernan (eds), *The Specter of Genocide*.

[17] Helen Fein, *Genocide: A Sociological Perspective* (London: Sage, 1993); Israel W. Charny (ed), *Genocide: A Critical Bibliographical Review* (London: Mansell, 1988); Frank Chalk and Kurt Jonassohn (eds), *The History and Sociology of Genocide* (New Haven: Yale University Press, 1990); Andreopoulos (ed.), *Genocide: Conceptual and Historical Dimensions*; Ben Kiernan, *Blood and Soil: A World History of Genocide and Extermination from Sparta to Darfur* (New Haven: Yale University Press, 2008).

of some spuriously positivistic attempt to nail down 'our' version of it. As the historian Charles Maier has noted, 'Taxonomy in the social sciences is always difficult, and often unfruitful.' To attempt to corral cases into a single paradigm is a Sisyphean conceit that ignores the inductive logic by which comparisons are made. Definitive answers cannot be expected when we know that 'an ideal type will not fit any individual case exactly: It's an abstraction from them all.'[18]

This collection is committed to probing the limits and the utility of the concept of genocide for historical understanding, and placing the crime back in its context(s) that may often include mass non-genocidal violence. We do this because the focus on upper case *Genocide* often entails a focus on outcomes rather than causes and processes that may or may not produce the mass killing which many think is the substance of genocide. The focus on specific types of outcomes that qualify as genocide is analogous to studying the peaks of mountains from above a cloudline that only particularly tall mountains penetrate, when a glimpse beneath the cloudline would illustrate that other mountains fell just short, and that the tallest mountains were connected to others contiguously or via foothills. Understanding the context in which genocide occurs is equivalent to viewing the landscape in a wider perspective.[19]

The volume seeks not simply to examine particular cases or ideologies of genocide, but to reflect in a more rounded way upon the relationship between genocide and broader historical trends, periods, and structures. The approach entails going beyond strictly comparative scholarship to something more consciously correlative and contextual. This approach can be operationalized at a number of levels, whether that of the individual group or polity, or of the supranational region, continent or even world. Martin Shaw's call for an international relations of genocide is an attempt to associate different episodes within an overall developmental pattern of interconnected state behaviour.[20] Michael Mann's *The Dark Side of Democracy: Explaining Ethnic Cleansing* (2005) sheds light on how a number of individual cases of genocide—occurring notably in ethnically plural societies passing through key developmental phases when the ethnopolitical identity and territorial integrity of the state is contested—might fit into such a framework; along the way, with

---

[18] Charles S. Maier, 'American among Empires? Imperial Analogues and Imperial Syndrome', *German Historical Institute Bulletin* 41 (2007), 21–2.

[19] This is also the rationale for a project conceived in 2004 by Mark Levene and Donald Bloxham and forthcoming as a series of ten monographs with Oxford University Press entitled *Zones of Violence*. The attempt to combine critical conceptual approaches with detailed regional history and empirical reconstruction is at the basis of Bloxham's *The Great Game* and his volume on the Holocaust in a continental context *The Final Solution: a Genocide* (Oxford University Press, 2009). Christian Gerlach, *Extremely Violent Societies* (Cambridge: Cambridge University Press, 2010) also sets individual cases into stimulating wider contexts.

[20] See his chapter in this volume.

reference to European settler societies in colonial contexts, he debunks the spurious notion that democracies do not engage in genocide, and thus the idea that the spread of (capitalistic) democracy is the antidote to genocide as well as war.[21]

It is Mark Levene, however, who has gone furthest in attempting an overall analysis of an international political economy that seems to have some inherent tendencies towards encouraging murderous intergroup conflict, and in putting that political economy in a distinct historical context, therefore fruitfully combining synchronic and diachronic elements. Levene's *Genocide in the Age of the Nation-State* (the first two of four volumes of which appeared in 2005) does not deny the instance of genocide in premodern times, but is concerned with the particular potentiality for genocide in a post-French revolution, post-industrial revolution world in which states engaged in increasingly desperate and unrestrained competition for sovereign autonomy and thus resources. As a prerequisite for the struggle they developed a heightened preoccupation with the loyalty and thus identity of their populations, which were at once a major source of potential strength and weakness. In this milieu, states reacted with increasing violence against heterogeneous elements perceived to be either holding back development because of particular cultural patterns or threatening state integrity by their split loyalties. Democratic and free market states contributed to the murderous dynamic quite as much as authoritarian/totalitarian regimes and states with command or *dirigiste* economies.

While we editors broadly concur with such structuralist and materialist interpretations, and have expanded upon our views elsewhere, by no means all of our authors would subscribe to the same views. We have included a number of scholars whose interpretations cohere with a classically liberal understanding of genocide, where the crime results above all from aberrant political ideologies and oppressive political systems, and where the problem of genocide can be solved by the reassertion of the healthy norms of international democratic society. Others of our contributors may well have no strong view on the matter, or no general view at all beyond their depiction of their own case(s), and all contributions can be read as self-sufficient, independent essays. In no way do we seek to impose our own editorial conception on our authors, and the fact that all can fit into the volume suggests that distinctions between philosophies of genocide scholarship are often more polarized in the abstract than in practice where, once again, the difference between opposing depictions of the same historical episode are matters of degree and nuance rather than anything else: in reality, all explanations eschew monocausality and embrace varying contexts and contingencies, just as even the most contingent or, again, the most structural explanations cannot account for anything without some reference to ideology and human agency.

---

[21] Michael Mann, *The Dark Side of Democracy: Explaining Ethnic Cleansing* (Cambridge: Cambridge University Press, 2005).

All we seek is to open up the debate about the relationship between individual acts of genocide and the wider political economy and norms of the worlds in which they occur, whether or not those worlds are coextensive with the actual globe (and many of our studies do not require such a broad unit of analysis). We implicitly ask to what extent common features of organized human life across large tracts of space and equally importantly *time*, and amongst the widest varieties of peoples and polities lend themselves to something like what we today call genocide. Such features include competition for land and resources, imperial expansion, warfare, subordination of populations along political or cultural lines, sovereignty disputes, security fears, accelerated socio-economic change, and the re-casting of traditional social hierarchies at moments of sudden flux such as revolution.

PLACING GENOCIDE IN HISTORICAL 'TIME'

Our part III on genocide in premodern and early modern times sheds light not just on common contextual settings for genocide across the ages but also on some continuities in the patterns of genocide's enactment. Alongside the murder of elite bearers of identity and the killing (or enslavement) of ordinary men capable of resistance, such measures include the kidnapping (and rape) of women and children for forced acculturation and the widespread destruction of cultural artefacts. While not universal, there is clearly a set of widely deployed genocidal pragmatics.

Contrary to the opinions of some scholars of the premodern world, and of states like Turkey that have a vested interest in denying the applicability of the term genocide to acts in their own past, it is therefore not anachronistic to discuss genocide *avant la lettre*, no more than it is anachronistic to apply the modern heuristic term 'feudalism' to the premodern past. Lemkin himself was convinced that genocide had always been a part of the human experience, and the UN Convention on the Prevention and Punishment of Genocide explicitly refers to its transhistorical character. What certainly have changed over time are the social cleavages on which genocide-like violence is perpetrated. It is in the enumeration of potential victim groups on select grounds of communal identity that the specifically mid-twentieth century context of the Genocide Convention is exposed, whatever the historical allusions of the document. To what extent we can use the Convention's terms concerning 'ethnic', 'national', and 'religious' groups (not to mention 'racial' [*sic*] groups) for different times in human history is open to a contestation that varies in intensity depending upon the period in question. That is true over and above the general recognition in today's historical and social scientific scholarship that all human communities of identity are constructed to one degree or another rather than simply 'given'.

If types of group vary over time, so too do ideas of how membership is constituted and, thus, how the group might be dismembered. Accordingly, discussing potential cases of genocide from beyond the realm of a Western-created modernity sometimes requires thinking along different lines of logic about group destruction. For instance, the early medieval practice of *strages gentium* that James Fraser describes in his chapter in our section on premodern and early modern genocide illustrates precisely how the destruction of a proportionally small number of certain elite signifiers of a group could be sufficient to represent the destruction of the group 'as such', to use the Convention's terms.

Given different ideologies, cleavages, and logics of genocide, does it therefore make sense to delineate 'modern' from 'premodern' genocide in the same way one might crudely delineate modern from premodern society? The answer depends upon how one understands the protean concept 'modernity'. An understanding that leans particularly upon modernity's material (economic and technical) aspects would of course allow that the development of surveillance, bureaucracy, central state strength, weaponry, etc., would create greater facility to pursue and murder 'enemies', and would equally allow that the increasing contact between different peoples and the more intensive and extensive exploitation of resources might provoke more and increasingly intense intergroup conflicts, but distinctions along these lines between modern and premodern are of degree rather than fundamental nature.

A comprehension of the peculiarities of modernity that more emphasizes cultural, intellectual, and philosophical shifts is encapsulated in the work of Zygmunt Bauman, which itself draws on deeper traditions in continental critical theory. Bauman provided the scholarship of modern genocide with one of its most powerful motifs when he invented the concept of the modern human society as garden, the modern state as gardener.[22] His conception of modernity incorporates its economic and technical aspects but those are subordinate to a post-Enlightenment cultural order embodied in growing secularism and a spirit of scientistic problem-solving. For Bauman, modernity is characterized by man's belief that he can reshape humankind in an image of perfectibility that in a more religious age was regarded as the sole preserve of God. Modern genocide is the radical application of this doctrine of perfectibility by one particular section of mankind against debilitating or imperfectible elements within and outside its collective body.

---

[22] Zygmunt Bauman, *Modernity and the Holocaust* (Ithaca, NY: Cornell University Press, 1989). His influence can be detected most clearly among the contributors to Amir Weiner's collection *Landscaping the Human Garden: Twentieth-Century Population Management in a Comparative Framework* (Stanford: Stanford University Press, 2003).

We do not seek to arbitrate one way or another over the matter of whether a Western-created modernity differs fundamentally, or only in degree, or only in certain ways, from 'premodernity'.[23] What we would observe is that it tends to be students of the modern, from Nietzsche to Foucault to Bauman, who invest most in modernity's putatively radical difference, whereas scholars of the premodern are as interested in continuities as changes, partly because they see so many premodern precursors of what modernists take to be quintessentially modern social, economic, and cultural developments. Medieval manifestations of genocide are, we believe, particularly interesting because the medieval period is often held up by theorists of the modern (and the postmodern) as modernity's 'other' in terms of intellectual, social, and political arrangements.[24]

On the matter of genocide, it is at least worthy of further discussion, then, that Len Scales's chapter adduces the example of a fourteenth-century Anglo-Irish notary in Dublin who advised his compatriots that 'when [the Irish] fall into your hands pluck them all up by the root, as the good gardener doth the nettle.' Here is no mere fleeting coincidence of vocabularies with Bauman's: the notary's injunction was made in the idiom of root and branch destruction in the interests of order and cleanliness, in a context where notions of filth and disease were equated not just with sin but with threat, and where difference, even among members of ostensibly the same religious faith, was by no means necessarily considered reconcilable.

GENOCIDE AND THE WORLD TODAY

However one elucidates the relationship of genocide to the prevailing cultural-philosophical order(s), it is demonstrably the case that in the contemporary world and for the foreseeable future the perpetrator–victim relationship is complicated by the existence of a distinctly modern 'world order'. This order, as manifested most obviously in occasional third party interventions, but more consistently and characteristically by partisan political and economic pressures that can be

---

[23] See the chapters by Ben Kiernan, Eric D. Weitz, Omer Bartov, and Marie Fleming in the section 'Genocide and Modernity' in Kiernan and Gellately (eds), *The Specter of Genocide*; the first volume of Levene's *Genocide in the Age of the Nation State*; A. Dirk Moses, 'Genocide and Modernity', in Stone (ed.), *The Historiography of the Holocaust*, 156–93; Martin Shuster's chapter in this volume; Donald Bloxham, 'Modernity and Genocide', *European History Quarterly* 38:2 (2008), 294–311; and the final chapter of Bloxham, *The Final Solution: A Genocide*.

[24] Elizabeth Deeds Ermath suggests modernity might be called 'postmedievalism' ('Ethics and Method', *History and Theory* 43 (2004), 69).

inflammatory as well as pacificatory, has been hailed as a potential panacea to genocide.[25] In assessing its prospects, we come to the final contribution of the volume.

In considering the relationship between genocide and the way the world order is set up, we seek to problematize the prospect of the 'international community' as benevolent policeman, intervening in genocidal situations and punishing génoci-daires. In this sense, we provide an implicit critique of the sort of picture painted by Samantha Power in her Pulitzer prize-winning 'A Problem from Hell': America and the Age of Genocide (2003). In Power's vision, the USA, as political and cultural leader of the international community (and, during the Cold War, of the 'free world'), exists in a solely reactive position vis-à-vis genocide. In her final analysis, all that is really needed to combat genocide is for the USA to assert its values with greater conviction and consistency, a greater determination to lead and an en-hanced preparedness to assume the human and financial costs of interventionist action. In a similar vein, the opening passage of the executive summary of Preventing Genocide, the report of the US 'Genocide Prevention Task Force', chaired by Madeleine Albright and William Cohen, declares that 'genocide and mass atrocities threaten American values and interests.' Such approaches focus, as it were, on America's 'sins of omission' rather than its 'sins of commission'. If we allow that genocide does indeed run against American values, it has frequently cohered with American interests, as we can see before the twentieth century in the expansion of the United States of America at indigenous expense, and during the twentieth century in American support for regimes engaged in genocide or 'poli-ticide' in, inter alia, Latin America, Indonesia, and Iraq, some of which are considered in this volume.

That which applies to American interests and the interests of so many other states past and present also applies to the international institutions that now have a greater potential than ever to intervene in and punish cases of genocide and related atrocity. Our last section (V) examines some of these institutions and their pro-spects. It examines them not simply in a responsive capacity, but in a way that considers what forms of political violence they tacitly permit. This tacit permission is distributed in two related ways. The first way is via the norms embedded in the structures of international law and international custom. Those norms have evolved partly in response to mass atrocity and partly in the interests of a state-based international system in which, whatever the fashionable rhetoric of account-ability, sovereign viability and extensive sovereign freedom of action within the domestic realm still remain hugely important structural features. The second way is through the power-political constellations—particularly in the form of great powers and their alliances—that shape and restrict the reach of ostensibly

[25] E.g. Gary Bass, Freedom's Battle: The Origins of Humanitarian Intervention (New York: Knopf, 2008).

supranational organizations like the UN and the ICC in accordance with matters of strategic and ideological interest. If genocide studies is to have any activist implications, the critical attention paid to transgressive regimes must also be extended to the states and organizations that create and (selectively) enforce the rules themselves. Some of those states also provide livings for the vast majority of genocide scholars.

The overall balance of the volume is as follows: beyond the present chapter, there are fifteen broadly thematic chapters in parts I, II, and V and sixteen more spatially and temporally delineated chapters in parts III and IV. All of the former are grounded more or less extensively in concrete examples; almost all of the latter reach further than individual instances and contain comparative and correlative elements.

Our authors have taken advantage of their broad remits such that, for instance, Christopher Browning writes not on 'the final solution' but on 'the Nazi empire'; Nicholas Werth writes on the murderous continuities as well as contrasts between Tsarist and Soviet policy in managing a diverse and rapidly modernizing imperial space; Daniel Feierstein considers a number of Latin American countries in the politico-spatial context of a concerted transnational anti-communist policy; Africa is divided up not according to individual genocides but according to zones and particular time periods that allow for internal and external comparison; genocides in Asia are divided into conceptual categories such as 'secessionist'; and so on. In this sense, there is not a clear divide between conceptualization and case study, simply a variation in the relationship between the theoretical and the empirical.

We have tried to be as balanced as possible in terms of chronological and geographical coverage. One of the novelties of the volume is the extensive space devoted to premodern cases, but in the modern period we have also sought to establish a distribution that is neither Eurocentric, neither biased towards the era of the two world wars, nor limited to the better known non-European cases. Inevitably some candidates for inclusion are not present, but this is not necessarily due to our myopia; a salutary lesson in putting the volume together was the difficulty in locating suitably qualified authors who were interested in addressing genocide in their area of expertise; we also suffered from the inevitable attrition involved in compiling a large collective volume, as some of our authors withdrew too late in the day to be replaced. We regret the absence of planned chapters on genocide and empire, war, and the question of genocide in medieval Eurasia. With the exception of the final one, most of the substantive issues that would have been raised in those missing chapters have been covered to one degree or another elsewhere in the book.

It is with particular regret that we had to forego a chapter on the relationship between economic developmentalism and genocide, since that would have furthered our interrogation of the structural violence inherent to the imperative of material progress upon which the modern world is constructed.[26] Nevertheless, the book concludes with a reflection on one of the most deleterious impacts of the ideology of developmentalism for homo sapiens: anthropogenic climate change and its ramifications in coming conflicts of resource scarcity and mass refugee movement.

We are grateful to all our authors for considering our often extensive suggestions for expansion and cross-integration of their material, and for the rewriting that we frequently requested. All responded with grace and professionalism. Each of their essays includes a select bibliography of relevant further material in English; the footnotes will provide additional specialist reading across the full range of relevant languages.

Donald Bloxham would also like to thank the Leverhulme Trust. In 2007 he was recipient of one of the Trust's Philip Leverhulme Prizes, which provided for two years of leave, part of which was spent editing this Handbook and writing his own contributions to it.

[26] Vinay Lal, 'The Concentration Camps and Development: The Pasts and Future of Genocide', *Patterns of Prejudice* 39:2 (2005), 220–43; Gerlach, *Extremely Violent Societies*; Nafeez Mosaddeq Ahmed, 'Structural Violence as Form of Genocide: The Impact of the International Economic Order', *Entelequia. Revista Interdisciplinar,* [online]. Accessed January 2009; available at http://www.eumed.net/entelequia

PART I

CONCEPTS

....

CHAPTER 1

RAPHAEL LEMKIN, CULTURE, AND THE CONCEPT OF GENOCIDE

....

A. DIRK MOSES

INTRODUCTION

....

'IN the beginning was Raphael Lemkin' is effectively how the conventional accounts of the genocide concept begin. As the coiner of the word and 'father of the genocide convention', his person is held to be coeval with the concept, so that biography replaces intellectual history. That biography is written teleologically as a heroic struggle against the odds, consummated in the 'United Nations Convention on the Punishment and Prevention of Genocide' in 1948, and invested with poignancy after his death, alone and exhausted in 1959, a martyr to the cause. His subsequent obscurity intensified the hagiographical imperative in the recent accounts to revive his memory and honor his achievement.[1] Enthusiasts have now devoted plays to Lemkin, and a book prize is given in his name. Reclaiming the lost son, the Polish

---

[1] Samantha Power, 'A Problem from Hell': America and the Age of Genocide (New York: Basic Books, 2002); William Korey, An Epitaph for Raphael Lemkin (New York: Blaustein Institute for the Advancement of Human Rights, 2002); John Cooper, Raphael Lemkin and the Struggle for the Genocide Convention (Houndmills: Palgrave MacMillan, 2008).

state named a conference room at the Ministry of Foreign Affairs after him in 2005, and then mounted a commemorative plaque on the house in which he had lived in Warsaw.[2]

For all that, a critical literature is still in its infancy. Lemkin remains obscure in the history of international law. The conferences dedicated to his memory invite the usual suspects, and mainstream journals of history and international relations generally eschew his term. To a great extent, 'genocide studies' has yet to break out of its self-imposed isolation.[3] Part of the problem is that Lemkin's revealing correspondence and invaluable unpublished manuscripts languish in archives in New York and Cincinnati, despite assurances that they will be made available to the public.[4] This problem is compounded by the priorities of the self-proclaimed 'pioneers of genocide studies'—those social scientists writing about genocide in the 1980s and 1990s—who paid Lemkin lip service for 'discovering' genocide but presumed to improve his definition without undertaking the necessary systematic reconstruction and explication of his ideas. Conceiving of themselves as activist-scholars on a mission to interdict genocide in the contemporary world, they were more interested in, say, penning crusading letters to the *New York Times* than embarking on the history of ideas.[5]

[2] In his speech dedicating the conference room in 2005, the Polish academic representing the Foreign Ministry identified Lemkin as a Pole and an American, but did not mention his Jewish identity: http://poland.usembassy.gov/poland/rotfeld_hall.html; http://www.msz.gov.pl/Address, by, Profesor,Adam,Daniel,Rotfeld,the,Ministry,of,Foreign,Affairs,in,honor,of,Raphael,Lemkin.,(Warsaw,, October,18,,2005),2410.html. The plays are Catherine Filloux, *Lemkin's House* (New York: Playscripts, 2005), and Robert Skloot, *If the Whole Body Dies: Raphael Lemkin and the Treaty against Genocide* (Madison, WI: Parallel Press, 2006).

[3] The only critical examinations of his work are Jürgen Zimmerer and Dominik Schaller (eds), *The Origins of Genocide: Raphael Lemkin as a Historian of Mass Violence* (London: Routledge, 2009); Bartolomé Clavero, *Genocide or Ethnocide, 1933–2007: How to Mark, Unmake and Remake Law with Words* (Milan: Giuffré Editore, 2008); Ann Curthoys and John Docker, 'Defining Genocide', in Dan Stone (ed.), *The Historiography of Genocide* (Houndmills: Palgrave MacMillan, 2008), 9–41; Martin Shaw, *What is Genocide?* (Cambridge: Polity, 2007); Anson Rabinbach, 'The Challenge of the Unprecedented: Raphael Lemkin and the Concept of Genocide', *Simon Dubnow Institute Yearbook* 4 (2005), 397–420. The German historian of Polish legal thought, Claudia Kraft, has also written lucidly about Lemkin; see note 45 below. In terms of international law scholarship, there is no mention of Lemkin in the much-cited Martti Koskenniemi, *The Gentle Civilizer of Nations: The Rise and Fall of International Law* (Cambridge: Cambridge University Press, 2002).

[4] Steven L. Jacobs of the University of Alabama has been cataloguing and editing 20,000 pages of Lemkin's papers for decades, but hardly any of it has been published. Most of Lemkin's papers are contained in three places: the Manuscripts and Archive Division of the New York Public Library (NYPL), 42nd Street, New York; the American Jewish Historical Society (AHJS), 15 West 16th Street, New York; and the Jacob Rader Marcus Center of the American Jewish Archives (JRMCAJA), 3101 Clifton Avenue, Cincinnati, Ohio. I have corrected his spelling in the quotations from the unpublished manuscripts.

[5] Samuel Totten and Steven L. Jacobs (eds), *Pioneers of Genocide Studies: Confronting Mass Death in the Century of Genocide* (Westport, CT: Greenwood Press, 2002). An important exception is Leo Kuper, who took Lemkin seriously in his *Genocide: Its Political Use in the Twentieth Century* (New Haven: Yale University Press, 1981).

Accordingly, Lemkin's ideas are not always well understood, whether by those who invoke him or by his critics. For some Holocaust specialists, his definition of genocide is too broad, illegitimately associating the Holocaust with other crimes by trivializing the former and miscategorizing the latter. For others, paradoxically, Lemkin's new word was modelled foursquare on the Holocaust, presuming, inaccurately, that he must have been referring exclusively to the Nazi extermination of Jews when he coined it during the Second World War.[6] Either way, the—upon reflection, extraordinary—assumption is that Lemkin did not properly understand genocide, despite the fact that he invented the term and went to great trouble to explain its meaning. Instead, most scholars presume to instruct Lemkin, retrospectively, about his concept, although they are in fact proposing a different concept, usually mass murder. To that end, even his texts have been bowdlerized to make genocide mean mass killing and/or resemble the Holocaust. Thus a rising star in the field quoted Lemkin as writing that the essence of genocide was the '*aim of annihilating the groups completely*', when Lemkin actually wrote 'of annihilating the groups themselves'.[7] The mix-up was all the more inexplicable because, on the same page as that from which this quotation is drawn, Lemkin made clear that total extermination was *not* necessary for genocide to occur:

Genocide has two phases: one, destruction of the national pattern of the oppressed group; the other, the imposition of the national pattern of the oppressor. This imposition, in turn, may be made upon the oppressed population *which is allowed to remain*, or upon the territory alone, after removal of the population and the colonization of the area by the oppressor's own nationals.[8]

For this reason, Lemkin tended to associate 'destruction'—a word he preferred to 'extermination'—with what he called 'crippling' a group: genocide, he wrote in 1946, is 'the criminal intent to destroy or cripple permanently a human group'.[9]

The lesson to be drawn from this persistent misquotation and misinterpretation of Lemkin is that his ideas, rather than solely his career, need to be studied carefully. For the fact is that genocide is a curious anomaly in the post-war regime

[6] Yehuda Bauer, 'The Place of the Holocaust in History', *Holocaust and Genocide Studies* 2 (1987), 211–15. According to Anton Weiss-Wendt, Lemkin 'incorporated a great many of offences in his, rather inclusive, interpretation of genocide' (personal communication, 20 November 2007).

[7] Scott Straus, 'Contested Meanings and Conflicting Imperatives: A Conceptual Analysis of Genocide', *Journal of Genocide Research* 3:3 (2001), 360. Emphasis in original. I am not suggesting such mistranscriptions are consciously committed. I am suggesting that they occur unconsciously because Lemkin's (mis)interpreters think that he *must* have intended genocide to mean total mass murder of an ethnic group.

[8] Raphael Lemkin, *Axis Rule in Occupied Europe: Laws of Occupation, Analysis of Government, Proposals of Redress* (Washington, DC: Carnegie Endowment for International Peace, 1944), 79. Emphasis added.

[9] Raphael Lemkin, 'Genocide as a Crime under International Law', *American Journal of International Law* 41:1 (1947), 147; cf. Caroline Fournet, *The Crime of Destruction and the Law of Genocide: Their Impact on Collective Memory* (Aldershot: Ashgate, 2007).

of international humanitarian law, which is dominated by the discourse of human rights with its emphasis on individuals, rather than the interwar focus on group rights manifested in the politically contentious minority rights protection provisions of the League of Nations.[10] As we will see below, it embodies the social ontology of 'groupism', because genocide is about the destruction of groups per se, not individuals per se. We have, then, the uneasy coexistence of rival languages of humanitarianism, though they are often conflated. To understand the language of group rights, we need to reconstruct Lemkin's thinking about genocide by placing it in various historical contexts.

Two Contextual Origins

As is well known, the Polish-Jewish jurist Raphael Lemkin (1900–59) invented the term genocide in 1943 for his book on Nazi imperialism, *Axis Rule in Occupied Europe*.[11] Its origins, however, go back much further. Three discourses, I suggest, were formative for the evolution of the concept. One was the social ontology of 'groupism' prevalent in the Eastern European context in which Lemkin was raised. The second was the Western legal tradition of international law critical of conquest, exploitative occupations, and aggressive wars that target civilians.

'Groupism'

Lemkin was a proponent of what the sociologist Rogers Brubaker calls 'groupism': 'the tendency to treat ethnic groups, nations, and races as substantial entities to which interests and agency can be attributed', that is, to regard them as 'internally homogeneous, external bounded groups, even unitary collective actors with common purposes'.[12] Others might say that he was a 'primordialist' who reified groups as 'given entities that are held constant throughout the analysis'.[13] This commitment baffles American liberals who can see in Lemkin's national cosmopolitanism

---

[10] Mark Mazower, 'The Strange Triumph of Human Rights, 1933–1950', *Historical Journal* 47:2 (2004), 379–98.

[11] Lemkin, *Axis Rule*. He coined the term in 1943, but the book was delayed for a year by contractual negotiations with the publisher.

[12] Rogers Brubaker, 'Ethnicity without Groups', in Andreas Wimmer et al (eds), *Facing Ethnic Conflicts: Towards a New Realism* (Lanham, MD, 2004), 35.

[13] Lars Cederman, 'Nationalism and Ethnicity', in Walte Carlnaes, Thomas Risse, and Beth A. Simmons (eds), *Handbook of International Relations* (London: Sage, 2002), 412.

only an anachronistic return to 'medieval organic imagery' or fundamental confu-sion.[14] Closer inspection reveals a coherent worldview.

What is the source of this worldview? As a boy, Lemkin reports, he had been first awakened to the persecution of human cultural groups by the story of the attempted extermination of Christians by the Roman emperor Nero. By learning about the travails of ethnic groups through the centuries—the Huguenots of France, Catholics in Japan, Muslims in Spain—he concluded that ethnic destruc-tion was a universal and enduring problem. The persecution of Jews was part of this sorry tale, and he was well aware of their suffering; the Jews of his region near Bialystok had suffered pogroms in 1906. But his sympathies were for people everywhere.

Why did Lemkin's sense of solidarity lead him to defend group rights as opposed to individual or human rights? Growing up in the multinational world of Eastern Europe, his cultural imaginary was irreducibly particular. Like the Polish romantic nationalists of the nineteenth century, he shared the national cosmopolitanism of Herder's adherence to the individuality principle and Mazzini's belief in the unique role of each people in the 'symphony of nations':[15]

The philosophy of the Genocide Convention is based on the formula of the human cosmos. This cosmos consists of four basic groups: national, racial, religious and ethnic. The groups are protected not only by reason of human compassion but also to prevent draining the spiritual resources of mankind.[16]

Undergirding the protection of group existence against extermination, then, is the communitarian assumption that nations and nationhood are intrinsically valuable because, unlike other human collectives such as political parties, they produce culture, endow individual life with meaning, and comprise the building blocks of human civilization.

It goes without saying that Lemkin's upbringing as a religiously conversant Jew flowed into his thinking. But how exactly? Did common Yiddish phrases form his social imaginary? 'May his name and memory be blotted out' was the standard saying about an enemy, itself derivative of the Biblical verse, 'I will utterly blot out the remembrance of Amalek' (Exodus 17:14; cf. Deuteronomy 25:19), the Amelek being the congenital enemy of ancient Jews. The Jewish festivals of Passover and Purim commemorate escapes from slavery and genocide, respectively; during the latter the name of the Persian king, Haman, a descendant of the Amelek, is met

[14] Steven Holmes, 'Looking Away', *London Review of Books*, 14 November 2002, and Michael Ignatieff, 'The Danger of a World without Enemies: Lemkin's Word', *The New Republic*, 21 February 2001.

[15] Andrzej Walicki, *Philosophy and Romantic Nationalism: The Case of Poland* (Oxford: Clarendon Press, 1982).

[16] Raphael Lemkin, 'Description of the Project', NYPL, Reel 3, Box 2, Folder 1.

with booing and other noise in order to 'blot' it out. We can only speculate exactly how these rituals impacted on Lemkin, but this background cannot be ignored in accounting for his worldview. The survival of Jews over the millennia, the mainte-nance of their traditions, their cultural flourishing in the lands of the former Polish-Lithuanian Commonwealth, where the vast majority of world Jewry lived and, equally, the intense consciousness that peoples and their memories could be entirely erased—these were the cultural milieu and drama in which Lemkin was steeped.

Interestingly, though, he was never a Zionist. Lemkin was drawn to Bundist notions of cultural autonomy because, like the Bundists, who were especially strong in Poland, he believed in multiethnic states with minority protection rather than monocultural states tied to specific plots of land that oppressed minorities. If he was attracted to Herder's romantic notion of cultural individuality, he was also wary of integral nationalism. Lemkin was likely influenced by Karl Renner, the non-Jewish Austro-Marxist, whom Lemkin wrote an effusive letter of praise as an inspiration for his ideas. Bundism drew heavily on Renner's thinking.[17]

Lemkin's was an ecumenical cosmopolitanism. Being a Polish patriot and advocate for all cultures never entailed renouncing his Jewish heritage or cultural rooting. His Jewish identity was not structured like a zero sum game. He always mentioned the genocidal persecution of the Jews by the Nazis in the same breath as the mass murder of Polish Christians, Roma, and other victims. Central was his attachment to the notion of 'spiritual nationality', a concept that most likely can be traced to Jewish sources as well as to Herder. Here are possible connections with the 'autonomism' of Russian-Jewish historian Simon Dubnow, who wrote of Jewish nationality that as 'a spiritual or historical-cultural nation, deprived of any possi-bility of aspiring to political triumph, of seizing territory by force or of subjecting other nations to cultural domination, it is concerned only with one thing: protect-ing its national individuality and safeguarding its autonomous development in all states everywhere in the Diaspora.'[18] Lemkin met the great historian during his flight from Poland; unlike Lemkin, he did not escape the Nazis.

Why was culture so central to Lemkin's conception of genocide? After the war, Lemkin drew on the anthropology of Sir James Frazer and Bronislaw Malinowski to flesh out his thinking. Malinowksi represented a special affinity. A fellow Pole, his brand of functionalist anthropology, so revolutionary and influential in Britain, was actually repackaging what Ernst Gellner calls 'East European populist

---

[17] Cooper thinks Lemkin was a Zionist, but the evidence he presents suggests he was a Bundist: Cooper, *Raphael Lemkin and the Struggle for the Genocide Convention*, 93.

[18] Simon Dubnow, *Nationalism and History: Essays on Old and New Judaism*, ed. and intro Koppel S. Pinson (Philadelphia: Jewish Publication Society of America, 1958), 97; Simon Rabinovitch, 'The Dawn of a New Diaspora: Simon Dubnow's Autonomism, from St. Petersburg to Berlin', *Leo Baeck Institute Yearbook* 50 (2005), 267–88.

ethnography invented in the service of nationalism, which had practised "going to the people" more as a moral and political, rather than methodological, principle.'[19] Malinoswki's theory of culture allowed Lemkin to cast his Eastern European primordialist intuitions in the language of modern social science.

From Frazer and Malinoswki, he took the proposition that culture derived from the precultural needs of a biological life. He called it 'derived needs' or 'cultural imperatives', but it was as constitutive for human group life as individual physical well being (i.e., 'basic needs'). Culture integrated society and enabled the fulfilment of individual basic needs because it constituted the systematic totality of a variety of interrelated institutions, practices, and beliefs. Culture ensured an internal equilibrium and stability. These 'so-called derived needs', Lemkin wrote, 'are just as necessary to their existence as the basic physiological needs.' He elaborated the point thus:

These needs find expression in social institutions or, to use an anthropological term, the culture ethos. If the culture of a group is violently undermined, the group itself disintegrates and its members must either become absorbed in other cultures which is a wasteful and painful process or succumb to personal disorganization and, perhaps, physical destruction.[20]

Consequently, he concluded, 'the destruction of cultural symbols is genocide.' To destroy their function 'menaces the existence of the social group which exists by virtue of its common culture.' This is pure Malinowski.[21]

Because culture incarnated the identity of peoples, Lemkin was a supporter of the national minority treaties of the League of Nations. Minorities should not be forcibly assimilated. As we will now see, the question of culture was also central to how Lemkin related to the second influential context, colonialism and imperialism.

Conquest, Occupation, and Cultural Change

The genocide concept is also the culmination of a long tradition of European legal and political critique of imperialism and warfare against civilians. All of the instances about which he wrote for his projected world history of genocide occurred in imperial contexts or involved warfare against civilian populations. Most of his case studies from the Eurasian land mass were taken from continental empires: the Roman Empire, the Mongols, the Ottoman Empire, Charlemagne and

---

[19] Ernst Gellner, *Language and Solitude: Wittgenstein, Malinowski and the Habsburg Dilemma* (Cambridge: Cambridge University Press, 1998), 120.

[20] Raphael Lemkin, 'The Concept of Genocide in Anthropology', NYPL, Box 2, Folder 2.

[21] Ibid.; Bronislaw Malinowski, *The Scientific Theory of Culture and Other Essays* (Chapel Hill: University of North Carolina Press, 1944), 36, 72–3.

the spread of German peoples eastwards since the Middle Ages.[22] Here is a typical statement from an article in the *Christian Science Monitor* in 1948:

The destruction of Carthage, the destruction of the Albigenses and Waldenses, the Crusades, the march of the Teutonic Knights, the destruction of the Christians under the Ottoman Empire, the massacres of the Herero in Africa, the extermination of the Armenians, the slaughter of the Christian Assyrians in Iraq in 1933, the destruction of the Maronites, the pogroms of Jews in Tsarist Russia and Romania—all these are classical genocide cases.[23]

Because genocide so often occurred in contexts of conquest and occupation, Lemkin was naturally drawn to the jurisprudence on this question.

This jurisprudence had a long pedigree. As the historian Andrew Fitzmaurice has shown, European theologians, philosophers, and lawyers have been debating the morality of foreign occupation since the Spanish conquest of the Americas in the sixteenth century. These Spanish intellectuals—above all, Bartolomé de Las Casas and Francesco de Vitoria—based their case on natural law that invested rights in Indigenous peoples. Hugo Grotius, Samuel Pufendorf, Emeric de Vattel, and Christian Wolff continued this line of critique. Nineteenth- and twentieth-century humanitarians who assailed the mistreatment of 'native peoples' by colonial authorities and settlers stood in this tradition.[24]

Twentieth-century jurists who defended indigenous rights, like Charles Solomon and Gaston Jèze, studied Vitoria carefully in making out their views. So did Lemkin, who likely knew Jèze in the 1920s. But Las Casas was his hero: his 'name has lived on through the centuries as one of the most admirable and courageous crusaders for humanity the world has ever known.'[25] Lemkin explicitly appropriated Las Casas' viewpoint in his study of the 'Spanish Colonial Genocide', a chapter in his projected world history of genocide. He called his book on the Nazi empire *Axis Rule in Occupied Europe* in order to place it in the tradition of criticizing brutal conquests. Genocide for Lemkin, then, was a special form of foreign conquest, occupation, and often warfare. It was necessarily imperial and colonial in nature. In particular, genocide aimed to permanently tip the demographic balance in favour of the occupier. In relation to the Nazi case, he wrote that 'in this respect genocide is a new technique of occupation aimed at winning the peace even though the war itself is lost.'[26] Any doubt that the roots of the genocide concept lie in the five-hundred-year

---

[22] E.g. Raphael Lemkin, 'Charlemagne', AJHS, P-154, Box 8, Folder 6. On the Mongols: JRMCAJA, Collection 60, Box 7, Folder 6. On Pan-German interest in colonizing Poland in the nineteenth century: JRMCAJA, Collection 60, Box 6, Folder 13.

[23] Raphael Lemkin, 'War against Genocide', *Christian Science Monitor*, 31 January 1948, 2. On the relationship between genocide and warfare, see Shaw, *What is Genocide?*.

[24] Andrew Fitzmaurice, 'Anti-Colonialism in Western Political Thought: The Colonial Origins of the Concept of Genocide', in A. Dirk Moses (ed.), *Empire, Colony, Genocide: Conquest, Occupation and Subaltern Resistance in World History* (New York: Berghahn Books, 2008), 55–80.

[25] Raphael Lemkin, 'Spain Colonial Genocide', AJHS, P-154, Box 8, Folder 12.

[26] Lemkin, *Axis Rule*, 81.

tradition of natural law-based critique of imperialism rather than solely in Lemkin's reaction to the Armenian genocide or Holocaust can be dispelled by his own words:

The history of genocide provides examples of the awakening of humanitarian feelings which gradually have been crystallized in formulae of international law. The awakening of the world conscience is traced to the times when the world community took an affirmative stand to protect human groups from extinction. Bartolomé de las Casas, Vitoria, and humanitarian interventions, are all links in one chain leading to the proclamation of genocide as an international crime by the United Nations.[27]

Lemkin, like Las Casas, did not oppose colonization or empire as such. He was typical of liberals in the first half of the twentieth century like J. A. Hobson and supporters of the League of Nations mandate system. Empire could be supported on humanitarian grounds if it served the interests of 'civilization'. After all, imperialism, however brutal at times, had also brought the spread of international law that Lemkin regarded as the central civilizational instrument to combat genocide.

Malinowski was useful here, too, because he offered a theory of cultural change that justified liberal imperial rule. Empires, humanely governed, contributed to human progress through 'diffusion', he implied. Diffusion amounted to intercultural exchange and was indentured to a theory of progress. It comprised

gradual changes occur[ing] by means of the continuous and slow adaptation of the culture to new situations. The new situations arise from physical changes, creative energies within the culture and the impact of outside influences. Without them the culture becomes static; if they appear but are not met with adaptation of the whole culture pattern, the culture becomes less integrated. In either case, it becomes weaker and may disintegrate entirely when exposed to strong outside influences. The rise and fall of civilizations have been explained on this general basis.[28]

Following Malinowski, Lemkin thought that cultural change was induced by exogenous influences, as weaker societies adopt the institutions of more efficient ones or become absorbed by them because they better fulfil basic needs.[29] An empire that promoted diffusion governed by 'indirect rule', Malinowski argued, because it supposedly enabled the autonomous indigenous acquisition of European institutions.[30]

[27] Raphael Lemkin, 'Proposal for Introduction to the Study of Genocide', NYPL, Reel 3, Box 2, Folder 1.
[28] Lemkin, 'The Concept of Genocide in Anthropology'. He cites Malinowski, *A Scientific Theory of Culture and Other Essays*; Arthur Toynbee, *A Study of History* (London: Oxford University Press, 1947); Ruth Benedict, *Patterns of Culture* (London: Routledge and Kegan Paul, 1935); Leo Louis Snyder, *Race: A History of Modern Ethnic Theories* (New York: Longmans, Green, 1939); Herbert Seligmann, *Race against Man* (New York: G. P. Putnam's Sons, 1939).
[29] Malinowski, *A Scientific Theory of Culture and Other Essays*, 61: 'the conveyance of a cultural reality from one culture to another' means that 'new needs are created' in the subject society.
[30] Paul T. Cocks, 'The King and I: Bronislaw Malinowski, King Sobhuza II of Swaziland and the Vision of Culture Change in Africa', *History of the Human Sciences* 13:4 (2000), 25–47.

Diffusion was a theory of cultural learning processes that justified liberal imperial rule by European powers.

How did he square this belief with his opposition to the heavy-handed assimilation of minorities he opposed in the new central European nation-states between the wars? 'Diffusion is gradual and relatively spontaneous,' Lemkin wrote, 'although it may lead to the eventual disintegration of a weak culture.'[31] The question was one of coercion. The absorption of 'weaker' cultures was not genocidal, although he also thought all cultural disappearances were a tragedy of sorts:

> Obviously throughout history we have witnessed decline of nations and races. We will meet this phenomenon in the future too, but there is an entirely different situation when nations or races *fade away* after having *exhausted their spiritual and physical energies*, and there is a different contingency when they are murdered on the highway of world history. Dying of age or disease is a disaster but genocide is a crime.[32]

Consequently, Lemkin was disturbed by occupations like German colonial rule in Africa that ultimately culminated in genocide in German South West Africa and German East Africa between 1904 and 1907. Their culture and members were assaulted in a concerted attack rather than fading away.[33] Plainly, Lemkin was as concerned with the loss of culture as with the loss of life. Accordingly, he urged the Nuremberg prosecutors not to confuse mass murder with genocide:

> It appears in light of this evidence that the term genocide is a correct one since the defendants aimed to destroy, cripple, or degrade entire nations, racial and religious groups. The terms mass-murder or mass-extermination in the light of hitherto produced evidence seems to be inadequate since they do not convey the racial and national motivation of the crime. [M]ass-murder or extermination do not convey the elements of selection and do not indicate the losses in terms of culture represented by the nation's victims.[34]

Criticisms that Lemkin's conception is imprecise or incoherent, and that therefore mass murder should be the definitional core of genocide, miss his point entirely.[35] Understanding Lemkin's assumptions, however, should not blind us to their problems. These primordialist assumptions meant that he had difficulties in conceiving of cultural hybridity and adaptation. The cultural options he envisaged in any encounter seemed to have been either genocide or total assimilation.[36] In keeping

[31] Lemkin, 'The Concept of Genocide in Anthropology'.

[32] Raphael Lemkin, 'The Principle of Diversity of Cultures', JRMCAJA, Collection 60, Box 7, Folder 7/12. Part 1, Chapter 2, Sec. I. II, II, 3. Emphasis added.

[33] Raphael Lemkin, 'The Germans in Africa', JRMCAJA, Collection 60, Box 6, Folder 9.

[34] Memorandum from Raphael Lemkin to R. Kempner, 5 June 1946. United States Holocaust Memorial Museum, R. Kempner Papers (RS 71.001).

[35] E.g. Stuart D. Stein, 'Conceptions and Terms: Templates for Analysis of Holocausts and Genocide', *Journal of Genocide Research* 7:2 (2005), 171.

[36] A cognitive theory of ethnicity, by contrast, would show how that category is a perspective on the world rather than a primordial, fixed, entity that engages in zero-sum relations with other ethnicities:

with this view, he tended to regard the encounter between European and Indigene as grossly asymmetric, thereby playing down both indigenous agency and the often-tenuous European grip on power, particularly in the initial stages of colonization. In German South West Africa, for instance, he did not see that the German governor was initially reliant on local chiefs. In fact, such reliance was most likely the norm, because collaboration with indigenous elites made imperial rule both cheap and efficient. In such cases, the imperial overlords cooperated with these elites rather than trying to Europeanize local culture. In the event, indirect rule, far from being a benign regime, often disrupted indigenous polities by promoting chiefly authority at the expense of other social actors or by fetishizing ethnic differences ('tribes'), which programmed these societies for genocidal conflict after decolonization.[37]

Lemkin's blindness to the question of survival and adaptation was rooted in his particular concept of culture. Despite his Eastern European preoccupation with peasant cultures (which Malinoswki had converted into anthropological 'field-work' among the natives), he seems to have equated national culture with high culture. Consider how he regarded the matter in this quotation:

All our cultural heritage is a product of the contribution of all nations. We can best understand this when we realize how impoverished our culture would be if the people doomed by Germany such as the Jews had not been permitted to create the Bible or give birth to an Einstein, a Spinoza; if the Poles had not had the opportunity to give the world a Copernicus, a Chopin, a Curie; the Greeks a Plato and a Socrates, the English a Shakespeare, the Russians a Tolstoy and a Shostakovich, the Americans an Emerson and a Jefferson, the Frenchmen a Renan and a Rodin.[38]

In this statement, the value of culture inhered in its elites who made contributions valuable for humanity as a whole. Genocide could occur when they were extermi-nated, and when libraries, houses of religious worship, and other elite institutions of cultural transmission were destroyed, even if the mass of the population survived and continued some hybrid popular culture. Here is what Lemkin wrote about the Maya in twentieth-century Mexico, centuries after their ravaging at the hands of the Spanish:

While the condition of the Indians has been improving since then, under a more progres-sive Mexican administration, their lot is still hard and their *cultural heritage has been irrevocably lost*. One million Indians still speak Maya dialect today. They still till the land as their forefathers had done but they have lost their civilized habits, their remarkable skills and knowledge long ago.[39]

Rogers Brubaker, Mara Loveman, and Peter Stamatov, 'Ethnicity as Cognition', *Theory and Society* 33:1 (2004), 31–64; Henry E. Hale, 'Explaining Ethnicity', *Comparative Political Studies* 37:4 (2004), 458–85.

[37] Mahmood Mamdani, 'Historicizing Power and Responses to Power: Indirect Rule and Its Reform', *Social Research* 66:3 (1999), 859–86.

[38] Memorandum from Lemkin to Kempner, 5 June 1946. See fn. 34.

[39] Raphael Lemkin, 'Yucatan', AJHS, P-154, Box 8, Folder 12. Emphasis added.

Clearly, this view is untenable today. Only white perceptions that 'real' Indians must be 'pure' prevented Europeans seeing that 'Indianness' was retained even while Indians adapted their culture and intermarried with others. Lemkin does not seem to have considered the possibility that genocide could be attempted, that much destruction could take place, and that cultural adaptation occurred nonetheless.

Formulating Genocide

Before he embarked on his world history of genocide after the Second World War, Lemkin was a lecturer in comparative law at the Free University of Poland and the Deputy Prosecutor of the District Court of Warsaw. In the late 1920s, he had become involved in the Polish Commission for International Juridical Cooperation, whose leading member, Emil S. Rappaport, was proposing that the League of Nations criminalize aggressive wars. Through this senior colleague, Lemkin was influenced by the proposal to make a certain class of crimes *delicta juris gentium*— offences against the law of nations, meaning grave threats to public international order that could be prosecuted anywhere under the principle of universal jurisdiction. At the first international conference for the unification of international law in Warsaw in 1927, these proposed crimes were piracy, counterfeiting of coins, producing a public danger, trade in women and children, trade in narcotics, and traffic in obscene publications. In subsequent years, the question of terrorism in relation to endangering public order was debated, and Lemkin was included in a commission to consider the matter and report at the Madrid meeting in 1933. He did not think the terrorism was a distinct crime, but rather comprised various criminal acts that individually constituted a public danger. To that list, he proposed to add barbarity, acts of vandalism, interrupting international communication, and propagating contagions.[40] He also wanted to expand the remit of the law from mere 'public danger', which 'threatens personally indeterminate individuals or an indeterminate quantity of the goods on a given territory'. In its stead, he suggested a 'general (transnational) danger [that] threatens the interests of several States and their inhabitants.'[41] In future decades, he advocated the genocide concept in these terms, namely that its elements were already crimes but that, taken together, it constituted a transnational danger.

'Barbarity' and 'Vandalism' are of relevance for genocide because of their focus on group protection. He had been indignant that the Turkish perpetrators of the Armenian deportations and massacres were able largely to escape prosecution, and

---

[40] Marc Segesser and Myriam Gessler, 'Raphael Lemkin and the International Debate on the Punishment of War Crimes, (1919–1948)', *Journal of Genocide Research* 7:4 (2005), 456–7.

[41] Raphael Lemkin, 'Acts Constituting a General (Transnational) Danger Considered as Offences against the Law of Nations', 1933: http://www.preventgenocide.org/lemkin/madrid1933-english.htm

appalled by the massacres of the Assyrian Christians in Iraq. Now it was time to criminalize them. 'Barbarity' combined acts against individuals and collectivities and thereby exceeded the concept of human rights:

In particular, these are attacks carried out against an individual as a member of a collectivity. The goal of the author [of the crime] is not only to harm an individual, but also to cause damage to the collectivity to which the later belongs. Offenses of this type bring harm not only to human rights, but also and most especially they undermine the fundamental basis of the social order.[42]

Such acts comprised 'massacres, pogroms, actions undertaken to ruin the economic existence of the members of a collectivity, etc.' He added other acts that linked the individual to the group, namely 'all sorts of brutalities which attack the dignity of the individual in cases where these acts of humiliation have their source in a campaign of extermination directed against the collectivity in which the victim is a member.' Individually, they violated the criminal codes of civilized nations, but taken together they endangered 'the entire social order' and therefore 'shake the very basis of harmony in social relations between particular collectivities'. For this reason, they were a transnational danger.[43]

This reasoning was also deployed for the other suggested crime of 'Acts of Vandalism'. It too was an 'attack targeting a collectivity' in 'the form of systematic and organized destruction of the art and cultural heritage in which the unique genius and achievement of a collectivity are revealed in fields of science, arts and literature'. He made the suffering of a particular people a transational danger by the postulate that 'The contribution of any particular collectivity to world culture as a whole forms the wealth of all of humanity,' such that vandalism was tantamount to an assault on 'world culture'. Revealing his perspective on civilizational progress, he noted that vandalism 'throws the evolution of ideas back to the bleak period of the Middle Ages' and 'shock[s] the conscience of all humanity'.[44] Remarkably early in his career, then, Lemkin highlighted the importance of culture to group life, but always in relation to a cosmopolitan vision of world civilization.

Ultimately, his report was not even considered at the Madrid meeting, which was preoccupied with terrorism, and his proposals were quickly forgotten.[45] They would become relevant ten years later when he adapted them in his famous book, *Axis Rule in Occupied Europe*. Why did he write it? When in exile in the United States as an academic and government advisor after 1941, he spread the word among his colleagues and superiors about the Nazis' exterminatory intentions toward European Jewry. Receiving a scant hearing, he resolved to publish the

---

[42] Ibid.
[43] Ibid.
[44] Ibid.
[45] Claudia Kraft, 'Völkermord als *delictum iuris gentium*: Raphael Lemkins Vorarbeiten für eine Genozidkonvention', *Simon Dubnow Institute Yearbook* 4 (2005), 79–98.

records of the German occupation he had been collecting, and devise a term for what Winston Churchill, soon after the German invasion of the Soviet Union, had called 'a crime without a name', namely, the 'extermination' of 'whole districts'. Like Lemkin, Churchill compared the Nazis 'to the Mongol invasions of Europe in the sixteenth century'. Nazism was a reversion to barbaric warfare.[46] Contrary to customary opinion, then, neither Lemkin nor Churchill were referring solely to the Holocaust of European Jewry; they meant the totality of the German campaign.

Completed in 1943 but published in November 1944, *Axis Rule* is a massive, 674-page book in which he first used and explained the meaning of genocide. What precisely he meant, however, has been a subject of some controversy. Is mass killing intrinsic to genocide? Indeed it is, many have asserted, and the Holocaust is prototypical of genocide.[47] Or is genocide a much broader term not conceptually indentured to the Holocaust, as others insist?[48] To elucidate Lemkin's intentions, we must consider this text as well as articles he wrote soon thereafter.

It is important to note that Lemkin devotes only one of twenty-six chapters in Parts One and Two of *Axis Rule* to genocide. Part Three, which comprises more than half the book, reproduces the German occupation decrees across Europe. The nine chapters of Part One are each devoted to a technique of occupation: administration, police, law, courts, property, finance, labour, legal status of the Jews, and genocide. This structure suggests that the book is not an analysis of genocide per se, but a study of German occupation in which genocide is a particular tool of conquest. Indeed, he writes, 'genocide is a new technique of occupation aimed at winning the peace even though the war itself is lost'.[49] Yet in the preface, he implies that all of the techniques were aspects of genocide, such that it forms the conceptual core of his book:

The picture of coordinated German techniques of occupation must lead to the conclusion that the German occupant has embarked upon a gigantic scheme to change, in favor of Germany, the balance of biological forces between it and the captive nations for many years to come. The objective of this scheme is to *destroy or to cripple* the subjugated people in their development so that, even in the case of Germany's military defeat, it will be in a position to deal with other European nations from the vantage point of numerical, physical, and economic superiority.[50]

A sentence later, however, he seems to restrict genocide to extermination, thereby distinguishing it from other techniques.

---

[46] Winston Churchill, *Winston S. Churchill: His Complete Speeches, 1897–1963*, ed. R. R. James, vol. 6 (New York/London: R. R. Bowker, 1974), 6474.

[47] Steven T. Katz, *Holocaust in Historical Context* (Oxford: Oxford University Press, 1994), 129; Yves Ternon, 'Reflections on Genocide', in Gerard Chaliand (ed.), *Minority Peoples in the Age of Nation-States* (London: Pluto Press, 1989), 127.

[48] Ward Churchill, *A Little Matter of Genocide* (San Francisco: City Lights Books, 1997), 67–75.

[49] Lemkin, *Axis Rule*, 81.

[50] Ibid. xi. Emphasis added.

The practice of extermination of nations and ethnic groups as carried out by the invaders is called by the author 'genocide,' a term deriving from the Greek word *genos* (tribe, race) and the Latin *cide* (by way of analogy, see homocide [*sic*], fratricide) and is treated in a chapter under the same name (Chapter IX).

So does genocide mean exterminating or 'crippling' a people? He begins Chapter Nine by declaring that genocide is 'the destruction of a nation or of an ethnic group'. But what does destruction mean? We know that he did not think it is consubstantial with the total disappearance of a people as a biological entity. Destruction can mean crippling, an interpretation supported by the references scattered throughout the book to non-murderous genocidal policies directed towards other peoples occupied by the Nazis.[51]

Plainly, he combined his original formulations, barbarity and vandalism, to form a new, more comprehensive concept. Vandalism—the destruction of cultural works—was now a technique of group destruction.[52] But is genocide a synonym for the forced assimilation of the conquered people? Apparently not. Terms like 'denationalization' or 'Germanization'—the imposition of the conqueror's 'national pattern' on the conquered people—were unsatisfactory, he continued, because 'they do not convey the common elements of one generic notion and they treat mainly the cultural, economic, and social aspects of genocide, *leaving out the biological aspects, such as causing the physical decline and even destruction of the population involved*.'[53] Was he hopelessly confused?

We need to recall Lemkin's conception of nationhood. Nations comprise various dimensions: political, social, cultural, linguistic, religious, economic, and physical/biological. Genocide is a 'coordinated plan of different actions' that attacks them 'with the aim of annihilating the groups themselves'. Annihilation cannot be reduced to mass killing, however. 'Generally speaking, genocide does not entail the immediate destruction of a nation, except when accomplished by mass killings of all members of a nation.'[54] And yet an essential aspect of nationhood is the physical/biological one. He thought the term 'Germanization' of the Poles inadequate, for example, because

it means that the Poles, as human beings, are preserved and that only the national pattern of the Germans is imposed upon them. Such a term is much too restricted to apply to a process in which the population is attacked, *in a physical sense*, and is removed and supplanted by populations of the oppressor nations.[55]

We do not seem closer to a clear answer.

---

[51] Ibid. 138–9, 196, 236–7.
[52] He referred explicitly to his 1933 proposals in ibid. 91.
[53] Ibid. 80. Emphasis added.
[54] Ibid. 79.
[55] Ibid. 80. Emphasis added.

Careful inspection of his writings reveals that, true to his concept of group life, he did not consider cultural destruction in isolation from attacks on the physical and biological elements of a group. Culture was inextricably interwoven with a broader assault encompassing the totality of group existence: 'Physical and biological genocide are always preceded by cultural genocide or by an attack on the symbols of the group or by violent interference with religious or cultural activities. In order to deal effectively with the crime of Genocide one must intervene at the very inception of the crime.'[56] Nazi mass murder, for instance, could not be separated from their attack on culture. 'Side by side with the extermination of "undesirables" went a systematic looting of artworks, books, the closing of universities and other places of learning, the destruction of national monuments.'[57]

In Lemkin's conception of it genocide affected all aspects of group life. 'Like all social phenomena,' he wrote later, 'it represents a complex synthesis of a diversity of factors.'[58] It was, therefore, 'an organic concept of multiple influences and consequences'.[59] As a total social practice, genocide comprised various techniques of group destruction. In *Axis Rule*, he outlined eight techniques used by the Nazis. They warrant listing in full because they illustrate his holistic conception of genocide, and demonstrate that mass killing was only one of a number of methods of group destruction. They are discussed here briefly in the order given by Lemkin.[60]

Political techniques refer to the cessation of self-government and local rule, and their replacement by that of the occupier. 'Every reminder of former national character was obliterated.'

Social techniques entail attacking the intelligentsia, 'because this group largely provides the national leadership and organizes resistance against Nazification.' The point of such attacks is to 'weaken the national, spiritual resources'.

Cultural techniques ban the use of native language in education, and inculcate youth with propaganda.

Economic techniques shift economic resources from the occupied to the occupier. Peoples the Germans regarded as of 'related blood', like those of Luxembourg and Alsace-Lorraine, were given incentives to recognize this kinship. There were also disincentives: 'If they do not take advantage of this "opportunity" their properties are taken from them and given to others who are eager to promote Germanism.'

---

[56] Raphael Lemkin, 'Memorandum on the Genocide Convention', AHJS, P-154, Box 6, Folder 5. Because attacks on cultural symbols were embedded in a general attack 'where cultural genocide appears to be merely a step towards physical extermination, there will certainly be no difficulty in distinguishing it from diffusion': Lemkin, 'The Concept of Genocide in Anthropology'.

[57] Raphael Lemkin, *Raphael Lemkin's Thoughts on Nazi Genocide: Not Guilty?*, ed. Steven L. Jacobs (Lewiston, NY, 1990), 299, 303.

[58] Raphael Lemkin, 'The Concept of Genocide in Sociology', JRMCAJA, Collection 60, Box 6, Folder 13, 1.

[59] Raphael Lemkin 'Description of the Project', NYPL, Reel 3, Box 2, Folder 1.

[60] This discussion of the eight techniques is taken from Lemkin, *Axis Rule*, 82–90.

Biological techniques decrease the birth rate of occupied people. 'Thus in incorporated Poland marriages between Poles are forbidden without special permission of the Governor . . . of the district; the latter, as a matter of principle, does not permit marriages between Poles.'

Physical techniques mean the rationing of food, endangering of health, and mass killing in order to accomplish the 'physical debilitation and even annihilation of national groups in occupied countries'.

Religious techniques try to disrupt the national and religious influences of the occupied people. In Luxembourg, the method entailed enrolling children in 'pro-Nazi youth organizations' so as to loosen the grip of Roman Catholic culture. Alternatively, in Poland, where no such assimilation was possible, the Germans conducted 'the systematic pillage and destruction of church property and persecution of the clergy,' in order to 'destroy the religious leadership of the Polish nation'.

Moral techniques are policies 'to weaken the spiritual resistance of the national group'. This technique of moral debasement entails diverting the 'mental energy of the group' from 'moral and national thinking' to 'base instincts'. The aim is that 'the desire for cheap individual pleasure be substituted for the desire for collective feelings and ideals based upon a higher morality.' Lemkin mentioned the encouragement of pornography and alcoholism in Poland as an example.[61]

What was the place of the persecution of Jews in this schema? This is an important question, because some scholars contend that when Lemkin wrote his book he 'did not yet fully comprehend the total planned annihilation of the Jewish people in Europe'.[62] Consequently, they maintain, Lemkin conflated the fate of Jews, whose total physical extermination the Nazis intended, with that of other nationalities, who were subject to violent denationalization. The latter is genocide but must be distinguished from the Jewish experience, which is a Holocaust. Lemkin's text reveals, however, that he was acutely conscious of the Nazis' radical plans for Jews. He devoted a specific chapter to Jews, outlining the 'special status' the occupiers created for them in every country they conquered. Nor was he unaware of the extermination camps: 'The Jewish population in the occupied countries is undergoing a process of liquidation (1) by debilitation and starvation; and (2) by massacres in the ghettos.' 'The Jews for the most part are liquidated within the ghettos, or in special trains in which they are transported to a so-called

---

[61] In a remarkable coincidence, Malinowski's adumbration of culture approximates almost exactly to Lemkin's facets of national life in his *Axis Rule*, published in the same year, 1944. 'From the dynamic point of view . . . as regards the type of activity, culture can be analyzed into a number of aspects such as education, social control, economics, systems of knowledge, belief, and morality, and also modes of creative and artistic expression' (*The Scientific Theory of Culture and Other Essays*, 150).

[62] Yehuda Bauer, 'The Place of the Holocaust in Contemporary History', in Jonathan Frankel (ed.), *Studies in Contemporary Jewry*, vol. 1 (Bloomington: University of Indiana Press, 1984), 204–5; Katz, *Holocaust in Historical Context*, 129–30 n 15.

"unknown" destination.' He was, in other words, well aware that the Jews were 'to be destroyed completely'.[63]

And yet, he included their experience in his 'one generic notion' of genocide. Why did he not distinguish the Jewish case from that of other victims of the Germans? Because he thought the various techniques of genocide issued in the same catastrophic end: the destruction of nationhood or group culture, one way or the other. Even if the Poles were not totally exterminated, Polish culture would be, and that fact represented as grave a loss to humanity as the loss of Jewish culture. That is what Lemkin meant by genocide.

FROM THE NUREMBERG TRIALS
TO THE GENOCIDE CONVENTION

The moral shock of Nazi policies led to celebrated developments in international law relevant to genocide, but the Nuremberg Trials were a diversion rather than a stepping stone. In 1945, the Americans favoured prosecuting war crimes and 'crimes against humanity', which included 'murder, extermination, enslavement, deportation, and other inhumane acts committed against any civilian population'. Thanks to the relentless lobbying of Lemkin, the indictment of the International Military Tribunal included 'deliberate and systematic genocide, viz., the extermination of racial and national groups ... particularly Jews, Poles, and Gypsies.' The British prosecutor, Sir Hartley Shawcross, added, seemingly following Lemkin, that 'Genocide was not restricted to extermination of the Jewish people or of the gypsies. It was applied in different forms to Yugoslavia, to the non-German inhabitants of Alsace-Lorraine, to the people of the Low Countries and of Norway.'[64] But, as Donald Bloxham has shown, the basic orientation of the Allies, particularly the British, was to play down as much as possible the racially specific dimension of Nazi crimes.[65] The priority was prosecuting the German leaders for waging an aggressive war ('crimes against peace'); persecutions of their own population were only salient insofar as they were connected to waging war.[66] Genocide was deployed as rhetorical flourish, and consequently none of the

[63] Lemkin, *Axis Rule*, 81.

[64] William A. Schabas, *Genocide in International Law: The Crime of Crimes* (Cambridge: Cambridge University Press, 2000), 36–8.

[65] Donald Bloxham, *Genocide on Trial: War Crimes Trials and the Formation of Holocaust History and Memory* (Oxford: Oxford University Press, 2001).

[66] Yves Beigbeder, *Judging War Criminals: The Politics of International Justice* (Houndmills: Palgrave MacMillan, 1999), 48.

Nazis was convicted of genocide, let alone for pre-war crimes, as a dismayed Lemkin noted.[67] For this reason, the United Nations, which was meeting in its first session when the first Nuremberg judgment was issued on 30 September/ 1 October 1946, decided that its definition of genocide should cover crimes committed during peacetime, and rejected the British suggestion that genocide be based on the 'Nuremberg Principles'.[68]

In December 1946, the General Assembly of the UN adopted a resolution affirming genocide as a crime denying 'the right of existence of entire human groups' that issued in 'great losses to humanity in the form of cultural and other contributions'.[69] This is pure Lemkin, and it comes as no surprise that he was a tireless lobbyist of UN delegates, many of whom had contact with him and his ideas. His reputation stood high. Britain's representative reminded all that, had his proposals been accepted in Madrid in 1933, the Nuremberg prosecutors would have been in a legally stronger position. Significantly, the term genocide was preferred to extermination so as to ensure that national destruction was not limited to mass killing.[70] He was then appointed as an expert to help formulate a draft convention (the 'Secretariat's Draft' of 1947). It defined genocide very broadly as acts committed with the 'purpose of destroying [a human group] in whole or in part, or of preventing its preservation or development'.[71] Lemkin is recorded as supporting the inclusion of this phase against objections that it was not an essential component of genocide.[72] He wrote: 'Cultural Genocide is the most important part of the Convention.'[73] The term 'cultural genocide' was also included in the subsequent Ad Hoc Committee's draft genocide convention.[74]

Lemkin has been fundamentally misunderstood by scholars of genocide who contend that he did not support the concept of cultural genocide.[75] But he was also a pragmatist and was prepared to compromise. In a letter to the *New York Times* as early as November 1946, he saw that cultural genocide would encounter strong objections from many UN delegates, for whom only mass murder 'shocked the conscience of mankind', as the General Assembly resolution on genocide put it a month later. Although he insisted that human groups 'can be destroyed through . . . disintegration of its spiritual resources', he added that,

---

[67] Power, 'A Problem from Hell', 49–50; Bloxham, *Genocide on Trial*, 67.

[68] Schabas, *Genocide in International Law*, 42.

[69] Lippman, 'The Drafting of the 1928 Convention', 7.

[70] Power, 'A Problem from Hell', 51–4.

[71] Neremiah Robinson, *The Genocide Convention: A Commentary* (New York: Institute of Jewish Affairs, 1960), 123.

[72] Schabas, *Genocide in International Law*, 179–80.

[73] Lemkin, 'Memorandum on the Genocide Convention'.

[74] Matthew Lippman, 'The Drafting of the 1948 Convention on the Prevention and Punishment of the Crime of Genocide', *Boston University International Law Journal* 3:1 (1985), 31.

[75] Representative of this misunderstanding is Helen Fein, *Genocide: A Sociological Perspective* (London: Sage, 1993), 9–11.

for the purposes of international legislation the definition must be limited to more basic elements, such as killing, mayhem, and biological devices, as, for example, sterilization. One should also limit oneself to such acts which are serious enough to be of international concern. Only acts undertaken habitually and systematically and deriving from an organized plan or conspiracy should be included.[76]

Legal assimilation was not cultural genocide, then, a conclusion that advantaged states which sought to assimilate their indigenous populations and other minorities after World War II. Lemkin's residual faith in Western civilization as the source of international humanitarian law may also have encouraged this narrower reading of cultural genocide. But in the end, even this restriction of cultural genocide's meaning was unsatisfactory for most UN delegates, who understood the Secretariat's Draft convention as equating the closing of libraries with mass murder. Many delegates were convinced by the Danish complaint that it showed 'a lack of logic and of a sense of proportion to include in the same convention both mass murder in gas chambers and the closing of libraries.'[77] Cultural genocide was eventually dropped from the final version of the convention.

Even so, the UN did not embrace mass murder as the primary mode of group destruction. In fact, it largely retained Article II of the Ad Hoc Committee Draft, which listed four genocidal techniques: (1) killing members of a group; (2) impairing their physical integrity; (3) inflicting measures and conditions aimed at causing their death; and (4) imposing measures intended to prevent births within the group.[78] The final convention includes a fifth element: the forced transfer of children from one group to another, originally in the subsection on cultural policies in the Secretariat's Draft, but now intended to complement the emphasis on the physical/biological consequences of genocidal techniques.[79] Mass murder, then, is only one of five techniques. Moreover, by stipulating an intention to destroy a group 'in whole or in part', the General Assembly affirmed Lemkin's argument that permanently crippling a group was genocidal. Clearly, what the UN defined as genocide was the first part of Lemkin's proposal in 1933, namely, barbarity. It excluded the equivalent of the second part, vandalism.

[76] Raphael Lemkin, Letter to the Editor, New York Times, 8 November 1946.
[77] Lippman, 'The Drafting of the 1948 Convention', 45.
[78] Robinson, The Genocide Convention, 132.
[79] Matthew Lippman, 'Genocide: The Crime of the Century: The Jurisprudence of Death at the Dawn of the Millennium', Houston Journal of International Law 23:3 (2001), 477.

CONCLUSION

Lemkin thought that the Nazi policies were radically new, but only in the context of modern civilization. Wars of extermination had marked human society from antiquity until the religious conflagrations of early modern Europe, after which the doctrine became normative that war is conducted against states rather than populations.[80] The Nazis, then, were at once an irruption of barbarism into civilization and 'the most striking and the most deliberate and thorough' of genocidal imperialists. 'They almost achieved their goal in exterminating the Jews and Gypsies in Europe.'[81] The Jewish experience is both distinctive in its extremity and part of a broader pattern. Given that forty-nine members of his family died in the Holocaust, his ecumenical approach to human suffering was at once astonishing and exemplary.

What of his legacy in relation to culture, so central to his concept of genocide generally? Briefly surveying the post-war legal regime reveals an ambiguous legacy. Although indigenous people often regard assimilation and development policies as genocidal or at least culturally genocidal, we know that they have no legal protection from the UN Genocide Convention. 'Cultural genocide' is of rhetorical effect only.[82]

Other legal instruments fill some of the gap. The International Labor Organization 'Convention (No. 169) concerning Indigenous and Tribal Peoples in Independent Countries' protects the individual and collective rights of such people. So does Article 27 of International Covenant on Civil and Political Rights (1966), which protects minority groups against assimilation:

In those States in which ethnic, religious or linguistic minorities exist, persons belonging to such minorities shall not be denied the right, in community with the other members of their group, to enjoy their own culture, to profess and practise their own religion, or to use their own language.

And although the reference to 'ethnocide' in the 'United Nations Declaration on the Rights of Indigenous Peoples' (2007) was removed, a number of articles in there still offer protection against those policies that an explicit article on cultural genocide would cover. Article 7 declares that

1) Indigenous individuals have the rights to life, physical and mental integrity, liberty and security of person.

---

[80] Lemkin, *Axis Rule*, 80.

[81] Raphael Lemkin, 'Genocide', *American Scholar* 15:2 (1946), 227–30.

[82] Alexandra Xanthaki, *Indigenous Rights and United Nations Standards: Self-Determination, Culture and Land* (Cambridge: Cambridge University Press, 2007), 114.

2) Indigenous peoples have the collective right to live in freedom, peace and security as distinct peoples and shall not be subjected to any act of genocide or any other act of violence, including forcibly removing children of the group to another group.

Article 8 lists very specific acts that are prohibited, such as forced population transfer, ethnic discrimination, forced assimilation, and land dispossession.[83]

And yet, while the UN described the new Declaration as 'an important standard for the treatment of indigenous peoples that will undoubtedly be a significant tool towards eliminating human rights violations against the planet's 370 million indigenous people and assisting them in combating discrimination and marginalization,' it is not a legally binding instrument, and it was objected to by the USA, New Zealand, Australia, and Canada, while many other countries abstained from the vote.[84] These classical settler societies with significant indigenous minorities could not accede to the articles on self-determination, control of resources on traditional land, including the right of veto against the state, the seeming uncertain definition of 'indigenous', the status of indigenous customary law, and the principle of special provisions for indigenous sections of the population. The United Kingdom spoke for many when it objected to the 'groupism' of the Declaration, and foregrounded the individualism of human rights.

The United Kingdom fully supported the provisions in the Declaration which recognized that indigenous individuals were entitled to the full protection of their human rights and fundamental freedoms in international law, on an equal basis to all other individuals. Human rights were universal and equal to all. The United Kingdom did not accept that some groups in society should benefit from human rights that were not available to others.[85]

What is more, the United Kingdom affirmed that it 'had long provided political and financial support to the socio-economic and political development of indigenous peoples around the world'.[86] The modern state is by definition a developmental one, and indigenous people can stand in the way of 'progress' and 'modernity'. They may claim that development, at least in some circumstances, is tantamount to cultural genocide and the state will deny it.

---

[83] United Nations Declaration on the Rights of Indigenous Peoples, Adopted by the General Assembly 13 September 2007: http://www.un.org/esa/socdev/unpfii/en/declaration.html

[84] United Nations Permanent Forum on Indigenous People, Frequently Asked Questions, United Nations Declaration on the Rights of Indigenous Peoples: http://www.un.org/esa/socdev/unpfii/documents/dec_faq.pdf

[85] United Nations General Assembly, GA/10612, press release on the Declaration: http://www.un.org/News/Press/docs/2007/ga10612.doc.htm

[86] Ibid.

It is unlikely that these legal instruments and declarations will protect indigenous people against development. Since the 'gold standard' of humanitarian emergencies is genocide, anything that does not resemble it falls beneath the radar of international public opinion. What is more, the general commitment to 'development', which appears in this declaration as well—of course, with the qualification that indigenous people should codetermine it—is hardly likely to 'shock the conscience of mankind' as legally defined genocide does or is supposed to. Lemkin might well consider indigenous people as weaker cultures who might be 'absorbed' by 'cultural diffusion'. He was not opposed to the spread of Western civilization; in fact, he saw the field of international law that he championed as the antidote to genocide, which he coded as barbarism. If his language now seems archaic, though, the tenacity of the indigenous identity claims and assertions shows that the language of individual human rights does not suffice for many people(s) since 1948.

Select Bibliography

Clavero, Bartolomé, *Genocide or Ethnocide, 1933–2007: How to Mark, Unmake and Remake Law with Words* (Milan: Giuffré Editore, 2008).

Cooper, John, *Raphael Lemkin and the Struggle for the Genocide Convention* (Houndmills: Palgrave MacMillan, 2008).

Korey, William, *An Epitaph for Raphael Lemkin* (New York: Blaustein Institute for the Advancement of Human Rights, 2002).

Kuper, Leo, *Genocide: Its Political Use in the Twentieth Century* (New Haven: Yale University Press, 1981).

Lemkin, Raphael, *Axis Rule in Occupied Europe: Laws of Occupation, Analysis of Government, Proposals of Redress* (Washington, DC: Carnegie Endowment for International Peace, 1944).

—— 'Key Writings of Raphael Lemkin on Genocide', ed. James T. Fussell, http://www.preventgenocide.org/lemkin/index.htm

Power, Samantha, *'A Problem from Hell': America and the Age of Genocide* (New York: Basic Books, 2002).

Schabas, William A., *Genocide in International Law: The Crime of Crimes* (Cambridge: Cambridge University Press, 2000).

Shaw, Martin, *What is Genocide?* (Cambridge: Polity, 2007).

Zimmerer, Jürgen, and Dominik Schaller (eds), *The Origins of Genocide: Raphael Lemkin as a Historian of Mass Violence* (London: Routledge, 2009).

CHAPTER 2

'ETHNIC CLEANSING' VERSUS GENOCIDE?

BENJAMIN LIEBERMAN

SINCE the 1990s, ethnic cleansing has become one of the most widely known forms of violence directed against groups. Ethnic cleansing is related to genocide, but ethnic cleansing is focused more closely than genocide on geography and on forced removal of ethnic or related groups from particular areas. The greatest overlap between ethnic cleansing and genocide takes place when forced removal of population leads to a group's destruction. This relationship between genocide and ethnic cleansing cannot be delineated in legal terms because there is no international convention that defines ethnic cleansing. Given the absence of any such legal definition, a historical approach is useful to outline the key elements of ethnic cleansing. Antecedents of ethnic cleansing can be traced back to the ancient world and to the Middle Ages. Ethnic cleansing emerged along multiple paths, both through policies to control border zones in large land empires and through practices employed by European settlers to push aside indigenous peoples. In the nineteenth and twentieth centuries, the rise of modern ethnic cleansing took place in several zones, including the old imperial lands of Central and Eastern Europe and Western Asia. Multiple waves of ethnic cleansing remade the ethnic and religious map of this region: the first ending shortly after the First World War, the second culminating and ending during and just after the Second World War, and the third at the end of the Cold War. This history of ethnic cleansing reveals the repeated use of coercion to forcibly remove particular groups from specified areas, but also several paradoxes. Ethnic cleansing is often a policy carried out by strong states to mould the population map, especially of border zones, but the breakup of such states also generates power struggles that can lead to ethnic cleansing. Thus, Norman Naimark refers to ethnic cleansing 'as a product of the most "advanced" stage in the development of the modern state', while Michael Mann argues new democracies are even more likely than 'stabile authoritarian regime' to carry out ethnic cleansing.[1] In yet another paradox ethnic cleansing often derives at least in part from ethnic and religious conflicts or through manipulation of such conflicts, but it is also sometimes advocated, at least in modified form, as a remedy for such conflict.

ORIGINS AND DEFINITION OF THE TERM ETHNIC CLEANSING

In the early 1990s, 'ethnic cleansing' entered the lexicon of terms closely associated with genocide. Language referring to the idea of clearing away groups had been used in previous conflicts, but the particular term ethnic cleansing only gained widespread attention during the wars for the former Yugoslavia. Though now widely condemned, the term 'ethnic cleansing' may actually have been coined by supporters of violent attacks designed to drive Bosnian Muslims out of mixed communities in the spring of 1992. It has also been suggested that Serb sources adopted a term previously employed by Serbs to describe Kosovar Albanian pressure against Serbs in Kosovo in the 1980s.[2] Almost from the start, the use of the term 'ethnic cleansing' caused controversy on the grounds that ethnic cleansing could function as a euphemism to cover up violence or to render it more harmless. But despite its provenance and potential for misinterpretation the term ethnic cleansing soon gained widespread recognition as a major form of violence directed against groups.

[1] Norman Naimark, *Fires of Hatred: Ethnic Cleansing in Twentieth Century Europe* (Cambridge, MA: Harvard University Press, 2001), 4; and Michael Mann, *The Dark Side of Democracy: Explaining Ethnic Cleansing* (Cambridge: Cambridge University Press, 2005), 4.

[2] Klejda Mulaj, 'Ethnic Cleansing in the Former Yugoslavia in the 1990s: A Euphemism for Genocide?', in Steven Béla Várdy and T. Hunt Tooley (eds), *Ethnic Cleansing in Twentieth-Century Europe* (Boulder, CO: Social Science Monographs, 2003), 695; Drazen Petrovic 'Ethnic Cleansing: An Attempt at Methodology', *European Journal of International Law* 5 (1994), 342–59; Naimark, *Fires of Hatred*, 3.

In October 1992, the UN Security Council requested that the Secretary General appoint a Commission of Experts to investigate reports of expulsion, deportation, and violence against individuals and property in the former Yugoslavia and especially in Bosnia Herzegovina. The Commission in a first interim report in February 1993 determined: 'Considered in the context of the conflicts in the former Yugoslavia, "ethnic cleansing" means rendering an area ethnically homogenous by using force or intimidation to remove persons of given groups from the area. "Ethnic cleansing" is contrary to international law.' Methods for carrying out ethnic cleansing included 'murder, torture, arbitrary arrest and detention, extra-judicial executions, rape and sexual assaults' as well as deportation and military assaults against civilians. In its final report in May 1994, the Commission described ethnic cleansing as 'a purposeful policy designed by one ethnic or religious group to remove by violent and terror-inspiring means the civilian population of another ethnic or religious group from certain geographic areas.' Subsequent definitions adopted similar language, referring to coerced and forced removal of a targeted group from a specific territory.[3]

Like genocide, ethnic cleansing focuses on applying force to a group, but the definition of ethnic cleansing is more closely related to geography. Ethnic cleansing refers to removal of a group from a particular area. It is a means for forced remaking of human landscape. Definitions of ethnic cleansing do not specify the type of area from which a targeted group is to be removed, but in practice ethnic cleansing often targets groups living in border areas with mixed populations. In the very case that gave rise to the term ethnic cleansing, Serb forces attacked ethnic and religious groups living next to Serbs along the borders of a prospective greater Serbia. It is in such regions that those responsible for ethnic cleansing are most likely to see their own group's power as contested or even threatened.

The term can refer to the forced removal not only of ethnic groups but also of similar related groups. Ethnicity typically denotes a group with an identity rooted in common culture or history, but the term may also refer broadly to a group seen as possessing a different and distinct identity from others. Ethnicity also overlaps with other forms of identity, most notably religion; however, the precise combination of factors that defines the identity of groups targeted for removal is less important than the relationship between perpetrators and victims. Typically, perpetrators identify those they force out as an inherently threatening group.

Ethnic cleansing is closely related to forced migration and population transfers. Forced migration is a broader term that includes ethnic cleansing, but that also covers population displacement from other causes, such as public works projects.

---

[3] Andrew Bell-Fialkoff, *Ethnic Cleansing* (New York: St. Martin's Griffin, 1996), 3; Naimark, *Fires of Hatred*, 3–5; Cathie Carmichael, *Ethnic Cleansing in the Balkans: Nationalism and the Destruction of Tradition* (London: Routledge, 2002), 1–2; Mann, *Dark Side of Democracy*; and Benjamin Lieberman, *Terrible Fate: Ethnic Cleansing in the Making of Modern Europe* (Chicago: Ivan R. Dee, 2006), xiii.

In organized population transfers, states agree on the transfer or exchange of particular groups across international boundaries. Rules arranged for transfer would in principle make population transfers less violent than other forms of expulsion. However, there are two reasons to question any strong distinction between population transfers and ethnic cleansing. First, transfers may fall short of rules for orderly migration. Second, population transfers even if conducted with concern for the security of civilians still rely on coercion. Entire groups are forced to leave simply on the basis of their identity. The most carefully organized population transfer would therefore amount to a form of ethnic cleansing.

ETHNIC CLEANSING, GENOCIDE, AND INTERNATIONAL LAW

Explaining the relationship between ethnic cleansing and genocide has caused controversy. Ethnic cleansing shares with genocide the goal of achieving purity but the two can differ in their ultimate aims: ethnic cleansing seeks the forced removal of an undesired group or groups where genocide pursues the group's 'destruction'. Ethnic cleansing and genocide therefore fall along a spectrum of violence against groups with genocide lying on the far end of the spectrum. The two are distinct where ethnic cleansing does not lead to destruction of groups, but extreme forms of ethnic cleansing overlap with genocide when the means employed to carry out ethnic cleansing lead to genocide. When high mortality through deportation or expulsion is predictable, intended, and expected it makes sense to refer to genocide rather than to ethnic cleansing or to both ethnic cleansing and genocide. The overlap between genocide and ethnic cleansing is greatest when genocide is conceived of as Raphael Lemkin originally described the term. Lemkin focused not only on actual mass killing, but also on what he described as 'destruction of the national pattern', and forced removal of a population from a given area can achieve that end.[4]

Ethnic cleansing and genocide are especially difficult to distinguish in the case of acts of genocide that take place within a campaign of ethnic cleansing. The Convention on the Prevention and Punishment of Genocide of 1948 lists acts of genocide that include 'killing members of the group'. Genocide most commonly describes campaigns of mass extermination that target entire groups, but the term

---

[4] Raphael Lemkin, *Axis Rule in Occupied Europe: Laws of Occupation—Analysis of Government - Proposals for Redress* (Washington, DC: Carnegie Endowment for International Peace, 1944), 79–80; and see the special issue of the *Journal of Genocide Research* 7 (December 2005), 441–559.

has also been used to refer to massacres that target all members of a particular group in a given area. The International Criminal Tribunal for the former Yugoslavia (ICTY) has employed the term genocide in this manner. In August 2001, the Trial Chamber in the case of Radislav Krstic determined that a genocide against Bosnian Muslims took place in July 1995 during the Srebrenica massacre in which women and children were deported and as many as eight thousand Bosnian Muslim men and boys were murdered. It found General Krstic guilty of genocide as well as other crimes, though an appeals chamber later determined that Krstic was not a direct perpetrator.[5]

As for genocide, debate over identifying ethnic cleansing often focuses on intent. Refugee movements or the flow of internally displaced people suggests the possibility of ethnic cleansing, but applying the term ethnic cleansing requires a judgment about organization and planning to encourage flight. Expulsion of civilians in wartime is covered by crimes of war, but leaving a war zone does not necessarily amount to ethnic cleansing if civilians flee because they fear insecurity and the risk of suffering grave harm. Their movement suggests ethnic cleansing, however, if they depart because they have good reason to fear that they will suffer attack because of their identity. In practice, ethnic cleansing often takes place by example: the sight of smoke rising from a burning village prompts flight from surrounding communities.

The basic elements of ethnic cleansing are widely understood, but ethnic cleansing, in contrast to genocide, has never been codified in international law. Instead ethnic cleansing is seen as a form of previously defined crimes. The Commission of Experts identified practices employed in ethnic cleansing as 'crimes against humanity' that 'can be assimilated to specific war crimes' and added 'that such acts could also fall within the meaning of the Genocide Convention'. Warfare for the former Yugoslavia therefore brought heightened scrutiny of ethnic cleansing without action to anchor the term ethnic cleansing directly into international law. The effect of this disjunction can be seen in the work of the ICTY. The ICTY is the legal body most responsible for punishing crimes associated with ethnic cleansing, but its proceedings have most often mentioned ethnic cleansing with the purpose of providing background to a case or evidence of another related crime. In court proceedings, ethnic cleansing has often appeared as a term within quotation marks. Indeed, an attorney for a defendant at the ICTY sought to use the absence of an international legal definition for ethnic cleansing as grounds to challenge the use of the term. Specifically, he objected to the prosecutor's use of the term, stating 'It does not exist in [the] Genocide Convention or in the international customary law.'[6]

---

[5] International Criminal Tribunal for the Former Yugoslavia, Case Number IT-98–33, http://www.un.org/icty/krstic/TrialC1/judgement/

[6] International Criminal Tribunal for the Former Yugoslavia, Case number IT-97–24-PT, http://www.un.org/icty/transe24Kovacevic/980227it.htm

HISTORY OF ETHNIC CLEANSING: ANTECEDENTS

In the absence of a definition of ethnic cleansing in international law, a historical approach can outline the development and key characteristics of ethnic cleansing. Like genocide, ethnic cleansing can be applied to events that occurred before any definition of the term. Genocide took place before Raphael Lemkin coined the term or the United Nations placed it into international law, and ethnic cleansing predated the 1990s. Indeed, antecedents of ethnic cleansing can be traced as far back as the ancient world. Deportations of civilians took place in Egypt, Mesopotamia, and the Hittite Empire. In the first millennium BCE, the Neo-Assyrian Empire regularly carried out mass deportations of people from conquered regions. Inscriptions tell, for example, of removing more than 27,000 people from Samaria to Assyria, and Sennacherib (705–681) was said to have deported 208,000 people from Babylon. Assyrian texts may have exaggerated the numbers forcibly removed, but Assyrian records recount hundreds of cases of deportations throughout the ancient Near East during and after the reign of Tiglath-pileser III (745–727 BCE). Deportation was also a major motif in Assyrian art. Motives for such deportations did not necessarily focus on obtaining ethnic purity, but included punishing rebels, acquiring labour and soldiers, resettling strategic areas, and urbanizing new and old cities.[7]

Antecedents of ethnic cleansing took several forms. During the Middle Ages and into the early modern era Europe experienced multiple cases of religious or confessional cleansing. Modern ethnic cleansing often targets victims on the basis of their religious as well as ethnic or racial identity, but medieval and early modern confessional cleansing focused still more strongly on religion. Both England and France expelled Jews, and Catholic monarchs who conquered the last Moorish realms of Spain in 1492 drove away Jews, or forced many Jews and Muslims to discard or hide their religious identity. In 1685, King Louis XIV's revocation of toleration for Protestants led French Protestants or Huguenots to scatter around the globe despite an official ban on their emigration.

PATHS TOWARD ETHNIC CLEANSING

Antecedents and early forms of ethnic cleansing emerged along different paths in Eurasia and in regions taken over by European settlers. In Europe and Western Asia

---

[7] Oded Bustenay, *Mass Deportation and Deportees in the Neo-Assyrian Empire* (Wiesbaden: Ludwig Reichert Verlag, 1979), 2–4, 7, 16, 19–30, 33–4, 41–59.

controlling border areas served as a major cause for deportation and colonization programmes. The Ottoman Empire employed a policy called *surgun* to exile selected groups. From the Empire's early years, Ottoman authorities periodically moved Muslim populations, often semi-nomadic peoples, to bolster the border in Turkey in Europe. These were primarily strategic initiatives aimed at converting independent populations into loyal and useful subjects of the Sultan.[8] The Ottoman Empire also used forced migration to repopulate Constantinople after capturing the city in 1453. Sultan Mehmed II moved Jews to Constantinople. Such programmes differed from modern ethnic cleansing in motive. Ottoman rulers who moved populations were much less guided by the pursuit of overall purity, whether religious, ethnic, or racial, than by strategic and economic goals. The Russian Empire also engaged in resettlement for strategic reasons. Thus, Russia in the eighteenth century periodically moved Muslim Crimean Tatars away from the front during times of war.[9]

In a very different path toward ethnic cleansing, European settlers displaced non-Western populations. There was no general policy of either killing or expelling every last non-Western population, but settler populations targeted specific peoples for expulsion. Numerous processes combined to force out Native American or Indian populations from lands in much of North America: signing treaties and buying land often functioned as the most effective ways to obtain native lands.[10] There was no single Indian relationship, either friendly or hostile, with settler populations. Indians traded with newcomers and complex hybrid identities emerged in border zones along the frontier. But force and the threat of force also drove Indians from contested regions. The Indian Removals carried out by the United States during the 1830s, which included the removal of Cherokees along the Trail of Tears, relied on a mixture of legality and coercion.[11] With most Indians removed from the eastern United States military campaigns pushed Indians out of areas on the edge of an expanding settler population along much of the Great Plains, and the United States ultimately pressed surviving populations into reservations.[12] This type of ethnic cleansing helped to remake the ethnic map of large areas of the United States.

---

[8] Yonka Köksal, 'Coercion and Mediation: Centralization and Sedentarization of Tribes in the Ottoman Empire', *Middle Eastern Studies* 42 (2006), 475.

[9] Michael Khodarkovsky, *Russia's Steppe Frontier: The Making of a Colonial Empire, 1500–1800* (Bloomington, IN: Indiana University Press, 2002).

[10] Stuart Banner, *How the Indians Lost Their Land: Law and Power on the Frontier* (Cambridge, MA: Harvard University Press, 2005).

[11] For a discussion of removals in a global context, see Patrick Wolfe, 'Settler Colonialism and the Elimination of the Native', *Journal of Genocide Research* 8 (2006), 391–2, 396–7, 399–400.

[12] Gary Clayton Anderson, *The Conquest of Texas: Ethnic Cleansing in the Promised Land* (Norman: University of Oklahoma Press, 2005).

In this form, ethnic cleansing is rooted in settler conquest and colonization.
Treatment of native populations was less organized toward a single purpose than
modern forms of ethnic cleansing in that campaigns to move groups such as
Indians generally lacked the ideological goal of obtaining absolute purity present
in some modern cases of ethnic cleansing. But policies toward natives along
shifting frontiers shared the coercive core of modern ethnic cleansing.

Contests for land and power in border zones most often targeted native popula-
tions but on occasion Europeans also expelled other European settlers. During the
Seven Years War Great Britain drove Acadian, French settlers, from their lands in
Nova Scotia.[13]

Another form of ethnic cleansing emerged in the nineteenth and twentieth
centuries in Central and Eastern Europe and Western Asia. Large land empires,
Austria-Hungary, Russia, and the Ottoman Empire, dominated most of this region,
and despite traditions of strategic and economic forced migration these empires
experienced limited effects from early forms of cleansing under settler regimes. The
Russian Empire advanced slowly into the north Caucasus in the nineteenth century
and shifted populations in an effort to pacify Chechen areas, and Russia cleared
Circassians out of the northwest Caucasus at a time when Russia saw this region on
the Black Sea coast as susceptible to the influence of foreign powers.[14] Russia
engaged in ethnic cleansing of Circassians, but neither Russia nor its fellow empires
pursued overall purity of population.

MODERN ETHNIC CLEANSING:
THE FIRST WAVE

From the late nineteenth into the twentieth centuries modern ethnic cleansing
remade the ethnic and religious map of much of Central and Eastern Europe and
Western Asia. Three massive waves of ethnic cleansing produced a shift toward
greater national homogeneity. By the First Balkan War of 1912–13 the Ottoman
Empire lost most of its possessions in Europe, and a combination of violent attack

---

[13] John Mack Faragher, *A Great and Noble Scheme: The Tragic Story of the Expulsion of the French Acadians from their American Homeland* (New York: Norton, 2005).

[14] Peter Holquist, '"To Count, to Extract, and to Exterminate": Population Statistics and Population Politics in Late Imperial and Soviet Russia', in Ronald Grigor Suny and Terry Martin (eds), *A State of Nations: Empire and Nation-Making in the Age of Lenin and Stalin* (Oxford: Oxford University Press, 2001), 116–19; and Brian Glyn Williams, 'Hijra and Forced Migration from Nineteenth-Century Russia to the Ottoman Empire: A Critical Analysis of the Great Crimean Tatar Emigration of 1860–1861', *Cahiers du Monde Russe* 41 (2000), 93.

and intimidation reduced the Muslim proportion of the population in several regions, including parts of Bulgaria and Macedonia. This first long wave of violence culminated during and immediately after the First World War. A second modern European wave of ethnic cleansing peaked during and immediately after the Second World War, and a third wave continued to remake the map of southeastern Europe and of parts of Transcaucasia at the end of the Cold War.

Modern ethnic cleansing shares several common features. Perpetrators repeatedly claim to be victimized by groups targeted for removal. The language used by perpetrators to describe victims can often be traced in part to long-term ethnic or religious tensions, but rapid radicalization often leads to ethnic cleansing. In some cases such radicalization leads all the way to genocide, but in others ethnic cleansing serves as the most ambitious method for removing supposedly threatening groups.

During the First World War varied authorities in both the Russian and Ottoman Empires resorted to forced migration of groups accused of insufficient loyalty or of outright betrayal. In the Russian Empire, the military command in the west moved Jews away from the war zone, ordering forced evacuation of up to one-fifth of the Empire's Jews, and Russian authorities also moved ethnic Germans away from the front. In the Ottoman Empire, leaders of the Committee of Union and Progress, the political party that had seized power just before the war, adopted policies of deportation, outright ethnic cleansing, and genocide. Many, though not all, Greeks, were deported from selected coastal regions of the Turkey, and in 1915 Armenians were deported from most of Turkey in a campaign of ethnic cleansing and genocide.

The persecution of Armenians during the First World War incorporated many of the chief features of ethnic cleansing. The Ottoman Empire had already experienced mass violence against Armenians, most notably with the massacres of Armenians carried out under Sultan Abdul Hamid II that peaked in 1895, but the First World War still brought unprecedented radicalization in anti-Armenian policy.

In this case ethnic cleansing led to genocide. Across Anatolia Armenians were ordered out of their homes and for the most part driven south into the deserts of Syria and Mesopotamia. As in many cases of ethnic cleansing, the campaign began in border areas, but it soon spread across most of the Ottoman Empire. This was a coordinated policy carried out against a group identified by both ethnicity and religion. There were a few exceptions to this policy in that the Armenian communities of the largest cities of the western empire, Smyrna (Izmir) and Constantinople (Istanbul), were not destroyed at this time, though Armenians living in Constantinople without their families and some political figures were targeted, and more sweeping deportations of Armenians were considered.[15] At the same time Turkish deportations of Armenians also led to genocide. Frequent

---

[15] Donald Bloxham, *The Great Game of Genocide: Imperialism, Nationalism, and the Destruction of the Ottoman Armenians* (Oxford: Oxford University Press, 2005), 78, 121.

massacres, especially of Armenian men, repeated assaults along routes southward, and the predictable lack of food and water in the desert heat caused the extermination of Armenians. This was ethnic cleansing so severe that it reached the level of genocide.

Ethnic cleansing continued after the First World War when the Ottoman Empire's final collapse generated nationalist power struggles. Greece landed an army in Turkey in 1919 starting a war that produced ethnic killing, deportations, and ethnic cleansing. Turkish Nationalists in the east of Anatolia deported Pontic Greeks, the Greeks who lived along the Black Sea Coast. In 1922, Turkish Nationalist victory prompted large-scale Greek flight. The Peace Conference at Lausanne reached agreement in 1923 for a Greek-Turkish population exchange under which Turks were moved from Greece to Turkey, and most Greeks were moved from Turkey to Greece, even though some of those moved ill fit the national categories of Greeks or Turks because the criteria for expulsion referred to religion rather than ethnic self-identification.[16] Killings and arson were common during the Greek-Turkish war, but the Lausanne population exchange was not genocide. The new immigrants suffered many hardships, but the intent was a national exchange. At the same time, the coercive nature of exchange meant that the Greek-Turkish population exchange amounted to ethnic cleansing.

MODERN ETHNIC CLEANSING: THE SECOND WAVE

The next major wave of modern ethnic cleansing reached a peak during the Second World War. Hitler spoke in the early days of World War II of creating a 'New Order'. He presented this as a way to better mark the boundaries between nationalities, but Germany almost immediately turned to forced migration to remake the ethnic map of much of Central and Eastern Europe as a zone under German and 'Aryan' domination. German authorities wished, for example, to make newly annexed areas of western Poland more German and in pursuit of this goal deported hundreds of thousands of Poles. With war against the Soviet Union, Himmler, the Head of the SS and of the Reich Commission for the Strengthening of Germandom (RKFDV), planned for even more ambitious programmes of deportation. Experts employed in drawing up a General Plan East proposed deporting

---

[16] Bruce Clark, *Twice a Stranger: The Mass Expulsions that Forged Modern Greece and Turkey* (Cambridge, MA: Harvard University Press, 2006).

millions of Slavs, including Poles, Ukrainians, and White Russians, far towards the east, but most plans were never carried out because of German defeat.

The Holocaust both incorporated and departed from ethnic cleansing. In terms of ultimate goals, the Holocaust was a genocide distinct from ethnic cleansing: the idea of exterminating all European Jews could not be satisfied by merely moving them. At the same time discussion of ethnic cleansing as one option for ridding Europe of Jews created one of several routes to genocide. During the early years of the Second World War, Nazi obsession with finding a final solution to the Jewish question in Europe, or the fact that Jews existed in Europe, generated a search for plans, including resettlement. The idea of sending European Jews to the island of Madagascar attracted attention, and Nazi racial experts also discussed forcibly moving Jews elsewhere, including to the far reaches of the Soviet Union. Some of these plans, if realized, would very probably have led to genocide, but the very failure to move forward with such schemes also propelled Germany's leaders toward genocide.[17]

Once the Holocaust began, mass murder carried out in towns and villages of the Soviet Union and in death camps in Poland soon superseded any policy of merely removing Jews from areas under German control, but in at least one region ethnic cleansing blended into genocide in a pattern reminiscent of the Armenian genocide. Research into the Armenian genocide has prompted a search for connections to the Holocaust both through Hitler's much discussed comment on the fate of Armenians and through research into the legacy of Germany's wartime alliance with Turkey, but the closest parallels to the Armenian genocide during the Holocaust can be found in areas where Romania initiated ethnic cleansing during the Second World War: Bessarabia and Northern Bukovina.[18] These were border regions with mixed populations taken from Romania by the Soviet Union in June 1940. Jews throughout Romania suffered pervasive anti-Semitism during the war years, and the Soviet takeover further radicalized antagonism against Jews. In Romania as in other regions along the eastern front, nationalists and government authorities accused Jews of having aided and abetted in the Soviet occupation. In June 1941, Romania under the leadership of Marshal Antonescu joined Nazi Germany in the invasion of the Soviet Union, retook Bessarabia and Northern Bukovina, and promptly carried out a policy of ethnic cleansing of Jews. Romanian forces massacred Jews and also drove Jews out of their homes. Indeed, Romanian officials used language almost identical to ethnic cleansing to refer to

---

[17] Götz Aly, 'Final Solution': Nazi Population Policy and the Murder of the European Jews, trans. Belinda N. Cooper and Allison Brown, (New York: Oxford University Press, 1999).

[18] Mark Levene, 'The Experience of Armenian and Romanian Genocide: 1915–16 and 1941–42', in Hans-Lukas Kieser and Dominik J. Schaller (eds), Der Völkermord an den Armeniern und die Shoah (Zurich: Chronos Verlag, 2002), 423–62.

their goals: they called for a policy of 'ground cleansing'.[19] Romanian forces at first forced surviving Jews into ghettos, but once Romania received a strip of territory on the east Bank of the Dniester termed Transnistria, Romanian gendarmes began to drive Jews east out of Bessarabia and across the Dniester. Some Jews were killed on route but many also died from starvation and disease during their first winter in Transnistria. As in the case of the Armenian genocide, extraordinarily violent deportations led to genocide. Of the 125,000 to 150,000 Jews forced into Transnistria only approximately 50,000 survived the war. Much as in the Armenian genocide, massacres, exposure, starvation, and disease predictably caused large numbers of deaths, though Jews forced into Transnistria in 1941 suffered from cold where Armenians at least in 1915 more often suffered from extreme heat.[20]

In several regions of eastern and southeastern Europe, extremist nationalist politics led to local wars of ethnic cleansing during the broader world war. In the Balkans, the Ustasha, a Croatian fascist movement placed in power after the German invasion of Yugoslavia in 1941, carried out a campaign of killings and expulsions against Serbs. A bitter war of ethnic cleansing also took place between Ukrainian and Polish armed bands in mixed Polish-Ukrainian border areas during the latter years of the Second World War.[21]

On the other side of the eastern front the Soviet Union also resorted to ethnic cleansing during the Second World War. The Soviet leadership built on pre-war practices: during the 1930s the USSR under Stalin deported selected groups, typically from ethnic groups that lived both within and outside of the borders of the USSR.[22] During the Second World War Soviet authorities swiftly deported entire populations accused of insufficient loyalty. It took only days to round up most Chechens and Ingush and Crimean Tatars in 1944. These were extraordinary displays of power by Soviet security forces, which surrounded villages, collected inhabitants, and sent them east to Central Asia and Siberia.[23]

The end and immediate aftermath of the Second World War produced a new surge of ethnic cleansing. As Germany faced imminent defeat many German civilians fled from areas including the Baltic and East Prussia rather than wait for the arrival of the Soviet army. In spring and early summer 1945 Czech and Polish

[19] Armin Heinen, 'Gewalt-Kultur: Rümanien, der Krieg, und die Juden (Juni bis Oktober 1941)', in M. Hausleitner, B. Mihok, J. Wetzel (eds), *Rumänien und der Holocaust: Zu den Massenverbrechen in Transnistrien 1941–1944* (Berlin: Metropol Verlag, 2001), 33–52.

[20] Raud Ioanid, *The Holocaust in Romania: The Destruction of Jews and Gypsies under the Antonescu Regime, 1940–1944*, foreword by Elie Wiesel (Chicago: Ivan R, Dee, 2000).

[21] Timothy Snyder, 'The Causes of Ukrainian–Polish Ethnic Cleansing 1943', *Past and Present* 179 (2003), 197–234.

[22] Terry Martin, 'The Origins of Soviet Ethnic Cleansing', *Journal of Modern History* 70 (1998), 813–61.

[23] Aleksandr M. Nekrich, *The Punished Peoples: The Deportation and Fate of Soviet Minorities at the End of the Second World War*, trans. George Saunders (New York: Norton, 1978); and Nikolaĭ Fedorovich Bougaĭ, *The Deportation of Peoples in the Soviet Union* (New York: Nova Science, 1996).

forces pushed Germans across the borders of Czechoslovakia and Poland. These have been termed 'wild expulsions' and fully meet the key criteria of ethnic cleansing. In August 1945, the United States, the United Kingdom, and the Soviet Union agreed at Potsdam to an organized transfer of ethnic Germans out of Poland, Czechoslovakia, and Hungary. According to the Potsdam agreement transfers were supposed to take place 'in an orderly and humane manner', but here again transfer amounted to ethnic cleansing: Germans were forced to leave many lands or communities that had long been German simply because of their identity. In all, 12 to 14 million ethnic Germans fled or were expelled or transferred.

MODERN ETHNIC CLEANSING: THE THIRD WAVE

During the height of the Cold War the pace of ethnic cleansing slowed but never stopped entirely. Recurrent violence between Greek and Turkish Cypriots created distinct Greek and Turkish zones and culminated in 1974 in the island's division along ethnic lines after a coup and Turkish invasion. As the Cold War approached its end, a new wave of ethnic cleansing gained international attention. In the former Yugoslavia, Bosnian Muslims, Croats, Serbs, and Kosovar Albanians all suffered ethnic cleansing. As war began in 1991 Serbs gained the upper hand in disputed mixed border areas of Croatia, and in 1992 Serb forces drove Bosnian Muslims and Croats out of contested areas of Bosnia-Herzegovina.[24] Bosnian Muslims and Bosnian Croat forces were nominally allies but fought against each other, producing still more ethnic cleansing in 1993 in western Herzegovina and in Central Bosnia. Bosnian Serb forces sought to complete the ethnic cleansing of Bosnia in 1995, attacking enclaves such as Srebrenica, an eastern Bosnian town that had been designated by the United Nations as a safe haven. But 1995 also saw a sudden turn of fortune with offensives by Croatian and by Bosnian Muslim forces and the ethnic cleansing of Serbs from regions including the Krajina border region of Croatia. Ethnic cleansing again struck the former Yugoslavia in 1999 with fighting for Kosovo, a region with a large Albanian majority. Serb forces at first carried out ethnic cleansing of Kosovar Albanians, but with the retreat of Serb forces in June 1999 Serbs left much of Kosovo.

At much the same time warfare in the Transcaucasus, the region south of the highest Caucus mountain chain in the Republics of Georgia, Armenia, and

---

[24] Roy Gutman, *A Witness to Genocide: The 1993 Pulitzer Prize-Winning Dispatches on the 'Ethnic Cleansing' of Bosnia* (New York: Macmillan, 1993).

Azerbaijan, also generated ethnic cleansing. Fighting over the Black Sea region of Abkhazia ended with Georgian defeat in 1993 and the ethnic cleansing of Georgians. In Armenia and Azerbaijan ethnic and religious conflict preceded the final Soviet breakup, and with the Soviet Union's end Armenian and Azerbaijani nationalist aspirations clashed most intensely in Nagorno Karabkah, an enclave with an Armenian majority within the borders of Azerbaijan. War for Nagorno Karabakh ended by 1994 with Armenian victory and the ethnic cleansing of Azerbaijanis.

Claims of victimization played a key role in generating ethnic cleansing in the former Yugoslavia and in the Transcaucasus. Perpetrators and their defenders presented ethnic cleansing as a defensive act against groups accused of presenting a dire threat. Serb forces, for example, emerged from the breakup of Yugoslavia with the greatest military might, but Serb nationalist ideology accused other groups of threatening Serb survival in a society where multiple groups had apparently lived in peace with each other for many years.

Such violence between groups that have long lived in close proximity presents one of the most puzzling aspects of ethnic cleansing. In mixed societies perpetrators of ethnic cleansing are likely to be familiar with the groups they seek to expel from a coveted region. Such relationships belie the notion that violence stems from ancient hatreds. In Yugoslavia, there was evidence of a past in which people of different religions and ethnic backgrounds lived peacefully alongside each other. At the same time, claims of past harmony also rested in part on myth. Intellectuals, the media, and selected politicians sharpened ethnic antagonisms in Yugoslavia during the 1980s, but they did not conjure up nationalist fears out of nothing. Marriages and other relationships across ethnic and religious lines were common, at least in parts of the country, but at the same time nationalist speeches and news coverage played on intense fear of the very same groups that typically drew on accounts of violence from the Second World War or from even further back in the more distant past.

PARADOXES OF ETHNIC CLEANSING: STATES AND STATE COLLAPSE

This capacity of residents of societies affected by ethnic cleansing to both trust and fear members of other ethnic and religious groups is one of several paradoxes of ethnic cleansing. Modern ethnic cleansing, for example, is both a tool with which states impose order and a result of the collapse of state power. Ethnic cleansing has functioned as an extreme form of population politics in which states impose simplified boundaries and ethnic categories on complex societies and pursue rationality at a high human cost. The very goal of moving groups across boundaries shows the imprint of states because states customarily draw up or at least maintain boundaries. Furthermore, the elasticity of ethnic identity points to the role of states in launching ethnic cleansing. In many cases, people moved through ethnic cleansing or population transfers only imperfectly fit into the identity of the groups targeted for removal. The population exchange carried out between Greece and Turkey, for example, saw the movement of Muslims who spoke varieties of Greek to Turkey, and conversely the movement of Christians who spoke Turkish to Greece. Such complex, mixed hybrid identities did not fit into the idealized scheme of nation-states.[25] Similarly in the aftermath of World War II significant populations of Central and Eastern Europe in areas such as Silesia could not be clearly identified as possessing a single ethnic or national identity.

As a form of violent social engineering, ethnic cleansing is closely associated with powerful dictatorships such as the Soviet Union and Nazi Germany. The Anfal campaign conducted by Saddam Hussein's Iraq against Kurds in 1989 also fits this model. Anfal combined ethnic cleansing and genocide in that Saddam's lieutenants worked to clear Kurds out of particular areas and also carried out large massacres, most notoriously with poison gas, that were identified by observers, including Human Rights Watch, as an act of genocide.[26]

Powerful states have pursued and carried out ethnic cleansing, but imperial breakup and collapse has also generated ethnic cleansing. A sequence of imperial decline and nationalist conflict propelled major waves of modern ethnic cleansing. Ottoman decline and breakup fed nationalist hopes of redeeming peoples conceived of as having suffered under a 'Turkish yoke' and fuelled efforts to construct nation-states out of mixed Ottoman lands. In the latter stages and at the end of the Second World War the breakup of a very different kind of empire again fed ethnic cleansing. The approach of German defeat encouraged ethnic cleansing by Polish and Ukrainian armed bands, and the final collapse of the Nazi empire led to expulsion, transfer, and the end of many German communities across Eastern and Central Europe. Finally, in the 1990s the breakup of powerful states played a key part in generating ethnic cleansing both in the former Yugoslavia and in parts of the former Soviet Union.

The breakup of empires can spur power struggles that lead to ethnic cleansing despite attempts to regulate the division of imperial lands. At a minimum partition in British India in 1947 and the end of the British Mandate in Palestine in 1948 led to large-scale forced migration. In South Asia, partition generated intense communal violence and the flight of some 12 to 13 million people. Much of the

[25] Renée Hirschon (ed.), *Crossing the Aegean: An Appraisal of the 1923 Compulsory Population Exchange between Greece and Turkey* (New York: Berghahn Books, 2003).

[26] Human Rights Watch, *Iraq's Crime of Genocide: The Anfal Campaign against the Kurds* (New Haven, 1995).

subcontinent remained relatively peaceful, but ethnic cleansing took place in particular regions including parts of the Punjab where Sikh armed groups attacked and expelled Muslims.[27] At the same time, Muslim groups attacked Hindus and Sikhs in West Punjab, though arson attacks and looting may well have proceeded from mixed motives.[28] In the case of Palestine, the British mandate ended in 1948 with the First Arab-Israeli War and the flight and expulsion of at least 700 thousand Palestinian refugees, though an Arab minority remained in the state of Israel after its independence. What remains disputed is the question of what produced this flight and the extent to which Zionist and eventually Israeli forces planned to drive out Palestinian Arabs. Debate in particular has centred on a plan created by the Zionist fighting force, the Haganah, named Plan Dalet or Plan D. This plan has been alternately described as a military operation carried out against Arab settlements behind Jewish lines or as a plan for expulsion.[29] The case for a centralized plan of ethnic cleansing remains subject to debate, but this may also be a case where Haganah forces discovered that they could carry out ethnic cleansing at the local and regional level as their offensive drove out large numbers of Arabs.[30]

PARADOXES OF ETHNIC CLEANSING: ETHNIC CLEANSING AND ETHNIC CONFLICT

The controversies over the partition reveal yet another paradox of ethnic cleansing. Partition or division of ethnically or religiously mixed states has been identified both as a cause of ethnic cleansing and as a possible remedy for ethnic cleansing. In particular, the 'security dilemmas' created when a group in a mixed society takes action that threatens another group's security provides a case for partition.[31]

---

[27] Ian Copland, 'The Master and the Maharajas: The Sikh Princes and the East Punjab Massacres of 1947', *Modern Asian Studies* 36 (2002), 657–704; *idem*, 'The Farther Shores of Partition: Ethnic Cleansing in Rajasthan 1947', *Past and Present* 160 (August 1998), 203–39; Yasmin Khan, *The Great Partition: The Making of India and Pakistan* (New Haven: Yale University Press, 2007), 130–1, 135–6.

[28] Paul Brass, 'The Partition of India and Retributive Genocide in the Punjab, 1946–1947: Means, Methods, and Purpose', *Journal of Genocide Research* 5 (2003), 82–3; and Khan, *Great Partition*, 159.

[29] On the case for intentional ethnic cleansing see Ilan Pappe, *The Ethnic Cleansing of Palestine* (Oxford: Oneworld Publications, 2006). For the most influential historian of the subject see Benny Morris, *The Birth of the Palestinian Refugee Problem Revisited*, 2nd edn (Cambridge: Cambridge University Press, 2004).

[30] On the Haganah offensives see Meron Benvenisti, *Sacred Landscape: The Buried History of the Holy Land since 1948*, trans. Maxine Kaufman-Lacosta (Berkeley, 2000), 117–18.

[31] On the debate over partition theory see Nicholas Sambanis, 'Partition as a Solution to Ethnic War: An Empirical Critique of the Theoretical Literature', *World Politics* 52 (2000), 437–83.

Finding boundaries in regions with mixed religious or ethnic groups has led to violence, but the search for solutions to persistent ethnic and / or religious conflict has also yielded the idea of separating hostile groups from one another. Whereas genocide has generally only been supported by perpetrators and their close allies, ethnic cleansing and closely related forms of population politics, especially organized population transfers or exchanges, have also been seen as useful means for resolving conflict.

Forced migration, including ethnic cleansing and related forms of coerced migration, emerged during the twentieth century as one of the chief solutions to persistent ethnic and religious tension and conflict. Such cleansing was not necessarily the first choice, but by the twentieth century it emerged as a widely used method for restructuring the ethnic and religious map in mixed borderlands in Europe and Western Asia. Between the First and Second World Wars democracies as well as dictatorships displayed growing interest in population transfers as a possible cure to salvage the nation-state. Thus, Czech President Eduard Benes, the last democratically elected leader in Central and Eastern Europe in the 1930s, considered population transfers as a way of reducing his country's German population, though only after years of Nazi manipulation of the Sudeten question.[32] The Great Powers also supported or at least tolerated forced migration as a means for removing the potential instability created by the presence of minority populations.[33] Democracies approved of the large population transfers in Central and Eastern Europe at the end of the Second World War. Meeting at Potsdam in the summer of 1945, Britain and the United States along with the Soviet Union agreed to the forced migration of most Germans residing outside the new boundaries of Germany. Churchill described himself as resisting the most sweeping demands for transfer of 8 or 9 million Germans, but still accepted the basic premise of mass population transfer. In 1944, he notably told the House of Commons, 'Expulsion is the method which, in so far as we have been able to see, will be the most satisfactory and lasting. There will be no mixture of populations to cause endless trouble . . . A clean sweep will be made.' In 1945, at Postdam he voiced reservations about moving eight or nine million Germans, but still spoke of accepting 'transfer' of 2–3 million Germans.[34] By this time, interest in ethnic cleansing crossed different types of states, political

---

[32] Detlef Brandes, *Der Weg zur Vertreibung, 1938–1945: Pläne und Entscheidungen zum 'Transfer' der Deutschen aus der Tschechoslowakie und aus Polen* (Munich: R. Oldenbourg, 2001), 5–6.

[33] Donald Bloxham, 'The Great Unweaving: The Removal of Peoples in Europe, 1875–1949', in Richard Bessel and Claudia Haake (eds), *The Removing of Peoples in the Modern World* (Oxford: Oxford University Press, 2008).

[34] Winston Churchill, *Triumph and Tragedy* (Boston: Houghton Mifflin, 1953), 658. For an account that stresses Churchill's doubts, see Alfred M. de Zayas, *Nemesis at Potsdam: The Anglo-Americans and the Expulsion of the Germans: Background, Execution, Consequences* (London: Routledge and Kegan Paul, 1977), 81–7.

systems, and ideologies. In Poland and Czechoslovakia groups with widely varied political views wanted Germans gone.[35]

Faced with the similar dilemma of creating nation-states in ethnically and religiously mixed regions, varied governments and political movements arrived at similar conclusions on the need to move entire peoples or at least large percentages of inconveniently placed ethnic or religious groups. Some embraced cleansing as a positive ideal; undemocratic states carried out the most violent ethnic cleansing. Ethnic cleansing was also likely to take place in new states and in the early phases of democratization.[36] There was then real disagreement about means and methods and about whether to move populations as a first or last option, but not about the usefulness of forcibly moving peoples across state boundaries.

International opinion began to turn against separating populations just as ethnic cleansing gained unprecedented attention with the breakup of Yugoslavia in the 1990s. The concept of 'ethnic partition' did not vanish in discussion of responses to nationalist conflict, but Yugoslavia's breakup brought both ethnic cleansing and increasing resistance to the very goals of forced migration of particular ethnic or religious groups.[37] International efforts to curb violence often proved inadequate with tragic consequences as at Srebrenica.[38] But the Dayton Peace Accords that ended hostilities in Bosnia-Herzegovina in 1995 represented a major move against the principles of ethnic cleansing consensus. It is easy to overlook the importance of what seems to be one of the most obvious elements of Dayton: the insistence on a right of return. The Dayton Peace Accords asserted, 'All refugees and displaced persons have the right freely to return to their homes of origin.' This was not always the norm after previous waves of forced migration. In the case of Israel the United Nations in 1949 in Resolution 194 called for the return of those refugees who wished to 'live at peace with their neighbours'. But with limited exceptions the Greek-Turkish population exchange of 1923 was compulsory, and in similar fashion, the Potsdam Protocol of 1945 saw the transfer of Germans as a necessity. Dayton, in contrast, sought to preserve the principle of a mixed society.

Ethnic cleansing after Bosnia faced more condemnation than ever before, but as genocide shows mere condemnation does not make mass violence impossible.

---

[35] Sebastian Siebel-Achenbach, *Lower Silesia from Nazi Germany to Communist Poland, 1942–1949* (New York: St Martin's Press, 1994), 33, 50; T. David Curp, *A Clean Sweep?: The Politics of Ethnic Cleansing in Western Poland, 1945–1949* (Rochester: University of Rochester Press, 2006); and Emilia Hrabovec, *Vertreibung and Abschub: Deutsche in Mähren 1945–1947* (Frankfurt am Main: Peter Lang, 1995), 41, 43.

[36] Mann, *Dark Side of Democracy*, 4.

[37] On 'ethnic partition,' see Jack L. Snyder, *From Voting to Violence: Democratization and Nationalist Conflict* (New York: Norton, 2000), 325.

[38] David Rohde, *Endgame: The Betrayal and Fall of Srebrenica, Europe's Worst Massacre since World War II* (New York, 1997).

Ethnic cleansing is deeply rooted in key developments of modernity: the rise of nations, the effort to categorize and define identities, the pursuit of purity, and both the power of governments and the emergence of mass politics. As such it may be a crime with both a past and a future.

SELECT BIBLIOGRAPHY

Bell-Fialkoff, Andrew, *Ethnic Cleansing* (New York: St Martin's Griffin, 1996).

Carnegie Endowment for International Peace, *The Other Balkan Wars: A 1913 Carnegie Endowment Inquiry in Retrospect*, with a new Introduction and Reflections on the Present Conflict by George F. Kennan (Washington, DC: Carnegie Endowment, 1993).

Carmichael, Cathie, *Ethnic Cleansing in the Balkans: Nationalism and the Destruction of Tradition* (London: Routledge, 2002).

Gutman, Roy, *A Witness to Genocide: The 1993 Pulitzer Prize-Winning Dispatches on the 'Ethnic Cleansing' of Bosnia* (New York: Macmillan, 1993).

Lieberman, Benjamin, *Terrible Fate: Ethnic Cleansing in the Making of Modern Europe* (Chicago: Ivan R. Dee, 2006).

Mann, Michael, *The Dark Side of Democracy: Explaining Ethnic Cleansing* (Cambridge: Cambridge University Press, 2005).

Naimark, Norman, *Fires of Hatred: Ethnic Cleansing in Twentieth-Century Europe* (Cambridge, MA: Harvard University Press, 2001).

Ther, Philipp, and Ana Siljak (eds), *Redrawing Nations: Ethnic Cleansing in East-Central Europe, 1944–1948* (Lanham, MD: Rowman and Littlefield, 2001).

Várdy, Steven Béla, and T. Hunt Tooley, (eds), *Ethnic Cleansing in Twentieth Century Europe* (Boulder: Social Science Monographs, 2003).

CHAPTER 3

....

GENDER AND GENOCIDE

....

ELISA VON JOEDEN-FORGEY

THE subject of gender in genocide is a relatively new research interest and still remains peripheral to the field of genocide studies as a whole. While most comprehensive treatments of genocide do not take gender seriously into consideration, significant new contributions by scholars such as Adam Jones and R. Charli Carpenter are changing this state of affairs.[1] Because genocide is a crime against groups, in which individuals are targeted due to their group membership, the assumption has long been that sex differentiation among the victims is of minor importance to the process as a whole. The genocides in Bosnia-Herzegovina and in Rwanda in the early 1990s, however, made clear the importance of gender constructs in genocide. Here the widespread and systematic rape of women and sexual exploitation of men, as well as the obvious use of gendered patterns of attack, were explicit parts of the perpetrators' genocidal strategies. Thus began a new moment in the study of genocide, one that has the potential to offer powerful tools for the prediction, prevention, and prosecution of genocide.

---

[1] R. Charli Carpenter, *Born of War: Protecting Children Sexual Violence Survivors in Conflict Zones* (Bloomfield, CT: Kumarian Press, 2007); 'Surfacing Children: Limitations of Genocidal Rape Discourse', *Human Rights Quarterly* 22:2 (2000), 428–77; 'Forced Maternity, Children's Rights, and the Genocide Convention', *Journal of Genocide Research* 2:2 (2000), 213–44; Adam Jones (ed.), *Gendercide and Genocide* (Nashville: Vanderbilt University Press, 2004); *Genocide: A Comprehensive Introduction* (London/New York: Routledge, 2006). See also Jones' Gendercide Watch website: http://www.gendercide.org

In this chapter I set out to demonstrate that a consideration of gender is crucial to our understanding of the crime, because genocide is an historical process that is, at its core, about group reproduction. As Helen Fein pointed out in a seminal essay on the subject, '[r]eproduction serves to continue the group; genocide to destroy it. Thus, perpetrators must either annul reproduction within the group or appropriate the progeny in order to destroy the group in the long run.'[2] While the perpetrators' ultimate aim is the material destruction of the target group, the means used to achieve this end tend to target men and women according to their perceived and actual positions within the reproductive process. Genocides are therefore characterized by highly symbolic and ritualized dramatizations of the perpetrator's obsession with demonstrating his or her destructive power over the target group's very life force. As part of the killing, then, one finds in all genocides a shared set of tortures involving generative symbols and institutions (reproductive organs, infants and small children, and the bonds that promote family coherence). In many cases, these symbols can be destroyed in ways that do not require the wholesale physical killing of all members of a group. In fact, it appears that the 'total' genocides, such as the Holocaust and Rwanda, are the exceptions; the norm is rather the sex-selective killing of specific members of a group combined with a host of strategies aimed at destroying the group's ability to survive into the future.

I will engage 'gender' as both a marker of biological sex and as a set of cultural practices and beliefs aimed at organizing relations of power between the sexes. Accordingly, I will treat gender as both 'a constitutive element of social relationships based on the perceived differences between the sexes' and 'a primary way of signifying relationships of power'.[3] Considering the experiences of men and women simultaneously can help us see genocide as a process that combines many different means of destruction in order permanently to undermine the future of a group. Although direct killing is a central part of the genocidal process, it is not the whole story. Studying gender in genocide can help identify frequently overlooked long-term causes of genocide as well as key problems faced by societies as they seek to rebuild in the wake of genocide.

MAKING GENDER VISIBLE

The study of gender in genocide opens up a new realm for the analytical discussion of genocide—the so-called 'private sphere', what Zainab Salbi, the founder of

---

[2] Helen Fein, 'Genocide and Gender: The Uses of Women and Group Destiny', *Journal of Genocide Research* 1:1 (1999), 43.

[3] Joan Wallach Scott, *Gender and the Politics of History* (New York: Columbia University Press, 1988), 42.

Women for Women International, calls the 'backline discussion'.[4] She points out that war and peace are usually understood solely according to the largely male 'frontline discussion' involving soldiers and politicians. But life is also, and perhaps primarily, lived in the 'backline discussion' of feeding families, raising children, and nurturing strong community bonds—things which, it must be said, are not exclusive to women. Genocide, like war, cannot be properly addressed without a serious and sustained investigation of the 'backline discussion' and the ways in which it influences the lead-up to genocide, the perpetration of genocide, and the search for justice and social healing after genocide. Indeed, the place of ordinary life is the primary focus of genocidal violence.

The foundation for an investigation of the 'backline discussion' was laid by women scholars of the Holocaust, who in the 1980s began to research the experiences of women survivors. Until then Holocaust research had reflected the gendered assumptions of historical scholarship wherein the history of men stood in for the history of humankind. Women's experiences were considered to be derivative of and ancillary to men's, and consequently of little importance to history. It was the testimony of male survivors that came to comprise the literary and historical canon of the Holocaust, despite the fact that women were a majority in the Jewish population of Europe before World War II.[5] Indeed, women wrote the majority of memoirs and testimonials in the first years after 1945,[6] despite having a lower survival rate overall.[7]

The importance of women to a full understanding of the Holocaust was recognized during the genocide itself by the noted Polish-Jewish historian Emmanuel Ringelblum, who studied Jewish women and mothers in the Warsaw ghetto while he too was incarcerated there with his family.[8] But it was not until feminist scholars began to investigate the lives of women in the Holocaust in the 1980s that gendered differences in experience began to be recognized.[9] Most scholars now accept that, in

---

[4] 'A Woman among Warlords: Interview with Zainab Salbi', *Wide Angle*, August 31, 2007, Daljit Dhaliwal, http://www-tc.pbs.org/wnet/wideangle/shows/warlords/interview/interview.pdf

[5] Raul Hilberg, *Perpetrators, Victims, Bystanders: The Jewish Catastrophe, 1933–1945* (New York: Harper Perennial, 1993), 127.

[6] Judith Tydor Baumel, *Double Jeopardy: Gender and the Holocaust* (London/Portland, OR: Vallentine Mitchell, 1998), 41.

[7] Hilberg, *Perpetrators*, 127, 130.

[8] Baumel, *Double Jeopardy*, 40.

[9] Lisa Pine, 'Gender and the Family', in Dan Stone (ed.), *Historiography of the Holocaust* (New York: Palgrave Macmillan, 2004), 364–82; Elizabeth R. Baer and Myrna Goldenberg (eds), *Experience and Expression: Women, the Nazis, and the Holocaust* (Detroit: Wayne State University Press, 2003); Atina Grossmann, 'Women and the Holocaust: Four Recent Titles', *Holocaust and Genocide Studies* 16:1 (Spring 2002), 94–108; Esther Fuchs (ed.), *Women and the Holocaust: Narrative and Representation* (Lanham, MD: University Press of America, 1999); Dalia Ofer and Lenore J. Weitzman (eds), *Women in the Holocaust* (New Haven, CT: Yale University Press, 1998); John Roth and Carol Rittner (eds), *Different Voices: Women and the Holocaust* (New York: Paragon House, 1993); Renate Bridenthal et al. (eds), *When Biology Became Destiny: Women in Weimar and Nazi Germany* (New York: Monthly Review Press, 1984).

Raul Hilberg's words, 'the road to annihilation was marked by events that specifically affected men as men and women as women.'[10]

The pioneering first two decades of work on women and the Holocaust focused on the ways that gender affected Jewish experiences under Nazi domination, and was strongly informed by the cultural feminist framework of the time. Cultural feminism tended to essentialize gender difference, celebrating women's 'special sphere' rather than investigating how gender categories and norms intersect with race, nationality, class to form identity and experience, as more recent treatments have begun to do. The cultural feminist analysis of the Holocaust was criticized for appearing to argue that women were *more* victimized than men because of their 'double burden' as Jews *and* as women (the assumption being that men carried 'merely' a single burden). It could also appear to ignore the sufferings of men by casting them as aggressors. And, in celebrating women's supposedly unique abilities to find coping mechanisms in times of crisis, an assertion that many women Holocaust survivors themselves made, cultural feminism at times suggested that women somehow transcended the horrors of the camp experience.[11]

Critics of the cultural feminist model worried further that the focus on sexism was overshadowing the core element of Nazi policy, which was its racist anti-Semitism. Cynthia Ozick remarked in a letter to Joan Ringelheim, '[t]he Holocaust happened to victims who were not seen as men, women, or children, but as Jews.'[12] Other scholars, such as Anna Hardman and Zoë Waxman, protested that cultural feminism ignored the variety and diversity of women's lives as well as the moments of antagonism and division between female victims.[13] Pascale Rachel Bos has argued that many of the gender differences that have been attributed to people's actual experiences are in fact differences in the way men and women construct memory.[14] Finally, Lawrence Langer has voiced scepticism about gender as an important variable in the context of the unspeakable suffering brought about by the Holocaust.[15]

What is clear from the research is that gender directly influenced people's experience of Nazi persecution at various moments within the overall pattern of destruction. Gender norms shaped how Jews in Germany and elsewhere responded to the Nazi threat.[16] Gender also shaped the specific nature of people's

---

[10] Hilberg, *Perpetrators*, 126.

[11] Joan Ringelheim, 'Women and the Holocaust: A Reconsideration of Research', in Roth and Rittner (eds), *Different Voices*, 387.

[12] Quoted in Baer and Goldenberg, *Experience and Expression*, xxviii.

[13] Pine, 'Gender and the Family', 372.

[14] Pascale Rachel Bos, 'Women and the Holocaust: Analyzing Gender Difference', in Baer and Goldenberg (eds), *Experience and Expression*, 23–52.

[15] Lawrence L. Langer, 'Gendered Suffering? Women in Holocaust Testimonies', in Dalia Ofer and Lenore J. Weitzman (eds), *Women in the Holocaust* (New Haven, CT: Yale University Press, 1998), 355.

[16] Pine, 'Gender and the Family'; Baumel, *Double Jeopardy*, 15.

vulnerabilities, which were, in significant respects, different for Jewish men and women. For example, rape and sexual exploitation are major themes in the memoirs written by women survivors but are barely mentioned by men. Myrna Goldenberg has well documented how women and girls faced the threat of sexual exploitation at every step of the process of destruction.[17] Although the Nazis imposed strict laws against 'race mixing', Jewish women were sometimes raped by German soldiers and SS men. They were raped in the camps by guards and sometimes by other inmates as well.[18] Girls who were placed into hiding also faced possible exploitation from their care givers.[19] The historian Nechama Tec found cases of Jewish women partisans who were sexually exploited and also raped by their comrades.[20] After liberation, women faced the additional threat of being raped by Soviet soldiers.[21] The very real threat of sexual exploitation that Jewish women faced from a variety of men alters the dominant image of the Holocaust as a 'closed' historical event by demonstrating the multiple trajectories of violence that coalesce in genocide and later feed back into post-genocide societies.

Apart from defining key differences in the way that men and women experienced persecution, feminist study of the Holocaust has shown that in both ideology and practice National Socialism was an expression of misogyny as well as racism.[22] When the Nazis targeted Jewish women, they often did so in specific ways based on women's deep symbolic association with life-giving powers, a theme that runs through the testimonials written by women survivors. Killing women, especially pregnant women, was a microcosm of genocide for Nazi murderers, since it allowed them to attack directly Jews' spiritual and biological future. Thus, women were killed at much higher rates than men upon arrival in the death camps.[23] In these camps pregnancy was treated with particular cruelty in accord with its potent symbolism. The SS appear to have reserved special tortures for pregnant women who were—in the case of Auschwitz—beaten 'with clubs and whips, torn by dogs, dragged around by the hair and kicked in the stomach with heavy German boots. Then, when they collapsed, they were thrown into the

---

[17] Myrna Goldenberg, 'Lessons Learned from Gentle Heroism: Women's Holocaust Narratives', *Annals of the American Academy of Political and Social Science* 548 (November 1996), 78–93.

[18] Olga Lengyel, *Five Chimneys: A Woman Survivor's True Story of Auschwitz* (Chicago: Academy Chicago, 1995), 199.

[19] Joan Ringelheim, 'Genocide and Gender: A Split Memory', in Ronit Lentin (ed.), *Gender and Catastrophe* (London/New York: Zed Books, 1997), 26–8.

[20] Nechama Tec, 'The Fate of Women', in *Defiance: The Bielski Partisans* (New York/London: Oxford University Press, 1994), 154–69.

[21] Isabella Leitner, 'Book Two: Liberation', *Isabella: From Auschwitz to Freedom* (New York/London: Anchor Books, 1994), esp. 89–91, 108–11.

[22] The classic studies of Nazi misogyny are Gisela Bock, *Zwangssterilisation im Nationalsozialismus: Studien zur Rassenpolitik und Frauenpolitik* (Opladen: Westdeutscher Verlag, 1986), and Claudia Koonz, *Mothers in the Fatherland: Women, the Family, and Nazi Politics* (New York: St Martin's, 1986).

[23] Hilberg, *Perpetrators*, 130.

crematory—alive.'[24] Women who gave birth in the camps were usually murdered immediately along with their infants. If the pregnancy and birth escaped the attention of the guards, other inmates were forced to kill the babies if they wished to save the mother.[25] Pregnant women caught up in *Einsatzgruppen* actions may have elicited particularly sadistic treatment from their killers as well.[26]

In addition to demonstrating the importance of misogyny to genocidal ideology, the study of gender and genocide also sheds light on the ways that perpetrators instrumentalize gender in the killing process. Even in what have been called 'gender neutral' genocides, such as the Holocaust and Cambodia, perpetrators treat the sexes differently, though not in ways that significantly affect overall survival rates.[27] In a careful study of gender and the Holocaust in Veszprém, Hungary, Tim Cole shows that while Jewish men aged 18 to 48 were much more likely to die as forced labourers before deportations to the death camps began, by 1944 many of them were able to avoid deportations, and almost certain death, precisely because of their labour power.[28] Most of the Jews deported were women, children, and the elderly. According to Raul Hilberg, men in general died much more quickly than women in the early phases of the Nazi occupation of Eastern Europe. This was largely because gender norms facilitated the treatment of civilian men as enemy combatants, providing a cover for their detention, forced labour, and massacre.[29] Men died at much higher rates in the ghettos, in part because of the hard labour they were forced to do.[30] Men may also have felt the responsibility to give up rations to their families or they may have succumbed more quickly to the ravages of malnourishment and starvation due to their body's faster metabolism in comparison with women.[31] Men also tended to 'die first' in the massacres committed by mobile killing squads in Poland, Russia, and Serbia because it was easier for soldiers and police reservists to rationalize and justify the killing of men, whom they identified as security threats.[32] Even Heinrich Himmler, who clearly had no qualms about killing Jewish men, needed an additional rationalization for killing Jewish women and children.[33]

[24] Gisela Perl, *I Was a Doctor in Auschwitz* (Salem, NH: Ayer, 1984), 80. Quoted from Goldenberg, 'Lessons Learned', 86.

[25] Ibid. 86.

[26] Raul Hilberg, *The Destruction of the European Jews* (New York: Holmes and Meier, 1985), 146.

[27] Fein, 'Genocide and Gender', 43–63.

[28] Tim Cole, 'A Gendered Holocaust? The Experiences of "Jewish" Men and Women in Hungary, 1944', in Randolph L. Braham and Brewster S. Chamberlin (eds), *The Holocaust in Hungary: Sixty Years Later* (New York: Columbia University Press, 2006), 54.

[29] Hilberg, *Perpetrators*, 128. He notes that there was a 'reversal of fortunes' after the development of the gas vans and the death camps, which made killing women and children psychologically less taxing on the killers.

[30] Ibid. Hilberg notes that many women were also forced to do hard labour, though perhaps in smaller numbers. See also Nechama Tec, *Resilience and Courage: Women, Men, and the Holocaust* (New Haven, CT: Yale University Press, 2003), 11.

[31] This latter possibility was suggested by Bos in 'Women and the Holocaust', 34.

[32] Hilberg, *Perpetrators*, 129.

[33] Roth, 'Equality, Neutrality, Particularity', 11.

ADDING MEN

The focus on men's gendered experience during genocide is very new. Up until recently, gender studies were preoccupied primarily with the lives of women, leaving men within the original framework of universal subjecthood and thereby unintentionally reaffirming the assumption of the gender-neutrality of men's lives. Among historians and other genocide scholars the initial focus on women can be explained very simply by the fact that gender studies were embraced by women scholars far earlier than by men. These scholars were interested in including women in historical narratives that had largely excluded them. It is therefore hard to argue, as some have, that men have been discriminatorily excluded from feminist scholarship on genocide.

The exclusion of male victims from international humanitarian attention is a different story. Rather than a product of feminism, however, this exclusion is the result of those patriarchal norms in international affairs that treat the term civilian as coterminous with 'women and children'.[34] These same patriarchal norms have ascribed to women a more peaceful nature, a theory that has had a measurable impact on scholarship on gender and violence. These two related beliefs—that women are by nature peaceful and that male victims are combatants—has exercised a direct, though often subtle, influence on the ways that observers measure atrocities. Attacks on women and children frequently appear to generate greater outrage than attacks on men, largely because attacks on men can be so easily explained away with reference to their supposed 'battle age'. Although public outrage at atrocities against women and children is usually short-lived (it has rarely translated itself into gender-sensitive priorities in war crimes tribunals or gender-sensitive economic development efforts in postgenocidal societies), it is nevertheless significant inasmuch as it can serve to bring a particular conflict to the forefront of international media attention. Alternately, génocidaires can use patriarchal traditions in international law semantically to hide their crimes behind putative counterinsurgency efforts, as the Government of Sudan has done in Darfur. The role played by gender constructs in genocide denial strategies is a subject that has yet to be researched.

Recognition that civilian men are primary targets of genocide is therefore crucial to any attempt to fashion an early warning system and end the impunity with which génocidaires have committed mass murder up to the present day. Adam Jones has shown that a policy of killing men first constitutes a 'tripwire or harbinger of fuller-scale root-and-branch genocides', an insight that should be

---

[34] R. Charli Carpenter, 'Innocent Women and Children': Gender, Norms and the Protection of Civilians (Burlington, VT: Ashgate, 2006).

very useful to an early warning system.[35] We have already discussed this pattern in the Holocaust. Jones notes that this pattern is also evident to varying degrees in the Armenian genocide, the genocides in Bosnia and Rwanda, in Kosovo, and in East Timor. In these cases men were killed first to radicalize the killers and habituate them to attacks on women and children. Sex-selective massacre may also be a means of 'decapitating' the family basis of the religious and social structure, much as the targeting of intellectuals is aimed at decapitating the institutional basis of the public life of a group. The massacre of 'battle-aged' men can be used to expose and render vulnerable the rest of the population.

For Jones, these sex-selective massacres, in addition to being harbingers of root-and-branch genocides, are also instances of 'gendercide'. Expanding upon the works of feminist writers, Jones defines gendercide as 'gender-selective mass killing' and argues that gendercide in and of itself is a form of genocide.[36] The term gendercide was first used by Mary Ann Warren, whose 1985 book of the same title examined instances in which women and girls were the targets.[37] Jones' work on gendercide seeks to bring to our attention the myriad ways in which men and boys are also vulnerable to sex-selective violence. His interventions have been a necessary reminder of the extent to which *civilian* men have been victims of mass murder throughout history.

There has been substantial debate about whether gendercide is itself a genocidal process. In Jones' edited volume *Gendercide and Genocide*, Stuart Stein and R. Charli Carpenter argue that gendercide is not genocide because it is not committed with the intent to destroy in whole or in part all members of a sex, as such.[38] The central question seems to be about the claims one would make about gendercide—is it a specific act within an ongoing genocide or is it a specific sort of violence unto itself that can be at times either genocidal in nature or used as a tool for genocide? Whatever one decides about gendercide as genocide, it seems clear that sex-selective killing can be an early warning sign of genocide as well as an act punishable by the Genocide Convention.

Two recent international court rulings on the Srebrenica massacre, where in July 1995 over 8,000 Bosnian Muslim men and boys were killed by Bosnian Serb forces under the command of the indicted Gen. Radko Mladic, support the notion of gendercide as genocide, though only in the limited sense that the gendercidal massacre at Srebrenica was embedded in a wider ethnic conflict. The International

[35] Adam Jones, 'Gendercide and Genocide', in Adam Jones (ed.), *Gendercide and Genocide* (Nashville, TN: Vanderbildt University Press, 2004), 23.

[36] For an overview of the concept of 'gendercide', see Jones, 'Gendercide and Genocide', 1–38. See also his Gendercide Watch website: http://www.gendercide.org.

[37] Mary Anne Warren, *Gendercide: The Implications of Sex Selection* (Totowa, NJ: Rowman and Allanheld, 1985).

[38] Stuart Stein, 'Geno and Other Cides: A Cautionary Note on Knowledge Accumulation', in Jones (ed.), *Gendercide and Genocide*, 196–229; R. Charli Carpenter, 'Beyond "Gendercide": Operationalizing Gender in Comparative Genocide Studies', in Jones (ed.), *Gendercide and Genocide*, 230–56. See also Jones' response, 'Problems of Gendercide: A Response to Stein and Carpenter', in *Gendercide and Genocide*, 257–71.

Criminal Tribunal for the Former Yugoslavia (ICTY) ruled in 2004 that the Srebrenica massacre was genocide, a ruling upheld by the International Court of Justice (ICJ) in 2007.[39] The presiding judge of the ICTY reasoned that Serb actions in Srebrenica constituted genocide for the following reasons: there was ample evidence of intent to destroy the Bosnian Muslim group in Srebrenica, the men and boys constituted a 'substantial part' of the group, and they were 'emblematic' of the group as a whole.[40] Significant in this finding is the concept of emblematic victims, which raises the importance of understanding gender constructs when making determinations of genocide. The judgment noted:

In addition to the numeric size of the targeted portion [of the group], its prominence within the group can be a useful consideration. If a specific part of the group is emblematic of the overall group, or is essential to its survival, that may support a finding that the part qualifies as substantial within the meaning of Article 4 [of the ICTY Statute].[41]

The court found that in a patriarchal society, the loss of 8,000 men within an immediate population of 40,000 would seriously hinder the future procreation of the group, potentially leading to its destruction.[42]

GENOCIDAL RAPE

When Serbia started its war with Bosnia in 1992 one of the major news stories coming out of the region was the systematic use of rape by the Serb forces to enforce a policy of 'ethnic cleansing', as it was then routinely called. The journalist Roy Gutman's articles in *Newsday* brought international attention to the mass rape of women during the war.[43] This was not the first time that newspapers focused on the brutality of rape during wartime, but it was the first time that women around the world were successful in organizing an international movement to have rape explicitly recognized and prosecuted as a war crime, a crime against humanity, and a crime of genocide.[44] The massive international effort to bring this about began

[39] ICTY, Prosecutor v. Krstić, 19 April 2004, www.un.org/icty/krstic/Appeal/judgement/index.htm; ICJ, Press Release, 26 February 2007.

[40] ICTY, Prosecutor v. Krstić, Parts II.A & II.B. See also ICTY, Press Release, 'Address by ICTY President Theodor Meron, at Potocari Memorial Cemetery', The Hague, 23 June 2004, http://www.un.org/icty/pressreal/2004/p860-e.htm

[41] ICTY, Prosecutor v. Krstić, 8.

[42] Ibid. 14.

[43] Roy Gutman, *A Witness to Genocide* (New York: Macmillan, 1993).

[44] Louise Chappell, 'Gender Mainstreaming in International Institutions: Developments at the UN Ad Hoc Tribunals and the International Criminal Court', *Paper Presented at the Annual Meeting of the*

with a ground-breaking article by Catherine MacKinnon, who argued early on in the war that rape was being used by Serb forces as a tool of genocide.[45] Her article was followed by books by Alexandra Sitglmayer (1994) and Beverly Allen (1996), each of which called attention to the particularly genocidal role that rape was playing in the violence.

It is estimated that between 20,000 and 50,000 women and girls were raped during the wars in the former Yugoslavia between 1991 and 1995. 'While all sides in the Bosnian conflict have committed rapes,' notes Joana Daniel-Wrabetz, 'Serbian forces appear to have used rape on the largest scale, principally against Muslim women.'[46] Usually rape was accompanied by various tortures, including branding with the Serbian cross, burning, slashing, beating, and threats of death against the women and their family members, especially their children. Rape frequently was used as a means of murder, but also served a policy of forced maternity to create more 'Serbian' children. Women's bodies were used to humiliate families and communities as the perpetrators raped girls in front of their parents or forced family members to rape each other.

Rape in Rwanda shared with rape in Bosnia these genocidal qualities, though here it was much more widespread and usually used as a means of murder. The estimates of the number of women raped reaches to 500,000, few of whom were allowed to survive.[47] While perpetrators used rape in this case primarily as part of a terrifying and drawn-out ritual of killing, some Tutsi women were also subjected to forced maternity under the logic that they would bear Hutu children, demonstrating the multiple and self-contradictory levels on which perpetrators pursue the destruction of the target group's reproductive powers.[48] Thousands of women survivors were rendered permanently disabled from the brutality of the rapes, many having been left incapable of bearing children. Furthermore, many assailants seem to have

International Studies Association, Hilton Hawaiian Village, Honolulu, Hawaii, 5 March 2005; Marsha Freeman, 'International Institutions and Gendered Justice', *Journal of International Affairs* 52:2 (1999), 513; Kelly Dawn Askin, 'Prosecuting Wartime Rape and Other Gender-Related Crimes under International Law: Extraordinary Advances, Enduring Obstacles', *Berkeley Journal of International Law* 21:2 (2003), 317.

[45] Catherine A. MacKinnon, 'Turning Rape into Pornography: Postmodern Genocide', *MS* 5 (July/August 1993), 24–30. MacKinnon's article was later published in Alexandra Stiglmayer (ed.), *Mass Rape: The War against Women in Bosnia-Herzegovina* (Lincoln/London: University of Nebraska Press, 1994), 74–81.

[46] Siobhan K. Fisher, 'Occupation of the Womb: Forced Impregnation as Genocide', *Duke Law Journal* 46:1 (1996), 109; Joana Daniel-Wrabitz, 'Children Born of War Rape in Bosnia-Herzegovina and the Convention on the Rights of the Child', in Carpenter (ed.), *Born of War*, 23.

[47] SURF-Survivor's Fund, 'Statistics of the Genocide', http://www.survivors-fund.org.uk/resources/history/statistics.php

[48] Human Rights Watch, *Shattered Lives: Sexual Violence during the Rwandan Genocide and its Aftermath* (New York: HRW, 1996); Jones, 'Gender and Genocide in Rwanda', in Jones (ed.), *Gendercide and Genocide*, 98–137; Marie Consolee Mukangendo, 'Caring for Children Born of Rape in Rwanda', in Carpenter (ed.), *Born of War*, 40–52.

knowingly infected raped women with HIV, thereby ensuring their eventual and untimely deaths even if they were to survive the genocide.[49]

In the face of heavy media attention on the use of rape in both the Bosnian and the Rwandan genocides, questions were raised about the best way to characterize these rapes. The controversy has revolved around the question of whether to conceptualize 'genocidal rape' as a special category of rape. Catherine MacKinnon sparked this debate when she argued that

rapes in the Serbian war of aggression against Bosnia-Herzegovina and Croatia are to everyday rape what the Holocaust was to everyday anti-Semitism: both like it and not like it at all, both continuous with it and a whole new departure, a unique atrocity yet also a pinnacle moment in something that goes on all the time.[50]

Several feminists have voiced concern about the high-profile public attention that has been focused on 'genocidal rape'. Rhonda Copelon has argued that '[t]he elision of genocide and rape in the focus on "genocidal rape" of Muslim women in Bosnia is ... dangerous,' because 'to emphasize as unparalleled the horror of genocidal rape is factually dubious and risks rendering the rape invisible once again.'[51] Susan Brownmiller also prefers not to treat rape in Bosnia as a special category of rape, commenting that 'Serbian land advances have been accomplished in the age-old manner of territorial aggression, with looting, pillage, and gratuitous violence that gets lumped under the rubric of atrocity.'[52] In a slightly different vein, former Executive Director of Human Rights Watch Aryeh Neier criticized the focus on genocidal rape for elevating the crime of rape in and of itself to genocidal proportions; in his words, unless the rape is committed with the intent of forcing pregnancy, it is 'inappropriate to single out one element, rape, and assert that it, by itself, constituted genocide.'[53]

The case for rape as a crime of genocide was made most forcefully in the case of forced pregnancy and maternity. The international law scholar Siobhan Fisher characterized the Serbian policy of forced maternity as a genocidal 'occupation of the womb'.[54] Writing on the Armenian genocide, Donald Bloxham has similarly identified forced marriage and sexual slavery as the 'colonization of the female body'.[55] Such policies are genocidal because the purpose is to force women to give birth to children from the perpetrator's group, thereby preventing them from

---

[49] Mukangendo, 'Caring for Children Born of Rape', 45.

[50] MacKinnon, 'Turning Rape into Pornography', 74.

[51] Rhonda Copelon, 'Surfacing Gender: Reconceptualizing Crimes against Women in Time of War', in Stiglmayer (ed.), Mass Rape, 197.

[52] Susan Brownmiller, 'Making Female Bodies the Battlefield', in Stiglmayer (ed.), Mass Rape, 180.

[53] Aryeh Neier, War Crimes: Brutality, Genocide, Terror and the Struggle for Justice (New York: Times Books, 1998), 186. Quoted in Carpenter, 'Surfacing Children', 439.

[54] Fisher, 'Occupation of the Womb', 124.

[55] Donald Bloxham, 'Internal Colonization, Inter-Imperial Conflict and the Armenian Genocide', in A. Dirk Moses (ed.), Empire, Colony, Genocide: Conquest, Occupation, and Subaltern Resistance in World History (New York: Berghahn Books, 2008), 338.

carrying children from their own group.[56] Many rapists in Bosnia and Rwanda plainly stated this intent while committing the rapes. While such logic confounds modern genetic understanding, it conforms to the highly patriarchal understanding of reproduction in each society, where fathers determine the ethnic identity of children. Fisher therefore argues that forced maternity conforms to subsection II (b), (c), and (d) of the Genocide Convention: 'Causing serious bodily or mental harm to members of the group', 'Deliberately inflicting on the group conditions of life calculated to bring about its physical destruction in whole or in part', and 'Imposing measures intended to prevent births within the group'.

Decisions by the international tribunals set up for Bosnia and Rwanda, established in 1993 and 1994, respectively, have upheld much of the scholarly work on genocidal rape. Fisher's interpretation of forced maternity was confirmed by both the International Criminal Tribunal for Rwanda (ICTR) in Prosecutor v. Akayesu and the ICTY in the Karadzic and Mladic decisions.[57] In Prosecutor v. Akayesu, the ICTR further found that rape and sexual violence 'constitute genocide in the same way as any other act as long as they were committed with the specific intent to destroy, in whole or in part, a particular group, targeted as such.'[58] While the Statute of the International Criminal Court (ICC) does not list sexual violence or rape as specific elements of the crime of genocide, the ICTY and ICTR decisions have set important precedents for trying gender-based violence as genocide.[59]

RELATIONAL VIOLENCE

The debate about the status of rape in genocide and whether it itself is genocidal neglects to consider the wider 'relational' context of much gender-based violence.[60] Rape in genocide is frequently part of an elaborate and sustained ritual on the part of perpetrators in which they focus not only on killing, raping, and expelling living members of a group but also on the intensive targeting of symbols of the group's life force.[61] Recognizing the wide-ranging targets of genocidal violence, Dirk Moses

---

[56] Fisher, 'Occupation of the Womb', 93.

[57] Mark Ellis, 'Breaking the Silence: Rape as an International Crime', *Case Western Reserve Journal of International Law* 38 (2006/2007), 232–35.

[58] ICTR, Prosecutor v. Akayesu, Case No. IT-96–4-T, 731.

[59] Rape is specifically recognized as a crime of war and a crime against humanity. Ellis, 'Breaking the Silence', 240.

[60] Jones, 'Gender and Genocide', 25.

[61] Elisa von Joeden-Forgey, 'Devil in the Details: 'Life Force Atrocity' and the Assault on the Family in Times of *Conflict*', *Genocide Studies and Prevention* 5 (forthcoming 2010).

has recently called genocide 'a "total social practice" that [affects] all aspects of group life'.[62] In such a context, rape can indeed be a crime of genocide. During genocide, people are usually targeted in terms of their familial roles, that is, the roles the perpetrators perceive them to play in the reproductive process of the group. So women and girls are tortured specifically as mothers, daughters, and sisters; similarly men and boys are targeted as fathers, sons, and brothers. In such cases, rape usually involves both inversion rituals (forcing family members to watch or participate in the torture and murder of loved ones) and ritual desecrations of sacred symbols of the group's generative force (such as sexual organs, infants and small children, and family bonds).[63] Common practices across genocides include killing infants in front of their parents, forcing family members to rape one another, destroying women's reproductive capacity through rape and mutilation, castrating men, eviscerating pregnant women, and otherwise engaging in ritual cruelties aimed directly at the spiritually sacred, biologically generative, and emotionally nurturing structures of family life.

The Armenian genocide is a key example of this genocidal pattern. Over and over again, perpetrators followed a family-based pattern of destruction. When villages were attacked, men were murdered and their surviving family members were raped, expelled, and killed. Perpetrators frequently engaged in inversion rituals and ritual desecrations in the process.[64] As in other cases, rape during the Armenian genocide served many purposes: it was part of the process of eliticide, the destruction of a group's leadership in order to sow confusion; it publicly demonstrated the perpetrators' mastery over the Armenian life force; it inflicted 'total suffering' on both the men and the women (and, presumably, the boys and girls) who were tortured in two ways—through violent attacks on their own bodies and by having to witness the immense suffering of their loved ones; and it compromised the future integrity of the group by sowing the seeds of psychic and familial dissolution.

Few scholars have recognized the central importance of relational violence to genocide, or its terrifying efficacy, even though it is a consistent characteristic of survivor testimony. The absence of a 'relational framework' in genocide scholarship, to use Adam Jones' phrase,[65] has ensured that some of the crimes common to genocide have languished in scholarly and legal obscurity. Most often these genocidal 'life force' atrocities are categorized simply as 'rape' in the literature. So, for example, atrocities listed as instances of sexual violence by the US State

---

[62] A. Dirk Moses, 'Empire, Colony, Genocide: Keywords and the Philosophy of History', in Moses (ed.), *Empire, Colony, Genocide*, 13.

[63] Joeden-Forgey, 'Devil in the Details'.

[64] Katherine Derderian, 'Common Fate, Different Experience: Gender-Specific Aspects of the Armenian Genocide, 1915–1917', *Holocaust and Genocide Studies* 19:1 (Spring 2005), 5.

[65] Jones, 'Gender and Genocide', 25.

Department's Atrocities Documentation Team in Darfur have included the following acts:[66]

- The killing of young children;
- The use of infants as weapons against their parents;
- The slashing of pregnant women's bellies and the murder of their babies; and
- The mutilation of women's reproductive organs, including their breasts.

We see here that the acts that go recorded by governments and NGOs as 'rape'
involve many kinds of tortures that are not synonymous with sexual violence.

An example from the Democratic Republic of Congo (DRC) demonstrates the
way that genocidal rape is part of an elaborate set of relational rituals aimed at the
total devastation of the life force of families and communities. A survivor named
Nadine told the American playwright Eve Ensler in 2007 about an attack on her
village that resulted in her gang rape and sexual enslavement. The unidentified
soldiers killed the village chief and his children, her parents, and her brother after
he refused to rape her. They then killed each of her three children—'They flung my
baby's body on the ground like she was garbage.' Nadine was gang-raped and
suffered complete rupture of her vagina and anus. While enslaved by the soldiers,
she witnessed the evisceration of a pregnant woman, whose baby was cooked and
force-fed to Nadine and the other enslaved women.[67] Although Nadine's story is
framed by a magazine article about rape, the crimes and the victims far exceed the
word. Her case demonstrates how some instances of the current violence in the
DRC are clearly genocidal.

Focusing on relational violence and life force atrocities draws in many other
instances of gross violations of human rights that do not easily conform to the
common understanding of genocide. During the 1971 war in Bangladesh, for example,
many of the estimated 200,000 rapes were accompanied by relational violence similar
to that found in Bosnia, Rwanda, and the DRC, including the evisceration of pregnant
women and the mutilation of fetuses.[68] Other instances include the Japanese Army's
attack on Nanking in World War II, its 'comfort women' system, and the recent war in
Sierra Leone.[69] Some of the election-related violence in the Rift Valley region in Kenya

[66] Kelly Dawn Askin, 'Prosecuting Gender Crimes Committed in Darfur', in Samuel Totten and
Eric Markusen (eds), *Genocide in Darfur: Investigating the Atrocities in the Sudan* (New York:
Routledge, 2006), 146–8.

[67] Eve Ensler, 'Women Left for Dead—and the Man Who's Saving Them', *Glamour Magazine*,
http://www.glamour.com/news/articles/2007/08/reallifedrama

[68] Yasmin Saikia, 'Beyond the Archive of Silence: Narratives of Violence of the 1971 Liberation War
of Bangladesh', *History Workshop Journal* 58 (2004), 275–87.

[69] Masahiro Yamamoto, *Nanking: Anatomy of an Atrocity* (Westport, CT: Praeger, 2000); James Yin
and Shi Young, *The Rape of Nanking: An Undeniable History in Photographs* (Chicago: Innovative
Publishing Group, 1996); Iris Chang, *The Rape of Nanking: The Forgotten Holocaust of WWII* (New
York: Basic Books, 1997); Yuki Tanaka, *Japan's Comfort Women: Sexual Slavery and Prostitution during
World War II and the US Occupation* (New York: Routledge, 2002); Kelly Dawn Askin, 'Comfort

in 2008 also has shown a genocidal logic, especially as regards the treatment of children.[70] Each of these cases is marked by distinct patters of inversion rituals and desecrations of symbols of the life force.

Determining what relationship such cases have to our understanding of genocide will rely on how we understand perpetrator intent. In Nanking, Japanese Imperial Army soldiers may have seen the city's inhabitants as symbolic stand-ins for the Chinese people as a whole. In the case of the Imperial Army's sex slavery system, it may be that some Japanese soldiers were opportunistically acting out their subjective genocidal fantasies against the Korean, Chinese, and Philippine peoples through their torture, mutilation, and murder of young women in the dark anterooms of the rape camps. In Sierra Leone, by contrast, it appears that perpetrators saw civilians *as such* to be the group to be targeted with genocide, since there was no clear ethnic logic to the attacks though life force atrocities were widespread. And in the DRC, where many different militia groups are involved in committing genocidal atrocities, it may be that genocidal atrocities have become a habitus, an unforeseen long-term consequence of the world's mishandling of the Rwandan genocide.

GENOCIDAL MASCULINITIES

The widespread nature of sexual violence against women and men during many genocides indicates that genocide is a crime intimately connected to particular concepts of masculinity.[71] Though much research remains to be done before we can determine exactly how this is the case, it seems clear that the ideologies and practices associated with genocide are in large part the products of the historical experience of men and their attempts to make meaning from this experience. It is certainly true, as Adam Jones has suggested, that the field of masculinity studies has the potential to yield insights specifically into the long-term cultural

---

Women: Shifting Shame and Stigma from Victims to Victimizers', *International Criminal Law Review* 1 (2001), 5–32; *The Women's International War Crimes Tribunal 2000 for the Trial of Japanese Military Sexual Slavery, Summary of Findings*, 12 December 2000; Amnesty International, *Sierra Leone: Rape and other Sexual Crimes against Girls and Women* (New York: Amnesty International, 2000); Human Rights Watch, *Sowing Terror: Atrocities against Civilians in Sierra Leone* (New York: Human Rights Watch, 1998); Amnesty International, *Democratic Republic of Congo, Mass Rape: Time for Remedies* (New York: Amnesty International, 2004); Jan Goodwin, 'Silence=Rape', *The Nation*, 8 March 2008.

[70] Xan Rice, 'Murder of the Children who Sought Sanctuary in Church', *The Guardian*, 3 January 2008.

[71] Ronit Lentin, 'Introduction: (En)gendering Genocides', in Ronit Lentin (ed.), *Gender and Catastrophe* (London/New York: Zed Books, 1997), 7.

developments that facilitate genocide and the perpetrators' intentions and motivations.[72]

One area that would benefit from sustained scholarly attention is the relationship between war and the development of a specifically genocidal form of masculinity. Such 'genocidal masculinity' is characterized by a concept of power that is dependent upon the destruction of those institutions and groups that the perpetrators believe set limits upon and constitute threats to the full expression of their masculine identity. Since genocide is a crime intimately linked with war,[73] the ways that men make sense of war and seek to cope with it should shed light on political, social, and cultural processes that can hasten the development and spread of particularly violent forms of masculine identity. Promising work has been done on this front regarding veterans of World War I in interwar Germany, especially the noted writer Ernst Jünger, who called war the 'male form of procreation'.[74] Andreas Huyssen has linked interwar fascist gender constructs like Jünger's to soldiers' 'traumatic experience of emasculation' during the war.[75] In his view, interwar fascism was a means of 'remasculinizing' the self by rejecting the feminized civilian and peacetime world and insisting on the liberatory and elevating power of violence, a construct that took on genocidal dimensions within the Nazi party.

Another promising line of enquiry is the relationship between institutions of male domination and genocidal ideology. Christopher Taylor highlighted the gendered nature of genocidal utopia when, writing on the Rwandan genocide, he described Hutu Power ideology as one that sought 'an imagined past condition of patriarchy as well as the perpetuation of Hutu dominance.'[76] The link between male domination within the perpetrator group and genocide against 'outside' groups is a common one, and usually expresses itself in terms of an ersatz patriarch (the leader, the party) who is both god and father in that he exercises final power over reproductive choices and determines who shall live and who shall die. This explains why political leaders who oversee genocides also often promote authoritarian and coercive reproductive policies within their own groups. Their efforts to erode institutions of autonomous generation among ethnic or national insiders (by reducing women to breeders, co-opting children, and forcibly separating family

---

[72] Jones, 'Gender and Genocide', 26–7.

[73] Martin Shaw, *War and Genocide: Organized Killing in Modern Society* (Cambridge: Polity Press, 2003).

[74] Ernst Jünger, *Der Kampf als inneres Erlebnis, Samtliche Werke* 2.1, vol. 7 (Stuttgart: Klett-Cotta, 1980), 50.

[75] Andreas Huyssen, 'Fortifying the Heart–Totally Ernst Jünger's Armored Texts', *New German Critique* 59 (Spring/Summer 1993), 9.

[76] Jones, 'Gender and Genocide in Rwanda', 101–102; Christopher C. Taylor, *Sacrifice as Terror: The Rwandan Genocide of 1994* (Oxford/New York: Berg, 1999), 151–79.

members) are intimately intertwined with their plans to destroy outside groups, in whole or in part.

The relationship between masculine identity and the behaviour of foot soldiers in genocide also warrants more in-depth research. Euan Hague has shown how the all-male rituals of genocidal rape in Bosnia-Herzegovina, for example, were a means of performing the potency of their Serbian national identity.[77] In his interpretation, when Serb soldiers raped Muslim and Croat women and men, girls and boys, they were exercising their masculinist domination over civilians that they identified specifically as *feminized* ethnic enemies, and this drama was a core feature of 'hetero-masculinist' constructions of Serbian national identity under Milošević.[78] Such an approach frames genocide as an expressive act that, in large part because of its gendered nature, requires constant recapitulation. Such an understanding helps explain why genocides tend to radicalize even further at the peripheries and expand to new victim groups.[79]

Finally, the ways that women find agency in these masculinist projects needs to be better explained. Roger W. Smith, discussing the high level of direct female participation in the Cambodian genocide, notes that '[i]f there had been a question about the capacity of women to participate in political murder and to exhibit elements of will and cruelty that, in the common imagination, are restricted to males engaged in warfare, Cambodia seems to have resolved it.'[80] He suggests that genocide in the Cambodian case 'occurred where gender distinctions had been eliminated'. However, despite the coercive gender neutrality of Khmer Rouge ideology, it is nevertheless historically part of a highly masculinized revolutionary tradition—Stalinism, to which the Khmer Rouge leaders had been introduced as students in France.[81] The Khmer Rouge's radical attempt to destroy all family ties, especially the bond between mothers and children, puts it squarely within the norm of masculinist genocidal ideology. The high level of participation of women does not change its hegemonic masculinity, though it shows it to be much more complex a phenomenon than we may otherwise assume. While genocide may not be an all-male crime, it remains a masculinist one.

---

[77] Euan Hague, 'Rape, Power and Masculinity: The Construction of Gender and National Identities in the War in Bosnia-Herzegovina', in Lentin (ed.), *Gender and Catastrophe*, 50–63.

[78] Hague, 'Rape, Power and Masculinity', 55.

[79] Robert Gellately, 'The Third Reich, the Holocaust, and Visions of Serial Genocide', in Robert Gellately and Ben Kiernan (eds), *The Specter of Genocide: Mass Murder in Historical Perspective* (Cambridge: Cambridge University Press, 2003), 241–63; Helen Fein, 'Genocide, Terror, Life Integrity, and War Crimes: The Case for Discrimination', in George J. Andreopoulos (ed.), *Genocide: Conceptual and Historical Dimensions* (Philadelphia: University of Pennsylvania Press, 1994).

[80] Roger W. Smith, 'Women and Genocide: Notes on an Unwritten History', *Holocaust and Genocide Studies* 8:3 (1994), 325–6.

[81] Eric D. Weitz, *A Century of Genocide: Utopias of Race and Nation* (Princeton/Oxford: Princeton University Press, 2003), 146–7.

GENDER AND THE DEFINITION OF GENOCIDE

When the Genocide Convention was drafted after World War II, international law—like the social sciences—was concerned with the 'public sphere', which was defined in gendered ways in opposition to the 'private sphere'. The definition of genocide reflects the public sphere emphasis of international law inasmuch as many of the experiences most common to women in genocides were not explicitly considered when crafting the convention's language. This includes rape, but also the host of other life force crimes common to genocidal destruction that occur in contexts that generally have been assumed to be 'private' (such as the household, the space of sexual intercourse and conception, and the relationships between family members). Life force crimes can be prosecuted under one or another of the elements of genocide listed by the convention, but to do so is artificially to tear apart phenomena that belong together. Taken as a whole these particular crimes demonstrate a patterned obsession with the destruction of the life force of a group and are aimed at the most sacred aspects of communal life.

Looking at genocide through the lens of gender therefore can help us see aspects of the crime that otherwise have remained 'hidden' by bringing together phenomena in a way that restores the internal logic of the original crime. Gender can help us see that genocide is, in its most basic form, a crime against the generative power of a group and the institutions that support it, especially the family. The perpetrators of genocide organize the destruction of a group by targeting members in accordance with the roles that they are perceived to play in the group's biological and social reproduction. Since the family is the basic unit of the reproduction of groups, and since perpetrators so often find their victims in family situations, the family and the roles that adhere to it are prime theatres for the enactment of genocidal intent.

When we look at victims in terms of their roles as members of families, we also are able to identify genocidal intent very early on in a conflict. Atrocities against the life force, which are so often focused on small groups like extended families, can be used as evidence of genocidal intent for the purpose of early warning and intervention. Furthermore, the family basis of much genocidal violence has the potential to offer us deeper insight into the longer term causes of genocide, particularly in terms of genocidal ideologies and the creation of conditions under which people are tempted to embrace and participate in genocidal killing.

Gender analysis problematizes definitions of genocide that rely on direct killing and numbers of dead, since focusing only on group members killed outright—the majority of whom are often men—can erase the genocidal intent behind the persecution of women in cases where they are allowed to go on living. The genocides in Bosnia and Rwanda, and the current violence in the DRC, point to the theoretical possibility of committing and achieving genocide solely through the systematic use of sexual violence against men and women alike. The immediate ideological precursors to the Nazi party—the Pan Germans—recognized such a possibility in 1905 by proposing mass sterilization programmes for unwanted groups that would result in their eventual annihilation.[82]

If the study of gender in genocide is important to an early warning system, it is equally important to rebuilding efforts in post-genocidal societies.[83] Gender analysis brings attention to the intentional ways in which families are disrupted and destroyed; therefore special emphasis will need to be placed on rebuilding families and fostering cohesion. This will require intensive public policy efforts to recognize and de-stigmatize male and female survivors of rape by giving due attention to the concentric circles of suffering caused by the relational nature of genocidal violence. Particular attention will need to be paid to women survivors who experience enormous structural vulnerability in post-genocidal societies in the form of social ostracism, impoverishment, and homelessness due to discriminatory customs of inheritance and limited occupational options. Many are forced to raise children alone, including children born of wartime rape and war orphans. Many are suffering from disabilities and illnesses related to genocidal violence. Many are unable to conceive or carry children, which can interfere with their ability to marry and thereby condemn them to a lifetime of economic hardship. Furthermore, studies indicate that violence against women increases in postwar contexts. In places like Bosnia, Rwanda, and Sierra Leone, where so many rapists have gone unpunished, women continue to live in fear of reprisals.

Gender analysis demonstrates that genocidal violence is part of a continuum of violence related to the mystery of life-giving and women's central place within it. In attempting the destruction of groups, which are, after all, microcosms of our collective humanity, génocidaires are pursuing a scenario of power that is gendered at its core. Recognizing the gendered nature of this crime holds out the promise of helping us not only to understand it better and to define it more precisely, but also to engage more successfully in genocide prevention—that aspect of the Genocide Convention that has eluded us for over six decades.

Select Bibliography

Allen, Beverly, *Rape Warfare: The Hidden Genocide in Bosnia-Herzegovina and Croatia* (London/Minneapolis: University of Minnesota Press, 1996).

[82] Josef Ludwig Reimer, *Ein pangermanisches Deutschland. Versuch über die Konzequenzen der gegenwärtigen wissenschaftlichen Rassenbetrachtung für unsere politischen und religiösen Probleme* (Berlin/Leipzig: Friedrich Luckhardt, 1905), 22–3; Elisa von Joeden-Forgey, 'Race Power, Freedom, and the Democracy of Terror in German Racialist Thought', in Richard H. King and Dan Stone (eds), *Hannah Arendt and the Uses of History: Imperialism, Nation, Race, and Genocide* (New York/Oxford: Berghahn Books, 2007), 21–53.

[83] These final comments are based on the essays included in Carpenter, *Born of War*.

Bridenthal, Renate, Atina Grossmann, and Marion Kaplan (eds), *When Biology Became Destiny: Women in Weimar and Nazi Germany* (New York: Monthly Review Press, 1984).

Carpenter, R. Charli, *Born of War: Protecting Children of Sexual Violence Survivors in Conflict Zones* (Bloomfield, CT: Kumarian Press, 2007).

Fein, Helen, 'Genocide and Gender: The Uses of Woman and Group Destiny', *Journal of Genocide Research* 1:1 (1999).

Grossmann, Atina, 'Women and the Holocaust: Four Recent Titles', *Holocaust and Genocide Studies* 16:1 (Spring 2002), 94–108.

Jones, Adam (ed.), *Gendercide and Genocide* (Nashville, TN: Vanderbilt University Press, 2004).

Koontz, Claudia, *Mothers in the Fatherland: Women, the Family and Nazi Politics* (New York: St Martins Griffin, 1988).

Lentin, Ronit (ed.), *Gender and Catastrophe* (London/New York: Zed Books, 1997).

Pine, Lisa, 'Gender and the Family', in Dan Stone (ed.), *Historiography of the Holocaust* (New York: Palgrave Macmillan, 2004), 364–82.

Smith, Roger, 'Women and Genocide: Notes on an Unwritten History', *Holocaust and Genocide Studies* 8:3 (Winter 1994), 315–34.

Stiglmayer, Alexandra (ed.), *Mass Rape: The War against Women in Bosnia-Herzegovina* (Lincoln/London: University of Nebraska Press, 1994).

Taylor, Christopher C., *Sacrifice as Terror: The Rwandan Genocide of 1994* (Oxford/New York: Berg, 1999).

CHAPTER 4

....

THE STATE AND GENOCIDE

....

ANTON WEISS-WENDT

INTRODUCTION

....

THIS chapter explores the connection between the state and genocide. My
contention is that no form of mass violence, and least of all genocide, erupts
spontaneously. It requires premeditation, usually by a government with a record
of gross human rights violations. Indeed, I argue, genocide is intricately linked to
the idea of the modern state, despite a body of scholarship that questions that
link. Non-state agents such as radical political parties or armed militias are usually
incorporated into the governing structure and therefore rarely perform on their
own. The state may deliberately use them as proxies to obfuscate the decision-
making process and thus to shift responsibility for the crimes committed. Even
though the ruling body may not always emphasize the state interests in genocide,
the painstaking reconstruction of the chain of command, where possible, inevitably points to the upper echelons of power as the original source of mass violence.
In some cases the subjects may not even be able to identify the leading individuals
who constitute the state. This, however, does not make the state less present at the
crime scene.

I use the conventional definition of state, as an organized political community
under one government. In case the forces in control of the government penetrate
through the entire state apparatus, including the civil service and military, this
political system becomes a 'regime'. The discussion of an 'ideal type of state' in my

opinion is as fruitless as the construction of an 'ideal type of genocide'. Neither the
state nor any of its constituencies possess certain innate characteristics that would
make it prone to violence. Like any other outcome of human activity, the crime of
genocide is developmental and can always be traced back to a particular set of
circumstances unique to a specific time and place.[1]

Until the early 1990s, the state had been considered as the prime, if not the only,
agent of genocide. The Yugoslav wars of secession and Rwanda genocide, however,
have bred dissent among scholars, some of whom began arguing that non-state
actors can at times perpetrate violence on a genocidal scale without the highest
authorities' sanction. This article asserts the original view, by deconstructing the
arguments that emphasize the role of military units and the ambiguity of dictatorship. The analysis of the centre–periphery interaction further affirms the primacy
of the state.

While acknowledging the role of the state in drafting and implementing the
policies of mass murder, some scholars also consider auxiliary agents of genocide.
This is particularly true with scholars examining earlier cases of premeditated mass
death. When dealing with the phenomenon of genocide beyond Nazi Germany,
Lemkin barely spent any time discussing the perpetrators. In his pioneering book,
Axis Rule in Occupied Europe, he used general terms such as 'occupant', 'oppressor',
or 'conqueror'. However, Lemkin's ambition to write a global history of genocide
demonstrates his intention to consider, among others, church authorities, local
warlords, and civil rulers as agents of genocide.[2] Thus his unpublished manuscript
includes a chapter of Spanish colonies in America abundant with references to
non-state agents of genocide. Lemkin held responsible for the crimes the local
administration, but also the colonists of New Spain, and sometimes their indigenous collaborators. Simultaneously, he emphasized that the Spanish government
never authorized slavery as such and actually tried to ameliorate the conditions of
the indigenous people.[3]

It is true that the UN Genocide Convention does not consider genocide a crime
planned and executed necessarily by the state. During the debates on the draft
Genocide Convention in 1947 and 1948, the attention was deliberately shifted away
from the state. The United States and the Soviet Union successfully countered the
joint United Kingdom and Belgian amendment proclaiming a state or government
the most likely offender. In the end, the British were forced to concede that states
had to carry only civil, not criminal responsibility following a violation of the

---

[1] Frank Chalk and Kurt Jonassohn (eds), *The History and Sociology of Genocide: Analyses and Case
Studies* (New Haven, CT: Yale University Press, 1990), 23.

[2] Raphael Lemkin, *Axis Rule in Occupied Europe: Laws of Occupation, Analysis of Government,
Proposals for Redress* (Washington, DC: Carnegie Endowment for International Peace, 1944), 79–93.

[3] Michael McDonnell and Dirk Moses, 'Raphael Lemkin as Historian of Genocide in the Americas',
Journal of Genocide Research 7:4 (December 2005), 510, 512.

convention.[4] This comes as no surprise, taking into consideration that the UN Genocide Convention was a result of a political compromise whose major goal was to safeguard the interests of the signing parties rather than accurately reflect on patterns of history.

When applying the concept of genocide to colonial Americas and Australia, historians tend to interpret the Genocide Convention in the light of Lemkin's writings. Thus, Ben Kiernan writes that some English settlers committed genocide in some parts of North America and later in Australia. He then adds that Virginia Indians on occasion paid the white settlers in kind. He attempts to differentiate by using the term 'genocidal massacres' instead of genocide. This enables him to argue that the so-called 'genocidal moments' can in equal measure be referred back to communal violence. Like Lemkin did fifty years earlier, Kiernan names particular governors, trade companies, and splinter groups that carried out, wittingly or unwittingly, partial genocide. At the same time, Kiernan does not let British colonial authorities and American federal officials off the hook, suggesting the crime of omission, and, indeed, legitimation by their general support of the colonization project.[5] Dirk Moses pursues a similar line of argumentation, discerning criminal intent from the enormous cost of Australia's colonization. The dramatic decline of indigenous population from 750,000 in 1788 to 31,000 in 1911 makes him implicate both central and local authorities in pursuing policies calculated to bring about their physical destruction, pursuant to Article II of the Genocide Convention. The more negotiating power the local settlers community had vis-à-vis the Colonial Office, the more radical the outcome, according to Moses.[6]

Despite the complex classification elaborated by social scientists—who distinguish between retributive, institutional, utilitarian, monopolistic, developmental, despotic, optimal, etc. genocide[7]—genocide is ultimately driven by ideology. In view of the intent to destroy, in whole or in part, tactical and integral functions of genocide become indistinguishable. Alternately, the act of physical or biological destruction of an entire group, no matter to what ends, is innately ideological in its

---

[4] William Schabas, *Genocide in International Law: The Crimes of Crimes* (Cambridge: Cambridge University Press, 2000), 419–23.

[5] Ben Kiernan, *Blood and Soil: A World History of Genocide and Extermination from Sparta to Darfur* (New Haven, CT: Yale University Press, 2007), 7, 14, 16, 35, 221–5, 232, 244–7.

[6] A. Dirk Moses, 'Genocide and Settler Society in Australian History', in Moses (ed.), *Genocide and Settler Society: Frontier Violence and Stolen Indigenous Children in Australian History* (New York: Berghahn Books, 2004), 24–36.

[7] Roger Smith, 'Human Destructiveness and Politics: The Twentieth Century as an Age of Genocide', in Isidor Wallimann and Michael Dobkowski (eds), *Genocide and the Modern Age: Etiology and Case Studies of Mass Death* (Syracuse, NY: Syracuse University Press, 2000 [1987]), 21–39; Kurt Jonassohn and Frank Chalk, 'A Typology of Genocide and Some Implications for the Human Rights Agenda', in ibid.; Helen Fein, *Genocide: A Sociological Perspective* (London: Sage Publications, 1993), 32–50.

intent. The traditional understanding of ideology as a rigid system of ideas and beliefs regarded as justifying action is usually augmented in the context of genocide by a pseudoscientific dogma. Obviously, violent ideology is not confined to the state and may exist on different levels down to radical splinter group, repressive communities, or individual fanatics. In fact, an ideology is usually a product of intellectuals. It does not mean though, contrary to what John Heidenrich has argued, that 'the bloodiest genocides of human history, especially in the twentieth century, were orchestrated by intellectuals.'[8] If it had not been for shrewd and fanatical politicians, Charles Darwin's postulate of survival of the fittest—to cite just one, classical example—would have remained nothing more than what it was, namely a theory. Nonetheless, accession to political power is a prerequisite for implementing that ideology, however important other forms of less formal power may be in shaping or stimulating genocide. In most cases, however, violent rhetoric and/or terror are a means of attaining power rather than a goal. From the vantage point of the rulers to be, resorting to genocide to hold sway is counterproductive. Even the most brutal among the actors concede the necessity of sustaining popular support. Therefore, genocide is rarely, if at all, used to build or take over the state. The policies of exclusion, segregation, and mass murder usually emerge from within the state that has already attained or striving to attain legitimacy by whatever means.

THEORETICAL APPROACHES

Social and political scientists were among the first scholars of genocide. Unsurprisingly, then, the scholars working in those fields have also developed a theoretical discourse on state and genocide. Helen Fein postulated that in order to uncover the origins of modern premeditated genocide we must first recognize it as organized state murder. Centrally planned and purposeful, genocide is instrumental to the perpetrators' ends, Fein argued. From the viewpoint of a ruling elite, genocide has a function that helps to legitimize the existence of the state. An ideology may justify eradicating peoples that do not fit into the new nation, by assimilating, expelling, or annihilating them. Fein put much emphasis on the rationality of the perpetrators, who allegedly weigh opportunities, costs, and sanctions before setting on a course of destruction. She established a straight connection between war and genocide, contending that the former reduces the deterrence against the latter.

---

[8] John Heidenrich, *How to Prevent Genocide: A Guide for Policymakers, Scholars, and Concerned Citizens* (Westport, CT: Praeger, 2001), 34.

This awards the perpetrators both freedom or action and post facto justification. Finally, she projected a higher risk of genocide in a situation of a crisis of national identity caused by the defeat in war.[9] Later on Fein broadened her theoretical framework, restating that genocide may be both a premeditated and improvised response to a problem or opportunity. Simultaneously, she began differentiating between the functions of group destruction, one of which is to eliminate a collectivity allegedly disloyal to the present regime and another to reinforce cohesion by restructuring the population.[10]

Frank Chalk and Kurt Jonassohn agree with Fein that genocide has always required a high degree of centralized authority and bureaucratic organization. However, they provide a different explanation, by assuming that most people are reluctant to slaughter innocent civilians en masse. Irving Horowitz, too, places the state at the centre of his analysis of genocide. He views genocide as the ultimate means of social control by a totalitarian state. Norman Cohn, counter Fein and Horowitz, views genocide not as a result of calculated action but as an attempt to realize fantasies of redemption, messianic and apocalyptic at the same time.[11] Jonnasohn tends to side with Cohn, by arguing that ideological genocides have been committed in the name of a fundamentalist religion, a millenarian political theory, or racial purity.[12] Barbara Harff, who has coined the term *politicide*, puts revolutionary upheavals in the same category as the defeat in war as a likely cause of genocide. For her, genocide is an instance of state terrorism.[13] Following Fein and Harff, Jack Nusan Porter emphasizes war or a defeat in war as one of the preconditions for genocide. The perpetrator can stigmatize victims as traitors and conceal mass murder as an extension of military warfare.[14]

During the past decade scholars have introduced several variables in the initial debate on the role of the state in genocide. Among the most important qualifications is the fact that the regimes rarely exercise absolute authority and that the ranks of genocide perpetrators include non-state actors claiming state authority. Harff has provided probably the most nuanced account of state-generated violence. A scenario leading to an ideological genocide involves a new elite coming to power, usually through a coup or revolution, with a radical vision of a new society

[9] Helen Fein, *Accounting for Genocide: Victims and Survivors of the Holocaust* (New York: Free Press, 1979), 7–9; Fein, *Genocide*, 36.

[10] Helen Fein, 'Scenarios of Genocide: Models of Genocide and Critical Responses', in Israel Charny (ed.), *Toward the Understanding and Prevention of Genocide: Proceedings of the International Conference on the Holocaust and Genocide* (Boulder, CO: Westview Press, 1989), 5.

[11] Fein, *Genocide*, 37, 42, 49.

[12] Kurt Jonassohn, *Genocide and Gross Human Rights Violations in Comparative Perspective* (New Brunswick, NJ: Transaction Publishers, 1993), 23; *idem*, 'What is Genocide?', in Helen Fein (ed.), *Genocide Watch* (New Haven, CT: Yale University Press, 1992), 24.

[13] Fein, *Genocide*, 38–9, 50.

[14] Jack Nusan Porter, *Genocide and Human Rights: A Global Anthology* (Lanham, MD: University Press of America, 1982), 15.

purified of unwanted or threatening elements. Besides exclusionary ideology, another factor contributing to escalation of conflict to genocidal levels is the narrow ethnic base of a regime. A situation in which the elite disproportionately represent one segment in a heterogeneous society may potentially lead to mass violence or even genocide. The elites are likely to safeguard their interests by designing policies of exclusion, prompting the under-represented groups to challenge them, and thus perpetuating the authorities' insecurity.

Harff notes that the Genocide Convention fails to take into account the possibility that non-state actors can and do attempt to destroy rival ethnic and political groups. However, mass murder is never accidental nor is it an act of individuals. According to her, genocide and politicide is carried out with the explicit or tacit approval of powers that be or those who claim state authority. Harff sums up her arguments as follows: 'any persistent, coherent pattern of action by the state and its agents that brings about the destruction of a collectivity, in whole or part, is prima facie evidence of authorities' responsibility.'[15]

Scott Straus appears to agree with Harff. He argues that state involvement exposes the causes and shapes the character of annihilation. It is essentially impossible to find a case of modern genocide occurring without state participation. The state can provide massive resources and coordinated planning required in a campaign of systematic destruction. A state project involves ideology and institutions. The questions that scholars should be asking are how do state officials decide on a policy of extermination, how do they convince a subject population to commit or condone genocide, and which institutional configurations induce the commission of the crime? At the same time, Straus doubts if the state is a necessary attribute in the definition of genocide. According to him, a campaign to eliminate a group of population launched by non-state actors should be equally considered genocide.[16] Among the first generation of genocide scholars, Leo Kuper is one who has accounted for all historical eventualities when he wrote that 'genocide is generally, though not exclusively, a state crime, committed by governments or with their knowledge and complicity.'[17]

The scholars mentioned above disagree on the degree of involvement of the state in genocide, without negating the relationship between the two. One particular historian, Christian Gerlach, however, has embarked on a mission to erase that link completely. Gerlach, who is best known for his works on the Holocaust, shifted the attention from the state to what he calls 'extremely violent societies'. Gerlach appears as the most radical critic of the theory of state, as it has developed in the

---

[15] Barbara Harff, 'No Lessons Learned from the Holocaust? Assessing Risks of Genocide and Political Mass Murder Since 1955', *American Political Science Review* 97:1 (February 2003), 57–70, quotation at 59.

[16] Scott Straus, 'Contested Meanings and Conflicting Imperatives: A Conceptual Analysis of Genocide', *Journal of Genocide Research* 3:3 (2001), 365.

[17] Leo Kuper, 'The Genocidal State: An Overview', in Pierre van den Berghe (ed.), *State Violence and Ethnicity* (Niwot: University Press of Colorado, 1990), 19.

field of comparative genocide studies. He downplays the state policies by emphasizing the importance of multicausality and context on the one hand and by
referring to methodological problems with the term genocide on the other. The
focus on the state and its attributes such as ideology, bureaucracy, and elites—
according to him—is a residue of the totalitarian, Eurocentric model. In his quest
for a new terminology Gerlach effectively substitutes a top-down approach to the
study of genocide by a one-dimensional model of explanation from below. For
example, in his interpretation, state and its functionaries act more as representatives of the larger population strata, making 'intent' irrelevant in establishing
whether genocide was perpetrated. By discarding intent to commit mass murder
and denying regimes the decision-making power, Gerlach shrugs off all the complexities of the term genocide, including implications of state involvement,
through his criticism of the function of prevention.[18] In the final analysis, the
phenomenon of participatory violence in no way excludes the intrinsic, structural
links between the authorities, various levels of state administration, and broader
masses. Indeed, a more sophisticated conception of intent and of the way it is
shaped at different levels could accommodate Gerlach's case studies within more
conventional conceptions of genocide.

Recent studies by Michael Mann and Mark Levene make a significant contribution to our understanding of mass violence, including the role of the state. Written
by a sociologist and a historian, respectively, *The Dark Side of Democracy* and *The
Meaning of Genocide* are remarkable books with novel theses worth comparing.
Mann and Levene take a different perspective discussing one and the same phenomenon, which they call by different names. Conspicuously, the subtitle of
Mann's book is 'Explaining Ethnic Cleansing', while Levene put as an overall title
for his four-volume study (of which two have appeared so far), *Genocide in the Age
of the Nation State*. The massive investigation into the roots of human destructiveness rendered interesting results.

Levene argues that we should examine the broader context in which genocide
has arisen in the modern world rather than the particularities of each instance of
genocide. As he also argues in his chapter in this volume, he links the phenomenon
of genocide with the emergence of Western powers and their expansion outside
Europe. Although the rise of the West was not identical with a comprehensive
programme of annihilation, it did create a cultural discourse that had made such
policy possible. In pursuit of that goal, the state set to organize its human resources
accordingly.[19] We are talking not about a totalizing state—Levene reminds the

---

[18] Christian Gerlach, 'Extremely Violent Societies: An Alternative to the Concept of Genocide',
Journal of Genocide Research 8:4 (December 2006), 458–65.

[19] Mark Levene, *Genocide in the Age of the Nation State*, vol i: *The Meaning of Genocide* (London:
I. B. Tauris, 2005), 155–6; idem, *Genocide in the Age of the Nation State*, vol ii: *The Rise of the West and
the Coming of Genocide* (London: I. B. Tauris, 2005), 103–19.

readers—but the homogenizing nation-state. Why nation-states target internal minorities is explained by the resentment of nationalist elites at the perceived cooperation of these minorities by external powers, especially former colonial powers, as in the case of the new Iraqi state's attack on the Assyrian population, whose men had been used by the British to maintain their rule of the Arabs there.[20]

The term 'pathological homogenization' introduced by political scientist Heather Rae may serve as a corrective to Levene's *longue durée* analysis. Echoing Levene, Rae contends that one of the methods of state-building throughout the modern period had been cultivating identification through exclusion of minority groups, often by violent means. Unlike the former, however, Rae states that pathological means of homogenization used in the past by state-builders had led to forced assimilation and expulsion, rather than outright genocide. The propensity for mass murder and genocide increased in the twentieth century along with the bureaucratic and technological capacity of the state.[21]

Mann isolates causation in specific types of violence by differentiating between different forms of mass violence and focusing more narrowly on the twentieth century. In the absence of a precise definition of ethnic cleansing, Mann uses the term inclusively, much like Norman Naimark before him. Whereas Levene explores the causal link between modernity, nation-state, and genocide, Mann draws a connection between modernity, democracy, and ethnic cleansing. His first argument is, that 'murderous cleansing is modern, because it is the dark side of democracy.' The extreme forms of ethnic cleansing require state coherence and capacity and therefore are usually directed by states. When it comes to a situation when a state slides towards ethnic cleansing, according to Mann, radicalization and factional split is more dangerous than disintegration. The novelty of his approach is that he considers different *levels* of perpetrator rather than merely identifying perpetrators. The top three levels include, respectively, radical elites operating party-states, paramilitaries, and the popular power base. The elites, militants, and core constituencies are interlinked and exercise power in three distinctive ways—top-down, bottom-up, and sideways respectively. Mann contends that ethnic refugees fleeing from threatened borderlands constitute one of the main core constituencies, as they are more dependent on the state for their subsistence and values. Unlike Levene, Mann differentiates between mass murder as a crime common throughout human history and murderous ethnic cleansing which is distinctively modern.[22] What Mann and Harff have to say about the relationship between modern state and genocide constitutes the core argument advanced in this chapter.

[20] Mark Levene, 'A Moving Target, the Usual Suspects and (Maybe) a Smoking Gun: The Problem of Pinning Blame in Modern Genocide', *Patterns of Prejudice* 33:4 (1999), 3–24.

[21] Heather Rae, *State Identities and the Homogenization of Peoples* (Cambridge: Cambridge University Press, 2002), 1–6, 14, 19, 212.

[22] Michael Mann, *The Dark Side of Democracy: Explaining Ethnic Cleansing* (New York: Cambridge University Press, 2005), 1–34, 70.

BUREAUCRACY

In their thinking of genocide, several social and political scientists referred to the state as the source of mass violence. Irving Horowitz went the farthest, proposing the following definition of genocide: 'a structural and systematic destruction of innocent people by a state bureaucratic apparatus'.[23] The idea of bureaucracy as a soulless machine that may acquire a life of its own modifies the notion of the destruction process. We do not any longer deal with the predictable situation in which the authorities see their order passed down the chain of command to be executed. Difficult to comprehend, the bureaucratic mood of operation makes the path to destruction more convoluted and thus less apparent. Set in motion by humans, it runs on autopilot. Although the outcome of this process rarely departs from the original vision of the leadership, the genocidal intent gets reinterpreted in terms of productivity and expediency. Internal tensions and power struggle inform the decisions of the officials on all levels of state bureaucracy much the same as they affect the clique. However independent in its decisions it may appear, bureaucracy is an extension of the state and therefore has only limited freedom of action. Regimes typically control the administrative bureaucracy through patronage and enforced ideology.

Most extensively, the role of state bureaucracy in genocide has been elaborated on the example of Holocaust. Raul Hilberg, who had come up with the concept of 'desk murderer', presented the linear model of operation of German state and party bureaucracy involved with the 'Final Solution of the Jewish Question'. According to Hilberg, a new agency was engaged every time its predecessor had failed the task. Karl Schleunes described the bureaucratic endeavour as a stopgap process in which several agencies worked on the 'problem' simultaneously. Neither Hilberg nor Schleunes doubted the role of Hitler as a prime behind-the-scene mover. Zygmunt Bauman moved the discussion into the realm of abstraction, talking about compartmentalization of tasks that stifle moral judgment. Building upon the research mentioned above, Götz Aly and Susanne Heim reached the farthest-reaching conclusion regarding the capacity of bureaucratic apparatus to further the mass murder agenda. In their interpretation, Nazi racial planers—or 'architects of genocide' as they called them—enjoyed almost unlimited freedom of action while mapping the future of the occupied East.[24] One step further and the intricate link between state as ultimate authority and bureaucracy as conduit of ascendancy would be severed. This is unlikely to happen,

[23] Irving Horowitz, *Genocide: State, Power and Mass Murder* (New Brunswick, NJ: Transaction Books, 1976), 18.

[24] Raul Hilberg, *The Destruction of the European Jews* (Chicago: Quadrangle Books, 1961); Karl Schleunes, *The Twisted Road to Auschwitz: Nazi Policy toward German Jews, 1933–39* (London: Andre Deutsch, 1970; Zygmunt Bauman, *Modernity and the Holocaust* (Ithaca, NY: Cornell University Press, 1989); Götz Aly and Susanne Heim, *Architects of Annihilation: Auschwitz and the Logic of Destruction* (London: Phoenix, 2003).

though, because state bureaucracy is and remains an essential part of power structure, also when it comes to genocide.

Donald Bloxham has arrived at a similar conclusion in his analysis of the role of bureaucracy in mass murder. As many other scholars, though, he began with a question: 'to what extent can bureaucracies themselves show the genocidal way as a result of their professional problem-solving abilities, leading rather than simply enacting policies decided on from above?' Bloxham observes that genocide, as predominantly a crime of state, is usually executed by the administration in the service of the state. He demonstrates on the example of Nazi Germany how an extremist political group managed to penetrate and subvert existing state organs, taking over the functions of the 'normative state'. A new bureaucracy thus created incorporates ideologically motivated young officials striving for rapid career ad-vancement and older authoritarian conservatives acquiescing to radical policies. Both groups perform in anticipation of rewards and at times personal security, which they can only receive from the state that employs them. By encompassing ideological engagement and systematic problem-solving state bureaucracies ulti-mately reflect regime values. The state is important in regulating popular versus organizational participation in mass violence, Bloxham concludes.[25] The escalation of political mass violence in the Soviet Union in the 1930s can be attributed in part to the bureaucratic mood of operation characteristic of the first socialist society.

When it comes to bureaucracy, the most peculiar feature of Stalinist terror was the quota system. The NKVD headquarters in Moscow provided local party and security police branches with the figures of how many thousands or tens of thousands of 'enemies of the people' or members of the 'enemy nationalities' should be deported from any given locality. In the process, local officials often appealed to their superior to increase the quotas, which had a snowball effect, particularly during the Great Terror of 1936–8. This phenomenon can be explained through the nature of the Soviet system on the one hand and protuberant instinct of survival on the other. Many historians see the planned economy (as opposed to market economy) as the grounding principle of the socialist system. Mass collectiv-ization and industrialization was the kernel of the First Five Year Plan introduced in the Soviet Union in 1928. Mass deportations of peasants and the famine could be viewed respectively as an intentional and unintentional consequence of social engineering. The expression 'fulfill and over-fulfill the Five-Year Plan' has persisted throughout the Soviet period. However, it was more than just material rewards and career advancement that made the officials in charge to perpetuate the class and ethnic cleansing. The erratic nature of Soviet terror—which puts it into the category of revolutionary terror but sets it apart from Nazi terror, for example—made no one safe, including the individuals who had administered it. An official

---

[25] Donald Bloxham, 'Bureaucracy and Organized Mass Murder: A Comparative Historical Analysis', *Holocaust and Genocide Studies* 22:1 (2008), 203–45.

who did not show enough zeal in exercising an assigned task, in this case population management, could potentially join the ranks of the unfortunate he or she had sent on paper to faraway destinations. Just consider the rotation within the NKVD organization whose former heads, Genrikh Yagoda and Nikolai Ezhov, were executed as 'the enemies of the people' in 1938 and 1940 respectively. Despite the arguments advanced by revisionist historians,[26] the element of fear was indeed omnipresent in the Soviet society in the late 1930s and early 1940s.

MILITARY

Some scholars have been subconsciously de-emphasizing the role of the state in genocide by drawing attention to the military as a self-governing body capable of generating violent impulses. The discourse usually centres on military leaders in the field or the military establishment at large. Particular instances of mass murder that have prompted the military-centred analysis range from colonial genocides such as German South West Africa to political genocides such as Indonesia. Those who consider the Gypsies, alongside with the Jews, the victims of Nazi genocide point to the indiscriminate shooting of the Ukrainian and Russian Roma by the Wehrmacht units in 1941.

Isabel Hull has argued in the case of German South West Africa that the extermination of the native populations in 1904–6 developed out of imperial military practices and was not ordered in Berlin. To ensure the unconditional implementation of his 'destruction order' from October 1904, Gen. Lothar von Trotha had first to establish total military control over the colony. By unseating the governor, who did not subscribe to his brutal policies, von Trotha felt free to circumvent the normal chain of command in the colonies. In his order to hunt down and starve the defeated Herero, von Trotha followed the nineteenth-century German military doctrine that prescribed the destruction of the enemy as a final goal of warfare. However, as Hull has explained, it was Kaiser Wilhelm who ordered 'to crush the uprising by all means'—a standard formulation used with regard to colonial revolts. It has as much to do with the personality of von Trotha, who had been known for a ruthless suppression of native uprisings prior to his appointment in German South West Africa.[27] In other words, he had arrived in Windhoek 'to do the job', as he understood it. Moreover,

---

[26] The strongest exponent of the 'push from below' theory is Robert Thurston, *Life and Terror in Stalin's Russia, 1934–1941* (New Haven, CT: Yale University Press, 1996).

[27] Isabel Hull, 'Military Culture and the Production of "Final Solutions" in the Colonies: The Example of Wilhelminian Germany', in Robert Gellately and Ben Kiernan (eds), *The Specter of Genocide: Mass Murder in Historical Perspective* (New York: Cambridge University Press, 2003), 144–62.

Governor Leutwein who had opposed von Trotha's extermination policy was himself a soldier experienced in putting down revolts. The General Staff that had installed von Trotha in his position convinced the Kaiser to reverse the 'destruction order'. As Hull writes, Bismarck's ultimate intention in masterminding a policy that had granted the military a free hand was to safeguard the monarchy. Therefore, it would be incorrect to present the German military, the General Staff, and specifically General von Trotha as acting *in opposition* to the central authorities. Rather, they discharged duties in accordance with contemporaneous norms and preconceptions and in anticipation of sanction from above. By the same token, the parliamentary debates and the public outcry caused by the inhuman treatment of colonial subjects in places like Tasmania and German South West Africa testifies to the emergence of pluralistic society in Europe rather than to a presumed goodwill of the European governments. Last but not least, both cases can be deemed transitional and as such hardly fitting into the pattern of modern ideologically driven genocide.

The emphasis on the military runs counter to a tendency of dissociating genocide from warfare. Many activists hailed as groundbreaking the clause in the Genocide Convention specifying that genocide can be committed not only in time of war but also in time of peace. This may be regarded a personal victory for Raphael Lemkin, who had failed to introduce the changes of genocide in the decision of the International Military Tribunal (IMT) in Nuremberg in 1946. The marginal treatment of the Holocaust in IMT proceedings was partially due to the Allied decision to tie the Nazi war crimes with the so-called crimes against the peace. Having taken the outbreak of the Second World War as a starting point for the legal investigation, the prosecution effectively excluded the 1930s policies of exclusion and discrimination—which had paved the way to genocide—from consideration.[28] The legal innovation that erased the distinction between the maltreatment of civilians in time of war and peace has led some social scientists to reject the link between war and genocide. According to Paul Bartrop, for example, five out of fifteen major genocides of the twentieth century that he has listed took place outside of a military conflict. He mentions specifically the 1932–3 famine in the Soviet Union, Indonesian massacres of 1965–6, Burundi killings in 1972, and routine executions in Cambodia between 1975 and 1979.[29] This and similar analyses ingrained in the quantitative method tend to disregard context. To the same extent to which the violent regimes invent enemies, they conjure up wars. This is particularly true in the case of communist dictatorships, which perpetuate the siege mentality.

The fear of losing control over the subject population, or even worse of being forced from power, is a potent factor when it comes to unleashing ethnic violence. Common

---

[28] Donald Bloxham, *Genocide on Trial: War Crimes Trials and the Formation of Holocaust History and Memory* (Oxford: Oxford University Press, 2001), 57–89.

[29] Paul Bartrop, 'The Relationship between War and Genocide in the Twentieth Century: A Consideration', *Journal of Genocide Research* 4:4 (2002), 519–32.

sense and history teach us that democracies are less prone to committing mass crimes than dictatorships. Much like in human relationships, the shrewd ways of gaining influence or misuse of office at the state level breed suspicion of those in power. Although the outside threat to the ruling clique may be real, more often than not it is imaginary. The regime perceives of a threat to its existence exaggerated. The statesmen in the 1930s Soviet Union and the 1970s Cambodia acted out of fear of war. Both countries were born into violence. Russia experienced a world war, a revolution, a civil war, a foreign intervention, and famine before Stalin began implementing mass collectivization and industrialization that conditioned the horrendous famine of 1932 and 1933, which struck Ukraine particularly hard. Confiscation of grain was part and parcel of a defence programme that was meant to ensure the Soviet Union's survival. Stalin was one of many old Bolsheviks who had been obsessed with hostile encirclement, border infiltration, and eventually full-scale war against the nascent socialist state. In Stalin's mind, whatever he did—including starving his own people—made the country stronger in the face of an inevitable military confrontation with the capitalist world. Magnified suspicion can at times border on paranoia. I mean political rather than individual paranoia, for Stalin had been clinically diagnosed with mental disorder to which his disastrous policies could have been attributed.

It was not substantially different in the case of the Khmer Rouge whose war rhetoric had become a self-fulfilled prophecy. Cambodia went through a foreign occupation during the Second World War, a struggle for independence, a civil war, and the American bombing prior to the communist takeover in 1975. The alienation from the Vietnamese patron soon escalated into the persecution of the Vietnamese minority, the incursion into the neighboring country's territory, and eventually defeat of Pol Pot's Cambodia at the hands of the Vietnamese. The impending war with the 'Western imperialism' and Vietnam served as an ultimate rationale for spreading terror within Cambodia. Thus, there exists a direct connection between war scare and cumulative radicalization. Simultaneously, it discredits the notion of total war as a conduit for genocide. It may be true in some cases—for example Ottoman Turkey, as Jay Winter has demonstrated,[30] and Nazi Germany—but not in others.

PARAMILITARIES

Mann considers the military as one of the four power networks—alongside with ideological, political, and economic factors—that may produce the rationale for

---

[30] Jay Winter, 'Under Cover of War: The Armenian Genocide in the Context of Total War', in Gellately and Kiernan (eds), *The Specter of Genocide*, 189–213.

genocide (Mann continually uses the term 'ethnic cleansing'). Armies, police forces, and irregulars are the main agencies of military power.[31] Whereas the armed forces are expected to protect the interests of the state, the paramilitaries often serve as an extension of the military, as it was the case in Indonesia, for example. Other times, the initiative to build irregular troops comes directly from the state authorities, without any mediation. Ottoman Turkey would be a good example of that. The shock units formed by political parties in their quest for power (though official justification is usually self-defence) represent the third type of auxiliaries. This kind of militia sprang up in Rwanda in the wake of the Arusha Accord and the Ndadaye assassination. Bands of armed men can also form spontaneously—or so it may appear at first glance—in secessionist territories, as it occurred in the Serb settled areas of Bosnia-Herzegovina. The most extensive use of irregular forces is possible under condition of prolonged military occupation, particularly in the territories that had experienced an enemy rule before. This phenomenon is usually described as collaboration, however imperfect is the term. Nazi Germany was fairly successful at raising local units amongst the Estonians, Latvians, Lithuanians, Ukrainians, and some Muslim peoples in the occupied Soviet territories. The state is eager to use militias, which it has clandestinely trained and armed, to simulate the condition of civil war. That disposition can afford two types of action, both beneficial to the state: denial or intervention. The officials may denounce the 'rumours' of state involvement, letting the bloodshed run its course. The role of militias in spearheading and/or meticulously carrying out mass murder is difficult to gauge due to the multiple chain of command, which can only be established with certainty post facto. The International Court's of Justice ruling in the case of Bosnia-Herzegovina against Serbia indirectly touched upon this problem. Some observers commented that the judgment from February 2007, which pronounced Serbia not guilty of the crime of genocide, could have been different if the government in Belgrade did not insist on withdrawing some important documents that had allegedly exposed the subordinate position of the Bosnian Serb administration vis-à-vis Milošević's regime.[32]

In the modern period, the use of proxies has been associated with the colonial conquest and the subsequent wars of liberation in Africa and Asia. During the Cold War the superpowers fought each other in the name of a superior ideology (at least nominally) by deploying indigenous troops that they had armed and trained. What might have looked as a conventional civil war to the outside world was planned and accounted for thousands of kilometres away. At times violence went out of hand: the armed units that were supposed to fight ideological warfare had split and regrouped along tribal lines, massacring each other instead of a designated enemy and their patrons. In certain cases, magnified manifolds, this scenario

---

[31] Mann, *The Dark Side of Democracy*, 32.
[32] See *New York Times*, 9 April 2007.

played out also in the context of genocide. While the United States sponsored the southerners in their fight against the Viet Cong, the Vietnamese communists supported the Khmer Rouge guerrillas in neighbouring Cambodia. Once the Khmer Rouge seized power in the country, they turned against their political backers and the Vietnamese people at large. No matter what is the political setup, the type of irregulars, or the extent of atrocities they commit, the traces inevitably go back to the state or the shadowy forces acting in its name. No scholar has succeeded so far in proving otherwise.

In Sudan and the former Yugoslavia the relationship between paramilitaries and the state is rather unambiguous. Thanks to compulsory military service, by 1990 the Yugoslav People's Army (JNA) numbered 185,000 men on active duty and half a million reservists. Up to three million men were subject to conscription by the Territorial Defence. Those who remained in the country when war broke out in 1991 had few choices. They could either join the armed forces or one of the militias that operated in Croatia and Bosnia-Herzegovina. While the federal state was falling apart, the nationalist authorities in Belgrade bet on paramilitaries, who could control territory and thus strengthen the Serbian state. Out of 10,000 Serb volunteers who fought in Bosnia, half had previously served in the Yugoslav People's Army. Unsurprisingly, then, the military controlled most of the militias, with the rest run by the State Security Service. The latter group of paramilitary units, including the notorious 'Tigers' under the command of Željko Ražnatović (Arkan), emphasized their connection with the Security Service. In some cases, though, the rank and file were unaware of that arrangement.[33]

Bosnian Serb forces and Serb paramilitaries account for most deaths in 1991–5 (with a high estimate put at 280,000). Evidence of central planning is in abundance. The JNA provided arms to the local Serbs in Bosnia-Herzegovina, and on several occasions participated in the atrocities. Paramilitary units were particularly efficient at carrying out the policy of ethnic cleansing when attached directly to regular Army units. Even though direct guidance for individual operations was normally exercised at the commander's level, the leadership set certain policy goals, allowing their subordinates the latitude to achieve them. If it were otherwise, Serbian political and military authorities in Bosnia and Belgrade would have made an effort to suppress local gunmen, as did the legitimate Bosnian government. The Belgrade leadership bears ultimate responsibility for the crimes committed, Norman Cigar insists. Milošević evidently provided financial and logistic support for some of the most brutal Serb militias operating in Bosnia, channelling it through Serbia's Ministry of Defence. According to a militia leader Vojislav Šešelj,

---

[33] Aleksandra Milićević, 'Joining the War: Masculinity, Nationalism and War Participation in the Balkans War of Secession, 1991–1995', *Nationalities Papers* 34:3 (July 2006), 266; Milićević, 'Paramilitaries and the State: The Case of Serbia', paper delivered at the 7th Convention of the International Association of Genocide Scholars, Sarajevo, 12 July 2007.

Milošević was in charge, even though he gave verbal rather than written orders. It is true that at a later point Milošević reined in some militias, including that of Šešelj. However, he did act only after he started viewing these groups as a political threat. Along with other state agencies and nationalist organizations, the Serbian Orthodox Church lent its hand in organizing, financing, and arming the infamous Serbian Volunteer Guard, as its leader Arkan had subsequently acknowledged. Arkan once stated that 'every member of paramilitary units must in the first place be responsible to the Serbian people and must respect the parliament and the president of the Republic.'[34]

The Sudanese authorities have been using militias as a counterinsurgency strategy since 1985. The government in Khartoum began mobilizing the Arab tribes against the Sudanese People's Liberation Army during the civil war in the south. Baggara Arab militias received arms and military training to strike against the Dinka and Nuba peoples suspected of supporting the rebels. The use of Arab militias enabled Khartoum not only to conserve its own, overstretched resources, but also to disguise its intervention as 'age-old tribal conflict'. Between 1985 and 2003, militias supported by military intelligence and aerial bombardment carried out a brutal policy of scorched earth, massacring, pillaging, and raping civilians. In 2003, Gen. Omar al-Bashir, who had seized power in the country fourteen years earlier, began using the same strategy in the Darfur region. The Sudanese army, untrained in desert warfare, was ineffective against the rebels, who used hit-and-run tactics. Experiencing humiliating defeats, the government of Sudan set out to crush rebellion in Darfur by arming militias from local Arab tribes, collectively known as *Janjaweed*. The Janjaweed struck against the civilian populations of those non-Arab tribes from which the rebels had largely drawn their recruits, that is, the Fur, Zaghawa, Massalit, and others. Arab militias resorted to a brutal practice of ethnic cleansing aimed at replacing the local population with Arab settlers, just as it had done in oil-producing areas of the south and the Nuba Mountains.[35]

A loosely organized Arab militia force, on horseback and camel, comprised some 20,000 men. Many criminals were released on the promise of joining the militia. This force was better trained, armed, and supplied than similar units in the past. The recruits were paid a decent salary considering the economic situation of the region. Many militiamen received regular army uniforms and insignias of ranks. More important, Khartoum coordinated the activities of its regular forces and those of Janjaweeds. Thus the government directed militia activities rather than merely condoned them. The most powerful militia leader, Musa Hilal, does not

---

[34] Norman Cigar, *Genocide in Bosnia: The Policy of 'Ethnic Cleansing'* (College Station: Texas A&M University, 1995), 36, 48–55, 64–5, 104; Benjamin Lieberman, *Terrible Fate: Ethnic Cleansing in the Making of Modern Europe* (Chicago: Ivan R. Dee, 2006), 307; Norman Naimark, *Fires of Hatred: Ethnic Cleansing in Twentieth-Century Europe* (Cambridge, MA: Harvard University Press, 2001), 161.

[35] Julie Flint and Alex de Waal, *Darfur: A Short History of a Long War* (London/New York: Zed Books, 2005), 24–5, 55–61, 64, 68–9.

even try to deny his links to the government in Khartoum, from which he receives marching orders. In fact, except for their sandals, turbans, and the emblem—an armed man on camelback—the Janjaweed are undistinguishable from regular troops. Hilal stated that he has raised a tribal militia at the request of the government to fight the rebellion in Darfur. Since the beginning of the aggression in Darfur, the Janjaweeds have become increasingly integrated into the Sudanese military structure. Many militia members have been incorporated into the police, security service, and various paramilitary organizations.[36]

DICTATOR, ONE-PARTY RULE, STATE

An intelligent doubt about the preponderance of the state in the genocide is rooted in the continuous debate in the social sciences between those who emphasize the role of individual and collective actors and those who accentuate institutional structures.[37] For some Holocaust historians it may sound like the old Intentionalist–Functionalist debate.

When it comes to initiating and sanctioning destruction, the visibility of leader makes him a natural subject of inquiry. Unable to comprehend the complex relationship between various levels of civil and military administration, survivors instinctively search for answers in the personality of a dictator, who is believed, and rightly so, to carry the burden of responsibility for committed atrocities. As with the previous discussions of bureaucratic, military, and paramilitary structures, the question is whether it is possible to dissociate the elites from the state. The evidence suggests a negative answer.

Despite the significant body of literature that examines the world's dictators from a comparative perspective, personality characteristics of the leaders associated with genocidal violence rarely match.[38] What they all do have in common is the quest for power. By explicating the synergy between the ruler and the ruled one can better understand the motives behind the crime. Leaders and the ruling elites are often motivated by self-interest. To achieve their goals, they may claim that the purpose

[36] Ibid. 36–41, 86, 101–14; Gerard Prunier, *Darfur: The Ambiguous Genocide* (Ithaca, NY: Cornell University Press, 2005), 97–109, 117, 134, 152–5; Joyce Apsel (ed.), *Darfur: Genocide before Our Eyes* (New York: Institute for the Study of Genocide, 2005), 23, 26, 33, 40, 54–5, 62–3, 67.

[37] George Andreopoulos, 'Introduction: The Calculus of Genocide', in Andreopoulos (ed.), *Genocide: Conceptual and Historical Dimensions* (Philadelphia: University of Pennsylvania Press, 1994), 8.

[38] See, for example, Ben Kiernan, 'Pol Pot and Enver Pasha: A Comparison of the Cambodian and Armenian Genocides', in Levon Chorbajian and George Shirinian (eds), *Studies in Comparative Genocide* (New York: St Martin's Press, 1999), 165–78.

of destruction is to bolster the power of an entire people. The ultimate skill of an authoritarian leader is to mobilize the population, by cultivating and channelling violent impulses. They strive to move a culture down a path of mass violence; they promote destructive ideologies, which can win them fanatical supporters; and they create critical infrastructure in the form of a bureaucracy and/or a military.[39]

The perception of a leader who single-handedly decides on genocide runs the danger of overlooking both structural factors and collective prejudices that may fuel the machine of destruction. The one scholar who rejects this thesis is Benjamin Valentino. Valentino argues that the violence is typically performed by a relatively small group of people, usually members of military or paramilitary organizations. Regime's leaders do not need to seek the broader public support, as they are capable of recruiting the few individuals to carry out genocide (Valentino uses a substitute term, 'mass killing'). Society at large comes to play a role in genocide mainly as passive onlookers, compliant with authority and indifferent to the fate of victims. A relatively small group of political or military leaders, according to Valentino, can wring the acquiescence to their radical policies even in societies actively opposed to them. He admits the factor of situational pressure only as far as it relates to leaders' strategic goals and beliefs. As an argument, he invites his critics to imagine the Great Terror without Stalin or the Holocaust without Hitler.[40]

The worn out Hitler–Stalin comparison does not suggest a one-man dictatorship in each and every instance of genocide. A single standing figure of a tyrant is not obvious in the case of Cambodia, is clearly missing in the case of Rwanda, and should be multiplied by three in the case of Ottoman Turkey. The Khmer Rouge genocide by all accounts lacked a charismatic leader. For quite some time, foreign observers were unable to tell who was actually running Democratic Republic of Kampuchea. Officially, Cambodia continued to be ruled by the government in exile headed by Norodom Sihanouk, until his forced removal in March 1976. Important decisions, however, were made by the mysterious body called Revolutionary Organization (*angkar padevat*). The Khmer cadre pledged absolute loyalty to the Organization, without necessarily knowing the leading personalities. The Khmer Rouge denied the authoritarian nature of their regime by stressing the collective nature of the leadership. For the same reason the names of the leaders of the 'Organization' were kept secret. Pol Pot went by the name Brother No. 1, Nuon Chea Brother No. 2, and so on.[41] The assassination of the Rwandan President, whose plane was shot down on April 6, 1994, in circumstances still unknown,

---

[39] Israel Charny, *How Can We Commit the Unthinkable? Genocide: The Human Cancer* (Boulder, CO: Westview Press, 1982), 193–9; Linda Woolf and Michael Hulsizer, 'Psychological Roots of Genocide: Risk, Prevention, and Intervention', *Journal of Genocide Research* 7:1 (2005), 106–8.

[40] Benjamin Valentino, *Final Solutions: Mass Killing and Genocide in the Twentieth Century* (Ithaca, NY: Cornell University Press, 2004), 2–7.

[41] David Chandler, *The Tragedy of Cambodian History: Politics, War, and Revolution since 1945* (New Haven, CT: Yale University Press, 1991), 246, 258.

propelled into power a group of relatives and close associates of Juvénal Habyar-imana who had reasons to seek his death. The interim government subsequently sworn in consisted of extremist Hutu politicians. However, it appears that those individuals were mere puppets in the hands of the actual génocidaires. The Committee of Union and Progress in Turkey was led by three men—Talat Pasha, Enver Pasha, and Djemal Pasha—who had collectively devised a policy leading to the demise of the Armenian minority.

The complex processes leading to genocide should not be reduced to a regime's leaders and their 'insanity'. Whether economic gain or territorial acquisition, revenge or security motivate a genocidal campaign against a certain group, the leaders of the regime believe in the justice of their cause and therefore are incapable of conceding that their policy was criminal. In that respect Talat Pasha, Hitler, Pol Pot, and even al-Bashir, all resemble each other. The closest that Stalin came to regret after the Great Terror in 1938 was his concession that some 'mistakes' were made.[42] Pol Pot had fought to the last against the government in Phnom Penh, however undemocratic it has been. Hitler preferred to go up in smoke but not to surrender to his mortal enemies, and Talat Pasha died unrepentant, cut down by a bullet of an Armenian assassin. Although genocide is almost always led by state elites, this is the end process of state disintegration, reconstitution, and radicalization.[43]

CONCLUSIONS

Scholars are reluctant to use qualifying adjectives such as 'terrible', 'horrendous', and 'inconceivable' when talking about genocide. These words lack the precise meaning and thus may impede the detached analysis. When all is said and done, however, we are left with no other choice but to acknowledge that genocide occurs when deadly calculus meets desperate and paranoid minds. Pogroms, massacres, ethnic cleansing, or even mass killings—all these violent acts may have their origin in popular culture, perpetuated and perpetrated by the masses. But not genocide! The plan to wipe out an entire group—'leaving none to tell the story', in the words of Alison des Forges—can only be born in the upper corridors of power, or alternatively to crystallize on its way up through the existing hierarchies. In either case, it requires the machine of state to implement the utopian vision of society.

---

[42] Hiroaki Kuromiya, *Stalin: Profiles in Power* (Harlow: Pearson-Longman, 2005), 126.
[43] Mann, *The Dark Side of Democracy,* 23.

Ideology, bureaucratic apparatus, political parties, the military, militias—these are the constituents of a state. These structures are complimentary, not exclusionary.

From the vantage point of the perpetrators, genocide is *contradictio in adjecto*. They believe that their nation is on the verge of collapse yet must regain its past glory. They belittle and dread the victim group at the same time. They delegate the delicate act of destruction to various agencies, while reserving the last word for themselves. They want to implicate in murder as many people as possible, without lessening their grip on power. They may be few, styled as many. The only element that remains constant through all phases of genocide is the presence of the state. Elites, political parties, bureaucracies, armed forces, and paramilitaries—all these entities can enter agential state, in isolation or in aggregate. However weak may appear the state, it serves as an invariable reference point in the case of genocide. With all the variables, detours, ambiguities, and exceptions accounted for, genocide is still primarily a crime of state.[44] The authoritarian system of governance implies that subordinate agencies and individuals can only carry out acts of genocide with the active or tacit consent of the senior leadership. Whenever genocide may appear to have been committed by individual actors in pursuit of their own goals, the latter inevitably act in concert with the government seeking to expand state control. In all circumstances, the central authorities remain clear stakeholders in the outcome of the genocide.[45]

SELECT BIBLIOGRAPHY

Bloxham, Donald, 'Bureaucracy and Organized Mass Murder: A Comparative Historical Analysis', *Holocaust and Genocide Studies* 22:1 (2008), 203–45.
—— *Genocide on Trial: War Crimes Trials and the Formation of Holocaust History and Memory* (Oxford: Oxford University Press, 2001).
Chalk, Frank, and Kurt Jonassohn (eds), *The History and Sociology of Genocide: Analyses and Case Studies* (New Haven, CT: Yale University Press, 1990).
Flint, Julie, and Alex de Waal, *Darfur: A Short History of a Long War* (London/New York: Zed Books, 2005).
Horowitz, Irving, *Genocide: State, Power and Mass Murder* (New Brunswick, NJ: Transaction Books, 1976).
Kiernan, Ben, *Blood and Soil: A World History of Genocide and Extermination from Sparta to Darfur* (New Haven, CT: Yale University Press, 2007).
Levene, Mark, *Genocide in the Age of the Nation State*, vol i: *The Meaning of Genocide* (London: I. B. Tauris, 2005).

[44] Frank Chalk, 'Redefining Genocide', in Andreopoulos (ed.), *Genocide* 60.
[45] Catherine Barnes, 'The Functional Utility of Genocide: Towards a Framework for Understanding the Connection between Genocide and Regime Consolidation, Expansion, and Maintenance', *Journal of Genocide Research* 7:3 (2005), 311, 313.

Mann, Michael, *The Dark Side of Democracy: Explaining Ethnic Cleansing* (New York: Cambridge University Press, 2005).

Rae, Heather, *State Identities and the Homogenization of Peoples* (Cambridge: Cambridge University Press, 2002).

Valentino, Benjamin, *Final Solutions: Mass Killing and Genocide in the Twentieth Century* (Ithaca, NY: Cornell University Press, 2004).

CHAPTER 5

GENOCIDE AND MEMORY

DAN STONE

INTRODUCTION

WE live in a memory-obsessed age. Western culture is suffused with autobiographies, especially with traumatic life narratives about the legacies of abusive childhoods. Tourism consists to a large extent of the consumption of 'heritage' such as castles and stately homes; memorials and museums increasingly dot the landscape; and commemorative events seem to occur with increasing frequency. The history of genocide is also affected by these broad cultural trends; indeed, in some respects it exemplifies them. The perpetration of genocide requires the mobilization of collective memories, as does the commemoration of it. For the individual victims of genocide, traumatic memories cannot be escaped; for societies, genocide has profound effects that are immediately felt and that people are exhorted (and willingly choose) never to forget. 'Dark tourism'—visits to death camps or other sites of mass murder—is fully integrated into the tourist trail.[1] Although thinkers as diverse as Friedrich Nietzsche, Ernest Renan, Paul Ricoeur, and Marc Augé might be right to suggest that forgetting is essential for the health of society, genocide is less amenable to willed oblivion than most events because of the deep wounds it creates; thus, in the memory politics that surround it, genocide can scar societies long before and long after its actual occurrence. This chapter

---

[1] J. John Lennon and Malcolm Foley, *Dark Tourism: The Attraction of Death and Disaster* (London: Continuum, 2000).

shows how genocide is bound up with memory, on an individual level of trauma and on a collective level in terms of the creation of stereotypes, prejudice, and post-genocide politics.

Before demonstrating the validity of these claims, it is necessary to say something about 'memory studies'. The basic premise of the study of 'collective memory' is not a quasi-mystical belief in the existence of a social mind, or that societies can be treated as organic wholes (in the manner supposed by many genocide perpetrators); rather, it is the basic claim that, in order to live meaningfully as a human being, that is, in order to have memories (for, as neurologists increasingly show, memory and selfhood are intrinsically linked), one must exist in a social setting. This claim, which has its origin in the work of French sociologists Emile Durkheim and Maurice Halbwachs, and perhaps reaches its zenith in Ricoeur's last major work, *Memory, History, Forgetting* (2000), overturns the intuitively appealing 'methodological individualism' of much twentieth-century thought, installing in its stead a 'methodological holism'. Whilst groups do not have memories in the neurological sense and thus there is no organic basis to the term 'collective memory', nevertheless, 'Collective memories originate from shared communications about the meaning of the past that are anchored in the life-worlds of individuals who partake in the communal life of the respective collective.'[2]

Thus collective memory becomes something that the historian or other scholar can study; memory can be a subject for critical historiography in the same way as gender or class. Historians can think theoretically about what collective memory is, how it is constructed and what it excludes, and they can provide detailed case studies, for example, in examining Italians' memories of fascism or the ways in which the My Lai massacre has been domesticated in American collective memory. Most often historians have focused on what Pierre Nora calls '*lieux de mémoire*', sites such as memorials, museums, or significant buildings (like the Panthéon in Paris, the Neue Wache in Berlin, or the Vietnam Veterans Memorial in Washington, DC), showing how a group's (usually a nation's) self-identity is anchored in these sites of memory. What such sites exclude becomes as relevant for understanding collective memory as the narratives they promote.

More recently, some historians have criticized this model for studying collective memory.[3] It is too easy to do, they say, because it is focused on material objects or aesthetic representations whose meaning can be shown to change over time as people interact with them differently in changed circumstances. For example, the meaning of Auschwitz to Catholic Poles living under communism before 1989 was

---

[2] Wulf Kansteiner, 'Finding Meaning in Memory: A Methodological Critique of Collective Memory Studies', *History and Theory* 41 (2002), 188.

[3] Alon Confino and Peter Fritzsche (eds), *The Work of Memory: New Directions in the Study of German Society and Culture* (Urbana: University of Illinois Press, 2002); Alon Confino, *Germany as a Culture of Remembrance: Promises and Limits of Writing History* (Chapel Hill: University of North Carolina Press, 2006); Kansteiner, 'Finding Meaning'.

different from the meanings that the camp acquired after the end of the Cold War once the site became internationalized. From being a site that acted for Poles as a metaphor for the evils of foreign occupation, Auschwitz became a key site in the Europeanization of Holocaust consciousness when, after the collapse of communism, its overwhelmingly Jewish victims were increasingly recognized. Far more meaningful than studying sites of memory, according to the critics, would be to trace the ways in which conflicts over memory affect social relations. In other words, we need to show how memory is linked with power. Doing so, argues Wulf Kansteiner, requires scholars of memory to think more carefully about their methodology. The scholarship, in his opinion, needs to delineate more clearly the distinctions between individual and collective memory and to think more about reception than about representation. It would benefit from adopting some of the vocabulary and methodology of media studies, with the result that collective memory would be understood as the result of the interaction of three 'types of historical factors: the intellectual and cultural traditions that frame all our representations of the past, the memory makers who selectively adopt and manipulate these traditions, and the memory consumers who use, ignore, or transform such artefacts according to their own interests.'[4]

But for historians memory is more than just a research topic.[5] Historians are also part of the broader culture, one that already fifteen years ago was diagnosed as suffering from a 'surfeit of memory'.[6] Critics of the memory culture argue that, like 'heritage', memory is exclusionary, reactionary, and nostalgic; at its worst, it can be accused in its quest for authenticity and 're-enchantment' of 'projecting "psycho-neurotic jargon" onto the memory of various national or (more often) ethnoracial groups.'[7] Memory is, *in fine*, one of the more dangerous tools of identity politics. Thus, scholars need to consider their own investments in memory politics, especially when writing about subjects like genocide. Interventions in, for example, debates about commemorative practices in Rwanda cannot be made on a whim. But finally, memory is inseparable from history, so that even when the current 'memory obsession' has passed, when the piles of confessional literature have been pulped and the commemorative ceremonies are unattended, still, as Ricoeur notes, memory will be the 'bedrock' of history. The fact that people can say that 'this has happened' remains the starting point for historiography.[8] Studying the links between genocide and memory means, then, examining the ways in which

---

[4] Kansteiner, 'Finding Meaning', 180.

[5] Kerwin Lee Klein, 'On the Emergence of Memory in Historical Discourse', *Representations* 69 (2000), 127–50.

[6] Charles S. Maier, 'A Surfeit of Memory? Reflections on History, Melancholy and Denial', *History and Memory* 5:2 (1993), 136–52.

[7] Klein, 'On the Emergence'.

[8] Paul Ricoeur, *Memory, History, Forgetting* (Chicago: University of Chicago Press, 2004 [orig. French 2000]). See also Dan Stone, 'Beyond the Menmosyne Institute: The Future of Memory after

collective memories of past humiliations or victories are mobilized in the present, showing how individuals and societies are traumatized by genocide, and analysing the ways in which post-genocidal commemorative practices sustain collective memories.

In 1950, Champetier de Ribes, the French Prosecutor, stated that Nazi crimes 'were so monstrous, so undreamt of in history throughout the Christian era up to the birth of Hitlerism, that the term "genocide" has had to be coined to define it.' As the legal scholar Alexander Greenawalt, who cites de Ribes, notes, the United Nations Genocide Convention (UNGC) was not merely a way of codifying individual guilt. The concept of genocide 'is as much about questions of history and collective memory'.[9] The background to the UNGC and questions of the definition of genocide are explored elsewhere in this *Handbook*; here I wish only to develop the point that genocide and memory are inseparable, for reasons of the cultural freight that the term contains as well as, more obviously, the enormity of the crime itself. In what follows, I will analyse the nature of this relationship.

MEMORY AS MOBILIZATION

It is tempting, when trying to understand perpetrators of genocide, to assume that they are convinced of their own superiority, that they are the arrogant bearers of an ideology that requires the merciless elimination of the weak. For example, one interpretation of the Holocaust suggests that behind the murder of the Jews lay a deeper desire to overthrow the moral law—represented by the Ten Commandments, the basis of Judeo-Christian civilization—and reinstate the right to commit genocide, as in the virile, martial societies of ancient Greece.[10] Such rhetoric is not hard to find, especially in colonial settings where the social Darwinist notion of superior races 'superseding' the inferior was common. Yet, in fact, most genocides result from processes of worsening national or imperial crisis that give rise to a feeling of massive insecurity or existential threat among the perpetrators. A curious, paradoxical logic is at work: genocide perpetrators commit the most horrific crimes in the belief—always exaggerated and sometimes outright fantastical—that they are defensive acts to ensure that they will not suffer the same fate. In

the Age of Commemoration', in Richard Crownshaw, Jane Kilby, and Anthony Rowland (eds), *The Future of Memory* (New York: Berghahn Books, 2010).

[9] Alexander K. A. Greenawalt, 'Rethinking Genocidal Intent: The Case for a Knowledge-Based Interpretation', *Columbia Law Review* 99:8 (1999), 2294.

[10] Gunnar Heinsohn, 'What Makes the Holocaust a Uniquely Unique Genocide?', *Journal of Genocide Research* 2:3 (2000), 411–30.

other words, barbaric actions are justified for fear of being subjected to barbaric actions. Germans in South West Africa (Namibia) 'did not commit massacres in the colonies because they were in a strong position and had the power to decide on life or death of the indigenous population. On the contrary, German settlers felt unsafe and were afraid to lose their existence.'[11] In some cases, as in Rwanda, a history of Hutu–Tutsi conflict from at least 1959 provided the background to genocide. In the Ottoman Empire, small numbers of Armenians joined revolution-ary movements that defied the state.[12] Yet in none of these cases was it necessary for the perpetrators to respond by seeking to slaughter the targeted population. What mobilized them to do so, what exacerbated the sense of threat to the point at which genocide became a viable and acceptable option, was fear underpinned by memo-ry: of former oppression or supposed treason. Specifically, collective memories of past suffering are almost always brought to bear on current crises, lending them cultural meaning—the weight of dead ancestors weighing on the minds of the living—and imbuing them with added ferocity. Memory fuels genocide.[13]

Stalin's Soviet Union and Pol Pot's Cambodia both illustrate the point. In the former, the construction of the 'Kulak', which began with Stolypin's reforms before 1917, revived fears of starvation and social conflict. Belief that peasants were hoarding food, which would lead to death on a massive scale for urban dwellers, then permitted massive oppression.[14] And in the latter, Khmer Rouge support was massively boosted by the effects of American bombing in the early 1970s. The response to this attack does not explain the ferocity of the 'auto-genocide' between 1975 and 1979, but memories of French colonial wars, Prince Norodom Sihanouk's contempt for the majority rural population, and the age-old fear of the Vietnamese certainly drove many ordinary Cambodians into the arms of the Khmer Rouge, as did the regime's revival of the grandeur of the Angkorian dynasty. As Ben Kiernan notes, 'The total reshaping of Cambodia under Pol Pot may be said to demonstrate the power of a myth.'[15]

---

[11] Dominik J. Schaller, 'From Conquest to Genocide: Colonial Rule in German Southwest Africa and German East Africa', in A. Dirk Moses (ed.), *Empire, Colony, Genocide: Conquest, Occupation, and Subaltern Resistance in World History* (New York: Berghahn Books, 2008), 311.

[12] Donald Bloxham, *The Great Game of Genocide: Imperialism, Nationalism and the Destruction of the Ottoman Armenians* (Oxford: Oxford University Press, 2005).

[13] See Mark Levene, *Genocide in the Age of the Nation State*. vol i: *The Meaning of Genocide* (London: I. B. Tauris, 2005), 196–202.

[14] Terry Martin, 'The Origins of Soviet Ethnic Cleansing', *Journal of Modern History* 70:4 (1998), 813–61; Nicolas Werth, 'The Crimes of the Stalin Regime: Outline for an Inventory and Classification', in Dan Stone (ed.), *The Historiography of Genocide* (Basingstoke: Palgrave Macmillan, 2008), 400–19; Werth in this volume.

[15] Ben Kiernan, 'Myth, Nationalism and Genocide', *Journal of Genocide Research* 3:2 (2001), 190. See also *idem*, 'Serial Colonialism and Genocide in Nineteenth-Century Cambodia', in Moses (ed.), *Empire, Colony, Genocide*, 205–28; *idem*, 'Roots of Genocide: New Evidence on the US Bombardment of Cambodia', *Cultural Survival Quarterly* 14:3 (1990); David P. Chandler, 'Seeing Red: Perceptions of Cambodian History in Democratic Kampuchea', in David Chandler and Ben Kiernan (eds), *Revolution*

The Rwandan example is equally full of such fears and fantasies, based on the memory of Hutu–Tutsi conflict from at least the Hutu Revolution of 1959 if not from the period of colonial rule (first German, then Belgian) from the late nineteenth century. Tutsi refugees and their children actively kept alive the memory of the land they had left (like Hutu refugees from Burundi in Tanzania),[16] so that even those young members of the RPF who had been born in Uganda and had never seen Rwanda felt that they were 'returning home' in 1994. And the memory of the colonial period, in which minority Tutsi domination was established according to the warped racial logic of the colonizers, was mobilized by Hutu extremists in the run-up to the genocide, especially as the framework for peace established by the Arusha Accords started collapsing.[17] Here the point about memory not as an organic phenomenon but as a key component of political power is especially clear. For although there had always been tensions between Hutus and Tutsis in Rwanda since the colonial period, when the Belgian authorities institutionalized the distinction as 'racial',[18] there was nothing like a permanent state of war between the two 'communities', which were, after the post-revolutionary violence of the early 1960s, in fact thoroughly mixed. Only with the threat of war did Hutu extremists revitalize the memory of pre-1959 Rwandan society, dominated by the Tutsi minority, and whip up fear among the Hutu population that they should eliminate the Tutsis because otherwise this same fate would be reserved for them. Indeed, as recent research shows, the speed with which certain parts of the country threw themselves into participating in genocide was determined less by the reception of infamous propaganda such as the 'Hutu Ten Commandments', *Kangura* magazine or Radio Télévision Libres des Milles Collines, than affinity to the ruling MRND party, proximity to the front line and fear of the approaching RPF.[19] And, indeed, the RPF made equally effective use of collective memories of expulsion and exile, with violent results both during and after the genocide. Since the RPF took power, the government has come under increasing

and Its Aftermath in Kampuchea: Eight Essays (New Haven, CT: Yale University Southeast Asia Studies, 1983), 34–56; Karl D. Jackson, 'Intellectual Origins of the Khmer Rouge', in *idem* (ed.), *Cambodia 1975–1978: Rendezvous with Death* (Princeton, NJ: Princeton University Press, 1989), 241–50.

[16] Liisa Malkki, *Purity and Exile: Violence, Memory and National Cosmology among Hutu Refugees in Tanzania* (Chicago: University of Chicago Press, 1995).

[17] For example, Nigel Eltringham, ' "Invaders Who Have Stolen the Country": The Hamitic Hypothesis, Race and the Rwandan Genocide', *Social Identities* 12:4 (2006), 425–46; René Lemarchand, 'Exclusion, Marginalization and Political Mobilization: The Road to Hell in the Great Lakes', *University of Copenhagen Centre of African Studies Occasional Paper* (March 2000).

[18] Mahmood Mamdani, *When Victims Become Killers: Colonialism, Nativism, and the Genocide in Rwanda* (Princeton: Princeton University Press, 2001); Edith R. Sanders, 'The Hamitic Hypothesis', *Journal of African History* 10:4 (1969), 512–32.

[19] Scott Straus, *The Order of Genocide: Race, Power, and War in Rwanda* (Ithaca, NY: Cornell University Press, 2006).

scrutiny by Western scholars who have grown suspicious of its 'harmonising perspective on pre-colonial society and history'. The fear that Rwandan memories of
both the pre-colonial period and the 1994 genocide are being instrumentalized—for
example, by labelling all Hutu refugees as génocidaires or by employing guilt
discourses in the international arena—not only maintains RPF power but 'perpe-
tuates violence in the Great Lakes.'[20]

Perhaps the most infamous example of such memory mobilization is the speech
given by Slobodan Milošević in 1989 at the site of the Battle of Kosovo Polje that took
place 600 years earlier on 28 June 1389. That battle (and that date—also the day of
Gavrilo Princip's shooting of Archduke Franz Ferdinand in 1914) is ingrained into
Serbian memory as a moment of military defeat at the hands of the Turks, but a
moment of moral victory, on the basis of Knez Lazar choosing a heavenly instead of
an earthly kingdom for the Serbs. As well as confirming the Serb nation's place in the
divine realm, the myth established the continuity of the Serb nation across the
centuries and confirmed Serbia's right to its ancestral lands in Kosovo.[21] It was also
the source of the 'betrayal syndrome'—Serb allegations that Muslims in Yugoslavia
are 'that part of themselves which betrayed the "faith of their forefathers."'[22] Milošević's speech is regularly cited as one of the key moments in his rise to power, and the
use of the legend of the battle a central component in his ethno-nationalist arsenal
and in the building of a nationalist consensus in Serbia. Although its significance can
be overstated, this manipulation of Serbian national memory—which of course
required grassroots activity to operationalize it, not Milošević alone—is key to
understanding the 'ethnic cleansing' that accompanied the Yugoslav wars of the
1990s and, especially, the violent efforts to expel ethnic Albanians from Kosovo at a
point when Serbia was already isolated as a pariah state in the eyes of the 'international community'. Extremists prevailed over moderates in Serbia because they
persuaded a large enough constituency that 'the powerful can fear the weak.'[23]

More important even than the myth of Kosovo, which represents Serbian 'deep
memory', was the memory of what had happened in World War II. In the 1990s, the

[20] Johan Pottier, *Re-Imagining Rwanda: Conflict, Survival and Disinformation in the Late Twentieth
Century* (Cambridge: Cambridge University Press, 2002), 130. See also Eric Stover and Harvey M.
Weinstein (eds), *My Neighbor, My Enemy: Justice and Community in the Aftermath of Mass Atrocity*
(Cambridge: Cambridge University Press, 2004); Gérard Prunier, *Africa's World War: Congo, the
Rwandan Genocide, and the Making of a Continental Catastrophe* (New York: Oxford University
Press, 2008).

[21] Florian Bieber, 'Nationalist Mobilization and Stories of Serb Suffering: The Kosovo Myth from
600th Anniversary to the Present', *Rethinking History* 6:1 (2002), 95–110; G. G. Raymond and S. Bajic-
Raymond, 'Memory and History: The Discourse of Nation-Building in the Former Yugoslavia',
Patterns of Prejudice 31:1 (1997), 21–30; Jasna Dragović-Soso, *'Saviours of the Nation': Serbia's
Intellectual Opposition and the Revival of Nationalism* (London: C. Hurst, 2002).

[22] Milica Bakić-Hayden, 'Nesting Orientalisms: The Case of Former Yugoslavia', *Slavic Review* 54:4
(1995), 927.

[23] Anthony Oberschall, 'The Manipulation of Ethnicity: From Ethnic Cooperation to Violence and
War in Yugoslavia', *Ethnic and Racial Studies* 23:6 (2000), 982–1001.

self-identification of Serbian and Croatian paramilitaries as Chetniks and Ustashe, respectively, was a conscious echo of the war, when 'Independent Croatia'—in reality, a Nazi puppet state under the leadership of the clerico-fascist collaborator Ante Pavelić—was responsible for the murder of tens of thousands of Serbs, Jews, and Romanies. No serious historian doubts that Serbs were subjected to a genocidal onslaught under the rule of Nazi-protected Croatia, but the manipulation of the figures of the dead in the 1980s and 1990s was a major contributor to the worsening of relations between the two major components of the Yugoslav federation. Croatia's neo-fascist president, Franjo Tudjman, was not only a Holocaust denier but a belittler of Serb suffering during World War II, and Serbian historians and politicians regularly exaggerated the numbers killed at Jasenovac and elsewhere in order to spread fear throughout the Serbian population (especially outside of the borders of Serbia) as Yugoslavia was breaking apart. A figure of 700,000 Serb deaths at Jasenovac was commonly heard in the 1980s, when the true figure is likely to have been about 100,000. This strategy was highly effective, as fear of becoming victims of genocide divided previously mixed communities into ethnically separate groups: 'Everyone was traumatized by all the talk of World War Two atrocities,' wrote Bogdan Denitch, 'even those who had seemed immune to nationalism.'[24] Reliable figures of the dead are still hard to come by, though the work of Tomislav Dulić, Robert M. Hayden, and others has done much to bring clarity to this fraught issue—but scholarship alone is of course insufficient to quell ultranationalist ideologies.[25]

The Holocaust can also to some extent be seen through this lens. Dirk Moses argues that the Holocaust should be understood using a framework in which genocide is seen as a combination of colonial expansion, security fears, and subaltern revenge. Hitler drew on the overseas colonial experience, especially in India and North America, for inspiration for his own vision of a colonized Europe. The treatment of Ukrainians, Poles, and other conquered nations certainly conforms to this colonial pattern, in which the 'natives' were to become a reservoir of slave labour. And the murder of the Jews, according to Moses, was in part a subaltern genocide, through which Hitler aimed to 'emancipate' Germany from perceived 'foreign occupation', that is, Jewish rule. Thus, whilst Slavic populations were

[24] Bogdan Denitch, *Ethnic Nationalism* (Minneapolis: University of Minnesota Press, 1996), 81, cited in Oberschall, 'The Manipulation', 990.

[25] Robert M. Hayden, 'Mass Killings and Images of Genocide in Bosnia, 1941–5 and 1992–5', in Stone (ed.), *The Historiography of Genocide*, 487–516; *idem*, 'Recounting the Dead: The Rediscovery and Redefinition of Wartime Massacres in Late- and Post-Communist Yugoslavia', in Ruby S. Watson (ed.), *Memory, Opposition and History under State Socialism* (Santa Fe: School of American Research Press, 1994), 167–84; Tomislav Dulić, *Utopias of Nation: Local Mass Killings in Bosnia and Herzegovina, 1941–42* (Uppsala: Uppsala University Press, 2005). On the figures from the 1990s, see Ewa Tabeau and Jakub Bijak, 'War-Related Deaths in the 1992–1995 Armed Conflicts in Bosnia and Herzegovina: A Critique of Previous Estimates and Recent Results', *European Journal of Population*, 21 (2005), 187–215; Research and Documentation Center, Sarajevo, *Human Losses in Bosnia and Herzegovina 91–95* (CD-Rom, 2006).

regarded as *Untermenschen* (subhumans), suitable for enslavement, the Jews were a source of fear, for they sought to take over the world, and their elimination was a project of 'national liberation'.[26] Genocide, in Moses' formulation, 'is as much an act of security as it is racial hatred'.[27] It is worth noting that this stress on Nazi fears of Jews—as opposed to the standard narrative that stresses Nazi racial theory and the need to rid the world of inferior 'non-Aryans'—provides common ground between scholars who incorporate the Holocaust into the new comparative genocide framework, and those who argue that the racial paradigm at the heart of the Nazi *Weltanschauung* ultimately owed less to race science than to a paranoid political conspiracy theory. This view suggests that the Nazis were not so much driven by their sense of superiority as by their fear of the power of 'the Jew'. Hence the lengths to which Goebbels went in his propaganda output to convince the German public that 'The Jews are guilty of everything!'[28] The source of this sense of existential threat was the 'stab-in-the-back' legend from 1918, the belief that Germany lost the Great War because the Jews had betrayed the country. Michael Geyer notes that 'The rhetoric of *Endkampf* [final battle] found its most potent enemy in the figure of the Jew.'[29] Indeed, the feeding through of the memory of 1918 into Nazi ideology is a textbook example of the power of traumatic memory, of what Mark Levene calls 'the perpetrator's "never again" syndrome'. 'They should not have staged 9 November 1918 with impunity', fumed Hitler to the Czech foreign minister in 1939, 'That day shall be avenged . . . The Jews shall be annihilated in our land.'[30]

POST-GENOCIDAL TRAUMATIC MEMORY

What happens after genocide? When communities are devastated, often all that is left is memory, and that a 'memory shot through with holes'.[31] Thus survivors turn

[26] A. Dirk Moses, 'Empire, Colony, Genocide: Keywords and the Philosophy of History', in Moses (ed.), *Empire, Colony, Genocide*, 34–40.

[27] A. Dirk Moses, 'Moving the Genocide Debate beyond the History Wars', *Australian Journal of Politics and History* 54:2 (2008), 264.

[28] See Jeffrey Herf, *The Jewish Enemy: Nazi Propaganda During World War II and the Holocaust* (Cambridge, MA: Belknap Press of Harvard University Press, 2006). Goebbels cited at 209. See also Doris L. Bergen, 'Instrumentalization of *Volksdeutschen* in German Propaganda in 1939: Replacing/Erasing Poles, Jews, and Other Victims', *German Studies Review* 31:3 (2008), 447–70 for an example of the manipulation of fears of German victimization at the hands of Poles.

[29] Michael Geyer, '*Endkampf* 1918 and 1945: German Nationalism, Annihilation, and Self-Destruction', in Alf Lüdtke and Bernd Weisbrod (eds), *No Man's Land of Violence: Extreme Wars in the Twentieth Century* (Göttingen: Wallstein, 2006), 47.

[30] Levene, *The Meaning of Genocide*, 197.

[31] Henri Raczymow, 'Memory Shot Through With Holes', *Yale French Studies* 85 (1994), 98–105.

inwards, and focus on themselves and the need for familial and community repair. This process is intrinsically related to memory, in the production of memorial books and monuments and, in interacting with the wider world, in attempts to bring what happened to general notice and to bring perpetrators to justice. If collective memory is essential for mobilizing perpetrators, it also underpins attempts to commemorate genocide in its immediate aftermath and to advocate on behalf of survivors in their quest for justice.

A large literature now exists on reparations, compensation, restitution, war crimes trials, truth commissions, and the developing international law on genocide since the founding of the International Criminal Court in 1999. In numerous contexts, from Guatemala to Poland, national commissions of inquiry have been set up to inquire into genocidal pasts. Austria's amnesia as regards its Nazi past was only an extreme example of a common phenomenon, and most European states have now 'discovered' the fact that Nazism and the Holocaust were part of their histories too. Since the Stockholm Forum in 2000, many European states have commissioned official investigations into their experience of and, often, collaboration with Nazi occupation and genocide. For example, the question of the extent of Nazi looting and of restitution for victims of the Holocaust has been an area of remarkable scholarly activity since the end of the Cold War.[32] Dan Diner has highlighted the relationship between memory and restitution in the light of the move to incorporate Holocaust Memorial Day into the European calendar and European cultural identity: 'a basic anthropological assumption' exists, thinks Diner, that presumes an 'organic interconnection between restituted property rights and the evocation of past memories, or vice versa: Restitution of property as the result of recovered memory.'[33] As he rightly notes, this link between memory and property is both plausible and problematic.

The issue of property and restitution provides a link between issues of memory that are victim community-focused and those aimed at the wider world. Perhaps post-genocide trials represent the purest form of the latter. The image of the twenty-two leading Nazis in the dock at Nuremberg is one of the most memorable of the twentieth century, and the memory of Nuremberg informs the currently developing international law on genocide and human rights.[34] Issues of

[32] Martin Dean, *Robbing the Jews: The Confiscation of Jewish Property in the Holocaust 1933–1945* (Cambridge: Cambridge University Press, 2008); Martin Dean, Constantin Goschler and Philipp Ther (eds), *Robbery and Restitution: The Conflict over Jewish Property in Europe* (New York: Berghahn Books, 2007).

[33] Dan Diner, 'Restitution and Memory: The Holocaust in European Political Cultures', *New German Critique* 90 (2003), 39–40. See also Dan Diner and Gotthard Wunberg (eds), *Restitution and Memory: Material Restoration in Europe* (New York: Berghahn Books, 2007).

[34] Donald Bloxham, *Genocide on Trial: War Crimes Trials and the Formation of Holocaust History and Memory* (Oxford: Oxford University Press, 2001); Mark Mazower, 'An International Civilization? Empire, Internationalism and the Crisis of the Mid-Twentieth Century', *International Affairs* 82:3 (2006), 553–66.

compensatory and/or corrective justice, as well as penal/retributive justice, are in evidence in different sorts of trials, depending on whether these deal with reparations or punishment. The Eichmann Trial exemplifies a deliberately orchestrated attempt to bring Holocaust memory into the centre of Israeli public (as opposed to private) consciousness, and the significance of post-genocide trials for memory work is not to be underestimated. Even though it is widely acknowledged that the punishment in such cases can never fit the crime—'The Nazi crimes, it seems to me, explode the limits of the law; and that is precisely what constitutes their monstrousness'[35]—the impact of such trials explains why they have been avoided in so many instances, from France to Cambodia, by the use of delaying tactics. Numerous scholars identify shortcomings in the UNGC, and some assert that these shortcomings have negative consequences for the establishment of collective memories of genocide;[36] but there is a good reason why the authorities often resist and place obstacles in the way of post-genocide trials.

When memory is the subject, the focus of attention is usually on commemorative practices, monuments, and museums. An enormous body of research now exists on Holocaust memorials and museums, of which there are many throughout the world.[37] But it is not only the Holocaust that provides material to test James E. Young's claim that monuments propagate an 'illusion of common memory'. The desire to memorialize traumatic events such as the Holocaust 'may actually spring from an opposite and equal desire to forget them', since the assumption that the monument is always there tends to encourage a lack of engagement with the issues.[38] A casual stroll through any major city, most of whose monuments remain unnoticed and, for the inhabitants, unidentifiable, suggests that Young has a point.

Apart from the question of whether genocide memorials too readily take their cue from representations of the Holocaust,[39] it is worth considering what forms of memory genocide memorials and museums are meant to encourage. One scholar suggests that 'fear of denial and scarcity of resources has resulted in the most graphic genocide memorial in history: that of Murambi' in Rwanda.[40] At the school where the massacre of several thousand Tutsis took place, the remains of

---

[35] Hannah Arendt to Karl Jaspers, 17 August 1946, in *Arendt/Jaspers Correspondence 1926–1969*, ed. Lotte Kohler and Hans Saner (San Diego: Harcourt Brace, 1992), 54.

[36] For example, Caroline Fournet, *The Crime of Destruction and the Law of Genocide: Their Impact on Collective Memory* (Aldershot: Ashgate, 2007); Gerry Simpson, *Law, War and Crime: War Crimes Trials and the Reinvention of International Law* (Cambridge: Polity, 2007).

[37] Dan Stone, 'Memory, Memorials and Museums', in *idem* (ed.), *The Historiography of the Holocaust* (Basingstoke: Palgrave Macmillan, 2004), 508–32.

[38] James E. Young, *The Texture of Memory: Holocaust Memorials and Meaning* (New Haven, CT: Yale University Press, 1993), 6–7.

[39] See David S. MacDonald, *Identity Politics in the Age of Genocide: The Holocaust and Historical Representation* (London: Routledge, 2008).

[40] William F. S. Miles, 'Third World Views of the Holocaust', *Journal of Genocide Research* 6:3 (2004), 388.

the dead were left as the monument, giving rise to a 'traumatic silence' amongst visitors. The same is true of the bones that function as memorials at Nyamata, Nyarabuye, and Ntarama, where 'the function of the memorials is not to obtain scientific evidence, but rather to produce an experience of memory.'[41] In Cambodia, the Tuol Sleng Museum of Genocidal Crimes and the Choeung Ek 'killing fields' site serve a similar function. They also aim to preserve the memory of genocide, but do so by shocking visitors (mostly Western tourists), partly by deliberately borrowing a Holocaust-inspired form of representation, and partly by instilling a new national narrative.[42] And given that most of the Khmer Rouge leaders have escaped the trials that belatedly began in November 2007 with the trial of Kaing Guek Eav (the head of Tuol Sleng, known as Comrade Duch), their memorial function is somewhat soured. In both countries, however, the significance of the genocides means that the public display of body parts has been permitted, contrary to usual custom, although one should bear in mind that 'the maintenance of a site to communicate its cursedness or ruination is itself a sustained act of intervention.'[43] The sheer mass of bones in these monuments provokes the shock and horror that are appropriate responses to genocide, but their anonymity means that they also recapitulate the logic of genocide: the reduction of individual human beings to representatives of a (perpetrator-defined) group. Hence the importance of local memorials and commemorative festivals in Cambodia.[44] And hence the great significance of naming in general, as seen in many memorial practices, from the post-Holocaust *yizker-bikher* (memorial books) to the recovery of names in Spain's *Todos los nombres* project.[45]

Remembering genocide, however, is only one side of the coin of responding to such traumatic events. The other is willed amnesia. The conscious turn to memory tends—though this is not always true—to require the passage of time, for in the immediate aftermath of genocide the scars are still too deep. Especially in instances where former perpetrators and surviving victims must live together in close

---

[41] Sara Guyer, 'Rwanda's Bones', *boundary 2* 36:3 (2009).

[42] Judy Ledgerwood, 'The Cambodian Tuol Sleng Museum of Genocidal Crimes: National Narrative', in David E. Lorey and Willian H. Beezley (eds), *Genocide, Collective Violence, and Popular Memory: The Politics of Remembrance in the Twentieth Century* (Wilmington, DE: Scholarly Resources, 2002), 103–22. See also Burcu Münyas, 'Genocide in the Minds of Cambodian Youth: Transmitting (Hi)stories of Genocide to Second and Third Generations in Cambodia', *Journal of Genocide Research* 10:3 (2008), 413–39; David P. Chandler, 'Cambodia Deals with its Past: Collective Memory, Demonisation and Induced Amnesia', *Totalitarian Movements and Political Religions* 9:2–3 (2008), 355–69.

[43] Paul Williams, 'Witnessing Genocide: Vigilance and Remembrance at Tuol Sleng and Choeung Ek', *Holocaust and Genocide Studies* 18:4 (2004), 242. On trials, see Jörg Menzel, 'Justice Delayed or Too Late for Justice? The Khmer Rouge Tribunal and the Cambodian "Genocide" 1975–79', *Journal of Genocide Research* 9:2 (2007), 215–33.

[44] Rachel Hughes, 'Memory and Sovereignty in Post-1979 Cambodia: Choeung Ek and Local Genocide Memorials', in Susan E. Cook (ed.), *Genocide in Cambodia and Rwanda: New Perspectives* (New Brunswick, NJ: Transaction, 2006), 257–80.

[45] Guyer, 'Rwanda's Bones'.

proximity, closing off memory, or at least trying to do so, is a meaningful way of dealing with the past. In Rwanda, for example, what is striking about Susanne Buckley-Zistel's interviews with people from across the country's diverse population is that, whilst they often referred to the 1994 genocide, 'the causes of the genocide and the decades of tension between Hutu and Tutsi were ignored.'[46] Precisely the years of tension from 1959 onwards that saw the mobilization of memory in the early 1990s were the years that had to be 'forgotten' (that is to say, left undiscussed), rather than the events of the genocide itself. Gacaca trials can address issues of who did what in the context of the genocide, but leaves the underlying causes unaddressed. Only time will tell whether the Rwandan government's attempt to switch the country from a Francophone to an Anglophone position, to remove ethnic markers from ID cards, to rewrite Rwandan history, and to advocate local as well as international forms of justice will help Rwandans to overcome these conflict-ridden memories.

In Bosnia, Cornelia Sorabji shows that memories of traumatic events continue 'to affect the social fabric', possibly sustaining the sort of hostility that fuelled conflict in the first place.[47] Sorabji correctly notes that the risk of analysing memory as a carrier of conflict is that it serves to perpetuate 'ancient hatreds' style arguments, which suggest that war in the Balkans is a more or less natural condition. Thus, she proposes to situate individuals and their memories—'real' or 'transmitted'—into the context of the politics of memory, that is, the broader framework of competing narratives at group or state level that seek to 'channel' people's memories in certain ways. For since 'collective memory' is not an organic process (there is no group mind), it follows that the inter-relationship between individuals ('memory users') and the group ('memory makers') needs to be analysed. One should not assume 'that human minds are endlessly manipulable and that schooling or the broadcasting of nationalistic commemorative ceremonies can fundamentally alter personal memories of strongly emotional, life-changing events such as violent bereavement.'[48]

Of course, one of the characteristics of traumatic memory is that it cannot be suppressed at will. It is by its very nature a memory that returns unexpectedly and uncontrollably to haunt individual victims and post-genocide societies. There is no need for memories of genocide to be 'recovered'—in the dubious manner of childhood abuse cases of the 1980s—since it has never gone away in the first place. Many scholars are now rightly critical of the view, fashionable in the 1990s especially in literary studies, that 'traumatic memory' is a widely applicable concept.

---

[46] Susanne Buckley-Zistel, 'Remembering to Forget: Chosen Amnesia as a Strategy for Local Coexistence in Post-Genocide Rwanda', *Africa* 76:2 (2006), 131.

[47] Cornelia Sorabji, 'Managing Memories in Post-War Sarajevo: Individuals, Bad Memories, and New Wars', *Journal of the Royal Anthropological Institute*, NS, 12 (2006), 1–18.

[48] Sorabji, 'Managing Memories', 2.

The idea that whole societies can be traumatized has been subjected to serious criticism, so that what we are generally left with is a more or less appropriate metaphor, not a concept that carries any of the precise, clinical meaning that it does when applied to individuals (when used carefully, and not just in the vernacular, as in 'what a traumatic day that was'). As Kansteiner notes, 'none of the existing concepts of Holocaust trauma is well suited to explain the effects of Holocaust representations on individuals or collectives who encounter the Final Solution only as a media event for educational or entertainment purposes.'[49] Still, in the case of societies that have experienced genocide, we are facing a situation where the concept of traumatic memory, if it has any use at all, is about as applicable as one can expect. This is why I noted at the outset that genocide is less amenable to willed amnesia than other events. What one actually sees, for example, in the cases of Bosnia or Rwanda mentioned above, is a form of repression, rather than a 'healthy forgetting' in the manner of Nietzsche. And what is repressed sooner or later returns, as we currently see the memory of the post-Civil War 'repression'—a somewhat coy term for what some historians actually consider a genocidal on-slaught—of the Nationalists' enemies in Spain.[50] The current tension in Bosnia and the desperate situation in the Democratic Republic of Congo, where estimates are that more than 5 million people have died in the post-1994 regional war, indicate that the politics of post-genocidal memories are matters of life and death.

COMMEMORATION AND MEMORY CONFLICTS

In February 2008, Kevin Rudd, the new Australian Prime Minister, made a decisive break with the politics of John Howard's conservative administration by making a public apology to the country's indigenous people for the suffering endured by the 'stolen children' and their families. This policy, which began in the early twentieth century and lasted until the 1960s, removed 'half-caste' children from Aboriginal communities, bringing them up in separated institutions with the explicit aim of assimilating Aborigines to 'white' culture. This was a change from the

[49] Wulf Kansteiner, 'Testing the Limits of Trauma: The Long-Term Psychological Effects of the Holocaust on Individuals and Collectives', *History of the Human Sciences* 17:2–3 (2004), 97; *idem*, 'Genealogy of a Category Mistake: A Critical Intellectual History of the Cultural Trauma Metaphor', *Rethinking History* 8:2 (2004), 193–221.

[50] Helen Graham, 'The Memory of Murder: Mass Killing, Incarceration and the Making of Francoism', in Alison Ribeiro de Menezes, Roberta Quance and Anne L. Walsh (eds), *Guerra y memoria en la España contemporánea/War and Memory in Contemporary Spain* (Madrid: Verbum, 2009, 29–49).

early-twentieth-century approach of biological absorption, or 'breeding out the black', which aimed to prevent white Australia from being threatened—so the fear went—by 'a large black population which may drive out the white'.[51] But whilst the official programme of biological absorption came to an end around 1940, the policy of child removal continued for several decades, devastating Aboriginal communities and leading Sir Ronald Wilson to proclaim in his 1997 *Bringing Them Home* report that the policy constituted genocide under article IIe of the UNGC. Whether this was an appropriate designation is in this context not the point (Rudd, incidentally, denies that it was genocide), so much as the fact that the subsequent furore revealed the way in which controversy about genocidal origins haunts 'national memory' generations after the cessation of frontier conflict.

The perpetration of genocide requires the mobilization of memory, as does its punishment, though in the latter case there is a prima facie argument that 'memory mobilizes itself'. Post-genocidal conflicts over memory, especially national memory, reveal another aspect of the question: memory can intervene in national politics in unexpected ways and present challenges to long-held and cherished national narratives. This is particularly true of settler societies, and is best illustrated by the Australian case. With the emergence of what its opponents pejoratively called 'black armband history', debates over Australian history overshadowed contemporary political debates concerning how best to deal with troubled Aboriginal communities. Conservative historians, most notably Keith Windschuttle, charged 'politically correct' historians not only with failing to appreciate the true nature of frontier conflict, in which mutual incomprehension rather than genocidal intent was at work, but also with deliberately exaggerating the numbers of Aborigines killed in massacres.[52] Even official efforts at reconciliation were 'framed in nation-building language which implicitly refused to accommodate indigenous aspirations of difference'.[53] The 'history wars' that followed the publication of Windschuttle's revisionist book have been described as an 'Australian *Historikerstreit*', a designation that is revealing, since the West German debate about the uniqueness of the Holocaust that took place in the 1980s broke no new historical ground but was fundamental to the self-image of the Federal Republic. So in Australia, debates about how best to describe the past go to the heart of national narratives. The challenge to the Australian story of mates pulling together to create the 'lucky country' is one that did not sit well with the cultural politics of the Howard government, which was not open to the fact that historians of early Australia

---

[51] Quoted in Robert Manne, 'Aboriginal Child Removal and the Question of Genocide, 1900–1940', in A. Dirk Moses (ed.), *Genocide and Settler Society: Frontier Violence and Stolen Indigenous Children in Australian History* (New York: Berghahn Books, 2004), 229, 237; Pat O'Malley, 'Gentle Genocide: The Government of Aboriginal Peoples in Central Australia', *Social Justice* 21:4 (1994), 46–65.

[52] Keith Windschuttle, *The Fabrication of Aboriginal History* (Sydney: Macleay Press, 2002).

[53] Damien Short, 'Reconciliation, Assimilation, and the Indigenous Peoples of Australia', *International Political Science Review* 24:4 (2003), 506.

were not arguing that the colonization of Australia was the same as the Holocaust, only that the similarities of the perpetrators' discourses of race and security in both cases ought to offer food for thought, particularly where current-day policies towards Aborigines are concerned.[54] But whilst debate rages in Australia—unlike in Germany—as to whether the country should be understood as a 'post-genocidal society', the fact that the colonization process was 'objectively lethal' for the Aborigines continues to be overlooked.[55] Irrespective of the statistics and other facts being debated by historians (and here the comparison with the *Historikerstreit* is unconvincing, for in West Germany no historians questioned whether genocide had occurred), the bigger point is that Australian collective memory was being deconstructed and reconstructed anew or, for conservative historians, being undermined by subversives bent on ridiculing national heritage.

Even long after genocide has taken place, memory wars can erupt when group narratives are felt to be under threat. The history of nation-building is inseparable from the 'memories' that nations create, in the shape of the narratives or monuments they construct. Indeed, collective memory does not emerge after the process has come to an end but is an essential part of the process whereby a group constitutes itself as a group; as Jens Bartelson notes, 'the coincidence of state and nation that we normally take to be the very culmination of a successful process of state formation had virtually been *remembered* into existence.'[56] The motives of memory, as James Young reminds us, are never pure.[57]

It is hardly surprising, then, that especially in societies founded on colonial settlement, challenges to positive national narratives are considered problematic. In Australia, whilst the official discourse has changed since the Rudd administration took office, historians such as Tony Barta fear that the 'public conversation' will remain dominated by a 'decent disposal' of the difficult questions. Nevertheless, by comparison with the United States, where the genocide question is still almost wholly ignored, even by prominent scholars of genocide, or Israel, where the memory of the Holocaust continues to poison relations with the Palestinians with devastating consequences, at least in Australia these memory conflicts are being

[54] Moses, 'Moving the Genocide Debate', 254–5. See also Patrick Brantlinger, ' "Black Armband" versus "White Blindfold" History in Australia', *Victorian Studies* 46:4 (2004), 655–74; Neil Levi, ' "No Sensible Comparison"? The Place of the Holocaust in Australia's History Wars', *History & Memory* 19:1 (2007), 124–56; Andrew G. Bonnell and Martin Crotty, 'Australia's History under Howard, 1996–2007', *Annals of the American Academy of Political and Social Science* 617 (2008), 149–65.

[55] A. Dirk Moses, 'An Antipodean Genocide? The Origins of the Genocidal Moment in the Colonization of Australia', *Journal of Genocide Research* 2:1 (2000), 89–106.

[56] Jens Bartelson, 'We Could Remember It for You Wholesale: Myths, Monuments and the Constitution of National Memories', in Duncan Bell (ed.), *Memory, Trauma and World Politics: Reflections on the Relationship between Past and Present* (Basingstoke: Palgrave Macmillan, 2006), 51.

[57] Young, *The Texture of Memory*, 2.

articulated in the public sphere.[58] 'Memory wars' have characterized the whole world since the end of the Cold War, from Romania to Argentina, South Africa to France. In post-genocidal societies, as we see in Bosnia or the DRC, such conflicts are potentially destabilizing and certainly have the power not only to inspire a cosmopolitan culture of human rights but also new outbursts of resentment and revanchism. The only sure conclusion is that memory cannot be ignored and that engagement with the issues—if not resolution of them—remains essential.

CONCLUSION

In a key article on the historical study of memory, Alon Confino asks: 'if the study of memory focuses creatively on how people construct a past through a process of appropriation and contestation, is the real problem not, perhaps, that people construct the past by using the term "memory" at all?'[59] There is, in other words, a danger of studying a phenomenon ('memory') by taking it as its own explanation. This problem, however, is not merely a methodological one of memory studies but a reflection of the complex place that 'memory' holds in contemporary societies. For memory is not simply synonymous with the way in which the past is represented in the present; it is itself constitutive of the present. Memory and identity go hand in hand.

Thus, irrespective of methodological problems, issues connected with memory will continue to resonate. Exclusivist, exclusionary memories remain powerful in many contexts; the generation of genocidal ideologies through the manipulation of memory is as much a possibility as it ever was. Indeed, memory wars by no means guarantee a peaceful resolution or mutually agreeable arbitration between competing versions of the past. As Peter Fritzsche notes, the reason that national memories 'remain so resonant' is 'not because they are more true, but because the narratives of collective guilt and collective victimization that they generate have the effect of recognizing and commemorating individual suffering in socially meaningful, if tendentious, ways.'[60] 'Memory studies' is not an academic game, but an investigation into a phenomenon that can be as dangerous as playing with fire. For this

---

[58] Tony Barta, 'Decent Disposal: Australian Historians and the Recovery of Genocide', in Stone (ed.), *The Historiography of Genocide*, 296–322; Alfred A. Cave, 'Genocide in the Americas', in ibid., 273–95; Avraham Burg, *The Holocaust is Over, We Must Rise from its Ashes* (Houndmills: Palgrave Macmillan, 2008).

[59] Alon Confino, 'Collective Memory and Cultural History: Problems of Method', *American Historical Review* 102:5 (1997), 1403.

[60] Peter Fritzsche, 'The Case of Modern Memory', *Journal of Modern History* 73:1 (2001), 117.

reason, memory cannot be avoided or swept aside. Despite the risks of perpetuating old divisions or reopening unhealed wounds, grappling with memory, especially after traumatic events like genocide, remains essential in order to remind the victims that they are not the worthless or less than human beings that their tormentors have portrayed them as. For nothing is more human, and thus more geared towards the generation of meaning where meaning is otherwise absent (or at least to 'keeping watch over absent meaning'),[61] than the broad spectrum of practices that come under the heading of 'memory'.

ACKNOWLEDGEMENT

My thanks to Donald Bloxham, Becky Jinks, and Dirk Moses for their comments on earlier versions of this chapter.

SELECT BIBLIOGRAPHY

Barayón, Ramón Sender, *A Death in Zamora* (Albuquerque: University of New Mexico Press, 1989).

Bizot, François, *The Gate* (London: Harvill Press, 2003).

Confino, Alon, and Peter Fritzsche (eds), *The Work of Memory: New Directions in the Study of German Society and Culture* (Urbana/Chicago: University of Illinois Press, 2002).

Eltringham, Nigel ed., 'Identity, Justice and "Reconciliation" in Contemporary Rwanda', Special issue of the *Journal of Genocide Research* 11:1 (2009).

Gray, Peter, and Kendrick Oliver (eds), *The Memory of Catastrophe* (Manchester: Manchester University Press, 2004).

MacDonald, David B., *Identity Politics in the Age of Genocide: The Holocaust and Historical Representation* (London/New York: Routledge, 2008).

Ricoeur, Paul, *Memory, History, Forgetting* (Chicago/London: University of Chicago Press, 2004).

Rousso, Henry, *The Vichy Syndrome: History and Memory in France since 1944* (Cambridge, MA: Harvard University Press, 1991).

Stone, Dan (ed.), *The Historiography of Genocide* (Basingstoke/New York: Palgrave Macmillan, 2008).

Suleiman, Susan Rubin, *Crises of Memory and the Second World War* (Cambridge. MA: Harvard University Press, 2006).

---

[61] Maurice Blanchot, *The Writing of the Disaster* (Lincoln: University of Nebraska Press, 1986), 42.

PART II

INTERDISCIPLINARY PERSPECTIVES

CHAPTER 6

....

THE LAW AND
GENOCIDE

....

WILLIAM A. SCHABAS

GENOCIDE is, first and foremost, a legal concept. Like many other terms—murder, rape, theft—it is also used in other contexts and by other disciplines, where its meaning may vary. Many historians and sociologists employ the term genocide to describe a range of atrocities involving killing large numbers of people. But even in law, it is imprecise to speak of a single, universally recognized meaning of genocide. There is a widely accepted definition, first set out in article II of the 1948 *Convention for the Prevention and Punishment of the Crime of Genocide*.[1] Like most legal definitions, its language is subject to various interpretations, and important controversies remain about the scope of the concept even within the framework of what is a concise and carefully worded definition. The crime of genocide has been incorporated within the national legal systems of many countries, where national legislators have imposed their own views on the term, some of them varying slightly or even considerably from the established international definition. As a result, even in law, one can speak of many definitions or interpretations of the concept of genocide.

The term itself was invented by a lawyer, Raphael Lemkin. He intended to fill a gap in international law, as it then stood in the final days of the Second World War. For more than two decades, Lemkin had been engaged at an international level in attempts to codify new categories of international crimes involving atrocities committed against vulnerable civilians. Even before Lemkin's time, international law recognized a limited number of so-called international crimes. As a general

[1] *Convention on the Prevention and Punishment of the Crime of Genocide* (1951), 78 UNTS 277.

rule, they were so designated not because of their shocking scale and extent, but for more mundane reasons, namely because they escaped the territorial jurisdiction of states. Piracy is the classic example, a crime committed on the high seas. Lemkin and others argued from a different perspective, proposing the recognition of international crimes where these represented serious human rights violations.

The beginnings of international prosecution for atrocities were already apparent at the time of the First World War, when Britain, France, and Russia warned that they would hold perpetrators to account for 'these new crimes of Turkey against humanity and civilization'. But the idea that a state could be held accountable for atrocities committed against its own nationals remained extremely controversial, and it was this gap in the law that Lemkin worked to fill. His initial proposal evidenced a much broader concept of genocide than what was eventually agreed to in the 1948 *Convention*. But Lemkin actively participated in the negotiations leading to the *Convention's* adoption, and while he would no doubt have hoped for a somewhat different result, he cannot be detached from the *Convention* definition. Indeed, following its adoption he campaigned aggressively for its ratification.

Lemkin's famous proposal, contained in a chapter entitled 'Genocide' in his book *Axis Rule in Occupied Europe*, called for the 'prohibition of genocide in war and peace'. Lemkin insisted upon the relationship between genocide and the growing interest in the protection of peoples and minorities manifested in several treaties and declarations adopted following the First World War. He noted the need to revisit international legal instruments, pointing out particularly the inadequacies of the Hague Convention of 1907, which he explained was 'silent regarding the preservation of the integrity of a people'. According to Lemkin,

the definition of genocide in the Hague Regulations thus amended should consist of two essential parts: in the first should be included every action infringing upon the life, liberty, health, corporal integrity, economic existence, and the honor of the inhabitants when committed because they belong to a national, religious, or racial group; and in the second, every policy aiming at the destruction or the aggrandizement of one of such groups to the prejudice or detriment of another.[2]

GENOCIDE AND CRIMES AGAINST HUMANITY

The legal concept of genocide was forged in the crucible of post-Second World War efforts to prosecute Nazi atrocities. Its development took place in conjunction with

[2] Raphael Lemkin, *Axis Rule in Occupied Europe: Laws of Occupation, Analysis of Government, Proposals for Redress* (Washington, DC: Carnegie Endowment for World Peace, 1944), 90–3.

that of other international crimes, especially crimes against humanity, with which it bears a close but complex and difficult relationship. The development and history of genocide as a legal concept cannot be properly understood without considering the parallel existence of crimes against humanity.

Although the participants in the UN War Crimes Commission, established in November 1943, and in the London Conference, which met from late June to early August 1945 to prepare the Nuremberg trial of the major war criminals, opted to use the term crimes against humanity in the prosecutions, they also employed the word genocide as if it was more or less synonymous. In his 'Planning Memorandum distributed to Delegations at Beginning of London Conference, June 1945', where Justice Robert Jackson outlined the evidence to be adduced in the Nuremberg trial, he spoke of '[g]enocide or destruction of racial minorities and subjugated populations by such means and methods as (1) underfeeding; (2) sterilization and castration; (3) depriving them of clothing, shelter, fuel, sanitation, medical care; (4) deporting them for forced labor; (5) working them in inhumane conditions.'[3] The indictment of the International Military Tribunal charged the Nazi defendants with 'deliberate and systematic genocide, viz., the extermination of racial and national groups, against the civilian populations of certain occupied territories in order to destroy particular races and classes of people, and national, racial or religious groups, particularly Jews, Poles, and Gypsies.'[4] The term 'genocide' was also used on several occasions by the prosecutors during the trial itself. Sir David Maxwell-Fyfe, the British prosecutor, reminded one of the accused, von Neurath, that he had been charged with genocide, 'which we say is the extermination of racial and national groups, or, as it has been put in the well-known book of Professor Lemkin, "a co-ordinated plan of different actions aiming at the destruction of essential foundations of the life of national groups with the aim of annihilating the groups themselves."'[5] Lemkin later wrote that '[t]he evidence produced at the Nuremberg trial gave full support to the concept of genocide.'[6]

Nevertheless, the *Charter of the International Military Tribunal* did not use the word genocide, nor does it appear in the final judgment issued on 30 September and 1 October 1946. The legal concept of crimes against humanity, as defined at Nuremberg, suffered from a very serious limitation, in that it was confined to atrocities committed in association with an aggressive war. This was quite intentional on the part of those who drafted the legal provisions governing prosecutions, especially the four great powers, the United States, the United Kingdom, France, and the Soviet Union. Indeed, extending international law from classic war crimes

[3] Report of Robert H. Jackson, *United States Representative to the International Conference on Military Trials* (Washington, DC: US Government Printing Office, 1949), 6.

[4] *France* et al. v. *Goering* et al., (1946) 22 International Military Tribunal (IMT) 45–6.

[5] (1947) 17 IMT, 61. See also: (1947) 19 IMT 497, 498, 509, 514, 531.

[6] Raphael Lemkin, 'Genocide as a Crime in International Law', *American Journal of International Law* 41 (1947), 145, 147.

involving battlefield offences and various forms of persecution of civilians in an occupied territory so that it would also cover atrocities committed by a government against its own civilian population was not only novel and unprecedented, it was also threatening to the very states who were organizing the prosecution. The distinctions were set out quite candidly by the head of the United States delegation, Robert Jackson, at a meeting of the London Conference on 23 July 1945:

It has been a general principle of foreign policy of our Government from time immemorial that the internal affairs of another government are not ordinarily our business; that is to say, the way Germany treats its inhabitants, or any other country treats its inhabitants is not our affair any more than it is the affair of some other government to interpose itself in our problems. The reason that this program of extermination of Jews and destruction of the rights of minorities becomes an international concern is this: it was a part of a plan for making an illegal war. Unless we have a war connection as a basis for reaching them, I would think we have no basis for dealing with atrocities. They were a part of the preparation for war or for the conduct of the war in so far as they occurred inside of Germany and that makes them our concern.[7]

Speaking of the proposed crime of 'atrocities, persecutions, and deportations on political, racial or religious grounds', which would shortly be renamed 'crimes against humanity', Justice Jackson indicated the source of the lingering concerns of his government:

[O]rdinarily we do not consider that the acts of a government toward its own citizens warrant our interference. *We have some regrettable circumstances at times in our own country in which minorities are unfairly treated.* We think it is justifiable that we interfere or attempt to bring retribution to individuals or to states only because the concentration camps and the deportations were in pursuance of a common plan or enterprise of making an unjust or illegal war in which we became involved. We see no other basis on which we are justified in reaching the atrocities which were committed inside Germany, under German law, or even in violation of German law, by authorities of the German state.[8]

There is little doubt that the British, the French, and the Soviets had reasons of their own to share these concerns. As a result, the definition of crimes against humanity in article VI(c) of the Nuremberg *Charter* requires that atrocities be committed 'in furtherance of or in connection with any crime within the jurisdiction of the International Tribunal'.[9] In its final judgment, the International Military Tribunal made a distinction between pre-war persecution of German Jews, which it characterized as 'severe and repressive', and German policy during the war in the occupied territories. Although the judgment frequently referred to events during

---

[7] 'Minutes of Conference Session of 23 July 1945', in *Report of Jackson, United States Representative,* 331.

[8] Ibid. 333 (emphasis added).

[9] *Agreement for the Prosecution and Punishment of Major War Criminals of the European Axis, and Establishing the Charter of the IMT,* annex, (1951) 82 UNTS 279.

the 1930s, none of the accused was found guilty of an act perpetrated prior to 1 September 1939, the day the war broke out.

Following the judgment, there was considerable outrage about the severe restriction upon the concept of crimes against humanity. A member of the Nuremberg prosecution team, Henry King, has described meeting Raphael Lemkin in the lobby of the Grand Hotel in Nuremberg in October 1946, a few days after the International Military Tribunal completed its work:

When I saw him at Nuremberg, Lemkin was very upset. He was concerned that the decision of the International Military Tribunal (IMT)—the Nuremberg Court—did not go far enough in dealing with genocidal actions. This was because the IMT limited its judgment to wartime genocide and did not include peacetime genocide. At that time, Lemkin was very focussed on pushing his points. After he had buttonholed me several times, I had to tell him that I was powerless to do anything about the limitation in the Court's judgment.[10]

The disappointment soon manifested itself in the UN General Assembly, which was meeting in New York. India, Cuba, and Panama proposed a resolution that they said would address a shortcoming in the Nuremberg trial by which acts committed prior to the war were left unpunished.[11] One of the preambular paragraphs in the draft resolution stated:

Whereas the punishment of the very serious crime of genocide when committed in time of peace lies within the exclusive territorial jurisdiction of the judiciary of every State concerned, while crimes of a relatively lesser importance such as piracy, trade in women, children, drugs, obscene publications are declared as international crimes and have been made matters of international concern.[12]

This paragraph never made it to the final version of Resolution 96(I), adopted in December 1946, because the majority of the General Assembly was not prepared to recognize universal jurisdiction for the crime of genocide. Nevertheless, the resolution, somewhat toned down from the hopes of those who had proposed it, launched a process that concluded two years later with the adoption of the *Convention for the Prevention and Punishment of the Crime of Genocide.*[13] Proposals that the *Genocide Convention* make reference to crimes against humanity as a related concept, or as some kind of broader umbrella under which the crime of genocide was situated, were rejected by the drafters so as not to create any confusion about the fact that genocide could be committed in time of peace as well as in wartime. This could not be said with any certainty about crimes against humanity at the time precisely because of the Nuremberg precedent.

---

[10] 'Remarks of Henry T. King, Jr., Case Western Reserve University School of Law, Genocide Conference', 27 September 2007, 1.

[11] UN Doc. A/C.6/SR.22.

[12] UN Doc. A/BUR/50.

[13] *Convention for the Prevention and Punishment of the Crime of Genocide*, 277.

Thus, the recognition of genocide as an international crime by the General Assembly of the United Nations in 1946, and its codification in the 1948 *Convention*, can be understood as a reaction to the narrow approach to crimes against humanity in the Nuremberg judgment of the International Military Tribunal. It was Nuremberg's failure to recognize the international criminality of atrocities committed in peacetime that prompted the first initiatives at recognizing and defining the crime of genocide. Had Nuremberg affirmed the reach of international criminal law into peacetime atrocities, the *Genocide Convention* might never have been adopted. The term 'genocide' might then have remained a popular or colloquial label used by journalists, historians, and social scientists but absent from legal discourse.

THE 1948 GENOCIDE CONVENTION

The *Convention for the Prevention and Punishment of the Crime of Genocide* was adopted unanimously by the UN General Assembly on 9 December 1948. It provides the following definition of the crime of genocide:

In the present Convention, genocide means any of the following acts committed with intent to destroy, in whole or in part, a national, ethnical, racial or religious group, as such:

(a) Killing members of the group;
(b) Causing serious bodily or mental harm to members of the group;
(c) Deliberately inflicting on the group conditions of life calculated to bring about its physical destruction in whole or in part;
(d) Imposing measures intended to prevent births within the group;
(e) Forcibly transferring children of the group to another group.

In one sense, the definition is considerably narrower than that of crimes against humanity, which can apply to a broad range of acts of persecution and other atrocities committed against 'any civilian population'. However, the definition is manifestly broader because of the absence of any requirement of a link with aggressive war.

Besides defining the crime, the *Convention* imposes several obligations upon states that ratify it. They are required to enact legislation to provide for punishment of persons guilty of genocide committed on their own territory. The legislation must not allow offenders to invoke in defence that they were acting in an official capacity. States are also required to cooperate in extradition when persons suspected of committing genocide elsewhere find refuge on their territory. They may not treat genocide as a political crime, which is an historic bar to extradition.

Disputes between states about genocide are automatically subject to the jurisdiction of the International Court of Justice.

The title of the *Convention* speaks of prevention, but aside from a perfunctory undertaking 'to prevent' genocide, there is nothing to suggest the scope of this obligation. In 2007, in a case filed by Bosnia and Herzegovina against Serbia, the International Court of Justice said there had been a breach of the *Genocide Convention* because Serbia failed to intervene with its allies, the Bosnian Serbs, so as to prevent the Srebrenica massacre of July 1995. The Court said that in view of Serbia's 'undeniable influence', the authorities should have 'made the best efforts within their power to try and prevent the tragic events then taking shape, whose scale, though it could not have been foreseen with certainty, might at least have been surmised'.[14] The judgment clarifies that the obligation to prevent extends beyond a country's own borders. The principle it establishes should apply to other States who take little or no action to respond when mass atrocity posing a risk of genocide is threatened. This pronouncement is in the same spirit as an emerging doctrine in international law expressed in a unanimous resolution of the UN General Assembly, adopted in 2005, declaring that States have a 'responsibility to protect' populations in cases of genocide, crimes against humanity, war crimes, and ethnic cleansing.[15]

The *Convention* specifies that genocide is to be prosecuted by the courts of the country where the crime took place or 'by such international penal tribunal as may have jurisdiction with respect to those Contracting Parties which shall have accepted its jurisdiction'. The original General Assembly resolution proposed by Cuba, India, and Panama called for recognition of universal jurisdiction over genocide. This would mean that the courts of any state could punish the crime, no matter where it was committed. The idea was rejected by the General Assembly in favour of an approach combining territorial jurisdiction and an international institution. The promised international court was not established for more than half a century, when the *Rome Statute of the International Criminal Court* entered into force on 1 July 2002.[16] Despite the *Convention*'s rejection of universal jurisdiction, in the *Eichmann* prosecution the Israeli courts decided that it was accepted by customary international law. Although no treaty authorizes universal jurisdiction over genocide, and there is as yet no determination of its legitimacy by the International Court of Justice, there now seems little doubt that it is permitted by international law. In 2006 and 2007, the International Criminal Tribunal for Rwanda authorized transfer of suspects for trial on the basis of universal jurisdiction with the approval

---

[14] *Case concerning Application of the Convention on the Prevention and Punishment of the Crime of Genocide (Bosnia and Herzegovina v. Serbia and Montenegro)*, Judgment, 26 February 2007, para. 438.

[15] '2005 World Summit Outcome', UN Doc. A/RES/60/1, para. 138.

[16] *Rome Statute of the International Criminal Court* (2002), 2187 UNTS 90.

of the UN Security Council, further evidence of the broad acceptance of universal jurisdiction over genocide.[17]

The *Genocide Convention* entered into force in 1951, after it had been ratified by 20 states. Approximately 140 states have now ratified the *Convention*. Several of them have limited their commitments in the form of reservations. Most of these are directed at excluding the jurisdiction of the International Criminal Court in the event of disputes about the application of the *Convention*.

The definition of genocide set out in article II of the *Convention* has frequently been criticized for its narrowness. For example, it applies to a limited number of protected groups, and it requires an intent directed at the ultimate physical destruction of the victimized group. There was disappointment when the International Court of Justice, in the *Bosnia and Herzegovina* case, dismissed attempts to broaden the definition by interpreting the words 'to destroy' so as to encompass the notion of 'ethnic cleansing'. The Court said that 'ethnic cleansing', which it described as the 'deportation or displacement of the members of a group, even if effected by force', was not necessarily equivalent to destruction of that group, and that destruction was not an automatic consequence of such displacement.[18] The relatively conservative approach to interpreting the definition, and a resistance to broadening the scope through judicial action rather than amendment of the *Convention*, is also reflected in judgments of the International Criminal Tribunal for the former Yugoslavia[19] and an authoritative report by a United Nations fact-finding commission.[20]

Nor has there been any serious effort at the political level to amend or modify the definition in Article II of the *Convention*. The ideal opportunity for such a development would have been the adoption of the *Rome Statute of the International Criminal Court*, when the definitions of the other core international crimes, crimes against humanity and war crimes, were quite dramatically modernized. But when it came to genocide, there were a few modest proposals, and these did not gain any traction during the negotiations.[21] At the Rome Conference, only Cuba argued for

[17] *Prosecutor* v. *Bagaragaza* (Case ICTR-2005–86-R11bis), Decision on Prosecutor's Request for Referral of the Indictment to the Kingdom of the Netherlands, 13 April 2007. For Security Council acquiescence, see UN Doc. S/PV.5697.

[18] *Case Concerning the Application of the Convention on the Prevention and Punishment of the Crime of Genocide (Bosnia and Herzegovina* v. *Serbia and Montenegro)*, Judgment, 26 February 2007, para. 190. See also the chapter by Lieberman in this volume.

[19] *Prosecutor* v. *Krstić* (Case IT-98–33-A), Judgment, 19 April 2004. Also *Prosecutor* v. *Stakić* (Case IT-97–24-T), Judgment, 31 July 2003; *Prosecutor* v. *Britanin* (Case IT-99–36-T), Judgment, 1 September 2004; *Prosecutor* v. *Blagojević* et al. (Case IT-02–60-A), Judgment, 9 May 2007.

[20] 'Report of the International Commission of Inquiry on Darfur to the United Nations Secretary-General, Pursuant to Security Council Resolution 1564 of 18 September 2004', Geneva, 25 January 2005, UN Doc. S/2005/60.

[21] 'Report of the Ad Hoc Committee on the Establishment of an International Criminal Court', UN Doc. A/50/22; para. 61; UN Doc. A/AC.249/1998/CRP.8, p. 2.; Herman von Hebel and Darryl Robinson, 'Crimes Within the Jurisdiction of the Court', in Roy S. Lee (ed.), *The International*

amendment of the definition, proposing it be expanded to include social and political groups.[22]

There is some evidence of innovation by national lawmakers when the provisions of the *Genocide Convention* are translated into domestic criminal legislation. The French *Code pénal*, for example, defines genocide as the destruction of any group whose identification is based on arbitrary criteria.[23] The Canadian implementing legislation for the *Rome Statute* states that '"genocide" means an act or omission committed with intent to destroy, in whole or in part, an identifiable group of persons, as such, that, at the time and in the place of its commission, constitutes genocide according to customary international law', explaining that the definition in the *Rome Statute*, which is identical to that of the *Convention*, is deemed a crime according to customary international law. The legislation adds, in anticipation: 'This does not limit or prejudice in any way the application of existing or developing rules of international law.'[24]

GENOCIDE AND CUSTOMARY INTERNATIONAL LAW

Although written conventions or treaties are fundamental as a source of public international law, binding norms may also be derived from custom, that is, a pattern of behaviour or practice that exists because the parties believe it to be required as a matter of legal obligation. Many rules and principles of international law exist in this manner, without any treaty being required. Classic examples include diplomatic immunities, the humane treatment of prisoners of war, and recognition that there is a maritime perimeter surrounding a country that forms part of its sovereign territory.

Shortly after the *Genocide Convention* was adopted, the International Court of Justice issued an advisory opinion to clarify whether states that had ratified the *Convention* but with reservations were actually party to the instrument. This was at least theoretically relevant to a determination of when the treaty entered into force, as this required twenty valid ratifications. The Court wrote that:

The origins of the Convention show that it was the intention of the United Nations to condemn and punish genocide as 'a crime under international law' involving a denial of the

---

Criminal Court: The Making of the Rome Statute, Issues, Negotiations, Results (The Hague/London/ Boston: Kluwer Law, 1995), 89 n 37.

[22] UN Doc. A/CONF.183/C.1/SR.3, para. 100.
[23] *Code Pénal* (France), Journal officiel, 23 July 1992, art. 211–1.
[24] Crimes against Humanity and War Crimes Act, 48–49 Elizabeth II, 1999–2000, C-19, s. 4.

right of existence of entire human groups, a denial which shocks the conscience of mankind and results in great losses to humanity, and which is contrary to moral law and to the spirit and aims of the United Nations. The first consequence arising from this conception is that the principles underlying the Convention are principles which are recognized by civilized nations as binding on States, even without any conventional obligation.[25]

This important statement is often cited as the judicial recognition of the prohibition of genocide as a customary legal norm, although the Court did not actually refer to it expressly in this way. There is much subsequent authority for the proposition that the prohibition of genocide, and the basic principles set out in the *Convention*, form part of customary international law.[26] According to the International Court of Justice, in its 2007 ruling in the *Bosnia and Herzegovina* case, the affirmation in article I of the *Convention* that genocide is a crime under international law means it sets out 'the existing requirements of customary international law, a matter emphasized by the Court in 1951.'[27] In 2006, the International Court of Justice said that the prohibition of genocide was 'assuredly' a peremptory norm (*jus cogens*) of public international law, the first time it has ever made such a declaration about any legal rule.[28] A peremptory or *jus cogens* norm is so fundamental to customary international law that it cannot be subject to derogation.

PROTECTED GROUPS

The definition in the 1948 *Convention* applies to 'national, ethnic, racial and religious groups'. The concept is broadly analogous to what, at the time the *Convention* was adopted, were considered as 'national minorities'. This was clearly the perspective of

---

[25] *Reservations to the Convention on the Prevention and Punishment of the Crime of Genocide* (*Advisory Opinion*), [1951] ICJ Reports 16, p. 23. Quoted in *Legality of the Threat or Use of Nuclear Weapons* (*Advisory Opinion*), [1996] ICJ Reports 226, para. 31; *Case Concerning the Application of the Convention on the Prevention and Punishment of the Crime of Genocide* (*Bosnia and Herzegovina v. Serbia and Montenegro*), Judgment, 26 February 2007, para. 161.

[26] *Prosecutor* v. *Sikirica* et al. (Case IT-95-8-I), Judgment on Defense Motions to Acquit, 3 September 2001, para. 55; *Prosecutor* v. *Musema* (Case ICTR-96-13-T), Judgment, 27 January 2000, para. 151; *Prosecutor* v. *Bagilishema* (Case ICTR-95-1A-T), Judgment, 7 June 2001, para. 54. The Australian High Court has written that '[g]enocide was not [recognised as a crime under customary international law] until 1948.' *Polyukhovich* v. *Commonwealth of Australia* (1991), 101 ALR 545, at 598 (*per* Brennan J.).

[27] *Case Concerning the Application of the Convention on the Prevention and Punishment of the Crime of Genocide* (*Bosnia and Herzegovina* v. *Serbia and Montenegro*), Judgment, 26 February 2007, para. 161.

[28] *Case Concerning Armed Activities on the Territory of the Congo* (*New Application: 2002*) (*Democratic Republic of the Congo* v. *Rwanda*), Jurisdiction of the Court and Admissibility of the Application, 3 February 2006, para. 64.

Raphael Lemkin and one of the other international experts who assisted the United Nations in preparing the first draft of the *Convention*, Vespasian Pella.[29]

During the negotiations, there was an important debate about whether to include political groups within the definition. Persecution on the grounds of membership in a political group had been recognized at Nuremberg as a crime against humanity. But the drafters of the *Genocide Convention*, Lemkin among them, quite decisively rejected the inclusion of political groups. Some of the subsequent literature on the subject has suggested that exclusion of political groups was the result of pressure from the Soviet Union, but a careful reading of the drafting history shows that opposition on this point was widespread.

In the first prosecution using a text derived from Article II of the *Convention*, identification of the victim group did not raise any legal difficulties. Israeli law avoided any discussion about the nature of 'groups' by simply reformulating the definition of genocide so as to refer to 'crimes against the Jewish people',[30] and nothing in the trial record suggests that Eichmann ever challenged the fact that the victims of Nazi atrocities were the 'Jewish people'.[31] The issue does not appear to have been particularly controversial in litigation concerning the conflict in Bosnia and Herzegovina. A Trial Chamber of the International Criminal Tribunal for the former Yugoslavia concluded that 'Bosnian Muslims' were a 'national group',[32] a finding that was not challenged on appeal and that was accepted by the Appeals Chamber.[33] After some initial uncertainty, probably driven by discomfort with the contemporary legitimacy of the concept of 'racial groups', Trial Chambers of the International Criminal Tribunal for Rwanda have taken judicial notice of the fact that the Tutsi, as well as the Hutu and the Twa, were ethnic groups within Rwanda at the time of the 1994 genocide.[34] In an innovative interpretation, a Trial Chamber of the International Criminal Tribunal for Rwanda held that the all 'stable and permanent groups' were protected by the *Convention*,[35] but its theory has had little resonance in subsequent case law.[36]

Generally, it is the perpetrator of genocide who defines the individual victim's status as a member of a group protected by the *Convention*. The Nazis, for example, had detailed rules establishing, according to objective criteria, who was Jewish and who was not. It made no difference if the individual, perhaps a non-observant Jew of mixed parentage, denied belonging to the group. As Jean-Paul Sartre wrote: 'Le juif est un

---

[29] Vespasien V. Pella, *La guerre-crime et les criminels de guerre, Réflexions sur la justice pénale internationale, ce qu'elle est ce qu'elle devrait être* (Neuchatel: Éditions de la baconnière, 1964), 80 n 1.

[30] Nazi and Nazi Collaborators (Punishment) Law, 1950 (Law 5710/1950), s. I(a).

[31] *A-G Israel* v. *Eichmann*, (1968) 36 ILR 5 (District Court, Jerusalem); *A-G Israel* v. *Eichmann* (1968), 36 ILR 277 (Supreme Court of Israel).

[32] *Prosecutor* v. *Krstić* (Case IT-98–33-T), Judgment, 2 August 2001, paras. 559–60.

[33] *Prosecutor* v. *Krstić* (Case IT-98–33-A), Judgment, 19 April 2004, para. 6.

[34] *Prosecutor* v. *Kajelijeli* (Case ICTR-98–44A-T), Judgment, 1 December 2003, para. 241.

[35] *Prosecutor* v. *Akayesu* (Case ICTR-96–4-T), Judgment, 2 September 1998, para. 652.

[36] 'Report of the International Commission of Inquiry on violations of international humanitarian law and human rights law in Darfur', UN Doc. S/2005/60, para. 501.

homme que les autres hommes tiennent pour juif.'[37] With considerable frustration, lawyers and courts have searched for objective definitions of the protected groups. But most of the judgments treat the identification of the protected group as an essentially subjective matter. For example, Trial Chambers of the International Criminal Tribunal for Rwanda have concluded that the Tutsi were an ethnic group based on the existence of government-issued official identity cards describing them as such.[38] A Trial Chamber of the International Criminal Tribunal for the former Yugoslavia wrote that 'the relevant protected group may be identified by means of the subjective criterion of the stigmatization of the group, notably by the perpetrators of the crime, on the basis of its perceived national, ethnical, racial or religious characteristics. In some instances, the victim may perceive himself or herself to belong to the aforesaid group.'[39] The prevailing view is that determination of the relevant protected group should be made on a case-by-case, relying upon both objective and subjective criteria.[40]

ETHNIC CLEANSING AND CULTURAL GENOCIDE

The *Convention* definition of genocide refers to the 'intent to destroy' without further precision. The five punishable acts that follow consist of a combination of physical, biological, and cultural attacks. For example, the fifth act of genocide in the definition, forcibly transferring children from one group to another, quite evidently does not involve their physical destruction. Rather, the elimination of a group is contemplated by destroying the cultural memory and the national language, through assimilation at a very young age. A literal reading of the definition can therefore support an interpretation whereby acts of 'ethnic cleansing' or of cultural genocide falling short of physical destruction would be punishable, a view that some judgments appear to support.[41]

When the *Convention* was being drafted, the punishable acts were divided into three categories, physical, biological, and cultural genocide. The UN General Assembly voted

---

[37] Jean-Paul Sartre, *Réflexions sur la question juive* (Paris: Gallimard, 1954), 81–4.

[38] *Prosecutor* v. *Kayishema* et al. (Case ICTR-95-1-T), Judgment, 21 May 1999, para. 98.

[39] *Prosecutor* v. *Brdanin* (Case T-99-36-T), Judgment, 1 September 2004, para. 683.

[40] *Prosecutor* v. *Brdanin* (Case IT-99-36-T), Judgment, 1 September 2004, para. 684. Also *Prosecutor* v. *Stakić* (Case IT-97-24-A), Judgment, 22 March 2006, para. 25; *Prosecutor* v. *Semanza* (Case ICTR-97-20-T), Judgment and Sentence, 15 May 2003, para. 317; *Prosecutor* v. *Kajelijeli* (Case ICTR-98-44A-T), Judgment and Sentence, 1 December 2003, para. 811; *Case Concerning the Application of the Convention on the Prevention and Punishment of the Crime of Genocide (Bosnia and Herzegovina* v. *Serbia and Montenegro)*, Judgment, 26 February 2007, para. 191.

[41] *Prosecutor* v. *Krstić* (Case IT-98-33-A), Partially Dissenting Opinion of Judge Shahabuddeen, 19 April 2004; *Prosecutor* v. *Blagojević* (Case IT-02-60-T) Judgment, 17 January 2005; *Jorgić* v. *Germany* (App. 74613/01), 12 July 2007, para. 47.

quite deliberately to exclude cultural genocide from the *Convention*.[42] It also rejected an amendment from Syria to include as an act of genocide behaviour that today might be called 'ethnic cleansing'. The Syrian amendment read: 'Imposing measures intended to oblige members of a group to abandon their homes in order to escape the threat of subsequent ill-treatment.'[43] When the General Assembly agreed to include forcible transfer of children, this was presented as an exception to the agreed upon exclusion of cultural genocide.[44] Consequently, a reading of the *Convention* definition that takes into account the intent of its drafters will tend to reject inclusion of cultural genocide and ethnic cleansing, and construe the words 'to destroy' as if they are modified by 'physically' and 'biologically'. On the other hand, a purely literal reading sustains the view that cultural genocide is comprised within the words 'to destroy'.

There are strong arguments for rejecting an approach to treaty interpretation that puts too much emphasis on legislative intent, particularly in the field of human rights law. Reliance upon the drafting history tends to freeze the provision, preventing it from evolving so as to take into account historical developments and changed attitudes. Be that as it may, courts to this day have shown great respect for the relatively narrow perspective adopted by the General Assembly in 1948. This tendency is only partially explained by an inherent conservatism, however. Just as the crime of genocide emerged in international law as a reaction to the limitations on crimes against humanity, more recently the law on crimes against humanity has evolved to such an extent that it can now cover acts of ethnic cleansing and cultural genocide, even when committed in peacetime. As a result, there is no 'impunity gap', and there is little or no pressure in a legal sense for the expansion of the definition of genocide by interpretation. Of course, there are important political prerogatives and much symbolism associated with the label 'genocide', and many victims are deeply disappointed when their own suffering is acknowledged as 'mere' crimes against humanity. They do not fully appreciate the importance of the legal distinctions, which are the result of a complex historical debate. Thus, while the distinction between genocide and crimes against humanity no longer has significant legal consequences, it remains fundamental in other contexts.

NUMBERS AND GENOCIDE

The 1948 definition of genocide speaks of destruction of a group 'in whole or in part'. It was a noble attempt by the drafters to reach consensus on the numerical

---

[42] UN Doc. A/C.6/SR.83.
[43] UN Doc. A/C.6/234.
[44] UN Doc. A/C.6/SR.82.

issue, but in reality the General Assembly used ambiguous terms and left their clarification to judges in subsequent prosecutions. Several theories have emerged with a view to circumscribing the notion of 'in part'. Because the terms appear in the preliminary paragraph of the definition, it is quite clear that they refer to the genocidal intent. As a result, the fundamental question is not how many victims were actually killed or injured, but rather how many victims the perpetrator intended to attack. Even where there is a small number of victims, or none at all—the *Convention* also criminalizes attempted genocide—the crime can be committed if the genocidal intent is present. The actual result, in terms of quantity, will nevertheless be relevant in that it assists in assessing the perpetrator's intent. The greater the number of actual victims, the more plausible becomes the deduction that the perpetrator intended to destroy the group, in whole or in part.

But there are other issues involved in construing the meaning of the term 'in part'. Could it be genocide to target only a few persons for murder because of their membership in a particular ethnic group? A literal reading of the definition seems to support such an interpretation. Nevertheless, this construction is rather too extreme, and inconsistent with the drafting history, as well as with the context and the object and purpose of the *Genocide Convention*. Two basic approaches to the scope of the term 'in part' have emerged, each adding a modifying adjective, 'substantial' or 'significant', to the word 'part'.

According to the Appeals Chamber of the International Criminal Tribunal for the former Yugoslavia, '[i]t is well established that where a conviction for genocide relies on the intent to destroy a protected group "in part," the part must be a substantial part of that group.'[45] Noting that the Nazis did not realistically intend to destroy all Jews, but only those in Europe, and that the Hutu extremists in Rwanda sought to kill Tutsis within Rwanda, the Appeals Chamber said: 'The intent to destroy formed by a perpetrator of genocide will always be limited by the opportunity presented to him. While this factor alone will not indicate whether the targeted group is substantial, it can—in combination with other factors—inform the analysis.'[46] In the factual context, the Appeals Chamber considered that the Bosnian Muslim community in Srebrenica constituted a 'substantial part' of the Bosnian Muslims as a whole, and that the attempt to destroy it amounted to genocide.[47]

Another approach takes more of a qualitative than a quantitative perspective, reading in the adjective 'significant'. There is nothing to support this interpretation in the drafting history of the *Convention*, and the idea seems to have been launched by Benjamin Whitaker in a 1985 report to the UN Sub-commission for the Protection and Promotion of Human Rights. He wrote that the term 'in part'

---

[45]   *Prosecutor* v. *Krstić* (Case IT-98–33-A), Judgment, 18 August 2004, para. 8.

[46]   Ibid. para. 13.

[47]   Ibid. para 22.

denotes 'a reasonably significant number, relative to the total of the group as a whole, or else a significant section of a group such as its leadership'.[48] Citing Whitaker's report, an expert body established by the UN Security Council in 1992 to investigate violations of international humanitarian law in the former Yugoslavia held that 'in part' had not only a quantitative but also a qualitative dimension. According to the Commission's chair, Professor M. Cherif Bassiouni, the definition in the *Genocide Convention* was deemed 'sufficiently pliable to encompass not only the targeting of an entire group, as stated in the convention, but also the targeting of certain segments of a given group, such as the Muslim elite or Muslim women.'[49]

This approach was adopted by the Prosecutor of the International Criminal Tribunal for the former Yugoslavia, in some of the initial indictments,[50] and was subsequently accepted by trial judges.[51] Although not explicitly endorsing the 'significant part' gloss on the *Convention*, the Appeals Chamber of the Tribunal considered the relevance to the Srebrenica Muslim community of the destruction of approximately 7,000 men. It referred to an observation of the Trial Chamber about the patriarchal character of Bosnian Muslim society in Srebrenica, and the consequent impact upon the future of the community that would result from the killing of its adult male population. 'Evidence introduced at trial supported this finding, by showing that, with the majority of the men killed officially listed as missing, their spouses are unable to remarry and, consequently, to have new children. The physical destruction of the men therefore had severe procreative implications for the Srebrenica Muslim community, potentially consigning the community to extinction.'[52] In other words, the adult males were a 'significant part' of a community, the Srebrenica Muslims, that was itself a 'substantial part' of the group as a whole, namely, Bosnian Muslims.

Genocidal Intent

In principle, what sets criminal law apart from other areas of legal liability is its insistence upon establishing that the punishable act was committed intentionally. At best, inadvertent or negligent behaviour lies at the fringes of criminal law, and will certainly not apply when the most serious crimes, including genocide, are

---

[48] Benjamin Whitaker, 'Revised and Updated Report on the Question of the Prevention and Punishment of the Crime of Genocide', UN Doc. E/CN.4/Sub.2/1985/6, para. 29.

[49] 'Final Report of the Commission of Experts', UN Doc. S/1994/674, para. 94.

[50] *Prosecutor* v. *Karadžić* et al. (Case IT-95–18-R61, IT-95–5-R61), Transcript of hearing of 27 June 1996, p. 15. Also *Prosecutor* v. *Jelisić* et al. (Case IT-95–10-I), Indictment, 21 July 1995, para. 17.

[51] *Prosecutor* v. *Jelisić* (Case IT-95–10-T), Judgment, 14 December 1999, paras. 82, 93; *Prosecutor* v. *Sikirica* et al. (Case IT-95–8-T), Judgment on Defense Motions to Acquit, 3 September 2001, para. 80.

[52] *Prosecutor* v. *Krstić* (Case IT-98–33-A), Judgment, 18 August 2004, para. 28.

concerned. As a rule, criminal legislation does not spell out a requirement of intent, as this stipulation is considered to be implicit. Exceptionally, the definition in the *Convention* refers to the intent of the perpetrator, which must be to destroy the protected group in whole or in part. There are actually two distinct intents involved, because the underlying genocidal act, for example killing or causing serious bodily or mental harm to a member of the group, must also be carried out intentionally.

Courts often refer to the 'specific intent' of genocide, or the *dolus specialis*, so as to distinguish it from non-genocidal killing. In principle, all crimes must be committed intentionally, in the sense that they are the result of an active mind operating consciously. The definitions of some crimes go beyond this general presumption, and state expressly that they must be committed with a special or specific intent. The assertion that genocide is committed when one of the punishable acts, killing for example, is perpetrated 'with intent to destroy' a protected group, leads to the observation that it is a crime of 'specific intent' or, according to jurists trained in continental law, one of *dolus specialis*. Application of this classic criminal law paradigm to genocide has resulted in what may be an exaggerated focus by some judges on the individual perpetrator, taken in isolation. The International Criminal Tribunal for the former Yugoslavia has adopted the view that an individual, acting alone, can commit an act of genocide to the extent that he or she engages in killing with a genocidal intent.[53] The problem with such analysis is that it loses sight of the importance of the plan or policy of a state or analogous entity. In practice, genocide within the framework of international law is not the crime of a lone deviant but the act of a state. The importance of a state policy becomes more apparent when the context shifts from individual prosecution to a broader and more political determination.

For example, in September 2005, the UN Security Council commissioned a study to determine whether genocide was being committed in Darfur. The resulting expert report did not seriously attempt to determine whether any single individual within Sudan had killed with genocidal intent. Rather, it examined the policy of the Sudanese government, stating: 'The Commission concludes that the Government of Sudan has not pursued a policy of genocide.'[54] The Commission said that there was evidence of two elements of the crime of genocide. The first was the presence of material acts corresponding to paragraphs in the definition of the crime set out in article II of the 1948 *Convention for the Prevention and Punishment of the Crime of Genocide*. It observed that 'the gross violations of human rights perpetrated by Government forces and the militias under their control' included reports of killing, causing serious bodily or mental harm, and deliberate infliction of conditions of

---

[53] *Prosecutor* v. *Jelisić* (Case IT-95–10-T), Judgment, 14 December 1999, para. 100.

[54] 'Report of the International Commission of Inquiry on Violations of International Humanitarian Law and Human Rights Law in Darfur', UN Doc. S/2005/60, para. 518.

life likely to bring about physical destruction. The second was the subjective perception that the victims and perpetrators, African and Arab tribes respectively, made up two distinct ethnic groups. But, said the Commission,

one central element appears to be missing, at least as far as the central Government authorities are concerned: genocidal intent. Generally speaking the policy of attacking, killing and forcibly displacing members of some tribes does not evince a specific intent to annihilate, in whole or in part, a group distinguished on racial, ethnic, national or religious grounds.[55]

Article III of the *Genocide Convention* establishes that in addition to criminal liability for the actual perpetrators of the crime, accomplices are also punishable. The transposition of concepts of complicity drawn from ordinary criminal law to the international setting of mass atrocity lacks some precision. In reality, it is the organizers and instigators of genocide who bear the greatest responsibility; the physical acts themselves are committed by individuals who are low in the hierarchy, and who may well be ignorant of the genocidal intent.

The statutes of the international criminal tribunals make provision for prosecution of the commander or superior where the acts themselves are committed by subordinates, even in the absence of evidence that actual orders or directions were given. This approach to liability, drawn from a notorious post-Second World War case,[56] has proven to be of only theoretical interest. The scenario whereby a superior is convicted for failing to prevent subordinates from committing genocide is implausible once it is understood that this is a crime that stems from a state or organizational plan or policy.

Many contemporary international criminal prosecutions are based upon a theory known as 'joint criminal enterprise'. It recognizes that atrocities that qualify as international crimes, including genocide, are committed by groups and organizations, acting with a common purpose. In practice, it means that the leaders or organizers will be held responsible for the crimes committed by their associates, even those that they did not specifically intend, to the extent that these were a reasonable and foreseeable outcome of the common purpose or joint enterprise.[57]

STATE RESPONSIBILITY

Although the definition of genocide is framed as a crime, implying that it applies only to individuals, the 1948 *Genocide Convention* imposes duties upon states to

---

[55] Ibid.

[56] *United States of America* v. *Yamashita* (1948), 4 LRTWC 1, pp. 36–7; In re Yamashita, 327 U.S. 1 (1945).

[57] *Prosecutor* v. *Britanin* (Case IT-99-36-A), Judgment, 3 April 2007, paras. 420–5.

prevent genocide and clearly envisages their liability before the International Court of Justice. Any doubts on this point were resolved in the February 2007 judgment of the International Court. There remains an ongoing debate among international lawyers as to whether states actually commit crimes. The Court avoided the question when it ruled that Serbia was liable for failing to prevent genocide, whether qualified as a crime or as an internationally wrongful act.

The Court also held that where charges of genocide are made, they must be established by proof 'at a high level of certainty appropriate to the seriousness of the allegation'.[58] This is a considerably more demanding standard than what would normally be applied in ordinary cases involving State responsibility before the International Court of Justice, and it appears to approximate the norm applied in criminal prosecutions. For example, the *Rome Statute of the International Criminal Court* says that '[i]n order to convict the accused, the Court must be convinced of the guilt of the accused beyond reasonable doubt.'[59] In adopting this approach, the International Court of Justice greatly reduced the likelihood of a result inconsistent with that of the international criminal tribunals. Its exigent standard of proof with respect to genocide virtually assured that the International Court of Justice, dealing with state responsibility, and the International Criminal Tribunal for the former Yugoslavia, dealing with individual responsibility, would remain very much on the same wavelength.

CONCLUDING REMARKS

First proposed by Raphael Lemkin in 1944 to fill a gap in the existing law that would adequately address Nazi crimes against minorities, especially European Jews, the crime of genocide was subsequently codified in the first important UN human rights treaty, the *Convention on the Prevention and Punishment of the Crime of Genocide*, adopted in December 1948. To a large extent, the *Convention* arose as a response to the inadequate codification of crimes against humanity at Nuremberg, which failed to address atrocities committed during peacetime. The *Genocide Convention* offered a definition of the crime that covered peacetime acts, but the General Assembly would only agree to this if the crime itself was defined rather narrowly.

---

[58] *Case Concerning Application of the Convention on the Prevention and Punishment of the Crime of Genocide (Bosnia and Herzegovina v. Yugoslavia)*, Judgment, 26 February 2007, para. 210.
[59] *Rome Statute of the International Criminal Court* (2002), 2187 UNTS 90, art. 66(3).

Over the years, the limited definition of genocide in the 1948 *Convention* has provoked much criticism and many proposals for reform. But by the 1990s, when international criminal law went through a period of stunning developments, it was the atrophied concept of crimes against humanity that emerged as the best legal tool to address atrocities. A gap in the law needed to be filled. Instead of enlarging the definition of genocide in order to accomplish this, the international community opted for an expanded view of crimes against humanity instead. As a result, genocide as a legal concept remains essentially reserved for the clearest of cases of physical destruction of national, ethnic, racial, or religious groups. An important ruling of the International Court of Justice of February 2007 confirms these observations about the stable and relatively conservative approach to genocide that is likely to prevail in the case law for many years to come.

Select Bibliography

Boot, Machteld, *Genocide, Crimes Against Humanity, War Crimes: Nullum Crimen Sine Lege and the Subject Matter Jurisdiction of the International Criminal Court* (Antwerp/Oxford/New York: Intersentia, 2002).

Drost, Pieter Nicolaas, *Genocide, United Nations Legislation on International Criminal Law* (Leyden: A. W. Sythoff, 1959).

Kress, Claus, 'The Crime of Genocide under International Law', *International Criminal Law Review* 6 (2006), 461–502.

Lemkin, Raphael, *Axis Rule in Occupied Europe, Laws of Occupation, Analysis of Government, Proposals for Redress* (Washington, DC: Carnegie Endowment for International Peace, 1944).

Mettraux, Guénaël, *International Crimes and the* ad hoc *Tribunals* (Oxford: Oxford University Press, 2005).

Robinson, Nehemiah, *The Genocide Convention: A Commentary* (New York: Institute of Jewish Affairs, 1960).

Schabas, William A., 'Genocide and the International Court of Justice: Finally, a Duty to Prevent the Crime of Crimes', *Genocide Studies and Prevention* 2:2 (2007), 101–22.

—— *Genocide in International Law*, 2nd edn (Cambridge: Cambridge University Press, 2009).

CHAPTER 7

··

SOCIOLOGY AND GENOCIDE

··

MARTIN SHAW

GENOCIDE is a crime of social classification, in which power-holders target particular populations for social and often physical destruction. Hence it can be
described as a peculiarly sociological crime, in which the activity of social
classification is perverted by pseudoscience. Not for nothing did the journalist
William L. Shirer describe the forever classifying National Socialists, whom he
observed first hand, as 'sociologists'.[1] Yet it was not sociologists who invented the
terminology for this crime, nor were they particularly open to the idea of 'genocide' when Raphael Lemkin first outlined it in *Axis Rule in Occupied Europe*. It was
the *American Journal of Sociology* that printed its 'harshest review', in which
Melchior Palyi astonishingly 'blamed Lemkin for his failure to explore the "exten-
uating circumstances" of Nazi behaviour.'[2]

It is true that sociology's history does not reveal quite the same depths as that of
its sister discipline, anthropology. 'Physical anthropologists, eugenicists, ethno-
graphers, and social anthropologists were equally busy during the first half of the
1940s,' Gretchen E. Schafft records, 'in "racial" studies, in Mendelian genetics, in
ethnographic studies of prisoners of war, and in sorting people by psychological
and physical characteristics. In these and in so many different ways they helped to

[1] William L. Shirer, *Berlin Diary: The Journal of a Foreign Correspondent 1934–1941* (London, 1941).
[2] Samantha Power, '*A Problem from Hell': America and the Age of Genocide* (London: Flamingo, 2003), 21.

determine the outcomes of the lives of their subjects.'[3] In occupied Poland, researchers carried out ethnographic research 'in conjunction with the SS, who provided protection for the scientists and ensured the compliance of the subjects. People were taken at gunpoint to collection places where they were measured, interviewed, and sometimes fingerprinted.'[4] But this involvement in genocide was not an aberration for social science. In the business of racial classification, 'one could move so easily from a study of differences to the conviction that differences could be gradated into a hierarchical value system.'[5] As Alexander Hinton has argued, there was something inherent in the concept of social classification that lent itself to this approach: 'Diverse ways of life were compressed into relatively stable categories, a homogenizing tendency that was paralleled by the anthropological typologies of race.'[6] This was a danger for sociology as well as anthropology.

It is true that during the Nazi era, according to Wolfgang Glatzer's history of the German Sociological Association, 'just about all reputable sociologists emigrated, especially those of Jewish origin', while some 'attempted to struggle through the years of the Third Reich without giving in to the Nazis'; only 'a third group adhered more or less openly to Nazi ideology, defining themselves as Volkish sociologists.'[7] Moreover Max Weber (who died in 1920) had dismissed race as a social category, pointing out that 'the possession of a common biological inheritance by virtue of which persons are classified as belonging to the same "race," naturally implies no sort of communal social relationship between them.'[8] And yet Weber's own earlier history demonstrated that sociologists were hardly immune to the degrading effects of the racial classifications that led to the anthropologists' collaboration. In the 1890s, he had advocated that the estates of the Prussian aristocracy, increasingly manned by cheaper Polish labour, should be recolonized with native German farmers to save the Reich from 'Polonization'. Weber even claimed that the danger of a Polish invasion lay in their 'physiological cleft' from the Germans. So when nearly half a century later Hitler expelled Poles (and Jews) in order to Germanize the areas of conquered Poland adjacent to Germany, he advanced an idea similar to one proclaimed by the man who would become known as the greatest modern sociologist.[9]

---

[3] Gretchen E. Schafft, 'Scientific Racism in the Third Reich: German Anthropologists in the Nazi Era', in Alexander Laban Hinton (ed.), *Annihilating Difference: The Anthropology of Genocide* (Berkeley: University of California Press, 2002), 119.

[4] Ibid. 128.

[5] Ibid. 124.

[6] Alexander Laban Hinton, 'The Dark Side of Modernity: Toward an Anthropology of Genocide', in *idem* (ed.), *Annihilating Difference*, 14.

[7] Wolfgang Glatzer, 'German Sociological Association', available at http://www.soziologie.de/#3.%20Die%20DGS%20und%20der%20NS

[8] Max Weber, *The Theory of Social and Economic Organization*, ed. Talcott Parsons (New York: Free Press of Glencoe, 1964), 138.

[9] Peter Thomas, 'Being Max Weber', *New Left Review*, 41 (Sept.–Oct. 2006).

Thus sociology has more to redeem than Palyi's review. And yet the consensus among the sociologists who have written about genocide is that until recently the discipline's subsequent record was astonishingly poor. Mostly genocide 'was largely overlooked or suppressed by social scientists until the 1970s'.[10] As Irving Louis Horowitz suggested, 'Many sociologists exhibit a studied embarrassment about these issues, a feeling that intellectual issues posed in such a manner are melodramatic and unfit for scientific discourse.'[11] Michael Mann, who has produced perhaps the most important sociological contribution to the study of genocide, confessed that his earlier work 'had neglected the extremes of human behaviour'. He 'had not thought much about good and evil'.[12] Textbooks continue to ignore or marginalize genocide even today. Zygmunt Bauman claimed: 'When measured against the work done by historians or theologians, the bulk of academic sociology looks more like a collective exercise in forgetting and eye-closing.'[13] Not surprisingly, he memorably concluded that 'the Holocaust has more to say about the state of sociology than sociology in its present shape is able to add to our knowledge of the Holocaust.'[14] His attack was fundamental:

The nature and style of sociology has been attuned to the selfsame modern society it theorized and investigated; sociology has been engaged since its birth in a mimetic relationship with its object—or, rather, with the imagery of that object which it constructed and accepted as the frame for its own discourse. And so sociology promoted, as its own criteria of propriety, the same principles of rational action it visualized as constitutive of its object. It also promoted, as binding rules of [its] own discourse, the inadmissibility of ethical problematics in any other form but that of a communally-sustained ideology and thus heterogenous to sociological (scientific, rational) discourse. *Phrases like 'the sanctity of human life' or 'moral duty' sound as alien in a sociology seminar as they do in the smoke-free, sanitized rooms of a bureaucratic office.*[15]

The historian Herbert Hirsch has seen these limitations as intrinsic to social science: 'It is unfortunate that Holocaust and genocide studies are being pressured into a phase of social science rationality... only to become bogged down in the elusive variable and definition, as everyday life becomes almost entirely eliminated from their concern.'[16] Nevertheless Bauman's work proved a starting point for sociological research, informed by the very humane values that Hirsch advocated, without abandoning his discipline's generalizing concerns. His agenda, 'to open up

[10] Helen Fein, 'Genocide: A Sociological Perspective', *Current Sociology* 38:1 (1990), 5.
[11] Irving Louis Horowitz, quoted ibid. 6.
[12] Michael Mann, *The Dark Side of Democracy: Explaining Ethnic Cleansing* (Cambridge: Cambridge University Press), ix.
[13] Zygmunt Bauman, *Modernity and the Holocaust* (Cambridge: Polity, 1989), 9–10.
[14] Ibid. 3.
[15] Ibid. 29. Emphasis in original.
[16] Herbert Hirsch, *Genocide and the Politics of Memory: Studying Death to Preserve Life* (Chapel Hill: University of North Carolina Press, 1995), 81.

the findings of the specialists to the general use of social science, to interpret them in a way that shows their relevance to the main themes of sociological inquiry, to feed them back into the mainstream of our discipline,'[17] has guided some significant scholars. Weber's own 'principles of rational action' could be utilized in critical analysis, explaining contextually the development of murderous intentions and violent means and their realization in political conflict.

Revisiting Concepts and 'Classification'

Sociologists have contributed particularly to the debate on the meaning of genocide. Some say we can have too much 'definitionalism', and that—whatever we call things—the important thing is concrete understanding. Nevertheless, words matter. As Weber put it: 'The apparently gratuitous tediousness involved in the elaborate definition of . . . concepts is an example of the fact that we often neglect to think out clearly what seems to be "obvious," because it is intuitively familiar.'[18] Lemkin invented 'genocide' because he wanted to describe—and highlight for countervailing action—a general class of violent actions. We do not have to adopt his terminology or definitions; indeed we cannot avoid modifying them. Yet if it was important that Lemkin introduced 'genocide', it is also important we are aware of how we change its meaning. If we use it in new ways, or introduce new terms to describe some of the phenomena it originally designated, we need to explain why. In any case, all serious concepts must be used coherently—with internal coherence of meaning as well as valid reference—and must be capable of explanation. For genocide studies to be coherent, the field must forge adequate concepts.

The answer to the misuse of classification is not, therefore, to abandon classification. We simply cannot do this: classification is an inescapable part of human cognition. Social scientists' classifications—like those of genocidists—are particular versions of this general human activity. Classification's danger is always, as Nigel Eltringham has suggested, that 'we "misplace concreteness" and set out to "prove" that our abstract concepts . . . really do *correspond* to reality, rather than being contingent approximations.'[19] Genocidists go a big step further in trying to *enforce* their social classifications, making reality correspond at the cost of lives. But victims, especially resisters, also advance their own categories. They assert *their*

---

[17] Bauman, *Modernity and the Holocaust*, xiii. Emphasis in original.
[18] Weber, *Theory of Social and Economic Organization*, 140.
[19] Nigel Eltringham, *Accounting for Genocide* (London: Pluto, 2004), 7.

understandings of their identities; they assert their status as 'victims', and as 'civilians.' And at the same time, resisters impose classifications on those who would classify *them*. They describe their persecutors' actions as 'genocide' and classify them as 'crimes'; they call their attackers 'perpetrators', 'criminals', and génocidaires. Social scientists mostly develop existing meanings rather than inventing new terms; we cannot avoid referring to categories developed by active participants. We need to make sense of perpetrators' intentions, but ultimately we should reject their absolutist and euphemistic categories—like 'ethnic cleansing'—and develop categories that articulate the experiences of victims, resisters, and bystanders.

LEMKIN'S OWN SOCIOLOGICAL FRAMEWORK

That Hirsch's concerns were in the end misplaced can be grasped even before we approach the writings of sociologists themselves. For violence against civilian populations always displays a 'social logic', which in turn demands to be critiqued or deconstructed by a critical 'sociology'. Although the founder of genocide studies was a lawyer by trade, his fundamental understanding of the phenomenon was sociological rather than legal or simply historical. Moreover, although there is much lip service to his achievements, there is little appreciation of how significant his distinctive understanding remains. Indeed the appreciation of Lemkin's work has suffered from his political success. It is to the Convention, rather than Lemkin himself, that even social scientists often refer in defining genocide. This tendency is unfortunate because, although Lemkin's was far from the last word, he offered a much more adequate sociological understanding. Moreover many authors, trying to improve on the Convention, have actually moved even further from Lemkin in ways that militate against sociological knowledge. Recovering the meaning of genocide for Lemkin is a necessary beginning for the sociology of genocide.

As is well known, from Lemkin's first formulations, when in 1933 he proposed a draft law banning 'barbarity', he was looking for a term and a law that brought together a whole *class* of violent and humiliating actions against members of collectivities. Genocide was not a specific type of violence, but a general charge that highlighted the common elements of many acts that 'taken separately' constituted specific crimes. Lemkin saw it as including not only organized violence but also economic destruction and persecution. What concerned him was precisely the 'common feature' of these types of action: their threat to the existence of a collectivity. When Lemkin finally introduced the term 'genocide' in 1944, he again warned against a narrow interpretation:

Generally speaking, genocide does not necessarily mean the immediate destruction of a nation, except when accomplished by mass killings of all members of a nation. It is intended rather to signify a coordinated plan of different actions aiming at the destruction of essential foundations of the life of national groups, with aim of annihilating the groups themselves.[20]

The nuances of the key word 'destruction' were indicated here by the difference between 'immediate destruction' of a nation and 'destruction of essential founda- tions' of its life. Lemkin was clear that genocide refers *generally* to the latter; 'immediate' destruction in the sense of 'mass killings of all members of a nation' was a specific type but did *not* define genocide. Lemkin's definition was exemplified in the substance of his book, where he wrote that 'the Nazi genocide was effected through a synchronized attack on different aspects of life of the captive peoples,' politically, socially, culturally, economically, biologically, religiously, physically, and morally.[21] Genocide, for the term's inventor, was a comprehensive process in which a power 'attacked' and 'destroyed' the way of life and institutions of peoples. 'Physical' genocide—especially mass killing—was only one dimension of the comprehensive 'attack'.

In contrast to Lemkin's original view, the Convention on the Prevention and Punishment of the Crime of Genocide—while maintaining something of his broad approach by defining genocide as a *range* of 'acts committed with intent to destroy, in whole or in part, a national, ethnical, racial or religious group, as such'—in practice narrowed it down by giving a restricted list of acts (killing, bodily and mental harm, conditions leading to physical destruction, restricting births, trans- ferring children) with greater emphasis on physical destruction. This was particu- larly evident in the third clause, where 'inflicting on the group conditions of life' was genocidal only in so far as it was 'calculated to bring about its physical destruction'. For Lemkin in contrast it was quite clear that 'a synchronized attack on different aspects of life' was genocidal *in itself*. The Convention laid stronger emphasis than Lemkin on physical and biological destruction, and less on broader *social destruction*. In contrast Lemkin—however much he wished to establish and enforce genocide law—offered a historical-sociological account. He was surely right that in order to understand genocide, we should see killing and physical harm as elements of the broader process of social destruction. Even the Nazis did not aim simply to kill subject peoples, not even the Jews: they aimed to destroy their ways of life and social institutions. It is implausible to reduce this aim to a 'means' of physical destruction, as the Convention implied. Indeed it was the other way round: when physical destruction came to be a distinct, eventually overriding end this was an extreme development of pre-existing Nazi policies of social

[20] Raphael Lemkin, *Axis Rule in Occupied Europe: Laws of Occupation, Analysis of Government, Proposals for Redress, Axis* (Washington, DC: Carnegie Endowment for International Peace, 1944), 79.
[21] Ibid. xi-xii.

destruction. Lemkin was correct to stress the integrated, multidimensional, nature of the attack, and not to fall (as later writers have) into the trap of separating physical violence from social destruction. In this sense his work, rather than the Convention, remains the essential starting point for sociological understanding.

Nevertheless Lemkin had not presented a fully plausible account of the relations of socially destructive ends and violent or murderous means. His listing of 'the field of physical existence' as just one aspect of Nazism's coordinated attack was too mechanical. He failed to clarify that while genocide involved much more than killing, violence in a broad sense and its threat lay behind all genocidal policies. *Although genocide could not be defined by a specific violent method like killing, the idea of social destruction necessarily entailed generally violent methods.* What else could social 'destruction' mean? The deficiency of Lemkin's listing approach meant that this relationship between violence and social destruction remained to be fully grasped.

THE SOCIOLOGICAL CONTRIBUTION ON THE CONCEPT OF GENOCIDE

After Lemkin, the social science of genocide was mostly neglected until the 1980s. The first major advance was Leo Kuper's wide-ranging study, which criticized the Convention, emphasized the importance of colonial genocide and introduced the crucial idea of 'genocidal massacre' to refer to localized mass killings.[22] After Kuper, however, many social scientists worked from the legal definition, which was an unusual way of defining a sociological concept. For example, Helen Fein closely followed the Convention when she proposed: 'Genocide is sustained purposeful action by a perpetrator to physically destroy a collectivity directly or through interdiction of the biological and social reproduction of group members, sustained regardless of the surrender or lack of threat offered by the victim.'[23] The idea that physical destruction of a group could either be 'direct' or be carried out through interdiction of reproduction faithfully reflected the Convention's specification of means. Likewise 'sustained purposeful action' resumed the Convention idea of intentional destruction. Yet Fein noted the difficulties of the latter, and that to 'avoid the whole question of inference of intent, [some authors] propose that we simply eliminate intent as a criterion.'[24] She disagreed with Tony Barta's alternative

[22] Leo Kuper, *Genocide: Its Uses in the Twentieth Century* (Harmondsworth: Penguin, 1981), 32.
[23] Fein, 'Genocide', 24.
[24] Ibid.

proposal of 'a conception of genocide which embraces *relations* of destruction'.[25] Accepting that the meaning of genocide was firmly lodged in the idea of destruction as the intentional, organized policy of particular actors, she argued that we cannot 'remove from the word the emphasis on policy and intention which brought it into being.' However, she insisted on a more usual understanding of 'intention':

Intent or purposeful action—or inaction—is not the same in law or everyday language as either motive or function. An actor performs an act, we say, with intent if there are foreseeable ends or consequences: for what purpose is different from why or for what motive is the act designed.[26]

We need, she proposed, 'the sociological concept of purposeful action' as a 'bridge' between the legal concept of intent and a broader understanding.[27]

Fein modified the Convention concept in three additional respects. First, she referred only to collectivities and groups in general, and did not reproduce the Convention's restriction to 'national, ethnical, racial and religious groups'. She saw the protected groups as 'basic kinds, classes, or sub-families of humanity, persisting units of society', and argued cogently that 'the specification of groups should be consistent with our sociological knowledge of both the persistence and construction of group identities in society' and 'should conform to the implicit universalistic norm and a sense of justice, embracing the right of all non-violent groups to co-exist.'[28] Second, by inserting the word 'physically' in her definition, she went even further than the Convention in narrowing the scope of the crime from Lemkin's original idea that genocide is 'a synchronized attack on different aspects of life of (captive) peoples' towards an exclusive emphasis on killing and other measures of 'biological' rather than social destruction. Third, Fein's phrase, 'sustained regardless of the surrender or lack of threat offered by the victim', emphasized genocide's separation from war: victims are destroyed even if they are not military threats.

A more distinctive sociological contribution came from Frank Chalk and Kurt Jonassohn, whose widely quoted definition stated: 'Genocide is a form of one-sided mass killing in which a state or other authority intends to destroy a group, as that group and members in it are defined by the perpetrators.'[29] In defining genocide simply as 'mass killing', Chalk and Jonassohn departed more radically from the Convention, identifying genocide with physical destruction even more narrowly than Fein, and moved still further from Lemkin's broad concept. Fein rightly criticized them for failing to allow for 'other forms of intentional biological destruction' and pointed out that specifying states as perpetrators

[25] Tony Barta quoted ibid. 16. Emphasis in original.
[26] Ibid. 19.
[27] Ibid. 20.
[28] Ibid. 24.
[29] Frank Chalk and Kurt Jonassohn, *The History and Sociology of Genocide: Analyses and Case Studies* (New Haven, CT: Yale University Press, 1990), 23.

was unnecessarily restrictive.[30] Even if states are commonly organizing centres, parties, settlers, paramilitaries, and others have also been responsible, thus it seems perverse to define genocide by the state (even with the let-out of 'or other authority').

However, it was Chalk and Jonassohn's definition of the victim group 'as that group and members in it are defined by the perpetrators' that was their most distinctive contribution. This was important for emphasizing that perpetrators work according to their own, often fantastical, ideas of 'enemy' groups. This idea brought into question the assumption made by Lemkin, the Convention, and Fein that groups necessarily exist 'objectively' or are defined by their own consciousness of their identity, and this is what genocidists aim to destroy. Since all agree that the genocidists' intention to destroy a group is the starting-point in defining genocidal action, it follows that it is *their* idea of that group which (first of all) counts in the process. As Fein suggested, Chalk and Jonassohn's definition involved the opposite danger of according too much significance to the ideas of the perpetrators:[31] it needs to be corrected to acknowledge the contending role of victims' self-perceptions. However, by recognizing the role of ideas in genocide, Chalk and Jonassohn opened up an important, indeed an unavoidable dimension.

They also gave new emphasis to the general separation of genocide from war. Their idea of 'one-sidedness' could be taken as meaning that genocide is something one party does to another without conflict or resistance. Clearly there is a fundamental sense in which one-sidedness *is* what genocide is about: everyone understands that its violence is targeted by an organized, armed power against a largely unarmed population. However, such violence has often been imposed in the context of conflict between organized forces (war) and often provokes resistance, and hence new conflict, so that the genocidal element of one-sided killing is often part of a situation of two- or many-sided conflict and violence. To define genocide as 'one-sided' killing was potentially misleading if it led scholars to miss these connections.

BIOPOWER, MODERNITY, AND THE HOLOCAUST

If writers like Fein, Chalk, and Jonassohn made distinctively sociological arguments central to the emerging field of genocide studies, their work did little to overcome the general sociological neglect. Only when major sociological writers

[30] Fein, 'Genocide', 13.
[31] Fein criticizes this aspect of Chalk and Jonassohn's definition: 'Genocide', 13.

turned their attention to genocide did the wider discipline began to take notice. No less a figure than Michel Foucault had implicated genocide in his arguments about the nature of power in modernity, when he commented: 'If genocide is indeed the dream of modern powers, this is not because of a recent return of the ancient right to kill; it is because power is situated and exercized at the level of life, the species, the race, and the large-scale phenomena of population.'[32] He clearly linked genocide to modern war,[33] and both to profound transformations of the mechanisms of power in modern times. Sovereign power was now

power bent on generating forces, making them grow, and ordering them, rather than one dedicated to impeding them, making them submit, or destroying them. There has been a parallel shift in the right of death, or at least a tendency to align itself with the exigencies of a life-administering power and to define itself accordingly. This death that was based on the right of the sovereign is now manifested as simply the reverse of the right of the social body to ensure, maintain or develop its life.[34]

For Foucault therefore genocide represented a manifestation of modern 'biopower', reflecting the fact that 'life and its mechanisms' had been brought 'into the realm of explicit calculations and made knowledge-power an agent of transformation of human life.'[35] The corollary of the state's management of life forces was a new management of death: 'One might say that the ancient right to *take* life or *let* live was replaced by a power to *foster* life or *disallow* it to the point of death.'[36]

However, if genocide is a manifestation of the general 'power over life', by which the state takes upon itself the task of regulating and maintaining its subjects' minds and bodies, we still need to ask why this is exercised in a genocidal manner. Foucault's explanation that genocide is the *other side* of the modern state's 'function of administering life' seems insufficient. His relatively unexamined idea of genocide appears overinfluenced by particular pseudoscientific, eugenic ideologies and the exceptionally rationalized murder of the extermination camps. Although totalitarian rulers did sometimes appear to be mobilizing power to raise and cull entire populations like livestock, scholars have shown that even their genocidal decisions were pragmatic, launched in contexts of political conflict and war. Elsewhere genocide has been influenced less by ambitious ideological concepts and even more by specific political aims. Genocide is practiced by regimes and armed groups that hardly have totalitarian ambitions or capabilities; conversely, today's Western states certainly 'manage life' but they do not practice genocide.

---

[32] Michel Foucault, *The Will to Knowledge: The History of Sexuality*, vol. 1, trans. R. Hurley (Harmondsworth: Penguin, 1998), 136–7.

[33] Ibid. 136–7.

[34] Ibid. 136.

[35] Ibid. 143.

[36] Ibid. 138.

Foucault's linkages were suggestive but they didn't explain the rise of genocide or why genocides are initiated.

Nevertheless, Foucault's formulations captured a widespread belief in the *enabling* implication of modernity. This view of modern society was seminally explored by Bauman, for whom 'the Holocaust was an outcome of a unique encounter between factors by themselves quite ordinary and common'[37] and 'a rare, yet significant and reliable, test of the hidden possibilities of modern society'.[38] He contended 'that every "ingredient" of the Holocaust—all those many things that rendered it possible—was normal . . . in the sense of being fully in keeping with everything that we know about our civilization, its guiding spirit, its priorities, its immanent vision of the world'.[39] Bauman specified this 'modern' focus in terms of mentality, technology, and organization, building on Raul Hilberg's conclusion that the machinery of destruction 'was structurally no different from organized German society as a whole. [It] was the organized community in one of its special roles'.[40] The Holocaust was a textbook case of 'scientific management', 'a paradigm of modern bureaucratic rationality'.[41] The department in the SS headquarters in charge of the destruction of European Jews entirely fitted Weber's description of modern administration:

in the last resort—*the choice of physical extermination as the right means to the task of* Entfernung [removal, elimination] *was a product of routine bureaucratic procedures*: means-end calculus, budget balancing, universal rule application. To make the point sharper still—the choice was an effect of the earnest effort to find rational solutions to successive 'problems,' as they arose in the changing circumstances. . . . *it arose out of a genuinely rational concern, and it was generated by bureaucracy true to its form and purpose.*[42]

Moreover, bureaucracy provided the 'moral sleeping pills' that made possible the Holocaust's 'technical-administrative success'.[43]

Yet like Foucault's idea, Bauman's concept of the Holocaust was over-rationalized. Although he recognized that only '[t]he *possibility* of the Holocaust was rooted in certain universal features of modern civilization; its *implementation* on the other hand, was connected with a specific and not at all universal relationship between state and society',[44] his account narrowed down its meaning and made it difficult to compare with other equally modern genocides. When he wrote that 'the Holocaust left behind and put to shame all its alleged pre-modern equivalents, exposing them as primitive, wasteful and ineffective by comparison. . . . It towers

---

[37] Bauman, *Modernity and the Holocaust*, xiii.
[38] Ibid. 12.
[39] Ibid. 8.
[40] Raul Hilberg, quoted ibid.
[41] Ibid. 149.
[42] Ibid. 17. Emphasis in original.
[43] Ibid. 26.
[44] Ibid. 82. Emphasis in original.

high over the past genocidal episodes in the same way as the modern industrial plant towers above the craftsman's cottage workshop,'[45] he focused entirely on the industrialized extermination of the Final Solution. We got little sense of the activities of the *Einsatzgruppen*, shooting huge numbers alongside improvised ditches and burning them alive in their villages. Yet this direct slaughter was the first phase of extensive mass murder, the decisive shift of gear that paved the way for Auschwitz.

The activities of the *Einsatzgruppen* were not only closer to premodern paradigms. They proved a more enduring model than the extermination camps for later génocidaires. In Rwanda, notoriously, machine guns and machetes proved quite as murderous as the gas chambers, without the need for bureaucracy on the German scale (although the organizers did employ modern political organization and mass media). In Bosnia, Serbian nationalists destroyed Bosniak and Croatian society while slaughtering only a minority, through intimidation, expulsion, torture, rape, and killing in improvised concentration camps. In contemporary destructions of indigenous peoples, the methods and organization have been much more basic than the Final Solution's. Not surprisingly, a student of these genocides has argued that Bauman's 'thesis linking genocide to a specific level of state formation, technological efficiency, rationality, and subjectivity is belied' by other examples.[46]

Such critiques have led to an alternative version of the modernity thesis. According to the social anthropologist Nancy Scheper-Hughes, genocide is not an exceptional, high-bureaucratic realization but an *endemic* feature of modernity. She suggested 'a genocide continuum' composed of 'small wars and invisible genocides' conducted 'in the normative social spaces of public schools, clinics, emergency rooms, hospital wards, nursing homes, court rooms, prisons, detention centers, and public morgues. The continuum refers to the human capacity to reduce others to nonpersons, to monsters, or to things, that gives structure, meaning and rationale to everyday practices of violence.' The human species had developed 'a genocidal capacity' seen in 'all expressions of social exclusion, dehumanization, depersonalization, pseudo-speciation that normalize atrocious behavior and violence toward others'.[47] The kernel of truth in this argument is that once we recognize the possibility of genocidal outcomes it is alarmingly easy to imagine how everyday social relations could facilitate them. But once again these can only be enabling conditions. The key question is, *in what circumstances can devaluing and dehumanization mutate into systematic, organized violence?* Since the former are common and the latter relatively exceptional, this kind of argument from modernity to genocide shares the over-abstraction of Bauman's version that it criticizes.

---

[45] Ibid. 89.

[46] Nancy Scheper-Hughes, 'Coming to Our Senses: Anthropology and Genocide', in Hinton (ed.), *Annihilating Difference*, 366.

[47] Ibid. 369.

A SOCIOLOGY OF 'ETHNIC CLEANSING'

In order to overcome this problem, a closer specification of causality is necessary, and this in turn implies a sociological engagement with the historical literature. There is, of course, a substantial literature of comparative genocide studies. Until recently sociology's contribution was very limited, but this has changed with Mann's ambitious sociology of 'ethnic cleansing'. Mann is an unrivalled practitioner of synthetic and comparative methods in historical sociology, and his richly sourced study provides—in reality for the first time—a comprehensive sociological explanation of the darkest side of modernity. He outlines eight theses that frame detailed case studies of New World genocides, Armenia, Nazism, Communism, Yugoslavia, and Rwanda.[48]

Mann's key argument is that 'murderous ethnic cleansing' is the dark side not simply of modernity but specifically of democracy. While all the four 'sources of social power'—economic, ideological, political, and military[49]—are involved, he offers 'essentially a political explanation'. His main case is that 'cleansing is a hazard of the age of democracy since amid multiethnicity the ideal of rule by the people began to intertwine the *demos* with the dominant *ethnos*, generating organic conceptions of the nation and the state that encouraged the cleansing of minorities.' Certainly 'cleansing' results less from democracy itself than from its *perversion*: 'Regimes that are actually perpetrating murderous cleansing are never democratic, since that would be a contradiction in terms.... Indeed as escalation proceeds, all perpetrating regimes become less and less democratic.' And 'regimes newly embarked upon democratization are more likely to commit murderous ethnic cleansing than are stable authoritarian regimes.' In fact, 'stabilized institutionalized democracies' are the least likely to commit 'cleansing', although they often have it in their pasts, the more violently where 'settler democracy' took hold: 'The more settlers controlled colonial institutions, the more murderous the cleansing.... It is the most direct relationship I have found between democratic regimes and mass murder.' Although Mann labels 'cleansing' a product of 'inter-group relations', he is clear that it is no simple product of ethnic *differences*: to become murderous these need political expression.

Yet although this is a political account, Mann shows that genocide is not simply statist. There are 'three main levels of perpetrator': radical elites running party-states, violent paramilitary bands, and 'core constituencies providing mass though not majority popular support'. Ordinary people 'are brought by normal social

---

[48] Mann, *The Dark Side of Democracy*, 2–9; all quotations in the following paragraphs are taken from these pages unless otherwise specified.

[49] Mann developed this fourfold typology of power in *The Sources of Social Power*, 2 vols (Cambridge: Cambridge University Press, 1986 and 1993).

structures into committing murderous ethnic cleansing', and they have many different motives. However, Mann recognizes that '[e]thnic cleansings are in their murderous phases usually directed by states, and this requires some state coherence and capacity.' Radical party elites are crucial because they homogenize diverse social forces, welding them into more cohesive blocs, and centralize normally fragmented state structures in the pursuit of exceptional goals. This happens through political struggle, and typically through a series of escalations. The *danger zone* exists 'when (a) movements claiming to represent two fairly old ethnic groups both lay claim to their own state over all or part of the same territory and (b) this claim seems to them to have substantial legitimacy and some plausible chance of being implemented.' Escalation to *the brink* happens

when one of two alternative scenarios plays out. [Either] The less powerful side is bolstered to fight rather than to submit . . . by believing that aid will be forthcoming from outside . . . [Or] The stronger side believes it has such overwhelming military power and ideological legitimacy that it can force through its own cleansed state at little physical or moral risk to itself.

Finally, going 'over the brink' into actual *perpetration* occurs 'where the state exercising sovereignty over the contested territory has been factionalized and radicalized amid an unstable political environment that usually leads to war.'

Mann's account challenges the absolutist concept of 'intention', echoing Fein's insistence on a flexible 'sociological concept of purposeful action'. He demonstrates convincingly that an entire historical episode of murderous politics, over many months or years, cannot be explained by singular intentionality: 'Murderous cleansing is rarely the original intent of perpetrators. . . . [It] typically emerges as a kind of Plan C, developed only after the first two responses to a perceived ethnic threat fail . . . To understand the outcome, we must analyze the unintended consequences of a series of interactions yielding escalation.' Instead of interpreting murder as the direct consequence of longstanding intentions, he emphasizes the contingency of violent outcomes: 'Out of . . . political and geopolitical crises radicals emerge calling for tougher treatment of perceived ethnic enemies. In fact, where ethnic conflict between rival groups is quite old, it is usually somewhat ritualized, cyclical and manageable. Truly murderous cleansing, in contrast, is unexpected, originally unintended, emerging out of unrelated crises like war.'

Although in this richness and complexity Mann's is a highly plausible sociological framework, problems remain. He disarms criticism by acknowledging that '[g]iven the messiness and uniqueness of societies, my theses cannot be scientific laws. They do not even fit perfectly all my case studies.' Yet the coherence of his detailed explanations too frequently appears to be, at least partially, at odds with his general theses. His 'ethnic competition' framework works well for Rwanda and former Yugoslavia, but it does not fit as well the major cases of twentieth-century political mass murder, such as the Holocaust. These very darkest episodes appear to have only tenuous connections to democracy. They are products, Mann acknowledges, of 'a few highly authoritarian regimes' that 'deviate' from the norm of stable authoritarianism, and 'mobilize majoritarian groups into a mass party-state mobilizing the people against "enemy" minorities'. Although Hitler had indeed perverted democracy, it is difficult to fit the Holocaust, Mann recognizes, into his pattern of ethnic competition. Germans and Jews were 'two fairly old ethnic groups', but it was hardly the case that they 'both laid claim to their own state over all or part of the same territory.' Likewise the extensive mass murders of Communist states are problematic. Mann plausibly describes many of them as *classicide*, because their targets were social classes, and explains them as 'mistaken revolutionary projects' rather than as ethnic conflict. But he also offers the perversion of socialism as a class variant of the more common ethnic perversion of democracy: 'socialist ideals of democracy also became perverted as the *demos* became entwined with the term *proletariat*, the working class, creating pressures to cleanse other classes.' Along with the perversion of national democracy, this was then a second 'general way in which democratic ideals were transmuted into murderous cleansing'. However, we may question whether the idea of the proletariat (working class) was really a moving force in creating 'pressures to cleanse other classes'.

A more fundamental question is whether Mann correctly identifies the main explanatory locus of murderous policies among his four types of power. He had earlier provided the clearest argument that political and military are two separate forms of power.[50] That murderous power *is* primarily military does not of course mean that its occurrence should be *explained* simply by military developments. Yet Mann's mainly political explanation is questionable. As he acknowledges, his theses connecting 'cleansing' to democracy 'apply beforehand, to the earlier phases of escalation of ethnic conflict'. It is military power that 'proves decisive in the later stages of the worst cases of ethnic cleansing. Armies, police forces, and irregular extrastate paramilitaries are the main agencies.' Indeed, he provides detailed arguments that *should* lead to a heavily 'military' explanation:

Most 20th-century cases of ethnic cleansing occurred during wars or during the chaotic transfer from war to peace.... Ideologically tinged wars reduce shared rules and convert civilians into enemies.... Civil wars and wars of secession with a strong ethnic component are dangerous for ethnic groups trapped behind enemy lines. The lure towards murderous ethnic cleansing increases when it can be accomplished at low military cost, with little fear of retaliation.... Military campaigns may generate tactical lure towards atrocities against civilians that were not originally intended.... Guerrilla warfare lures guerrillas to kill civilians.... These [and others] are all features of military power that may produce murderous cleansing.[51]

50 Ibid. i.10–11.
51 Mann, *The Dark Side of Democracy*, 32.

Yet at the most general level of Mann's analysis, in formulating his theses and locating his explanation in political power, this role of war is strangely neglected. So we need to go further: genocide generally (although not always) arises from and is carried out through war. Most genocide is actually part of genocidal war.[52] Murderous politics do not arise primarily from political power relations, but out of political power that is fundamentally conditioned by military power: out of the interactions of political and military power.

THE PROBLEM OF CONCEPTUAL PROLIFERATION

The limitations of Mann's framework are conceptual as well as analytical. Although 'ethnic cleansing' and 'genocide' are highly contested terms, he does not fully justify the adoption of 'cleansing' as a master concept. This is unfortunate, since the term is widely rejected as a perpetrator euphemism unsuitable for social-scientific use. As Norman Naimark, a historian who uses the term, remarks: 'There is nothing "clean" about ethnic cleansing. It is shot through with violence and brutality in the most extreme form.'[53] Mann defines it as 'the removal by members of one [ethnic] group of another such group from a locality they define as their own.' His insistence that 'murderous cleansing' is a subtype gives credence to the notion that removal can be non-murderous or non-violent—a manifestation of political but not military power. Yet, the wholesale removal of a population group from their homeland is generally involuntary, resisted, and enforced through extreme coercion. The forms and extents of violence vary greatly, but ethnic removal generally falls under Lemkin's original concept of genocide as 'the destruction of a nation or of an ethnic group'.[54]

Mann has adopted the 1990s reinvention of genocide as 'ethnic cleansing' and the corresponding narrowing of genocide itself to the intentional murder of all the members of a group. His work in this sense fits into a wider pattern of scholarship, as well as political and legal commentary, that adopts a narrow concept of genocide as exclusively defined by premeditated mass killing, and therefore uses other terms—not only 'ethnic cleansing' and 'classicide' but also 'ethnocide', 'politicide', 'gendercide', 'cultural genocide', 'urbicide', etc.—to refer to aspects of what Lemkin considered under a broad definition of genocide. 'Genocide' then refers to a

---

[52] For more support for these assertions, see my *War and Genocide* (Cambridge: Polity 2003), Chapter 2.

[53] Norman Naimark, *Fires of Hatred: Ethnic Cleansing in Twentieth-Century Europe* (Cambridge, MA: Harvard University Press, 2001), 193.

[54] Lemkin, *Axis Rule*, 79.

specific type of political violence, rather than a broad class of violent actions, and another term is needed to act as the master concept that Lemkin originally intended 'genocide' to be. In Mann's case, 'ethnic cleansing', refined as 'murderous cleansing', assumes this broad role; but non-sociological writers have produced other proposals, such as Rudolph Rummel's idea of 'democide'.[55] From the point of view of genocide studies, there is a strong case that the many new '-cide' terms are unimaginative imitations of Lemkin's original word, and that these '-cides' should be understood as ways of referring to the many *sides* of genocide. Certainly, the rapid conceptual proliferation has been accompanied by confusion over the meanings and relationships of terms, rather than improved understanding. Understood broadly and sociologically, suitably refined and expanded, 'genocide' itself can provide a coherent framework for understanding the range of organized violence targeted specifically at civilian populations.[56]

Towards a Structural Concept of Genocide

However, if the idea is to function in this fashion, genocide studies need a new phase of conceptual discussion to overcome the present state of contestation and confusion. While many case studies, historical and contemporary, adopt conflicting definitions according to the circumstances of particular cases, and others either implicitly or explicitly use the Holocaust as a standard (although one case could never act as an adequate definition of the general concept), there is a strong need for greater conceptual clarity. This is a task to which sociology can make a crucial contribution. As Weber suggested, there is a crucial difference between explanations of individual events and those of general phenomena, which defines the respective roles of the interrelated subjects of history and sociology. Sociology is 'a generalizing, regularity-seeking discipline, rather than an "idiographic" one, and its method [is] essentially typological,' although it is also 'interdefined' with history, and facilitating 'the causal analysis of singular historical phenomena'.[57] Therefore as Thomas Burger has put it, the difference between sociology and history 'is not just one of degree.... For the task of sociology is

---

[55] Rudolph Rummel, *Death by Government* (Brunswick, NJ: Transaction Publishers, 1997).

[56] The argument in this and the preceding paragraph is developed in my *What is Genocide?*, chs 4 and 5.

[57] Weber, *Theory of Social and Economic Organization*, 161. Thus many argue that history and sociology need to be combined in a 'sociological history' or a 'historical sociology'. See C. Wright Mills, *The Sociological Imagination* (London: Oxford University Press, 1959); Philip Abrams, *Historical Sociology* (Shepton Mallet: Open Books, 1982).

the construction of a special kind of general concept whereas the goal of history is the formation of individual concepts.'[58] Moreover, without clear definitions, words would be 'vague thought-images created to meet the unconsciously felt need for adequate expression whose meaning is only concretely felt but not clearly thought out.'[59] Clearly, defined terms enabled 'the conceptually clear description of *individual* historical developments, whenever this is necessary and the merely felt mental picture is too unprecise [*sic*] for a particular purpose in question.'[60]

From the point of view of sociological concept formation, genocide studies are mostly stuck at the first stage, of defining the phenomenon by the subjective meaning of the action for the actors themselves (and of course for a particular group of actors, the 'perpetrators'). Moreover, we have seen that there has been a tendency, heavily influenced by the legal discourse, to identify this subjective meaning with a rarefied concept of a singular, absolute 'intention'. Sociologists like Fein and Mann have provided a more satisfactory way of understanding intention, but this is only a beginning. As Weber explained, understanding the subjective meaning of action (in his well-known term *Verstehen*) is not in itself an analytical method, but a starting point from which it is necessary to proceed to causal explanation through the development of *structural* concepts of the *relationships* between actors. So we need not just a way of representing the subjective meaning of actions, but models, 'mental constructs, consisting of a number of elements standing in particular relationships to each other, which are designed to represent, for descriptive purposes, a specific segment of empirical reality and the interdependencies existing in it.'[61] Genocide should be defined not only by the 'intentions' of 'perpetrators', but by the social relationships between them and the 'victim' group, including the relations within each of these categories of actor, and relations to other actors, conventionally described as 'bystanders'. The patterns of these relationships define genocide not just as a type of social action ('committed' by 'perpetrators'), but as a *structure* of *conflict* between actors. This approach will lead us, of course, to transcend ideas of genocide as 'one-sided' action, for although genocide is certainly a very asymmetrical type of conflict, the responses of the targeted group, for example resistance, and of other actors, for example in armed intervention, are also of crucial importance to understanding it. Only if genocide is generally understood as a structural form will it be possible to develop coherent explanations. Grasping genocide itself as a structure will enable it to be seen in relation to other structures—cultural, economic, political, and military—within which genocidal relations develop.

---

[58] Thomas Burger, *Max Weber's Theory of Concept Formation: History, Laws and Ideal Types* (Durham, NC: Duke University Press, 1987), 138. Emphasis added.

[59] Ibid. 136.

[60] Ibid.

[61] Ibid. 177. Emphasis in original.

I have therefore proposed that we need to define genocide as a type of unequal social *conflict* between two sets of actors, which is conditioned in the first instance by the type of *action* carried out by the more powerful side. Thus genocide as a structure should be understood as 'a form of violent social conflict or war, between armed power organizations that aim to destroy civilian social groups and those groups and other actors who resist this destruction'. Genocidal action (or genocide as action, a sense closer to previous understandings) can be defined as 'action in which armed power organizations treat civilian social groups as enemies and aim to destroy their real or putative social power, by means of killing, violence and coercion against individuals whom they regard as members of the groups.'[62]

THE DESTRUCTION OF 'GROUPS'

Sociology has also helped clarify the vexed question of the 'group' element of genocide. Although some have proposed that any mass killing should be seen as genocide, the idea of group destruction has been central to the concept. Indeed it is difficult to see how intentional harm against a large number of people could not be informed by a 'group' idea. In legal and other discourse, there has been a great deal of discussion of different types of group—whether the 'ethnic, national, racial, and religious' groups of the Convention refer to different categories, or are different ways of describing the same thing; and whether 'political', 'social' ('class') and other groups should be added to the protected list. Sociologists have, as we have seen, short-circuited this discussion by proposing a *generic* concept of group (Fein) and adding that attacked groups are *subjectively* defined by perpetrators (Chalk and Jonassohn). So we can say that genocide involves the attempt to destroy a group of people, regardless of how far groups defined by perpetrators correspond to 'real' groups that are intersubjectively recognized by their members or objectively identifiable by observers. I have argued that the one commonality of all target groups in genocide is that they are all essentially *civilian* populations, largely unarmed in the face of armed violence.[63]

However, the 'group' element leads to another key issue, the relationship between group 'destruction' and harm towards individuals. Lemkin's use of the common suffix '-cide' suggested that the destruction of groups was similar to the killing of individuals denoted by established terms like infanticide and patricide.

---

[62] Shaw, *What is Genocide?*, 154.
[63] Ibid. Chapter 8.

Genocide involved the 'killing' of a social group, as the UN General Assembly made clear when it asserted, 'Genocide is a denial of the right of existence of entire human groups, *as homicide is the denial of the right to live of individual human beings.'*[64] Yet this powerful analogy, like all analogies, had a potential to mislead. At that time, there was a greater propensity than today to consider societies as organisms, in which the functioning of the whole determined the activities of the parts, and the well being of the individual was subordinated to the whole. This view was formulated most starkly in fascist, Stalinist, and indeed genocidal ideologies, but there was a more general belief in the holistic nature of national societies and individuals' subordination to them. This holistic tendency was represented in sociology, too, but in reality human groups or societies were not so like biological organisms. Human societies were constituted through social relations between individual human beings: 'societies' and 'groups' are ways of thinking about how these relations bind individuals together. As Weber had written,

For other cognitive purposes . . . it may . . . be convenient or even indispensable to treat social collectivities . . . as if they were individual persons. . . . But for the subjective interpretation of action in sociological work these collectivities must be treated as *solely* the resultants and modes of organization of the particular acts of individual persons, since these alone can be treated as agents in a course of subjectively understandable action.[65]

Since social groups are not like individuals, it follows that 'destroying' them is not like killing embodied human beings, either. We have seen that there is a powerful trend in genocide theory to reduce 'destruction' to its 'physical' and 'biological' dimensions. The logical conclusion is that genocide is seen simply as mass killing. However, this position is sociologically incoherent even in its own terms. Because groups are social constructions, they can be neither constituted nor destroyed simply through the bodies of their individual members. Destroying groups must involve a lot more than simply killing, although killing and other physical harm are rightly considered important to it. The discussion of group 'destruction' is obliged, then, to take seriously Lemkin's 'large view of this concept'[66]—discarded in genocide's reduction to body counts—which centred on social destruction. A more appropriate way of interpreting group destruction is therefore to see it as involving a nexus between the destruction of collective ways of life and institutions and bodily and other harm to individuals.

---

[64] UN General Assembly Resolution 96(I), 11 December 1946, quoted by William A. Schabas, *Genocide in International Law* (Cambridge: Cambridge University Press), 45. Emphasis added.

[65] Weber, *Theory of Social and Economic Organization*, 101.

[66] Schabas, *Genocide in International Law*, 228.

CONCLUSION

This chapter has argued that sociology can make central contributions to genocide studies. As a generalizing, concept-forming discipline it can help clarify the still-contested meaning of genocide and clarify some of its theoretical difficulties. Through historical-sociological work it can contribute to the comparative study of genocides. So far its contributions have been modest, but some important work has begun to overcome the sharply critical judgements of the discipline made by Zygmunt Bauman and others two decades ago. There is reason to believe that the terrible crimes of social classification that have marred modernity are at last beginning to receive an appropriate response from those whose professional concern is the critical analysis of social forms.

SELECT BIBLIOGRAPHY

Bauman, Zygmunt, *Modernity and the Holocaust* (Cambridge: Polity, 1989).

Chalk, Frank, and Kurt Jonassohn, *The History and Sociology of Genocide: Analyses and Case Studies* (New Haven, CT: Yale University Press, 1990).

Fein, Helen, 'Genocide: A Sociological Perspective', *Current Sociology* 38:1 (1990).

Horowitz, Irving Louis, *Taking Lives* (New Brunswick, NJ: Transaction Books, 1979).

Kuper, Leo, *Genocide: Its Political Uses in the Twentieth Century* (Harmondsworth: Penguin, 1981).

Mann, Michael, *The Dark Side of Democracy: Explaining Ethnic Cleansing* (Cambridge: Cambridge University Press, 2005).

Shaw, Martin, *War and Genocide* (Cambridge: Polity, 2003).

—— *What is Genocide?* (Cambridge: Polity, 2007).

CHAPTER 8

POLITICAL SCIENCE AND GENOCIDE

SCOTT STRAUS

INTRODUCTION

THE discipline of political science has been an important arena for scholarly innovation about the study of genocide. Political scientists penned several landmark qualitative and quantitative comparative studies of genocide; political scientists have proposed several influential theories of genocide; and political scientists have been instrumental in broadening the concept of genocide. More generally, genocide is almost always a *political* phenomenon. The occurrence of genocide is usually closely tied to the state, either directly when national governments act as the chief instigator and perpetrator of violence or indirectly when national governments enable private actors or local officials to commit mass violence. Genocide is also political in that the origins and dynamics of the phenomenon generally entail struggles for power, the containment of threat, and control over the distribution of goods and property. These are political processes, and thus a discipline devoted to the study of politics has a set of natural advantages when approaching the study of genocide.

At the same time, the actual fit between political science and genocide studies has hardly been seamless. For many years, the study of genocide remained firmly at the margins of the discipline, as some of the first political scientists to study genocide attest.[1] That began to change in the 1990s, with the onset of several high-profile cases and a general geopolitical shift after the end of the Cold War. The net result is that analysis of genocide as a political phenomenon—and related topics such as genocide prevention, intervention to stop genocide, and justice after genocide—have received considerably more visibility in the discipline.

Nonetheless, despite this increased attention, there is a not a standard political science paradigm when it comes to studying genocide. As a discipline, political science is theoretically and methodologically diverse, and what can be said of the discipline may also be said of political scientists' studies of genocide. More specifically, no theoretical consensus with regard to the structural conditions, triggers, or causal dynamics that drive, facilitate, or accelerate genocidal violence has emerged. There is also not a standard research design that emerges from political science; rather, political scientists have developed multiple different approaches to the study of genocide, ranging from single-country studies, to comparisons of a limited number of countries, to cross-national quantitative studies. Some political scientists focus their explanations on macro-social conditions and states; others focus on micro-level dynamics and units of analysis. In short, the diversity that characterizes the discipline characterizes political scientists' approaches to the study of genocide.

Given the absence of theoretical and methodological convergence in the discipline, this chapter focuses attention on three major themes in considering the relationship between political science and genocide studies. In the first substantive section, the chapter discusses the evolution of genocide studies within the discipline and expands on the points raised above. In the second section, the chapter identifies seminal contributions that have emerged from some four decades of political science studies of genocide. In particular, I isolate five major areas of innovation and concentration:

1) A methodological emphasis on the comparative method, including both quantitative and qualitative studies;
2) A move to broaden the concept of genocide using related but different terms;
3) A theoretical emphasis on regime type;
4) A theoretical emphasis on political leaders' decision-making calculus—more specifically, political scientists have been in the forefront of developing rationalist explanations of genocide; and
5) A theoretical emphasis on the connections between warfare and genocide.

---

[1] Herbert Hirsch, 'Studying Genocide to Protect Life', in Samuel Totten and Steven Jacobs (eds), *Pioneers of Genocide Studies* (New Brunswick, NJ: Transaction Publishers, 2002), 113–27; Roger Smith, 'Who Is My Neighbor?', in ibid. 179–93.

In the third substantive section, I present some general critiques of political science approaches and suggest avenues for future research in the discipline.

Before going forward, a few caveats are in order. The first is that the chapter is not comprehensive. The main focus of the chapter is on political science explanations of the origins and dynamics of genocide, with a bias towards political scientists who consider genocide as a transhistorical and cross-national phenomenon. Moreover, the focus is on aggregate contributions from political scientists and thematic areas of emphasis—I do not seek to review every political science theory of genocide. That means certain studies will not be discussed. It also means that whole topics covered by political scientists will not receive sustained attention. One major analytic emphasis among political scientists not discussed in the chapter concerns the opportunities and obstacles that attend the prevention of genocide and efforts to stop genocidal processes once they have begun. Often this literature goes under the heading of 'humanitarian intervention', and in addition to scholars of international law political scientists have been in the forefront of studies of humanitarian intervention.[2] Another major area of research concerns the aftermath of genocide, in particular the study of different judicial mechanisms of accountability for genocide crimes. The literature generally operates under the heading of 'transitional justice', and political scientists have been instrumental in this area as well.[3] I do not focus on either the humanitarian intervention literature or the transitional justice literature for two main reasons. First, to keep the chapter manageable, I concentrate on methodological and theoretical approaches to

---

[2] Some of the most important work by political scientists on humanitarian intervention include Michael Barnett, *Eyewitness to a Genocide: The United Nations and Rwanda* (Ithaca, NY: Cornell University Press, 2002); Timothy Crawford and Alan Kuperman (eds), *Gambling on Humanitarian Intervention: Moral Hazard, Rebellion and Civil War* (New York: Routledge, 2006); Herbert Hirsch, *Anti-Genocide: Building an American Movement to Prevent Genocide* (Westport, CT: Praeger, 2002); J. L. Holzgrefe and Robert Keohane (eds), *Humanitarian Intervention: Ethical, Legal, and Political Dilemmas* (New York: Cambridge University Press, 2003); Roger Smith (ed), *Genocide: Essays toward Understanding, Early-Warning, and Prevention* (Williamsburg, VA: College of William and Mary/Association of Genocide Scholars, 1999); Benjamin Valentino, 'Still Standing By: Why America and the International Community Fail to Prevent Genocide and Mass Killing', *Perspectives on Politics* 1:3 (2003), 565–76; Thomas Weiss, 'Halting Genocide: Rhetoric vs. Reality', *Genocide Studies and Prevention* 2:1 (2007), 7–30; Nicholas Wheeler, *Saving Strangers: Humanitarian Intervention in International Society* (Oxford: Oxford University Press, 2003).

[3] For some examples of political scientists who study justice mechanisms, see Gary Bass, *Stay the Hand of Vengeance: The Politics of War Crimes Tribunals* (Princeton: Princeton University Press, 2000); Leigh Payne, *Unsettling Accounts: Neither Truth Nor Reconciliation in Confessions of State Violence* (Durham, NC: Duke University Press, 2008); Victor Peskin, *Trials and Tribulations: The Politics of War Crimes Tribunals in the Balkans and Rwanda* (New York: Cambridge University Press, 2008); Kathryn Sikkink and Ellen Lutz, 'The Justice Cascade: The Evolution and Impact of Foreign Human Rights Trials in Latin America', *Chicago Journal of International Law* 2:1 (2001), 1–33; Kathryn Sikkink and Carrie Booth Walling, 'The Impact of Human Rights Trials in Latin America', *Journal of Peace Research* 44:4 (2007), 427–45; and Jack Snyder and Leslie Vinjamuri, 'Trials and Errors: Principle and Pragmatism in Strategies of International Justice', *International Security* 28:3 (2003), 5–44.

explaining why genocide occurs, which is a major focus in the political science literature. Second, the now-extensive literatures on humanitarian intervention and transitional justice are not limited to the prevention of genocide, but pertain to sometimes different phenomena, such as humanitarian crises that emerge from state collapse or apartheid.

A second caveat is that political science is not an exclusive domain for the themes and contributions discussed in the chapter. The general rise in prominence of genocide studies in political science is analogous to other kin disciplines, including history, sociology, and anthropology. Moreover, there is considerable overlap of thematic and methodological concerns in sociology and history. Sociologists and historians, for example, have developed comparative approaches to the study of genocide. Nonetheless, if not exclusive domains, the areas highlighted in the chapter are intellectual zones where political scientists have made distinctive and repeated contributions. These are the areas where political scientists have left and are likely to continue to leave their mark on the study of genocide.

The Study of Genocide and the Discipline of Political Science

During the past decade, there has been a general growth of interest in genocide, and the political science discipline is not an exception to that trend.[4] Papers on different aspects of genocide are now common at the discipline's major annual conferences (such as the American Political Science Association and the International Studies Association). In the past decade, studies of genocide have been published in the major university presses for political scientists, as well as in some of the discipline's flagship journals, notably the *American Political Science Review, International Organization,* and *World Politics*. I explore below some reasons for the upsurge of scholarly interest among political scientists. However, it is important to note that as genocide studies first developed in the 1970s and 1980s, the topic remained largely marginal to the discipline. The point is not that political scientists were absent from the early stages of the development of genocide studies—many were quite instrumental—but rather that the study of genocide had very limited visibility within the discipline.

The reasons why the study of genocide was initially marginal are instructive. First, however rigorous and systematic scholars may wish to make the study of

---

[4] Scott Straus, 'Second-Generation Comparative Research on Genocide', *World Politics* 59:3 (2007), 476–501.

genocide, concern with the topic has almost inevitable normative dimensions. While not alien to political science, normatively driven inquiries are not always welcome within a discipline that prides itself on value-neutral, social scientific scholarship. Second, until the mid-1990s, the topic of genocide was not prominent in foreign policy or major media outlets, and political scientists often take their cue from topics of general policy and public interest. Moreover, genocide as an outcome remained for many political scientists strongly associated with the Holocaust. As a perceived singular, single, and historical case, the Holocaust did not attract substantial interest as representative of a broader phenomenon.[5] Third, as an international crime codified in a UN Convention and as originally coined by a jurist (Raphael Lemkin), the concept of 'genocide' had strong legal origins and connotations, which in turn inhibited political science scholarship on genocide. Finally, genocide studies emerged as (and remains) an interdisciplinary area of research. Political scientists are not uniformly disinterested in interdisciplinary areas of inquiry, but the interdisciplinary character of genocide studies kept the topic at some distance from the centre of the discipline.

A marked change became apparent in the mid-1990s for a number of reasons. First, the broader geopolitical context changed with the end of the Cold War. A number of topics that were once somewhat marginal to political science became topics of increased interest and analysis, including international human rights, humanitarianism, civil war, and political violence. The interest in genocide is part of this broader scholarly trend. Second, several high-profile conflagrations, which the press, policymakers, and courts frequently labelled as 'genocide', were prominent in the mid-1990s and later in the 2000s. The primary cases were the Balkans series of wars in the mid- to late 1990s; the 1994 violence and civil war in Rwanda; and Darfur in the mid-2000s. Each of these cases commanded significant public and policy interest, and the result is that the topic of genocide was brought to the attention of a wide array of scholars. The cases in turn generated political-science-type questions concerning the causal dynamics that drive genocide and the attendant search for commonalities among disparate cases. Finally, attention to genocide became increasingly prominent in international politics. To take a few examples: in 2004, the UN Security Council established a special advisor on the prevention of genocide; in 2006, the United States incorporated genocide prevention into the country's National Security Strategy; and in 2008 a coalition of prominent US-based think tanks and non-governmental organizations produced

---

[5] Alan Zuckerman, 'Political Science and the Jews: A Review Essay on the Holocaust, the State of Israel, and the Comparative Analysis of Jewish Communities', *American Political Science Review* 3:4 (1999), 935–45.

a high-level report on genocide prevention chaired by Madeleine Albright (a former Secretary of State) and William Cohen (a former Secretary of Defense).[6]

The newfound attention to genocide should not be overstated. Genocide is not a top foreign policy concern or a top concern in international forums like the UN Security Council or General Assembly. Genocide remains one of dozens of topics analysed by political scientists who study international politics. And the public and press concern with specific cases is episodic. Nonetheless, the topic commands considerably more visibility and legitimacy than it ever has, and that has contributed to a large upsurge of research and political science publications.

THEMATIC AREAS OF FOCUS AND INNOVATION

In this section, I discuss four-and-a half major areas of focus and innovation in how political scientists approach the study of genocide. I also raise questions and concerns about each of the areas. In order, the areas of focus are:

1) The comparative method (including attendant conceptual creativity—the 'half' alluded to previously);
2) A theoretical interest in regime type;
3) A theoretical interest in rationalist explanations; and
4) A theoretical interest in the relationship between warfare and genocide.

The Comparative Method (and Conceptual Innovation)

Political scientists often seek to make generalizations about the causal factors that drive a particular outcome, and a principal tool by which political scientists identify generalizable causal patterns is the comparative method. The approach is foundational for one of the main subfields within the discipline, that of comparative politics, and indeed many political science studies of genocide are the product of scholars within the subfield. The comparative method is also common and important for scholars of international relations, which represents the other pillar of political science studies of genocide.

Political scientists' use of the comparative method to examine genocide takes many forms. One is to examine a particular case and to make comparative generalizations on the basis of that case. The method is evident in analysis of some seminal cases, in particular Rwanda, the former Yugoslavia, and to an extent the

---

[6] The report may be downloaded at http://www.usip.org/genocide_taskforce/index.html

Holocaust.[7] A second comparative approach receiving increased use in the discipline is to make within-country comparisons, in particular by comparing villages or regions.[8] The approach has the advantage of holding macro-level, national factors constant while examining variation across regions, time periods, and individuals. However, the most common comparative approach for political scientists who study genocide and arguably within the broader discipline is to make comparisons for which countries are the units of analysis. Even this approach is varied: some political scientists conduct qualitative studies of a handful of countries; other political scientists engage in qualitative research, but where a dozen or more cases are compared; and finally some political scientists treat genocide as a quantifiable dependent variable and use statistical methods to test hypotheses.

Examples of each of these different approaches are evident in the political science scholarship on genocide, ranging from the earliest studies to the most contemporary. Leo Kuper's 1981 book, *Genocide: Its Political Use in the Twentieth Century*, is a founding work of scholarship in the genocide studies field.[9] Kuper, a political scientist, makes a number of wide-ranging observations in the book, including durable insights about the politics of ratifying the UN Genocide Convention as well as observations about obstacles to intervention. Kuper also advances an argument that the structural condition that underlies different cases across the twentieth century is the presence of deep divisions in plural societies. The claim is that persistent social cleavages are the wellspring of the enmity, dehumanization, and distrust that fuel genocide. To substantiate the claim, Kuper uses the comparative method of the second type described above: he presents a number of short case histories at a general level. He then observes empirical and causal patterns and draws out his argument about deep divisions.

Another seminal work in the genocide studies field is a focused comparison of the Holocaust and the Armenian genocide by political scientist Robert Melson.[10] In analysing two cases, rather than multiple ones at a general level, Melson is able to examine the cases in greater depth and to identify dynamic processes within each case. Melson concludes that two major structural factors underlie the cases.

---

[7] For examples, see V. P. Gagnon, *The Myth of Ethnic War: Serbia and Croatia in the 1990s* (Ithaca, NY: Cornell University Press, 2005); Daniel Jonah Goldhagen, *Hitler's Willing Executioners: Ordinary Germans and the Holocaust* (New York: Random House, 1996); and Mahmood Mamdani, *When Victims Become Killers: Colonialism, Nativism, and the Genocide in Rwanda* (Princeton: Princeton University Press, 2001).

[8] For example, see Lee Ann Fujii, *Killing Neighbors: Webs of Violence in Rwanda* (Ithaca, NY: Cornell University Press, 2009), and Scott Straus, *The Order of Genocide: Race, Power, and War in Rwanda* (Ithaca, NY: Cornell University Press, 2006).

[9] Leo Kuper, *Genocide: Its Political Use in the Twentieth Century* (New Haven, CT: Yale University Press, 1981).

[10] Robert Melson, *Revolution and Genocide: On the Origins of the Armenian Genocide and the Holocaust* (Chicago: University of Chicago Press, 1992).

First, he argues for the importance of a prior revolution; revolutions have multiple effects, but principally they redefine and divide political communities into authentic and undeserving populations. Second, Melson argues that war is significant. In wartime, states link enemies of the revolution to external wartime enemies, thereby increasing the risk that the domestic 'enemies' will be targeted for elimination. Melson's argument about war remains influential and echoes more contemporary research on genocide. Focused comparison is also found in recent studies by political scientists Jacques Sémelin and Manus Midlarsky, each of whom analyses three cases in depth and generates an argument on the basis of the comparison.[11]

While political scientists have been in the forefront of qualitative comparative research on genocide, the method is evident in kin disciplines. In their seminal book for the genocide studies field, for example, historian Frank Chalk and sociologist Kurt Jonassohn employ a methodological approach similar to that of Kuper. They present a fairly general account of multiple different cases, which, in their case, date to antiquity.[12] Melson's use of focused comparison of a small number of cases is the methodological choice in important works by historian Eric Weitz, psychologist Erwin Staub, and sociologist Michael Mann.[13]

The final comparative method discussed here, quantitative cross-national studies of genocide, is more distinctive among political scientists. Sociologist Helen Fein has done quantitative research, comparing Jewish victimization rates across Nazi-occupied territories during the Holocaust.[14] However, the method is fairly rare outside political science. Among the most influential political science quantitative studies is that of Barbara Harff. In her quantitative research, Harff conceptualizes genocide as analogous to 'politicide' (systematic mass murder of a political group). In an influential study in the *American Political Science Review*, Harff analysed more than 30 cases of genocide and politicide between 1955 and 2001. She concludes that six main risk factors help explain the onset of genocide and politicide. The factors include not only upheaval, but also the existence of prior genocides or politicides; elite 'exclusionary ideology'; autocratic regimes; ethnic

---

[11] Manus Midlarsky, *The Killing Trap: Genocide in the Twentieth Century* (New York: Cambridge University Press, 2005); Jacques Sémelin, *Purifier et détruire: Les usages politiques des massacres et génocide* (Paris: Le Seuil, 2005) (translated as *Purify and Destroy: The Political Uses of Massacre and Genocide*, trans. Cynthia Schoch (New York: Columbia University Press, 2007)).

[12] Frank Chalk and Kurt Jonassohn, *The History and Sociology of Genocide: Analyses and Case Studies* (New Haven, CT: Yale University Press, 1990).

[13] Michael Mann, *The Dark Side of Democracy: Explaining Ethnic Cleansing* (New York: Cambridge University Press, 2005); Ervin Staub, *The Roots of Evil: The Origins of Genocide and Other Group Violence* (New York: Cambridge University Press, 1989); Eric Weitz, *Century of Genocide: Utopias of Race and Nation* (Princeton: Princeton University Press, 2003).

[14] Helen Fein, *Accounting for Genocide: National Responses and Jewish Victimization during the Holocaust* (Chicago: University of Chicago Press, 1979).

minority rule; and low trade openness.[15] A similar quantitative approach is also found in the work of political scientist Matthew Krain, who bases his analysis on an earlier data set of genocide and politicide put together by Harff and Ted Gurr. Krain refers to his dependent variable as 'state-sponsored mass murder', and he argues that 'political opportunity structure', especially civil war, is the key determinant.[16]

A different approach is found in the work of political scientist Benjamin Valentino. Like Harff and Krain, Valentino moves away from a strict focus on genocide and anchors his research on the concept of 'mass killing', which refers to events in which 50,000 civilians or more died in a five-year period.[17] In co-authored quantitative work (discussed in greater depth below), Valentino examines mass killing events in the twentieth century, arguing that mass killing is most commonly associated with counterinsurgency.[18] Yet another approach is that of Rudolph Rummel, who quantifies what he calls 'democide', which includes genocide and other forms of state-orchestrated violence against civilians.[19] In his book, Rummel generates statistical counts of the numbers of dead across numerous instances of democide in the twentieth century. In his study, quantification is less a method for testing hypotheses cross-nationally, and more for determining the volume of civilian death across different cases.

Two related but more sophisticated data sets on large-scale violence against civilians have since been created. The first is the 'One-Sided Violence' data set coming out of the Uppsala Conflict Data Program. Authors Kristine Eck and Lisa Hultman define 'one-sided violence' as 'civilians that are deliberately and directly targeted by governments or non-state groups'.[20] For data collection, the authors employ a computer program that collects articles on individuals killed or injured from five major international news media sources from 1989 to 2004. A similar data collection project comes out of the University of Kansas, led by political scientist Philip Schrodt. The Political Instability Task Force Worldwide Atrocities Dataset captures any incident reported in four major media outlets in which at least five civilian deaths were killed for a nominally political purpose.[21]

---

[15] Barbara Harff, 'No Lessons Learned from the Holocaust? Assessing Risks of Genocide and Political Mass Murder since 1955', *American Political Science Review* 97:1 (2003), 57–73.

[16] Matthew Krain, 'State-Sponsored Mass Murder: The Onset and Severity of Genocides and Politicides', *Journal of Conflict Resolution* 41:3 (1997), 331–60.

[17] Benjamin Valentino, *Final Solutions: Mass Killing and Genocide in the Twentieth Century* (Ithaca, NY: Cornell University Press, 2004).

[18] Benjamin Valentino, Paul Huth, and Dylan BalCH-Lindsay, ' "Draining the Sea": Mass Killing and Guerrilla Warfare', *International Organization* 58 (2004), 375–407.

[19] Rudolph Rummel, *Death by Government* (New Brunswick, NJ: Transaction Publishers, 1994).

[20] Kristine Eck and Lisa Hultman, 'One-Sided Violence against Civilians in War: Insights from New Fatality Data', *Journal of Peace Research* 44:2 (2007), 235.

[21] The media outlets are the Agence France-Press, the Associated Press, the *New York Times*, and Reuters. For more information, please visit http://web.ku.edu/keds/data.dir/atrocities.html

As these examples make clear, quantitative approaches to the study of genocide generally entail collecting evidence on more than just genocide cases. One reason is that there are not enough genocide cases to support a quantitative study of genocide only. Genocide is thus paired with another outcome or treated as one example of a broader phenomenon. That necessity has meant political scientists have engaged in important conceptual innovation around the term genocide, and here again we see a distinctive contribution from the discipline. Harff, for example, pairs genocide with the concept of politicide; Krain refers to 'state-sponsored mass murder'; Valentino treats genocide as one form of mass killing; Rummel considers genocide as one type of democide; Eck and Hultman conceptualize genocide within the context of one-sided violence; and Schrodt and his collaborators embed genocide within the study of 'atrocity'. The move in this direction—to think of genocide within a broad class of violence against civilians—is sensible, as I argue in the Conclusion.

As promising as qualitative and quantitative comparative research is, several problems are apparent.[22] One common problem is that cases treated as similar are in fact quite different. This is particularly evident in quantitative studies that code heterogeneous events—ones that vary considerably in duration, magnitude of violence, character of violence, socio-economic context, and historical period— as having the same value. On the quantitative side, the Eck and Hultman study and the Worldwide Atrocities data set present particularly attractive options for obviating some of the problems associated with unit heterogeneity. These data sets allow genocide to be conceptualized along a continuous, rather than a dichotomous, scale;[23] they link the study of genocide to the broader phenomenon of organized violence against civilians; they make observations on many more cases than other studies do; and they identify a transparent and consistent method of data collection. In short, for quantitative approaches to the study of genocide—which is one of the distinctive contributions of the political science literature—there is an advantage to disaggregating the outcome as a form of deliberate violence against civilians and collecting data along those lines.

For qualitative comparative studies, an area that has not received enough attention is the study of 'non-genocide' or 'negative' cases. The modal qualitative comparison is to examine cases of genocide that happen in different periods and in different regions to discover commonalities among them. However, not enough attention has been paid to the many cases that existing theory would suggest could result in genocide but do not. Comparing genocide cases to non-genocide cases is also a method for pairing cases that have fewer macro-level differences between

[22] The points made in this section are similar to those made in Straus, 'Second-Generation Research'.

[23] Krain also measures the 'severity' of state-sponsored mass murder; however, severity is measured in terms of the duration of the violence, not the magnitude of violence in terms of numbers killed.

them. In other words, political scientists who study genocide qualitatively would do well to compare more similar countries and enabling circumstances, but countries and circumstances that have variation on the outcome of interest. Doing so will help ideally to isolate the factors that drive genocide.

Regime Type

A trademark of political science is the study of the state, and a natural extension among political scientists who study genocide (and related outcomes) concerns how regime type does and does not influence the occurrence of genocide. In one of the earliest general books on genocide, political scientist Irving Louis Horowitz argues that the concentration of power is central to why genocide occurs. 'Genocide is the operational handmaiden of a particular social system, the totalitarian system,' writes Horowitz.[24] Horowitz's claim is deepened in Rummel's work, in which he argues that 'absolute power' constitutes the structural origin of democide. For both Horowitz and Rummel, a democratic system where there are checks and balances on power serves as one of the best antidotes to genocide. Harff similarly identifies authoritarian regimes as one of the six key risk factors that can lead to genocide.[25]

The relationship between regime type and violence outcomes is a long-standing concern in political science. Horowitz's reference to the link between genocide and totalitarianism is clearly indebted to the work of Hannah Arendt, a political philosopher who famously wrote about totalitarianism in Nazi Germany and the Soviet Union.[26] Like the idea that deep divisions and enmity between groups is a wellspring for genocide, the idea that genocide is more likely in dictatorial states has a certain common-sense resonance. It seems intuitive mass killing would be more likely where power is concentrated among the few and where citizens do not enjoy broad democratic rights.

Nonetheless—and despite regime type being a distinctive concern among political scientists—there are a number of concerns with the argument. Several authors publishing in the past decade or so, in particular Krain, Valentino, and Mann, have raised specific concerns with the argument. One concern is simply a problem of timing: authoritarian regimes are often long-standing, yet genocides occur in particular moments or periods of time. The causal factor is static, yet genocide is a dynamic outcome. Another concern is that there are many more authoritarian states than genocides. While one could argue that authoritarian political structures

[24] Irving Louis Horowitz, *Genocide: State Power and Mass Murder* (New Brunswick, NJ: Transaction, 1976), 36.

[25] Harff, 'No Lessons Learned'.

[26] Hannah Arendt, *The Origins of Totalitarianism* (New York: Meridien, 1959).

are a necessary condition for genocide to occur, they are certainly not sufficient. A third concern is empirical. In his statistical tests, Krain does not find support for the hypothesis that the concentration of power affects the onset of state-sponsored mass murder. Mann argues that non-authoritarian states also commit what he calls 'murderous ethnic cleansing', and they do so in the name of democracy. Mann identifies transitional regimes—ones moving between authoritarian and democratic—as the most likely political conditions to trigger genocide. Indeed, the most recent cases of genocide are an uneven fit with the authoritarian/totalitarian argument: in the Balkans and in Rwanda, the regimes that committed genocide and mass violence were in the midst of democratic transitions and made ethnic nationalist claims in the name of majoritarian rule.

Rationalist Explanations

A third area of distinctive contribution by political scientists is what might be called a 'rationalist' approach to the study of genocide. Rationalist paradigms are common in the discipline. That is, rather than being the product of irrational, megalomaniacal leaders or the product of deeply prejudiced masses, the major claim is that genocide is the outcome of deliberate, strategic actions of elites. This type of rationalist argument is especially pronounced and well articulated in the contemporary work of Valentino. However, the framework is not new to Valentino. In a piece published in the late 1980s, political scientist Roger Smith, for example, talks of how genocide is 'calculated to achieve the ends of the perpetrator'.[27] In 1990s work, political scientist George Andreopolos advances the notion of a 'calculus of genocide'; René Lemarchand talks of the 'rationality of genocide'; and Krain discusses how changing political contexts shape strategies that elites use against challengers, in some cases facilitating state-sponsored mass murder.[28] In other words, a rationalist framework—albeit with different inflections and different levels of emphasis—is a recurring theme among political scientists who study genocide.

The rationalist framework is, as noted above, most influentially presented in Valentino's work. In a 2004 book, *Final Solutions*, Valentino's central theoretical claim is that genocide and mass killing are the products of 'strategic' decisions by leaders.[29] He argues that analysis should focus at the elite level; mass publics, he

---

[27] Roger Smith, 'Human Destructiveness and Politics: The Twentieth Century as an Age of Genocide', in Isidor Walliman and Michael Dobkowski (eds), *Genocide and the Modern Age: Etiology and Case Studies of Mass Death* (Westport, CT: Greenwood Press, 1987), 23.

[28] George Andreopoulos, 'Introduction: The Calculus of Genocide', in *idem* (ed.), *Genocide: Conceptual and Historical Dimensions* (Philadelphia: University of Pennsylvania Press, 1994), 1–28; René Lemarchand, 'Rwanda: The Rationality of Genocide', *Issue: A Journal of Opinion* 23:2 (1995), 8–11; Krain, 'State-Sponsored Mass Murder', 333.

[29] Valentino, *Final Solutions*.

submits, are not necessary to perpetrate large-scale violence. Genocide and mass killing are chosen as the best available means to achieve leaders' most important political and military goals. In subsequent co-authored work, Valentino pushes the analysis further through collecting data and quantifying mass killing events in the second-half of the twentieth century. Valentino and his collaborators argue that mass killing is most common as counterinsurgency—as a response to guerrilla warfare. In their words, mass violence is an effort to 'drain the sea', depriving rebels the cover and support they need to challenge a state militarily.[30]

There are multiple implications of the rationalist approach. One is that the remedy—genocide prevention—is not to reshape society but rather to change elite incentives (or to change elites). Another implication is that a strongly emphasized strategic framework moves analysis away from seeing genocide as the product of deep divisions, enmity, pathology, and social stress. Valentino's work, in which strategic calculation is the primary prism by which to understand genocide, is thus quite different from the work of Leo Kuper. A third implication is the 'normaliza-tion' of genocide studies in that genocide and mass killing are not outside the ambit of strategic, rational calculations that analysts perceive in other circumstances. A related claim is made by Martin Shaw, who, as I discuss below, similarly wants to 'normalize' the study of genocide by embedding it in the study of war.[31] Outside political science, the theme is found elsewhere in contemporary scholarship, notably the work of historian Donald Bloxham.[32]

Despite the welcome normalization of the study of genocide, there are important tensions and problems with rationalist approaches. Genocide and mass killing are, at a minimum, risky, extreme, and expensive responses to threats. They cost money and reputation; in the contemporary world, they invite prosecution; and, more-over, genocidal and mass killing policies often fail: the architects of mass violence in the late Ottoman Empire, Germany, Serbia, and Rwanda all lost power immediately after their genocidal policies. Genocide is also deliberate—by definition, genocide is in the realm of intentional, calculated, usually state-led violence. That being the case, identifying the conditions that push political elites to promulgate highly risky policies and pinpointing the kinds of objectives that push elites to extremes is a research priority. Valentino emphasizes 'final solutions': elites choose mass vio-lence after other policies have failed. He also points to different scenarios and conditions, in which elites choose mass violence such as guerrilla warfare but also ethnic conflict, and communist revolution. Rationalist approaches thus help make genocide understandable and analysable, but rationalist approaches need to specify

[30] Valentino et al, ' "Draining the Sea" '.
[31] Martin Shaw, *What is Genocide?* (Cambridge: Polity, 2007).
[32] Donald Bloxham, *The Great Game of Genocide: Imperialism, Nationalism, and the Destruction of the Ottoman Armenians* (Oxford: Oxford University Press, 2005).

why political leaders opt for quite risky action and when the promotion of genocide seems rational.

Warfare and Genocide

Valentino's research points towards another recurring theme in the political science literature on genocide. Indeed, if there was a common environment that political scientists emphasize as conducive to genocide, that environment would be armed conflict. The argument is most apparent in the work of Martin Shaw, a scholar of international relations (whose orientation and writing clearly overlap with sociology). Other political scientists reference the importance of armed conflict, even if armed conflict is not the dominant focus. The emphasis in the work of French political scientist Jacques Sémelin, for example, is on ideological constructs that lead to mass violence and genocide. However, Sémelin argues that armed conflict is a condition that creates anxiety and uncertainty, prompting political elites to redefine political communities in ideological terms that can lead to genocide. A linkage between war and genocide is found explicitly, as noted above, in the work of both Melson and Krain. In Harff's early research, war is a type of social upheaval that can lead to genocide.[33] In my research on Rwanda, I argue that war was a critical factor that shaped the origins and perpetration of the genocide; I also argue warfare shaped why political elites chose mass violence in Darfur.[34] Outside political science, other scholars such as Mann and Weitz reference armed conflict as a condition that has a causal relationship to genocide, even if, again, armed conflict is not their focus. In sum, the emphasis on a connection between armed conflict and genocide is a recurrent and distinct, though not exclusive, emphasis in the political science literature on genocide.

The claim that war and genocide are interrelated is most pronounced in Shaw's work. In two distinct books, Shaw makes a strong and explicit connection between war and genocide.[35] In the first, *War and Genocide*, Shaw argues that genocide is a distinct form of war and that the logic of warfare is intimately connected to the logic of genocide. He contends that genocides are committed when an organized armed force considers civilians to be enemies in war, and he links the prevalence of genocide to a broader trend of 'degenerate' warfare. In a second book, Shaw extends some of his observations about the connection between war and genocide,

---

[33] Barbara Harff, 'The Etiology of Genocides', in Isidor Walliman and Michael Dobkowski (eds), *Genocide and the Modern Age: Etiology and Case Studies of Mass Death* (Westport, CT: Greenwood Press, 1987), 41–59.

[34] Straus, *The Order of Genocide*; Scott Straus, 'Rwanda and Darfur: A Comparative Analysis', *Genocide Studies and Prevention* 1:1 (2006), 41–56.

[35] Martin Shaw, *War and Genocide: Organized Killing in Modern Society* (Cambridge: Polity, 2003); Shaw, *What Is Genocide?*

but also examines and rethinks both the foundations of the concept of genocide and how genocide should be studied. Shaw concludes that genocide is a 'form of violent social conflict' in which armed groups seek to destroy civilian social groups.[36] In so doing, Shaw argues that genocide should be treated as a generic concept, and he contends that genocide and 'genocidal action' should not be considered exceptional, but rather connected to the more common phenomena of war and conflict.

The theme of war and genocide is also evident in Midlarsky's work, also a specialist in international relations. However, Midlarsky sees genocide as exceptional, or at least highly infrequent. In the book, Midlarsky analyses three cases of genocide in the twentieth century: the Armenian genocide, the Holocaust, and the Rwandan genocide. Like other political scientists, his primary theoretical focus is on the decision-making calculus of leaders, arguing that genocide is the product of 'imprudent realpolitik' brought on specifically by loss, usually territorial, in wartime. By 'imprudent', Midlarsky emphasizes that the response to loss is 'disproportionate' to a perceived provocation or threat.[37] Thus, Midlarsky adds a dimension of irrationality or at least unwise decision-making in the name of state interests. In that there is an important distinction from Valentino and others who stress the deliberate, strategic origins of genocide. Midlarsky also brings in an international dimension, arguing that leaders of states that commit genocide are facilitated by allies abroad. In sum, Midlarsky's precise theoretical innovations vary from Valentino and Shaw, as does his methodology and case selection, but the connection between war and genocide is a running theme for all three contemporary scholars—and thereby echoing the earlier research of political scientists Robert Melson and Barbara Harff.

As robust as the connection between warfare and genocide is, the mechanisms and reasons why armed conflict and genocide are connected are subject to different interpretation. In the work of Valentino and his co-authors, the emphasis is on the strategic use of mass violence to destroy insurgents' civilian support bases. Mass killing is a deliberate military strategy to defeat guerrillas who have strong civilian support or who pose a major threat to a regime. Shaw argues in general that war and genocide are entwined, such that genocide cannot be separated conceptually or in explanatory terms from war. He argues more specifically that in war a 'power organization' is more likely to define civilian populations as 'enemies' and that 'power organizations' tend to be militarized or at least that political power and military power are closely connected.[38] In Sémelin's hands, war contributes to defining some groups as internal enemies, and war increases uncertainty and

---

[36] Shaw, *What Is Genocide?*, 154.
[37] Midlarsky, *The Killing Trap*, 94.
[38] Shaw, *What Is Genocide?*, 147.

vulnerability, which can lead to the use of violence.[39] For Midlarsky, war creates conditions of state insecurity, and loss in war can lead to disproportionate responses. In my work on Rwanda, I argue that war shaped the logic of genocide, legitimized violence, created uncertainty and insecurity, thereby empowering hard-liners over moderates, and led specialists in violence (soldiers, paramilitaries, and militias) to enter the domestic political arena.

In sum, the political science literature indicates that war matters, but the questions of how and why war matters remain an area for future research. Existing theory highlights, variously, war type and dominant strategy (guerrilla versus conventional warfare), the entwining of military and political arenas in war, the effects of uncertainty and insecurity produced in war, and the labelling of civilian populations as 'enemies' in war. However, an empirical problem in the war–genocide linkage is that most civil and international wars do not lead to genocide. Shaw argues that a theory of genocide should explain a range of organized violence against civilians in war. Shaw wants to embed theories of genocide within a broader universe of cases of what he calls 'genocidal action'. At the same time, it is important to recognize differences in outcomes—that is, there is an important empirical difference between 'genocidal action' that leaves several hundred civilians dead and 'genocidal action' in which hundreds of thousands are killed. Thus, understanding why some armed conflicts lead to limited violence against civilians while others lead to large-scale violence against civilians and genocide is a critical question, but one that remains underdeveloped.

CONCLUSIONS AND NEW DIRECTIONS

In the development and evolution of genocide studies, political science has made significant and lasting contributions. As (most often) a crime of state and a function of policy choices and social mobilization, the fit between the study of genocide and the discipline should come as no surprise. Nonetheless, the existing political science literature is far from theoretical, conceptual, or methodological convergence with regard to both the origins of genocide and how to study it. Given the complexity of the outcome, as well as the growing yet still comparatively small amount of political science research on genocide, the absence of consensus is not necessarily a weakness. Rather, the lack of consensus presents an opportunity for future research that seeks to build on the insights of past work. In the conclusion, I take a step in that direction by making some observations about gaps in the

---

[39] Sémelin, *Purifier et détruire*, 172, 178.

existing literature and by suggesting some avenues for future political science research on genocide.

The first observation is that the study of genocide (and mass killing) has been strangely cloistered from studies of kin phenomena, in particular the use of violence in war. As noted above, the empirical and theoretical intersections between genocide and armed conflict are strong. There exists a very large and rapidly growing political science literature on civil war and the use of violence in wars, both international and domestic.[40] That literature has major theoretical implications for the study of genocide, but in large respect the connections remain underexplored. For example, in his seminal research on violence in civil war, Stathis Kalyvas distinguishes between 'discriminate', targeted violence and 'indiscriminate', widespread violence.[41] Kalyvas' attention to information and relative control in the context of armed conflict carries direct potential insight into the dynamics of genocide. More generally, his use of the concept of 'indiscriminate' is certainly akin to how some scholars conceptualize 'genocide' and related terms, such as mass killing and politicide. Political scientists who study genocide thus need to be in greater theoretical engagement with this work, and vice versa. Similarly, in quite different research on international conflict, Alexander Downes analyses the determinants of 'barbarism'—intentional targeting and violence against civilians in wartime.[42] Like 'indiscriminate violence', large-scale, intentional violence against civilians is not far from the concept of genocide. Yet there remains little theoretical engagement between the research on intentional targeting of civilians in international war and genocide. Another example is that of 'asymmetric' warfare, which designates the overwhelming power of one side in an armed conflict.[43] Given the connections between war and genocide and that victims in genocide often have disproportionately less resources than perpetrators, examining the two phenomena would be worthwhile. Researchers who examine these phenomena might underscore differences between genocide and 'asymmetric' war, barbarism, or indiscriminate violence in war, but doing so would sharpen theory on genocide and initiate a scholarly conversation with students of related phenomena.

The second observation is the need for greater attention to methodological concerns. 'Methodology' is meant broadly, including attention to concepts, hypothesis generation, and research design. While there remain quite different concepts in use (from genocide, to mass killing, to politicide, to democide) within

[40] Stathis Kalyvas, 'Civil Wars', in Carles Boix and Susan Stokes (eds), *Handbook of Political Science* (New York: Oxford University Press, 2007), 416–34.

[41] Stathis Kalyvas, *The Logic of Violence in Civil Wars* (New York: Cambridge University Press, 2006).

[42] Alexander Downes, *Targeting Civilians in War* (Ithaca, NY: Cornell University Press, 2008).

[43] Ivan Arreguín-Toft, *How the Weak Win Wars: A Theory of Asymmetric Conflict* (New York: Cambridge University Press, 2005).

the political science literature, most scholars examine a large-scale outcome. But a relatively underexplored avenue would be to disaggregate the concept, identifying researchable dimensions of genocide (or related terms). Doing so would connect research to the literature on violence, but doing so also could lead to a focus on escalation, mobilization, or the coordination of power.[44] In short, disaggregating genocide into smaller, researchable, but salient questions offers an avenue for potential future research. Research design broadly conceived is another obvious area of greater thinking. Given that genocide is relatively infrequent, what is the best way to study the phenomena? How should negative cases be incorporated into the analysis? How should (positive and negative) cases be selected? In what ways might a multi-method (quantitative/qualitative) research design be employed? How might insights from game theory apply to the study of genocide? Could genocide be formally modelled? What types of data are needed to test hypotheses? What would an empirical research on genocide look like beyond the existing cross-national data on occurrence or level of violence in cases? These and other methodological questions are essential for advancing political science explanations of genocide, but to date they have received fairly little self-conscious reflection in the political science literature.

The third observation is the relative absence of critical thinking about explanation and causation. The most common causal model in political science is to look for macro-level structural conditions that give rise to genocide. However, consistent with the suggestion to disaggregate, theory might focus on a specific dimension of genocide, such as escalation or explaining the difference between low violence and high violence. Similarly, the question of specifying connections between top- and bottom-level policy is an area worthy of greater research. How do national and local levels interact? How do domestic and international dimensions interact? What explains the specific timing of when leaders decide to implement a policy of genocide? Another under-represented area concerns theorizing constraint. That is, much theory focuses on conditions and incentives that would push leaders to promulgate genocide. Much less attention is on the conditions that restrain leaders from the use of mass violence.[45] In short, political scientists might consider the trade-offs in explaining genocide as a macro phenomenon or in explaining certain dimensions of genocide.

---

[44] In their works, Mann and Sémelin move in this direction as does Donald Bloxham in 'Organized Mass Murder: Structure, Participation, and Motivation in Comparative Perspective', *Holocaust Genocide Studies* 22 (2008), 203–45.

[45] This is work that I have begun: see Scott Straus and Daniel Knudsen, 'The Costs of Genocide: Theorizing Restraint and Negative Cases in the Study of Mass Violence', unpublished manuscript, Department of Political Science, University of Wisconsin; available upon request.

SELECT BIBLIOGRAPHY

Harff, Barbara, 'No Lessons Learned from the Holocaust? Assessing Risks of Genocide and Political Mass Murder since 1955', *American Political Science Review* 97:1 (2003), 57–73.

Horowitz, Irving Louis, *Genocide: State Power and Mass Murder* (New Brunswick, NJ: Transaction, 1976).

Krain, Matthew. 'State-Sponsored Mass Murder: The Onset and Severity of Genocides and Politicides', *Journal of Conflict Resolution* 41:3 (1997), 331–60.

Kuper, Leo, *Genocide: Its Political Use in the Twentieth Century* (New Haven, CT: Yale University Press, 1981).

Melson, Robert, *Revolution and Genocide: On the Origins of the Armenian Genocide and the Holocaust* (Chicago: University of Chicago Press, 1992).

Midlarsky, Manus, *The Killing Trap: Genocide in the Twentieth Century* (New York: Cambridge University Press, 2005).

Rummel, Rudolph, *Death by Government* (New Brunswick, NJ: Transaction Publishers, 1994).

Sémelin, Jacques, *Purifier et détruire: Les usages politiques des massacres et génocide* (Paris: Le Seuil, 2005).

Shaw, Martin. *War and Genocide: Organized Killing in Modern Society* (Cambridge: Polity, 2003).

—— *What is Genocide?* (Cambridge: Polity, 2007).

Straus, Scott, 'Second-Generation Comparative Research on Genocide', *World Politics* 59:3 (2007), 476–501.

Valentino, Benjamin. *Final Solutions: Mass Killing and Genocide in the Twentieth Century* (Ithaca, NY: Cornell University Press, 2004).

——, Paul Huth, and Dylan Balch-Lindsay, '"Draining the Sea": Mass Killing and Guerrilla Warfare', *International Organization* 58 (2004), 375–407.

....

CHAPTER 9

ANTHROPOLOGY AND GENOCIDE

....

KEVIN LEWIS O'NEILL

In the broadest of terms, anthropology is the study of humanity, but more practically (although perhaps stated in a more obtuse way), anthropology is the study of culture—the attitudes, behaviours, and practices that constitute a given community. Anthropology's method of choice has long been ethnography, which is a qualitative research technique that places anthropologists amidst particular cultures for extended periods of time to conduct formal and informal interviews, to observe everyday life, and to examine archival materials when they are available. Traditionally, Western anthropologists have pursued ethnographic research in distant, far-off places to make the argument that 'those people over there' are either quite different or remarkably similar to 'us over here'. With an eye to the colonial subplots that these assumptions carry, anthropology has changed considerably over the past few decades, applying its deft ethnographic touch to such slippery objects of study as globalization, nationalism, and technology.

Amidst this new wave of anthropology, an emerging object of study continues to come into focus: genocide. While anthropology has long been silent on the topic, recent scholarship has proven that a tremendous amount can be learned from a comparative perspective when researchers interview and observe survivors, perpetrators, aid workers, and government officials in genocidal and post-genocidal contexts. The result has been an anthropology of genocide that has been slow to start but is now quickly emerging as a particularly evocative subfield of not just anthropology but also genocide studies. The anthropology of genocide, in fact, lends analytical clarity and empirical rigour (as well as emotional texture) to a range of issues, including truth, memory, and representation in post-genocidal spaces.

Anthropology's growing interest in genocide has a number of roots, including a continued interest in both modernity and globalization as well as violence and terror; a shift from small village studies to research that examine the state-level dynamics in situations of upheaval, flux, and violence; and a greater commitment to reflexivity, historicity, and engaged anthropology. The questions that now constitute anthropology's growing interest in genocide include: What happens to people and the societies in which they live during and after genocide? How are the devastating events experienced and remembered on the individual and collective levels? How do these memories intersect and diverge as governments in post-genocidal states attempt to produce a more monolithic 'truth' about the past? Another important cluster of questions reads: How are representations of a violent past structured by one's positioning as a survivor, perpetrator, journalist, or ethnographer? And what are the epistemological, ethical, and empirical entangle-ments in which researchers find themselves enmeshed in post-genocidal contexts? The formation of these anthropological questions builds from several other intel-lectual developments such as critical assessments of ethnography, nationalism, violence, and refugees, but nonetheless continues to extend far beyond these issues in rather creative and thought-provoking ways.

Ethnography, Nationalism, Violence, Refugees

The anthropology of genocide has been able to develop as rapidly as it has because of at least four vibrant anthropological literatures. They are critical reflections on ethnography, nationalism, violence, and refugees. With regard to ethnography, anthropologists have become keenly aware that their method of analysis does not represent knowledge in an objective sense, but rather produces knowledge from a subjective perspective.[1] Ethnography is not only limited in its scope but is also a powerful tool of knowledge production that too often carries an overextended weight of authority. In critical response, contemporary ethnographic practices in cultural and social anthropology stress that every representation is historical and contestable, that anthropological observations are not the result of either an

---

[1] Renato Rosaldo, *Culture and Truth: The Remaking of Social Analysis* (Boston: Beacon Press, 1989).

omniscient perspective or absolute scientific clarity.[2] While it would be possible to see this epistemological anxiety as a threat to any study of genocide (because of its affinity to cultural relativism),[3] it is important to stress that attention to these issues actually strengthens the anthropology of genocide with a unique sensitivity to questions of representation, allowing the anthropologist of genocide to situate a survivor or perpetrator's testimony not only historically but also along lines of ethnicity, class, and gender, for example.[4]

The anthropology of genocide has also gained a great deal from anthropological considerations of the nation-state. Given the nation-state's centrality in genocidal processes, anthropologists have found it productive not to assume that the nation-state exists with as much density as other social scientific perspectives might suggest. While political scientists, for example, might tend to focus on the role of the Guatemalan nation-state during acts of genocide against indigenous populations, the anthropologist might also ask how committing acts of genocide contributed to the formation of a national identity—how acts of extraordinary violence construct the cultural boundaries that determine who is and who is not a Guatemalan. The anthropological contribution here is the idea that acts of genocide are cultural practices that contribute to the formation of the nation-state as an 'imagined community', in the words of Benedict Anderson.[5] Anderson famously argues that a nation is a socially constructed community constituted by those who see themselves as a part of that group, and that a range of cultural developments and practices contribute to the formation of the modern nation-state as an imagined community. While Anderson focuses on print capitalism's ability to foster a common vernacular (and, in turn, a common national identity), anthropologists of genocide explore genocidal acts as an equally potent (if not more dramatic and especially heinous) means to imagine the nation. It is important to note, however, that this process of identity construction can only continue during the very process of genocide. Radicalization develops further among the perpetrators even as they commit the act. Genocide can sometimes be a way of testing limits and accidentally discovering how far perpetrators can go.[6]

---

[2] James Clifford and George Marcus (eds), *Writing Culture: The Politics and Poetics of Ethnography* (Berkeley: University of California Press, 1986).

[3] Thomas Cushman, 'Anthropology and Genocide in the Balkans: An Analysis of Conceptual Practices of Power', *Anthropological Theory* 4:1 (March 2004).

[4] Beatriz Manz, *Paradise in Ashes: A Guatemalan Journey of Courage, Terror, and Hope* (Berkeley: University of California Press, 2004).

[5] Benedict Anderson, *Imagined Communities: Reflections on the Origin and Spread of Nationalism* (London: Verso, 1983).

[6] Bette Denich, 'Dismembering Yugoslavia: Nationalist Ideologies and the Symbolic Revival of Genocide', *American Ethnologist* 21:4 (May 1994), 367–90; Robert M. Hayden, 'Imagined Communities and Real Victims: Self-Determination and Ethnic Cleansing in Yugoslavia', *American Ethnologist* 23:4 (November 1996), 783–801.

Third, the anthropology of genocide builds on the field's increasingly sophisti-cated approach to violence, which continues to explore the topic on at least two different scales. The first is a routine, even everyday, kind of violence, which includes identity politics.[7] The violence of racial or class-based slurs, even assaults, allows anthropologists to understand how individuals slog through the kind of habitual violence that ultimately 'primes', in the words of Alex Hinton, genocidal events.[8] The second is an increasing attention to more large-scale events, such as state-sponsored violence, and the cultural practices and occasions that constitute these large events.[9] Implied in these two levels of analysis is the anthropological effort to situate violence historically, noting that violence neither emerges nor is experienced *ex nihilo.* Rather, violence is imagined and performed amidst thick historical and cultural contexts. Anthropology's emphasis on human experience as well as how violence becomes situated within a culture (and situated differently by different people within that culture) allows anthropologists to gain purchase on not just genocide's cultural complexity but also genocide's emotional depth. Violence, for the anthropologist, exists as an odious form of cultural expression.[10]

Finally, anthropology's growing attention to refugees has allowed the field to gain an added (and rather productive) perspective on genocide studies. Anthro-pology, it has been noted, long assumed a tight relationship between culture and space.[11] For quite some time, anthropologists could assume (in seemingly uncom-plicated ways) that Rwandans, for example, live in Rwanda and amidst Rwandan culture. This perspective has historically resulted in studies that elide the reality of displacement, diaspora, and deterritorialization. Yet, genocidal events displaced tens of thousands of Rwandans, for example, making 'Rwandan culture' a rather complicated object of ethnographic study. Rwandans as refugees literally shifts the content and context of what might be understood as Rwandan culture.[12] Anthro-pological approaches to genocide have since adjusted, building on an ethnographic attention to those people who are in constant motion—who live at the margins and amidst the borders of transnational contexts. A vivid example of this approach comes from Liisa Malkki's ethnographic research with Hutu refugees who lived in

---

[7] Arthur Kleinman, 'The Violences of Everyday Life: The Multiple Forms and Dynamics of Social Violence', in Veena Das, Arthur Kleinman, Mamphela Ramphele, and Pamela Reynolds (eds), *Violence and Subjectivity* (Berkeley: University of California Press, 1997), 226–41.

[8] Alex Laban Hinton, *Why Did They Kill?: Cambodia in the Shadow of Genocide* (Berkeley: University of California Press, 2005); Veena Das, 'Language and Body: Transactions in the Construction of Pain', in Arthur Kleinman, Veena Das, and Margaret Lock (eds), *Social Suffering* (Berkeley: University of California Press, 1997), 67–91.

[9] Nancy Scheper-Hughes and Philippe Bourgeois (eds), *Violence in War and Peace: an Anthology,* (London: Basil Blackwell Press, 2004).

[10] Neil Whitehead (ed.), *Violence* (Santa Fe, NM: School of Advanced Research Press, 2004).

[11] Akhil Gupta and James Ferguson, 'Beyond "Culture": Space, Identity, and the Politics of Difference', *Cultural Anthropology* 7:1 (February 1992), 6–23.

[12] Rogers Brubaker, *Ethnicity without Groups* (Cambridge, MA: Harvard University Press, 2004).

Tanzania after the 1972 genocide in Burundi.[13] Malkki's work details how Hutu refugees understood the refugee category from their own perspective. As persons who had long owned (in an emotional sense) the category of the refugee by living in refugee camps and by self-identifying as refugees, Malkki demonstrates how the Hutu saw themselves as a nation in exile.[14] As will be detailed below, those persons displaced by genocide fit squarely within today's conceptualization of an anthropology of genocide.

ANTHROPOLOGY AND GENOCIDE

It is difficult but important to recount the fact that before an anthropology of genocide can be outlined in any detail, one needs to recognize the historical relationships that have existed between anthropology and genocide. Given that acts of genocide themselves gain legitimacy from ideologies that mix nationalism with ethnicity to produce a threatening kind of difference, it may come as no surprise that anthropology—a field of study that has been historically interested in not only origin myths but also nationalism and ethnicity—has contributed to genocidal activities. Anthropology's participation in the Holocaust is one well-documented case in point.

Bettina Arnold, for example, explains how archaeological research contributed to the justification of genocide in Nazi Germany through the construction of difference.[15] Arnold makes the argument that archaeology's cultural capital—its authoritative voice as well as its ability to contribute to the ideological underpinnings of political systems—placed the practice of archaeology at the centre of German National Socialism. National Socialists, she reports, employed archaeological research to define and reify nationalist and ethnic identities in Germany. National Socialists, for example, saw race as the defining quality for one's membership in the Germanic community and this construction of race depended most heavily upon the material record: 'In the nineteenth and early twentieth centuries, Germany was where Germans were or could be shown to have been.

[13] Liisa Malkki, 'Speechless Emissaries: Refugees, Humanitarianism, and Dehistoricization', *Cultural Anthropology* 11:3 (August 1996), 377–404.

[14] Liisa Malkki, *Purity and Exile: Violence, Memory, and National Cosmology among Hutu Refugees in Tanzania* (Chicago: University of Chicago Press, 1995).

[15] Bettina Arnold, 'Justifying Genocide: Archaeology and the Construction of Difference', in Alex Laban Hinton (ed.), *Annihilating Difference: The Anthropology of Genocide* (Berkeley: University of California Press, 2002), 95–116. See also Bettina Arnold and Henning Hassmann, 'Archaeology in Nazi Germany: The Legacy of the Faustian Bargain', in Phillip Kohl and Clare Fawcett (eds), *Nationalism, Politics and the Practice of Archaeology* (Cambridge: Cambridge University Press).

Germans established territory by occupying it and leaving a distinctive material record of their presence.'[16] Archaeological research under the Third Reich was thus able to construct its own imagined community and sphere of moral obligation through the material record, while at the same time justifying the Holocaust through the mapping of ethnicity and racial superiority. Through the creation and maintenance of origin myths, archaeology facilitated both nationalism and genocide.

As for cultural anthropology, Gretchen Schafft's *From Racism to Genocide* details how anthropologists contributed to the needs of the Nazi state by allowing their research on race to inform Nazi political views.[17] While some argue that Schafft's argument is overstated,[18] she insists that this kind of collaboration took place on several different levels. Anthropologists, much like the archaeologists of Arnold's work, helped to solidify the German Reich, both through the creation of an imagined community rooted in the past and with the production of a future, even purer, gene pool. This kind of genocidal purification project took place by way of anthropologists—scientists of race—who participated in sterilization campaigns. Much of this research on race, Schafft argues, was meaningless, given that 'there were no standards by which to judge Jewishness, so no conclusions ever could have been drawn from the morphological measurements.'[19] Yet, anthropologists did not act alone, or at least with their own funding. Schafft's work also establishes the transatlantic connections vis-à-vis international philanthropic agencies, such as the Rockefeller Foundation, that supported anthropological research on race during the Third Reich—even when it was obvious what kind of violence this research supported.

This kind of anthropological rationalization of genocide, sadly, does not pertain only to the Holocaust. Nancy Scheper-Hughes, for example, points towards the anthropological justification of apartheid and its genocidal dimensions as well as Alfred Kroeber's silence in the face of the genocide that took the lives of Californian Indians.[20] In a dramatic sentence, Scheper-Hughes writes, 'Modern anthropology was built up in the face of colonial genocides, ethnocides, mass killings, population die-outs, and other forms of mass destruction visited on marginalized peoples whose lives, suffering and deaths have provided us [anthropologists] with a livelihood.'[21] The argument, if not a plea, is for anthropologists to become not only

[16] Arnold, 'Justifying Genocide', 97.

[17] Gretchen E. Schafft, *From Racism to Genocide: Anthropology in the Third Reich* (Urbana: University of Illinois Press, 2004).

[18] Dan Stone, 'Review: From Racism to Genocide: Anthropology in the Third Reich', *H-Net Reviews in the Humanities & Social Sciences* (March 2005).

[19] Schafft, *From Racism to Genocide*, 32.

[20] Nancy Scheper-Hughes, 'Coming to our Senses: Anthropology and Genocide', in Hinton (ed.), *Annihilating Difference*, 348–81.

[21] Scheper-Hughes, 'Coming to our Senses', 348.

more cognizant of the violence that surrounds them while in the field, which is a challenge that present-day anthropologists have continued to meet to an increasing extent, but also to engage genocide head-on as an object of study. This final call to research and action constitutes what is now understood as the anthropology of genocide.

FORENSIC, ACTIVIST, CRITICAL

Central to the anthropology of genocide is the notion that socially and historically located cultural practices construct genocidal and post-genocidal contexts and that these practices are best observed through qualitative research methods. Indeed, one of the major ways in which anthropology contributes to the field of genocide studies is through the ethnographic method of data collection. Extended, face-to-face engagements with communities yield textured, thick descriptions that more macroanalyses of genocide overlook. To this end and through these means, contemporary formations of the anthropology of genocide have taken three distinct forms. They are forensic anthropology, activist anthropology, and anthropology as cultural critique. Each approaches a relatively common question from three distinct methodological approaches. The overarching question is: What do cultural practices and lived experiences look like in genocidal and post-genocidal contests—spaces where trauma, grief, and fear, as well as power and state control, frame and at times define the contours of everyday life for survivors and perpetrators alike?

Attending to this question, many (if not all) anthropologists of genocide maintain that their work is politically engaged. The research often aims to contribute to those who work on and in post-genocidal contexts, ranging from scholars in the field of genocide studies and human rights to staff workers at non-governmental organizations, aid workers, and development officers. Because of anthropologists' field experience and attunement to local understandings, they have a great deal to offer interdisciplinary discussions about genocide. This is to say that while scholars in other fields have conducted excellent analyses of the macro-level factors facilitating genocide, fewer have been able to approach genocide from this type of a local perspective.

Forensic anthropology, for example, is a branch of applied anthropology that assists in the identification of deceased individuals whose remains are unrecognizable because of extensive burns, mutilation, or decomposition. Traditionally used in legal and academic settings, forensic anthropology has become increasingly involved with not only issues of human rights but also genocide.[22] Forensic anthropologists now work within post-genocidal contexts to discover, document, and detail clandestine gravesites. They often work with reconciliation commission groups and transitional justice teams, documenting past abuses.

The work of Victoria Sanford, for example, details the role of the Guatemalan Forensic Anthropology Foundation (GFAF) in the exhumation of clandestine graves.[23] The GFAF's forensic work documents a state-sponsored genocide that left some 200,000 Mayan dead and discarded—buried throughout the Guatemalan highlands in mass gravesites. Denied not only their lives but also a culturally appropriate burial, murder victims of the Guatemalan genocide continue to be exhumed by forensic anthropologists so that they can be properly buried by their community. Alongside this project, forensic anthropologists are also committed to the careful documentation of each body and its markings, for the purposes of formal reconciliation and litigation.

Typifying the kind of political role that forensic anthropologists now play in post-genocidal contexts, Sanford's work makes a series of larger theoretical arguments that are themselves rooted in the persistent but nonetheless muddied work of forensic anthropology. Through participant-observation with forensic anthropologists, Sanford suggests that 'the transformation of a private memory creates a public space, however small, where survivors learn to speak; it breaks down to externally imposed understandings and chips away at the power structures imposed through silent negotiation of life-shattering events.'[24] Sanford articulates the promise of forensic anthropology—the hope that clarifying the past will foster a just future.

Forensic anthropology's hope and practice builds from and is related to a second anthropological approach to genocide: activist anthropology. At its most basic, activist anthropology, to quote Charles R. Hale, means 'a method through which we affirm a political alignment with an organized group of people in struggle and allow dialogue with them to shape each phase of the process, from conception of the research topic to data collection to verification and dissemination of the results.'[25] Activist anthropology's call to action prompts anthropologists to use their data to assist a particular community or organization—to be an engaged observer.[26] With regard to the anthropology of genocide from an activist's

---

[22] Christopher Joyce and Eric Stove, *Witnesses from the Grave: The Stories Bones Tell* (London: Little, Brown, 1991); William Maples and Michael Browns, *Dead Men Do Tell Tales: The Strange and Fascinating Case of a Forensic Anthropologist* (Pella, IA: Main Street Books, 1995).

[23] Victoria Sanford, *Violencia y Genocidio en Guatemala* (Guatemala: F&G, 2003); *eadem, Buried Secrets: Truth and Human Rights in Guatemala* (New York: Palgrave Macmillan, 2003).

[24] Sanford, *Buried Secrets*, 12.

[25] Charles R. Hale, 'Activist Research v. Cultural Critique: Indigenous Land Rights and the Contradictions of Politically Engaged Anthropology', *Cultural Anthropology* 21:1 (2006), 97.

[26] Victoria Sanford and Asale Angel-ajani (eds), *Engaged Observer: Anthropology, Advocacy, and Activism* (New Brunswick, NJ: Rutgers University Press, 2006).

perspective, practising activist anthropology has meant giving witness to genocidal and post-genocidal events and making these events public. 'Giving a voice to the voiceless' is one approximation of activist anthropology in genocidal and post-genocidal contexts.

Human rights activism, for example, largely rests on the power of testimony— one of the most central elements of anthropological data. Anthropologists, for example, often leave their respective field sites with hundreds of hours of recorded testimonies that provide a local perspective and, possibly, some emotional texture to a particular object of study. Testimony, simply put, is a convincing genre of anthropological data. The same is true when building a legal case for prosecuting genocide. Ever since the Holocaust, human rights activists have used testimony as a powerful tool for both litigation and reconciliation.[27] And, more recently, activist anthropologists have worked with truth commissions to interview survivors and perpetrators, documenting with ethnographic detail genocide's lived experience— in Cambodia, Rwanda, Guatemala, and Bosnia, for example. Their work makes and re-makes a commitment to applying ethnographic data for communities who otherwise would remain either silent or forever under-represented.

Finally, the anthropology of genocide's third manifestation fits squarely within what is commonly known as cultural critique, 'an approach to research and writing in which political alignment is manifested through the content of the knowledge produced, not through the relationship established with an organized group of people in struggle.'[28] The anthropology of genocide as cultural critique oftentimes deconstructs genocidal events by way of discourse theory, historical analysis, and critical theory. As part of this growing engagement with the anthropology of genocide, a number of anthropologists began writing about genocide, particularly after the genocides of the 1990s in the former Yugoslavia and Rwanda. However, to date, the nascent anthropological literature on genocide (as critique) has been published in diffuse forums—articles, book chapters, and a handful of ethnographies. Two edited volumes by Alex Hinton, however, provide a more systematic effort at constructing an anthropology of genocide.[29]

Hinton's edited volumes, in fact, provide the clearest and most sophisticated examples of what an anthropology of genocide looks like when imagined from the perspective of cultural critique. In the introduction to one of Hinton's volumes, he argues that 'Within genocide studies, much work has focused on the macro-level processes, exploring how genocide is linked to historical, political, economic, and structural factors. Similarly, journalists have published powerful accounts of the

---

[27] Shoshana Felman and Dori Laub, *Testimony: Crises of Witnessing in Literature, Psychoanalysis, and History* (London: Routledge Press, 1992).

[28] Hale, 'Activist Research v. Cultural Critique', 98.

[29] Hinton (ed.), *Annihilating Difference*; idem (ed.), *Genocide: An Anthropological Reader* (Malden: Blackwell, 2002).

origins and experience of genocide.'[30] An anthropology of genocide, Hinton then suggests, does both tasks at one and the same time; an anthropology of genocide shuttles between the macro (the relationship, for example, between notions of modern progress and acts of genocide from a historical perspective) and the micro (genocide as a local process, as an ethnographic problematic). Hinton's ultimate point is that anthropology's strengths—for example, its ability to link the construction of binaries, otherness, and meta-narratives to the texture of lived experiences—allow scholars to see genocide anew in challenging and critically insightful ways.

Hinton argues with much reference to anthropological literature that modernity has motivated genocidal violence. Modern notions of progress combined with the means to engage in systematic attempts at annihilation have resulted in genocidal violence. And, closely related to the question of modernity for Hinton is the issue of difference-making. He writes, 'Group identities are premised on the existence of an "other" from which "we" is distinguished, often in terms of an ethnocentric set of binary oppositions.'[31] Modernity's meta-narratives, Hinton continues, supply those in power with the cultural grids from which they can distinguish between civilized and savage as well as between good/evil, moral/immoral, and order/disorder. Invoking the work of famed anthropologist Mary Douglas,[32] Hinton speaks about the cultural manufacturing of difference and purification, noting that difference is necessary but not sufficient to produce genocide.

A growing number of book-length manuscripts reflect Hinton's vision. One example worth reviewing, even if only briefly, is Christopher C. Taylor's *Sacrifice as Terror*.[33] The book provides a symbolic analysis of violence and terror during the years prior to the 1994 Rwandan genocide. In a semi-autobiographical tone, Taylor historicizes the Rwandan genocide, demonstrating that the long-held cultural distinction between Hutu and Tutsi had been manipulated and warped by Eurocentric stereotypes introduced during colonialism. Alongside a strong plea to anthropologists to be critical of such cultural constructions, Taylor then details how these kinds of divisions patterned Rwandan violence. He makes the argument that the violence itself was structured by cultural assumptions and legitimated by them also. Gender, for example, played a significant role. Taylor makes the claim that, during the genocide, women were important agents and symbols of violence. As agents, women played important roles on both sides during the conflict. As symbols, Taylor notes how gender contributed to the construction of ethnic difference. Amidst the genocide, women existed as symbols of potential purification but

---

[30] Hinton (ed.), *Genocide*, 3.

[31] Ibid. 9.

[32] Mary Douglas, *Purity and Danger: An Analysis of the Concepts of Pollution and Taboo* (New York: Routledge, 1991).

[33] Christopher C. Taylor, *Sacrifice as Terror: The Rwandan Genocide of 1994* (Oxford: Berg, 1999).

also tools manipulated to reassess patriarchy. Taylor's argument has been tempered by Scott Straus's *The Order of Genocide*, which makes the point that there is a historicity to when difference is rendered toxic in a genocidal sense.[34]

Taylor's commitment to structural, symbolic, and discursive analyses typifies the anthropology of genocide as cultural critique—the kind of analysis that champions genocide's victims and deconstructs the cultural and historical relationships that make genocide possible. The same can be said of Alex Hinton's own book-length manuscript, *Why Did They Kill?*[35] Hinton investigates the Khmer Rouge's rise to power and the genocidal outcome of the Democratic Kampuchea regime. He provides an ethnographic analysis of the perpetrators' motivation to kill—to participate in genocide—in a way that does not reduce agency to ideology. The central observation is that local, cultural frameworks melded with state ideologies, forming a world vision that allowed perpetrators to kill. One of Hinton's contributions, then, is to demonstrate that genocide is not understood as a mere event from an ethnographic perspective, but as a process that complicates more traditional understandings of state-sanctioned genocidal violence.

TRUTH, MEMORY, REPRESENTATION

In the end, it is safe to say that the anthropology of genocide is only in its beginning stages. Important now is how this young field will begin to read across the lines that scholars have already drawn, and also beyond the analytic categories that the field of anthropology uses to understand genocide. One provocative line of analysis is anthropological research that addresses truth, memory, and representation in post-genocidal contexts. The focus here is on discursive privileging and moments of silencing that complicate and constitute issues of truth and falsity in post-genocidal contexts. One of the clearest examples of this muddied new frontier comes from the construction of genocide's definition.[36]

Polish jurist Raphael Lemkin sought to create new international law. Writing in the shadow of the Holocaust, Lemkin wanted to give a name to acts of mass murder. He ultimately took the Greek *genos* (race, tribe) and the Latin *cide* ('killing') to coin

---

[34] Scott Straus, *The Order of Genocide: Race, Power, and War in Rwanda* (Ithaca, NY: Cornell University Press, 2006).

[35] Alex Laban Hinton, *Why Did They Kill?: Cambodia in the Shadow of Genocide* (Berkeley: University of California Press, 2005).

[36] Kevin Lewis O'Neill and Alex Laban Hinton, 'Representation and/in Post-Genocidal Contexts: An Introduction', in *idem* (eds), *Genocide: Truth, Memory, and Representation* (Durham: Duke University Press, 2009).

the term 'genocide'. As Lemkin's own writings evidence, the word intended to denote a crime that involved 'a coordinated plan of different actions aiming at the destruction of essential foundations of life of national groups, with the aim of annihilating the groups themselves.'[37] Of interest here are the social processes that adjusted the definition, both its meaning and scope. In 1948, for example, Resolution 96-I became international law, with genocide referring to 'acts committed with intent to destroy, in whole or in part, a national, ethnical, racial or religious group, as such.' As the text makes clear, these acts include both outright 'killing' and 'causing serious bodily or mental harm' or creating 'conditions of life' intended to physically destroy the members of a group. The definition of genocide in Resolution 96-I also encompassed attempts to eliminate a group's survival by 'preventing births' or 'forcibly transferring [their] children' to another group. Yet, it is important to note that several key elements of Lemkin's original conceptualization of genocide were left out of Resolution 96-I.[38]

How? United Nations delegates debated the wording of the Convention for two years.[39] Certain types of groups ('national, ethnical, racial, or religious') were included. Others, such as economic and political groups, were eventually excluded for a variety of reasons ranging from the conceptual (i.e., some argued that political and economic groups were not 'enduring') to the pragmatic (i.e., many states feared interference in their internal political affairs and some, such as the Soviet Union, feared accusations they had committed genocide against such groups).[40]

Similarly, in *Axis Rule in Occupied Europe*, Lemkin argues that there was a range of other factors omitted. Those include political, social, cultural, economic, biological, physical, religious, and moral 'techniques of genocide'.[41] While physical, biological, and cultural acts appeared in the initial draft of the Convention, the broader sense of 'cultural genocide' was eliminated from the final text.[42] Cultural genocide, for example, includes curtailing or banning a language, traditional socialization practices, artistic endeavours, ritual practices, social institutions, and so forth. The framers of the 1948 Convention on Genocide erased these aspects from the text for conceptual/ legal reasons (some argued that cultural genocide was already prohibited in international law) and practical reasons (colonial powers, for example, likely feared accusations of cultural genocide). There were similar debates over issues of motivation/ intent, the scale of destruction, and punishment/enforcement.[43]

---

[37] Raphael Lemkin, *Axis Rule in Occupied Europe; Laws of Occupation, Analysis of Government, Proposals for Redress* (Washington, DC: Carnegie Endowment for International Peace, 1944), 79.

[38] O'Neill and Hinton, 'Representation and/in Post-Genocidal Contexts'.

[39] Leo Kuper, *Genocide: Its Political Use in the Twentieth Century* (New Haven, CT: Yale University Press, 1981), 23.

[40] O'Neill and Hinton, 'Representation and/in Post-Genocidal Contexts'.

[41] Lemkin, *Axis Rule in Occupied Europe*, 82.

[42] Kuper, *Genocide*.

[43] O'Neill and Hinton, 'Representation and/in Post-Genocidal Contexts'.

The very conception and legal definition of genocide was forged in a highly politicized atmosphere, one that resulted in inclusions and exclusions and a moral gradation of atrocity. The destruction of political groups, while abhorrent, was written out of the Genocide Convention and became something else, an implicitly lesser crime; cultural genocide similarly dropped from sight, eventually reemerging as 'ethnocide'. Yet, it is precisely these sorts of processes of inclusion and exclusion that the anthropology of genocide now turns.

One forward-looking example comes from Alex Hinton and Kevin Lewis O'Neill's edited volume on truth, memory, and representation.[44] The volume represents anthropology of genocide's continued interest in post-genocidal contexts. While some of the chapters grapple with the formal definition of genocide directly, most carry these themes far and wide to consider how genocide is itself represented and remembered in a variety of contexts. Along these lines, the book examines several cases commonly regarded as genocide and other cases in which there is contestation over the term, ranging from the North–South conflict in Sudan to Guatemala, where debate continues over whether civil conflict reached genocidal proportions. The Guatemalan case also illustrates how such views change over time, as many more people came to view the violence against indigenous Mayans as genocide following the findings of the Historical Clarification Commission in 1999. These more contested cases are revealing about the ways in which horrific violence is represented, remembered, and linked to truth claims about genocide.

Accordingly, the essays in the volume do not just explore the relationship of genocide to truth, memory, and representation, but also are concerned with how discourses about genocide, truth, memory, and representation are interlinked. Conerly Casey's chapter, for example, addresses the talk of genocide in Nigeria.[45] While some scholars suggest that Nigeria has been the site of genocide or genocidal massacres, others would argue genocide has not taken place there. It is a struggle over definitions, criteria, and key terms. What is genocide? And how does a grieving community define it? In response, Casey's chapter explores the ways in which discourses about genocide in Nigeria are bound up with issues of representation, memory, and truth claims, particularly with regard to the media. Central to Casey's chapter is the idea that the media disrupts the temporality of history, creating entangled representations of social reality. In media-saturated places such as Northern Nigeria, Casey argues, youths' uncertain experiences of local conflicts become placed next to regional and global media images of political unrest. The result is an affective citizenship that becomes constituted by historical ruptures, such as violence. Casey's intent is to make clear that media representations play an especially

---

[44] Hinton and O'Neill, *Truth/Memory/Representation and Genocide.*
[45] Conerly Casey, 'Mediated Hostility: Media, "Affective Citizenship", and Genocide in Northern Nigeria', in Hinton and O'Neill (eds), *Genocide.*

important role in the construction of political belonging among Nigerian youths who are (or who may become) perpetrators in genocidal massacres.

At the same time, the anthropology of genocide is directly concerned with issues of truth, memory, and representation in the aftermath of what most people would agree is genocide. Central to the growing anthropological study of genocide, in fact, is the idea that the 'truth' of genocide often becomes a power-laden tool over which politicians, activists, and the international community wrestle by asserting and contesting representations cobbled together from the often fragmented and clash-ing memories of survivors, perpetrators, witnesses, and bystanders. While scholars can make distinctions between truth, memory, and representation for the sake of analytical clarity, these divisions frequently become problematic on the ground. This conceptual unsteadiness can be troubling for those who want to definitively explain how, why, and when mass murder takes place.

The stakes are high in this area, as various individuals, groups, governments, and institutions vie to map out a narrative of the past that legitimates their agendas or desire for justice, to assert or reject the right to legal redress for and moral outrage about 'the crime of all crimes', and to acknowledge or disavow memories, experi-ences, suffering, and losses linked to mass murder. These often fiery debates rage around us in the world today, ranging from the Turkish government's continuing denials of the Armenian genocide to the debate over whether genocide is taking place in Darfur. There is also the case of denial in which various Western govern-ments seek a 'balanced' or qualified view about their complicities in colonial projects.[46] As noted earlier, another example is the debate over whether Guatema-la's civil war (1960–96) was genocidal. What the field aims to appreciate, however, is not whether Guatemala's civil conflict was genocidal itself, but how Guatemala's two truth commission reports represent genocide. Moreover, the question that the anthropology of genocide now addresses is how such truth commission reports function as machines of documentation—how they collect, analyse, edit, and publish extraordinary amounts of data that form seemingly comprehensive his-tories of human rights abuses. A close textual analysis, for example, demonstrates that Christian imaginations motivate representations of genocide in Guatemala.[47]

While acknowledging that such tribunals and truth commissions are often very important to people who have been the victims of mass atrocity, the anthropology of genocide suggests a new trajectory—one that demonstrates that there are inevitably 'grey zones' and silences that are erased from these 'official' accounts. This new line of analysis lingers on the disorderliness of genocide as well as the inevitable incompleteness of any attempt to remember and represent the truth of

---

[46] Stanley Cohen, *States of Denial: Knowing about Atrocities and Suffering of Others* (Malden, MA: Blackwell, 2001).

[47] Kevin Lewis O'Neill, 'Writing Guatemala's Genocide: Christianity and Truth and Reconciliation Commissions', *Journal for Genocide Research* 7:3 (September 2005), 310–31.

mass killings, systematic torture, and the deliberate attempt to annihilate a single group of people from the face of the earth. This line of analysis takes into account genocide's 'psychic imprints of terror', in the words of Leslie Dwyer, that destabilize everyday life for many living after genocide.[48]

Conclusion

Rather than seeking complete truths, full memories, and factual representations, the anthropology of genocide encourages scholars of genocide to focus on the cultural work that practices of truth, memory, and representation do in genocidal and post-genocidal contexts and how that work differs from one social and historical space to another. This, again, is not to say anthropologists are not concerned with the lived reality of genocide, or that anthropologists are somehow dismissive of debates over whether genocide occurred in a given region. Given ethnography's insistence on an engaged research that places anthropologists amidst zones of terror and abandonment, an argument could be made that anthropologists are some of the most empathetic observers and critics of genocide. By definition, anthropologists of genocide witness; they listen. Anthropologists also demonstrate that scholars of genocide must rely on their imaginations to understand the incomprehensible and in a way that uncovers how and why truth, memory, and representation exist as entangled efforts in spaces of such traumatic and horrific acts of mass violence.

Select Bibliography

Das, Veena, Arthur Kleinman, Mamphela Ramphele, and Pamela Reynolds (eds), *Violence and Subjectivity* (Berkeley: University of California Press, 1997).

Hinton, Alex Laban, *Why Did They Kill?: Cambodia in the Shadow of Genocide* (Berkeley: University of California Press, 2005).

—— (ed.), *Annihilating Difference: The Anthropology of Genocide* (Berkeley: University of California Press, 2002).

—— (ed.), *Genocide: An Anthropological Reader* (Malden: Blackwell, 2002).

—— and Kevin Lewis O'Neill (eds), *Genocide: Truth, Memory, and Representation* (Durham, NC: Duke University Press, 2009).

[48] Leslie Dwyer, 'The Intimacy of Terror: Gender and the Violence of 1965–66 in Bali', *Intersections: Gender, History, and Culture in the Asian Context* 10 (August 2004).

Malkki, Liisa, *Purity and Exile: Violence, Memory, and National Cosmology among Hutu Refugees in Tanzania* (Chicago: University of Chicago Press, 1995).

Sanford, Victoria, *Buried Secrets: Truth and Human Rights in Guatemala* (New York: Palgrave Macmillan, 2003).

Scheper-Hughes, Nancy, and Philippe Bourgeois (eds), *Violence in War and Peace: An Anthology* (London: Basil Blackwell Press, 2004).

Taylor, Christopher C., *Sacrifice as Terror: The Rwandan Genocide of 1994* (Oxford: Berg, 1999).

Whitehead, Neil (ed.), *Violence* (Santa Fe, NM: School of Advanced Research Press, 2004).

CHAPTER 10

SOCIAL PSYCHOLOGY AND GENOCIDE

PAUL A. ROTH

Hier ist kein Warum.

Primo Levi[1]

[T]he International Military Tribunal (IMT) at Nuremberg introduced conspiracy and membership in a criminal organization as charges that transcended individual involvement by what could be seen as 'guilt by association.' In the minds of their American authors, one of the main purposes of these charges was to find a legal basis for...'a ghoulish *embarras de richesse*': the large number of perpetrators—estimated at the time at hundreds of thousands—in numerous branches of the German executive, bureaucratic and economic apparatus.

Jürgen Matthäus[2]

Understanding perpetrator and perpetration is *the* essential element to understanding genocide. Other 'lessons' are ancillary.

Donald Bloxham[3]

---

[1] Primo Levi, *Survival in Auschwitz.*

[2] Jürgen Matthäus, 'Historiography and the Perpetrators of the Holocaust', in Dan Stone (ed.), *The Historiography of the Holocaust* (New York: Palgrave Macmillan, 2004), 199.

[3] Donald Bloxham, 'From Streicher to Sawoniuk: the Holocaust in the Courtroom', ibid. 414.

> We will not have come to terms with the past until the causes of what
> happened then are no longer active. Only because these causes live on
> does the spell of the past remain, to this very day, unbroken.
>
> Theodor W. Adorno[4]

THIS chapter examines what purports to be a core standing problem in the explanation of genocide, viz. how to account for the large number of people willing to participate in mass murders. Yet this core status notwithstanding, I contend that research in social psychology has already answered the question of 'perpetrator production'. Recruiting people to be perpetrators proves to be alarmingly easy. In addition, the application of social psychology to genocide has also become entangled in an ongoing moral debate, a debate that focuses on whether an emphasis on the extrinsic predictors of behaviour fits at all well or comfortably with a sense that people should be held morally (and legally) responsible for the choices they make.[5] This chapter argues as well that social psychology neither casts a pall of inevitability over such events nor provides moral exculpation for those involved.

In what follows, I use the phrase 'situationist social psychology', 'situationism', and cognate terms to designate a research tradition that emphasizes how situational variables most often prove determinative of individual and group behaviour. 'Situational' contrasts with 'dispositional', i.e., an emphasis on factors specific to the psychology of an individual. The paradigm takes a person's immediate context—the 'situation' in which one finds oneself—as a highly reliable predictor of behaviour. The key factor in terms of 'defining the situation' concerns the group or social norms that implicitly or explicitly govern expected behaviour in the situation. *Experiments in this tradition place people in contexts where the usual norms have been changed or expectations must be challenged.* The emphasis on situation implies that social stability (the following of certain standards of behaviour) should be understood as a function of the 'normative stability' of the contexts in which a person happens to be. Changes in normative expectations change behaviour. More generally, the paradigm teaches how people have a powerful tendency to conform to stated or implied norms in social and institutional contexts.

---

[4] Theodor W. Adorno, 'What Does Coming to Terms with the Past Mean?', in Geoffrey H. Hartman (ed.), *Bitburg in Moral and Political Perspective* (Bloomington, IN: Indiana University Press, 1986) 129. This essay was originally published in German in 1959.

[5] For a somewhat equivocal view of the relation between the social psychology and moral theory, see John M. Doris and Dominic Murphy, 'From My Lai to Abu Ghraib: The Moral Psychology of Atrocity', *Midwestern Studies in Philosophy* 31 (2007), 25–55. See also the special issue of the journal *Metaphilosophy* devoted to the topic, 'Genocide's Aftermath: Responsibility and Repair', *Metaphilosophy* 37 (2006), 299–543.

Experimental work in situationist social psychology has taught troubling yet important lessons.[6] Although the key research has been much discussed for close to four decades, its implications remain underappreciated. A reason for the lack of uptake of this research might be the unpleasantly shallow picture it suggests of what actually guides human behaviour, for the experiments suggest that people simply adapt to the norms present in the situation in which they find themselves and do not 'carry over' previous standards. But the lessons of situationism prove too valuable to let lie idle.[7]

The 'situationist' paradigm in social psychology pioneered by Kurt Lewin and developed experimentally by Solomon Asch, Stanley Milgram, and Philip Zimbardo can be shown to have broad and somewhat surprising application to historical cases of genocide.[8] This serendipitous marriage of social science and historical research represents a type of model for how the details of historical research (often thought to resist extrapolation to other cases) fits well with the generalizing proclivities of social science. Yet the relevant social psychological parameters fit a wide range of historical cases. Surprise (or horror) arises insofar as the experimental data demonstrate how relatively easily a substantial number of people can be co-opted for the purpose of assisting in mass murder.

Definitional issues regarding what does or does not count as genocide will not be examined in this essay. By focusing instead on how people transform into perpe-trators, the definitional or conceptual debates surrounding genocide assume no more than legalistic status. As a legal type, definition may matter for purposes of, e.g., mobilizing international support. But some suggestion that an event called into existence by definitional fiat can then serve as the basis for comparative analysis is a thin reed on which to rest any claim to science: 'Concepts determine case selection, which in turn shapes causal inference.'[9] Yet for concepts such as that of genocide, definitions create the cases. And for cases so stipulatively created, no reason exists for assuming that they then fit into any causal order.[10]

---

[6] For an excellent overview and characterization of work in this tradition, see Lee Ross and Richard E. Nisbett, *The Person and the Situation* (Boston: McGraw Hill, 1991). A recent updating of research in this area can be found in Philip Zimbardo, *The Lucifer Effect: Understanding How Good People Turn Evil* (New York: Random House, 2008).

[7] Works such as, e.g., Ervin Staub, *The Roots of Evil* (New York: Cambridge University Press, 1989) overtheorize genocide and yet add nothing of predictive value.

[8] Christopher R. Browning's work provides the compelling model. See his now classic book, *Ordinary Men: Reserve Police Battalion 101 and the Final Solution in Poland* (New York: HarperPerrenial, 1993). For a defence of Browning's use of the social psychological research, see my 'Beyond Understanding: The Career of the Concept of Understanding in the Human Sciences', in Stephen P. Turner and Paul A. Roth, eds., *The Blackwell Guide to the Philosophy of the Social Sciences* (Malden, MA: Blackwell, 2003) and 'Hearts of Darkness', *History of the Human Sciences* 17 (2004), 211–51.

[9] See Scott Straus, 'Contested Meanings and Conflicting Imperatives: A Conceptual Analysis of Genocide', *Journal of Genocide Research* 3 (2001), 359.

[10] See my 'Historical Explanation', *Journal of the Philosophy of History* 2 (2008), 214–26.

The social psychological experiments suggest a focus instead on comprehending the construction of a corps of perpetrators. The victims may be almost randomly chosen once one understands how perpetrators can be readily recruited. What makes conditions conducive to mass-producing perpetrators of acts such as genocides?[11] Posing the problem this way helps highlight two distinct philosophical components inseparable from the social psychological task of explaining participation in mass murder. One concerns the motivational question—what could account for a choice to behave in the way that genocidal killers and mass murderers do? The second concerns the relation of any proposed explanation and that of responsibility. Since explanations typically speak to causes, and causes can readily be understood to mitigate agency—freedom of or responsibility for choice—it might appear that the more one explains, the less people can be held responsible. However, properly understood, situationist accounts explain and yet require no diminution of attribution of responsibility.

The first section sets a philosophical frame for discussions of explanations of genocide. The second section examines how certain results from social psychology nicely accord with and support this frame. The third and final section looks at Ian Hacking's accounts of 'making up people' as enriching and supporting the theoretical lessons informed by the empirical work.

GENOCIDE AND 'THOUGHTLESS' BEHAVIOUR

The social trauma of the Second World War and its political aftermath were never far from the minds of European philosophers of that time. What seem to be philosophical abstractions turn out to connect to grim political concerns. For example, take Jean-Paul Sartre's declaration that 'Existence precedes essence.' Essences constitute a thing's nature, what it must be. Existence without a prior essence permits a type of freedom. One's own choices can then determine who or what one will be. But if a lack of an essence makes existential freedom possible, it also makes people at core unreliable. For nothing need determine how one acts. 'Tomorrow . . . some may decide to set up Fascism, and the others may be cowardly

---

[11] Regarding how definitional concerns have had some interesting ramifications in moral, legal, and historical debates, see Ann Curthhoys and John Docker, 'Defining Genocide', in Stone (ed.), *The Historiography of Genocide*, 9–41. As with so much else, Arendt anticipates these definitional concerns. Genocide, she argued, represents a new break in the moral order. 'Nothing is more pernicious to an understanding of these new crimes . . . than the common illusion that the crime of murder and the crime of genocide are essentially the same' (Hannah Arendt, *Eichmann in Jerusalem*, rev and enlg edn (New York: Penguin Books, 1977), 272).

and muddled enough to let them do it. Fascism would then be the human reality, and so much the worse for us.'[12] War revealed the ambivalent legacy of postulating human freedom subject to no moral imperatives.

Writing about a decade and a half after Sartre, Adorno too ponders what the experience of the Second World War reveals with regard to a 'social weakening of personal autonomy'.[13] Both worry in light of that experience about who will choose to resist oppression. Revelations surrounding perpetrator behaviour and the death camps in the intervening decade and a half sharpens this worry about whether or how people will in fact exercise autonomy. In this context, Adorno famously asks, 'What Does Coming to Terms with the Past Mean?' Do enduring but unaddressed social conditions continue to exist that incline people to political oppression and mass murder? Has post-war society comprehended the social conditions that caused or abetted the horrific acts? Insofar as these conditions persist, they leave in place the forces that ultimately produce, for example, genocides. Only by bringing these processes to collective self-awareness might their hold be broken. The proliferation of genocides through the second half of the twentieth century suggests that the social determinants remain in place.

Adorno's essay touches on two themes that remain relevant to any attempt to explain why genocide-like events recur. The first concerns his emphasis on 'objective conditions'—the social situations in which people find themselves—as having explanatory priority over individual 'subjective' factors. This suggested focus on objective situation (however cashed out) shall be termed the 'choice problem'—what determines how people act? The choice problem typically seeks answers regarding motivation—why people would choose to do what they did. The second concerns the affective character—a need to explain the enthusiasm often manifested by those inflicting the pain. This is the 'smile problem'.[14] The very questions suggest how social psychology might inform a philosophical anthropology. Answers to these problems would presumably indicate whether conditions could be altered so as to make genocidal behaviour less likely and if so how.

The concerns of Sartre and Adorno connect to yet a third figure whose philosophical writings attempt to comprehend how people behaved under conditions of

[12] Jean-Paul Sartre, 'Existentialism is a Humanism', in George Sher (ed.), *Moral Philosophy* (New York: Harcourt Brace Jovanovich, 1987), 480–1.

[13] Adorno, 'What Does Coming to Terms with the Past Mean?', 117.

[14] Adorno echoes both worries in the following remark. '[T]he past one wishes to evade is still so intensely alive. National Socialism lives on, and to this day we don't know whether it is only the ghost of what was so monstrous that it didn't even die off with its own death, or whether . . . the readiness for unspeakable actions survives in people, as in the social conditions that hem them in' (Adorno, 'What Does Coming to Terms with the Past Mean?', 115). Social conditions are one thing; people's 'readiness for unspeakable actions' quite another. See also Roth, 'Beyond Understanding', 322 and 'Hearts of Darkness', 226–36. Daniel Jonah Goldhagen takes the smile problem as key to explaining the Holocaust. See his *Hitler's Willing Executioners: Ordinary Germans and the Holocaust* (New York: Vintage, 1997).

occupation and oppression. Hannah Arendt too takes the choices made by perpetrators not as reflecting their individual quirks, but as revelations about us all.
Schooled in the same philosophical tradition as were Sartre and Adorno, her oft-
quoted and yet widely misunderstood remark about the 'banality of evil' with
respect to Eichmann reflects a shared concern about the nature and conditions
of choice.

How could Eichmann deny recognition to others of a common humanity, and so
of moral worth? Her answer—recognizable to anyone in the Kantian tradition
from which she comes—identifies Eichmann's failure as one of refusing responsibility for his choices by letting others determine the ends of action. Sartre and
Adorno and Arendt all share with Kant the view that our ability to will—to
choose—separates us from beasts in the field. Other animals cannot but behave
as instinct dictates; only humans can will to act against instinct. Eichmann fails this
essential test of one's humanity, for he uses reason only to follow rules others have
made for him.

It was sheer thoughtlessness—something by no means identical with stupidity—that
predisposed him [Eichmann] to become one of the greatest criminals of that period. And
if this is 'banal' and even funny, if with the best will in the world one cannot extract any
diabolical or demonic profundity from Eichmann, that is still far from calling it common-
place.... That such remoteness forms reality and such thoughtlessness can wreak more
havoc than all the evil instincts taken together which, perhaps are inherent in man—that was,
in fact, the lesson one could learn in Jerusalem. But it was a lesson, neither an explanation of
the phenomenon nor a theory about it.[15]

A literal failure to 'think for himself' marks him as thoughtless, as behaving as if a
being who could not recognize and follow the moral law. Human will allows us
only this choice, i.e., to follow the dictates of reason over that of animal nature. If
one holds their will in abeyance, behaviour cannot be original—something other
than a product of instinct or animal nature. If not original, then banal. The
consequences of any failure of will thus can provide a lesson, an example of the
consequences of indifference to aligning action to our human nature. But nothing
can compel humans to act against instinct, i.e., freely.

Evil becomes banal once the actions that produce it lack just this type of Kantian
thoughtfulness, i.e., becomes a mere following of ends given by others and not by
reason. Arendt specifically comments upon Eichmann as manifesting a 'strange
interdependence of thoughtlessness and evil'. Indeed, when she speaks explicitly of
Eichmann as personifying the 'banality of evil', it is in the context of 'forgetting' he
was at his own death sentence, i.e., faced with his own mortality. This proves to be a
defining moment. For in the philosophical tradition to which Arendt belongs, such
a 'forgetting' comes significantly freighted. Recognizing oneself as human involves

---

[15] Arendt, *Eichmann in Jerusalem*, 288.

always being confronted with the fact of one's own mortality. Losing sight of this just is losing sight of what defines us as human—our common fate and our capacity to choose. *Eichmann's crime, Arendt contends, consists precisely in this special thoughtlessness.*[16]

The substitution of technical reasoning—bureaucratic, economic, technological—for considerations about the best conditions for humans characterizes contemporary thoughtlessness about the ends of action. Arendt worries theses issues most thoroughly. For her, the disconnect that arises between thinking and willing signifies the area of most concern in contemporary life. By letting ends set by things and institutions go proxy for those freely chosen, banality ensues. Insofar as modern technology makes masses of people economically unnecessary and to the extent technology allows for the ready mobilization of killers, the world stage has been set for a 'new' crime to emerge.

So what begins as an extremely abstract pronouncement about humankind's lack of essence and the nature of free choice becomes, when filtered through the related musings of Adorno and Arendt, a question about the material conditions that engender 'thoughtless' action. Arendt, in particular, suggests that the Holocaust results from this type of thoughtless behaviour. In this regard, the oft-discussed connection between Arendt's invocation of the 'banality of evil' and work in social psychology must be seen in light of how experimental settings can readily induce just such 'thoughtless' behaviour.

INDUCING 'THOUGHTLESS BEHAVIOUR' AND CREATING PERPETRATORS

Can one experimentally create situations so as to induce such 'thoughtless' behaviour? Note that what calls for explanation concerns not only the production of perpetrators, but also their 'disappearance'. That is, characteristics of genocides in the twentieth century include the large number of perpetrators, their wantonness, and their later return to live undisturbed among the populace. If one considers the political furor accompanying, e.g., the residential locations of sex offenders, the reassimilation of perpetrators appears strikingly anomalous.[17]

In emphasizing the importance of situational factors, the salient feature concerns how the experiments effectively construct scenarios that require people to challenge norms (decide against a group or an authority figure) or forge normative

---

[16] Arendt, *Eichmann in Jerusalem*, 252, 279.
[17] This point struck Arendt as well. Ibid. 16–19.

limits (e.g., how to modulate or enact the authority one has over others).[18] So, for example, people will identify a shorter line as the longest in a set if a majority of others in their group do or choose to inflict pain despite having no prior history of a willingness to do so.[19] The core point demonstrated by these experiments concerns the power of the 'conformity effect'—the amazing willingness of people to simply assimilate the norms of the situations in which they find themselves. Experiments in the 'Asch paradigm' provides replicable demonstrations of how this powerful 'conformity effect' trumps other factors as a predictor of behaviour.[20]

An interesting and important feature of the classic experiments in the Asch–Milgram–Zimbardo line is that in each case the outcomes proved contrary to the prior expectations of the experimenters.[21] In Asch's experiments, pressure to conform presumably arises merely from the implied challenge of contravening those who have already announced a decision. Milgram's justly celebrated extension of this experimental paradigm explored whether this proclivity to conformity to a real or imagined norm would be manifest if the choice involved inflicting pain or possible harm on others.

In earlier writings, I emphasized how these experiments could be brought to bear on two key explanatory problems noted in the introduction—the 'choice problem' and the 'smile problem'. The choice problem can be characterized as follows: why do so many people with no prior history of brutalization or murder participate, at one level or another, in the killing operations involved in genocides and mass murders?[22] The smile problem connects to the choice problem. For if the choice problem asks why people did these acts voluntarily, the smile problem

---

[18] Material in this and the subsequent three paragraphs borrow from my discussion in 'Hearts of Darkness', 217–20.

[19] For a detailed account of Asch's experiments in this vein and important related work, see Zimbardo, *The Lucifer Effect*, esp. Chapter 12. An extensive overview and summary presentation of the relevant research can also be found in Philip Zimbardo, 'Transforming Good People into Perpetrators of Evil: Can We Reverse the Process?', *Ricerche di psicologia* 28 (2005), 1–52.

[20] See the helpful and historically broad accounts of this research tradition and its influence on social psychology in Ross and Nisbett, *The Person and the Situation*.

[21] In *The Lucifer Effect*, Zimbardo devotes over 200 pages to elaborating the details of the Stanford Prison Experiment (SPE). From his discussion one learns that there is a web site devoted just to the SPE, http://www.prisonexp.org, one devoted to Zimbardo's book featuring his extensive retrospective analysis of the material, http://www.LuciferEffect.com ('Lucifer Effect' t-shirts can be purchased from this site), and one devoted to Zimbardo himself, http://www.zimbardo.com. Given that the SPE (unlike, e.g., the Milgram experiment) was effectively a one-time occurrence that occurred 37 years ago, it yet remains a focus of much attention. Much more so than the Milgram experiment, the SPE poses ethical obstacles to its replication. But see S. H. Lovibond, X. Mithiran, and W. G. Adams, 'The Effects of Three Experimental Prison Environments on the Behaviour of Non-convict Volunteer Subjects', *Australian Psychologist* 14 (1979), 273–87. Their results strikingly confirm those of the SPE. 'It is clear that our Standard Custodial regime induced ordinary people with little knowledge and no experience of prisons, to behave in much the same way as prisoners and officers in real prisons' (283; see also 278). See discussions of the SPE and replications in Zimbardo, *The Lucifer Effect*, 250–5.

[22] See my discussion in 'Beyond Understanding', 320.

points to the disconcerting fact that many do so with apparent enjoyment. Simply put, those inflicting harm appeared to enjoy it.[23]

A close analysis of Milgram's work and Zimbardo's establishes that the situational analysis accounts in all essentials for the number of perpetrators and their otherwise incomprehensible brutality. The experiments compellingly demonstrate that a 'conformity effect' suffices to predict both the extent of participation (and thus obviate any apparent problem of choice) and the sadistic enthusiasm that individuals invest in roles to which accidents of experimental design (or of fate) have assigned them (and thus solve the smile problem).

Milgram's work bears primarily on questions of choice; Zimbardo's addresses issues related to the smile problem.[24] To briefly summarize, the 'Milgram experiment' (and its variants) involves subjects who believe that they are administering electric shocks to someone as part of a learning experiment. The core of this experiment concerns the extent to which subjects continue to inflict the electric shocks despite pleas, screams, cries, etc. from the supposed victim. In some variations, in excess of 60% of subjects regularly deliver up to maximum shocks (450 volts). *No coercion of the subject exists other than the norm requiring someone to 'obey' the experiment's protocols.*

Zimbardo was the chief architect of the Stanford Prison Experiment (SPE). This involved arbitrarily assigning college students (pre-screened for personality abnormalities) to roles as prisoners or as guards. The experiment had to be terminated after only a few days because of the brutality invested by guards in their roles and the debilitating psychological effects on those assigned to be prisoners. The chief theoretical point was to establish how structures, roles, or situations trump dispositional factors as determinants of behaviour. This the experiment did in compelling fashion. The famously unexpected result concerned the pleasure people took in exercising arbitrary power over others. For by experimental design in the SPE the roles were left underspecified just for the purpose of seeing how those assigned the role 'filled them in'. As Zimbardo states in that essay, 'The third feature

---

[23] Emphasis on the smile problem constitutes the core of Goldhagen's critique of Browning's use of social psychology to explain perpetrator behaviour. In the view of some social psychologists, it remains a standing objection to the explanatory reach of Milgram's work. See, e.g., Arthur G. Miller, 'What Can the Milgram Obedience Experiments Tell Us about the Holocaust?: Generalizing from the Social Psychology Laboratory', in *idem* (ed.), *The Social Psychology of Good and Evil* (New York: Guilford Press, 2004), 193–239, but esp. 212–16. Note how the chief criticisms of the explanatory power of Milgram emphasize what I term the smile problem. Quite inexplicably, although Zimbardo has an essay in the Miller anthology, his work receives no discussion in the other essays, and Miller himself does not connect or emphasize the joint importance of using Milgram and Zimbardo together for purposes of explanation. For my introduction and discussion of the smile problem, see 'Beyond Understanding', 322. See also 'Hearts of Darkness', 226–36.

[24] For an excellent summary of work done by Milgram and the many replications of his results, see Thomas Blass, 'The Milgram Paradigm after 35 Years: Some Things We Now Know about Obedience to Authority', in *idem* (ed.), *Obedience to Authority: Current Perspectives on the Milgram Paradigm* (Mahwah, NJ: Lawrence Erlbaum Associates, 2000), 35–59. See also Zimbardo, *The Lucifer Effect.*

of the study was the novelty of the prisoner and guard roles: Participants had no prior training in how to play the randomly assigned roles. Each subject's prior societal learning of the meaning of prisons and the behavioural scripts associated with the oppositional roles of prisoner and guard was the sole source of guidance.'[25] Zimbardo's design strongly suggests that cruelty will simply emerge; it does not have to be planned for. The smile problem asks how people can take pleasure in inflicting pain, especially when accidents of circumstance account for their position to do so. The SPE and related research indicate that the mere ability to do this engenders pleasure for many in doing so.[26]

Taken together, these experiments indicate that it requires little incentive to recruit people for unsavory purposes. What appear as explanatory puzzles arise only because such behaviour does not appear to be the norm. But confusion arises if one takes a *choice* of norms as explaining the stability of the situations, as opposed to seeing stability as a product of mere *conformity* to norms. When for whatever reason stability disappears, people will simply adapt to what they take to be expected of them. In short, the work of Milgram and Zimbardo retrodictively account for general behaviour of people under the Nazis and make (or should have made) what happened at Abu Ghraib predictable.[27]

A third puzzle also can be solved by the situationist account—the 'nasty neighbour problem'. The nasty neighbour puzzle arises insofar as one might assume that a general populace would not desire known mass murderers to continue to live undisturbed in their midst. But, as Arendt notes for the German case and has been seen in later cases of genocides, the general populace reabsorbs perpetrators with seeming complacency.[28] Indeed, I am unaware that this has been recognized as an explanatory *problem* by social psychologists or historians examining perpetrator behaviour.

In tracing different accounts of perpetrator behaviour that have marked the historical literature about the Holocaust, Mark Roseman notes that one model

[25] See Philip G. Zimbardo, 'A Situationist Perspective on the Psychology of Evil: Understanding How Good People Are Transformed into Perpetrators', in Miller (ed.), *The Social Psychology of Good and Evil*, 39.

[26] For a detailed analysis of just why this solves the choice problem, see Roth, 'Hearts of Darkness', 232–3. Regarding the smile problem, see 233–6. Important here is related work by Zimbardo on deindividuation. See account in *The Lucifer Effect*.

[27] The social psychology explains the events recounted in Victor Klemperer, *I Will Bear Witness*, 2 vols (New York: Random House, 1998).

[28] Arendt, *Eichmann in Jerusalem*, 16. For a detailed study which brings particular empirical force to Arendt's observation, see Dick de Mildt, *In the Name of the People: Perpetrators of Genocide in the Reflection of Their Post-War Prosecution in West Germany* (Boston: Martinus Nijhoff. 1996). For a personal perspective, see Katharina von Kellenback, 'Vanishing Acts: Perpetrators in Postwar Germany', *Holocaust and Genocide Studies* 17 (2003), 305–29. Mark Roseman also raises this issue in 'Beyond Conviction? Perpetrators, Idea, and Action in the Holocaust in Historiographical Perspective', in Frank Biess, Mark Roseman, and Hanna Schissler (eds), *Conflict, Catastrophe and Continuity: Essays on Modern German History* (New York: Berghahn Books, 2007), 83–103.

emphasizes just a form of the nasty neighbour puzzle.[29] But while Roseman does not embrace this specific model, he acknowledges it as one of the standing explanatory challenges regarding perpetrator behaviour:

Yet Arendt and others had grasped an essential problem that continues to be posed to us by the Nazi regime, and which lies at the core of [historian Hans] Mommsen's analysis too—namely, how a body of men could operate with such comprehensiveness and relentlessness right up to the last minute, and then let go of the program, like that, as if it had never been theirs.[30]

As with the choice and smile problems, situational analyses offers a resolution of the nasty neighbour puzzle. That is, the situation explains why people readily become killers, indeed even killers who relish their work. Altering it then also accounts for the otherwise counter-intuitive result that these very same people not only reintegrate peaceably in their respective societies, but also that they can be accepted as if they posed no threat.

Although the nasty neighbour puzzle has not figured prominently in debates regarding explanations of perpetrator behaviour, it should. For too often those committing the crimes simply melt back into the general populace. In this regard, recent work indicates that there appears nothing remarkable about the particular backgrounds from which the perpetrators of the Holocaust, for example, were drawn.[31] Somewhat oddly, given that the number of perpetrators in the German case has been estimated at up to 250,000, the investigator focuses on about 1,500 cases, drawing only from those tried for a war crime. Not too surprisingly, he finds a disproportionate number of 'real Nazis'—committed party members with a long history of Nazi association—in this group. But what light does this shed on how the mass of perpetrators were co-opted?

More relevantly, Scott Straus attempts to find a way to accurately estimate the number of perpetrators in the Rwandan genocide.[32] The numbers are large, both in absolute terms and in terms of the relative proportion of the population. This detailed effort at quantifying the number of perpetrators and bystanders appears consistent with numbers developed for the Holocaust case. I have elsewhere provided a detailed analysis of the Milgram experiments that show why the percentages of obedient subjects suffices to provide the needed number of perpetrators just by virtue of a tendency to obey authority. The question of choice ceases

---

[29] Roseman, 'Beyond Conviction?', 91.

[30] Ibid. 99. Roseman and I differ sharply on Arendt on banality.

[31] Michael Mann, 'Were the Perpetrators of Genocide "Ordinary Men" or "Real Nazis"? Results from Fifteen Hundred Biographies', *Holocaust and Genocide Studies* 14 (2000), 334–5. For an account at variance both with Mann's and my own, see Donald Bloxham, 'Organized Mass Murder: Structure, Participation and Motivation in Comparative Perspective', *Holocaust and Genocide Studies* 22:2 (2008), 203–45.

[32] Scott Straus, 'How Many Perpetrators Were there in the Rwandan Genocide? An Estimate', *Journal of Genocide Research* 6 (2004), 85–98.

to matter. By demonstrating what people will do simply sidesteps any question of whether they could have chosen otherwise.[33] Put another way, situations do not necessitate behaviours. But the tendency to conform makes this freedom to choose moot. A type of herd mentality effectively trumps any actual ability to behave otherwise.

There remains in the social psychological literature an unfortunate tendency to equate situationist explanations with 'judgmental dopes', as caricatures of people blindly shaping themselves to situations. For example, a recent article discusses straight-faced and with endorsement a reading of the Arendtian notion of banality and thoughtlessness as equivalent to asserting the 'Nazi killers were unwitting minions',[34] and that the experiments were meant to show that the people involved were 'amoral automatons'.[35] Thus does the situationist paradigm come to be labelled 'reductionist'.

Arendt, Milgram, and Zimbardo played a critical part in taking us beyond reductionist explanations of tyranny as a simple product of pathological individuals. But now, their reductionist explanations of tyranny as a simple product of pathological situations—the banality-of-evil hypothesis—seem equally untenable. Instead, . . . an interactionist understanding that sees the social psychology of individual tyrants and collective tyranny as interdependent and mutually reinforcing.[36]

But the foregoing only reflects a fundamental misreading of these texts. *Nothing in the Milgram experiments or in the SPE makes the situation inherently pathological. The 'pathology' consists in the thoughtless investment people make in roles handed them by an accident of fate.* Arendt's Kantian-inflected notion of banality resonates deeply with what Milgram and Zimbardo demonstrate empirically.

In an effort to reject what he characterizes as 'strong situationism', Leonard Newman maintains that controversies featuring disputes between situational and dispositional variables are passé. Rather, 'It has long been recognized that people and their traits and the situations in which they find themselves *interact*.'[37] Yet the problem with distinguishing this model from the situationist also becomes immediately if unwittingly apparent. For while interactionists maintain that traits and situations mutually effect one another, Newman adds that 'Traits will express

[33] Roth, 'Hearts of Darkness', 232 ff; *idem*, 'Beyond Understanding', 319–26.

[34] S. Alexander Haslam and Stephen Reicher, 'Beyond the Banality of Evil: Three Dynamics of an Interactionist Social Psychology of Tyranny', *Personality and Social Psychology Bulletin* 33 (2007), 615–22, esp. 617–19.

[35] Ibid. 619. Donald Bloxham discusses some of these readings of Arendt in 'Organized Mass Murder'.

[36] Haslam and Reicher, 'Beyond the Banality of Evil', 621.

[37] Leonard S. Newman, 'Beyond Situationism: The Social Psychology of Genocide and Mass Killing', in Helgard Kramer (ed.), *NS-Täter aus interdisziplinärer Perspektive* (München: Martin Meidenbauer, 2006), 110.

themselves in some situations and not others.'[38] Indeed, one does not even need to do any new experiments to prove this. The old experiments suffice for that purpose. 'In fact, if you look carefully at the results of those studies [Asch, Milgram, Zimbardo], the evidence is right there. Not everyone obeys, not everyone conforms, and not everyone gets swallowed up into a role.'[39] True enough. But what then could be Newman's point regarding how to distinguish between situationism and interactionism? The data from the classic situational experiments only made claims about how a certain percentage of people would respond. 'Interactionism' proves indistinguishable from what it proposes to replace.[40]

Surprisingly, Newman appears to concede the point, for he drops the idea that specific traits interact in particular ways, and instead emphasizes that situations can later alter the traits that people initially have. He cites literature that indicates that even though individuals might be aware that they create a certain situation, e.g., a stench caused by unsanitary conditions that perpetrators established, people will nonetheless 'blame the victim'. He sums this up as follows: '*People are not only affected by situations; they also change those situations.* The process is bi-directional. In addition, people are not always aware of how they have changed situations, and when they are, they do not always take their influence into account.'[41] Indeed, Christopher Browning's now classic *Ordinary Men* offers clear and graphic demonstrations of this bidirectional process of influence. But this simply shows the extent to which the situationist paradigm already incorporates the dynamic aspect on which interactionism insists. Likewise, Newman explicitly raises the smile problem as if it were a difficulty for situationism, whereas in fact the ability to deal also with this issue proves to be a situationist strength.[42]

Mass murder has become a feature of the twentieth century. Arendt's concern that genocides represent a new break in the moral order implicates the newly evolved technologies. Insofar as certain technologies—e.g., those of mass communication—help to engineer changes in the perceived normative framework, technology abets thoughtlessness in the Kantian sense. Even in cases where the actual means of killing remain relatively primitive, e.g., Rwanda, the use of such technologies allows for the ready mobilization and manipulation of would-be perpetrators. Technology makes *practical* obstacles to mass murders for those in the

---

[38] Leonard S. Newman, 'Beyond Situationism: The Social Psychology of Genocide and Mass Killing', in Helgard Kramer (ed.), *NS-Täter aus interdisziplinärer Perspektive* (München: Martin Meidenbauer, 2006), 110.

[39] Ibid.

[40] Newman does appreciate how Arendt has been misread by social psychologists, See Leonard S. Newman, 'The Banality of Secondary Sources: Why Social Psychologists have Misinterpreted Arendt's Thesis' (2001, unpublished talk).

[41] Newman, 'Beyond Situationism', 115.

[42] Ibid., 111–13; see Roth, 'Beyond Understanding', and 'Hearts of Darkness'.

changed situation disappear.[43] Research and history show that prior norms will not provide sufficient constraint.

'THOUGHTLESSNESS' IN (FURTHER) THEORETICAL PERSPECTIVE

The work in social psychology has profound implications, in turn, for philosophical anthropology—our understanding of the type of beings that we are. And, in fact, these empirical and theoretical considerations have been further extended through some of the important and innovative work done by Ian Hacking on 'making up people'.[44] Hacking explores how categories of people or medical classifications of them come into being (e.g., suicides, the normal, child abuse, multiple personality disorder). By what processes, he asks, do human kinds become sorted into recognized types that bureaucrats and others then use as bases for how to treat people?

In raising these questions, he goes to the heart of how social science might be possible, for scientific generalizations typically utilize categories (kinds) of entities. The generalizations, that is, apply to like items, and the relevant likenesses mark out the properties by which to sort things into kinds. The stability of generalizations thus presumes a stability of the kinds. If one seeks generalizations about human behaviour, the question to be answered concerns what makes for stable human kinds.

Hacking develops examples from a fascinating range of areas—homosexuality considered both as a medical category and as a 'life style', multiple personality disorder, suicides. In each case, he examines the technological, social, and scientific factors surrounding the emergence of each of these ways of categorizing individuals. So, for example, he shows how innovations in classifying and counting made possible by the development of statistical analysis abets efforts to measure the 'health' of

[43] For related reflections, see A. Dirk Moses, 'Genocide and Modernity', in Stone, *The Historiography of Genocide* (ed.), 166–70.

[44] Key essays by Hacking in this regard include 'Making Up People', in Thomas Heller, Morton Sosna, and David Wellbery (eds), *Reconstructing Individualism* (Stanford: Stanford University Press, 1986), 222–36; 'Multiple Personality Disorder and its Hosts', *History of the Human Sciences* 2 (1992), 3–31; 'World Making by Kind-Making: Child Abuse for Example', in Mary Douglas and David Hull (eds), *How Classification Works* (Edinburgh: Edinburgh University Press, 1992), 180–238; 'The Looping Effects of Human Kinds', in Dan Sperber, David Premack, and Ann J. Premack (eds), *Causal Cognition* (Oxford: Clarendon Press, 1995), 251–83; *Rewriting the Soul: Multiple Personality and the Sciences of Memory* (Princeton: Princeton University Press, 1995); 'Between Michel Foucault and Erving Goffman: Between Discourse in the Abstract and Face-to-Face Interaction', *Economy and Society* 33 (2004), 277–302.

societies, and so ultimately to classify and count suicides. The emergence and growth of multiple personality disorder as a diagnostic category likewise links with the evolution of the definition of child abuse from physical to primarily sexual abuse. Childhood sexual abuse becomes by definition a key part of the etiology of multiple personality disorder. So as one is found pervasive, so is the other. Likewise, the homosexual considered as a distinct medical and social type also proves to be of recent historical origin. In all cases, a drive to medicalize problems (and so make them into individual and not social problems) or create scientifically certified categories of social misfits (as with multiple personality disorder) suggests how individuals can be at the mercy of others for ways to think about themselves, and how bureaucratic or social imperatives trump what the available evidence actually establishes.

But the ways in which people become classified by existing institutional arrangements also manifest what Hacking calls 'looping effects'. These involve cases where people come to inhabit a classificatory category that has been created. *Hacking's looping effect, I suggest, should be seen as a manifestation of what has been discussed above as the conformity effect.* Hacking's work points to the presence of institutionally pervasive pressures to conform to the ways in which one is diagnosed or sorted as a type of person. The categories do not need a prior reality, so to speak. Once they have an institutional context, people will make them 'real' and populate the categories.

As a philosopher of science, Hacking has a keen awareness of the stakes here in exploring how human kinds come to be, change, and perhaps fade away. 'I could develop the argument that what I call human kinds are at the historical root of sociology—the science of normality and deviance.'[45] This looping effect becomes another way to theoretically account for how people come to 'make real' roles they never envisioned themselves as inhabiting. In this regard, the implicit concern involves whether one takes the designation of a certain type of behaviour—'perpetrator', for example—as the name of a kind. Taken as a kind, one assumes common properties, and looks for elements all the individuals share. But the distinction between the notions of looping and that of situations indicates that the common elements may be largely or wholly extrinsic to the individuals involved. People readily become perpetrators by falling prey to situational factors. Looping effects indicate that the behaviour in question involves more than the conformity effect, but also the self-definition of the actor. The conformity effect does not imply looping, while the looping effect indicates how categories can be taken up by those so categorized.[46]

In short, looping effects point to a power of categorization that goes beyond what the conformity effect demonstrates. Categories matter existentially, so to speak. People come to inhabit and so perpetuate and make real the categories by which they are classified. But their ultimate significance as historical or social

---

[45] Hacking, 'Looping Effects', 360.

[46] Hacking readily acknowledges the immense influence that the work of Michel Foucault has had on his approach to these issues.

artefacts remains distinct from the power of the conformity effect. If perpetrators adopt and adapt a categorization of themselves as perpetrators, they will internalize kind-like attributes.

Thus one way in which some human kinds differ from some kinds of thing is that classifying people works on people, changes them, and can even change their past. The process does not stop there. The people of a kind themselves are changed. Hence 'we', the experts, are forced to rethink our classifications. Moreover, causal relationships between kinds are changed. . . . This is not because we have found out more about the natural disorder, but because people who see themselves as having this human disorder now find in themselves memories of trauma, often traumas of a kind that they could not even have conceptualized twenty years ago. . . . This in turn generates a looping effect, because people of the kind behave differently and so are different. That is to say the kind changes, and so there is new causal knowledge to be gained.[47]

Otherwise, what makes them perpetrators is only conformity.

A dramatic illustration of Hacking's looping effect can be found in Zimbardo's description of the well-known case where a schoolteacher, Jane Elliott, discriminated among her students by an arbitrarily chosen characteristic, e.g., eye color. The students quickly realize that discrimination exists and determine the group to which they belong. They then behave as either those entitled to privilege or those who expect the worst. A key feature of this incident concerns how the children came to occupy categories of a kind of person who was being discriminated against. Though simple in structure, the case indicates the power of categorization and how adaption to contextual norms induces a looping effect, i.e., creates and sustains certain patterns of behaviour.[48]

As Hacking insists, his account of looping effects goes beyond what, e.g., labelling theory suggests insofar as the individual may shape the category in which placed, and in doing so alters both the kind and what there is to know about the kind in question. In labelling theory a certain normative tag (e.g., 'delinquent') comes to be applied to certain behaviours. In Hacking's case, however, the emphasis concerns how people 'fill out' institutionally specified but otherwise underdetermined social roles. In many interesting cases, behaviours become tagged as representing a category in advance of any determination that they reflect common properties or causes. But this calls into existence institutionally designated but vaguely articulated kinds. Actual individuals then come to adapt to and inhabit these categories, making them real after the fact, so to speak.

Hacking suggestively juxtaposes in a complementary fashion the philosophical approaches of Michel Foucault (concerned with structures of power as structures of knowledge) and sociologist Erving Goffman, who in his turn did classic studies of self-construction within institutional frameworks and in face-to-face interactions.[49]

---

[47] Hacking, 'Looping Effects', 369.
[48] The case is described by Zimbardo in *The Lucifer Effect*, 283–4.
[49] Hacking, 'Between Michel Foucault and Erving Goffman'.

By combining Foucauldian macroanalyses of how power influences structures of everyday life and Goffman's microanalyses of the environment of 'closed institutions'—asylums, hospitals, boarding schools—Hacking provides a compelling picture of how certain types of social norms become institutionalized and sustained even in the absence of conscious decisions by people to accept these norms. The net effect sketches how the constraints of a physical space and the assigned but indeterminate roles that people must work out within them determine who people can be.[50]

The emphasis on how people come to inhabit the roles offered them emphasizes the existential insight that constraints allow for the discovery of who we are. For in the process of filling out a role, one learns and defines in a literal sense who one is.

Does one feel different, has one a different experience of oneself, if one is led to see oneself as a certain type of person? Does the availability of a classification, a label, a word or phrase, open certain possibilities, or perhaps close off others? . . . It seemed to me that a new way of describing people does not only create new ways to be, but also new ways to choose—in the existentialist philosophy, new ways to choose who one is.[51]

Marx famously observed that 'Men make their own history, but they do not make it just as they please; they do not make it under circumstances chosen by themselves, but under circumstances directly encountered, given, and transmitted from the past.'[52] Hacking looks to update just this view by supplementing Marx's broad sweep with the finer grained analyses of Foucault and Goffman.

I want instead to draw on both the archaeological and the sociological approach to better understand the ways in which the actual and possible lives of individuals are constituted. . . . This is not because how we are can be freely chosen, but because the choices that are open to us are made possible by the intersection of the immediate social settings . . . and the history of that present.[53]

The unifying point linking the thinkers discussed concerns the importance of choices. People create themselves within institutional spaces and categories not of their making. In this regard, Hacking's work extends our understanding of how

---

[50] Erving Goffman, *Asylums: Essays on the Social Situation of Mental Patients and other Inmates* (Garden City, NY: Anchor Books, 1961). Hacking puts the point of comparison this way: 'Goffman analyzed, by a series of ideal types, the ways in which human roles are constituted in the face-to-face interactions within an institution setting, and how patterns of normality and deviance work on individual agents—and how the agents change those norms, by a sort of feedback effect. Foucault's archaeologies establish the preconditions for and the mutations between successive institutional forms. His later genealogies are closer to how the historical settings work on people to form their potentialities, but never indicate how this happens in daily life. Goffman does that in rich detail, but gives no hint of how the surrounding structures themselves were constituted' ('Between Michel Foucault and Erving Goffman', 288).

[51] Ibid. 285.

[52] Karl Marx, 'The Eighteenth Brumaire of Louis Bonaparte', in Lewis S. Feuer (ed.), *Marx and Engels: Basic Writings on Politics and Philosophy* (New York: Anchor Books, 1959), 320.

[53] Hacking, 'Between Michel Foucault and Erving Goffman', 288.

the conformity effect ranges over medical categories and social institutions. It helps replicate the categories created by which to count, classify, and treat people.

Perpetrators may be unwittingly made by circumstance, but the same can be said for many other types of people. My argument has been to establish that the ability of the situationist approach to deal successfully with the choice problem and the smile problem implies that the affective dimensions of genocidal behaviours—the alarming enthusiasm people bring to these roles—needs (alas) no special, or especially deep, explanation. The nasty neighbour problem and its proposed solution, i.e., that people implicitly recognized that role-determined behaviour does not constitute a general threat once the general circumstances have changed, adds I suggest an additional measure of credence to the results. To the best of my knowledge, no other explanatory proposal put forward so neatly resolves all three of these problems. These activities, rather, reflect all too well the sort of elements involved in 'making up people'.

That these problems all find explicit anticipation in Arendt's *Eichmann in Jerusalem* underscores the ways in which philosophy and social science remain curiously tied together, at least on this issue. For on the one hand, the social scientific resources exist for explaining why people would suddenly become murderers on a mass scale, pursue this with grisly abandon, and then return to 'normal' lives when circumstances change. On the other hand, the empirical work appears to generate a type of moral revulsion or psychological resistance to the idea that people can just be so malleable. But perhaps a key to lessening the likelihood of creating perpetrators resides precisely in coming to terms with acknowledging the fact that though people can choose against conformity effects, relatively few will.

ACKNOWLEDGEMENTS

I thank Donald Bloxham, Yves Gingras, Colin Koopman, Dirk Moses, and Renee C. Winter for their comments on earlier drafts of this essay.

SELECT BIBLIOGRAPHY

Adorno, Theodor W., 'What Does Coming to Terms with the Past Mean?', in Geoffrey H. Hartman (ed.), *Bitburg in Moral and Political Perspective* (Bloomington, IN: Indiana University Press, 1986).

Browning, Christopher R., *Ordinary Men: Reserve Police Battalion 101 and the Final Solution in Poland* (New York: Harper Perennial, 1993).

Hacking, Ian, *Rewriting the Soul: Multiple Personality and the Sciences of Memory* (Princeton: Princeton University Press, 1995).

—— 'Between Michel Foucault and Erving Goffman: Between Discourse in the Abstract and Face-to-Face Interaction', *Economy and Society* 33 (2004), 277–302.

Moses, A. D., 'Structure and Agency in the Holocaust: The Case of Daniel Jonah Goldhagen', *History and Theory* 37:2 (1998), 194–219.

Roth, Paul A., 'Beyond Understanding: The Career of the Concept of Understanding in the Human Sciences', in Stephen P. Turner and Paul A. Roth (eds), *The Blackwell Guide to the Philosophy of the Social Sciences* (Malden, MA: Blackwell, 2003).

—— 'Hearts of Darkness,' *History of the Human Sciences* 17:2–3 (2004), 211–51.

Stone, Dan (ed.), *The Historiography of the Holocaust* (New York: Palgrave Macmillan, 2004).

Zimbardo, Philip, *The Lucifer Effect: Understanding How Good People Turn Evil* (New York: Random House, 2008).

CHAPTER 11

PHILOSOPHY AND GENOCIDE

MARTIN SHUSTER

§1

SURPRISINGLY few philosophers have written about genocide, leading to the question of what it would mean to pose genocide as a philosophical problem. In the course of this chapter, I will review some of the ways philosophers have addressed genocide and then, by using the work of Max Horkheimer and Theodor W. Adorno, suggest an alternative way in which they can proceed further. The first question to pose, then, is why have philosophers been prone *not* to discussing genocide?[1] Answering this question will go a long way in helping to understand what philosophy can and cannot do in analysing genocide.

Many philosophers fall into two broad camps: those who feel uncomfortable addressing genocide, and those who do not see any particular philosophical problem in the occurrence of genocide. The former tend to feel as if a philosophical intervention into genocide would be unfruitful owing to the complexities involved: either that they lack the requisite empirical knowledge or that they need to gain clarity on a variety of 'smaller' issues involving perhaps ethics, social/political philosophy, and/or the philosophy of action (just to name a few areas); all of

---

[1] Kenneth Seeskin raised this question in 1992 about the Nazi genocide and philosophy, but the point still stands today and with respect to the study of genocide as such. See his review of Berel Lang's *Act and Idea in the Nazi Genocide*: Kenneth Seeskin, 'Lang, *Act and Idea in the Nazi Genocide*', *The Jewish Quarterly Review* 88, no. 1–2 (1992), 273.

these issues would need to be properly worked through before tackling the 'big' issue of genocide.

Alternatively, or coextensively, it may be the case that philosophers simply do not see a *particular* philosophical problem in the occurrence of genocide. For example, one of the most notable monographs to come out on evil in recent years treats genocide as an example of atrocity,[2] different in scale, scope, and/or degree, but not in kind from other evils.[3] On such a view, an understanding of evil implicitly addresses itself to understanding genocide. One could repeat this procedure with other issues such as racism, murder, and so forth: genocide is implicitly addressed by considering these other issues. Drawing a connection between philosophy and genocide can then be either too easy or too difficult.

Another way of addressing genocide, but not dealing with it as a particular problem, is to see genocide as representative of some deeper problem, for example, nihilism or relativism. Certain readings of Martin Heidegger take this to be his position: that the Holocaust (and presumably other genocides) is simply a manifestation of a deeper nihilism,[4] which itself is simply a stage in the 'destiny of Being' (*Seingeschick*).[5] Alternatively, genocide may be seen as exemplifying or illustrating some more basic philosophical problem. For example, one may ask about the exact parameters of moral responsibility and then adduce a particular instance within a specific genocide as revealing some feature about moral responsibility.[6] With these sorts of approaches, it is often irrelevant which particular genocide is being discussed or whether the perpetrator in question is from the Nazi *Waffen-SS* or Hutu *interahamwe*. While this generality may or may not be problematic for the study of genocide *as such* (see my discussion of the Nazi genocide in the next section), the chief issue with the approaches just outlined is that they are not really insights into genocide, at least no more than discussions of murder generate insights into suicide—that is, such discussions are and are not insightful (they are insofar as suicide is a species of murder, but they are not insofar as the differences between the two seems to be precisely the point). Furthermore, it should be noted that defining philosophy is as problematic as defining genocide

---

[2] See Adam Morton, *On Evil* (New York: Routledge, 2004).

[3] Emil Fackenheim criticized this sort of approach to the Nazi genocide in *To Mend the World* (Bloomington: Indiana University Press, 1994), 11.

[4] For a concise overview of Heidegger's thought vis-à-vis nihilism, see Robert B. Pippin, *Modernism as a Philosophical Problem: On the Dissatisfaction of European High Culture*, 2nd edn (Oxford: Blackwell, 1999), 114–44.

[5] See Richard Wolin, *The Terms of Cultural Criticism: The Frankfurt School, Existentialism, Poststructuralism* (New York: Columbia University, 1995), 142. For a compelling rebuttal of Wolin and readings akin to his, see Philippe Lacoue-Labarthe, *Heidegger, Art, and Politics: The Fiction of the Political*, trans. Chris Turner (Oxford: Basil Blackwell, 1990). There is here an added question of Heidegger's relation to the Nazi genocide in the context of Nazism. See §6.

[6] See, for example, Geoffrey Scarre's 'Moral Responsibility and the Holocaust', in Eve Garrard and Geoffrey Scarre (eds), *Moral Philosophy and the Holocaust* (Burlington: Ashgate, 2003), 103–16.

(see below): the philosophical enterprise itself is often a contested or multifaceted mode of inquiry,[7] spanning a variety of approaches and orientations.

§2

Before suggesting an alternative way in which philosophers can contribute to the study of genocide (§§7–10), I would like, in the several sections that follow, to review the various species of ways in which philosophers have specifically addressed genocide. I should mention that when discussing genocide, philosophers like many scholars have often focused on the Nazi genocide. This attention is not unjustifiable,[8] but I do think that it can be dangerous by giving one the false sense that whatever one says about the Nazi genocide can thereby be said of genocide as such. That is one issue; another is that the uniqueness of the Nazi genocide has itself become a topic of inquiry, with some stressing its uniqueness.[9] I do not enter this debate in any fashion here, except only to say both that I view the Nazi genocide as an act of genocide and that concerns about the applicability of philosophical insights gleaned from an analysis of the Nazi genocide must be addressed on a case by case basis in order to determine their applicability to genocide as such.

This point about the status of Nazi actions vis-à-vis genocide and their uniqueness or lack thereof naturally suggests one of the first areas of inquiry pursued by philosophers: the definition of genocide itself. There are different ways of framing this question: one may inquire about the definition itself—what does it mean to commit an act of genocide? What other terms does it presuppose for its efficacy? How does it differ from ethnic cleansing or mass murder? Or, alternatively, one may ask about the nature of the groups targeted by perpetrators—what sorts of

---

[7] For some of the issues, see Richard Rorty, 'Analytic and Conversational Philosophy', in *idem* (ed.), *Philosophy as Cultural Politics: Philosophical Papers*, vol. 4 (Cambridge: Cambridge University Press, 2007), 120–31.

[8] Particularly, since *historically* the event often is taken to be a watershed event. See Christopher Browning, *Nazi Policy, Jewish Workers, German Killers* (Cambridge: Cambridge University Press, 2000), 32. The question here, of course, is whether the same is true *philosophically*.

[9] See Alan Rosenberg, 'Was the Holocaust Unique? A Peculiar Question?', in Isidor Walliman and Michael N. Dobkowski (eds), *Genocide and the Modern Age* (New York: Greenwood, 1987), 145–61. Also, Kenneth Seeskin, 'What Philosophy Can and Cannot Say about Evil?', in Alan Rosenberg and Gerald E. Myers (eds), *Echoes from the Holocaust* (Philadelphia: Temple University, 1988). More recently, Norman Geras also takes up this issue in 'In a Class of its Own?', in Garrard and Scarre (eds), *Moral Philosophy and the Holocaust*, 25–57.

groups can be the victims of genocide?[10] Obviously, these questions are related: one's definition informs what sorts of groups fall under its purview and one's understanding of victim groups informs one's definition. This is furthermore complicated by the fact that genocide is largely a legal term,[11] and so already some legal framework is implicitly presupposed. I mention this here at the outset because it is not at first obvious why philosophers should be any more qualified to define or comment on genocide in this definitional capacity than jurists or social scientists. One way to refine this point is to distinguish between two approaches to genocide definition. On one hand, one can be doing work with genocide definition in order to find ways to link particular events together or as a precursor to a typology of genocide. In proceeding this way one must be able to cogently distinguish genocide from ethnocide (or 'cultural' genocide), take stock of various proposed definitions, perhaps account for its misuse, and so forth. On the other hand, however, one could be working with the definition in order to make sense of what it would mean for an agent to have the intention of genocide. These two approaches are not mutually exclusive, but the former is largely a task best left to jurists, historians, and social scientists, since they are more equipped to proceed in such a fashion,[12] while the latter is eminently ripe for philosophical discussion. Indeed, the notion of intention—a philosophical mainstay since philosophy's inception—underpins the two parameters (act and group membership) mentioned above.

§3

Several distinct questions emerge with a consideration of intention in the context of genocide. First, is the question of whether perpetrators can intend to do evil: that is, do we take it that genocide perpetration involves wanting to do evil or are the perpetrators acting on (ultimately incoherent or mistaken) utilitarian grounds (i.e. are they ultimately assuming that they are acting for the good)?[13] Related to this

[10] Compare to Berel Lang, *Act and Idea in the Nazi Genocide* (Chicago: University of Chicago Press, 1990), 6.

[11] For two differing positions on whether genocide is fundamentally a legal or a sociological term, see William A. Schabas, 'The Law and Genocide' and Martin Shaw, 'Sociology and Genocide', both in this volume.

[12] Two overviews of the issues involved in such an approach are Mark Levene, *Genocide in the Age of the Nation State*, 4 vols, vol i: *The Meaning of Genocide* (London: I. B. Tauris, 2005); and Scott Straus, 'Contested Meanings and Conflicting Imperatives: A Conceptual Analysis of Genocide', *Journal of Genocide Research* 3:3 (2001), 349–75.

[13] Lang, *Act and Idea in the Nazi Genocide*, 26.

question is the question of what perpetrators must ultimately think of victims. Is it the case that it is truly possible to treat victims as not human? Or is it the case that any treatment, no matter how inhuman, fundamentally presupposes a victim's human agency?[14]

A not wholly unrelated, even broader question centres on the very nature of intention itself. First, one may ask whether and to what extent it is possible to separate—prior to the act—intentions from actions.[15] Second, and related, the way an action is understood is dependent on the way in which it is described: the same action may be susceptible to more than one correct description.[16] It is possible, then, that the same action could turn out to be intentional or unintentional, depending on the way in which it is described; furthermore, descriptions themselves then become a site for philosophical discussion, particularly in the context of genocide. It may be that the whole view of selves as discrete monads expressing 'inner' states via 'outer' acts is itself problematic and that the self is itself a fundamental social achievement, its inner and outer components being inseparable from its existence in a social space.[17]

From a certain perspective, then, debates like those that took place between functionalists and intentionalists seem unusually contrived, with both sides starting with not only unconvincing, but also unexamined views of individuals and acts.[18] Further, the relative reconciliation between the two groups seems almost accidental, with neither having examined the expansive philosophical literature on the topic.[19]

Likewise, read with these issues in mind, Hannah Arendt's work then becomes the obverse side of this discussion.[20] The *banality of evil* is an affirmation not only of the fundamentally social nature of selfhood, but also a powerful comment on all of the issues raised here. In addition to the trivial point that genocide requires a particular social backdrop to its execution, I take Arendt to argue that 'thoughtlessness' is a particular, modern way of comporting oneself towards or navigating

[14] Berel Lang, 'The Concept of Genocide', *Philosophical Forum* 16:1–2 (1984/5), 10–13. Also see Stanley Cavell, *The Claim of Reason: Wittgenstein, Skepticism, Morality, and Tragedy* (Oxford: Oxford University Press, 1979), 375–8.

[15] Lang, *Act and Idea in the Nazi Genocide*, 24.

[16] See Donald Davidson, 'Actions, Reasons, and Causes', in *Essays on Actions and Events* (Oxford: Oxford University Press, 2001).

[17] Terry Pinkard, *Hegel's Phenomenology: The Sociality of Reason* (Cambridge: Cambridge University, 1996), 142.

[18] Berel Lang makes an analogous point in 'Philosophy's Contribution to Holocaust Studies', in Garrard and Scarre (eds), *Moral Philosophy and the Holocaust*, 6.

[19] Two excellent overviews of the philosophical issues involved in analysing intentions are G. E. M. Anscombe, *Intention* (Ithaca, NY: Cornell University, 1969); and Alfred Mele (ed.), *The Philosophy of Action* (Oxford: Oxford University Press, 1997).

[20] For a more elaborate treatment of Arendt from social psychological perspective, see Paul A. Roth, '*Hier ist kein Warum*: Philosophical Reflections on the Social Psychology of Genocide', in this volume.

the world, one that involves seeing people and things in a distinct light and one that in no way abrogates responsibility, at least no more than the almost automatic actions of a virtuous person preclude them from moral praise.[21] Read in this light, then, the earlier *Origins of Totalitarianism* has a strong link to *Eichmann in Jerusalem*: the former provides the theoretical backdrop for the latter, laying out the social and ethical structures and conditions for the destruction of human spontaneity, while the latter explores the moral psychology of a perpetrator in such a state of affairs.[22] Furthermore, it is precisely at this point that Michel Foucault's and Giorgio Agamben's work on *biopolitics*—the idea that the modern sovereign has power not just over subjects but power of administration over the biological process as such (i.e., power over life, not just death)—connects to our discussion.[23] If we find Arendt's reading of totalitarianism as the project of the destruction of human spontaneity compelling,[24] then biopolitics becomes the (or arguably, *a*) means of completing the account, of sketching its stakes and logic.[25] Through biopower, the involvement of a state in the regulation of ever more levels of human life down to bodily control, reproduction, and ultimately consciousness, a state strives to radically alter the nature(s) of its subjects, thereby transforming the very makeup of the state from the 'ground up'.

§4

As I mentioned earlier, however, intentions are only one side of the coin; scholars have focused as well on elaborating the notion of victim groups as a way of linking act/intention and genocide. One way to do this is to elaborate a thesis of 'social death', wherein what is produced is a 'meaninglessness of one's life and even of its termination'.[26] Social death is a state of affairs where one is 'no longer able to pass

---

[21] Compare to John McDowell's position on virtue: John McDowell, *Mind, Value, and Reality* (Cambridge: Harvard University Press, 1998), 77–221.

[22] Richard J. Bernstein, *Hannah Arendt and the Jewish Question* (Cambridge, MA: MIT Press, 1996), 137–53. For an opposing view, see Dana Villa, 'Conscience, the Banality of Evil, and Idea of a Representative Perpetrator', in *Politics, Philosophy, Terror: Essays on the Thought of Hannah Arendt* (Princeton: Princeton University Press, 1999), 39–61.

[23] See Giorgio Agamben, *Homo Sacer: Sovereign Power and Bare Life* (Stanford: Stanford University, 1998), Michel Foucault, *The History of Sexuality*, vol. 1 (New York: Vintage, 1978), 135–59.

[24] See Hannah Arendt, *The Origins of Totalitarianism* (London André Deutsch, 1986), 437–60.

[25] For more on this, see J. M. Bernstein, 'Intact and Fragmented Bodies: Version of Ethics "after Auschwitz"', *New German Critique* 33:1 (2006), 40.

[26] Claudia Card, 'Genocide and "Social Death"', *Hypatia* 18:1 (2003), 73.

along build upon ... traditions, cultural developments ... and projects of earlier generations.'[27] By focusing on the consequences for victim groups, the social death view is able to account for a meaningful distinction between mass murder and genocide, but only at the expense of collapsing the distinction between ethnic cleansing and genocide (already fragile and partial as it is).[28] On this view, what is important is the 'social health' of a particular group.[29] Stress is taken off 'mere' physical well being (although this too is important) and put onto the various items that feed into providing a meaningful life for agents (such social goods as relation-ships, goals, and traditions). Furthermore, it is precisely the assault on these social components that makes social death intolerable, ultimately distinguishing geno-cide from mass murder of individuals as individuals. The chief issue with this view is that although perverse, it may nonetheless be true that genocidal suffering may contribute to the flourishing of social health (indeed, one can imagine robust communities created solely due to such suffering). If one finds this depraved and points to the great bodily harm (and mass death) involved in such suffering, then one is invoking a standard above and beyond that of social death, and so the original intention of the thesis loses its potency. All of this points to the funda-mentally normative character of what is used to anchor this view: that social death is an evil precisely because it is intolerable—but 'intolerable' is itself a contested term that pushes those invoking it to instance some other justification or justifica-tory standard.[30]

§5

The focus on victim groups above goes hand in hand with three other broad areas of inquiry that philosophers have pursued: trauma, memory, and the limits and status of representation. Often drawing on the connections between these three, one can ask about the experience of and relationship between trauma and memory; and in doing so, one may ask about the limits of representation.

[27] Ibid. Card is drawing on the work of Orlando Patterson; see Orlando Patterson, *Slavery and Social Death* (Cambridge, MA: Harvard University Press, 1982).

[28] In defending Card, Mohammed Abed embraces this conclusion. See Mohammed Abed, 'Clarifying the Concept of Genocide', *Metaphilosophy* 37:3–4 (2006), 308–30.

[29] This phrase is mine.

[30] For more on this, see Adam Morton, 'Inequity/Iniquity: Card on Balancing Injustice and Evil', *Hypatia* 19:4 (2004), 199.

Generally, discussion of this point can be mapped onto two opposing poles,[31] consisting of realists and antirealists.[32] In discussing the Nazi genocide, for example, Zygmunt Bauman is able, via a realist account (an account that purports to provide a sufficient theoretical explanation that posits a more or less ascertainable correspondence between its terms and the empirical reality to which its terms allude), to make the genocide intelligible using a sociological framework.[33] Alternatively, Elie Wiesel has argued that the Nazi genocide simply cannot be explained, that it ultimately 'transcends history'.[34] In turn, Giorgio Agamben has attempted to draw the implications of looking at the relationship as a fundamentally contradictory or *aporetic* one: where the notion of testimony is precisely the relation between being compelled to bear witness to an event that fundamentally cannot be witnessed.[35]

Attempting to bypass this debate, some have tried to ignore this broader question of the relationship between these two poles and instead have focused on analysing issues that transcend or saturate these poles. For example, philosophers since Augustine have inquired about the nature of memory, and it is quite possible that genocide either introduces some sort of particular nuance on the topic or raises fundamental issues about or in relation to it.[36] Or the experience of trauma or suffering as such may fundamentally alter one's constitution of experience and/ or the self (whether experientially, phenomenologically, or otherwise).[37] Indeed, in exploring this area, one quickly notices that the three topics mentioned in the beginning of this section are difficult to unweave: they point towards one another.[38] Although a difficulty, this is also precisely where more 'genocide'-themed philosophy precisely pushes back towards 'mainstream' philosophical concerns with the nature of the self, the philosophy of mind, and so forth.

---

[31] For an overview, see Michael Rothberg, 'Introduction', to *Traumatic Realism: The Demands of Holocaust Representation* (Minneapolis: University of Minnesota Press, 2000).

[32] For an example of the former, see the aforementioned Hannah Arendt, *Eichmann in Jerusalem* (New York: Viking Press, 1963). For an example of the latter, see Arthur A. Cohen, *The Tremendum* (New York: Continuum, 1981).

[33] Zygmunt Bauman, *Modernity and the Holocaust* (Ithaca, NY: Cornell University, 2000).

[34] Irving Abramson (ed.), *Against Silence: The Voice of and the Vision of Elie Wiesel* (New York: Holocaust Library, 1985), 158, Elie Wiesel, 'Trivializing the Holocaust: Semi-Fact and Semi-Fiction', *New York Times*, 16 April 1978.

[35] Giorgio Agamben, *Remants of Auschwitz* (New York: Zone, 1999), 13. See also Sara Kofman, *Smothered Words*, trans. Madeleine Dobie (Evanston: Northwestern University Press, 1998), 36.

[36] For an overview, see Robert Eaglestone, *The Holocaust and the Postmodern* (Oxford: Oxford University Press, 2004), especially 72–101.

[37] Adorno has been read as developing this thread. For more on this point, see Raymond Geuss, 'Suffering and Knowledge in Adorno', *Constellations* 12:1 (2005), 3–20. The aforementioned Rothberg book, *Traumatic Realism*, attempts to think through a realist account under the aspect of trauma.

[38] Ruth Leys's genealogical analysis of trauma superlatively illustrates precisely this point; see Ruth Leys, *Trauma: A Genealogy* (Chicago: University of Chicago, 2000).

§6

The approaches sketched in §§3–5 manage to tease philosophical threads out of genocide, but it may be possible that the enterprise of philosophy itself—as such—is causally connected to genocide. There are many ways to establish this connection: one can argue that certain thinkers (e.g. Heidegger or Nietzsche) endorsed philosophical positions that directly led to, encouraged, or justified genocide.[39] Or one may argue that the whole of the philosophical tradition is analogously related to genocide (whether as direct input or as intellectual precursor); that is, that the philosophical tradition itself carries a kernel of thinking or proposes an orientation to the world that is somehow explicitly or implicitly genocidal.[40] However one draws this connection, under this rubric, some sort of, generally causal, connection is established between a particular philosophical position and genocide.

There are many problems with this sort of approach. First is that it commonly elides the distinction between complicity and causality (and, furthermore, does not even distinguish between degrees of complicity).[41] Second, there is the danger of mere *reductio ad Hitlerum*, that is, of mere guilt by association. Third, and most important, however, is that crucial differences on both ends of discussion, on the pole of genocide or philosophy, are simply overlooked or elided. On the pole of genocide, this approach can fundamentally miss the specificity of genocide and perpetrators, lumping very diverse groups of perpetrators together, ignoring their individual differences in motivation for, role in, and history amidst genocide.[42] In order to draw analogues between X ideology and Y philosophy, one must posit a coherent ideology X, but what genocide study has revealed is that genocides often only have vague (or confused or diverse or multifaceted) ideologies behind them

[39] See, e.g., Hubert Kiesewetter, *Von Hegel zu Hitler: Die politische Verwirklichung einer totalitären Machtstaatstheorie in Deutschland, 1815–1945* (Frankfurt am Main: Peter Lang, 1974); Abir Taha, *Nietzsche, Prophet of Nazism: The Cult of the Superman—Unveiling the Nazi Secret Doctrine* (Bloomington: AuthorHouse, 2005), Richard Wolin, *The Politics of Being* (New York: Columbia University Press, 1990); idem, *The Seduction of Unreason: The Intellectual Romance with Fascism from Nietzsche to Postmodernism* (Princeton: Princeton University Press, 2006). See also fn 5 above.

[40] See, e.g., David Patterson, 'The Complicity of Modern Philosophy in the Extermination of the Jews', in Dennis B. Klein, et al. (eds), *The Genocidal Mind: Selected Papers from the 32nd Annual Scholars' Conference on the Holocaust and the Churches* (St Paul: Paragon House, 2005), 32–63, idem, *Open Wounds: The Crisis of Jewish Thought in the Aftermath of Auschwitz* (Seattle: University of Washington Press, 2006).

[41] For more on this, see David E. Cooper, 'Ideology, Moral Complicity and the Holocaustm', in Garrard and Scarre (eds), *Moral Philosophy and the Holocaust*, 9–24.

[42] See Peter Haas's critique of David Patterson in John K. Roth (ed.), *Ethics after the Holocaust: Perspectives, Critiques, and Responses* (St. Paul: Paragon House, 1999), 177–80.

and that the variety of agents involved in genocide are often operating at different levels of influence vis-à-vis ideology (if at all).[43]

Analogously, scholars may perform the same selective procedure at the philosophical end of the discussion: they may cast their philosophical figures in hackneyed or uncritical terms, ignoring certain sources in favour of others, or simply approaching the sources they do pick with a lack of subtlety.[44] For scholars who urge a relationship between not just a particular philosopher, but the whole philosophical tradition, these two dangers are compounded by a third. Often, scholars who posit the case must oppose the philosophical tradition *to* something—in some cases it is religion,[45] or in others it is an alternate or revised conception of philosophy.[46] The danger here is that oppositions of this sort are difficult to delineate let alone maintain, particularly as the scholars in question are—presumably—incapable of fully transcending the philosophical traditions which they implicate in genocide; at the very least, it is not so easy to *think through* such an opposition, as opposed to merely posit it (such oppositions perhaps may be maintained, but they are generally marshalled with insufficient resources).[47]

In addition, the analogy to the approach sketched in §1 should by now be apparent. This approach proceeds largely by taking genocide as an instantiation of a deeper difficulty: whether it is a problem with the philosophical tradition as such or a problem with a particular philosopher who makes, by association or appropriation, certain segments or types of society susceptible to genocide perpetration. These issues, however, are insufficiently contextualized—historically and philosophically—and thereby genocide is seen to arise—at least philosophically— out of thin air. If, for example, we take Nietzsche's *will to power* to be the force that

[43] For more on this point with respect to the Nazi genocide, see Donald Bloxham and Tony Kushner, *The Holocaust: Critical Historical Approaches* (Manchester: Manchester University Press, 2005), 61–176. For Rwanda, see Scott Straus, *The Order of Genocide: Race, Power, and War in Rwanda* (Ithaca, NY: Cornell University Press, 2008), 65–153. Analogous procedures can be performed with all of the major genocides of the twentieth century.

[44] Figures like Kant, Hegel, and Nietzsche are notoriously misrepresented in this literature. All three figures had a very complex relationship, e.g., to Judaism. For a corrective on Hegel and Nietzsche, see Yirmiyahu Yovel, *Dark Riddle: Hegel, Nietzsche, and the Jews* (Cambridge: Polity, 1998). As well, for Nietzsche, see Weaver Santaniello, *Nietzsche, God, and the Jews: His Critique of Judeo-Christianity in Relation to the Nazi Myth* (Buffalo: State University of New York Press, 1994). In order to deal with Kant's relationship to Judaism, one would need to take seriously Kant's developments in the *Opus Postumum*, as I intend to in future work.

[45] E.g., for David Patterson, it is a particular gloss of Judaism. See Patterson, *Open Wounds*, 32–63.

[46] I will come to this shortly, but I have in mind thinkers like Adorno and Levinas.

[47] For more on some of the issues with this and the opposition between Judaism/Greek thought (of which David Patterson makes so much of), see Leora Batnitzky, *Leo Strauss and Emmanuel Levinas: Philosophy and the Politics of Revelation* (Cambridge: Cambridge University Press, 2006), 5–8. See also the classic piece by Derrida, 'Violence and Metaphysics', in *Writing and Difference* (Chicago: University of Chicago, 1978), 79–154. On the point of philosophy and religion, see Hent de Vries, *Philosophy and the Turn to Religion* (Baltimore: Johns Hopkins University Press, 1999).

drives genocide, then it remains entirely unanswered not only why the *will to power* must manifest itself in this fashion, as opposed to, e.g., 'mere' mass murder or *pogromic* violence or disciplinary force or whatever, but also why the *will to power* became a compelling philosophical position in such a context in the first place. Just as historical analyses of genocide must be situated in a broader matrix of Western history and civilization, so too must philosophical analyses be deployed in a similar expansive but nonetheless historicized context.[48]

§7

One way to respond to the above problems of contextualization is to attempt to connect the project of Enlightenment with genocide. There are others, but I focus on the Enlightenment precisely for its suggestiveness and its scope.[49] On such a move, genocide becomes a structural fixture within the evolution of the broader landscape of our political, economic, and social systems and commitments. This proposal, of course, is a very complicated procedure. First, 'Enlightenment' is a contested term. Second, making sense of the relation—if any—between Enlightenment and genocide is notoriously difficult.[50] In part, this has to do with the relationship between ideas and events: in a certain sense, it is obviously true that the Enlightenment had a hand in what came after it—but in this sense, it is trivial, as trivial as pointing out that metallurgy or the principle of non-contradiction had a hand in genocide. In another sense, it is patently unbelievable to assert that the Enlightenment as a series of events had anything to do with genocide.

The key, then, is in how we gloss our terms ('genocide' included, see §2). The concerns here can be separated most broadly into historical and philosophical ones. The historical issues include *locating* the Enlightenment: was there a coherent

[48] For an argument for the necessity of such a historical contextualization as well as an example of it, see Levene, *Genocide in the Age of the Nation State.*

[49] A related approach would be to connect genocide to modernity. For an overview, see A. Dirk Moses, 'Genocide and Modernity', in Dan Stone (ed.), *The Historiography of Genocide* (Houndmills: Palgrave Macmillan, 2008), 156–92. See also Martin Shaw's discussion of Zygmunt Bauman in his 'Sociology and Genocide', in this volume. As well, one could focus on capitalism; see Moishe Postone's 'Nationalsozialismus und Antisemitismus: ein theoretischer Versuch', in Dan Diner (ed.), *Zivilisationsbruch: Denken nach Auschwitz* (Frankfurt am Main: Fischer, 1988), 242–254; Moishe Postone, *Time, Labor, and Domination: A Reinterpretation of Marx's Critical Theory* (Cambridge: Cambridge University Press, 1993).

[50] For an overview, see John Docker, 'The Enlightenment, Genocide, Postmodernity', *Journal of Genocide Research* 5:3 (2003), 339–60.

Enlightenment programme? Who were its chief figures, time periods, and locales?[51] The philosophical issues include, implicitly, these historical issues as well as the problem of accounting for the scope of the enlightenment: if enlightenment thinking is taken in a broad enough sense, then it includes the very project of philosophy itself, and if that is the case, then it becomes difficult—if not impossible—to use philosophy to criticize its own shortcomings. Indeed, there arise then crucial and complex issues centring on autonomy.[52] Ultimately, if a mode of thinking itself is at stake—as opposed to any particular historical period—then questions of method must be explicitly addressed. Horkheimer and Adorno's *Dialectic of Enlightenment* (*DE*) is fruitful in this context; I turn to it in the following sections.[53]

§8

....

When one looks at *DE*, however, it is not at first obvious that the account therein has anything at all to do with genocide. Indeed, Horkheimer and Adorno write in the Preface that they 'had set out to . . . explain why humanity, instead of arriving at a truly human condition, is sinking into a new type of barbarism' (*DE* xiv/16).[54] Of course, this question is so broad as to border on vacuous, so Horkheimer and Adorno quickly revise their intentions as 'merely' inquiring about the 'self-destruction of enlightenment' (*DE* xvi/18). As per §7, this question brings to the fore the problem of how to understand 'enlightenment' in *DE*. Adorno and Horkheimer urge the reader not to understand the enlightenment in *DE* as designating a

---

[51] For more on these issues and others surrounding the Enlightenment, see Peter Gay, *The Enlightenment: The Rise of Modern Paganism* (New York: W. W. Norton, 1995), *idem*, *The Enlightenment: The Science of Freedom* (New York: W. W. Norton, 1996), Jonathan I. Israel, *Radical Enlightenment: Philosophy and the Making of Modernity* (Oxford: Oxford University Press, 2002), *idem*, *Enlightenment Contested: Philosophy, Modernity, and the Emancipation of Man* (Oxford: Oxford University Press, 2009).

[52] For an elaboration of this point, see Pippin, *Modernism as a Philosophical Problem*.

[53] The English edition cited is Max Horkheimer and Theodor W. Adorno, *Dialectic of Enlightenment, Philosophical Fragments*, ed. Mieke Bal and Hent de Vries, trans. Edmund Jephcott (Stanford: Stanford University Press, 2002). The German cited is Max Horkheimer, *Gesammelte Schriften*, 19 vols (Frankfurt am Main: S. Fischer, 1987), vol. v. Henceforth, *DE*. All citations in this piece will follow the format of English/German.

[54] Translation modified. Indeed, this opening claim seems precisely to countermand the advice of their friend Benjamin. In his eighth thesis, Benjamin wrote: 'The current amazement that the things we are experiencing are "still" possible in the twentieth century is *not* philosophical. This amazement is not the beginning of knowledge—unless it is the knowledge that the view of history which gives rise to it is untenable.' See Walter Benjamin, 'Theses on the Philosophy of History', in *Illuminations* (New York: Shocken Books, 1968), 253–65.

historical period, but rather a process (*DE* 1/25).[55] In order to make sense of the continual reference to the entirety of the Western philosophical and extra-philosophical tradition, we must understand this 'process' maximally as involving not a critique of culture detailing the various failings of some ill-defined 'Enlightenment Project',[56] but rather as involving a philosophical interrogation of the most basic elements of thinking which aims to enlighten, where such thinking is taken in the broadest possible terms. As Horkheimer and Adorno write: 'Enlightenment understood in the widest sense as the advance of thought, has always aimed at liberating human beings from fear and installing them as masters' (*DE* 1/25). This notion of enlightenment designates an outlook that spans a variety of temporal and spatial boundaries.

If we take enlightenment in this sense, then, we need to sketch, at least in broad terms, some of the claims that Horkheimer and Adorno do make about enlightenment, particularly in the specific relationship that they propose between enlightenment and myth. Adorno and Horkheimer write:

Enlightenment has always regarded anthropomorphism, the projection of subjective properties onto nature, as the basis of myth. The supernatural, spirits and demons, are taken to be reflections of human beings who allow themselves to be frightened by natural phenomena. According to enlightened thinking, the multiplicity of mythical figures can be reduced to a single common denominator, the subject. (*DE* 4/28)

Furthermore, they propose that ultimately 'enlightenment . . . wanted to dispel myths, to overthrow fantasy with knowledge' (*DE* 1/25). In this sense, the idea is that 'the mind, conquering superstition, is to rule over disenchanted nature' (*DE* 2/26). Knowledge, then, is power. What is more, it is a power that 'knows no limits, either in its enslavement of creation or in its deference to worldly masters' (*DE* 2/26). So much so that if it is allowed to develop unchecked by anything external, enlightenment turns on everything, including the things that it professed to hold dear. All ideas, but most notoriously professedly universalistic ideas like human rights, become suspect and take on a mythical light (*DE* 3/27). Every 'definite theoretical view is subjected to the annihilating criticism that it is only a belief, until even the concepts of mind, truth, and, indeed, enlightenment itself have been reduced to animistic magic' (*DE* 7/33). As Horkheimer and Adorno point out, 'in the authority of universal concepts enlightenment detected a fear of the demons through whose effigies human beings had tried to influence nature in magic rituals' (*DE* 3/27).[57] Indeed, 'no difference is said to exist between the totemic animal, the dreams of the spirit-seer, and the absolute Idea' (*DE* 3/27). Ultimately, 'anything

---

[55] For more on this, see Simon Jarvis, *Adorno: A Critical Introduction* (Cambridge: Polity Press, 1998), 24–6.

[56] James Schmidt, 'What Enlightenment Project?,' *Political Theory* 28:6 (2000), 734–57.

[57] Translation modified.

which does not conform to the standard of calculability and utility must be viewed with suspicion' (*DE* 3/28). In short, 'enlightenment is totalitarian' (*DE* 3/28).

Continuing with the political metaphor, Horkheimer and Adorno write, 'enlightenment stands in the same relationship to things as the dictator to human beings. He knows them to the extent that he can manipulate them' (*DE* 6/31). Since enlightenment is merely the removal of fear of the unknown, then humans only 'believe themselves free of fear when there is no longer anything unknown' (*DE* 11/38). To achieve this goal, the self ultimately equates truth in general with classifying thought (*DE* 10/36). Fate, then, which enlightenment sought to combat in its battle against mythology, returns, with a vengeance (*DE* 8–9/34–5). As Horkheimer and Adorno point out, 'abstraction, the instrument of enlightenment, stands in the same relationship to its objects as fate, whose concept it eradicates: as liquidation' (*DE* 9/36). Fate returns in the form of science: where fate once explained everything as pre-ordained, science performs the same procedure via lawful repetition within universal laws (*DE* 8/35). Furthermore, they write, again invoking a political metaphor, that 'the distance of subject from object, the presupposition of abstraction, is founded on the distance from things which the ruler attains by means of the ruled' (*DE* 9/36). Through distance from the particular object to abstraction in the form of universality, enlightenment reverts to the very mythology that it sought to overcome. Indeed, we have returned precisely to where we have started: everything is 'reduced to a single common denominator', namely, 'the subject' (*DE* 4/29). Not only that, but Horkheimer and Adorno further claim that myth itself is already enlightenment since myth as well sought to 'report, to name, to tell of origins . . . therefore to narrate, record, explain' (*DE* 5/30). Moreover, since myths are continually collected and recorded, they themselves in the end become proper teachings and rituals. For this reason, myth ultimately 'becomes enlightenment' (*DE* 6/31). Indeed, mythology actually 'set in motion the endless process of enlightenment', since 'magic like science is concerned with ends' (*DE* 7/33). In short, then, 'just as myths already entail enlightenment, with every step enlightenment entangles itself more deeply in mythology' (*DE* 8/34).

According to Horkheimer and Adorno, this dialectic then precisely presupposes genocide—as an institution—as its teleological conclusion. As Adorno writes later in *Negative Dialectics* (*ND*): 'Genocide is the absolute integration. It is on its way wherever men are leveled off—"polished off," as the German military called it—until one exterminates them literally, as deviations from the concept of their total nullity. Auschwitz confirmed the philosopheme of pure identity as death' (*ND* 362/355).[58] Anything that is unable to be integrated is eliminated.

---

[58] The English edition cited is Theodor W. Adorno, *Negative Dialectics*, trans. E. B. Ashton (New York: Continuum, 1973). The German is Adorno, *Gesammelte Schriften*, 20 vols. (Frankfurt am Main: Suhrkamp Verlag, 1984), vol v. All citations in this piece will follow the format of English/German.

There is, however, a very deep question here about the *necessity* of this dialectic. Even if we grant Horkheimer and Adorno the myriad premises involved in their argument, it is still not apparent that all rationality—whether in the form of myth *or* enlightenment—*must* be so totalizing. Why precisely is genocide the teleological conclusion to this process? Even if we grant Adorno the premise 'that objects do not go into their concepts without leaving a remainder' (*ND* 5/15), that is, that there will always be something that cannot and will not be integrated, why precisely must this something be eliminated as opposed to, e.g., marginalized (apartheid) or disempowered (slavery) or spatially rather than 'existentially' eliminated (ethnic cleansing or exile)? While I do think that Horkheimer and Adorno have answers to these questions, elaborating them is beyond the scope of this chapter; rather, I would like to suggest an alternative way of instantiating the relationship between philosophy and genocide.

§9

It is imperative that philosophers start with the fact of genocide (itself already a mediated term denoting a variety of connected data). From this we should work backwards, not with the aspiration of being able to determine causally what prompted genocide, but rather with the intention of developing, at least provisionally, some account that can make sense of genocide within a broader philosophical picture, only in order *then*—and this is the crucial step—to be able to suggest some deeper or more fundamental area of philosophical inquiry as following *from* this account.[59] As an example, I would point out that a neglected significance of *DE* is that Horkheimer and Adorno mean to cast suspicion on the inviolability of any sort of philosophical justification: any ultimate philosophical ground or justification becomes suspect in light of their claims about reason via the elaboration of their dialectic.[60] The philosophical problem of genocide—if there is one—is not, then, that it occurs, but rather that we can make no ultimately justifiable argument for why it should not occur. Richard Rorty raises an analogous point when he writes the following:

all vocabularies, even those which contain the words which we take most seriously, the ones most essential to our self-descriptions—are human creations . . . this would mean giving up the idea that liberalism could be justified, and Nazi or Marxist enemies of liberalism refuted, by driving the latter up against an argumentative wall—forcing them to admit

---

[59] Hannah Arendt takes this approach in *Origins of Totalitarianism*. For more on this, see Robert Pippin's 'Hannah Arendt and the Bourgeois Origins of Totalitarian Evil', in Alan D. Schrift (ed.), *Modernity and the Problem of Evil* (Bloomington: Indiana University, 2005), 149.

[60] A notable exception to this neglect is J. M. Bernstein, *Adorno: Disenchantment and Ethics* (Cambridge: Cambridge University Press, 2001).

that liberal freedom has a 'moral privilege' which their own values lacked . . . any attempt to drive one's opponent up against a wall in this way fails when the wall against which he is driven comes to be seen as one more vocabulary, one more way of describing things.[61]

Indeed, to push Rorty's point further,[62] our liberal vocabulary (vocabulary used here in the aforementioned Rorty-ian gloss) has as much dissimilarity as it does similarity to, e.g., the vocabulary of the Third Reich.[63] For Horkheimer and Adorno, the disturbing implication of *DE* is that not merely totalitarian regimes, but rather the whole gamut of Western thinking is perhaps complicit, or at the very least, intimately close to the practice of genocide. Indeed, their account is fundamentally opposed to any reading of history that sees genocide as a barbaric or regressive tendency, as a deviation from modern Western civilization, or as something opposed to proper, progressive, enlightened thought. Ultimately, for them, not only is the dualism between the two naïve, but halting genocide is not simply getting people to be 'more Western', or 'more enlightened' or 'more like us'—these dualisms may themselves precisely be part of the problem.[64] Ultimately, then, *DE* contextualizes the practice of genocide in a broader Western framework. Where scholars are performing this procedure in a contextualized historical framework, by studying the complex historical web of global interests, narratives, and material conditions that contributes to, props up, or perhaps encourages genocide,[65] we should see Horkheimer and Adorno as initiating a fundamentally similar procedure, only in a philosophical register. It is in this vein that we should understand Adorno's 1959 claim, a claim he made after having returned to Germany, 'I consider the survival of National Socialism *within* democracy to be potentially more menacing than the survival of fascist tendencies *against* democracy.'[66] The problem, though, is not relativism or that we precisely have these competing vocabularies,[67]

---

[61] See Richard Rorty, *Contingency, Irony, and Solidarity* (Cambridge: Cambridge University, 1989), 53.

[62] It may be the case that there is something to be said about how, when, and why vocabularies change and that Rorty's position that it is all contingency is dogmatic: see Pippin, *Modernism as a Philosophical Problem*, 69.

[63] It is in this tenor that we should read Peter J. Haas, *Morality after Auschwitz* (Philadelphia: Fortress Press, 1988), Claudia Koonz, *The Nazi Conscience* (Cambridge, MA: Harvard University Press, 2003).

[64] In this sense, we can see it as the philosophical counterpart to historical studies such as Levene, *Genocide in the Age of the Nation State*; and Michael Mann, *The Dark Side of Democracy: Explaining Ethnic Cleansing* (Cambridge: Cambridge University Press, 2005).

[65] See ibid.

[66] Theodor W. Adorno, *Critical Models: Interventions and Catchwords*, trans. Henry W. Pickford (New York: Columbia University Press, 1998), 90.

[67] For an analysis of the connection between relativism and genocide, see Michael Freeman, 'Speaking about the Unspeakable: Genocide and Philosophy', *Journal of Applied Philosophy* 8:1 (1991), 3–17.

but rather that we have these competing vocabularies and they are in such *close proximity* to each other.[68]

Ultimately, given that these competing vocabularies are bound to rub against each other and given that such friction and disagreement is ultimately a constitutive part of any community,[69] I want to suggest that the question becomes: given this proximity and inherent friction of vocabularies, how does or can disagreement lead to cohesion or unity without silencing certain segments of society or without manifest conflict with others? Ultimately, how do we achieve community? This question, I want to urge, though is not a question *explicitly* about how to structure or organize our communities, but rather is a question about the very possibility of community. Given the failure of any cognitive model to show conclusively the necessity of a global community,[70] how is it that we can achieve a solidarity that would countenance the claims of *any* segment of the global population, not just those segments closest to us (whether spatially or otherwise)? Again, this is not, at this point, a question about the empirical specifics of any particular community, or of community as such. (Indeed, it may be the case that the notion of a 'global community' is itself problematic and that we should be after 'communities' in the plural.) Such empirical matters are deeply important, particularly given the omnipresence, historically, of the notion of community to the execution of genocide, but answers to these empirical concerns, however, can only be properly justified after the theoretical ground, centring on how to gloss the idea of duties or commitments to one another, has been cleared.

§10

It is in this tenor that we should understand the later Adorno's stress on education 'after Auschwitz' (Adorno's stress on the Holocaust should be taken with the caveat vis-à-vis this point in §4) and his insistence on a new categorical imperative.[71] As

---

[68] This issue could be framed as drawing out certain stakes of Davidson's argument that there can be no differing conceptual schemes. See Donald Davidson, 'On the Very Idea of a Conceptual Scheme', in *Inquiries into Truth and Interpretation*, 2nd edn (Oxford: Clarendon, 2001), 183–99. Also, see *idem*, 'A Coherence Theory of Truth and Knowledge', in *Subjective, Intersubjective, Objective* (Oxford: Clarendon, 2001), 137–54. Of course, there are deep differences between Rorty and Davidson, see Robert Brandom (ed.), *Rorty and His Critics* (Oxford: Blackwell, 2000), 65–81.

[69] This is a broad claim that I cannot properly contextualize and justify here, but Stanley Cavell has explored this issue in various texts. In particular, see his *The Claim of Reason: Wittgenstein, Skepticism, Morality, and Tragedy* (New York: Oxford University Press, 1979); and *Conditions Handsome and Unhandsome* (Chicago: University of Chicago, 1990).

[70] I take this to be a consequence of the argument of *DE*, although I have not made this argument explicitly.

[71] See Theodor Adorno, 'Education after Auschwitz', in *Critical Models*, 191–204.

he writes, 'Hitler has forced (*aufgezwungen*) a new categorical imperative upon humans in the condition of their unfreedom: to arrange their thoughts and actions so that Auschwitz will not repeat itself, so that nothing similar will occur' (*ND* 362/ 358).[72] Adorno's' new imperative poses many questions, not the least of which is what one should think of such a new imperative after 'a century of genocide'.[73] What is at least as interesting, if not more so, is that Adorno continues with the following:

> This imperative is as rebellious towards its justifications as the given one of Kant's. To deal with it discursively would be an outrage [*Frevel*]: for it causes us to feel, bodily, the moment of the moral addendum [*Hinzutretenden am Sittlichen*]. Bodily, because it is now the practical abhorrence of the unbearable physical agony to which individuals are exposed even with individuality about to vanish as a form of mental reflection. It is only in the unvarnished materialistic motive that that morality [*Moral*] lives on.' (*ND* 362/358)[74]

Adorno's stress seems precisely to be on an 'a-cognitive' (as opposed to non-cognitive) model of solidarity,[75] one that works along some sort of material axis, with the experience of raw bodily suffering prompting a response. This is what I take Adorno to mean by the 'unvarnished materialistic motive': the somatic experience of bodily suffering is to call forth an immediate response from an agent. To attempt to anchor this response in grounds or logical forms (as philosophy does) is to 'mock' the 'urgency' of this call (*ND* 285–6/280–3). Of course, it is notoriously difficult to determine how to 'cash out' this proposal of Adorno's,[76] since it precisely brings to the fore all of the methodological issues touched on earlier. Furthermore and most difficult, if we opt for this a-cognitive approach, how do we make sense of it philosophically?

To conclude, philosophers can ultimately contribute to genocide studies by trying their hands at these sorts of questions, formulating others in this vein, and all the while keeping the context (philosophical and historical) in which such questions arise in mind. The question of genocide—the philosophical problem of genocide—is really a cluster of problems that serves to highlight the systemic and structural nature of genocide. Indeed, if we see genocide as a wretched, but all too common means of resolving or incorporating conflicts,[77] then it becomes

---

[72] Translation modified.

[73] Samuel Totten and William S. Parsons (eds), *A Century of Genocide: Critical Essays and Eyewitness Accounts*, 3rd edn (New York: Routledge, 2008).

[74] Translation modified.

[75] There is an affinity between Adorno's proposal and Rorty's position in *Contingency, Irony, and Solidarity*. Where the two differ is that Rorty flatly says, 'there is no answer to the question, "Why not be cruel"—no noncircular theoretical backup for the belief that cruelty is horrible' (xv). Adorno would agree with Rorty, but would argue that there is such a backup along a material axis. Understanding this axis is precisely the challenge.

[76] For an attempt, see Bernstein, *Adorno*, 263–457.

[77] See Stanley Cavell's account of morality in *The Claim of Reason*, 269.

crucial to explore the deepest, most structural and systematic causes for conflict. Genocide, then, re-enters the philosophical frame as a distinctly modern, but nonetheless ultimately human possibility—one that has a particular genealogy and one that can be explored via its underpinnings in a complex network of philosophical commitments and positions.

ACKNOWLEDGEMENTS

Parts of this chapter were written under the auspices of a Diane and Howard Wohl Fellowship at the Center for Advanced Holocaust Studies, US Holocaust Memorial Museum, 2007–8. Thanks to the Center staff and fellows, as well, thanks to editors of this volume for their comments and suggestions.

SELECT BIBLIOGRAPHY

Agamben, Giorgio, *Homo Sacer: Sovereign Power and Bare Life* (Stanford: Stanford University, 1998).

Arendt, Hannah, *Eichmann in Jerusalem* (New York: Viking Press, 1963).

—— *The Origins of Totalitarianism* (London André Deutsch, 1986).

Card, Claudia, 'Genocide and Social Death,' *Hypatia* 18:1 (2003), 63–79.

Eaglestone, Robert, *The Holocaust and the Postmodern* (Oxford: Oxford University Press, 2004).

Garrard, Eve, and Geoffrey Scarre (eds), *Moral Philosophy and the Holocaust* (Burlington: Ashgate, 2003).

Horkheimer, Max, and Theodor W. Adorno. *Dialectic of Enlightenment, Philosophical Fragments*, trans. Edmund Jephcott, ed. Mieke Bal and Hent de Vries (Stanford: Stanford University Press, 2002).

Lang, Berel, *Act and Idea in the Nazi Genocide* (Chicago: University of Chicago Press, 1990).

Levene, Mark, *Genocide in the Age of the Nation State*. 4 vols (London: I. B. Tauris, 2005).

Pippin, Robert B., *Modernism as a Philosophical Problem: On the Dissatisfaction of European High Culture*, 2nd edn (Oxford: Blackwell, 1999).

Roth, John K. (ed.), *Ethics after the Holocaust: Perspectives, Critiques, and Responses* (St. Paul: Paragon House, 1999).

Rothberg, Michael, *Traumatic Realism: The Demands of Holocaust Representation* (Minneapolis: University of Minnesota Press, 2000).

PREMODERN AND EARLY MODERN GENOCIDE

CHAPTER 12

....

GENOCIDE IN THE ANCIENT WORLD

....

HANS VAN WEES

EUROPEAN literature begins with a story of genocide: the destruction of a city and its entire population in the legendary Trojan War. In a chilling episode of the *Iliad*, the commander-in-chief of the Greek army, Agamemnon, notices his brother hesitating to kill a Trojan captive, so:

He ran up to him, shouting his orders:

'Menelaos!...Not a single one of them must escape sheer destruction at our hands. Not even if a mother carries one in her belly and he is male, not even he should escape. All together they must be exterminated from Troy, their bodies untended and invisible.'

With these words the hero swayed his brother's mind, since he gave seemly advice.[1]

Modern readers find it hard to accept that genocide could be called 'seemly' (*aisima*), but although the *Iliad* sympathizes deeply with the sad fate of individual Trojans, it also places the blame for the war squarely on the Trojans' collective shoulders and there can be no reasonable doubt that for Homer the annihilation of the Trojans was a legitimate goal of war.[2]

---

[1] Homer, *Iliad* 6.54–65. (Translations from Greek and Latin are author's own; the Bible is cited from the Revised Standard Version; the sources of translations from other ancient languages are indicated in the notes.) This paper has benefited from the valuable comments and suggestions of Amélie Kuhrt, Karen Radner, and the editors.

[2] Hans van Wees, *Status Warriors* (Amsterdam: Gieben, 1992), 176–81; contra e.g. Simon Goldhill, 'Supplication and Authorial Comment in the *Iliad*: Iliad Z 61–2', *Hermes* 118 (1990), 373–6; Naoko Yamagata, '*Aisima pareipon*. A Moral Judgement by the Poet?', *La Parola del Passato* 45 (1990), 420–30.

The massacre of all Troy's male inhabitants and the enslavement of its women and children was fictional, but it had many counterparts in ancient history. It was almost the normative form of genocide—the use of that term will be justified shortly—in ancient Greece and some other parts of the ancient world, although mass enslavements and mass executions which made no distinctions of gender or age are also widely attested. The Greeks' reasons for treating the Trojans so brutally were typical of the motivations for genocide in antiquity: it was usually an act of 'conspicuous destruction', a display of force designed to assert the power and status of the perpetrator in the face of a perceived challenge. Ancient genocide sometimes had a religious dimension, but 'ethnic' or racial antagonism rarely if ever played a part.

Ancient history spans four millennia, from about 3500 BC to AD 500, a geographical range from Spain to Afghanistan, and a vast number of distinct societies and cultures, many of which changed dramatically over the centuries. Even if one concentrates on the first millennium BC, as this chapter does, largely omitting the civilizations of the Bronze Age and later Rome, to speak of 'genocide in antiquity' therefore entails extreme generalization. Yet broad patterns do emerge, and it is both possible and worthwhile to analyse in general terms the ideology, practice, and historical development of genocide in the ancient world.

'CUTTING OPEN PREGNANT WOMEN':
THE RHETORIC OF GENOCIDE

The evidence for genocide in antiquity ranges from highly rhetorical celebrations or condemnations of the annihilation of an enemy to laconic notices about the destruction of cities, and its value is often hard to assess. Is a claim that the enemy was 'utterly destroyed' a record of genocide or a hyperbolic boast of overwhelming victory? What does it mean when cities are said to be 'razed to the ground', when so many of these places reappear in the sources only a few years later, as if nothing had happened? We do not always have enough evidence to answer such questions. Yet even when we cannot tell what reality lay behind the words, the rhetoric is valuable because it reveals ancient ideologies of genocide.

A case in point is the horrific image of victorious besiegers who 'cut open pregnant women', which is occasionally found in Assyrian and Babylonian poems, repeatedly conjured up in the Bible, and implied in Agamemnon's exhortation to his brother. Its earliest appearance is in an Assyrian poem which probably glorifies a military victory of Tiglat-Pileser I, c.1100 BC:

> He slits the wombs of pregnant women; he blinds the infants.
> He cuts the throats of their strong ones. . . .
> Whoever offends the god Asshur will be turned into a ruin.[3]

The message here and in the biblical parallels is that enemies of all ages will be eliminated: adults killed by the sword, children blinded so as to render them helpless (or, elsewhere, beaten to death), and foetuses ripped from their mother's wombs. The sentiment is precisely that of Agamemnon: not even the unborn should be allowed to escape. In the *Iliad*, it is specifically male foetuses which are to be destroyed, and the Assyrian and Hebrew texts, too, seem to allude to the massacre of men ('the strong ones').[4]

The extermination of males of all ages is presented as legitimate punishment for offending Asshur or Yahweh. By contrast, the prophet Amos proclaims that God will punish the Ammonites who cut open pregnant women in the town of Gilead in Israel merely in order to 'enlarge their border'. Used in the naked pursuit of power, without religious justification, this form of genocide seemed unacceptable to a number of biblical authors.[5]

Did this brutal rhetoric correspond to an equally brutal practice? One could not, of course, selectively kill only male foetuses; the pregnant women and their unborn girls, too, would die. But conceivably this consequence was seen as acceptable 'collateral damage' of the symbolically important extermination of all males. Annalistic accounts of the events sung by poets and predicted by prophets, however, do not suggest that the entire male population was annihilated, even when it might have suited their purposes to make this claim.[6] As for the *Iliad*, the motif of killing unborn boys appears once only, and never again in the whole of Greek literature, which suggests that it was a piece of extreme rhetoric rather than a Greek genocidal practice. It may in fact have been a borrowing from the Near East by Greek raiders and mercenaries, which even as a rhetorical conceit proved too strong for later Greek tastes. This form of genocide thus served as the ultimate threat, boast, and accusation for centuries in the ancient world, but may never have been perpetrated.

An even more extreme example is the ideology of extermination set out in the laws of war formulated in Deuteronomy, and allegedly put into practice by the

---

[3] VAT 13833, rev. 3–6: text and translation in Mordechai Cogan, ' "Ripping Open Pregnant Women" in the Light of an Assyrian Analogue', *Journal of the American Oriental Society* 103 (1983), 755–8.

[4] The closest biblical parallels are Hosea 14.1 on Samaria and 2 Kings 8.11–13 on Israel; elsewhere the foetus-killing motif appears on its own, but is presumably to be understood as the culmination of the whole genocidal programme, not as an isolated atrocity (contra Paul Kern, *Ancient Siege Warfare* (Bloomington: Souvenir Press, 1999), 84; cf. Amélie Kuhrt, 'Women and War', *Nin* 2:1 (2001), 7–8).

[5] Amos 1.13; cf. the implied criticism of the usurper Menahem's genocidal war in 2 Kings 15.16, with Cogan, ' "Ripping Open Pregnant Women" ', and Kern, *Ancient Siege Warfare*, 7–8.

[6] See e.g. Cogan, ' "Ripping Open Pregnant Women" ', 756, for Tiglat-Pileser; 2 Kings 13.1–25; 17.5–21, for the fall of Samaria/Israel.

Israelites in their occupation of the Promised Land. The law demands that any city
of non-believers within this God-given territory should be struck with a 'ban'
(*herem*), which entails that:

You shall save alive nothing that breathes, but you shall utterly destroy them, the Hittites
and the Amorites, the Canaanites and the Perizzites, the Hivites and the Jebusites, as the
Lord your God has commanded.[7]

The meaning of 'everything that breathes' fluctuated. When the army killed all the
men of the Midianites but took the women, children, and animals as booty, Moses
angrily told the soldiers to execute all the boys and adult women as well, sparing
only virgin girls and livestock. Usually, the ban did not spare virgin girls either, and
in some instances, such as Joshua's sack of Jericho or Saul's destruction of the
Amalekites, the ban required even cattle, sheep, donkeys, and camels to be slaughtered. The law did, however, categorically exempt trees.[8] The stories of Moses and
Saul both spelled out the message that the killing of livestock was an unpopular
measure but a religious necessity to be enforced regardless.[9]

The genocidal campaigns claimed for the early Israelites, however, were largely
fictional: the intrinsic improbability and internal inconsistencies of the account in
Joshua and its incompatibility with the stories of Judges leave little doubt about
this. Much of the biblical ideology of the ban was in fact formulated later, in the
seventh century BC,[10] yet it was neither unique nor entirely a later literary invention. In an inscription of *c.*810 BC, Mesha, king of Moab, Israel's old enemy, boasts
that he massacred the population of a town, 7,000 men, women, and children: 'for
[the god] Ashtar-Kemosh I had it put to the ban.' We need to be wary of taking this
claim at face value, since Mesha also made the quite unwarranted boast that, as a
result of his campaigns, 'Israel utterly perished forever.'[11] But the similarity between his words and those found in biblical accounts does show that even if the
events were not historical, the ideology of legitimate genocide which underlies
these stories did exist, and may occasionally have been put into practice.

At the other extreme of the rhetorical range, we have one-word notices that so-
and-so 'sacked' or 'destroyed' a city, without any elaboration on what happened to
its people, or bald statements that a defeated people were 'sold into slavery'.

---

[7] Deuteronomy 20.16–17; cf. 13.12–16.

[8] Numbers 31.14–18 (Midianites); Joshua 6.20–21 (Jericho); 1 Samuel 15.3 (Amalekites). Livestock
spared: Joshua 8.2, 27; 11.14. Trees exempt: Deuteronomy 20.19–20.

[9] Detailed analysis in André Lemaire, 'Le hérem dans le monde ouest-sémitique', in Laila Nehmé
(ed.), *Guerre et conquête dans le Proche-Orient ancien* (Paris: J. Maisonneuve, 1999), 79–92; Susan
Niditch, *War in the Hebrew Bible* (Oxford: Oxford University Press, 1993).

[10] For introductions to these source problems, see n. 9 above, and Amélie Kuhrt, *The Ancient Near
East*, vol ii (London: Routledge, 1995), 417–37; Robert Carroll, 'War in the Hebrew Bible', in John Rich
and Graham Shipley (eds), *War and Society in the Greek World* (London: Routledge, 1993), 25–44.

[11] 'The Moabite Stone': Mark Chavalas, *The Ancient Near East: Historical Sources in Translation*
(Malden/Oxford: Blackwell, 2006), no. 126; cf. Niditch, *War in the Hebrew Bible*, 31.

Sometimes such elliptic statements simply reflect the brevity of our sources, but even otherwise detailed accounts often say little more. The surviving Greek and Roman historians mostly belong to a school of thought which did not like to elaborate on the suffering caused by war, partly as a matter of general historiographical principle, but also because they often felt that a destroyed or enslaved city *deserved* its fate and did not deserve the sympathy which a description of its misery would evoke.[12] Such attitudes are almost the opposite of the celebrations of force in some Near Eastern texts, and leave us with a record that may understate rather than exaggerate the frequency and extent of destruction. But this record is in its own way a no less telling expression of the common ancient view that in certain circumstances the annihilation of a community could be a legitimate, desirable, and even necessary course of action.

THE CITIES OF MEN: TARGETS FOR ANNIHILATION

The victim of a campaign of destruction was typically the population of a single city, and the question arises whether this counts as genocide. We should certainly exclude from this category the countless sieges which caused huge damage and loss of life but did not end with the elimination of the besieged city's entire population. Also to be excluded are massacres committed by soldiers running amok and wiping out entire towns, without being ordered to do so, or indeed in defiance of orders to stop killing. But where the population of a city was executed or permanently dispersed by the design of military or political authorities, the label 'genocide' surely is appropriate even if a city does not easily fit into the categories of 'national, ethnical, racial or religious group' defined by the United Nations as potential victims of genocide. In the ancient world, towns and cities—most ranging in size from a few thousand to several tens of thousands of inhabitants and the largest few reaching six-figure populations—were by far the most significant social, economic, and political entities. City-states predominated in large parts of the Mediterranean and the Near East; many ancient empires took the form of hierarchical alliance systems in which one city-state set itself above others. Where city-states prevailed, the inhabitants of a town constituted in effect a 'national' group, the destruction of which can reasonably be described as genocide.

---

[12] Both factors play a part in Polybius' classic discussion of the sack of Mantinea in 223 BC (*History* 2.56.7–12; cf. Victor d'Huys, 'How to Describe Violence in Historical Narrative', *Ancient Society* 18 (1987), 209–50).

City-states were often part of wider 'ethnic' groups—unlike in the modern world where ethnic groups are usually a subordinate part of nation-states. The citizens of Sparta were not only Spartiates, but also shared with the other inhabitants of the region the name 'Lacedaemonians'; they claimed a shared origin with many other cities as 'Dorians'; and at the highest level of ethnic identity they counted themselves as 'Hellenes', Greeks. Rome shared with neighboring city-states an identity as 'Latins'; the city-states of central Italy which we know as Etruscan called themselves collectively 'Rasenna'; and so forth. These identities emerged and faded over time, but were meaningful to those who claimed to share them, and generally entailed a sense that they had a language, customs, and cults in common.[13] The destruction of an ethnic group above the level of the city-state was seldom if ever sought in the ancient world, though the alleged wars of extermination between Israelites, Moabites, and other groups of ethnically affiliated cities in the Levant, noted above, may be an exception.

Where city-states were not the predominant form of political organization, broader ethnic identities were of primary importance, as they were, for example, among the Persians, Thracians, and Macedonians, with their 'tribal' subdivisions, and in Egypt. One might say that destroying a single settlement could not count as 'genocide' in a region where the main group affiliations were to a larger ethnic unit, but I would argue that towns, and even villages, everywhere had sufficiently distinctive identities for their annihilation to constitute a form of genocide. The extinction of larger ethnic groups as such was probably never envisaged, although the armies of Alexander the Great in India, and the legions of Caesar in Gaul, massacred on such a large scale that they must have come close to wiping out entire tribes.[14]

The massacre of all inhabitants of a city was quite rare, though not unknown. More common was the killing of all men, or all men of military age, while the women and children were led away to be sold as slaves. This is described as standard procedure for dealing with a city captured by force in a range of texts from Deuteronomy and the *Iliad* to Livy's history of Rome.[15] Some scholars have

[13] Ethnicity: Jonathan Hall, *Ethnicity in Greek Antiquity* (Cambridge: Cambridge University Press, 1997); *idem, Hellenicity: Between Ethnicity and Culture* (Chicago: University of Chicago Press, 2002); Irad Malkin (ed.), *Ancient Perceptions of Greek Ethnicity* (Cambridge, MA.: Harvard University Press, 2001); and relevant chapters in Tim Cornell and Kathryn Lomas (eds), *Gender and Ethnicity in Roman Italy* (London: Accordia, 1997).

[14] See A. B. Bosworth, *Alexander and the East* (Oxford: Oxford University Press, 1996), 133–65. Appian, *Gallic History* 2, claimed that Caesar killed 1 million and enslaved 1 million Gauls, out of a total population of 4 million; Caesar himself reports, e.g., the sale into slavery of 53,000 Atuatuci (*Gallic War* 2.33.6–7).

[15] Deuteronomy 20.12–15 (cities outside the Promised Land); *Iliad* e.g. 6.448–65; 9.591–5; 22.62–8; Livy 21.13.9. See W. Kendrick Pritchett, *The Greek State at War*, vol v (Berkeley: University of California Press, 1991); Pierre Ducrey, *Le traitement de prisonniers de guerre dans la Grèce antique* (Paris: Boccard, 1968; new edn 1999); Mars M. Westington, 'Atrocities in Roman Warfare to 133 BC', PhD dissertation, University of Chicago, 1938, 68.

imagined that men were killed because they were 'more difficult to control than women and children', so that enslavement was not feasible.[16] This is hardly a tenable view, given that countless men were in fact reduced to chattel slavery and other forms of forced labour throughout antiquity and beyond. Conversely, the youngest children and the elderly were spared despite being no use as slaves: they would often find no buyer and be left to die of exposure, hunger, or attack by wild animals. On one occasion, a Roman army actually butchered the young and the old but made slaves of the adult men.[17] Instead, if a distinction by gender and age was made, it was because communities were conceived of as consisting essentially of adult men. Women, children, and the aged were mere dependants. The death of the men amounted to the annihilation of the community; killing the others was not necessary.

We have good contemporary evidence for instances of genocide which took this sharply gendered form, as we shall see, but the impression created by literary sources that it was standard practice is probably misleading, since quite a range of different treatments of sacked cities is attested. A common Roman practice, for instance, appears to have been to engage initially in a period of indiscriminate slaughter—'one may often see not only the corpses of human beings, but dogs cut in half and the dismembered limbs of other animals'—until the commander gave the signal to stop; then survivors of both sexes and all ages were systematically rounded up to be sold, which in one notorious campaign produced a total of 150,000 slaves from 72 settlements in Epirus. Similar mass enslavements occurred with some frequency in the Greek world.[18] Not even nuclear families would be kept together when they were sold into slavery, so the result was complete dispersal of a community. The irrevocable destruction of a group in this way could be counted as a form of genocide, even if few were killed.

Rape did not play the ancillary part in genocidal campaigns which it has played in more recent history. A few brief and rather euphemistic references leave no doubt that many women, and indeed young men, were raped during the sack of cities, but our sources tend to treat this as an incidental and distasteful aspect of siege warfare. Unlike killing and enslavement it was not a matter of public policy. A concerted campaign of rape may just be hinted at in the *Iliad* when the Greeks are

---

[16] Kern, *Ancient Siege Warfare*, 23, citing I. J. Gelb, 'Prisoners of War in Early Mesopotamia', *Journal of Near Eastern Studies* 32 (1972), 72.

[17] Left to die: Xenophon, *Agesilaos* 1.21–2; cf. Tacitus, *Histories* 3.33.1. Killed: Livy, *Ab urbe condita* 42.63.10–11.

[18] Roman practice: Polybius, *History* 10.15.4–16.9, who speaks only of 'booty', but this clearly included people (see Adam Ziolkowski, '*Urbs Direpta*, or How the Romans Sacked Cities', in Rich and Shipley (eds), *War and Society in the Greek World*, 69–91); Epirus: ibid. 30.16; Livy, *Ab urbe condita* 45.34.5; Pliny, *Natural History* 4.39. For mass enslavement in general, see Hans Volkmann, *Die Massenversklavungen der Einwohner eroberter Städte in der hellenistisch-römischer Zeit*, 2nd edn (Stuttgart: Franz Steiner, 1990).

told: 'Let no one be in a hurry to go home until he has slept with the wife of a Trojan, in revenge for the shocks and sobs of Helen' (2.354–6). But this could be explained instead as a reference, not to rape as it was understood then, but to soldiers having sex with Trojan women who were allocated to them as slaves—a form of sexual coercion which was regarded as legitimate, and which allowed men to establish a form of control over women which was far more lasting and comprehensive than a brief and limited exercise of power through ad hoc sexual violence. Near Eastern sources say even less on the subject than Greek and Roman sources do.[19]

The physical site of the city was another target for destruction. Towns are forever being 'burnt down' and 'razed to the ground' in ancient records, and in many cases this may be no more than a formulaic reference to the damage done in the course of the siege and haphazard vandalism by pillaging soldiers. A common theme in Near Eastern texts is the turning of a defeated city's territory into an uninhabitable wasteland by 'sowing it with salt', planting it with weeds, or covering it with brimstone and pitch,[20] but this could surely have been done only symbolically, on a small scale, if at all. Deliberate flooding as a punishment is also attested, though not very reliably. In the Greek and Roman world cultivation of the territory of a destroyed city might be forbidden, sometimes by dedicating it to a god, so that the land 'reverted to a sheep-walk'.[21]

The purpose of the physical destruction of buildings and land is made clear in an inscription which claims that Sennacherib of Assyria flooded Babylon in 689 BC, 'so that it might be impossible in future days to recognize the site of that city and its temples.' The destruction of a Spanish town, Ilurgia, in 206 BC, is described in similar terms: the Romans wanted to 'erase the memory' of their enemy. Conversely, to leave buildings standing was regarded as leaving a 'tomb and monument' to the former inhabitants, and the Romans are said to have left the walls and houses of another Spanish town, Astapa, intact as a mark of respect for a community that

---

[19] For the Greek and Roman evidence, see Elisabeth Vikman, 'Sexual Violence in Warfare, Part I: Ancient Origins', *Anthropology and Medicine* 12:1 (2005), 21–31; Kern, *Ancient Siege Warfare*, 154–62, 235–6, 345–7; ancient attitudes to rape generally: Susan Deacy and Karen Pierce (eds), *Rape in Antiquity* (London/Swansea: Classical Press of Wales, 1997). Omission of women from classical historiography of war: Simon Hornblower, 'Warfare in Ancient Literature: The Paradox of War', in Philip Sabin et al. (eds), *The Cambridge History of Greek and Roman Warfare*, vol i (Cambridge: Cambridge University Press, 2007), 42–7. Near-absence from Near Eastern evidence: Kern, *Ancient Siege Warfare*, 80–3.

[20] Sowing with salt: e.g. Judges 9.45; other evidence collected in Moshe Weinfeld, *Deuteronomy and the Deuteronomic School* (Winona Lake: Eisenbrauns, 1992), 110–16; R. T. Ridley, 'To Be Taken with a Pinch of Salt: The Destruction of Carthage', *Classical Philology* 81 (1986), 140–6.

[21] Flooding: see below. 'Sheep-walk': Isocrates, *Orations* 14.31 (Kirrha, *c.*590 BC); Diodorus of Sicily, *The Library* 15.63.1; Strabo, *Geography* 7.5 (315); Dionysius of Halicarnassus, *Roman Antiquities* 2.16.1. The story of the 'cursing' of Carthage's territory is discussed by Ridley, 'To Be Taken with a Pinch of Salt'.

had committed mass suicide rather than surrender.[22] The idea that the victims should vanish without a trace was extended in Greek literature even to the non-burial of the dead: hence Agamemnon's demand in the *Iliad* that the Trojans' corpses should be left 'untended and invisible', that is, without tombs to keep their memory alive. Extermination of the people was not enough: ideally, even the evidence of their existence had to be obliterated.

ALTERNATIVES TO ANNIHILATION: GENOCIDE IN CONTEXT

The prominence of warfare in the historical record of the ancient world, the brutal rhetoric of many of the sources, and the suggestion found in authors such as Thucydides and Plato that states were engaged in a permanent war of all against all conspire to create the impression that ancient cities and states were always out to destroy one another. They were not, of course. International relations in the ancient world were complex, with a wide range of recognized relationships between states, including kinship and friendship, as well as formal treaty obligations, and sophisticated diplomatic mechanisms, from inviolable envoys and ambassadors, via exchanges of letters and gifts, to international arbitration. Despite some modern claims to the contrary, peace was always considered the norm and ideal, even if it was often interrupted by the necessary evil of war.[23] When war did break out, its goals usually stopped well short of annihilating the enemy, and we need to consider the full range of options which an ancient state had in dealing with a hostile city before we can try to determine why sometimes a city-state, kingdom, or empire chose to resort to genocide.

From as early as the third millennium BC, wars were often concluded with pacts of non-aggression or treaties of equal alliance, sometimes on terms which

[22] Babylon: J. A. Brinkman, 'Sennacherib's Babylonian problem: an interpretation', *Journal of Cuneiform Studies* 25:2 (1973), 89–95 (translation, 94); Kuhrt, *The Ancient Near East*, 582–7. Ilurgia: Livy, *Ab urbe condita* 28.20.5–7. 'Monument and tomb': Livy 31.29.11; cf. 26.16.11–12. Astapa (206 BC): Appian, *Punic Wars* 6.33 (a different account in Livy 28.22–3).

[23] For a brief survey of ancient international relations, see Hans van Wees, 'Peace and the Society of States in Antiquity', in Jost Dülffer and Robert Frank (eds), *War, Peace and Gender* (Essen: Klartext, 2009); David Bedermann, *International Law in Antiquity* (Cambridge: Cambridge University Press, 2001). On Greece and Rome, see also the relevant chapters in Anja Hartmann and Beatrice Heuser (eds), *War, Peace and World Orders in European History* (London: Routledge, 2001), and in both volumes of Sabin et al. (eds), *The Cambridge History of Greek and Roman Warfare*. On the Near East, see especially Mario Liverani, *International Relations in the Ancient Near East, 1600–1100 BC* (Basingstoke: Palgrave, 2001); on Assyria, see Bustenay Oded, *War, Peace, and Empire: Justifications for War in Assyrian Royal Inscriptions* (Wiesbaden: Ludwig Reichert Verlag, 1992).

required close cooperation. Alternatively, war might end with an unequal treaty, imposing military obligations on the defeated side; the Romans in addition confiscated some of the land of their new allies.[24] The most powerful states went beyond alliance-making to impose outright subjection. Egyptian, Assyrian, and Persian kings demanded tribute as a token of submission; regular taxes and other duties replaced, or were added to, such obligations as conquests were consolidated. The Romans similarly created subject 'provinces' rather than allies when they expanded beyond Italy.[25] In all such cases, communities were left wholly intact, apart of course from any casualties suffered in combat, and often retained a high degree of local autonomy as well, losing little more than their international standing.

More violent measures begin with the elimination of a city's leadership, which was particularly common in dealing with 'rebels', i.e. cities which in some way offended against the terms of their subordination, or sometimes simply refused to be subordinated. Tension between a ruling class and the rest of the population was a constant feature of political and social life in Greek cities, and in order to strengthen or regain control over their subject allies, classical Athenians and Spartans exploited such divisions by executing or exiling hostile or rebellious political elites.[26] They had precursors in the Near East, such as Sennacherib's treatment of rebels in Ekron and Jerusalem, a few years before his demolition of Babylon. In Ekron, the elite were theatrically executed, some commoners enslaved, and the rest spared. Biblical accounts of the siege of Jerusalem emphasize that Sennacherib's representatives refused to negotiate with the elite alone, and insisted on announcing the terms of surrender in Hebrew so that the common people would understand—evidently an attempt to exploit internal divisions. Exiling or executing the ruling elite alone later became the Romans' standard procedure in dealing with rebellious cities.[27]

---

[24] See previous note, and in addition: Polly Low, *Interstate Relations in Classical Greece: Morality and Power* (Cambridge: Cambridge University Press, 2007); Hans van Wees, *Greek Warfare: Myths and Realities* (London: Duckworth, 2004), 12–15; Stephen Oakley, 'The Roman Conquest of Italy', in Rich and Shipley (eds), *War and Society in the Greek World*, 9–37; and a comparative study by Barry Strauss, 'The Art of Alliance and the Peloponnesian War', in Charles D. Hamilton and Peter Krentz (eds), *Polis and Polemos* (Claremont: Regina Books, 1997), 127–40.

[25] Subjection: e.g. Oded, *War, Peace and Empire*; tribute: e.g. Karen Radner, 'Abgaben an den König von Assyrien aus dem In- und Ausland', in H. Klinkott et al. (eds), *Geschenke und Steuern, Zölle und Tribute* (Leiden/Boston: Brill, 2007), 213–30. Roman provinces: e.g. Andrew Lintott, *Imperium Romanum* (London/New York: Routledge 1993), 16–42.

[26] For the classical period, see Hans-Joachim Gehrke, *Stasis* (Munich: Beck, 1985); Andrew Lintott, *Violence, Civil Strife and Revolution in the Classical Greek City* (London: Routledge, 1982); for archaic Greece, see Hans van Wees, '*Stasis*, Destroyer of Men', in Cedric Brélaz and Pierre Ducrey (eds), *Sécurité collective et ordre public dans les sociétés anciennes* (Vandoeuvres: Fondation Hardt, 2008), 1–48.

[27] Ekron: Daniel Luckenbill, *Ancient Records of Assyria and Babylonia*, vol ii (Chicago: University of Chicago Press, 1927; reprinted 1989), nos. 211–12. Jerusalem: 2 Kings 18.26–8; 2 Chronicles 32.18; Isaiah 36.11–13. Rome: e.g. Westington, 'Atrocities in Roman Warfare to 133 BC', 86–107.

In a famous passage, Thucydides has the Athenian assembly debate the pros and cons of killing only the responsible members of the ruling class versus massacring the entire population of Mytilene, an allied city which had revolted. The argument in favour of the former is essentially that it will in the long run be more profitable not to destroy the whole community, and the view that material advantages, rather than moral qualms, militated most strongly against genocide, may have been widely shared. The Athenians decided in the end to kill 'only' a thousand leading Mytileneans.[28]

Elsewhere, elites were driven into exile or deported. The Athenians in 506 BC expelled 'the Horsemen' who ruled Chalcis, and in 338 BC the Romans forced the senators of Velitrae to go and live 'on the other side of the Tiber'. Deportation and resettlement of local elites was common practice in the empires of the Near East: the 'Babylonian exile' of the priests and ruling class of Judah from 586 to 537 BC is only the best known instance of many. Settlers from other parts of the empire usually replaced the deportees.[29]

Not just elites, but whole communities might be driven from their homes. The victors sometimes let a defeated enemy vacate their city unmolested when they surrendered, typically allowing them to bring literally only the clothes on their backs.[30] Large-scale deportations are well attested in the Near East, where Assyrian kings in particular moved tens of thousands of people from one end of the empire to the other. Communities were usually not deported in their entirety: some families were selected for deportation while others stayed behind. This relocation did much to weaken local communities, of course, but they were not destroyed and the deportees were kept together as a group as much as possible. They were 'counted as Assyrians' in their new homes rather than reduced to slavery. The Persians, judging by Greek accounts, did deport entire communities—where possible, as on islands, soldiers marched in a linked chain across the territory to ensure that not a single person avoided capture—but again kept them intact. The people of Eretria, deported a few days before the battle of Marathon and put to work scooping petroleum from a well, still formed a distinct, Greek-speaking community deep in Persian imperial territory two generations later.[31]

Genocide, in short, was far from the only or normal outcome of hostile inter-group relations in the ancient world. Quantifying its relative frequency compared with other ways of dealing with enemy cities is not possible, but we do have enough information to show that mass executions were far rarer than mass enslavement. In

---

[28] Thucydides, *History* 3.36–50, with Simon Hornblower, *A Commentary on Thucydides*, vol. i, books I-III (Oxford: Oxford University Press, 1991), 420–41.

[29] Chalcis: Herodotus, *Histories* 5.77.2; Velitrae: Livy, *Ab urbe condita* 8.14. Assyria: Bustenay Oded, *Mass Deportations and Deportees in the Neo-Assyrian Empire* (Wiesbaden: Reichert, 1979), 43–5.

[30] See van Wees, *Greek Warfare: Myths and Realities*, 261 n 44.

[31] Assyrians: analysis in Oded, *Mass Deportations and Deportees in the Neo-Assyrian Empire*, and J. Nicholas Postgate, 'Ancient Assyria: a Multi-Racial State', *Aram* 1 (1989), 1–20 (reprinted in Postgate, *The Land of Assur and the Yoke of Assur* (Oxford: Oxbow, 2007). Persians: Herodotus, *Histories* 3.149; 6.31, 119.

his first campaign, Sennacherib claimed to have sacked eighty-nine fortified towns and 820 villages, yet he boasted about the extermination of the population of only one town, Hirimme.[32] The pattern for Roman wars of expansion in the third and second centuries BC is similar. In the Third Samnite War (298–290 BC), at least eleven cities and 40,000 people were enslaved by the Romans, but not a single massacre is recorded. The First Punic War (264–241 BC) saw the enslavement of five cities in Sicily, and of 27,000 North Africans from an alleged 200 or 300 villages, but only one mass killing (at Lipara, 252) and one near-massacre at Myttistratos (257). After surviving Hannibal's invasion of Italy, the Romans enslaved many settlements during their counter-offensive in North Africa, but perpetrated only one mass killing (at Locha, 203). The statistics for their wars of conquest in Spain, Greece, and the Near East are comparable. Numerous other campaigns enslaved people in their tens of thousands but at no point attempted to exterminate the inhabitants of any settlement.[33]

The relative rarity of mass murder suggests that it was not just a by-product of randomly brutal warfare but an option deliberately chosen in particular circumstances. This brings us back to the question of what motivated genocidal actions by ancient states and armies.

Conspicuous Destruction: Profit, Power, and Genocide

On 19 December 51 BC, Cicero, then governor of Cilicia, wrote a letter to his close friend Atticus in which he gave a jocular account of enslaving a small town in his remote province:

At the time of the Saturnalia festival, the Pindenissetans surrendered themselves into my power, on the fifty-seventh day after we began our siege of them. 'What the devil? The Pindenissetans? Who are they?,' you may say. 'I have never even heard the name.' Well, what am I supposed to do? Can I turn Cilicia into Aetolia or Macedonia? . . . We went to Pindenissus, a well-defended settlement of the Free Cilicians which has been under arms

---

[32] Luckenbill, *Ancient Records of Assyria and Babylonia*, nos. 234 (with different numbers), 261, 267, 272, 274; Hirimme: ibid. nos. 235, 266, 276, 303. Cf. the analysis of Assyrian records in Kern, *Ancient Siege Warfare*, 69–75.

[33] Spain: at least eight fortified towns and numerous villages enslaved; a single massacre at Ilurgia, 206; Greece and the Near East: nine cities enslaved, all men massacred at Antipatreia, 200. The above is based on evidence collated by Volkmann, *Die Massenversklavungen der Einwohner eroberter Städte in der hellenistisch-römischer Zeit*, and Ziolkowski, '*Urbs Direpta*', 83–4. Note that the ancient record is far from complete.

as long as anyone can remember. The people are savage and fierce and in every way prepared to defend themselves. [With great effort but without loss of life,] we finished the business. A jolly Saturnalia—also for the soldiers, to whom I handed over the booty except the captives. The slaves were sold on the third day of the Saturnalia. At the time of writing, the proceeds on my dais stand at about 120,000 sesterces.[34]

From the mock-solemn opening sentence to the modest sum recorded at the end, Cicero self-deprecatingly stressed the trivial nature of the event (which left no trace in the historical record outside his letters). He felt no need to explain his reasons for selling the population into slavery or for attacking the town, except to hint at their refusal to submit to Roman authority.

Cicero was aware that his victory was insignificant, but he wanted public recognition all the same, and even set his sights on a triumphal procession, the highest military honour. He therefore recorded details of his campaign in a second letter, which he sent to Cato, one of the most powerful men in Rome, asking him to propose public honours on his behalf:

I led the army to Pindenissus . . . Because this place was located in a very elevated and well-defended spot, and was inhabited by people who had never submitted to any king, and because they had also taken in refugees [from an earlier battle] and were eagerly awaiting the arrival of the Parthians, I came to the decision that it was a matter of upholding the reputation (*existimatio*) of the empire to crush their impertinence, so that the spirit of others who are hostile to our empire might be more easily broken.

He added that 'they came into my power by coercion when every part of their city had been either demolished or set on fire.' That enslavement was their fate is not even mentioned.[35] Here, Cicero offers three reasons for sacking the city: to punish the people of Pindenissus for taking sides with Rome's enemies, the Parthians, who were rumoured to be planning an invasion; to punish them for more generally showing disrespect towards the Roman empire; and to deter others from acting with similar disloyalty and disrespect. The very difficulty of capturing the place, in its mountainous location, becomes a reason for its destruction: it serves as demonstration of Rome's power to coerce any community, however inaccessible and defiant. These letters are worth quoting at length because it is rare to have a perpetrator's private account of an act of genocide, and because Cicero alludes to many of the reasons for mass enslavement and mass killing which we commonly encounter in ancient texts.

The material profit to be made from selling people into slavery, in Cicero's case evidently at best a secondary reason, seems the primary motivation of several earlier Roman campaigns. Operations in Sardinia and Istria in 177 flooded the market with up to 85,000 slaves and gave rise to the expression 'Sardinians for sale!'

---

[34] Cicero, *Letters to Atticus* 5.20.1 and 4.
[35] Cicero, *Letters to his Friends* 15.4.10.

to describe an abundance of cheap goods, and neither in these campaigns nor in the mass enslavement of 150,000 Molossians from Epirus only ten years later do we know of any particular justification for such severity. It is significant that the victims inhabited regions where levels of urbanization were low, which made the population 'savages', in Roman eyes, as well as vulnerable to attack. The Romans seem to have regarded such people as legitimate targets for slave-raiding on a massive scale. The Greeks similarly developed a notion that all non-Greeks were 'barbarians' whose enslavement was a kind of hunting, and as such in no need of special justification.[36] In some cases, then, the annihilation of communities was not a goal in itself, but merely an incidental consequence of a ruthless pursuit of profit. The question of intent, however, is academic: slave-raiding states could not fail to realize that the ultimate result of their actions would be genocide.

One suspects that profit was always a significant motive for mass enslavement, even when quite different formal reasons were adduced. At the very least, when a state considered how to retaliate against an enemy or punish a subject city, the prospect of material gain must often have swung the balance in favour of enslavement rather than massacre—which is why the former was so much more common than the latter. By the same token, however, the decision to massacre was inhibited by economic, as well as moral and political, concerns. The choice was not between killing an enemy and letting him or her go, but between selling captives at a profit or executing them and going empty-handed. When Menelaus hesitated to kill a Trojan, this was not due to any humanitarian feelings but because it would cost him the 'infinite ransom' which a living prisoner might bring. The Israelites needed reminding repeatedly that putting an enemy to the ban meant forgoing all booty of slaves, livestock, and valuables. Conversely, we are told, the only way to stop furious Roman soldiers massacring the people of Myttistratus was to promise that they could keep as personal booty anyone whom they caught and did not kill.[37]

If the profit motive encouraged enslavement but discouraged killing, only when it was countered by even more powerful motivations did states resort to genocidal massacres. An endless variety of such motivations is mentioned in ancient sources, but the majority have at least one feature in common: those perpetrating the massacre saw themselves as inflicting revenge or punishment for what one may call an 'aggravated' challenge to their power and status as a community and/or to the power of a god whose cause they champion. A few typical scenarios will have to suffice to illustrate this point.

---

[36] For Sardinia and Istria, see Volkmann, *Die Massenversklavungen der Einwohner eroberter Städte in der hellenistisch-römischer Zeit*, 27, 54–5. For Epirus, see n. 18, above. For ancient attitudes to enslavement, see Peter Garnsey, *Ideas of Slavery from Aristotle to Augustine* (Cambridge: Cambridge University Press, 1996).

[37] Menelaus: Homer, *Iliad* 6.43–53. Israelites: above, at n. 9–10. Myttistratus: Zonaras, *Historical Epitomes* 8.11.10; cf. Polybius, *History* 1.24.11; Diodorus of Sicily, *The Library* 23.9.4.

First, imperial powers sometimes destroyed small independent towns on the grounds that their very independence constituted an affront which made the empire look weak. This is the main reason adduced by Cicero for his enslavement of Pindenissus, and elsewhere the same principle is cited to justify a massacre. In Thucydides' 'Melian Dialogue', the Athenians explain bluntly why they must incorporate the small, neutral island of Melos into their naval empire: 'Since you are islanders, and weaker than the others, you cannot be allowed to escape from those who rule the sea.' When the Melians refused to submit, the Athenians killed the men, and enslaved the women and children.[38] The same reasoning probably lay behind Sennacherib's destruction of Hirimme, another small town which had so far refused to submit to any king.[39] Resistance to imperial power is evidently a worse offence for a small town than for a large city. Refusal to submit implies that the opponent regards himself as somehow the 'equal' of the empire, which is more insulting when it comes from an insignificant little town than from a serious rival. The destruction of defiant small towns was therefore not just a matter of con- solidating imperial power, but of upholding status. The demands of power politics might have been satisfied by merely forcing Pindenissus, Melos, Hirimme, and their like to submit to imperial authority, but the demands of status required that they be destroyed to wipe out the insult.

A second scenario involves the destruction of a roughly equal opponent who is regarded as in some way too persistent in his hostility. For instance, while relations between Athens and most of its rivals alternated between hostility and alliance, the Athenians saw the neighbouring Aeginetans as implacable enemies, who had started hostilities in the dim past and kept attacking without provocation. In 431 BC, the Athenians drove the Aeginetans out of their island, forcing the refugees to find new homes all over Greece; a large group settled in Thyrea. Not content with this result, in 424 BC the Athenians sent a fleet to attack Thyrea, which they captured, looted, and burned down. All Aeginetans captured alive were taken to Athens, where a formal decision was made to execute every last one 'on account of the hostility which they had always shown in the past.'[40] In much the same way, the Romans came to regard the Carthaginians as an exceptionally bitter and relentless enemy, which may explain their eventual destruction of Carthage and enslavement of its people in 146 BC. Power-political motivations clearly played a prominent role, but it is striking that the Aeginetans and Carthaginians were destroyed at a time when they no longer posed a serious threat to their old rivals, however dangerous

[38] Thucydides, *History* 5.97, 101, 116.4 (cf. 4.122.5–6), with Simon Hornblower, *A Commentary on Thucydides*, vol iii, books V.25–VIII.109 (Oxford: Oxford University Press, 2008), 216–25.

[39] Their defiance is noted: Luckenbill, *Ancient Records of Assyria and Babylonia*, no. 266; cf. 276.

[40] Thucydides, *History* 2.27; 4.57; for the Athenian tradition of an age-old feud with Aegina, see Herodotus, *Histories* 5.81–9, written around the time of the events described above.

they might once have been. Their annihilation was strongly symbolic: a demon-stration by Athens and Rome of how great a superiority they now enjoyed.[41]

Also common was a third scenario: the destruction of a formerly friendly or allied city which was deemed to have committed a particularly heinous act of treachery, which seriously endangered the city betrayed. This situation features in another of Thucydides' set-pieces, the 'Mytilenean Debate', concerning a proposal to execute all the men and enslave the women and children of Mytilene. This city had changed sides in the middle of major war, raising the spectre of a general defection to Sparta of all Athens' allies; its destruction, it was argued, would act as a deterrent to other would-be rebels. For similar reasons, the Romans massacred or enslaved more Italian cities than at any other time during the wars in which they came closest to defeat. In the Second Samnite War (326–304 BC), they killed the inhabitants of four towns, killed all the men in a fifth, and enslaved the population of a further two; during Hannibal's invasion of Italy, they enslaved at least 14 Italian and Sicilian towns, and massacred the people of two more. In each case, the victims had either changed sides or were suspected of being about to do so.[42] Here we have genocide carried out for calculated political effect, as a means of deterrence and intimidation. It was used in much the same way in campaigns of conquest, as in Cicero's mini-war against Pindenissus: harsh treatment of the first town to offer any resistance served to frighten others into submission.

Yet political pragmatism was not always the whole story even in these cases. A major argument used in favour of the massacre of all men of Mytilene, according to Thucy-dides, was that this ally's betrayal did not just create a serious threat to security but entailed a serious breach of trust, because relations between Athens and Mytilene had been unusually close and privileged. 'They were not ruled by Athens, like the others,' but retained autonomy 'and were treated with the highest respect by us.' Their betrayal was all the more culpable because there was evidence that they had been planning to defect for a long time. 'We should never have treated them with more respect than anyone else,' he adds, 'then they would not have become so arrogant; for it is human nature to despise those who show deference and to admire those who concede nothing.'[43] Once again, emotive matters of status creep into the picture alongside political calculation: a failure to reciprocate respect and friendship calls for violent retaliation.

A final scenario is the annihilation of a community as punishment for a religious offence. This principle is widely attested, but seems to have been more often an additional justification for genocide than a major motivation in its own right. In Greece, the so-called Amphictyons, a league of states in charge of the oracle of Apollo

---

[41] The Athenians did not occupy the Aeginetans' land in Thyrea, and the Romans left the territory of the Carthaginians untouched for more than a decade, so their destruction brought no material benefit.

[42] Mytilene: Thucydides, *History* 3.37.2, 39.7–8, 40.4–7. Rome: the evidence is again collated by Volkmann and Ziolkowski, as cited in fn 33, above; the latter, however, questions the evidence for the Second Samnite War.

[43] Special status of Mytilene: Thucydides, *History* 3.36.2, 39.2 and 5.

at Delphi, swore an oath that they would 'uproot' any city which committed offences against the sanctuary, and tradition claimed that in 591 BC they destroyed the town of Kirrha for acts of aggression against the oracle.[44] Even earlier, the inscription which recounts Sennacherib's destruction and flooding of Babylon in 689 also states that the victorious king retrieved cult images which had been taken from Assyria by the Babylonians 418 years earlier. The implication is that Babylon was being punished for this ancient act of sacrilege. But none of the other records of Sennacherib's campaigns against Babylon mention either this religious offence or the punishment of destruction, although they hint at plenty of other political and personal reasons why the king might have dealt harshly with the city.[45] At the other end of antiquity, when the Persian king Sapor II was shot at during his siege of Amida in AD 359 and an arrow damaged his cloak, he responded 'as if the enemy had committed sacrilege' and set about trying to destroy the city.[46] The sarcastic tone of the Roman eyewitness who reports this shows that he did not take this episode seriously—but it also shows how widely accepted was the idea that genocide was suitable punishment for an act of collective sacrilege.

Cities might in theory also be destroyed for breaking divinely sanctioned rules, rather than direct offences against gods or god-like rulers. The sack of Corinth and the flooding of Sybaris are said to have been provoked by these cities' violation of respectively Romans and Crotoniat diplomatic envoys, regarded as sacrosanct.[47] The *Iliad* implicitly justifies the annihilation of Troy by showing the Trojans accumulating offences with a religious dimension: they threaten to kill Menelaus when he visits Troy on a diplomatic mission, they break the divinely sanctioned bond of hospitality in abducting his wife, and finally they break a truce which they had sworn to uphold on pain of destruction by the gods.[48] Since all treaties and truces and many other aspects of international relations in the ancient world were under the protection of the gods, it was rarely difficult to accuse an opponent of a religious offence. Near Eastern empires, moreover, generally saw themselves as implementing the will of their chief gods, such as Asshur for the Assyrians or Auramazda for the Persians, so that any opposition to their power was by definition an offence against these divinities.[49] Religious offences alone, however, without other aggravating circumstances, were not often adduced as a reason for genocide.

---

[44] The oath and Kirrha: Aeschines *Orations* 2.115; 3.107–9; and n. 25, above (doubts about the historicity of the oath seem to me unjustified: Hans van Wees, 'The Oath of the Sworn Bands', in Andreas Luther et al. eds., *Das frühe Sparta* (Stuttgart: Steiner Verlag, 2006), 139–42).

[45] Babylon's religious offence: Luckenbill, *Ancient Records of Assyria and Babylonia*, no. 341; other accounts: see Brinkman (n. 22, above).

[46] Ammianus Marcellinus, *Histories* 19.1.5, with Josh Levithan, 'Emperors, Sieges and Intentional Exposure', in Edward Bragg et al. (eds), *Beyond the Battlefields* (Newcastle: Cambridge Scholars Publishing, 2008), 37–8.

[47] Corinth: Livy, *Epitome* 52; Sybaris: Strabo, *Geography* 6.1.13.

[48] Breaking oath: Homer, *Iliad* 3.67–4.222; quotation: 3.298–301; cf. 4.235–9; 7.351–3. Threats to ambassador: 11.123–5, 139–42; cf. 3.205–24. Discussion: van Wees, *Status Warriors*, 176–81.

[49] Assyrians: Oded, *War, Peace and Empire*; Persians: Kuhrt, *The Ancient Near East*, 676–82.

The exception, as noted above, were the wars of extermination under the ban developed in the Levant. Here the idea that the actions of a king and his people represented the will of their supreme god was pushed further, to the point where any opposition to their power could be treated as a serious religious offence which demanded the annihilation of the enemy as a sacrifice to the offended god, be he Yahweh of Israel or Ashtar-Kemosh of Moab.

Extraordinary as the concept of the ban was, it rested on the same fundamental premise as more common legitimations of genocide in the ancient world: a challenge to the power of a community and/or its gods must be answered with a display of force in proportion to the seriousness of the challenge and may require an act of 'conspicuous destruction' which completely eliminates the challenger. What determined the seriousness of a challenge was partly its impact on security and power politics, but often its symbolic significance and impact on status counted at least as heavily. A challenge from a treacherous friend, an inveterate enemy, or a low-status opponent required a harsher response than an otherwise equally dangerous challenge from an open and equal rival. The more powerful a community, the more it might be inclined to demand respect in proportion to its status and to respond violently to even the slightest, least dangerous, challenge. The same was true of gods, who were imagined as responding to offences with greater force in proportion to their vastly greater power. A god as uniquely powerful as Yahweh and a people as closely identified with their god as the Israelites could therefore almost be expected to exterminate anyone who stood in their way: they pushed common ancient attitudes to their more-or-less logical and most brutal extreme.

Conclusions: Genocide and its Limits

Intentional genocide was perpetrated, and legitimate, according to ancient sources, when a community had committed a serious offence which called for the ultimate punishment. The form and extent of the destruction wrought is often difficult to determine because the ancient rhetoric of genocide variously over- or understated the damage done, and the explanations for genocide offered in ancient texts equally need to be treated with caution, since they are unlikely to tell the full story. Some might argue that the sources' emphasis on the symbolic, religious, and status-related nature of offences does not tell the true story at all, and that the extermination of communities must in reality have been motivated by a search for more power, resources, and territory. In support of that view, one might point out that the ideology of genocide was most widely accepted, and genocidal campaigns most common, among cities and states engaged in rapid military expansion. Macedonian armies, for instance, destroyed many cities during their campaigns in Greece and in the Persian Empire under Philip II and Alexander III the Great, but once these conquests had been consolidated into three fairly stable new kingdoms, a century went by without a single genocidal campaign being recorded.[50] The Romans enslaved and massacred on a huge scale while they extended their power across the Mediterranean, but once their control was established, very few further acts of genocide are attested. Conversely, scruples about genocidal warfare began to be much more forcefully articulated in Greece only when continuing warfare no longer led to significant expansion, as a de facto balance of power was achieved in the fifth and especially fourth century BC.[51] Yet there are enough instances of genocide which did not result in any political advantage or material gain for the perpetrators—the Athenian massacre of the Aeginetans in Thyrea is a striking example—to show that it was not always merely an excuse for expansionism.

I would argue that we must accept at least the basic premise of the sources: whatever its political or economic motivations, genocide was always also, and sometimes mainly, an act of 'conspicuous destruction' which served to display the power of the perpetrators and to restore or enhance their status. And a concern with status might not only lead to the destruction of a city which brought its destroyers no additional power or wealth, but also, just occasionally, save a city when purely political and economic reasons might have favoured its destruction, as when the Spartans after a long and bitter war spared Athens in deference to the city's eminent international status, or when Caesar decided not to wipe out Massilia, 'more on account of the reputation (*nomen*) and antiquity of their state than because it had done anything to deserve this from him'.[52] Genocide was most commonly perpetrated by the most aggressively expansionistic states not only because such states pursued their own material interests with more ruthless calculation, but also because they pursued prestige more competitively and with greater emotional intensity than others. Those who aimed for the highest possible status in the world order were least able to tolerate any challenge to their honour and most willing to eliminate without a trace those who seemed to show insufficient respect.[53]

---

[50] Admittedly, the history of this century is not particularly well attested.

[51] Ethical debate: e.g. Ducrey, *Le traitement de prisonniers de guerre dans la Grèce antique*, 313–32; Volkmann, *Die Massenversklavungen der Einwohner eroberter Städte in der hellenistisch-römischer Zeit*, 71–91.

[52] Caesar, *Civil War* 2.22. Athens: Xenophon, *Hellenica* 2.2.19–20.

[53] Role of honour in international relations: Greece: J. E. Lendon, 'Homeric Vengeance and the Outbreak of Greek War', in Hans van Wees (ed.), *War and Violence in Ancient Greece* (London/Swansea: Classical Press of Wales, 2000), 1–30; van Wees, *Greek Warfare*, 19–33. Rome: J. E. Lendon, *Empire of Honour* (Oxford: Oxford University Press, 1997), 74–7 (cities within empire); Susan Mattern, *Rome and the Enemy* (Berkeley: University of California Press, 1999), 171–222.

SELECT BIBLIOGRAPHY

Deacy, Susan, and Karen Pierce (eds), *Rape in Antiquity* (London/Swansea: Classical Press of Wales, 1997).

Ducrey, Pierre, *Le traitement de prisonniers de guerre dans la Grèce antique* (Paris: Boccard, 1968; new edn 1999).

Kern, Paul, *Ancient Siege Warfare* (Bloomington: Souvenir Press, 1999).

Niditch, Susan, *War in the Hebrew Bible* (Oxford: Oxford University Press, 1993).

Oded, Bustenay, *Mass Deportations and Deportees in the Neo-Assyrian Empire* (Wiesbaden: Reichert, 1979).

—— *War, Peace and Empire: Justifications for War in Assyrian Royal Inscriptions* (Wiesbaden: Ludwig Reichert Verlag, 1992).

Sabin, Philip, Hans van Wees, and Michael Whitby (eds), *The Cambridge History of Greek and Roman Warfare*, vols i–ii (Cambridge: Cambridge University Pess, 2007).

van Wees, Hans, *Greek Warfare: Myths and Realities* (London: Duckworth 2004).

Vikman, Elisabeth, 'Sexual Violence in Warfare, Part I: Ancient Origins', *Anthropology and Medicine* 12:1 (2005), 21–31.

Volkmann, Hans, *Die Massenversklavungen der Einwohner eroberter Städte in der hellenistisch-römischer Zeit*, 2nd edn (Stuttgart: Franz Steiner, 1990).

....

CHAPTER 13

EARLY MEDIEVAL EUROPE

THE CASE OF BRITAIN AND IRELAND

....

JAMES E. FRASER

As far as the influential sixth-century historian Gregory of Tours was concerned, the history of fifth-century Gaul (roughly modern France) boiled down to tales of saints and their powers (*virtutes sanctorum*) and tales of genocides (*strages gentium*), literally 'the slaughter of peoples'. The Venerable Bede might have said the same thing, two centuries later, about seventh-century Britain. Flourishing in Northumbria, the kingdom of the northern English, the great scholar wrote that, three generations before his own, 'a great *strages* was conducted of both the Church and the nation (*gens*) of the Northumbrians.' The perpetrator of this *atrocitas* against the men, women, and children of Bede's nation was a British (which is to say Welsh-speaking) king, Caedualla, who 'for a long time raged through all their kingdoms, meaning to wipe out (*eradere*) the whole English race (*genus*)'. His allegation reads like unambiguous genocide, and Bede, like Gregory, would have scoffed at any suggestion that his society was incapable of *strages gentium*. This chapter assesses his assumptions. Its focus is early medieval Britain and Ireland. From time to time, Insular attitudes are considered against a broader backdrop, but a British case study is sufficient to answer the central research question relating to early medieval genocide. Although Len Scales has taken important steps towards introducing medievalists to genocide studies (and vice versa), that question remains, at present, rather basic and fundamental: did *strages gentium* happen?[1]

Britain is an ideal place to confront this question. It retained next to nothing of the state apparatus inherited in part by the barbarian kingdoms that supplanted Roman administration in the Latin West, and perpetuated in the Greek East. As such, there can be no question of applying modern, or indeed classical templates for understanding state-sponsored genocide, which might be applicable to the interesting Byzantine evidence. The island was also sharply segregated along ethno-linguistic lines, which tended to be rather blurrier elsewhere in Europe, and less likely to become flashpoints of violence. Moreover, students of early medieval Britain have been talking about genocide for many years, or at least wondering about it, in attempting to understand the coming of the Anglo-Saxons, the growth and expansion of their culture and political pre-eminence, and, latterly, a similar Gaelic expansion in the Scottish north. The lack of any decisive resolution to these debates suggests that concrete and unambiguous evidence for early medieval acts meeting the criteria for genocide outlined in the UN Convention on the Prevention and Punishment of the Crime of Genocide will always elude us, wherever we might seek them. For the most part we find ourselves stumbling back into the laps of Bede and his fellow commentators, seeking to understand their descriptions of *strages gentium* for what they are and are not; and also for what they reveal about early medieval conceptions surrounding the destructions of peoples.[2]

IDENTIFYING GENOCIDE: THE PROBLEM
OF BIBLICAL MODELS

Our problems in establishing whether genocides actually took place in Western Europe in this epoch are legion, as scholarship surrounding the *adventus Saxonum* has shown. That can hardly occasion surprise: it is difficult enough to amass decisive proof of genocides only years or generations old, never mind *strages gentium* from early medieval Britain. Certainly Bede's description of the ethnic

---

[1] Gregory: *Historiarum libri X*, ii.prol. (Bruno Krusch and Wilhelm Levison (eds), *Gregorii Turonensis Opera* 1: *Libri historiarum X*, Monumenta Germaniae Historica: Scriptores Rerum Merovingicarum, 2nd edn (Hanover: Hahn, 1937–51)). Bede: *Historia ecclesiastica gentis Anglorum*, ii.20 (Bertram Colgrave and R. A. B. Mynors (eds), *Bede's Ecclesiastical History of the English People* (Oxford: Oxford University Press, 1991)). Scales: Len Scales, 'Bread, Cheese and Genocide: Imagining the Destruction of Peoples in Medieval Western Europe', *History* 92 (2007), 284–300.

[2] Ethnic segregation: Alex Woolf, 'Apartheid and Economics in Anglo-Saxon England', in N. J. Higham (ed.), *The Britons in Anglo-Saxon England* (Woodbridge: Boydell and Brewer, 2007), 116.

carnage wrought by Caedualla is nothing like as clear-cut as it first appears. He wrote one hundred years later, with all of the accusatory, one-sided indignation that investigators have come to expect of victims of alleged atrocities and their descendants. In the previous chapter of his *Ecclesiastical History*, he had been jubilant in the face of genocide. The perpetrator that time was Aeðilfrith, the 'very brave' pagan king of Bede's own Northumbrian people, whom he reports had 'laid waste (*uastauit*) the British *gens*', subduing and occupying its districts, 'having exterminated or subjugated the natives (*exterminatis uel subiugatis indigenis*)'. Translating Bede's Latin verb *exterminare* as 'to exterminate' may not, however, be accurate. It implies mass murder to us, when the early medieval Latinist probably understood *exterminare* to mean 'to drive [something] beyond (*ex*) the boundaries (*termini*) [of something else]'. In a later quotation, we shall see Bede associating acts of *exterminatio* with bloodbaths, but its usage here is ambiguous, more likely to refer to population displacement than massacres.[3]

Now, for our purposes it may matter little whether Aeðilfrith massacred his British victims in the course of depopulating their devastated home districts. Either outcome amounts to the violent physical removal of a people from its territory, and deserves consideration as an act of genocide, as the UN Genocide Convention defines that crime as intended destruction in whole or in part. However, we must accept that translation problems and the hindsight of witnesses introduce layers of complexity and difficulty in interrogating our sources about genocide. Another problem is that nothing would be more inappropriate than to evaluate Bede's morality using our own inadmissible moral compass. His condemnation of genocide as *atrocitas* when visited upon his own people by Britons looks hypocritical and chauvinistic to our eyes, if perhaps predictable, alongside his triumphalist estimation of the reverse case. His moral position was more complex, however, than accusations of hypocrisy allow. Bede reflected on Aeðilfrith's achievement with recourse to allusions to the Bible, the source of his morality as a devout monk and one of the foremost experts of the age in biblical studies. The king, he wrote, 'might be compared with Saul, who was once king of Israel', on account of his treatment of the Britons; and he also felt that Jacob's blessing of Benjamin his son was suitable for application to Aeðilfrith's brutalization of them: 'Benjamin shall ravin as a wolf; in the morning, he shall devour the prey, and at night he shall divide the spoil.' For modern non-specialists, increasingly, such biblical allusions represent obscure asides, even unwelcome interruptions of a lively narrative. However, they are often vital clues, revealing to the specialist a great deal about what a writer like Bede was thinking as he attempted to evaluate an historical episode.[4]

Why did this particular scripture spring to Bede's mind in contemplating Aeðilfrith's British genocide? The Israelite tribe of Benjamin was regarded by

[3] Bede: *Hist. eccl.*, i.34.
[4] Ibid. Jacob: Genesis 49:27.

Christian scholars at the time as emblematic of St Paul, a wolf who had ravined in the morning (by persecuting Christians early in his career), but who had divided the spoil in the evening (by evangelizing among the gentiles after his conversion). Bede's underlying point, in making this connection, was thus to imply that the British genocide perpetrated by Aeðilfrith had been, ultimately, for the greater good, like the victimization of those Christians whom Paul had persecuted on his road to conversion. The eighth-century reader was encouraged to see extermination of Britons as part of the trajectory that saw the Northumbrians convert eventually to the Christian religion of their victims (like Paul did), and then outdo them as exemplary believers (like Paul did). Perversely, from the standpoint of modern ethics, it seems that Bede was looking upon the Britons as bit-players in their own genocide: his biblical allusion makes the story all about the Northumbrian English, whose brutality prior to hearing the gospel heralded their later redemption and greatness as a Christian nation.

Even that is not the whole story. There was a deeper association between the Benjamites, genocide, and redemption that influenced the formulation of Bede's doctrine relating to Aeðilfrith. There is a biblical account of a Benjamite genocide perpetrated by their fellow Israelites, who banded against them on account of their wickedness. The result was a great battle, on the first and second days of which the Israelites were 'massacred' (*occiderunt*) by the Benjamites: these successes were the 'ravining in the morning' which Jacob had foreseen. On the third day, however, having called upon God for aid, the Israelites turned the tables on the 26,000 Benjamites, and 'the Lord smote (*percussit*) them before the eyes of the sons of Israel, and they destroyed 25,100 men of them.' The Israelites then smote (*percusserunt*) all the Benjamite cities with such slaughter that the tribe would have died out, had not maidens been forcibly removed from a neighbouring people in order to provide them with wives. Like Paul, the Benjamites had required to be disempowered in order to see the light. From Bede's perspective, his own Northumbrian *gens* had shared that same requirement, as his linking it to Benjamin shows.[5]

That conclusion brings us back to the first genocide outlined in this essay—the Northumbrian one perpetrated by a cruel Briton. This *strages* Bede clearly reckoned to be another stop on his people's road to their Damascus. For him, like other thinkers in early medieval Europe, genocide was a key divine method of dealing with wayward *gentes*. As a cleanser, it was surpassed only by the Flood—the ultimate biblical case of *strages gentium*. The vulgate Bible refers no less than seventy-four times to groups that, like the Benjamites, experienced *percutio*, 'smiting'. God typically plays the role of advocate, and even instigator of the carnage,

---

[5] Bede, Benjamin, and St Paul: J. M. Wallace-Hadrill, *Bede's* Ecclesiastical History of the English People: *A Historical Commentary* (Oxford: Oxford University Press, 1988), 48. Benjamite genocide: Judges 20–1.

intending it as a just punishment. Since Bede likened Aeðilfrith with Saul, we might as well consider an example from that king's story:

So Saul took the kingship over Israel, and he fought against all his enemies . . . and wherever he turned, he kept on conquering (*superabat*). And he gathered a host and smote (*percussit*) the Amalekites, delivering Israel from the hands of those who had plundered them . . . Samuel said to Saul . . . 'This is what the Lord of Hosts says . . . Go now, smite (*percute*) the Amalekites and totally destroy everything that belongs to them. Do not spare them. Put to death men and women, children and infants, cattle and sheep' . . . Then Saul smote (*percussit*) the Amalekites . . . Agag, king of the Amalekites, he took alive, and all his people he totally destroyed (*interfecit*) with the edge of the sword. But Saul and the people spared Agag, and the best of the sheep and the cattle . . . Then the word of the Lord came to Samuel, saying, 'I am sorry that I have made Saul king, because he has turned away from me, and has not carried out my instructions.'

Here genocide is God's revenge upon the Amalekites for victimizing the Israelites, satisfaction eluding him because the carnage falls short of utter extermination. The underlying morality here of feud or vendetta—Guy Halsall's 'customary vengeance'—was fully embraced by early medieval societies: injury and insult were to be avenged, violently if necessary, and irredeemable malefactors invited obliteration. A closer look at Bede's testimony reveals that the newly converted Northumbrians whom Caedualla destroyed had, as Bede believed, apostatized against Christianity. That kind of abject treachery was punishable by violent retribution in ordinary society, and by genocide where God was concerned.[6]

As regards the central question of this essay, we must note that social and theological truths arguably encouraged Bede to ascribe appropriate genocidal ambitions to Caedualla's devastating campaigns, whether or not the British king had himself espoused them. This problem haunts the early medievalist at every turn where genocide is concerned. As Scales has established for the medieval epoch entire, 'tales of inter-ethnic bloodshed' could '[project] clear-cut ethnic purges onto outbreaks of violence which must often have been both more limited in scope and more complex in character,' particularly where a biblical parallel waited in the wings, to which events could be likened. By introducing such a biblical dimension to his history, Bede was conveying to his readers a multifaceted understanding of why the Northumbrians, chastened like the Benjamites, had quickly returned to the Christian fold after apostasy, with greater resolve and commitment. We have already seen that he gives the game away in his account of Aeðilfrith's British genocide, showing that he had concluded that such persecution had been a

6 Savagery as cleanser: e.g. J. M. Wallace-Hadrill, *The Long-Haired Kings* (London: Methuen, 1962), 61–2. Saul and the Amalekites: 1 Samuel 14:47–15:11. Customary vengeance: Guy Halsall, 'Violence and Society in the Early Medieval West: An Introductory Survey', in *idem* (ed.), *Violence and Society in the Early Medieval West* (Woodbridge: Boydell Press, 1998), 22–6; Wallace-Hadrill, *Long-Haired Kings*, 122–8. Bede: *Hist. eccl.*, iii.1. Biblical dimension of medieval notions of genocide: Scales, 'Bread, Cheese and Genocide', 294–5.

necessary Pauline step towards conversion and outstripping these Christians sub-sequently in the enterprises of evangelization and reformation. Elsewhere, Bede confirms such a reading of this account by levelling explicit accusations of wicked-ness at the Britons: they had unjustly withheld Christianity from the Anglo-Saxons (in contrast to the later Anglo-Saxon thirst for mission); and they were being more obstinate against reform than any other Insular people (in contrast with the leading reformist role played by the Anglo-Saxons). Here, again, genocide was theologically appropriate. Bede may therefore be suspected of concluding that it had actually taken place on the conjoined understanding that, on the one hand, God ought to have willed it, no less than he had willed the *percutio* of the Amalekites, and, on the other, that Aeðilfrith had been just the Saul for the job.[7]

IDENTIFYING GENOCIDE: THE PROBLEM
OF HISTORIOGRAPHICAL MODELS

The important general points for genocide historians in all of this are twofold. On the one hand, early medieval accounts of genocide can be problematic. On the other, and as Scales has argued, despite modern assumptions about the intrinsic modernity of genocide, the medieval assumption was that *strages gentium* was intrinsic to the age. The foregoing discussion is emphatically not to say that Aeðilfrith and Caedualla had not, in their turn, dealt harshly or brutally with their victims. It is not even to say that neither of them wished or succeeded in 'acts committed with intent to destroy, in whole or in part, a national, ethnical, racial or religious group,' as the UN Genocide Convention defines genocide. Admitting the possibility is one way to explain the Anglo-British hostility characteristic of both Northumbrian and North British early medieval writings. However, these texts tend to date from many generations after 'first contact', and on the whole are probably a far better guide to contemporary 'historicized' antagonisms, the roots of which were being sought in older times (and indeed projected into them), than to the ethnic attitudes of those older times themselves. Scholars find themselves in the unsatisfying position of being unable to rule out the possibility of real acts of genocide, having no particular reason to do so, but unable as well to place a great deal of weight on Bede's descriptions as proofs.[8]

---

[7] Scales, 'Bread, Cheese and Genocide', 286–7. Bede's accusations: *Hist. eccl.*, i.22, iii.1, v.23.

[8] Anglo-British relations: e.g. David Rollason, *Northumbria, 500–1100: Creation and Destruction of a Kingdom* (Cambridge: Cambridge University Press, 2003), 57–109, especially 93 ff (Northumbrian focus).

In addition to influences exerted upon his historiographical methodology by his biblical learning, Bede was following in an established historiographical tradition which had long since concluded that the coming of the Anglo-Saxons to Britain involved genocide visited upon a wicked British nation for its sins against God. The architects of that tradition were not Anglo-Saxon, but British. Gildas, who flourished in the middle third of the sixth century, argued in a text used by Bede that the Britons, having alienated Rome through treason, left themselves vulnerable to barbarian 'assaults and massacres'. God had granted them a respite, but because they embraced wickedness, wishing 'to purge his family, and to cleanse it from such an infection of evil', God brought the Anglo-Saxons to Britain, 'in just punishment'. Here again all of the same caveats raised against Bede apply: for the same reasons, it was a natural assumption that a wicked nation (once identified) should justly be pulverized at God's pleasure. Early medieval commentators were, as Paul Fouracre has observed, attuned to 'the manifestly vigorous execution of divine judgement'. Gildas was explicitly marshalling his apocalyptic account as a stern warning to his fellow Britons, with the implication that, by mending their ways, they would find the strength from God to rid Britain of the Anglo-Saxon menace in a great counter-genocide. It would be difficult to find any era of Christian civilization in which such talk did not resonate, from Gildas's time to our own. His influence upon Bede's notion 200 years later of Anglo-British genocide and counter-genocide at the opening of Northumbrian history is obvious.[9]

WAS GENOCIDE ALL IN THE MIND IN THE EARLY MIDDLE AGES?

Given the uncertainties surrounding what seemed, at the outset, to be pretty unambiguous allegations of genocide by a careful historian like Bede, whose work continues to be admired today, as well as the open question of what genocide might look like in the archaeological record, students of early medieval genocide find themselves in a difficult position. Not without reason, genocidal conventional models for understanding early Insular history, arising from naïve readings of such textual evidence, have been abandoned, and there are numerous Continental

[9] Gildas: *De excidio Britanniae*, i.15, i.19, i.22, i.24 (Michael Winterbottom (ed.), *Gildas: The Ruin of Britain and Other Documents* (London/Chichester: Phillimore, 1978), 87–142). Later medieval accounts with some of the same imagery: Scales, 'Bread, Cheese and Genocide', 288–9. Paul Fouracre, 'Attitudes towards Violence in Seventh- and Eighth-Century Francia', in Halsall (ed.), *Violence and Society*, 60–75, at 63.

parallels. However, the findings of genetic research have recently seen genocide, or at least mass population displacement, return from the cold as a subject for scholarly deliberation in early British history. At the same time, medievalists, early and late, are increasingly willing to contemplate genocide as an aspect of medieval life and society, as well as of medieval thought.[10]

Apart from what they thought, then, did early medieval people actually commit acts 'with intent to destroy, in whole or in part, a national, ethnical, racial or religious group'? This question returns us to the problem of Latin terminology. It is clear that the biblical *percutiones* of the Amalekites and Benjamites constitute genocide by anybody's reckoning, and it need not be doubted that Bede had precisely the same horrors in mind when he wrote about Anglo-British massacres (*strages*), brutality (*atrocitas*), and devastation (*uastatio*). At the very least, then, early medieval commentators can be said both to have been familiar with the concept of genocide, and to have perceived *strages gentium* as quite possible, both in thought and in deed, within the sociological and technological confines of the times. Such perceptions must carry greater weight than modern preconceptions about what such societies, lacking advanced technological weapons of mass destruction, were capable of.

Bede and Gildas expected to horrify and to edify through their lurid descriptions of ethnic carnage, economic devastation, and depopulation. They expected these to be accepted as true accounts of the past, chilling proofs of God's earnest will that all people should live according to his word and laws. There is nothing to suggest that they expected readers to find them far-fetched; indeed, attempts to horrify and edify depend on an ability to play on genuine and present fears. Neither were their audiences exclusively erudite biblical scholars fully versed in contemporary forms of text-criticism, reading on a multiplicity of levels, so that surface features paled into insignificance. Bede dedicated his work to his king, and a draft was sent to the royal court in advance 'for perusal and criticism'. Gildas names and shames a series of kings in the second person, as if the sermon was intended for their eyes: 'what are you doing, Aurelius Caninus,' he wrote for example; 'are you not being engulfed by the same slime as the man I have just spoken about?' Although one would not wish to press the point too far, nor a long way down the social scale, notions of secular illiteracy in the early medieval epoch can be exaggerated, even in Britain and Ireland. The Carolingian historian Nithard was active as a military leader, with a strong sense of God's role in affecting outcomes on battlefields. We may take it that in general terms the military elites who ruled and dominated early medieval realms

---

[10] Continental historiographical parallels: e.g. Bryan Ward-Perkins, *The Fall of Rome and the End of Civilization* (Oxford: Oxford University Press, 2005). Genetics: Mark G. Thomas et al., 'Evidence for an Apartheid-Like Social Structure in Early Anglo-Saxon England', *Proceedings of the Royal Society B* (doi: 10.1098/rspb.2006.3527 (2006)); Martin Richards et al., 'Genetics and the Origins of the British Population', *Encyclopedia of Life Sciences* (forthcoming), provides some welcome caveats.

were no strangers to genocidal rhetoric and historical models, biblical or otherwise, whether or not they understood them on all of the levels that the clerical intelligentsia did. As a result, we cannot dismiss the possibility that such familiarity encouraged genocidal ambitions, or for that matter ambitions calculated to prevent genocide being inflicted upon their people.[11]

With this in mind, let us turn to the eighth-century annalist, connected with the great monastery in the Hebridean island of Iona in Atlantic Scotland, who was familiar as a monk with the biblical models known to Bede and Gildas, to guide him in his choice of terminology. This man recorded a *percutio* in 741, inflicted upon the Dál Riata, the leading Gaelic people in the West Highlands of Scotland, by a Pictish king from the north-east lowlands, only about ten years after Bede wrote. Similarly, a *percussio* of the district of Dyfed in south-west Wales a century before was recorded by a British annalist. These records could not be more terse or dispassionate, and could scarcely be less informative. At the same time, they are precious for their contemporaneity. Their writers had neither the time nor the inclination to assimilate these elusive events within the grander narratives of a Bede or a Gildas. This situation may be contrasted with the more problematic hindsight of the *Anglo-Saxon Chronicle*, compiled more than a century after Bede, which envisioned the early wars between Anglo-Saxon and Briton as race wars peppered with genocidal episodes. Thus at *Anderitum* in the 490s, that chronicle records, a successful siege by two Anglo-Saxon kings was followed by a massacre, in which they 'killed all who lived in there; there was not even one Briton left there.' The chronicle is not by any means a contemporary witness to this alleged carnage, and Asser's description, based on it, of an Anglo-Saxon genocide of Britons on the Isle of Wight is even less reliable. Our eighth-century chronicler, however, was a contemporary witness to his *percutio Dáil Riata*.[12]

Early medieval Latinists had a range of terms available to them to describe devastating military campaigns, and *percutio*, although it is very common in the Bible, is very rare in Insular usage as applied to such campaigns. All that really prevents us from concluding that these *percutiones* are contemporary records of acts of genocide or ethnic cleansing like the biblical examples are our own preconceptions, though of course it cannot ever be proven that these annalists equated

---

[11] Bede: *Hist. eccl.*, preface. Gildas: *De excid.*, i.30.

[12] Insular *percutiones*: *Annals of Ulster*, 741.10 (Seán Mac Airt and Gearóid Mac Niocaill (eds), *The Annals of Ulster (to A.D. 1131)* (Dublin: Dublin Institute for Advanced Studies, 1983)); *Annales Cambriae*, 645.1 (Edmond Faral (ed.), *La Légende Arthurienne: études et documents*, vol iii (Paris: H. Champion, 1929), 44–50). Anglo-Saxon Chronicle: *Anglo-Saxon Chronicle*, s. a. 491 (e.g. Susan Irvine (ed.), *The Anglo-Saxon Chronicle: a Collaborative Edition 7* (MS E) (Cambridge: D. S. Brewer, 2004)). Asser: 'Life of King Alfred', §2; W. H. Stevenson (ed.), *Asser's Life of King Alfred, Together with the Annals of St. Neots, Erroneously Ascribed to Asser* (Oxford: Clarendon Press, 1904); for discussion, see Simon Keynes and Michael Lapidge (eds.), *Alfred the Great: Asser's Life of King Alfred and Other Contemporary Sources* (London: Penguin, 1983), 230.

percutio with genocide. Similarly, Bede had a further tale of genocide to tell, involving a different Caedwalla, an Anglo-Saxon king of Wessex this time, which may be regarded as more compelling evidence of genocide than the examples already discussed. 'After Caedwalla had gained possession of the kingdom,' he wrote, 'he also captured the Isle of Wight . . . ; and he endeavoured to exterminate (*exterminare*) all the natives by merciless slaughter (*ac stragica caede*), and to replace them by men from his own kingdom.' Here, as promised above, we find Bede linking *exterminatio* with *strages.* He was describing events that had taken place when he was thirteen years old, not generations earlier. Moreover, involving as they do two groups of Anglo-Saxon pagans, they are not bedevilled by the Anglo-British dimension which problematizes our accounts above. Indeed, unlike in those cases, Bede supplied no explanation or justification of Caedwalla's aggressive ethnic purge of the Isle of Wight, presumably because it was self-explanatory and insufficiently remarkable to invite further comment.[13]

Early medieval populations enjoyed no intrinsic rights to exist or flourish: they were entitled to expect instead, at God's pleasure, to be harvested by enemies bent on devastation, pillage, killing, rapine, and enslavement. All indications are that secular society accepted that might was right, not least because it was a condition bestowed by God. The Irish wisdom text *Audacht Moraind* concerned to outline princely virtue, idealized princes who were just, merciful, and supportive of their own people, and who kept them safe. Its author accordingly saw bloodshed at home as 'a vain destruction of all rule'. In contrast, he urged the 'true' prince to 'remove the shame of his cheeks by arms in battle against other lands'. In that context, far from requiring moral justification, aggression and bloodshed were moral imperatives whereby 'the prince's truth' could be tested and proven.[14]

GENOCIDE AND THE QUESTION OF IDENTITY

These factors encourage acceptance that, in these instances, we have accounts of real acts tantamount to genocide in early medieval Britain. Can we draw the same conclusion about the Hebrides and Orkney, obliterated (*deletae sunt*) in 671 and 681 respectively, possibly by the same Pictish king each time? Among these different examples of contemporary records, only in the Dalriadic one in Scotland can we be confident that the victims were a particular 'national, ethnical, racial or religious

---

[13] Bede: *Hist. eccl.*, iv.16. Self-evident nature of ethnic violence: Scales, 'Bread, Cheese and Genocide', 285–6.

[14] Might was right: e.g. Fouracre, 'Attitudes Towards Violence', 67. *Audacht Moraind*: Fergus Kelly (ed.), *Audacht Moraind* (Dublin: Dublin Institute for Advanced Studies, 1976).

group', distinct from the perpetrators. This problem is compounded by the fact that it is not always clear how groups (and thus potential perpetrators and victims of genocide) went about distinguishing one *gens* from another. This question has been the subject of a very considerable body of research, the size and scope of which can come as something of a surprise to non-specialists. Nationalist historiography of the nineteenth and twentieth centuries understandably regarded the collapse of the Roman Empire and the rise of the earliest medieval realms of Western Europe as a pivotal moment in the genesis of the nations which became the great powers of Europe and the colonial world. Unsurprisingly perhaps, given the uses to which such historiography could ultimately be put in informing the nationalist and racist ideologies which shaped the great and terrible wars and colonial projects of the age, the evidence relating to the formation, function, and perception of ethnicity in the early Middle Ages is fraught with sometimes acute controversy which must be passed over here.[15]

The Latin terminology associated with ethnicity (*gens* and *natio* in particular) envisions ethnic identity as 'kinship "writ large"', marking early medieval people out, in human sciences terms, as 'primordialists' who believed that ethnicity was largely a function of 'the givens of birth'—ties of blood (real and imagined) to kin and *gens*, homeland, language, and culture. Yet individual identities were also influenced by situational concerns, as any number of examples show. Early medieval communities thus possessed flexible means of ascertaining their sameness with, or difference from other groups, and could shift the goalposts to suit their immediate situation. Thus the obliteration of pagan Anglo-Saxon communities on the Isle of Wight by the forces of a pagan Anglo-Saxon king of Wessex was capable of being envisioned as a struggle between two quite distinct groups, however much they might, in other situations, invite consideration as constituents of a single race. The potential for such situationality in early medieval ethnicity, including the role of kings in identifying otherness, raises the particular issue of 'ethnogenesis', and the sometimes bitter scholarly dispute surrounding the paradigmatic theoretical model formulated by Reinhard Wenskus to explain the creation of peoples in early medieval times. Wenskus envisioned new post-Roman ethnic groups as coalescing around a coherent group of aristocrats, which he called a *Traditionskern*, a 'core of tradition', and concluded that its sacred traditions preserved ethnic traits of great antiquity that were transferred outwards to the entire *gens* which it had come to dominate. On this model, the behaviour of kings and other social elites is the principal engine which shaped, stabilized, and overturned early medieval ethnic solidarities.[16]

---

[15] Hebridean episodes: *Annals of Ulster*, 672.2, 682.5.

[16] Early medieval ethnicity: Patrick J. Geary, 'Ethic Identity as a Situational Construct in the Early Middle Ages', *Mitteilungen der Anthropologischen Gesellschaft in Wien* 113 (1983), 15–26; for a more general statement on medieval ethnicity, see Scales: 'Bread, Cheese and Genocide', 290. Primordialism:

'*Traditionskern* ethnogenesis theory' has not gone unchallenged, and criticism has revolved in particular around the notion of the 'core of tradition'. The critique has considerably more to commend it than the paradigm, with the result that we are not required to accept that ethnic consciousness within the early medieval *gens* emanated from an elite core. It is an important point for the study of genocide. Had Wenskus's theory held true, the destruction of the *Traditionskern* would have emerged as sufficient *ipso facto* to bring about 'ethnonemesis', the eradication of the *ethnos*. Such a conclusion does not seem to be justified. Our texts do indicate, none the less, that the leaders of a community enjoyed an intimate relationship with its ethnic identity. A famous passage from an Irish legal tract from the period observes that 'a people (*túath*) is no people, without scholar, church, poet, and king.' The sentiment chimes with that aspect of early medieval thought that encouraged Wenskus, and those who have since embraced his theory, to adopt their elitist notion that the roots of ethnic consciousness were planted in an elite *Traditions-kern*. Fortunately, the Irish sentiment also chimes with Scales's observations from a later medieval perspective that, in medieval thought

> to strip a people of its identity, in the form of its rights and liberties, was to render it incapable of its own defence, and thus expose it to the gravest of perils . . . [A people] was conceivable as a community of a shared identity, rooted in law and privilege. To forfeit these was to stand helpless before an implacably hostile world. From disenfranchisement and loss of common identity to physical annihilation . . . was but a short step.

On this showing, that early medieval Irish lawyers regarded communities as non-peoples without a scholar, a church, a poet, and a king had nothing (necessarily) to do with any sense that elites were the engine that drove ethnic consciousness, *Traditionskern*-fashion. The point was instead that a *túath* or people was regarded as something 'rooted in law and privilege', which, if it lacked scholar, church, poet, and king, was in no position to protect and uphold the rights and liberties involved, and so could not be recognized as possessing such entitlements in the first place.[17]

Siân Jones, *The Archaeology of Ethnicity: Constructing Identities in the Past and Present* (London/New York: Routledge, 1997), 56–83. Insular examples of situational identity: Adomnán, *Vita sancti Columbae*, i.2 (Alan O. Anderson and Marjorie O. Anderson (eds), *Adomnán's Life of Columba*, 2nd edn (Oxford: Oxford University Press, 1991)); Bede: *Hist. eccl.*, iv.22 (see also James Campbell, *Essays in Anglo-Saxon History* (London/Ronceverte: Hambledon Press, 1986), 86–7). Wenskus: Reinhard Wenskus, *Stammesbildung und Verfassung: das Werden der frühmittelalterlichen gentes* (Cologne: Böhlau, 1961). Synopses and evaluations of 'ethnogenesis' paradigm: Andrew Gillett (ed.), *On Barbarian Identity: Critical Approaches to Ethnicity in the Early Middle Ages* (Turnhout: Brepols, 2002), esp. 1–18, 39–68, 221–39.

17 Irish legal tract: Fergus Kelly, *A Guide to Early Irish Law* (Dublin: Dublin Institute for Advanced Studies, 1988), 4. Scales, 'Bread, Cheese and Genocide', 292.

GENOCIDE AND THE PURGATION OF ELITES

It follows naturally from such thinking that, *Traditionskern* or no *Traditionskern*, elite purges in the early Middle Ages could, in many cases, double as ethnic ones in the imagination, since disempowerment could threaten a community's capacity to uphold and defend the common customs, laws, and privileges which it believed set it off from other groups. In other words (and although it was certainly not intended as such), the Irish sentiment could, if it was widely appreciated, have provided something of a formula for genocide in early medieval Europe. The ninth-century Frankish biographer Einhard would seem to have been thinking along similar lines to the Irish jurists, when he envisioned the destruction of Avar elites by Charlemagne as equating to the depopulation of Avar-held Pannonia. This link between ethnicity and protection of laws and privileges offers something of an explanation, too, of instances where the *gens* seems to be equated with the army in the early Middle Ages, with the corresponding point that massacres of warriors could have been intended, and understood at some level, as genocidal acts. It may be that we have an Insular example. After a battle in Ireland in 738 between the powerful Uí Néill kingdoms and the Laigin of Leinster, the Laigin king 'was beheaded by a battle-sword', and the Uí Néill 'in unaccustomed fashion, routed, trampled, crushed, overthrew and destroyed their Laigin adversaries, so much so that almost the entire enemy was well nigh annihilated.'[18]

The biblical *percutiones* discussed above bear no relation either to elite purges or to massacres confined to military men. Early medieval commentators could at least envisage genocide as mass murder on the kind of horrific scale that we tend to associate with it today, and could also justify it with the help of moral theology. It may therefore be that we would recognize as genocidal acts the rare *percutiones* on Insular record in this period. In contrast, the purging of elites probably fails to register today as genocide, but did not fail to do so then, and seems to have been fairly common in early medieval Britain. Bede's account of the genocide visited upon the denizens of the Isle of Wight by Caedwalla of Wessex conveniently weds the purgation of elites with extermination:

I think that I must not pass over in silence the fact that among the first fruits of the island who believed [i.e. converted to Christianity] and were saved were two boy-princes (*regii pueri*) ... When the enemy was approaching the island they escaped by flight and crossed over [to the mainland] ... They thought they could remain concealed from the victorious king; but they were betrayed and condemned to death.

---

[18] Armies as nations: Michael Kulikowski, 'Nation versus Army: A Necessary Contrast?', in Gillett (ed.), *On Barbarian Identity*, 69–84. Avars: Einhard, *Vita Karoli magni*, §13 (Oswald Holder-Egger (ed.), *Einhardi Vita Karoli Magni*, Monumenta Germaniae Historica: Scriptores Rerum Germanicarum 25 (Hannover: Hahn, 1911)). Uí Néill and Laigin: *Annals of Ulster*, 738.4.

The implications of the full account are that Caedwalla succeeded in his genocidal agenda, which featured as its centrepiece the killings of these young princes. His account of the other Caedualla, the British king who strove to eradicate the Northumbrians, is also characterized by the flights of princes, adult and child, to the courts of foreign kings whence none returned, as well as by the executions of those who had failed to elude capture. Princely exile is a recurrent feature of regime change in Bede's Britain, suggesting that purges were an anticipated aspect of political change. Men like Aeðilfrith, Caedualla, and his later namesake may not, in fact, have visited upon their victims levels of elite carnage which differed greatly from the normal amounts of blood shed when dynasty replaced dynasty through the usual course of succession custom. It may have been their otherness, rather than bloodthirstiness in excess of the norm, which encouraged the sense that genocide had taken place.[19]

GENOCIDE AND RELIGIOUS OTHERNESS

In the cases of both Aeðilfrith, a pagan exterminating Christians, and Caedualla, a Christian wiping out apostates, religion was a prominent element of their otherness, at least for Bede. In his own day, Bede continued to see the religious otherness of the Britons as a key factor in their ongoing troubles with the Anglo-Saxons, observing that 'they oppose ... the whole state of the catholic church by their incorrect Easter and their evil customs,' and so were 'opposed by the power of God and man alike', with the result that 'they have been brought partly under English mastery.' Scholars have debated the reasons for Bede's infatuation with the seventh-century Insular schism over observances like the correct calculation of the date of Easter, but here he indicated that it helped to explain why God endorsed Anglo-Saxon subjugation of British communities. Similar thinking underlies the problematic note, in a later medieval chronicle relating to the extinction of the Picts in northern Britain, that they had been 'annihilated' (*deleuit*) because 'God, by reason of their wickedness, deigned to make them alien from and void of their heritage.'[20]

If the early medieval Insular world was capable of looking upon genocidal suppressions of religious groups as righteous acts against the wicked, the most

[19] Bede: *Hist. eccl.*, ii.20; iii.1; iv.16; iv.22.

[20] Bede: *Hist. eccl.*, v.23. Picts: *Chronicle of the Kings of Alba*, §2 (Marjorie O. Anderson (ed.), *Kings and Kingship in Early Scotland*, 2nd edn (Edinburgh/London: Scottish Academic Press, 1980), 149–53).

infamous attempt to destroy one in the age was perpetrated by Charlemagne on the Continent in and after the 770s. In 775, according to a contemporary chronicle, three years after destroying and pillaging one of their shrines, he began all-out war on 'the treacherous and treaty-breaking *gens* of the Saxons', intending that it should be 'either defeated and forced to accept the Christian religion, or entirely exterminated (*tollerentur*)'. Charlemagne's biographer Einhard wrote that this war was *atrocius*, full of atrocities, lasting over thirty years until the victorious king 'transported some 10,000 men...and dispersed them in small groups, with their wives and children, into diverse parts of Gaul and Germany.' This depopulation, attested as well in a contemporary chronicle, was intended to ensure that the Saxons would 'be united with the Franks and become one people with them'. As news of Charlemagne's war spread, an Anglo-Saxon abbot wrote to him, entreating him to 'increase [his] righteous zeal for their conversion, suppress the worship of idols, [and] cast down the buildings of their temples', that he might 'find a rewarder in heaven in him whose name and knowledge [Charlemagne] will have spread on earth'. Thus was the moral rectitude of the Saxon genocide confirmed on the grounds of religious persecution, as Bede had envisioned for his Northumbrian examples, where motives of border security, imperialism, persecution, and *strages gentium* were similarly inextricably intertwined. The same mix of factors was surely involved in Charlemagne's campaigns against the Avars, which according to Einhard left their lands 'completely uninhabited'; in the suppression of a Saxon rebellion 'in a great bloodbath (*nimia caedes*)' two generations later; and in Ireland in 902, when the pagan Scandinavian community which had captured and settled at Dublin fifty years earlier was 'driven from Ireland' by a conspiracy of Uí Néill and Laigin kings, 'and escaped half dead after they had been wounded and broken'. The famous expulsion of Irish settlers from Dyfed by a dynasty of North Britons soon after the end of Roman Britain, recorded in a ninth-century text, is, however, almost certainly pseudo-historical.[21]

---

[21] Charlemagne and the Saxons: *Annales regni Francorum, s. a.* 772, 775–6, 804 (Friedrich Kurze (ed.), *Annales regni Francorum* (741–829), Monumenta Germaniae Historica: Scriptores Rerum Germanicarum 6 (Hanover: Hahn, 1895)); Einhard, *V. Karoli*, §7; see also e.g. Henry Mayr-Harting, 'Charlemagne, the Saxons, and the Imperial Coronation of 800', *English Historical Review* 111 (1996), 1113–33. Anglo-Saxon approbation: Dorothy Whitelock (ed.), *English Historical Documents c.500–1042*, 2nd edn (London/New York: Methuen, 1979), 832–3. Avars: Einhard, *V. Karoli*, §13. Saxon *caedes*: Nithard, *Historiae*, iv.6 (Ernst Müller (ed.), *Nithardi Historiarum Libri IIII*, Monumenta Germaniae Historica: Scriptores Rerum Germanicarum 44 (Hanover: Hahn, 1907)). Scandinavians: *Annals of Ulster*, 902.2. Dyfed: Alex Woolf, 'The Expulsion of the Irish from Dyfed', in Karen Jankulak and Jonathan M. Wooding (eds.), *Ireland and Wales in the Middle Ages* (Dublin: Four Courts Press, 2007), 102–15.

BRUTALITY AND DEHUMANIZATION
AS MORAL GREY AREAS

Clerical commentators were of course capable of looking upon brutality as a hallmark of wickedness. Bede certainly did so with regard to Caedualla. Yet for early medieval clergy there was nothing intrinsically immoral about horrific violence, up to and including genocide. Context was everything. Gildas celebrated how Roman soldiers, arriving in Britain to deliver the provincials from barbarian invaders, 'laid low a great number', and 'planted in their enemies' necks the claws of their sword-points', so that they 'caused among them a slaughter like the fall of leaves'. A psalm which his hagiographer said was sung by the Irish St Columba outside the gates of a royal Pictish fortress exhorts kings to 'ride forth victoriously on behalf of truth, humility and righteousness', that 'peoples (*populi*) shall fall beneath your feet.' Gildas's lurid details relating to the 'dreadful and devastating onslaughts' endured by the Britons at the hands of barbarians, in which 'a quick end saved [men] from the miserable fate which awaited their brothers and children,' were intentionally apocalyptic. Yet the apocalypse reflects, as well as exaggerating, warfare as it was practised in Britain when Gildas wrote. From a modern perspective war crimes drip from the pages of early medieval chronicles, but our witnesses, as often as not, present such details as the products of divine or natural justice. In that respect, their treatment of *strages gentium* forms a subgroup of clerical treatment of war more generally, in which notions of war crimes were rather different than our own. Nithard provides particularly revealing ninth-century insight, recording that after a battle in which he had fought on the winning side, a convocation of bishops found that the victors 'had fought for justice and equity alone, as God's judgement had made clear' in the granting of victory. Each man among them was found to be 'an instrument of God, free from responsibility', save any who 'knew that he had either counseled or committed anything . . . from wrath or hatred or vainglory or any passion'. In the early Middle Ages, war crimes were thought crimes.[22]

The UN Genocide Convention is not solely concerned, of course, with attempts to obliterate groups directly through violent atrocities. There are also questions of inflicting 'mental harm' on them, and creating 'conditions of life' calculated to eliminate them. It is too difficult to know the minds of early medieval people well enough to comment on the psychological effects of ethnic victimization. It may be worth raising, however, the subject of dehumanization. In his biography of Charlemagne, Notker related stories in which Franks spoke of Scandinavians as

---

[22] Attitudes towards violence: e.g. Fouracre, 'Attitudes towards Violence', 62–3. Gildas: *De excid.*, i.15–19. Adomnán: *V. sanct. Columbae*, i.37; Psalm 45 (*Vulg.* lxiv). Nithard, *Hist.*, iii.1.

'dog-heads' (*cynocephales*), of Slavs and Avars as 'tiny birds' (*aviculae*), and of one Slavonic group as 'tadpoles' (*ranunculi*) and 'worms' (*vermiculi*) who died 'squealing their incomprehensible tongue'. Non-Latinate readers will have missed the additional belittling implications of the -*culi*/-*culae* endings of some of these words, emphasizing the wretchedness of these dehumanized enemies. Gildas provides the most picturesque Insular examples, with recourse to ugly imagery all too familiar to us today, speaking of the Britons' aggressive Insular neighbours as 'dark throngs of worms (*vermiculi*) which wriggle out of narrow fissures in the rock when the sun is high,' or as 'greedy wolves (*lupi*), rabid with extreme hunger, which, dry-mouthed, leap over into the sheepfold when the shepherd is away.' Much later, Bede's older contemporary Stephen of Ripon referred to Pictish rebels against Northumbrian domination as 'bestial peoples' (*populi bestiales*) and as 'swarms of ants' (*formicarum greges*).[23]

That such descriptions may be thought offensive seems to be confirmed by Bede, whose discretion prevented him from adopting the dehumanizing epithets favoured by Gildas and Stephen, despite having otherwise made use of their works as sources of historical information. Dehumanizing rhetoric is not genocide, but is regarded by modern commentators as intrinsic to the process, or at least as preparation for the righteous extermination of such inhuman pests. Something more sinister may have been on the cards in a West Saxon law code dating from Bede's lifetime. Here, as Alex Woolf has argued, the fact that the honour prices compensating British nobles and normal freemen were set respectively at just 50 and 60 per cent of those of their Saxon counterparts may have had a much greater and more devastating effect even than the classification of Britons as second-class citizens in Wessex. As Woolf theorizes, 'the imbalance ... may hold within it the very key to the disappearance of the Britons' in much of lowland Britain:

If, for example, a hypothetical English and British nobleman ... got into a series of disputes with one another and were dealt with fairly by the courts ... then all compensations paid by the Briton to the Englishman would be twice the value of those paid to him by his opponent. The end result would be that the property and finally the land [held by the Briton] would pass to the Englishman.

If Woolf's theory correctly encapsulates the long-term effects of such stark legal segregation, which he terms 'apartheid' unreservedly, we are looking here at something of a blueprint for the eradication of the Britons. However, it is unlikely that such eradication was envisaged or intended, so that it cannot really be

---

[23] Notker, *Gesta Karoli*, ii.12–13 (Hans F. Haefele (ed.), *Notker der Stammler: Die Taten Karls des Großen*, Monumenta Germaniae Historica: Scriptores Rerum Germanicarum, Nova Series 12 (Hanover: Hahn, 1959)); for discussion, see Matthew Innes, 'Memory, Orality and Literacy in an Early Medieval Society', *Past and Present* 158 (1998), 3–36, at 27–8. Gildas: *De excid.*, i.16, i.19. Stephen, *Vita sancti Wilfrithi*, §19 (Bertram Colgrave (ed.), *The Life of Bishop Wilfrid by Eddius Stephanus* (Cambridge: Cambridge University Press, 1927)).

regarded as genocide through the creation of conditions of life calculated to destroy a group. It is more likely to have been the natural result of a system devised in order to emphasize the political superiority of Anglo-Saxon groups within a polity which included British ones, while at the same time recognizing the wisdom of preserving the legal rights of the latter in order to stave off resistance. As such, this scenario may stand as an example of the kinds of indirect damage which could, in the early Middle Ages, be inflicted by dominant groups upon submissive ones, as a result of a tendency to devalue and dehumanize those regarded as outsiders.[24]

CAPTIVES, SLAVES, AND DEPOPULATION

Similar indirect damage could be inflicted upon early medieval groups through the forcible transfer of women and children into other groups, a genocidal crime recognized by the UN Genocide Convention. In 697, Adomnán of Iona formulated and promulgated a *Law of Innocents*, embraced in Ireland and northern Britain. Its purpose was to discourage the victimization of *innocentes* or non-combatants—principally women, children, and clerics—by the armed classes of Insular society whose arms were emblematic of their free status. The effects of the law are unknowable. What is important for our purposes is that it anticipates that victimization of women and children was rampant. Indeed, the text of the law provides some chilling details about men, women, and children being butchered, mutilated, and degraded by warriors in horrific ways. These details are much more convincing than Notker's fanciful tale of Charlemagne rounding up the children of one unnamed people and 'shortening by a head' all who exceeded the height of a sword. Taking *innocentes* captive seems to have been fairly common. Sometimes, the intention was to ransom them back to their home communities. Early Irish law cast no moral aspersions upon the killing of unransomed captives; and the Church (which did) was inclined to intervene and ransom them.[25]

An alternative to murder was enslavement. Bede tells the tale of a warrior nobleman who tries but fails to pass himself off to his captors as a country

---

[24] Dehumanizing rhetoric and genocide: Rowan Savage, '"Disease Incarnate": Biopolitical Discourse and Genocidal Dehumanisation in the Age of Modernity', *Journal of Historical Sociology* 20:3 (2007), 404–40. Woolf, 'Apartheid and Economics', 127–9 (for genetic support, see Thomas et al., 'Evidence for an Apartheid-Like Social Structure').

[25] Adomnán, *Cáin Adomnáin*, §§33–6, 40, 44, 46, 50 (Máirín Ní Dhonnchadha, 'The Law of Adomnán: a Translation', in Thomas O'Loughlin (ed.), *Adomnán at Birr, AD 697: Essays in Commemoration of the Law of the Innocents* (Dublin: Four Courts Press, 2001)), 53–68. Notker, *Gest. Karoli*, ii.12. Kelly, *Guide to Early Irish Law*, 128–9.

bumpkin, receives a stay of execution for his honest admission of his true identity, and is sold into slavery to foreign buyers. People could be harvested for enslavement more actively. The famous St Patrick described a slave raid in which newly converted Irish women and men 'were butchered and slaughtered with the sword' by the retinue of a Christian British king, and others 'were removed and carried off to faraway lands'. There they were sold into slavery, 'who were freeborn', although the raiders had evidently enslaved some of the women themselves. Patrick's indignant reaction was roused, not by the raid as such, but by the fact that he had not been given an opportunity to redeem the captives, who had been enslaved rather than being kept safe for ransoming. As a youth in his native Britain, Patrick had himself been a victim of a similar raid and was removed to Ireland along with youths of both sexes, where he was enslaved. Communities denuded of their women and children in this way (to say nothing of bodies of normal freemen) could face a bleak future: the Benjamites discussed above avoided annihilation only because their Israelite conquerors replaced their massacred women with others captured from abroad. Here again, however, whether the intention was ever to threaten a group's existence is an open question. In neither of the cases involving himself is there any hint in Patrick's testimony of specific genocidal motives behind, or consequences from, the transportation of women and children. That being said, cross-cultural anthropological analysis of this question suggests that 'non-state' societies like these recognized at some level its genocidal potential, if only on a local scale. All that can really be said with confidence is that, where genocidal motives existed in early medieval Europe, tactics like these were well known and available for scattering a population among several captors, and undermining its reproductive future.[26]

FINAL THOUGHTS: GENOCIDE AND THE EARLY MEDIEVAL MIND

Scholars have good reason to baulk at the application of a term like 'genocide,' with all its twentieth-century moral and legal baggage, to early medieval episodes of violence, depopulation, and displacement which would otherwise seem to meet the criteria for genocide enumerated in the UN Convention on the Prevention and Punishment of the Crime of Genocide. Yet that Convention observes in its

[26] Bede: *Hist. eccl.*, iv.22. Patrick, *Epistola*, §§3, 7, 10, 13, 15, 16, 22 (A. B. E. Hood (ed.), *St. Patrick: His Writings and Muirchu's Life* (London/Chichester: Phillimore, 1978), 35–8). Patrick, *Confessio*, §§1, 16 (Hood (ed.), *St. Patrick*, 23–34). Anthropology: Lawrence H. Keeley, *War before Civilization* (Oxford: Oxford University Press, 1996), 48.

Preamble 'that at all periods of history genocide has inflicted great losses on humanity,' and our examination of the early medieval evidence from Britain and Ireland suggests that this period at least need not be excluded from such an assertion. Historians having long since abandoned judgemental evaluations of past societies according to anachronistic ethics; no early medieval person or people was guilty of the *crime* of genocide. It is an alien modern concept which early medieval people would have struggled to comprehend. For them, *strages gentium* were an integral part of the natural order of things ordained by God, the ultimate judge of humanity, whose sentences could include the smiting of individuals and whole peoples. Even had they any conception of crimes against humanity, to have questioned God's sentence of *percutio* was to commit Saul's crime against him; and a crime against God was always going to outweigh other considerations in early medieval Europe.

Whether or not we absolve them from guilt, early medieval Europeans may have something to contribute to genocide studies today. The evidence shows that concepts of ethnic obliteration, and what constituted it, were variable, depending upon class and social standing, and extended well beyond the comparatively narrow confines of actual physical slaughter. It may be particularly important that disempowerment and defencelessness could be regarded as annihilation, the social theory of the age envisioning an intimate and mutually reinforcing relationship between elites and ethnicity. If modern social theories disagree with early Irish law that a group's scholars, churches, poets, and king represent the pillars of its peoplehood, worthy of strenuous protection, they may routinely identify other entities and institutions whose endangerment is liable to occasion indignation for seeming to be a threat against a community's very existence. A consideration of genocide in the early Middle Ages thus reinforces for us that genocide and social theory are inextricably linked in every age, and that genocide may take on a number of guises over time and space, the shape and conception of a given society shaping the formula for its obliteration. Is existing legislation sufficiently flexible to take adequate account of the variation in social theories which characterizes humanity today? If not, we may be failing to provide adequate protection against annihilation to threatened groups and communities, especially those whose social theories may have more in common with early medieval thought than the West.

SELECT BIBLIOGRAPHY

Colgrave, Bertram, and R. A. B. Mynors (eds), *Bede's Ecclesiastical History of the English People* (Oxford: Oxford University Press, 1991).

Geary, Patrick J., 'Ethnic Identity as a Situational Construct in the Early Middle Ages', *Mitteilungen der Anthropologischen Gesellschaft in Wien* 113 (1983), 15–26.

Gillett, Andrew (ed.), *On Barbarian Identity: Critical Approaches to Ethnicity in the Early Middle Ages* (Turnhout: Brepols, 2002).

Halsall, Guy (ed.), *Violence and Society in the Early Medieval West* (Woodbridge: Boydell Press, 1998).

Keeley, Lawrence H., *War before Civilization* (Oxford: Oxford University Press, 1996).

Kelly, Fergus, *A Guide to Early Irish Law* (Dublin: Dublin Institute for Advanced Studies, 1988).

Ní Dhonnchadha, Máirín, 'The Law of Adomnán: A Translation', in Thomas O'Loughlin (ed.), *Adomnán at Birr, AD 697: Essays in Commemoration of the Law of the Innocents* (Dublin: Four Courts Press, 2001), 53–68.

Richards, Martin et al., 'Genetics and the Origins of the British Population', *Encyclopedia of Life Sciences* (forthcoming).

Scales, Len, 'Bread, Cheese and Genocide: Imagining the Destruction of Peoples in Medieval Western Europe', *History* 92 (2007), 284–300.

Thomas, Mark G. et al., 'Evidence for an Apartheid-Like Social Structure in Early Anglo-Saxon England', *Proceedings of the Royal Society B* (doi: 10.1098/rspb.2006.3527 (2006)).

Wallace-Hadrill, J. M., *The Long-Haired Kings* (London: Methuen, 1962).

Ward-Perkins, Bryan, *The Fall of Rome and the End of Civilization* (Oxford: Oxford University Press, 2005).

Winterbottom, Michael (ed.), *Gildas: The Ruin of Britain and Other Documents* (London/Chichester: Phillimore, 1978).

Woolf, Alex, 'Apartheid and Economics in Anglo-Saxon England', in N. J. Higham (ed.), *The Britons in Anglo-Saxon England* (Woodbridge: Boydell and Brewer, 2007), 115–29.

CHAPTER 14

··

CENTRAL AND LATE MEDIEVAL EUROPE

LEN SCALES

··

The wicked shall be turned into hell, and all the nations that forget God

Psalm 9:17

NEW ORDER: GENOCIDAL FANTASIES, EUROPEAN TRANSFORMATIONS

··

FOR some, genocide is Europe's peculiar gift to the world. Others insist that, far from being atavistic, genocide is a crime of—as well as against—civilization.[1]

---

[1] For a radical claim for the (premodern) European origins of genocide see Ward Churchill, *A Little Matter of Genocide: Holocaust and Denial in the Americas 1492 to the Present* (San Francisco: City Lights Books, 1997); for genocide and civilization: Michael Mann, *The Dark Side of Democracy: Explaining Ethnic Cleansing* (Cambridge: Cambridge University Press, 2005), Ch. 1; Eric D. Weitz, 'The Modernity of Genocide: War, Race, and Revolution in the Twentieth Century', in Robert Gellately and Ben Kiernan (eds), *The Specter of Genocide: Mass Murder in Historical Perspective* (Cambridge: Cambridge University Press, 2003), 53–4.

Where, then, to place those centuries—between, approximately, the years 1000 and 1500—in which, if some very distinguished medieval historians are to be believed, European civilization itself was formed? On the whole, sunny vistas still prevail here—especially on that formative period between the eleventh and thirteenth centuries, which is sometimes called the 'high' Middle Ages. Here was a Europe of cathedrals and universities, of mind and spirit, in which the peaceful arts prospered in growing towns, new orders of monks sought a foretaste of heaven on earth, and the values of chivalry began to soften the violence of the Dark Age warlord. 'Humanism' found a home already in the twelfth no less than the fifteenth century. A 'Europe of sensibility' was being born, which 'brooked no internal boundaries'.[2] Where to look for the dark side? Was there, from the present volume's perspective, a 'dark side' at all? The history of genocidal thought and action in medieval Europe remains unwritten. Perhaps that is because there is none to write.

There is indeed a history to recount, and the formation of European literate culture, or civilization, must be given a central part in it. So, too, however, must the developing structures of power upon which civilizations rest; and the history of power in medieval Europe is one of new divisions as well as emergent unities. An eleventh-century illustrated gospel book, now in the Pierpont Morgan Library in New York, shows Christ cleansing the Temple with a whip.[3] It might stand as emblematic for much of what was to follow in the period—and what follows in these pages. The book was made for Countess Matilda of Tuscany, close ally of Pope Gregory VII (1073–85), whose radical vision of a society transformed under papal headship did so much to set Latin Europe on new foundations. The image signals some salient characteristics of the dawning era: a preoccupation with purity and a mission to purge the impure; a new decisiveness in setting boundaries and ruling both in and out; a growing facility in discrimination—understood both as discernment and disfavour; a quest for perfectible *Christian* communities; and a willingness to seek these ends by force. In each of these developments, culture and power were bound up together. They were elements in a 'Europe of sensibility' that induced its inhabitants to build up, not tear down, walls. People grew increasingly sensible of *difference*—of the threats which it seemed to pose, but also of their own capacity to meet those perceived threats with violence. The earthly paradise was not for all, and if some were to be gathered in, others must needs be cast out.

The Catholic Church under its reforming popes led the way in separating sheep from goats, while also introducing into European life a new stress on the general, the total, the all-encompassing. These same principles are also to be observed at

---

[2] Jacques Le Goff, *The Birth of Europe 400–1500*, trans. Janet Lloyd (Oxford: Blackwell, 2005), 42; and for an influential older account, R.W. Southern, *The Making of the Middle Ages* (London: Hutchinson, 1953).

[3] Malcolm Barber, *The Two Cities: Medieval Europe 1050–1320* (London: Routledge, 1992), facing 192.

work in the development of political communities of various kinds in the centuries after 1000—among them the European kingdoms and the Christian peoples (*gentes, nationes*) to which it was widely believed these kingdoms gave constitutional form.[4] Peoples claimed a central part in the political assumptions of medieval Western Europeans—just as they did in the Bible, from which the political vocabulary of the Latin Middle Ages was to a large extent drawn.[5] Medieval writers believed that humanity was fundamentally divided on ethnic lines. Its social building blocks were communities held together by ties of blood and shared origin, though also displaying common cultural attributes, ranging from language and law to elements such as dress, hairstyle, food, and manner of war. Common blood also took visible form in stature, physique, and skin colour. That the ethnic unities which medieval observers claimed to perceive were in fact cultural constructs hardly needs stating—but then, they always are. There seems no reason, therefore, to shrink from ascribing to medieval people fully fledged notions of ethnicity (we might also say 'race') and—when these were linked to political titles—nationhood.[6] For their articulation, medieval writers commanded a substantial and flexible terminology, in Latin and the vernacular tongues, and the manner in which they applied this is often strikingly close to modern usage. If it is also frequently vague, question-begging, and contradictory, that, too, will scarcely surprise the student of modern nationalist discourse. The period after the first millennium is marked by the emergence in embryonic form of a Europe of sovereign 'nation-states'—political communities which combined claims to constitutional autonomy and territorial integrity with a population base conceived as ethnically homogeneous.[7] By 1300 this process was, as we will see, entering a crucial and in some ways ominous phase.

The world of Latin Europe in the central and late Middle Ages was an increasingly interconnected one, shaped by the development of communications channels and media more intensive and sophisticated than before. The size of surviving document archives and the number of known manuscript books show a marked increase for the centuries after the first millennium. To a heightened degree, this was a textual, a black-and-white world, in which words themselves became instruments of power—instruments which, with the expanding study of law, philosophy,

[4] Susan Reynolds, *Kingdoms and Communities in Western Europe 900–1300*, 2nd edn (Oxford: Oxford University Press, 1997), ch. 8.

[5] For the biblical rhetoric of nation see Regina M. Schwartz, *The Curse of Cain: The Violent Legacy of Monotheism* (Chicago: University of Chicago Press, 1997), esp. ch. 4.

[6] For the medieval terminology see Robert Bartlett, 'Medieval and Modern Concepts of Race and Ethnicity', *Journal of Medieval and Early Modern Studies* 31 (2001), 39–56, as well as Reynolds, *Kingdoms and Communities*, 256–61.

[7] For a single example: Colette Beaune, *The Birth of an Ideology: Myths and Symbols of Nation in Late-Medieval France*, trans. Susan Ross Huston (Berkeley: University of California Press, 1991).

and theology, literate Europeans were wielding with a new confidence, precision, and transformative effect.

These various changes, in religion, politics, and culture, were in their turn made possible by the transformation of economic life and social organization in the centuries following the first millennium.[8] Europe's population rose steadily: on some estimates, between two- and threefold overall between 1000 and the Black Death (1348–50). The population of France may have grown from around five to perhaps fifteen million over the same period. All such figures carry a large margin of uncertainty. Not in doubt, however, are the consequences of demographic growth. Vast areas of land were cleared for agriculture to sustain the burgeoning population, forests were felled, marshes drained, and thousands of new villages established. Towns grew in size and number, proliferating across landscapes in which urban life was previously largely unknown. In Westphalia, east of the Rhine in northern Germany, only six towns were to be found before 1180: by 1350 there were 138 (though mostly small). Trade routes, bearing a swelling traffic of people, news, and rumour, as well as goods, now linked towns to their rural hinterlands, and entire regions to each other, to the farthest ends of Europe, and to the world beyond. Money, unfamiliar to many at the millennium, became ubiquitous in the following centuries. And with its increased circulation came the powerful, disturbing responses that, underpinned by the Church's teachings and sanctions, it evoked: fascination at its mysteriously transformative effect; and deep fear of that same evident power to change (and taint?) all that it touched.

By the late Middle Ages, Europe's most economically advanced regions were heavily urbanized. In 1300, northern Italy boasted cities with populations in excess of 100,000. By the same date, between fifteen and twenty per cent of English men and women were living in towns. In the fifteenth century, the urban element in the population of Flanders was over a third. Urban centres, and the values and mentalities which they nurtured, now offered a potent challenge to the landed, aristocratic order which had developed across medieval Europe—and a strong attraction to those rural peasantries whose landlords aspired to hold them in subjection. Tensions and conflicts between town and country, but also within the towns themselves, were heightened after the mid-fourteenth century by the sharp and protracted population fall which recurrent bouts of plague visited on much of Europe. Despite these changes, however, the human landscape across the Continent was marked by sharp regional contrasts. While late medieval Brabant (in the

---

[8] For what follows see: William Chester Jordan, *Europe in the High Middle Ages* (London: Alan Lane, 2001), Ch. 1; Wim Blockmans and Peter Hoppenbrouwers, *Introduction to Medieval Europe, 300–1550*, trans. Isola van den Hoven (London: Routledge, 2007), Ch. 5; N. J. G. Pounds, *An Economic History of Medieval Europe*, 2nd edn (London: Longman, 1994), esp. 248–9; R. H. Britnell, *Britain and Ireland 1050–1530: Economy and Society* (Oxford: Oxford University Press, 2004), 138; Peter Moraw, *Von offener Verfassung zu gestalteter Verdichtung: Das Reich im späteren Mittelalter 1250 bis 1490* (Berlin: Propyläen, 1985), 49, 50.

north-west, bordering Flanders) sustained around forty-five inhabitants to every square kilometre, an equivalent space in the Polish bishopric of Poznań was still home to just two people. Europe's margins long remained relatively empty—and continued to beckon incomers, of diverse status and of more and less pacific intent, from the more densely settled heartlands.

Medieval people thought genocidally. This was partly a consequence of their disposition radically to simplify their world, its past and imagined future, into a story of peoples. Because it was a dynamic story, in which some peoples rose and prospered, others necessarily fell, and even disappeared. Vanishing 'like the Avars' was a familiar enough motif for it to be applied proverbially by a twelfth-century Russian chronicler.[9] And because earthly life in medieval accounts was filled with violence, the fall of peoples was also violent. Illustration of this view may be found in the numerous legendary accounts of the origins of European nations.[10] Although a handful of these date from the early Middle Ages (and the origin of the genre itself is Roman), their number increases sharply from the eleventh and twelfth centuries. It was not invariably through violence that, in these legends, Europe's peoples attained their medieval homelands; but bloodshed is a common enough motif to indicate a characteristic mode of thought. From Bavaria to Brittany and beyond, the forebears of medieval populations were repeatedly portrayed as immigrant warrior bands that had won their territories in a remote past by destroying or expelling the indigenous peoples whom they discovered upon arrival. The tale of the settlement of Britain, recounted by Geoffrey of Monmouth in the twelfth century and repeated and elaborated thereafter, has the Trojan émigré Brutus and his companions purging the rich isle of Albion of its aboriginal giants. In the settlement myth of the continental Saxons, the Thuringians were present in the Saxons' land first and were removed, through a combination of killings and expulsions, to make way for the newcomers. The Scottish origin legend, as it is encountered in the early fourteenth century, has the ancient Scots occupying their homeland 'having first driven out the Britons and altogether destroyed the Picts'.[11] Thereafter, the victors commonly renamed the conquered land from their own leader or some reputed ancestor, in this way remaking its identity and obliterating what had gone before. In names were concentrated a people's status, titles, and claims, and therefore, in one important sense, its very existence.

---

[9] Quoted in Timothy Reuter, 'Whose Race, Whose Ethnicity? Recent Medievalists' Discussions of Identity', in *idem*, *Medieval Polities and Modern Mentalities*, ed. Janet L. Nelson (Cambridge: Cambridge University Press, 2006), 102. The Avars were an obscure but historical central European people, which disappeared for largely unexplained reasons at some time late in the first millennium.

[10] Susan Reynolds, 'Medieval *Origines Gentium* and the Community of the Realm', *History* 68 (1983), 375–90; for ethnic destruction in the legends, Len Scales, 'Bread, Cheese and Genocide: Imagining the Destruction of Peoples in Medieval Western Europe', *History* 92 (2007), 295.

[11] A. A. M. Duncan, *The Nation of Scots and the Declaration of Arbroath (1320)* (London: Historical Association, 1970), 34.

Such tales are revealing in a number of ways. For one thing, they reflect the earlier roots of medieval beliefs about the relations between different peoples. One of these was in the authority of Antiquity. The legend of Troy offered an example of how, through ethnic destruction and dispersal, new peoples might come into being. More pervasively, there was the template for ethnic history set out in the Old Testament. This precedent had a special importance in portraying the migration and settlement of one particular, divinely favoured, people and the slaughter and eviction of others as according with God's plan. It was therefore not only inevitable but right that some peoples should prevail and others face oblivion. The idea had already received famous and influential formulation by Bede in the eighth century, in his account of the triumph of the English over the native peoples of Britain,[12] but it was to attain new prominence and applicability after the millennium, in an age which emphasized in novel ways the organically Christian quality of political communities. Underlying all was a vision, inherited from the early Middle Ages and perpetuated through epic and heroic tales, of the feuding and mutual undoing of kindreds, clans, and, by natural extension, peoples in obscure yet vividly evoked indigenous pasts. The aestheticization of violence found in heroic literature, where the most elaborate metaphors were reserved for warriors, their weapons, and the harm they wrought, was to live on in a new and heightened ideological framework in the age of the Crusades.

It is no accident that legends recounting the settlement and overthrow of peoples proliferated in Western Europe when they did. They belong to an age which brought a new urgency and confidence to the tasks of explaining, labelling, classifying, and distinguishing. Between the eleventh and the fourteenth centuries, a great deal of broadly ethnographic lore, on subjects ranging from the reputed origins of Islam to the nature and habitation of the fabled 'monstrous races' of mankind, passed into circulation among literate Europeans: primarily, though not exclusively, members of the clergy.[13] The revived interest in classical learning during the twelfth century both extended the quantity of knowledge available about the world and its peoples and enriched the conceptual vocabulary for their analysis. The fruits of these developments are evident in ethnographic writings such as those of Gerald of Wales in the late twelfth century on the Celtic peoples of the British Isles.[14] The impulse to give account (though not necessarily seek understanding) of other peoples was quickened by the Crusades against Turks and other Muslims and against the pagan peoples of northern Europe. The rise of the Mongols in the thirteenth century not only confronted Westerners with the

[12] *Bede's Ecclesiastical History of the English People*, ed. Bertram Colgrave and R. A. B. Mynors (Oxford: Clarendon Press, 1969), 202–5.

[13] John Block Friedman, *The Monstrous Races in Medieval Art and Thought* (Cambridge, MA: Harvard University Press, 1981); John Tolan, *Saracens: Islam in the Medieval European Imagination* (New York: Columbia University Press, 2002).

[14] Robert Bartlett, *Gerald of Wales, 1146–1223* (Oxford: Clarendon Press, 1982).

shock of a strange and terrifying ethnic Other but also, before long, opened up routes through Asia along which some Europeans were able to attain directly an expanded vision of a multifariously peopled world.

Because medieval people regarded ethnicity as an active and fundamental historical presence, they characteristically simplified and exaggerated, sometimes to the point of fictionality, its role in the events and developments with which they linked it. Genocidal thought therefore occupies a more substantial place in European history in this period than do genocidal acts, however broadly conceived. And medieval ideas of what constituted a people's destruction were very broad. Writers seldom had in mind only systematic mass killing—though killing was nearly always, directly or indirectly, a part of their picture, and they were quite capable of imagining it being done systematically. In many cases, the actions which they invoked are more akin to modern notions of ethnic cleansing than the organized mass murder which some would now regard as the main object of the term genocide. These actions, real or imagined, characteristically envisaged the forcible creation of ethnically homogeneous landscapes through processes involving various combinations of compulsory resettlement, eviction, exile, and actual slaughter. Often, however, they clearly meant by a people's 'extermination' or 'elimination'—terms by no means rare in medieval writings—little more than its political disenfranchisement, the lopping-off (by means more or less bloody) of its native ruling elite, or the suppression of its means of common defence. Used rhetorically, the language of ethnic destruction might refer to developments in themselves no more violent than subjection to foreign rulers, the dominance of aliens at court, or the violation of alleged native privileges, customs, or laws. None of this, however, should be interpreted as meaning that medieval people were not serious in using such language, or that its use need not be taken seriously by modern readers. To act in ways which undermined a people's standing within a competitive economy of peoples or (much the same thing) to threaten the continuation of its name was potentially to act genocidally. Such acts portended real and grave consequences. By stripping a people of the tangible lineaments of common being—indeed, of its historical and constitutional charters to be—they marked the start of a path which might well lead quickly to enslavement, murder, and oblivion. This was not an unrealistic way of thinking; and the trajectory of destruction which it anticipates was indeed mapped out by more than one ethnic group in this period.

It was not that medieval Europeans imagined the history of relations between different peoples *only* as violent, or thought that good could never come of their interaction. Some origin myths depict immigrant bands intermarrying with indigenous populations, thereby bringing forth offspring who represented a happy blending of the supposedly distinctive qualities of each people. A collection of maxims from twelfth-century Hungary contends that a multiethnic kingdom is stronger than one resting only upon a single language and

law.[15] Characteristically, however, medieval writers' judgements on the consequences of ethnic mixing were less favourable. For the fourteenth-century
chronicler Thomas Gray, the political fickleness of the English was a regrettable
consequence of their being 'a mixture of diverse nations'. The mutual enmity
which seemed readily to arise when different peoples came together likewise
argued for their being kept apart. Such antipathies appeared for some to have an
inveterate quality. For the German chronicler Ekkehard, the coming-together of
German and Frankish knights on the First Crusade only brought to light their
'natural enmity'.[16]

Ancient natural barriers between different European peoples were indeed being
undermined, in a more mobile and interconnected age, of which the Crusading
movement is a prime manifestation. But this seems only to have encouraged in
some quarters a heightened insistence on their naturalness and the need for their
maintenance. The thirteenth-century chronicler and cartographer Matthew Paris,
on a celebrated map of Britain, gave much prominence to the Hadrianic and
Antonine walls, with labels denoting the peoples they had 'once' kept apart.
Other ethnic barriers, meanwhile, had a more urgent and continuing relevance.
High-medieval world maps (*mappae mundi*) took pains to depict the great wall
which it was believed Alexander the Great had built in the Caucasus, to pen up the
cannibalistic peoples of Gog and Magog.[17] Heroic and salutary feats of ethnic
engineering were for medieval observers a hallmark of the great ruler. Yet the
prophetic scheme of Christian history also disclosed to them that such barriers
would not stand for ever, for it was necessary that the genocidal scourge of the
'unclean peoples' at some time be unleashed upon Christendom.

Rulers, Territories, and the Changing
Map of Peoples

The ethnographic turn and the quest for common origins were impelled by shifts
in the political map involving both the formation of political communities
within Europe and the dealings of European powers with their neighbours in
a wider world. In this climate, origin legends had an importance beyond mere

[15] Benedykt Zientara, 'Foreigners in Poland in the 10th–15th centuries: Their Role in the Opinion of
the Polish Medieval Community', *Acta Poloniae Historica* 29 (1974), 5–6.

[16] *Sir Thomas Gray, Scalacronica 1272–1363*, ed. and trans. Andy King, *Publications of the Surtees
Society* 209 (Woodbridge: Boydell, 2005), 95; Ludwig Schmugge, 'Über "nationale" Vorurteile im
Mittelalter', *Deutsches Archiv für Erforschung des Mittelalters* 38 (1982), 446 n 28.

[17] P.D.A. Harvey, *Medieval Maps* (London: British Library, 1991), 27, 74.

antiquarianism. They were claims to power and constitutional independence: manifestos, in short, for ethno-political survival where this seemed imperilled. In an age of political expansion and consolidation, there were some who found in the brutally dog-eat-dog world which they evoked, where the genocidally ruthless prevailed, tracts for their own times. The Scottish origin myth was recounted in response to English pretensions, in the age of Edward I (1272–1307), to suppress and swallow up the hitherto-distinct kingdom of Scots. An imaginative vision of the actual fate of those who went down before the onset of conquering kings was unfolded early in the thirteenth century by Gervase of Tilbury, an Englishman writing for the German emperor Otto IV. Gervase told of how Henry II (1154–89) had intervened in Ireland, reordering social relations there, 'though not without the shedding of much blood of English and Britons'. A new civilization had thereby dawned in the island, 'once the foul Irish race had been expelled'.[18] In Scotland, too, 'a succession of holy kings' had introduced beneficial changes, but only after 'the Scots, men of a foul way of life' were driven out. Of course, no such mass expulsion had occurred in either land. Yet, mistaken as they are, Gervase's claims are highly significant, indicating how developments even in the very recent past might be understood—or rather, radically misunderstood—in terms of the self-same model of violent ethnic replacement found in the origin myths. Socio-political reordering meant also a new *ethnic* order. Re-shaking the kaleidoscope of peoples, moreover, pertained especially to kings.

Far-reaching developments were indeed afoot; and at Europe's expanding high-medieval margins these took on a particular character. If contemporaries simplified the role of ethnicity within them and exaggerated its importance and consequences, their reactions nevertheless illuminate the experience of social and political change for those caught up in it—and the material responses, which for some, those changed facts of life seemed to invite. Between the eleventh and fourteenth centuries, population growth, migration, and the transplantation to Europe's frontier zones of legal systems, technologies, and social and political institutions previously developed at its Western continental core enabled the establishment of societies which some historians have termed colonial.[19] At Europe's western and eastern extremities, incoming warrior elites founded their dominance over indigenous communities both upon new, overmastering technologies of violence (notably those associated with the armoured heavy cavalryman) and upon self-justifying doctrines of cultural superiority. New power relationships were therefore bound up

[18] Robert Bartlett, *England under the Norman and Angevin Kings 1075–1225* (Oxford: Clarendon Press, 2000), 101.

[19] For what follows see generally Robert Bartlett, *The Making of Europe: Conquest, Colonization and Cultural Change 950–1350* (Harmondsworth: Penguin, 1993). These developments have been placed within a longer term view of the development of interethnic violence by Mark Levene, *Genocide in the Age of the Nation State*, vol ii: *The Rise of the West and the Coming of Genocide* (London: I. B. Tauris, 2005), 29–34.

with changed relations between peoples and cultures—though the interconnections were in reality more complex and varied than the remarks of medieval writers mostly allow us to suspect. Nevertheless, the expansion of certain peoples was indeed in some respects at the expense of others. And it accorded with their familiar habits of thought when contemporary and later observers diagnosed a harsh fate for the losers. Such commentators were not always remote or ignorant. Helmold of Bosau (d. after 1177), who chronicled the conversion of the Baltic Slavs and the settlement of Germans and Flemings in their lands, could scarcely have been better informed. Himself a priest at work on the Slav-German frontier when the movement was at its height, he knew personally many of the main participants. For Helmold too, immigration and social change inevitably meant ethnic replacement:

Now ... because God gave plentiful aid and victory to [Henry the Lion, duke of Saxony] and to the other princes, the Slavs have been everywhere crushed and driven out. A people strong and without number have come from the bounds of the ocean, and taken possession of the territories of the Slavs. They have built cities and churches and have grown in riches beyond all estimation.[20]

Helmold's account of his times is not (here in contrast to Gervase of Tilbury's) fundamentally wrong: not only was the ethnic composition of his region changing: coercion and, at least locally, forced displacements were indeed part of the story. But in its bald ethnic essentialism it is certainly misleading. Nevertheless, it was the first draft of a history that would harden to orthodoxy in the years that followed. In the fifteenth century, the Church reformer and historiographer Dietrich of Niem, himself a native Saxon, would shift part of the by-then mythologized story further back in time. For Dietrich, the Frankish conqueror Charlemagne (768–814) had already destroyed and expelled the Slavs from lower Saxony, 'apart from a handful, who down to the present day dwell in certain rural hamlets, mostly in marshy places, though under perpetual servitude to the Saxons'.[21]

Yet nothing was fixed for ever. Since all medieval peoples tended in their own estimations to rate as doughty warriors, there was no remaking of the ethnic map that might not in its turn be undone by some heroic future act of collective violence. As early as the ninth century, the *History of the Britons* (perhaps wrongly) associated with the name of Nennius was holding out the prophetic hope that the red British serpent would chase from the island the white of the Saxon interloper. The same hope was still alive at the end of the twelfth when, according to Gerald of Wales, the Welsh were drawing from the prophecies of Merlin the expectation 'that both the nation (*natio*) and name of the [English] foreigners shall

---

[20] *The Chronicle of the Slavs by Helmold, Priest of Bosau*, ed. and trans. Francis Joseph Tschan (New York: Columbia University Press, 1935), 235–6.

[21] Hermann Heimpel, *Dietrich von Niem (c. 1340–1418)* (Münster: Regensbergsche, 1932), 261.

be expunged' from their land.[22] Those who moved between the lines on Europe's colonial frontiers could turn to their advantage the hopes and fears of both camps. As a fourteenth-century Irish poet explained to the first earl of Desmond:

In the [English] foreigners' poems we promise that the Irish shall be driven from Ireland; in the Irishmen's poems we promise that the foreigner shall be routed across the sea.[23]

By the troubled fifteenth century, such fears, resting on wildly mythologized recollections of high-medieval migrations and ethno-demographic shifts of the kind we have glimpsed already, might become a basis for explicit agitation. A manifesto of the Czech Hussites (1420) rallied its audience to arms against their German neighbours with a warning that 'just as they did to our tongue on the Rhine, in Misnia, in Prussia, and drove it out, the same they intend to do to us and to occupy the places of the banished.'[24]

The two or three centuries which follow the millennium can accurately be called an age of kings. The number of European kingdoms itself grew substantially as also did the capabilities of royal government and the claims advanced in the names of rulers and peoples. The empire-building pretensions of kings, and of quasi-regal figures like Henry the Lion of Saxony (d. 1195), lay at the heart of many of those premonitions and allegations of violent ethnic change which recur in writings from the time. The medieval habit of mapping ethnicity onto constitutional formations meant not only the emergence of new 'peoples' within new realms but also, in a climate of political and dynastic flux, the spectre of obliteration for others. The viewpoint which conceived of political revolution as ethnic destruction was given classic formulation by the chronicler Henry of Huntingdon, for whom the Norman Conquest of England was an implementation of God's judgement on the sinful English, namely that they should cease to exist as a people. In twelfth-century imagination, a people's undoing did not need to involve mass killing. It might do, however: another chronicler, Orderic Vitalis, tells of a plot which came to the notice of King Stephen 'to kill all the Normans on a fixed day and hand the government of the kingdom over to the Scots.'[25] Not all were prepared to accept

---

[22] *Nennius, British History and the Welsh Annals*, ed. and trans. John Morris (London: Phillimore, 1980), 30–1; R. R. Davies, 'The Peoples of Britain and Ireland 1100–1400 II: Names, Boundaries and Regnal Solidarities', *TRHS* 6th ser. 5 (1995), 4.

[23] Katharine Simms, 'Bards and Barons: The Anglo-Irish Aristocracy and the Native Culture', in Robert Bartlett and Angus MacKay (eds), *Medieval Frontier Societies* (Oxford: Clarendon Press, 1989), 181.

[24] František Šmahel, 'The Idea of the "Nation" in Hussite Bohemia', *Historica* 16/17 (1968/9), 222.

[25] *Henry, Archdeacon of Huntingdon, Historia Anglorum: The History of the English People*, ed. and trans. Diana Greenway (Oxford: Clarendon Press, 1996), 412–13; and for Orderic, John Gillingham, 'Henry of Huntingdon and the Twelfth-Century Revival of the English Nation', in Simon Forde, Lesley Johnson and Alan V. Murray (eds), *Concepts of National Identity in the Middle Ages* (Leeds: University of Leeds, 1995), 76.

divine judgement as binding or view the settlement of 1066 as irreversible: inter-ethnic violence might write its own, new histories.

At Europe's margins, changing topographies of peoplehood and power came together with the expanding resources, claims, and possibilities of kingship. By the thirteenth century, rulers of the more highly developed kingdoms were possessed of both the means and the will to reorder in some detail the ethnic landscapes of their realms. Between the 1220s and 1240s, Frederick II of Hohenstaufen (d. 1250) relocated the entire Muslim population of his Sicilian kingdom—perhaps numbering between 15,000 and 30,000 people—to the mainland town of Lucera. We have not yet quite heard the last of the Muslims of Lucera. A more modest example of ethno-social engineering illuminates what the king stood to gain. In 1295, Edward I founded an English settler-borough beside his castle at Beaumaris, deep in newly conquered Wales. The population of a native township on the site was forcibly resettled twelve miles away. The pattern was repeated elsewhere in Wales around the same time, amounting to a not insignificant re-shaking of the pattern of peoples there.[26] Economic advantage, defence and security, and the visible display of dominance by a quasi-imperial conqueror might all alike recommend a royal policy of local ethnic displacement.

When the king's actions benefited his peers and native-born followers, all might be well. But matters were not always so simple and the position of kings themselves in relation to the settlement movements of the twelfth and thirteenth centuries could prove troublingly ambivalent. On the one hand, it had been customary since the earliest times for rulers to draw useful or prestigious foreigners to their realms and courts—a practice whose extension the economic opportunities of the age strongly favoured. On the other, the idea of kings as fathers to their (ideally, ethnically cohesive) peoples was at this time finding increasingly powerful expression. There was nothing new about foreign favourites at court drawing the resentment of native elites; but now, in European frontier regions, those high-status interlopers were just one element within a larger, socially diverse immigration process. In this climate, alien courtiers seemed in the eyes of some to be malevolent harbingers of a radically new ethnic order. A Polish chronicler of the early fourteenth century believed that Germans brought in to advise the young princes of Głogów had incited them 'to exterminate the entire Polish nation, both clergy and laity, and especially the knights'.[27] Such fancies took wing the more readily when a ruler harnessed aliens to local development projects like Edward I's in Wales. Certain kings of Bohemia earned a dark name among the Czech-speaking political classes for using Germans in this way. Přemysl Otakar II (1253–78) had resettled

---

[26] Julie Anne Taylor, '*Lucera Sarracenorum*: A Muslim Colony in Medieval Christian Europe', *Nottingham Medieval Studies* 43 (1999), 110–25; R. R. Davies, 'Colonial Wales', *Past and Present* 65 (1974), 3–23.

[27] Quoted in Zientara, 'Foreigners in Poland', 20.

with Germans the suburb beneath Prague castle, at the myth-laden heart of his realm, on one account by expelling the native residents. Within little more than a generation of his death, indigenous myth-making had turned the king's unpatriotic act into a full-scale plan to hand his kingdom over to the Germans. In the febrile atmosphere of the Hussite agitations of the fifteenth century, the same and worse was being reported of the cosmopolitian Charles IV of Luxembourg (1347–78). Charles had 'thought to settle the Czech land with the German race, of which he himself came, and gradually root out the Czechs from it.'[28]

Such spectres drew substance both from an awareness of what kings by the late Middle Ages were capable of doing and from some strikingly ethnocentric ideas about what they might and should do. In the more governmentally sophisticated realms, such perceptions and assumptions came together relatively early. A twelfth-century estimation of the powers (and intentions) of the English monarchy is glimpsed in Henry of Huntingdon's depiction of the St Brice's Day massacre of 1002, in which, according to the Anglo-Saxon Chronicle, 'all the Danish men in England' had been killed at the behest of King Æthelred II.[29] The sparseness of contemporary evidence makes this instance of genocide by royal command hard to judge; but historians have argued for its likely modest extent. Henry, however, presents it as a coordinated act of government, underpinned by the systematic dispatch of royal letters to every town in the realm. His picture, while unlikely to be accurate, was certainly prophetic, and by the end of the thirteenth century some royal bureaucracies were capable of targeting unpopular or controversial groups with police actions of chilling scope and suddenness. 'You have achieved in one day what the Pharaohs of ancient Egypt failed to do,' was one chronicler's response to Edward I's expulsion of the Jews from England. For the poet Geoffrey of Paris, the actions instituted by Philip IV of France (1285–1313) against Jews, Templars, and others merged into a single vision of royal purge: 'Jews, Templars and Christians | Were caught and put in bonds, | And driven from one country to another.'[30] The Capetian imitators of Christ were cleansing the regnal Temple with a whip.

The late medieval wars that those formidable royal bureaucracies came to sustain led some to perceive in the kingdoms of Europe, however unrealistically, instruments of organized mass violence portending the outright ethnic obliteration of their neighbours. Edward I's celebrated claim of 1295, that the French king was

---

[28] For Otakar see Jörg K. Hoensch, *Přemysl Otakar II. von Böhmen: Der goldene König* (Graz: Styria, 1989), 103; *Kronika Neplachova*, ed. J. Emler, *Fontes rerum Bohemicarum* 3 (Prague: Spolku Historického v Praze, 1882), 476; for Charles IV, Šmahel, 'The Idea of the "Nation" ', 126 n 118.

[29] *Henry, Archdeacon of Huntingdon, Historia Anglorum*, ed. and trans. Greenway, 340–1; *The Anglo-Saxon Chronicle*, ed. Dorothy Whitelock (London: Eyre and Spottiswoode, 1961), 86.

[30] Robin R. Mundill, *England's Jewish Solution: Experiment and Expulsion, 1262–1290* (Cambridge: Cambridge University Press, 1998), 1; E. A. R. Brown, '*Persona et Gesta*: The Case of Philip the Fair', *Viator* 19 (1988), 237: 'Christians' is here doubtless being used as a catch-all term for the king's political opponents.

preparing an invasion in order to 'delete' the English tongue, was to be the first of several such pieces of rhetorical scaremongering set down in the name of late medieval English kings.[31] In France, where some regions suffered the protracted ravages of war, the late medieval vision of destruction attained Biblical proportions: a late fourteenth-century tapestry portrays the English kings as crowned and mounted Apocalyptic locusts, emerging from the bottomless pit to devour the land (Revelation 9.1–11).[32] As will shortly become clear, the totality of this vision of destruction was characteristic of an important strand in medieval ethno-religious thought, as was also its polarizing quality, pitting holy kings and chosen peoples against personified evil—dehumanized, bestial, and unclean.

The notes of extremism, and the harnessing to violent acts of a violently ethnocentric rhetoric, also infused other elements of late medieval life. The richness and the character of the surviving sources may admittedly make the fourteenth and fifteenth centuries appear to us more distinct from what had gone before than they actually were. It is clear, however, that reports and predictions of large-scale bloodshed were also underlain by new currents and tensions in social and religious life. The prospect of organized mass killing was periodically in the air in various contexts, not always related to ethnicity. Some radical religious groups believed a general slaughter of the clergy to be imminent, while both lords and peasant communities in various parts of Europe confronted from time to time the seemingly impending prospect of fundamental and bloody social upheaval. Where members of different ethnic groups were involved, movements and conflicts with complex origins were easily seen as struggles between implacable rival peoples. Such perceptions came to the fore especially in the towns, whose spectacular growth in number and size across much of Europe was one of the most enduring legacies of the post-millennium period. Towns, with their complex and periodically acute social tensions and power rivalries, penned up natives and aliens together in closely confined spaces under conditions apt to render the outsider both visible and vulnerable.

The hothouse urban environment encouraged the invocation of ethnic divisions to explain conflicts stemming in part from other discontents: economic, political, devotional, local, or even professional. Alien university masters and students might be forced out, as several hundred Germans were from Prague in 1409. Foreign garrisons were massacred—as in Palermo in 1282 or Bruges in 1302.[33] In various

---

[31] William Stubbs, *Select Charters and other Illustrations of English Constitutional History*, 9th edn (Oxford: Clarendon Press, 1913), 480.

[32] See René Planchenault, *L'Apocalypse d'Angers* (Paris: Caisse Nationale des Monuments Historiques, 1966).

[33] Peter Moraw, 'Das Mittelalter', in F. Prinz (ed.), *Deutsche Geschichte im Osten Europas: Böhmen und Mähren* (Berlin: Siedler, 1993), 154–5; Steven Runciman, *The Sicilian Vespers: A History of the Mediterranean World in the Later Thirteenth Century* (Harmondsworth: Penguin, 1960), ch. 13; J. F. Verbruggen, *The Battle of the Golden Spurs (Courtrai, 11 July 1302: A Contribution to the History of Flanders' War of Liberation, 1297–1305*, trans. David Richard Ferguson (Woodbridge: Boydell, 2002), 25.

parts of Europe, barriers were now being raised, with towns making it harder for foreigners to settle or practise crafts, or excluding them altogether. Bouts of economic hardship and political instability were liable to be attended by outbreaks of violence against resident foreign merchants, seamen, or artisans. Occasionally, these attained major proportions and left substantial numbers dead, as did the attacks on 'Flemings' in the south and east of England in 1381.[34] The 'great rising' in June of that year was a response to the perceived corruption and incapacity of English royal government, particularly in its handling of the war with France. Its background, however, lay in the disintegration of social hierarchies and the legal relationships that underpinned them in the circumstances of sharp demographic downturn, falling rents, and rising labour costs which followed the Black Death. The anti-alien violence which accompanied the rising, particularly the killing of many foreign artisans and merchants in London, illustrates clearly how urban spaces might act to draw social and political discontents to a focus in interethnic bloodshed.

Often, admittedly, such late medieval bloodshed was the outcome of mere riots or drunken brawls. Increasingly, however, if contemporary reports are to be believed, the voice of the people was to be heard on such occasions, clamouring for a general destruction of the foreigner. 'Death to the French!' 'Kill all Flemings!' Those same reports tell also of the homely watchwords that conspirators coined to affirm their solidarity and to tongue-tie and expose the alien in their midst. Without question, our sources commonly exaggerate the destructiveness of such disorders and simplify the role of ethnicity in them; but this exaggeration itself reveals much about contemporary moods. And where popular disturbances attracted more than local support, modest revisions to the ethnic map bequeathed by high-medieval migration might indeed result. The revolt of Owain Glyn Dŵr in early fifteenth-century Wales induced some inhabitants of the English boroughs to take flight for England. Local ethnic displacement was more substantial where social and political tensions were combined with religion, as they were in fifteenth-century Bohemia, resulting in the purging of German communities from a number of towns, including the capital.[35]

By this time, contending political and social groups were able to hurl at each other stereotyped vocabularies of ethnocentric abuse of much radicalism and menace. Compiling lists of the supposed good and (particularly) bad qualities of different peoples was nothing new: as a literary exercise it went back to Antiquity. The classification of peoples began, however, to shed its dry schoolbook quality during the twelfth century, in context of a broader interest among educated

---

[34] Rodney Hilton, *Bond Men Made Free: Medieval Peasant Movements and the English Rising of 1381* (London: Temple Smith, 1973), 195–8.

[35] R. R. Davies, *The Revolt of Owain Glyn Dŵr* (Oxford: Oxford University Press, 1995), 275; Moraw, 'Das Mittelalter', 163–4.

Europeans in the nature of humanity, coupled with a revived application of Antique notions of the barbarian.[36] These developments were taking place at a time when colonization and state-building were lending such cultural pursuits a keen political edge, and developments in the Church underpinning them with a new facility in judging and condemning. Against this background, certain peoples—particularly those which found themselves locked in violent competition with their neighbours—came to be subjected to negative portrayals more eloquent and absolute than before, backed by a new doctrinal authority, and bearing an underlying call to destruction. Definitions of humanity emphasizing reason, cultivation, and order were deployed to portray enemies and subject populations as less than fully human. The Irish, in English accounts, were 'wild', the Scots 'bestial men'. The Germans were 'dog-heads'—semi-humans, evoking the monstrous beings supposed to inhabit the earth's arid margins. The lives of such ones were surely cheaper than those of the fully human. The English in fourteenth-century Ireland were accused of saying that it was no more a sin to kill an Irishman than a dog.[37] To monstrosity and sub-humanity were added associations of filth, pollution, and parasitism. The Czechs were a 'putrid odour' to the Bohemian king Sigismund (1419–37), while for a fourteenth-century Czech pamphleteer their German rivals were 'wolves in the fold, flies on the food, serpents in the bosom, harlots in the house'.[38]

That a land should be cleansed of such pollutants appeared axiomatic; and a luxuriating imagery of weeds and vermin indicated not only problems, but solutions. 'When [the Irish] fall into your hands pluck them all up by the root, as the good gardener doth the nettle,' urged a fourteenth-century Dublin notary.[39] Talk of beasts—the Irish as hares, for example—led on naturally to talk of hunting. The task could seem the more urgent since beastliness and hybridity were no neutral states. Monsters (as their supposed Latin cognates, *monstro, moneo,* made clear) were signs and warnings: they spoke of sin. For Gerald of Wales, it was the propensity of the Irish for bestial, incestuous, and other illicit sex that explained the proliferation of malformed people in their land. But to some, the image of their

[36] W. R. Jones, 'The Image of the Barbarian in Medieval Europe', *Comparative Studies in Society and History* 13 (1971), 376–407.

[37] *Die Königsaaler Geschichts-Quellen mit den Zusätzen und der Fortsetzung des Domherrn Franz von Prag,* ed. J. Loserth, Fontes rerum Austriacarum: Oesterreichische Geschichtsquellen I.8 (Vienna: Oesterreichische Akademie der Wissenschaften, 1875), 164 (dog-heads); *Irish Historical Documents 1172–1922,* ed. Edmund Curtis and R. B. McDowell (London: Methuen, 1943), 43.

[38] Thomas A. Fudge, *The Magnificent Ride: The First Reformation in Hussite Bohemia* (Aldershot: Ashgate, 1998), 269; Wilhelm Wostry, 'Ein deutschfeindliches Pamphlet aus Böhmen aus dem 14. Jahrhundert', *Mitteilungen des Vereins für Geschichte der Deutschen in Böhmen* 53 (1915), 229.

[39] James F. Lydon, 'Nation and Race in Medieval Ireland', in Simon Forde, Lesley Johnson, and Alan V. Murray (eds.), *Concepts of National Identity in the Middle Ages* (Leeds: University of Leeds, 1995), 107. For the imagery of vermin and pollution in modern racist rhetoric see Zygmunt Bauman, *Modernity and the Holocaust* (Ithaca, NY: Cornell University Press, 1989), 66–72.

neighbours spoke of things beyond sin: active malevolence, imminent danger. The vocabulary of interethnic defamation thus merged at its extreme end with one of absolute evil. Heretics were also routinely compared to parasites; the encroaching Mongols too were a monster people, their wickedness encoded in misshapen bodies. Bohemia's Germans were for one Czech author an 'accursed tribe', as utterly outside the fold as Muslims or Jews.[40] To speak in this way of wayward and unclean races was to invoke an Old Testament template—one which pointed towards the extirpation of the wicked by the chosen under their divinely blessed leaders.[41]

PEOPLES ACCURSED OF GOD: VIOLENCE AND THE CHRISTIAN FRONTIER

It was when the language of ethnic distinction became overlaid with that of divine favour and disfavour that fantasies of the destruction of peoples most often found a measure of material fulfilment. The Reform movement in the eleventh-century Church offered western Europeans not only the vision of a purified Christian community and distinct criteria for inclusion and exclusion, but a strong imperative to act for its creation. And action was from the outset conceived in part as a cleansing struggle between peoples. A chronicle account of Pope Urban II's speech of 1095 inaugurating the First Crusade has him appeal to the Franks as a people divinely chosen. The Muslim occupiers of the Holy Places, on the other hand, were 'an accursed race, a race utterly alienated from God'.[42] While the mass slaughter of Muslims was not a specific aim of the Crusaders, a degree of territorial purification was. Not only Muslims and Jews, but all who were not Latin Christians were initially purged from Jerusalem following the city's fall in 1099 and forbidden to dwell there. While some native Christians were subsequently readmitted, the bar to Jews and Muslims remained. And if outright mass killing proved to be but a partial and temporary phenomenon, it certainly occurred. Not only were many of Jerusalem's Muslims and Jews put to the sword when the city fell; large-scale slaughter of non-Christians continued in other Palestinian cities upon their capture by the

---

[40] Asa Simon Mittman, 'The Other Close at Hand: Gerald of Wales and the "Marvels of the West" ', in Bettina Bildhauer and Robert Mills (eds), *The Monstrous Middle Ages* (Cardiff: University of Wales Press, 2003), 97–112; Alfred Thomas, 'Czech-German Relations as reflected in Old Czech literature', in Bartlett and MacKay (eds), *Medieval Frontier Societies*, 202.

[41] See Schwarz, *Curse of Cain*, esp. ch. 2.

[42] Robert of Reims, cited in Edward Peters (ed.), *The First Crusade: The Chronicle of Fulcher of Chartres and Other Source Materials*, 2nd edn (Philadelphia: University of Pennsylvania Press, 1998), 27.

Latins throughout the first decade of the twelfth century. Moreover, in a manner which was to be characteristic of crusading warfare, Western commentators celebrated the killing of non-Christians, and talked up the body count. When Jerusalem fell, men rode through blood up to their knees and the bridle bits of their horses. 'Has anyone ever seen or heard of such a slaughter of the infidel race?', wondered one chronicler. 'God alone knows the number for no one else does.'[43]

The same large and general acts, the same absolute distinctions between damned and saved, were transferable to other Christian frontiers. Henry of Livonia tells how in 1227 'all the people of both sexes' were baptized on Ösel (Saaremaa) in the Gulf of Riga, following the island's conquest by a crusading army. The Christian priests 'watered the nations by the font, and their faces with tears'. It was not to last. Another chronicler explains how in 1260 the island's inhabitants 'broke away and left not a single Christian alive in all their territories'. 'Later', he adds, 'many of them were destroyed for doing this.'[44] Bloodshed followed quickly on the watering of the gentiles—and each was conceived as a general act. The manner of thought was characteristic; so too the scale of violence. 'Kill them *all*; Truly, God will know his own!' The words, attributed to a papal legate at the massacre of the population of Béziers (1209) during the Albigensian crusade, may never have been uttered; but the writer who set them down just a few years afterwards captured the spirit of time and context.[45] Crusaders shed blood with hopeful hearts and easy consciences, and the chivalric norms curbing some of the extremities of war at Europe's core counted for much less on a religious frontier. The population in some parts of Prussia may have fallen for a time by between twenty and fifty per cent during the Teutonic Order's destructive conquest—part holy war, part strategic land-grab—in the thirteenth century.[46] Crusading doctrine, to its proponents, stiffened the soldier's will against pragmatism and backsliding. It made of him also an ethnic warrior. St Bernard of Clairvaux sought to rouse up the German nobility for a crusade against the Baltic Slavs with the injunction that they should 'take vengeance on the [pagan] peoples and exterminate them from the land of our Christian name'. There was to be no peace 'until, with God's aid, either the [heathen] rite itself or the population [*natio*] has been destroyed.'[47]

[43] Hans Eberhard Mayer, 'Latins, Muslims and Greeks in the Latin Kingdom of Jerusalem', *History* 63 (1978), 175–92; *Petrus Tudebodus, Historia de Hierosolymitano Itinere*, ed. John Hugh Hill and Laurita L. Hill (Paris: Paul Geuthner, 1977), 142.

[44] *The Chronicle of Henry of Livonia*, trans. and intro. by James A. Brundage (Madison: University of Wisconsin Press, 1961), 245; Richard Fletcher, *The Conversion of Europe: From Paganism to Christianity 371–1386 AD* (London: HarperCollins, 1997), 501.

[45] Mark Gregory Pegg, *A Most Holy War: The Albigensian Crusade and the Battle for Christendom* (Oxford: Oxford University Press, 2008), 77.

[46] Hartmut Boockmann, *Deutsche Geschichte im Osten Europas: Ostpreußen und Westpreußen* (Berlin: Siedler, 1992), 138.

[47] Hans-Dietrich Kahl, 'Crusading Eschatology as Seen by St Bernard in the Years 1146 to 1148', in Michael Gervers (ed.), *The Second Crusade and the Cistercians* (New York: St Martin's Press, 1992), 42–3.

The resulting expedition—the 'Wendish Crusade' of 1147—predictably took a different and far more limited course than that urged by the zealot Bernard. Nevertheless, his conception of the Crusade as a radical contest of *peoples* is affirmed by others. Helmold of Bosau writes as often of Slavs and Saxons as he does of pagans and Christians. Most religious frontiers were also cultural and ethnic ones, and religion itself readily conceived as an attribute of peoplehood, reflecting shared character and identity. A story survives of how a group of Livonians in the late twelfth century decided to wash off their recent baptism with the waters of the River Dvina and thus send their Christianity back to the land of the Saxons, whence it came. It was not therefore only for Bernard that religious non-conformity dictated ethnic destruction. It was as a race of heretics that, for the German Dominican Johann Falkenberg (writing *c*.1412), all Poles merited extermination.[48] The doctrines of Church reformers and Crusade preachers were by the late Middle Ages furnishing western Europeans with a powerful conception of *Christian* community, within which the presence of alien groups looked increasingly unacceptable.

The power of this doctrine to reshape the ethnic landscape became particularly apparent with its growing assimilation to the political sphere. By the thirteenth century, princes and their learned apologists were increasingly harnessing invocations of sacred community to notions of shared political allegiance and legal doctrines exalting the power of monarchs within their consolidating realms. Their exclusionary potential was realized earliest on the frontier. The fall of Seville to the king of Castile in 1248 was followed by the wholesale expulsion of its Muslim population. In thinly populated frontier zones, such changes were apt to prove only temporary. At Europe's core, however, they would be more secure. The last Crusader strongholds in the Latin East fell in 1291; but at exactly that time rulers were acting with a new resolve to build their own purified Christian holy lands on European soil. It marked a significant new departure when the entire Muslim population of Minorca was enslaved following the island's fall to the Aragonese in 1287. In 1300, the deeply devout Charles II of Naples (nephew of one royal saint and father to another) sold into slavery the Muslims of Lucera. The city was henceforth to be a Christian space, protected by the Virgin Mary.[49] The Promised Land had come home; but this only served to highlight the obligation upon those

---

[48] *Chronicle of Henry of Livonia*, trans. and intro. Brundage, 34; Hartmut Boockmann, *Johannes Falkenberg, der Deutsche Orden und die polnische Politik* (Göttingen: Vandenhoeck and Ruprecht, 1975), ch. 2.

[49] Richard Fletcher, *The Cross and the Crescent: Christianity and Islam from Muhammad to the Reformation* (London: Alan Lane, 2003), 112 (Seville); for Minorca and Lucera see David Abulafia, 'Monarchs and Minorities in the Christian Western Mediterranean around 1300: Lucera and Its Analogues', in Scott Waugh and Peter Diehl (eds), *Christendom and Its Discontents: Exclusion, Persecution and Rebellion 1000–1500* (Cambridge: Cambridge University Press, 1996), 234–63.

(Christian) Israelites to whom it rightly belonged to destroy the unclean Canaanite peoples whose presence still befouled it.

THE TEMPLE AND THE WHIP: THE JEWS IN A CHRISTIAN EUROPE

A thirteenth-century *mappa mundi* portrays the figure of Christ as physically merged with a created and peopled world.[50] The centuries after the first millennium saw Christ drawn closer to humanity, which in turn became conceivable as a Christian body—or, politically, as a community of Christian peoples under their kings. Christ's body and blood lent legitimacy and affirmed common bonds; but they also became an increasingly extensive charter for shedding the blood of those not of that body (-politic). The communities of Jews, which by the eleventh century were already numerous and widely scattered through Europe, would in the period which followed become the object of the most virulently genocidal rhetoric and the most extensive and radical violence to be suffered by any European ethnic group. And yet, unique though these were in scope, intensity, and consequences, they also resemble in certain ways the patterns of abuse and coercion which we have discovered underlying other medieval interethnic conflicts. Latin Christians wrote about Jews in a (highly abusive) language of race. For Peter the Venerable (d. 1156) they were a 'wretched people'. The chronicler Guibert of Nogent portrays Crusaders in 1096 wondering why they were making an arduous journey to the East when 'the Jews, of all races the worst foes of God, are before our eyes.'[51] Jews became the subject of a repertoire of defamatory stereotypes which mirrored and extended those which Christian peoples applied to each other. Jews too were likened to vermin. They were less than fully human, assimilated by physiognomy (as also were Muslims) to the 'monstrous races'; they were associated with demons and with the baser animals: in bestiaries, the hyena was a Jew prototype. Jews acted as a community—to Christian polemicists, an encompassing, malevolent, and conspiratorial community. As a people, they were linked by blood to other accursed races: for Matthew Paris, the Mongols were the ten Lost Tribes, whose destructive onset was in concert with their kinsmen within Christendom.[52]

---

[50] Harvey, *Medieval Maps*, 28.

[51] Jeremy Cohen, 'Christian Theology and Anti-Jewish Violence in the Middle Ages: Connections and Disjunctions', in Anna Sapir Abulafia (ed.), *Religious Violence between Christians and Jews: Medieval Roots, Modern Perspectives* (Basingstoke: Palgrave, 2002), 47, 49.

[52] Debra Higgs Strickland, *Saracens, Demons and Jews: Making Monsters in Medieval Art* (Princeton: Princeton University Press, 2003), 133–6, 147–8; Sophia Menache, 'Tartars, Jews, Saracens and the Jewish-Mongol "Plot" of 1241', *History* 81 (1996), 319–42.

They came, moreover, increasingly to be associated, by a variety of commentators, with *general* schemes of pollution and violence, inviting in turn violent general responses. In 1321, wild rumours associated the Jews of Languedoc in a well-poisoning conspiracy with lepers (who wished *all* people to be leprous) and with outside Muslim powers.[53] With the high-medieval humanization of the figure of Christ and the Christianization of human communities went a growing tendency to depict Jews as not only deicidal but genocidal. Their supposed practice of mistreating consecrated communion hosts was not only a re-enactment of the Crucifixion on Christ's miraculous body; it was an attack on the unity of Christ and his people.

There were still some within Christian Europe who came to the Jews' defence: distinguished churchmen, popes among them, who reiterated the traditional defence of the Jews' presence in Christendom as divinely willed and spoke against the wilder anti-Judaic fantasies. Over time, however, their arguments proved less and less able to prevail against rival currents, also drawing on Christian justifications, which urged the Jews' exclusion or destruction. It was from fear of their 'extermination', explained Pope Innocent IV in 1247, that Jews in Germany had sought his aid.[54] The fear was by this date an increasingly realistic one.

The earliest major attacks on Jewish communities in Europe had been during the First Crusade, and subsequent expeditions were also attended by localized bouts of bloodletting. However, it was from the later thirteenth century that anti-Jewish violence in Europe took on new proportions. It is estimated that several thousand may have perished in the agitations which convulsed parts of Germany in 1298, inspired by host-desecration charges. However, bloodshed of a quite new extent and thoroughness was attained in the massacres which heralded the arrival of the Black Death in central Europe during the years 1348–50. In town after town, well-poisoning rumours became a pretext for the systematic killing of entire Jewish communities. Nearly a thousand may have died in the German town of Erfurt alone. In some places—Basel, Strasbourg, Constance—the Jews were forced into specially constructed houses to be burned. A contemporary chronicler claimed that it took six days to burn Strasbourg's Jews on account of their number. 'And I could believe', he mused, 'that the end of the Hebrews had come.'[55]

Elsewhere in Europe, princes had already by this date taken steps of their own to reaffirm the Christian character of their realms, by means of the mass expulsion of

---

[53] Malcolm Barber, 'Lepers, Jews and Moslems: The Plot to Overthrow Christendom in 1321', *History* 66 (1981), 1–17.

[54] Edward A. Synan, *The Popes and the Jews in the Middle Ages* (New York: Collier-Macmillan, 1965), 114–15.

[55] Michael Toch, *Die Juden im mittelalterlichen Reich* (Munich: Oldenbourg, 1998), 60 (for 1298); František Graus, *Pest, Geißler, Judenmorde: Das 14. Jahrhundert als Krisenzeit* (Göttingen: Vandenhoeck and Ruprecht, 1987), 168–214; Rosemary Horrox (ed. and trans.), *The Black Death* (Manchester: Manchester University Press, 1993), 208–10.

their Jewish populations. Whereas Church reformers and heretics had pursued their rival visions of a purged and purified Christian heaven on earth, Catholic monarchs now laid more limited plans for building 'heaven in one country'. England's Jews were forced out by Edward I in 1290. The Jews of France, who had suffered temporary expulsions and other oppressions under previous kings, were systematically driven from the realm by Philip IV in 1306. As many as 100,000 people may have been compelled to leave.[56] The pattern was repeated in other late medieval realms, down to the mass expulsion of the large Jewish populations of the Iberian kingdoms at the end of the fifteenth century. In part, princes now acted in this way because, as we have seen, they had attained the governmental means to do so. More importantly, however, some rulers had come by this time to view the purification of their realms as a sacred duty. There was henceforth to be just one— organically Christian—Chosen People, rightfully occupying the holy soil of its own sovereign kingdom under its rightful and anointed king. Read as a constitutional text, the Bible itself had come to represent, for the peoples of medieval Europe and for their rulers, the most powerful, and fatally empowering, collective origin myth of all.

RULED OUT: EXCLUSIONARY IMPULSES AND THE MAKING OF EUROPE

The existence of peoples in Europe in the central and later Middle Ages reflected the facts of power: for contemporaries, ethnic communities were axiomatically political ones. To imperil a people's political status, as embodied in its privileges, laws, common institutions, in the power of its members to *act* politically, and more numinously in their sense of shared prestige and distinctiveness within a world of peoples, was to act genocidally. In a period which saw extensive changes to the European political map, the spectre of such acts never seemed far remote. Where the interactions of different peoples were most intensive, stress-laden, and ideo- logically and politically charged—on the frontier, at the courts of princes, or in the great towns—acts of ethnic destruction were anticipated, and in some quarters sought, most keenly. Medieval people were prone to simplify and exaggerate the role of ethnicity in the conflicts of their day. Consequently, the destruction of peoples—even in their own broad understanding of that phenomenon—did not occur nearly as often as they expected. Despite this, their diagnosis of its causality

---

[56] William C. Jordan, *The French Monarchy and the Jews: From Philip Augustus to the Last Capetians* (Philadelphia: University of Pennsylvania Press, 1989), 202.

and likely course was fundamentally correct. When entire populations were indeed subjected to systematic violence, enslavement, or eviction, those acts were usually preceded—often over a protracted period—by other seemingly lesser ones, which served to strip the group of its political and legal independence: its autonomous right to *be*. 'The king's Jews' necessarily waited on the king's will; and his will was by the late Middle Ages taking, across much of Europe, an increasingly ethnocentric turn.

The pattern was not bound to be repeated everywhere, of course. Political and legal marginalization did not have to lead to collective oblivion: it did not do so, for example, in late medieval Ireland or post-conquest Wales. Outright ethnic destruction was most likely to occur where political subjugation was reinforced by fundamental religious difference. Pagans, Muslims, and Jews, but also, in an age of sharpened conceptions of religious orthodoxy, adherents of (for their opponents) false forms of Christianity, were singled out for extreme solutions. For the rest, the history of this long period is partly one of how, through more intensive and precisely defined interactions, different imagined ethnic groups evolved forms of coexistence and mutual accommodation. Nevertheless, Europeans were also by the end of the Middle Ages more practised and accomplished ethnic discriminators and excluders, in thought and deed, than they had been in earlier times. Their world was one of more sharply defined and cohesive communities, in which the alien was more conspicuous, more readily and vehemently named, and less easily accommodated: a world which sought unities and was keenly sensible of the problems of coping with multiplicity. Their power fundamentally to rule out, and conviction that such ruling-out was needful, ultimately derived in large part from those same currents of social change, religious reform, and intellectual renewal which had also provided a foundation for the period's most startling cultural achievements and advances—as some would say, for European civilization itself.

SELECT BIBLIOGRAPHY

Bartlett, Robert, *Gerald of Wales, 1146–1223* (Oxford: Clarendon Press, 1982).
——— *The Making of Europe: Conquest, Colonization and Cultural Change 950–1350* (Harmondsworth: Penguin, 1993).
——— and Angus MacKay (eds), *Medieval Frontier Societies* (Oxford: Clarendon Press, 1989).
Fletcher, Richard, *The Conversion of Europe: From Paganism to Christianity 371–1386 AD* (London: HarperCollins, 1997).
——— *The Cross and the Crescent: Christianity and Islam from Muhammad to the Reformation* (London: Alan Lane, 2003).
Forde, Simon, Lesley Johnson, and Alan V. Murray (eds), *Concepts of National Identity in the Middle Ages* (Leeds: University of Leeds, 1995).

Friedman, John Block, *The Monstrous Races in Medieval Art and Thought* (Cambridge MA: Harvard University Press, 1981).

Gillingham, John, *The English in the Twelfth Century: Imperialism, National Identity and Political Values* (Woodbridge: Boydell, 2000).

Moore, R. I., *The Formation of a Persecuting Society: Power and Deviance in Western Europe, 950–1250* (Oxford: Blackwell, 1987).

Reynolds, Susan, *Kingdoms and Communities in Western Europe 900–1300*, 2nd edn (Oxford: Oxford University Press, 1997).

Strickland, Debra Higgs, *Saracens, Demons and Jews: Making Monsters in Medieval Art* (Princeton: Princeton University Press, 2003).

CHAPTER 15

....

COLONIAL LATIN AMERICA

....

NICHOLAS A. ROBINS

INTRODUCTION

....

THE conquest of Latin America resulted in the deaths of tens of millions of individuals, primarily as a result of disease and forced relocation into more concentrated settlements, as well as through exterminatory attacks on those who resisted Iberian domination. Severe exploitation aggravated the process through overwork, nutritional deficits, and reduced resistance to illnesses generally. Paralleling this process were concerted efforts to destroy the religious and cultural fabric of native societies through the systematic destruction of sacred objects, the death of indigenous religious leaders, and the prohibition of native rites. Indian rebellions against colonial rule could also take the form of subaltern genocides in which the oppressed seek the extermination of their overlords. The study of genocide in colonial Latin America challenges many prevailing conceptualizations in genocide studies. Among these are the construction of intent in defining genocidal outcomes, the role of the state in genocides, and the relative military capacities of victim groups.

Understanding the incidence and breadth of genocide in colonial Latin America is conditioned by several factors, the two most salient being controversies over the size of pre-conquest populations and the role of intent. Related to these are the impact of diseases on the native population, relative to other factors such as forced labour and migration, and conflicting conceptualizations of genocide. These factors are explored below within the context of colonial Latin American genocides.[1]

The work of Raphael Lemkin, who coined the term genocide in *Axis Rule in Occupied Europe*, is generally associated with the Jewish Holocaust. What is less widely recognized, however, is that Lemkin developed many of his ideas in the wider context of colonialism. Indeed, colonialism was inherent to the concept as developed by Lemkin, who wrote that 'Genocide has two phases: one, destruction of the national pattern of the oppressed group: the other, the imposition of the national pattern of the oppressor' that may be done through the 'colonization of the area by the oppressor's own nationals'.[2] Lemkin recognized the vital role of culture in the maintenance and perpetuation of individual and collective identity, and viewed deliberate cultural destruction as a form of genocide.'[3]

In referring to the 'methods' of what he called 'cultural' genocide, Lemkin included 'desecration and destruction of cultural symbols, destruction of cultural leadership, destruction of cultural centers, prohibition of cultural activities, [and] forceful conversion'. Other means included 'physical' genocide, such as 'massacre and mutilation, deprivation of livelihood, slavery', and 'biological' genocide which included 'separation of families, sterilization, destruction of foetus [*sic*]'.[4] Like many who wrote after him, Lemkin's understanding of genocide in Latin America was informed by romantic notions of pre-Hispanic civilizations (such as the Aztecs having a 'fairly democratic government') and heavy reliance on the writings of the Dominican friar Bartolomé de Las Casas.[5]

DEMOGRAPHIC IMPLOSION AND GENOCIDE

The conquest and ensuing domination of Latin America was intimately linked to the spread of pathogens to which the native populations in the region initially had little or no resistance. Beginning with the arrival of Columbus in the New World in 1492, the Spanish conquistadors established their dominance first in Hispaniola

[1] For a wider framing of the definitional debate and their relation to colonial and modern genocides, see A. Dirk Moses, 'Conceptual Blockages and Definitional Dilemmas in the "Racial Century": Genocides of Indigenous Peoples and the Holocaust', *Patterns of Prejudice* 36:4 (2002), 7–36.

[2] Michael A. McDonnell and A. Dirk Moses, 'Raphael Lemkin as Historian of Genocide in the Americas', *Journal of Genocide Research* 7:4 (2005), 501; Raphael Lemkin, *Axis Rule in Occupied Europe* (Washington, DC: Carnegie Endowment for International Peace, 1944), 79.

[3] Raphael Lemkin, 'The Concept of Genocide in Anthropology', cited in McDonnell and Moses, 'Raphael Lemkin as Historian', 514.

[4] McDonnell and Moses, 'Raphael Lemkin as Historian', 504.

[5] Ibid. 505, 515.

and Cuba before successively extending their control to what is today Panama in 1510, to Mexico in 1521 and subsequently to the rest of Central America. From there, they advanced southward to present day Peru in 1532, and thence to contemporary Bolivia, Ecuador, and much of South America.

Once released in the region, disease often spread in advance of the conquerors, and facilitated their conquest. In the case of Peru, it appears that smallpox had spread south from Panama in 1524, eight years before the arrival of Pizarro, killing the Inca Huayna Capac and much of the population and setting off the civil war which facilitated the Spanish conquest of the region. In the case of Brazil, after the Portuguese claimed the region in 1500 and an initial focus on brazilwood extraction, sugar production relying heavily on slaves imported from Africa came to dominate.[6]

Estimates of the pre-conquest population in Latin America tend to vary widely, a result of a virtual absence of pre-contact baseline population data, inaccurate censuses in the colonial period, and differing methodologies. In such situations, errors can quickly become compounded. To the extent that there were native population records on the eve of conquest, with very few exceptions they did not survive, either being lost, or as in many cases, deliberately and systematically destroyed by the Spaniards.

Once established in the region, the colonists did conduct censuses to determine tribute levies; however, challenges in logistics and coordination took their toll on accuracy. In addition, most surveys were limited to individuals of tribute age (males between eighteen and fifty years old), and as a result any extrapolation requires an estimate of average family size. Royal authorities were reluctant to conduct censuses, not only due to their cost and complexities, but because they recognized that, until the eighteenth century, the native population had been declining. Hence, an accurate census would in many cases result in a reduction of tribute and other levies on native communities, and this colonial officials clearly wanted to avoid.[7]

Further complicating modern efforts to determine pre-conquest populations are methodological differences that can yield widely varying results. Approaches that examine the 'carrying capacity' of the land, the native crops grown on it, and the caloric intake of the indigenes are especially useful at a micro level, but, as with

[6] Henry F. Dobyns, 'An Outline of Andean Epidemic History to 1720', *Bulletin of the History of Medicine* 37:6 (1963), 494, 497; Heraclio Bonilla, '1492 y la población indígena de los Andes', in Heraclio Bonilla, Robin Blackburn, et al. (eds), *Los conquistados: 1492 y la población indígena de las Americas* (Bogotá: Tercer Mundo Editores/ Facultad Latinoamericana de Ciencias Sociales, 1992), 106; Nicolás Sánchez-Albornoz, *The Population of Latin America: A History*, trans. W. A. R. Richardson (Berkeley: University of California Press, 1974), 61.

[7] Nicholas A. Robins, *Priest-Indian Conflict in Upper Peru: The Generation of Rebellion, 1750–1780* (Syracuse: Syracuse University Press, 2007), 17.

other approaches, extrapolation can lead to significant inaccuracies.[8] Archaeological approaches face many challenges, not the least of which is data literally concealed beneath the ground.[9] When there is pre-conquest population data for an area, and a subsequent colonial census, one can generate a depopulation ratio. While valuable, such an approach can be limited by differing or uncertain age ranges for pre-conquest tribute payers and generally small sample sizes.[10]

More widely applicable are approaches that examine mortality from disease in a known context, and then apply that to the area under study. For example, if smallpox is known to kill thirty per cent of a population without immunity in one area, this ratio can be applied elsewhere. Altitude, and the cooler climate associated with it, as well as population densities play important roles in the spread of diseases and are factors which must be taken into account. The picture is further clouded in the not uncommon situation where there is uncertainty concerning exactly what disease was afflicting the indigenes. Despite these shortcomings, this approach yields more reliable results than those based on carrying capacity or archeology.[11] The final and perhaps most accurate approach is that based on post-conquest census projections, where there are two comparable censuses and a rate of depopulation can be calculated and retroactively applied.[12]

As the preceding indicates, one must approach estimates of pre-contact populations with considerable caution. Despite the differing approaches and their inherent limitations, there is a general convergence among historical demographers indicating that between 1492 and 1600, approximately ninety per cent or more of the native population in Latin America perished.[13] In central Mexico, for example, utilizing the carrying capacity approach and depopulation ratios, Woodrow Borah and Sherburne Cook estimated that the population was 25,200,000 in 1518, but by 1605 it had fallen to 1,075,000, a drop of approximately ninety-six per cent.[14] In a critique of their research and utilizing the carrying capacity approach, Brooks

---

[8] Noble David Cook, *Demographic Collapse: Indian Peru, 1520–1620* (Cambridge: Cambridge University Press, 1981), 18, 28.

[9] For a discussion of the broader limitations of this approach, see ibid. 30–40.

[10] Ibid. 41–2, 54.

[11] Ibid. 59, 62, 64.

[12] Ibid. 107.

[13] Noble David Cook, *Born to Die: Disease and New World Conquest, 1492–1650* (Cambridge: Cambridge University Press, 1998), 206; C. T. Smith, 'Depopulation of the Central Andes in the 16th Century', *Current Anthropology* 11:4–5 (1970), 459; Sherburne F. Cook and Woodrow Borah, *Essays in Population History: Mexico and California*, vol iii (Berkeley: University of California Press, 1979), 1. This discussion focuses on Mexico and Peru; however, for other regions in Latin America, see Cook, *Born to Die*; Sánchez-Albornoz, *Population of Latin America*; Dobyns, 'Outline of Andean Epidemic History'; and Alfred Crosby, *The Columbian Exchange: Biological and Cultural Consequences of 1492* (Westport, CT: Greenwood Press, 1972).

[14] Woodrow Borah and Sherburne Cook, *The Aboriginal Population of Central Mexico on the Eve of the Spanish Conquest* (Berkeley: University of California Press, 1963), 4–5, 88–90; Cook and Borah, *Essays in Population History*, 1.

argues that the pre-contact population was 5,000,000, which yields a decline of a not much less catastrophic eighty per cent.[15]

In the Andes, smallpox may have killed one-half of the population before the Spanish conquest of the region.[16] In the area of present day Peru, N. D. Cook utilizes census projections to conclude that the population in 1530 was approximately 9,000,000; however, by 1580 only between 600,000 and 1,000,000 indigenes remained, a collapse of approximately ninety-three per cent. As in Mexico, he notes that disease and mortality rates were higher on the coast, where populations were more densely concentrated and temperatures higher. Indeed, on the Peruvian coast the Indians were 'almost completely wiped out'.[17]

Despite differing methodologies, their respective limitations, and the differences they yield, there is little debate over the scale of the demographic implosion which resulted from the conquest of what came to be called Latin America. It does, however, raise questions over the relationship between native exploitation and the population collapse. Furthermore, and of significant importance for the field of genocide studies, it raises the issue of intent. To what varying extents did the colonists want to dominate and exploit the indigenes or exterminate them?

FORCED LABOUR, INTENT, AND THE DEMOGRAPHIC DISASTER

While historical demographers have focused on the agency of disease in the massive death associated with the conquest, others, while recognizing the role of disease, stress the brutality and dislocation associated with various forced labour systems, and their concomitant impact on the native population, impacts which were exacerbated by hopelessness and suicide.[18] Disease and exploitation were clearly interrelated. Deliberate, state-mandated policies forcing natives to live in concentrated settlements, such as missions and Spanish-style towns, and other policies that subjected them to harsh and abusive labour conditions had a tragically synergistic effect in promoting depopulation. Overwork reduced the ability of the

---

[15] Francis Brooks, 'Revising the Conquest of Mexico: Smallpox, Sources and Populations', *Journal of Interdisciplinary History* 24:1 (1993), 1–2, 5, 7.

[16] Dobyns, 'Outline of Andean Epidemic History', 494, 497; Bonilla, '1492 y la población indígena de los Andes', 106; Sánchez-Albornoz, *Population of Latin America*, 61.

[17] Cook, *Demographic Collapse*, 114.

[18] See, for example, David Stannard, *American Holocaust: Columbus and the Conquest of the New World* (New York: Oxford University Press, 1992), and Ward Churchill, *A Little Matter of Genocide: Holocaust and Denial in the Americas 1492 to the Present* (San Francisco: City Lights Books, 1997).

body to fight infections, lowered life expectancy, and sometimes killed on the spot, and diseases spread much more rapidly in close quarters. Forcing indigenes to labour in climates to which they were not accustomed, especially in the hot lowlands where disease was more prevalent, was often a death sentence. Although mortality among populations with no resistance to new diseases would have been extremely high in non-exploitative conditions, exploitation unquestionably aggravated the situation. In so weakening the native population, and with it their ability to resist colonial rule, it also served the imperial objective perpetuating domination.

A brief review of colonial labour systems illustrates these dynamics. Although Indians could only be technically enslaved, and thus sold as such, when they disavowed the authority of the Spanish king, in practice, however, there emerged an array of forced labour systems which resulted in de facto Indian slavery. Among such systems was the *encomienda* system, in which a Spaniard, usually but not always a conquistador or his descendant, was granted rights to Indian tribute in a specific area. This was not a grant of land, but of labour, and the beneficiary, or *encomendero*, undertook the obligation of 'Christianizing' the Indians. Often this Christianizing was nothing more than a quick, mass baptism devoid of any previous catechism. Fearing the emergence of a New World nobility, the Spanish crown sought to eliminate this system with the implementation of the New Laws of 1542.[19]

Replacing the *encomienda* system was that of the *repartimiento*, in which royal authorities became responsible for the assignment of Indian labour to the colonists. Other systems included bonding the native to an agricultural estate through inheritable debt. The Crown also instituted systems of corvée labour in which rotating groups of Indians were forced to work for a limited term on projects of public benefit under specific conditions, which were, however, consistently ignored by the colonists. Other systems included penal labour and wage labour, the latter of which often became a form of debt peonage.[20]

There is no dispute concerning the coercive nature of Indian labour systems in colonial Latin America, and the fact that many died as a result of them. They were designed to induce the natives to produce a surplus and to forcibly extract it from them. Whatever the specific system, it was rigorously reinforced by recourse to the lash, pillory, prison, and taking family members as hostages for debts, among other means. The larger question, however, is the impact that such systems had on the total native population.[21]

Despite the clear role of disease in the demographic disaster, some authors seek to establish the intention of the colonists to exterminate native populations by

[19] C. H. Haring, *The Spanish Empire in America* (New York: Harbinger, 1947), 40–41, 51.
[20] Peter Bakewell, *Miners of the Red Mountain: Indian Labor in Potosí, 1545–1650* (Albuquerque: University of New Mexico Press, 1984), 69; Donald Wiedner, 'Forced Labor in Colonial Peru', *The Americas* 16:4 (1960), 377; Haring, *The Spanish Empire in America*, 15.
[21] Robins, *Priest-Indian Conflict*, 69–76.

focusing on exploitation or purposeful extermination as the leading cause of Indian depopulation. More polemical than scientific, their approach borders on dismissing the effects of disease, averring for example that labour abuses in the Andes 'precipitated the demographic crisis' or confuse mercury mining with silver mining.[22] Others, while recognizing that disease played a role, focus on the abuses committed against natives to argue that the Spanish engaged in a 'deliberate racist purge' or policy of 'systematic extermination' against them.[23] There is no question as to the brutality of the system implemented by the Spanish, but by minimizing the role of disease one gets a distorted picture of what actually happened.

The debate concerning the relative weight of disease versus deliberate abuses in the depopulation equation is important as it concerns intent. In the case of the Spanish conquest of the Americas, the invaders sought riches and the means to extract them. The domination of the native population was central to this strategy, black slaves generally only being introduced in areas where the native population had been exterminated, such as Hispaniola and Cuba, or could not otherwise survive. The survival of the empire and its extractive systems depended heavily upon the survival of the indigenes, as surplus producers, and paradoxically, upon their continuing weakness so as to forestall uprisings. While the colonial enterprise demanded natives for labour, the multifaceted extractive systems that coerced this labour also maintained them in a position of physical weakness. Although there were numerous colonial policies that were genocidal and will be discussed below, the Spanish sovereigns sought the domination of the natives, not their physical extinction, and issued a host of edicts, routinely ignored in the colony, in an effort to preserve the labour force. As Latin American population history has made clear, however, an absence of intention to kill does not mean an absence of massive death.

Although genocidal intent, and even knowledge, were lacking in terms of the spread of pathogens, the same cannot be said concerning armed resistance to conquest. Such resistance occurred at two levels, the establishment of the Spanish in the region, and the expansion of the frontier, both of which in Lemkin's view would be considered 'physical genocide'.[24] In the former case, the invaders were vastly outnumbered, and were quick to resort to massacres both as a means to achieve immediate military victory and to instill terror and panic in the wider population.[25] Such efforts led to the deliberate and systematic slaughter of non-combatants, and the enslavement and usually relocation of those who survived.

Once established in the region, early colonial authorities had sizeable numbers of soldiers who were often idle and the cause of disturbances. Opening new frontiers

---

[22] Teresa Cañedo-Arguelles Fábrega, *Potosi: La version aymara de un mito europeo. La minería y sus efectos en las sociedades andinas del siglo XVII (La Provincia de Pacajes)* (Madrid: Editorial Catriel, 1993), 45; Stannard, *American Holocaust*, 74, 89, 91; Churchill, *A Little Matter of Genocide*, 87–8.

[23] Stannard, *American Holocaust*, xii; Churchill, *A Little Matter of Genocide*, 86.

[24] McDonnell and Moses, 'Raphael Lemkin as Historian', 506.

[25] Ibid. 506–7.

was a way to rid Spanish settlements of disruptive and potentially dangerous elements, and at the same time offered the possibility of bringing new territory, and subjects, into the realm. As an Indian group legally became rebels once they had ignored a formal call for submission, and rebels against the Crown could legally be enslaved, expansion of the frontier, and the suppression of Indian rebellions, provided a continuing pretext for both genocidal massacres and enslavement. Those who resisted were often subject to onslaughts 'by fire and blood' which had as their objective the physical elimination of the rebel group and the enslavement of any survivors. Thus, for Indians the choices were few indeed. One alternative was integration into the Spanish realm, and subjection to ethnocidal policies which sought the cultural destruction of the indigenes. The other option was resistance, which elicited a deliberate response from the Spaniards which sought the elimination and/or enslavement of their adversaries.[26] Migration from conquered areas often entailed a change in climate which could be deadly in lowland areas, and also could leave the refugees at the mercy of established groups in the region.

ETHNOCIDE AND THE EXTIRPATION OF NATIVE RELIGIOUS PRACTICES

To the physical genocide that resulted from deliberate extermination of specific groups which resisted Iberian domination was added a host of other genocidal policies systematically inflicted upon the indigenes. In this context, clerics, both secular and regular, became a vortex of ethnocide, or the destruction of culture and its repositories. Many policies were patently ethnocidal and concerned the introduction of Catholicism to the region in the sixteenth and seventeenth centuries. Although Indians were exempt from the loathed Holy Office of the Inquisition, they were no less subject to religious persecution. Native religions and their cultural underpinnings were the focus of well-organized campaigns of extirpation, often involving killing native religious authorities and the systematic destruction of native places of worship and sacred documents.[27]

As Duviols notes in the Andean context, the goal was to 'destroy every vestige of the pagan religion, both in objects and in the spirit of the Indians', and to Lemkin,

---

[26] Charlotte Gradie, *The Tepehuan Revolt of 1616: Militarism, Evangelism, and Colonialism in Seventeenth-Century Nueva Vizcaya* (Salt Lake City: University of Utah Press, 2000), 33.

[27] McDonnell and Moses, 'Raphael Lemkin as Historian', 514.

such acts constituted 'cultural genocide'.[28] Extirpation campaigns were formal and systematic affairs, and mixed violent and peaceful means. Often, Indians were first given an opportunity to confess concerning their beliefs, practices, and the locations of shrines. Those who were less forthcoming, or unconvincing, were subjected to torture. Such techniques were often effective, and resulted in the gathering up and destruction of shrines and other items associated with native worship, and the concealment of their ashes or shards. Those found guilty of idolatry were often flogged and/or had their head shaved as a form of humiliation, and were forced to attend catechism to complete the process.

Apart from the perceived spiritual dividends of Catholicism, extirpation campaigns could yield silver and gold, further inflaming the zeal with which such campaigns were undertaken.[29] Indeed, such was the fervour with which such operations were conducted that occasionally the residents of a village would flee before the arrival of the extirpation committee. Other times, those leading the campaign were charged with excesses, such as unlawfully seizing Indian lands and destroying houses.[30] To give an idea of the yield of such efforts, by 1559 in the region of Huaylas, Peru, Augustinian extirpators reported destroying over 5,000 native religious artefacts.[31]

Despite such attacks, native religions often survived, although in adaptive, syncretic forms. Part of this was due to the fact that a fragment of a native religious object was believed to retain its complete power, and some natural religious sites, such as hills and mountains, simply could not be destroyed.[32] While some traditional practices continued furtively, others melded into Catholicism, and the polytheistic nature of native belief systems imbued it with an important degree of adaptability.[33] Ironically, in their efforts to destroy native religions, idolatry campaigns could help preserve information concerning native rites for future generations. For example, books that essentially were training manuals for extirpators often contain extensive information concerning native beliefs and practices. Gleaned through hostile eyes, such vestiges are often all that remain of pre-conquest beliefs.[34]

Although such campaigns were not always successful in eradicating native religious beliefs and practices, they did help frame the terms of a modus vivendi

---

[28] Pierre Duviols, *La destrucción de las religiones andinas (Conquista y colonia)* (Mexico City: UNAM, 1977), 423; McDonnell and Moses, 'Raphael Lemkin as Historian', 508, 511.

[29] Duviols, *La destrucción de las religiones andinas*, 9, 249–59, 373–7, 424.

[30] Ibid. 405–18, 422.

[31] Ibid. 430.

[32] Ibid. 436; Nicholas Griffiths, *The Cross and the Serpent: Religious Repression and Resurgence in Colonial Peru* (Norman: University of Oklahoma Press, 1996), 8, 26.

[33] Duviols, *La destrucción de las religiones andinas*, 437.

[34] See, for example, Pablo Joseph de Arriaga, *The Extirpation of Idolatry In Peru*, trans. L. Clark Keating (Lexington: University of Kentucky Press, 1968).

between the two spiritual, and cultural, worlds. Once established in a region, some priests were willing to tolerate a degree of discreet idolatry. For example, saint's days celebrations often served as a cover for continuing traditional rites. Part of this tolerance reflected an acceptance of reality; in other cases it was a tacit agreement of mutual tolerance of forbidden practices, such as priestly promiscuity or their engagement in commercial enterprises. Other times, it reflected a fear among clerics that a lack of tolerance could result in their own death, especially through poisoning as natives often were forced to serve as cooks for the priest, among other duties.[35] Nevertheless, in Indian villages the priest embodied spiritual, economic, and political power, with the desirability of a parish often being a function of its economic potential. Any overt challenge to clerics was dealt with harshly, through flogging, incarceration, banishment, seizure of goods, or accusations of idolatry.[36]

Beyond extirpation campaigns, ethnocide often took more discreet but not less destructive forms. Rural clergy were especially important in this regard due to their close contact with the natives. Coerced conversions and participation in Catholic rituals, involuntary marriages, and massive forced relocation into new settlements and missions all had among their objectives the destruction of native religions. Although efforts to impose monogamy inhibited native reproduction, forced relocation was especially detrimental to native populations, as higher population concentrations greatly facilitated the spread of disease.[37] The exploitation and abuse suffered by Indians at the hands of their priests, as well as their frequent hypocrisy regarding sexual activity, alienated many from the Catholic faith, even when they ascribed supernatural powers to it.[38]

To the genocidal massacres of conquest, and the ethnocide of forced religious conversion, was added forced migration which would be considered by Lemkin as physical genocide through the 'deprivation of livelihood'.[39] Forced migration occurred at three levels: migration into new, state-mandated settlements, migration to fulfill state-mandated labour obligations, such as the mita in Peru, and migration to avoid such demands. In the cases of mercury production in Huancavelica in Peru and silver mining in Potosí (in present-day Bolivia), certain provinces were assessed a quota of labourers to provide for a fixed length of time. Because their token wage, if paid, was below a subsistence level, many travelled with their families who also worked in the area as ore sorters, vendors, and domestic servants. While many in the mines succumbed to cave-ins, falls, toxic gasses, and other accidents, others were so weakened that they never fully recovered or maimed such that they

[35] Duviols, *La destrucción de las religiones andinas*, 401–3.

[36] Griffiths, *The Cross and the Serpent*, 161, 245, see also Robins, *Priest-Indian Conflict*, 69–76.

[37] Cook, *Demographic Collapse*, 89, 253.

[38] Kenneth Mills, *Idolatry and Its Enemies: Colonial Andean Religion and Extirpation, 1640–1750* (Princeton: Princeton University Press, 1997), 254–6, 284–5.

[39] McDonnell and Moses, 'Raphael Lemkin as Historian', 506, 507–8.

could not earn an income or work the land. Those sent by overlords to the hot
climes of the coca plantations often quickly perished from disease.

Those that did not die under conditions of forced labour often had little reason to
return home, as many who did found they had lost access to their lands. Worse, as the
labour levies were based on grossly outdated censuses, many Indians in Peru would
also find that they would be forced to return for another labour turn in the mines in
only two or three years, as opposed to the theoretical seven for the mita. As a result,
many, ironically, stayed in the silver mining city Potosí where wages and tasks for non-
conscripts were better than many other places. Others migrated to provinces that were
not subject to the labour draft, and where they also paid less tribute.[40]

Other factors affecting native populations included widespread miscegenation,
often forced and sometimes not, which reduced the native population and led to
the emergence of a new group, mestizos (those of Indian and Spanish heritage),
who often assumed positions of authority over the natives. Furthermore, children
were routinely seized in lieu of debts. If the debt, now converted in effect into a
ransom, was not paid, the child was forced to work it off. This effort to pay off the
debt could easily become an open-ended process, as charges for their upkeep could
be applied to the debt, and they could remain in permanent bondage. Such
practices, due to their effects on the family unit and reproduction, were considered
by Lemkin to be examples of 'biological' genocide.[41]

It is clear that the indigenes in Latin America did not simply suffer genocide,
they suffered genocides: physical, biological, and cultural.[42] The unintentional
spread of disease was part and parcel of this process as it facilitated the conquest
and the human and cultural destruction which ensued. Concerning the exploitation of the natives, at the level of Crown policy in Spain, there were a plethora of
laws specifically designed to protect the Indians from a wide variety of abuses
which the Crown was aware were routinely committed. Such laws, however, were of
little effect, not only because of the exploitative nature of the colonial system and
the flexibility given to local officials by the Crown, but also because the laws
concerning the Indies were riddled with contradictions and ambiguities. Just as
there were laws that sought to temper the degree of exploitation, others permitted
forced migration, familial dissolution, coerced relocation, and efforts to exterminate native religions, practices, and culture.[43]

[40] Peter Bakewell, *Miners of the Red Mountain: Indian Labor in Potosí, 1545–1650* (Albuquerque:
University of New Mexico Press, 1984), 69; Jeffrey A. Cole, *The Potosí Mita, 1573–1700. Compulsory
Indian Labor in the Andes* (Stanford: University Press, 1985), 26–28.

[41] McDonnell and Moses, 'Raphael Lemkin as Historian', 507.

[42] Ibid. 504.

[43] On this topic, see for example, Silvio Zavala, *El servicio personal de los indios en el Peru*, vol i
(Mexico City: El Colegio de Mexico, 1978); Roberto Levillier, *Don Francisco Toledo, supremo
organizdor del Perú* (Buenos Aires: Espasa-Calpe, S.A., 1940), and Ruben Vargas Ugarte, *Pareceres
juridicos en asuntos de indias (1601–1718)* (Lima: CIP, 1951).

Policies concerning religion had multiplicative effects that went well beyond forcible conversions. As with private individuals, religious orders owned land and often encroached on that of native communities, reducing their ability to provide for themselves. Local clergymen also routinely demanded unremunerated services from their parishioners, and drained them of any surplus they may have through forced participation in religious services and confraternities. Furthermore, forced marriages and the imposition of monogamy eliminated choice and restricted population growth. Finally, the forced relocation of Indians to Spanish-style towns not only uprooted them from places which had religious significance to them, but also facilitated the spread of disease and further spurred depopulation. The clergy had a disproportionate role in native ethnocide not only due to systematic efforts to destroy native belief systems and the culture that surrounded them, but also because they were the only non-Indian legally allowed to reside in native communities.

NATIVE RESISTANCE AND SUBALTERN GENOCIDE

Given the nature of the system under which the natives lived, and died, it should come as little surprise that rebellions against colonial rule could assume a genocidal character. Such cases of 'subaltern genocide', or genocides from below where subject populations seek the extermination of their oppressors, were the exception rather than the rule in the continuum of resistance. Most rebellions were short, local affairs against a specific individual, such as a priest or governor, or against a policy, such as tribute assessments, forced purchase of goods, or religious fees. On occasion, however, such uprisings were broader in scope and objectives.[44]

One such subaltern genocidal rebellion was the Tepehuan uprising in present-day Mexico, which lasted from late 1616 until it was finally suppressed in 1620. Hundreds of Hispanic settlers and their slaves perished in the rebellion, in addition to several clerics.[45] This rebellion erupted in a context of severe depopulation from disease, which was exacerbated by forcing populations to live at missions.[46] In 1615,

---

[44] For detailed case studies of such subaltern genocides, see Nicholas Robins, *Native Insurgencies and the Genocidal Impulse in the Americas* (Bloomington: Indiana University Press, 2005) and *Genocide and Millennialism in Upper Peru: The Great Rebellion of 1780–1782* (Westport, CT: Praeger, 2002). Most recently, see Nicholas Robins and Adam Jones (eds), *Genocides by the Oppressed: Subaltern Genocide in Theory and Practice* (Bloomington: Indiana University Press, 2009).

[45] Daniel Reff, 'The "Predicament of Culture" and the Spanish Missionary Accounts of the Tepehuan and Pueblo Revolts', *Ethnohistory* 42:1 (1995), 63; Gradie, *The Tepehuan Revolt of 1616*.

[46] Reff, 'The "Predicament of Culture" ', 71.

a dire situation for the Tepehuans was made worse as a result of a drought and famine.[47] As elsewhere, native religious leaders were powerless to change the course of events and saw their prestige decline. As the missionaries were equally unable to stop the spread of disease, many natives saw little reason to remain Christians.[48] Indeed, over time, many Indian groups began to associate Catholic rituals with 'evil spells that resulted in death and disease.'[49] The leader of the Tepehuan revolt, Quautlatas, commanded his followers not only to kill those of Iberian origin, but anyone who had converted to Christianity. To inspire his followers, he assured them that those who fell in battle would be resurrected within a week of their victory, adding that the elderly would be young again.[50] In addition, he promised that reascendant native deities would forever prevent the Spanish from returning by sending storms to sink their ships.[51]

Another subaltern genocidal uprising was the 1680 Pueblo Revolt in present-day New Mexico. The Franciscan order, backed by military force, was instrumental in advancing the Spanish presence northward in Mexico. In the Pueblo region, while nominally subject to civilian authorities, they wielded considerable autonomy and power. As in other regions of Latin America, by the mid-seventeenth century, the sedentary Indians of the region had experienced a population collapse from disease of well over ninety per cent, and suffered consistent and systematic attacks against traditional religion and customs. A long-planned and well-coordinated revolt erupted in 1680, led by a medicine man known only as Popé.[52]

On the night of 10 August 1680, the natives of the region rose up, killing almost all non-Indians they captured. Those who could fled to Santa Fe, the district capital, where they took refuge with the governor. Soon besieged, they were vastly outnumbered by their adversaries, who cut off their water supply. With surrender as the only other option, the Hispanics made a bold attack on the Indians, killing many and creating enough disarray among the rebels to allow them to begin an exodus southward. Eventually, they made it south of the Rio Grande, and tallied their losses. Of approximately 2000 settlers in the region, 401 people had been killed, all but ninety-five of them being women and children. In addition, the rebels had destroyed thirty-four villages along with many ranches and agricultural estates. For the next twelve years the Pueblo Indians would live free of Spanish control.[53]

---

[47] Gradie, *The Tepehuan Revolt of 1616*, 150.

[48] Reff, 'The "Predicament of Culture" ',71; idem, *Disease, Depopulation and Culture Change in Northwestern New Spain, 1518–1764* (Salt Lake City: University of Utah Press, 1991), 277.

[49] Reff, *Disease, Depopulation and Culture Change*, 273.

[50] Reff, 'The "Predicament of Culture" ',70; idem, *Disease, Depopulation and Culture Change*, 273; Gradie, *The Tepehuan Revolt of 1616*, 149.

[51] Gradie, *The Tepehuan Revolt of 1616*, 149.

[52] Andrew Knault, *The Pueblo Revolt of 1680: Conquest and Resistance in Seventeenth-Century New Mexico* (Norman: University of Oklahoma Press, 1995), 153–5, Robins, *Native Insurgencies*, 27–9.

[53] Robins, *Native Insurgencies*, 30–4.

The objectives of the rebels were plainly stated by many.[54] For example, the insurgent leader Alonso Catiti called upon followers 'to assemble in order to go to the Villa to kill the governor and all who were with him'. Others were inspired by the call 'to kill the friars, the alcalde mayor and the other persons' in Santa Fe, while others simply did 'not want religious or Spaniards'.[55] These were not idle observations; only women were among the few prisoners taken by the rebels. Not only did the Indians seek to exterminate the interlopers, they sought to systematically remove all vestiges of Spanish rule. Popé and other leaders prohibited anything of Spanish origin, including crops, Christian names, and the practice of Catholicism. Those who had been baptized were commanded to engage in ritual bathing to remove the perceived taint of baptismal waters, and all those who had been forced by the friars into marriages were declared free from matrimony. Native objectives were also expressed at a symbolic level, such as by the destruction of church bells, which had commanded them to work and worship, the piling of dead friars on altars, and the scalping of statues of Christ.[56]

Although ultimately defeated, the Great Rebellion of Peru and Upper Peru (present-day Bolivia) of 1780–2 was no less genocidal and in fact was the largest regional challenge to Spanish rule in the Americas before the independence wars. In the years leading up to the rebellion, the Indian exploitation had been growing more severe. Not only were new taxes on Indian staples levied and aggressively collected, but Spanish provincial governors had increasingly expanded their system of forcing the Indians to purchase goods at highly inflated prices under the *repartimiento de mercancías* system. The clergy, seeing their economic and political power under attack by the Bourbon monarchy, increased their own efforts to strip the Indians of any surplus through increasing the number of saint's days celebrations, and the fees associated with them. Priests also issued more frequent demands for unremunerated labour, routinely charged extortionate fees for services, and utilized funeral charges as a means of taking from the deceased any property they may have had. Finding no effective redress in colonial courts and having little hope of a better future other than that offered by millennial prophecies, in 1780 a storm of genocidal violence swept the region.[57]

The insurgency was a loosely confederated series of uprisings, the first of which erupted in Chayanta, in what is today south central Bolivia. Initially led by Tomás Catari, a hereditary leader denied the leadership of his village, his brothers Dámaso and Nicolás led an even more violent phase after his death. Calling for the

---

[54] For a discussion of the intentionality of rebel actions and their relation to their broader objectives in this and the Great Rebellion of Peru and Upper Peru, see ch. 4 of Robins, *Native Insurgencies*, 68–95.

[55] Ibid. 72.

[56] Ibid. 142–5.

[57] Scarlett O'Phelan Godoy, *Rebellions and Revolts in Eighteenth Century Peru and Upper Peru* (Colonge: Bohlau Verlag, 1985), 109, 119, 148, 207, 260, 270–80.

elimination of civil taxes, religious fees, forced labour, and coerced purchases, the insurgents killed those who opposed them. Initially, mestizo village overlords were targeted; however, as the rebellion progressed and radicalized, those of lighter skin in general were systematically killed. Usually, the rebels would isolate a village, while the defenders took refuge in the local church. They would then attack the town, storm the church, and kill those inside. On some occasions, women would be spared to serve the rebels, as were some men who could serve as scribes or operate or repair weapons.

Similar grievances led to similar events in the region of Cuzco, present-day Peru, where the rebellion was led by José Gabriel Túpac Amaru, the hereditary leader of the village of Tungasuca. Villages were attacked and people systematically killed on the basis of race and ethnicity before the tide turned against them following a brief siege on Cuzco, the ancient Inca capital, in January 1781. The city of La Paz, capital of present-day Bolivia, was also besieged between March and October 1781 by another rebel, Túpac Catari. Approximately 10,000 people, or one-third of the city's population, perished, mostly from starvation, before royalist forces finally broke the siege.[58]

As in the Pueblo Revolt, the exterminatory nature of this insurgency was evident not only in the systematic slaughter of whites and those of lighter skin, but in the rebels' frequent efforts to destroy objects associated with the Catholic Church. Statues of Christ were denuded and thrown into pyres, monstrances deliberately shattered, and many priests killed who did not flee their parishes in time. Overall, the ferocity and exterminatory nature of the insurgency was highest in Upper Peru and increased with time and distance from nominal, and more conservative, leaders such as Túpac Amaru and Tomás Catari. Prophecies promising the return of native rule were frequently reinforced by a belief that not only had native deities finally risen to expel the invaders, but that those who fell in battle would resurrect and enjoy the utopia they were creating.[59]

Subaltern genocides offer important insights into how native peoples perceived ethnicity and race, as opposed to how it was viewed by the colonial elite. Unlike colonial legislation that utilized a detailed progenitor-based system to categorize and regulate racial categories, rebels in these movements employed a more 'empirical' approach in which race and colour were considered in a wider context.[60] While the light skin of Spaniards and Creoles clearly identified them as 'white', mestizos and even Indians were also marked for death based on such factors as their dress, occupation, religious orientation, and the primary language they spoke. Cultural markers such as these generally reflected one's position in the hierarchy of colonial

---

[58] Robins, *Native Insurgencies*, 38–50.

[59] Nicholas A. Robins, *Genocide and Millennialism in Upper Peru: The Great Rebellion of 1780–1782* (Westport, CT: Praeger, 2002), 202–5.

[60] For an example of such categorization in Brazil, see Patrick Wolfe, 'Land, Labor, and Difference: Elementary Structures of Race', *American Historical Review* 106 (2001), 896.

exploitation. As a result, for example, a mestizo who served in a position of authority as an overseer or tax collector and who wore Spanish-style clothing would not be considered a native in rebel eyes. But simply being mestizo was in and of itself often insufficient to mark one for death, a tendency epitomized by the fact that Túpac Amaru was a mestizo.[61] Cultural orientations, and their physical expression, were central in defining indigenous identity, and often who lived and who died.[62]

Such cases of subaltern genocides call into question widely held views of genocide. For example, such uprisings were the means to establishing an Indian state, not an expression of state policy. Furthermore, genocidal movements are not bound to any specific time period, and subaltern genocides demonstrate that genocides are not always from above or about the strong over the weak. Although in many genocides the victim group does not possess the military or organizational means of defeating their adversaries, in cases of subaltern genocide such as the Great Rebellion (or the 'Sepoy Mutiny' in British-ruled India), the insurgents were confronting a formally organized and better armed military force. Unlike genocides from above, subaltern perpetrators of genocide often were defeated by their enemies.

Subaltern genocide also challenges prevailing concepts of leadership. While that of the Pueblo revolt was highly centralized, that of the Great Rebellion (and later the Caste War of Yucatan) was highly fragmented, confederational, and far from bureaucratic. In some cases, such as with Tomás Catari in Upper Peru and Túpac Amaru in Peru, despite their charismatic appeal, the objectives of the formal leadership were considerably more limited in scope and generally more conservative than that of those who operated in their name. This led to them having minimal operational control in areas outside of their immediate command, and as a result they became largely nominal to the rebellions that they are credited with leading. In contrast, local level leaders had prominent roles in these uprisings and were central in the perpetration of genocide.[63]

CONCLUSION

Exploring the genocides of conquest and colonization in Latin America highlights the shortcomings of conventional definitions of genocide. According to some interpretations of the 1948 UN Convention on genocide, it is possible to have a

---

[61] Robins, *Genocide and Millennialism*, 59, 195.
[62] Robins, *Native Insurgencies*, 4, 8–9, 76–7.
[63] Ibid. 118–24.

'genocide' free of death. Actions 'causing serious bodily or mental harm to members of the group' are legally considered genocide, yet can be interpreted as not necessarily involving mass killing even when the object is the destruction of a group. Likewise, although in a broader intellectual context, deliberate cultural destruction, or ethnocide, and the deliberate elimination of languages, or linguicide, are also often considered genocide.[64] On the other hand, the unintended extinction or near extinction of a people from disease, a literal genocide and what could also be termed 'collateral genocide', is not considered genocide according to the UN Convention.

While the debate over the role of intentionality in genocide will no doubt continue, the empirical reality of the Latin American case supports an approach to genocide in which intent, whether specific or general, is only one component of a complex, interrelated, and often impersonal process.[65] Intentional policies and events, such as genocidal massacres to aid conquest, forced relocation of subjects, deprivation of livelihood, separation of families, and systematic cultural destruction, were facilitated by an unintended, demographic collapse of monumental proportions. That genocidal colonial policies and practices reflected the norms of their times did not mitigate their effect on the population, nor does it make them any less genocidal. Furthermore, the emphasis on intent, and the UN Genocide Convention generally, is focused on establishing a judicial basis to punish present and future perpetrators. Applying such modern standards to historical processes only serves to limit, not deepen, our understanding of them.[66]

SELECT BIBLIOGAPHY

Borah, Woodrow, and Sherburne Cook, *The Aboriginal Population of Central Mexico on the Eve of the Spanish Conquest* (Berkeley: University of California Press, 1963).
Churchill, Ward, *A Little Matter of Genocide: Holocaust and Denial in the Americas 1492 to the Present* (San Francisco: City Lights Books, 1997).

[64] Frank Chalk and Kurt Jonassohn, 'The Conceptual Framework', in *eidem* (eds), *The History and Sociology of Genocide: Analyses and Case Studies* (New Haven: Yale University Press, 1990), 9–10.

[65] Concerning such divisions within genocide studies and the primacy ascribed to the Holocaust, see Moses, 'Conceptual Blockages', and on the role of impersonal processes in genocides, see Vinay Lal, 'The Concentration Camp and Development: The Pasts and Future of Genocide,' *Patterns of Prejudice* 39:2 (2005), 220–43.

[66] Concerning the debate on this topic, see the following three articles in the *Journal of Genocide Research* 10:1 (2008): Tony Barta, 'With Intent to Destroy: On Colonial Intentions and Genocide Denial,'; Norbert Finzsch, 'If it Looks Like a Duck, If It Walks Like a Duck, If It Quacks Like a Duck', and David Stannard, 'Déjà Vu All Over Again'. See also Isidor Walliman and Michael Dobkowski (eds), *Genocide and the Modern Age: Etiology and Case Studies of Mass Death* (Westport, CT: Greenwood Press, 1987).

Cook, Noble David, *Demographic Collapse: Indian Peru, 1520–1620* (Cambridge: Cambridge University Press, 1981).

Duviols, Pierre, *La destrucción de las religiones andinas (Conquista y colonia)* (Mexico City: UNAM, 1977).

Gradie, Charlotte, *The Tepehuan Revolt of 1616; Militarism, Evangelism, and Colonialism in Seventeenth-Century Nueva Vizcaya* (Salt Lake City: University of Utah Press, 2000).

Griffiths, Nicholas, *The Cross and the Serpent: Religious Repression and Resurgence in Colonial Peru* (Norman: University of Oklahoma Press, 1996).

Las Casas, Bartolomé de, *Brevissima relación de la destrucción de las Indias.* (Bayamón, Puerto Rico: Universidad Central de Bayamón, 2000).

Moses, A. Dirk, 'Conceptual Blockages and Definitional Dilemmas in the "Racial Century": Genocides of Indigenous Peoples and the Holocaust', *Patterns of Prejudice* 36:4 (2002), 7–36.

Robins, Nicholas, *Native Insurgencies and the Genocidal Impulse in the Americas* (Bloomington: Indiana University Press, 2005).

Stannard, David, *American Holocaust: Columbus and the Conquest of the New World* (New York: Oxford University Press, 1992).

CHAPTER 16

....

RETHINKING GENOCIDE IN NORTH AMERICA

....

GREGORY D. SMITHERS

SINCE the 1940s, American historians have been reluctant to incorporate Raphael Lemkin's concept of genocide into the narrative of the United States' history. This reluctance is in large measure a reflection of the context in which Lemkin's concept of 'genocide' entered popular and political discourse in America. The word genocide became part of the American vernacular with the onset of Cold War politics in the late 1940s and early 1950s.[1] As the world grappled with the magnitude of the atrocities visited upon the European Jewish population by the Nazi regime and contended with the emergence of the 'Communist bloc' under the leadership of the Soviet Union, most Americans found it difficult to see how Lemkin's neologism had anything to do with their own nation's history.[2] And yet, Lemkin's concept of genocide, like the colonial origins of the United States, was rooted in the often-violent encounters between European colonists and Native Americans. In the wake of *Axis Rule in Occupied Europe* (1944), Lemkin arrived at his broad-reaching definition of genocide after studying the historical impact of colonialism on

---

[1] In the United States, lawmakers worried that ratification of the UN Convention on Genocide would expose the federal government to charges of genocide against Native Americans and African-Americans. Lawrence J. LeBlanc, *The United States and the Genocide Convention* (Durham: Duke University Press, 1991), 26, 64.

[2] Ibid. 6–7, 50.

indigenous peoples throughout the Americas. In North America, English settler colonialism left indigenous Americans struggling to survive European diseases for which they lacked immunity, and grappling to understand the significance of cultural, social, environmental, and economic changes that settler colonialism brought to the east coast of North America. As recent scholarship has recognized, the legacy of settler colonialism in North America continued to impact Native Americans long after the Founding Fathers drafted and passed a national constitution.[3] It is in the context of settler colonialism that the concept of genocide needs to be re-examined in relation to North American history.

Lemkin defined genocide as the 'destruction of a nation or of an ethnic group'. He coined the term from the ancient Greek word *genos*, meaning 'race' or 'tribe', and the Latin *cide*, or 'killing'. In Lemkin's mind, the genocide of a people did not have to occur in one instance, for the most important factor in defining a genocidal event was intent, or the existence of 'a coordinated plan of different actions aiming at the destruction of essential foundations of the life of national groups, with the aim of annihilating the groups themselves'. The issue of intent has divided American historians. Some, as we will see, define intent broadly, and refer to both the cultural and biological destruction of indigenous people. Other scholars argue that American history lacks evidence of coordinated government efforts to commit genocide on any group of people.[4] During the early years of the Cold War, the idea that English colonial authorities or the US Government had ever acted with genocidal intentions toward Native Americans undermined the notion of American exceptionalism, and struck at the heart of America's self-identification as a beacon for liberty and freedom in the face of Communist oppression.[5]

During the civil rights era of the 1960s, historians began to challenge the traditional historical interpretations of American exceptionalism. New insights emerged that reassessed racial, ethnic, and gender relations in US history.[6] These studies focused on the violent and often genocidal aspects of colonial encounters between the British and American Indians. Historians such as Francis Jennings,

---

[3] Michael A. McDonnell and A. Dirk Moses, 'Raphael Lemkin as Historian of Genocide in the Americas', *Journal of Genocide Research* 7:4 (2005), 501–29. See also Ann Laura Stoler, 'Tense and Tender Ties: The Politics of Comparison in North American History and (Post) Colonial Studies', *Journal of American History* 88:3 (2001), 829–65.

[4] Raphael Lemkin, *Axis Rule in Occupied Europe: Laws of Occupation, Analysis of Government, Proposals for Redress* (1944; New York: Howard Fertig, 1973), 79. See also Samantha Power, *'A Problem from Hell': America and the Age of Genocide* (New York: Harper Perennial, 2002), 42.

[5] John K. White, *Still Seeing Red: How the Cold War Shapes the New American Politics* (Boulder, CO: Westview Press, 1997), 5; William E. Odom and Robert Dujarric, *America's Inadvertent Empire* (New Haven: Yale University Press, 2004), 226.

[6] Seymour M. Lipset, *American Exceptionalism: A Double-Edged Sword* (New York: W. W. Norton, 1996); Ian Tyrell, 'Making Nations/Making States: American Historians in the Context of Empire', *Journal of American History* 84:3 (1999), 1015–43; David W. Noble, *Death of a Nation: American Culture and the End of Exceptionalism* (Minneapolis: University of Minnesota Press, 2002).

Roy Harvey Pearce, Richard Drinnon, Winthrop Jordan, George Fredrickson, and Roger Daniels enriched our understanding of the various aspects of Western racism and the impact of racially motivated violence that targeted Native American, African-American, and Asian American peoples. Like settler societies in Australasia and southern Africa, the colonies that became the United States in 1789 (the year that George Washington became the first President of the United States) were a product of complex sociocultural, economic, and geopolitical motives that helped European and American colonizers structure settler colonial society in North America. As Richard Cole Harris informs us, 'Colonialism has more than one voice'; understanding these complex and sometimes contradictory voices goes a long way to explaining 'genocidal episodes' in the settler colonial history of North America, and particularly the United States.[7]

SETTLER COLONIALISM IN ENGLISH NORTH AMERICA

The sixteenth- and seventeenth-century motives for English colonization along the eastern seaboard of North America were multifaceted and complex. Historically specific and geographically contingent factors, such as the sociopolitical context of early modern Europe, the hope of a New World ripe with socioeconomic opportunities, and changing European perceptions of Native American peoples, all played a role in shaping settler colonialism in English North America. Puritans and Separatists, for example, fled religious persecution in England and Europe, an experience that shaped their collective ambition to establish economically profitable settlements characterized by political self-rule in the New England frontier.[8] With the rapid decline of New England's Native American population due to the ravages of disease, thousands of acres of forests, meadows, and marshlands were left 'relatively unoccupied'.[9] Puritan missionaries hoped to convert Native Americans, or 'praying Indians' as the missionary John Eliot called them, to Christianity (a conversion that Lemkin labelled 'cultural genocide'), while settlers aimed to fill these 'empty' spaces with their version of settler colonial civilization, carving out of

[7] Richard Cole Harris, *Making Native Space: Colonialism, Resistance, and Reserves in British Columbia* (Vancouver: University of British Columbia Press, 2002), 46; A. Dirk Moses, 'Conceptual Blockages and Definitional Dilemmas in the "Racial Century": Genocides of Indigenous Peoples and the Holocaust', *Patterns of Prejudice* 36:4 (2002), 28.

[8] Ray Allen Billington, *American History before 1877* (Totowa, NJ: Rowman and Littlefield, 1965), 16–17.

[9] Daniel Vickers, *A Companion to Colonial America* (Malden, MA: Blackwell, 2003), 55.

the New England wilderness the towns, villages, and farms that comprised the material foundation for a Christian society in the New World.[10] Settler colonialism in New England therefore involved what Alfred Crosby has called the 'demographic takeover' of New England, the reorganization of land use, and for the surviving indigenous inhabitants, the gradual restructuring of traditional social, economic, and political folkways.[11]

English settlements and plantations also emerged in the mid-Atlantic, the Carolinas, and Chesapeake Bay during the seventeenth and eighteenth centuries. In the Chesapeake, small farms and plantations dotted the landscape along the James River to the mouth of the Chesapeake Bay. The Chesapeake experienced slow and uneven economic development for much of the seventeenth century. As a result, the colonies of Virginia and Maryland remained tottering frontiers of settlement. Not until the cultivation of tobacco emerged as a cash crop during the late seventeenth century, an economic development that led to pressure for ever larger tracts of land in the Chesapeake occupied by Native Americans, and worked increasingly by African slaves, did the colonial economy develop and significant territorial expansion begin.[12] The demographic heterogeneity that emerged in seventeenth-century Virginia, as in other English settler colonies, meant that the Old World social, economic, and political frameworks that defined epistemological categories such as master and servant, or landowner and lessee, were rethought to meet the historical and geographic demands of settler colonialism in the North American colonies.[13]

Demographic heterogeneity, a defining characteristic of English settler colonialism in North America, necessitated an elaborate system of colonial regulation of human behaviour. To the English in North America, racial and ethnic cosmopolitanism was an impediment to the growth of politically stable settler communities

---

[10] Daniel Gookin, *Historical Account of the Doings and Sufferings of the Christian Indians, in the Years 1675, 1676, 1677* (1836; New York: Arno Press, 1972), 434–40, *passim*; Kristina Bross, *Dry Bones and Indian Sermons: Praying Indians in Colonial America* (Ithaca, NY: Cornell University Press, 2004), 21; John Docker, 'Are Settler-Colonies Inherently Genocidal? Re-reading Lemkin', in A. Dirk Moses (ed.), *Empire, Colony, Genocide: Conquest, Occupation, and Subaltern Resistance in World History* (New York: Berghahn Books, 2008), 86. 89, 95.

[11] Alfred W. Crosby, *Germs, Seeds and Animals: Studies in Ecological History* (Armonk, NY: M. E. Sharpe, 1994), 29; David Scott, *Conscripts of Modernity: The Tragedy of Colonial Enlightenment* (Durham: Duke University Press, 2004), 44.

[12] Lorena S. Walsh, 'Slave Life, Slave Society, and Tobacco Production in the Tidewater Chesapeake, 1620–1820', in Ira Berlin and Philip D. Morgan (eds), *Labor and the Shaping of Slave Life in the Americas* (Charlottesville: University Press of Virginia, 1993), 170.

[13] Reinhart Koselleck and Keith Tribe, *Futures Past: On the Semantics of Historical Time* (New York: Columbia University Press, 2004), 256; Ian Tyrell, 'Beyond the View from Euro-America: Environment, Settler Societies, and the Internationalization of American History', in Thomas Bender (ed.), *Rethinking American History in a Global Age* (Berkeley: University of California Press, 2002), 170–1.

and a source of social anxiety.[14] As a result, colonialists, particularly English colonial authorities, articulated a binary logic in which settler colonial civilization was imagined and created in opposition to the chaos of the American wilderness. This binary logic became increasingly elaborate as English settler colonies developed and expanded territorially during the eighteenth century, ultimately helping settlers to structure and organize wilderness spaces with a combination of town planning, trade relations with other Europeans as well as Native Americans, and the delineation of a social hierarchy that by the American Revolution was overtly racial and white supremacist in nature.[15] As Eyal Ben-Ari and Yoram Bilu observe, 'space and place are central organizing principles in all complex societies.'[16] To Ben-Ari's and Bilu's observation we must add that English colonists in North America adapted Old World economic, political, and social structures to order their New World existence. Recognition of the commitment of English settlers to these ideals, and the colonial structures that they helped to establish, moves us towards an understanding of how English colonists rationalized anti-Indian violence, or even genocidal actions.

The historian Patrick Wolfe has presented one of the most sustained frameworks for understanding settler colonialism. Wolfe argues that 'Settler colonies were (are) premised on the elimination of native societies.'[17] In an influential 2001 essay in the *American Historical Review*, Wolfe presents a 'typology of strategic phases' for understanding settler colonialism. These phases include 'confrontation', which for indigenous peoples involves the loss of life through disease and violent conflict with settlers; 'carceration', or the removal and segregation of indigenous peoples away from settler society; and 'assimilation', which can involve biological and/or cultural assimilation of indigenous peoples with settler populations.[18] Wolfe argues that 'the recalcitrant persistence of extraneously constituted indigenous societies'—be they Australian Aborigines or North American Indians—posed a serious problem to settler colonialism.[19] Settlers, coveting the land that indigenous peoples occupied, turned settler colonialism into a 'zero-sum contest over land on which

---

[14] A. G. Roeber, 'The Origins of Whatever Is Not English among Us: The Dutch-Speaking and the German Speaking Peoples of Colonial British America', in Bernard Bailyn and Philip D. Morgan (eds), *Strangers within the Realm: Cultural Margins of the First British Empire* (Chapel Hill: University of North Carolina Press, 1991), 226; Michael Hechter, Debra Friedman, and Satoshi Kanazawa, 'The Attainment of Social Order in Heterogeneous Societies', in Michael Hechter (ed.), *Theories of Social Order: A Reader* (Palo Alto, CA: Stanford University Press, 2003), 331.

[15] George M. Fredrickson, *White Supremacy: A Comparative Study in American and South African History* (New York: Oxford University Press, 1981), 5.

[16] Eyal Ben-Ari and Yoram Bilu, 'Introduction', in *eidem* (eds), *Grasping Land: Space and Place in Contemporary Israeli Discourse and Experience* (Albany: SUNY Press, 1997), 6–7.

[17] Patrick Wolfe, *Settler Colonialism and the Transformation of Anthropology: The Politics and Poetics of an Ethnographic Event* (London: Cassell, 1999), 2.

[18] Patrick Wolfe, 'Land, Labor, and Difference: Elementary Structures of Race', *American Historical Review* 106:3 (2001), 871.

[19] Ibid. 874.

conflicting modes of production could not ultimately coexist'.[20] In the United States, however, historians of colonial North America and the republic of the United States have generally overlooked Wolfe's framework.

Part of the reason that American historians have neglected Wolfe's analysis lies in the well-established and nuanced historiography of English–Indian relations and colonial violence in colonial North America.[21] American historians have analysed in great detail the complexity of colonialism during the seventeenth and eighteenth centuries, observing that European settlers, traders, militiamen, and explorers arrived in colonial North America with very different motives. Some, such as French and Spanish traders, were motivated by a desire to seek their fortune in the Americas.[22] It was therefore in the best interest of traders, and the trickle of settlers to regions as diverse as Quebec, New England, the Chesapeake, and the Mississippi and Arkansas, to cultivate trade and diplomatic relations with indigenous Americans. In this vast colonial context, the 'elimination' of the 'native' was not a viable option if trade, let alone settler colonialism, was to take root in North America. Kathleen Duval has demonstrated that indigenous Americans in the Arkansas Valley believed that 'Incorporating alien [European] peoples proved to be an effective means of maintaining and increasing power', while 'Colonial administrators generally delineated the boundaries of their empires by referring to the native peoples with whom they had forged alliances'.[23] This historiography suggests that there existed no predetermined 'structural' rationale for violence or even genocide in colonial North America; rather, early settler colonialism in North America was a messy business, as Old World cultural ideals and socioeconomic structures were forced to adapt to new landscapes and were *creolized* because Native Americans held the upper hand, at least

[20] Ibid. 868. See also Patrick Wolfe, 'Settler Colonialism and the Elimination of the Native', *Journal of Genocide Research* 8:4 (2006), 398.

[21] Of an enormous historiography, see Richard White, *The Middle Ground: Indians, Empires, and Republics in the Great Lakes Region, 1650–1815* (Cambridge: Cambridge University Press, 1991); Kathleen Brown, 'Native Americans and Early Modern Concepts of Race', in Martin Daunton and Rick Halpern (eds), *Empire and Others: British Encounters with Indigenous Peoples, 1600–1850* (Philadelphia: University of Pennsylvania Press, 1999), 79–100; Karen Ordahl Kupperman, *Indians and English: Facing off in Early America* (Ithaca, NY: Cornell University Press, 2000); Ann Marie Plane, *Colonial Intimacies: Indian Marriage in Early New England* (Ithaca, NY: Cornell University Press, 2000); James H. Merrell, 'The Indians' New World: The Catawba Experience', in Stanley N. Katz, John M. Murrin, and Douglas Greenberg (eds), *Colonial America: Essays in Politics and Social Development* (Boston: McGraw Hill, 2001), 301–28; Jenny Hale Pulsipher, *Subjects unto the Same King: Indians, English, and the Contest for Authority in Colonial New England* (Philadelphia: University of Pennsylvania Press, 2005); Alan Taylor, *The Divided Ground: Indians, Settlers and the Northern Borderland of the American Revolution* (New York: Alfred A. Knopf, 2006).

[22] J. H. Elliott, *Empires of the Atlantic World: Britain and Spain in America, 1492–1830* (New Haven, CT: Yale University Press, 2006); Christopher Scmidt-Noware, *The Conquest of History: Spanish Colonialism and National Histories in the Nineteenth Century* (Pittsburgh: University of Pittsburgh Press, 2008).

[23] Kathleen Duval, *The Native Ground: Indians and Colonists in the Heart of the Continent* (Philadelphia: University of Pennsylvania Press, 2006), 8, 24, 26, 188–90.

initially, in terms of military strength, access to economic resources, and political power. As Daniel Richter presciently observes, 'British-American Indian relations during the long eighteenth century defy a single narrative.'[24]

How, then, might we attempt to understand anti-Indian violence and episodes of genocide in English colonial North America? While an ever growing historical literature informs us that English colonists, like Spanish and French colonists, forged socioeconomic networks and cultural identities that were adapted to the New World, the English colonists maintained a dogged determination to see themselves, and the settler communities they were creating, as English in political, social, and economic form. Confronted with the racial and ethnic heterogeneity of settler colonialism in North America, English colonists quickly developed a deep sense of anxiety about their collective identity, political independence—from both England and local indigenous peoples—and their economic prosperity.[25] In this respect, Michael Zuckerman argues that the 'early colonists were at once more free and more controlled, more concerned about themselves and more sensitive to the opinions of others, than their European forebears had been; and those who came after them...sought simultaneously a new purity of personal identity and a new consummation of conscious community.'[26] In the binaries of civilization and wilderness that colonists hoped would structure settler colonial life, and in the settler's often-frustrated hopes for the future acquisition of land, economic security, and political independence, the seeds of anti-Indian violence and genocide germinated.

NATIVE AMERICANS AND THE QUESTION OF COLONIAL GENOCIDE

American historians routinely begin their assessments of settler colonialism by pointing to the devastating consequences of disease among indigenous American peoples. Alfred Crosby's now famous description of 'virgin soil epidemics', or

[24] Daniel K. Richter, 'Native Peoples of North America and the Eighteenth-Century British Empire', in P. J. Marshall (ed.), *The Oxford History of the British Empire: The Eighteenth Century* (Oxford: Oxford University Press, 2001), 347.

[25] See for example Jean M. O'Brien, *Dispossession by Degrees: Indian Land and Identity in Natick, Massachusetts, 1650–1790* (New York: Cambridge University Press, 1997), 10; James Horn and Philip D. Morgan, 'Settlers and Slaves: European and African Migrations to Early Modern British America', in Elizabeth Mancke and Carole Shammas (eds), *The Creation of the British Atlantic World* (Baltimore: Johns Hopkins University Press, 2005), 39–40.

[26] Michael Zuckerman, 'Identity in British America: Unease in Eden', in Nicholas Canny and Anthony Pagden (eds), *Colonial Identity in the Atlantic World, 1500–1800* (Princeton: Princeton University Press, 1987), 130.

outbreaks of diseases to which Native Americans had no previous exposure and were 'therefore immunologically almost defenseless', have led historians to estimate that Native American populations declined by as much as ninety per cent within a century of first contact.[27] Russell Thornton argues that after suffering the debilitating consequences of disease in the colonial era, the Native American population continued to decline during the nineteenth century, falling from 600,000 in 1800, to 228,000 by 1890.[28]

Observing the death of indigenous people from disease in New England, John Winthrop observed in 1629 that 'God hath consumed the Natives wth a great plague in those parts soe as there be few inhabitants left.'[29] Such comments have led some historians to speculate that disease transfer was an example of the genocidal consequences of settler colonialism in North America. According to Steven Katz, Native American depopulation from disease was an unintentional consequence of settler colonialism. He argues that 'the greatest demographic disaster in history, the depopulation of the New World, for all its death and terror, was largely an unintended tragedy, a tragedy that occurred despite the sincere and indisputable desire of Europeans to keep the Indian population alive'.[30] According to Katz, the spread of European diseases and the death of Native American populations was not

[27] Alfred W. Crosby, 'Virgin Soil Epidemics as a Factor in the Aboriginal Depopulation in America', *William and Mary Quarterly* 3rd ser. 33:2 (1976), 289; Alfred Cave, 'Genocide in the Amercias', in Dan Stone (ed.), *The Historiography of Genocide* (Hampshire: Palgrave Macmillan, 2008), 273.

[28] Russell Thornton, 'Aboriginal Population Size of North America', in Michael R. Haines and Richard H. Steckel (eds), *A Population History of North America* (New York: Cambridge University Press, 2000), 24. See also Henry F. Dobyns, 'Disease Transfer at Contact', *American Review of Anthropology* 22 (1993), 275–6; James Mooney, 'The Aboriginal Population of America North of Mexico', in John R. Swanton (ed.), *Smithsonian Miscellaneous Collections*, vol 80 (Washington, DC: US GPO, 1928), 1–40; William Cronin, *Changes in the Land: Indians, Colonists, and the Ecology of New England* (New York: Hill and Wang, 1983), 88; Henry F. Dobyns, *Their Number Become Thinned: Native American Population Dynamics in Eastern North America* (Knoxville: University of Tennessee Press, 1983); Russell Thornton, 'Aboriginal North American Population and Rates of Decline, ca. A. D. 1500–1900', *Current Anthropology* 38:2 (1997), 310–15; Melissa L. Meyer and Russell Thornton, 'Indians and the Numbers Game: Quantitative Methods in Native American History', in Colin G. Calloway (ed.), *New Directions in American Indian History* (Norman: University of Oklahoma Press, 1992), 5–30.

[29] Winthrop quoted in Peter C. Mancall (ed.), *Envisioning America: English Plans for Colonization of North America, 1580–1640* (Boston: Bedford/St. Martin's, 1995), 137.

[30] Steven T. Katz, *The Holocaust in Historical Context*, vol i: *The Holocaust and Mass Death before the Modern Age* (New York: Oxford University Press, 1992), 20. Native American historians have taken exception to this view, seeing a seamless connection between what they interpret as the impact of disease and the ensuing cultural and physical genocide of Native American peoples. See George E. Tinker, *Missionary Conquest: The Gospel and Native American Cultural Genocide* (Minneapolis: Fortress Press, 1993), 4–5; Ward Churchill, *A Little Matter of Genocide: Holocaust and Denial in the Americas, 1492 to the Present* (San Francisco: City Lights Books, 1997), 137–43. See also Edward D. Castillo's preface in Clifford E. Trafzer and Joel R. Hyer (eds), *Exterminate Them! Written Accounts of Murder, Rape, and Enslavement of Native Americans during the California Gold Rush* (East Lansing: Michigan State University Press, 1999), x.

an intentional effort to perpetuate genocide.[31] In contrast, Ward Churchill refers to settler colonialism in North America as 'the American holocaust', and David Stannard similarly portrays the European colonization of the Americas as an example of 'human incineration and carnage'.[32]

Over the past forty years, American historians have endeavoured to move beyond the polemical debate about disease transfer in an effort to understand the nuances of settler rationalizations for the often-violent treatment of Native Americans.[33] A closer recognition for the importance of chronology has been critical to such analysis. For example, the historian Karen Kupperman has observed that the initial encounters between northeastern Native Americans and English settlers were not characterized by violence, but mutual curiosity and a desire for trade, something particularly important to the survival of English settlements.[34] To the west, Richard White's analysis of Algonquin–French encounters in the Great Lakes region notes that 'campaign[s] of genocide' against indigenous peoples did not occur until long after the early years of contact, years characterized by the mutual search for trade allies.[35] Kupperman and White remind us that settler colonialism in North America occurred in uneven chronological and geographical phases. What is important is that only after traders and settlers established the foundations of permanent settler communities, as Wolfe's framework suggests, did competition for land and natural resources intensify, and some of the most extreme examples of settler colonial violence emerged.

Chesapeake Bay settlers provide us with an early example of frontier violence. Between 1607 and 1644, scholars point out that a series of 'wars' were fought between the English and the Powhatan Indians. These battles were sparked by the aggressive aspirations of English traders, the desire of settlers for land and natural resources, and the sense among the Powhatan that the English were not conforming to local trade practices and land-use agreements.[36] By 1622 the English in Virginia had become particularly nervous about the intentions of local Indians

---

[31] M. Annette Jaimes offers a sustained analytical rethinking of disease transfer and genocide in her *The State of Native America: Genocide, Colonization, and Resistance* (Boston: South End Press, 1992), 31–3.

[32] David E. Stannard, *American Holocaust: The Conquest of the New World* (New York: Oxford University Press, 1992), xi, 62, 69.

[33] R. David Edmunds, 'The Indian in the Mainstream: Indian Historiography for Teachers of American History Surveys', *History Teacher* 8:2 (1975), 242–62; Reginald Horsman, 'Well-Trodden Paths and Fresh Byways: Recent Writing on Native American History', *Reviews in American History* 10:4 (1982), 234–44.

[34] Kupperman, *Indians and English*, 173, *passim*. See also Norbert Finzsch, '"The Aborigines . . . were never annihilated, and still they are becoming Extinct": Settler Imperialism and Genocide in Nineteenth-Century America and Australia', in Moses (ed.), *Empire, Colony, Genocide*, 254.

[35] Richard White, *Middle Ground: Indians, Empires, and Republics in the Great Lakes Region, 1650–1815* (New York: Cambridge University Press, 1991), 25, 168.

[36] April Lee Hatfield, *Atlantic Virginia: Intercolonial Relations in the Seventeenth Century* (Philadelphia: University of Pennsylvania Press, 2007), 24.

after Powhatan warriors murdered several Englishmen. To the English, these murders reflected the increasingly aggressive stance that the Powhatan were assuming towards them. In this uneasy colonial context, settlers needed little prodding to take up arms after they received orders from the Virginia Company 'to root out [the Powhatan Indians] from being any longer a people . . . Wherefore, as they have merited, let them have a perpetual war without peace or truce, and, although they have desired it, without mercy, too.'[37]

A similar pattern of mutual suspicion and violence emerged in other North American colonies. In 1644, Dutch authorities in New Amsterdam (later renamed New York) hired John Underhill to burn and slaughter some five hundred Native Americans after settlers became nervous about 'unprovoked' attacks on colonial communities.[38] Violent clashes with Native Americans produced in settlers a growing suspicion of the 'wild' frontier Indians, a psychology that in moments of extreme stress or anxiety resulted in a determination to exterminate the local indigenous populations. In 1763, for example, Pennsylvania settlers, led by the infamous Paxton boys, surrounded and killed twenty peaceful Susquehannock Indians after a period of heightened settler anxiety.[39]

One of the most controversial historical case studies of English–Indian violence occurred in New England between 1636 and 1637. The Pequot War had its origins in the Pequot Indians determination to prevent rival Indian tribes—particularly the Narragansett—from attaining more favourable trade relations with Dutch and English traders in the Connecticut River Valley. Pequot leaders felt that the emergence of the Massachusetts Bay Colony, and its increasing trade with rival Indian tribes, squeezed the Pequot out of a position of dominance with European traders. This loss of influence proved irksome to Pequot leaders and worried Dutch merchants. The Dutch attempted to shore up trade relationships with Indian tribes by drafting formal agreements. For example, in 1633 the Dutch–Pequot Agreement was designed to give the Dutch access to trade with Indian tribes other than the Pequot. This trade arrangement rankled Pequot warriors, and prompted them to assault and kill traders from the rival Narragansett tribe. A series of Dutch–Pequot reprisals and counter-reprisals ensued, culminating in Pequot warriors mistaking the captain of an English trading vessel, John Stone, and six of his crew, as

---

[37] James Mooney, 'The Powhatan Confederacy, Past and Present', *American Anthropologist* 9 (1907), 138; John Esten Cooke, *Virginia: A History of the People*, 6th edn (Boston: Houghton, Mifflin, 1885), 124–5; Hatfield, *Atlantic Virginia*, 234; Ben Kiernan, *Blood and Soil: A World History of Genocide and Extermination from Sparta to Darfur* (New Haven, CT: Yale University Press, 2007), 219–25.

[38] John J. Anderson and Alexander Clarence Flick, *A Short History of the State of New York* (New York: Maynard, Merrill, 1902), 31.

[39] James H. Merrell, *Into the American Woods: Negotiators on the Pennsylvania Frontier* (New York: Norton, 1999), 16, 37–9.

Dutchmen.[40] The raid and subsequent murder of Stone and his crew prompted Massachusetts Bay authorities to send a military party under the leadership of John Endecott to ensure the peace of the colonists 'by killing the barbarians'.[41]

It is at this point that historians express a wide range of views about the historical significance of the Pequot War. Specifically, historians disagree over the nature of the Puritan attack on a Pequot village at West Mystic, Connecticut, on 26 May 1637. At West Mystic, English soldiers and their Narragansett allies killed approximately four hundred Pequot men, women, and children, and also burned the Pequot village. The English hoped that this attack would cripple the Pequot. The following year the English attempted to seal the fate of the Pequot. The Treaty of Hartford extinguished the legal right of surviving Pequot Indians from using their tribal name or attaining access to ancestral lands. Through a combination of violence and legal manoeuvring, the Puritans helped to establish English settler colonial patterns of economic, political, and social practices designed to separate the Indians from the English, and ultimately exterminate indigenous peoples from the land that settlers coveted.[42]

Steven Katz argues that the Pequot War was neither genocidal nor racially motivated. He insists that because Indian warriors and English soldiers fought together against the Pequot, the Pequot War was therefore non-racial in character.[43] Moreover, the regrouping of the Pequot by 1650 proved that genocidal intent did not motivate the English.[44] In a forceful response, Michael Freeman argues that the violence of the Pequot War and the subsequent Treaty of Hartford did indeed reflect Puritan intentions to commit both biological and cultural genocide.[45]

[40] Jennings, *Invasion of America*, ch. 13; Neal Salisbury, *Manitou and Providence: Indians, Europeans, and the Making of New England, 1500–1643* (New York: Oxford University Press, 1984), 214–25; Adam J. Hirsch, 'The Collision of Military Cultures in Seventeenth-Century New England', *Journal of American History* 74:4 (1988), 1194–6; Alden T. Vaughan, *New England Frontier: Puritans and Indians, 1620–1675*, 3rd edn (Norman: University of Oklahoma Press, 1995), ch. 5; Alfred A. Cave, *The Pequot War* (Amherst: University of Massachusetts Press, 1996), 56–8, 72–3.

[41] Cave, *The Pequot War*, 109.

[42] Jennings, *Invasion of America*, 220–6; Vaughan, *New England Frontier*, 144–7; Salisbury, *Manitou and Providence*, 221–3; Hirsch, 'The Collision of Military Cultures', 1202–3; Cave, *Pequot War*, 146–51; Wilbur R. Jacobs, 'British-Colonial Attitudes and Policies toward the Indian in the American Colonies', in Howard Peckham and Charles Gibson (eds), *Attitudes of Colonial Powers toward the American Indian* (Salt Lake City: University of Utah Press, 1969), 95.

[43] Steven T. Katz, 'The Pequot War Reconsidered', *New England Quarterly* 64:2 (1991), 206–24. Katz takes aim at what he labels Frances Jennings's 'genocidal thesis', and Richard Drinnon's 'genocidal intentions' argument in his *Facing West*. Francis Jennings, *The Invasion within: Indians, Colonialism, and the Cant of Conquest* (Chapel Hill: University of North Carolina Press, 1975).

[44] Katz, 'Pequot War Reconsidered', 222–3.

[45] Katz rejects the bulk of Freeman's argument by insisting that acts of genocide must be defined by the criteria of 'actualized intentions'. Steven T. Katz, 'Pequots and the Question of Genocide: A Reply to Michael Freeman', *New England Quarterly* 68:4 (1995), 641–9, esp. 648; Michael Freeman, 'Puritans and Pequots: The Question of Genocide', *New England Quarterly* 68:2 (1995), 290.

Borrowing the words of one Puritan captain, Freeman insists that the English intent was 'to cut off the remembrance of them [the Pequot] from the earth'.[46]

The Pequot War, as was the case with the Powhatan massacre in Virginia, highlighted one of the most important patterns in English–Indian relations: as settlers established communities and sociopolitical hierarchies developed, the presence of Native American peoples elicited a nagging sense of vulnerability and a growing racialized distrust of American Indians, and sparked outbursts of anti-Indian violence. In the cases of the Powhatan massacre and Pequot War, the perception of imminent Indian attacks prompted English aggressions with the objective of protecting settler society by eliminating the threat posed by the Native American warriors. Therefore, the actions of Virginian and Puritan settlers can be interpreted as offensive actions to defend an emerging settler colonial order that settlers imagined themselves creating. This was why John Winthrop claimed that 'we went not to make war upon them [the Pequots], but to do justice, etc.'[47] To Puritan leaders, as with colonial officials in the mid-Atlantic and Chesapeake, doing 'justice' meant eliminating the Indian threat to settler society.[48] Thus, imbedded in the fluid economic structures, developing political hierarchies, and colonial culture of eighteenth-century North America was an increasingly explicit belief that exterminating Native American peoples could indeed be seen as a 'just' means for settler colonialism to expand from the Atlantic to the Pacific Ocean.

THE AMERICAN REPUBLIC AND THE QUESTION OF GENOCIDE

By the mid-eighteenth century, settler colonial patterns of settlement, colonial politics, and economic exchange informed Anglo-American expansion into the southern and western frontiers of North America. In the south and southwest in particular, settler colonial expansion involved the dispossession of Native Americans and the forced labour of African-American slaves, factors that united all white Americans in a socioeconomic community of common interest. The historian Norbert Finzsch refers to American territorial expansion after the Revolutionary War as 'settler imperialism', or 'a process of constant deterritorialization and reterritorialization'.[49] American settler imperialism was in many ways influenced by the social and legal precedents

---

[46] Freeman, 'Puritans and Pequots', 280, 285, 289.

[47] Ronald Dale Karr, ' "Why Should You Be So Furious?": The Violence of the Pequot War', *Journal of American History* 85:3 (1998), 903; Kiernan, *Blood and Soil*, 325–6.

[48] Karr, ' "Why Should You Be So Furious?" ', 904.

[49] Finzsch, ' "The Aborigines . . . were never annihilated" ', 261.

set in eighteenth-century North America. For example, as early as 1732, the Preamble to the Georgia Charter explicitly stated that 'Our provinces in North America have been frequently ravaged by Indian enemies.'[50] Adding to the racial anxiety that accompanied Anglo-American settler expansion was the ever present fear of slave revolts. For instance, in the wake of the Stono rebellion in South Carolina in 1739, colonial officials observed that the uprising of African-American slaves reminded settlers that 'every one that had a life to lose were in the most sensible Manner shocked at such Danger daily hanging over their Heads.'[51] So important was white supremacy to the social order in settler colonial North America that the Revolutionary War between the colonists and Britain unleashed a new wave of anti-Indian and anti-Negro sentiment. Indeed, rather than sooth racial anxieties, political independence from Britain magnified them. Thus, in 1790 the US Congress passed legislation that defined citizenship on the basis of race. The Naturalization Act stated that

all free white persons who, have, or shall migrate into the United States, and shall give satisfactory proof, before a magistrate, by oath, that they intend to reside therein, and shall take an oath of allegiance, and shall have resided in the United States for one whole year, shall be entitled to the rights of citizenship.[52]

The emergence of a racially defined American republic in North America added a level of ideological intensity to colonial patterns of frontier violence and the Anglo-American quest for territorial and economic aggrandizement. Standing in the path of a republican settler colonial empire that stretched from the Atlantic to the Pacific were the Native American communities of the south, southwest, the Great Plains, and the west. American explorers, ranchers, settlers, and gold-seekers took to the United States' frontiers of settlement their hopes and dreams for a better life, and a moral repugnance for indigenous peoples that expressed itself, in the words of one recent scholar, as the 'beastilization' of Native Americans.[53] It is in the nineteenth- and twentieth-century context of Anglo-American expansion that Patrick Wolfe's 'eliminationist' framework best helps us understand the often-genocidal violence and government policies associated with the Cherokee 'Trail of Tears' in the late 1830s, and military expeditions against American Indians from the southeast, Great Plains, and the Pacific coast that resulted in such events as the Mountain Meadow Massacre in Utah (1857), the Bannock River Massacre in Idaho

[50] Matthew Frye Jacobson, *Whiteness of a Different Color: European Immigrants and the Alchemy of Race* (Cambridge, MA: Harvard University Press, 1998), 24.

[51] Peter H. Wood, 'Anatomy of a Revolt', in Mark M. Smith (ed.), *Stono: Documenting and Interpreting a Southern Slave Revolt* (Columbia: University of South Carolina Press, 2005), 59.

[52] Jacobson, *Whiteness of a Different Color*, 22.

[53] Karl Jacoby, '"The Broad Platform of Extermination": Nature and Violence in the Nineteenth-Century North American Borderlands', *Journal of Genocide Research* 10:2 (2008), 249–67; *See also* Ned Blackhawk, *Violence over the Land: Indians and Empires in the Early American West* (Cambridge, MA: Harvard University Press, 2006), 172–3.

(1860), and the many postbellum 'expeditions' against the Sioux in Wyoming and Nebraska, and the Ute in Colorado, to name just a few examples.[54]

One of the clearest examples of how indigenous communities were adversely impacted by the disease and settler violence that accompanied Anglo-American expansion was in California. Albert Hurtado observes that Spanish colonialism in California led to the dramatic decline of the Indian population from approximately 300,000 to 200,000 between 1769 and 1821. By the end of the 1850s, and in the wake of the California Gold Rush, the Native American population teetered around 30,000. The rapid decline in California's Native American population was the result, Hurtado argues, of 'disease, starvation, homicide, and a declining birthrate'.[55] Thus, California's indigenous communities struggled to endure European diseases and violence, first from Spanish colonists and missionaries moving north from south and central America, and by the mid-nineteenth century, Anglo-American colonists migrating from the east to the west coast of North America.[56] Hurtado's statistics portray a settler colonial context in which the mere survival of California's indigenous communities hung in the balance.

The citizens and political leaders of the United States had coveted California and other lands west of the Mississippi for much of the nineteenth century.[57] The discovery of gold in the 1840s added an additional material motivation in the drive to colonize the west and eliminate Native Americans from land rich in natural resources.[58] As the number of US migrants increased in California in the 1840s and 1850s, a written record of anti-Indian racism and violence emerged.[59] This

---

[54] See for example William L. Anderson, *Cherokee Removal: Before and After* (Athens: University of Georgia Press, 1991); Dee Brown, *Bury My Heart at Wounded Knee: An Indian History of the American West* (New York: Henry Holt, 1970); Jerry Keenan, *Encyclopedia of American Indian Wars, 1492–1890* (New York: W. W. Norton, 1999); Peter Cozzens, *Conquering the Southern Plains: Eyewitnesses to the Indian Wars, 1865–1890* (Mechanicsburg, PA: Stackpole Books, 2003); Jeffrey Ostler, *The Plains Sioux and U. S. Colonialism from Lewis and Clark to Wounded Knee* (Cambridge/New York: Cambridge University Press, 2004); Benjamin Madley, 'Patterns of Frontier Genocide 1803–1910: The Aboriginal Tasmanians, the Yuki of California, and the Heroero of Namibia', *Journal of Genocide Research* 6:2 (2004), 167.

[55] Albert L. Hurtado, *Indian Survival on the California Frontier* (New Haven: Yale University Press, 1988), 1, 66–8, *passim*; Kiernan, *Blood and Soil*, 350–1.

[56] Douglas Monroy, 'Guilty Pleasures: The Satisfaction of Racial Thinking in Early-Nineteenth-Century California', in Paul Spickard (ed.), *Race and Nation: Ethnic Systems in the Modern World* (New York: Routledge, 2005), 33–52.

[57] Estwick Evans, *A Pedestrious Tour, of Four Thousand Miles, through the Western States and Territories, during the Winter and Spring of 1818. Interspersed with Brief Reflections upon a Great Variety of Topics: Religious, Moral, Political, Sentimental, &c. &c.* (Concord, NH: Joseph C. Spear, 1819), 198; James M. McCaffrey, *Army of Manifest Destiny: The American Soldier in the Mexican War, 1846–1848* (New York: New York University Press, 1994), 67–8; Hurtado, *Indian Survival*, 86–7; John S. D. Eisenhower, *So Far From God: The U. S. War with Mexico, 1846–1848* (Norman: University of Oklahoma Press, 2000), 19, 172, 269, 286;

[58] Hurtado, *Indian Survival*, 97, ch. 6; Alan G. Bogue, 'An Agricultural Empire', in Clyde A. Milner II, Carol A. O'Connor, and Martha A. Sandweiss (eds), *The Oxford History of the American West* (New York: Oxford University Press, 1994), 275–313; H. W. Brands, *The Age of Gold: The California Gold Rush and the New American Dream* (New York: Anchor Books, 2002).

[59] Madley, 'Patterns of Frontier Genocide', 169.

literature was framed by a belief in the 'White man' being both racially superior to the California Indians and the embodiment of civilization. In contrast, California's Indian population embodied a 'savage' impediment for settlers to overcome in their desire to exploit the natural resources of California.[60] Writing in 1854, the historian Elisha Smith Capron argued that Spanish missionary efforts to bring 'civilization' to California's Indians had failed. Capron wrote:

The general characteristics of the Indians of Upper California may be inferred, with much correctness, from what has been said respecting the missions. It is very certain that the reverend fathers would not have been able, with the means they had, and the system they pursued in California, to tame the spirit and enslave the bodies of the tall, athletic, haughty-souled savages of the more northern and eastern country.[61]

Missionary efforts to Christianize California's Indians falls under what Lemkin called a 'subtle kind of cultural genocide'.[62] 'Cultural genocide' included such practices as taking Indian children from their parents and placing them in mission schools, imposing lessons in Christianity and Western forms of economic practices, and most significantly, teaching indigenous children a European language so that linguistic ties with indigenous cultural traditions would be forever severed.[63] With the lessons of Spanish colonialism in California and Anglo settler expansion in the eastern United States to draw upon, Anglo-Americans understood implicitly that the success of settler imperialism, or what I have labelled elsewhere 'republican settler colonialism', hinged on their ability to control, transform, and if necessary, eliminate both the untamed wilderness and the Native American peoples.[64]

Anglo-Americans in California articulated a progressive, forward-looking conception of their envisioned settler colonial civilization. They did this, in part, by ascribing negative racial stereotypes to California Indians. For example, the Indian Agent E. A. Stevenson argued in 1853: 'Many of them [California Indians] being without any settled place of habitation; and many of them have already imbibed the very worst vices of civilization, and are becoming vitiated and degraded, a pest and nuisance to the

---

[60] Madley, 'Patterns of Frontier Genocide', 177.

[61] Elisha Smith Capron, *History of California: From Its Discovery to the Present Time: Comprising a Full Description of its Climate, Soil, Rivers, Towns, Beasts, Birds, Fishes, State of Its Society, Agriculture, Commerce, Mines. &c.* (Boston: John P. Jewett, 1854), 19.

[62] Docker, 'Are Settler-Colonies Inherently Genocidal?', in Moses (ed.), *Empire, Colony, Genocide*, 90.

[63] Bernard W. Sheehan, *Seeds of Extinction: Jeffersonian Philanthropy and the American Indian* (New York: W. W. Norton, 1974), 139–41; Blanca Tovias, 'Navigating the Cultural Encounter: Blackfoot Religious Resistance in Canada (c. 1870–1930)', in Moses (ed.), *Empire, Colony, Genocide*, 271; Gregory D. Smithers, 'The "Pursuits of the Civilized Man": Race and the Meaning of Civilization in the United States and Australia, 1790s–1850s', *Journal of World History* 20:2 (2009), 245–72.

[64] Smithers, 'The "Pursuits of the Civilized Man"', 247.

localities where they resort.'[65] White Americans insisted that the California Indians were immoral savages because they lacked the intelligence to moderate their behaviour.[66] Quite simply, the Indians represented an uncivilizable impediment to white settlement and a threat to the safety of white settlers. As a result, Anglo-American settlers expressed a determination 'to exterminate these merciless foes, or drive them from us'.[67]

California settlers believed they were under siege from 'savage' Indians. According to one nineteenth-century historian, the Anglo-American settlers knew from their own experience that acts of Indian aggression were a product of the 'character of the Indian—a mischievous disposition and desire for plunder' that convinced settlers that they needed to 'either unite and exterminate the Indians in their neighborhood or withdraw from it altogether'.[68] However, by the mid nineteenth-century, with gold to be discovered, land to be farmed, and racial 'science' reinforcing the Anglo-American belief in white supremacy, settlers came to the conclusion that California's Indians presented an innate biological and sociocultural threat from within the expansionist republic. Republican settlers, therefore, wrote often about the anxiety that California's indigenous inhabitants were causing them. Most Anglo-Americans agreed. California's natives were 'wild Indians', most being 'in the habit of killing great numbers of hogs and cattle and stealing provisions and other articles from the houses and camps of the whites'.[69] The alleged harassment of white settlers by California Indians continued unabated for three decades after gold fever ended. One settler, Walter Van Dyke, informed Governor Stanford in 1862 that the white residents in his county 'have been so harassed and frightened by the Indians that many had been forced out of fear to leave their homes'. Van Dyke echoed the racialized anxieties harboured by most white Californians, and opposed any government scheme to protect Native Americans on reserves. According to Van Dyke, 'It is impossible, utterly so, to keep these Indians on any reservation'; therefore, it was not only 'a waste of time but a swindle on the Government and an insult and injury to our people to continue this plan'.[70]

California governors heard this message from their citizens on a regular basis. Because white Californians felt utterly unprotected from what they saw as

[65] Robert F. Heizer (ed.), *The Destruction of California Indians* (Santa Barbara: Peregrine Smith, 1974), 14. The quotation 'White man' was Stevenson's, and is typical of the racialized language of American settlers and officials to California.

[66] These sentiments, as Benjamin Madley observes, were articulated in the face of white settlers kidnapping Indian women and children. See Madley, 'Patterns of Frontier Genocide', 178.

[67] James J. Rawls, *Indians of California: The Changing Image* (Norman: University of Oklahoma Press, 1984), 178.

[68] Theodore Henry Hittell, *History of California*, 4 vols (San Francisco: N. J. Stone, 1898), iii.904.

[69] Citizens of Tehema County to Governor Weller, May 29, 1859, Folder F 3753: 348, Military Department, Indian War Papers, 1850–1880, MF 3:6 (22), roll 3, California State Archives, Sacramento, California [hereafter Indian War Papers, CSA]; Heizer, *The Destruction of California Indians*, 130.

[70] Walter Van Dyke to Governor Stanford, November 25, 1862, F 3753: 623, MF 3:6 (24), roll 3, Indian War Papers, CSA. See also Traftzer and Hyer (eds.), *Exterminate Them!*, 40, 44.

unprovoked Indian attacks, many settlers decided to take matters into their own hands and dispensed a brand of frontier justice designed to force the Indians off their homelands and into the mountainous regions of California. The Sierra, for example, presented a bleak prospect for many tribes, as hunger and the desperate quest for survival forced Indians to act in ways that whites deemed threatening and uncivilized.[71] The Native American struggle for survival did not register with most settlers, nor did it engender sympathy from the governors of California, for most supported the genocidal inclinations of the white population. In 1851, Governor Burnett gave official voice to the genocidal intent of settler violence against the California Indians, stating: '[T]he white man, to whom time is money, and who labors hard all day to create the comforts of life, cannot sit up all night to watch his property... after being robbed a few times he becomes desperate, and resolves upon a war of extermination.' According to Burnett, 'A war of extermination will continue to be waged between the races until the Indian race becomes extinct.'[72] John McDougal, Burnett's successor in the governor's office, made the genocidal intent of the State of California even clearer. McDougal warned that the State would 'make war upon the [Indians] which must of necessity be one of extermination to many of the tribes'.[73]

Not all California governors—or settlers for that matter—supported these genocidal intentions.[74] Governor Weller, for instance, insisted that the State's responsibility was 'not to wage a war of extermination against the Indians', but to protect lives and property.[75] Unfortunately for Weller, the official sanction that his predecessor gave to genocidal operations had become entrenched in settler culture and behaviour. For example, in November 1850, William Rogers, who had been directed by the California governor to form a militia of two hundred men, reported the discovery of fifteen dead Mowok. Rogers reported that there existed 'numerous Trails Marked with Blood', suggesting the death toll could have been much higher. Even more brutal, the *Daily Alta California* reported in 1852 that in Trinity County a 'rancheria of 148 Indians, including women and children, was attacked, and nearly the whole number destroyed'.[76] These accounts highlight what one contemporary reported was 'a deliberate design to exterminate the Indian race'.[77]

[71] Heizer (ed.), *The Destruction of the California Indians*, 282. See also Frank H. Baumgardner, *Killing for Land in Early California: Indian Blood at Round Valley: Founding the Nome Cult Indian Farm* (New York: Algora, 2005), 2.

[72] Hurtado, *Indian Survival*, 134–6; Edward D. Castillo, 'Preface', in Trafzer and Hyer (eds), *Exterminate Them!*, x; Kiernan, *Blood and Soil*, 351–2.

[73] Hurtado, *Indian Survival*, 134, 136.

[74] Madley, 'Patterns of Frontier Genocide', 179. Baumgardner, *Killing the Land in Early California*, 11.

[75] Governor Weller to Capt. W. Jarboe, October 23, 1859, F 3753: 399, Indian War Papers, MF 3:6 (22), roll 1, CSA; Baumgardner, *Killing for Land in Early California*, 160.

[76] Heizer (ed.), *The Destruction of the California Indians*, 249.

[77] Ibid. 254.

The genocidal intent of California settlers and government officials was acted out in numerous battles and massacres (and aided by technological advances in weaponry, especially after the Civil War), in the abduction and sexual abuse of Indian women, and in the economic exploitation of Indian child labourers.[78] While the California government proved reluctant to pass laws that would have protected California Indians from white attacks, the federal government responded with a combination of indifference and incompetence. The response—or lack there of—from the California and federal officials sent white settlers the message that no official obstacle would impede their efforts to culturally and physically destroy the California Indians. The intent behind settler attacks on California's Native American population was therefore unequivocal: assert white supremacy and exterminate the Indians. According to an anonymous correspondent to the *Daily Alta California* in 1851, 'God has given us in California a goodly heritage' and the 'well-known energy and enterprise of the Anglo-Saxon race' was claiming its Providential inheritance from the California Indians.[79] By the early twentieth century, the American educator and journalist Henry Kittredge Norton articulated the Anglo-American belief that the West had been cleared of indigenous communities and successfully colonized by republican settler societies. Kittredge claimed that 'nowhere are there any Indian neophytes to be seen, for with a few exceptions the descendents of the California Indians are in their graves, literally exterminated by the onward march of a stronger race'.[80]

CONCLUSION

Colonial North America in the seventeenth and eighteenth centuries constituted an ever growing number of racially and ethnically heterogeneous sites of trade, exploration, and settlement. As Europeans ventured westward into the North American wilderness, territorial expansion, changing land-use patterns, new economic networks, and different systems of coerced labour all motivated settlers to think and act with different colonial motives that contributed to a sense of instability and flux in settler communities. What bound Europeans together, and provided the ideological and political basis for ordering settler societies, was an increasingly explicit racialized anxiety and disgust for Native Americans. The

---

[78] Ibid. Chs. 6–9 provide primary source accounts of such activities. See also Lt. Edward Dillen to Maj. W. W. Mackall, January 27, 1860, F 3735: 423, Indian War Papers, MF 3:6 (23), roll 2, CSA.

[79] Traftzer and Hyer (eds), *Exterminate Them!*, 42.

[80] Henry Kittredge Norton, *The Story of California from the Earliest Days to the Present*, 2nd edn (Chicago: A. C. McClurg, 1913), 142.

settlers' sense of disgust was important to the genocidal intentions behind different forms of colonial violence. Certainly, by the Revolutionary era white Americans saw Indian attacks on their communities as examples of a 'savage' and 'treacherous' race engaging in unprovoked pillaging.[81] As David Hollenbach explains, 'repeated exposure to images of violence . . . can give rise to public moral disgust, leading to a haughty sense of superiority, [and] a deepened perception of divisions between the civilized "us" and the savage "them".'[82] This binary logic lay at the centre of a developing colonial order of civilized settlers and uncivilized Indians (and Africans, for that matter), and led to phases of officially sanctioned efforts to exterminate the 'natives', as was the case at Fort Mystique, or inspired frontier settlers anxious to defend *their* land and homes from Indian attacks to violently strike out against indigenous people with the intent of exterminating the threat posed to settler colonial society.[83]

By the time of the early republic and antebellum era, the cultural, legal, economic, and social precedents established by colonial relations between settlers and Indians led frontier settlers and government officials to adopt a loose mixture of official military incursions against indigenous warriors, or inspired the type of frontier exterminatory violence that state and federal officials sanctioned either in word or through inaction in California.[84] In numerous other sites across the American republic's vast western frontier, a combination of military and settler violence placed many indigenous communities on the edge of extinction by the early twentieth century. Much research remains to be done on the genocidal violence visited upon the Native American peoples of the Great Plains and southwest.[85] By placing this analysis in a settler colonial framework, as suggested by scholars such as Patrick Wolfe and Ian Tyrell, the death and destruction experienced by Native Americans in the half decade after the American Civil War (1861–5) emerges less as an anomalous moment in US history, and comes into focus as an important example of the transnational drive of Western settler colonial powers to dispossess the world's indigenous peoples, reorder nature by imposing Western political and economic structures on the landscape, and if necessary, eliminating

[81] Gregory D. Smithers, *Science, Sexuality, and Race in the United States and Australia, 1780s–1890s* (New York: Routledge, 2008), ch. 1.

[82] David Hollenbach, *The Common Good and Christian Ethics* (Cambridge: Cambridge University Press, 2002), 237.

[83] Kiernan, *Blood and Soil*, 234.

[84] Benjamin A. Valentino, *Final Solutions: Mass Killings and Genocide in the Twentieth Century* (Ithaca, NY: Cornell University Press, 2004), 50–1.

[85] Excellent new research is being done, for example, by Ostler, *The Plains Sioux*, 15, 39, *passim*; Rob Harper, 'Looking the Other Way: The Gnadenhutten Massacre and the Contextual Interpretation of Violence', *William and Mary Quarterly* 3rd ser. 64:3 (2007), 621–44; Kiernan, *Blood and Soil*, ch. 8; Madley, 'Patterns of Frontier Genocide'; Ned Blackhawk, *Violence over the Land: Indians and Empires in the Early American West* (Cambridge, MA: Harvard University Press, 2006); Jacoby, ' "The Broad Platform of Extermination" '.

indigenous people from the land.[86] As Richard Cole Harris observes, the 'geographical core' of settler colonialism—to which I include the United States—was 'about the displacement of people from their land and its repossession by others'.[87] This basic analytical premise inspired what Ben Kiernan refers to as the 'selective threat of genocide' against Native Americans, a threat that resulted in various forms of organized and spontaneous acts of violence since the seventeenth century was driven by the intent to exterminate the American 'natives'.[88]

FURTHER READING

Anderson, William L., *Cherokee Removal: Before and After* (Athens: University of Georgia Press, 1991).

Baumgardner, Frank H., *Killing for Land in Early California: Indian Blood at Round Valley: Founding the Nome Cult Indian Farm* (New York: Algora, 2005).

Blackhawk, Ned, *Violence over the Land: Indians and Empires in the Early American West* (Cambridge, MA: Harvard University Press, 2006).

Brown, Dee, *Bury My Heart at Wounded Knee: An Indian History of the American West* (New York: Henry Holt, 1970).

Brown, Kathleen, 'Native Americans and Early Modern Concepts of Race', in Martin Daunton and Rick Halpern (eds), *Empire and Others: British Encounters with Indigenous Peoples, 1600–1850* (Philadelphia: University of Pennsylvania Press, 1999), 79–100.

Cave, Alfred, *The Pequot War* (Amherst: University of Massachusetts Press, 1996).

Jacoby, Karl, '"The Broad Platform of Extermination": Nature and Violence in the Nineteenth-Century North American Borderlands', *Journal of Genocide Research* 10:2 (2008): 249–67.

Madley, Benjamin, 'Patterns of Frontier Genocide 1803–1910: The Aboriginal Tasmanians, the Yuki of California, and the Heroero of Namibia', *Journal of Genocide Research* 6:2 (2004), 167–92.

Merritt, Jane T., *At the Crossroads: Indians and Empires on a Mid-Atlantic Frontier, 1700–1763* (Chapel Hill: University of North Carolina Press, 2003).

Smithers, Gregory D., *Science, Sexuality, and Race in the United States and Australia, 1780s–1890s* (New York/London: Routledge, 2009).

[86] Wolfe, 'Land, Labor, and Difference'; Tyrell, 'Beyond the View of Euro-America', 170; Smithers, 'The "Pursuits of the Civilized Man"'.

[87] Harris, *Making Native Space*, xxiv.

[88] Kiernan, *Blood and Soil*, 322.

PART IV

GENOCIDE IN THE
LATE MODERN
WORLD

....

CHAPTER 17

GENOCIDE AND MASS VIOLENCE IN THE 'HEART OF DARKNESS'

AFRICA IN THE COLONIAL PERIOD

....

DOMINIK J. SCHALLER

INTRODUCTION

....

IN autumn 2001, representatives of the Namibian Herero filed lawsuits against the government of the Federal Republic of Germany, the Deutsche Bank, and two other German companies at the US Federal Court. The so-called Herero People's Reparation Corporation claimed reparations in the amount of US$4 billion because of these companies' alleged involvement in a military campaign in the former German colony of South West Africa between 1904 and 1908 that had resulted in the deaths of almost 80,000 Africans and the destruction of the traditional Herero society. The Herero were the first African people to demand reparations for colonial policies in terms of genocide.[1] The lawsuit and the associated discussions about German colonial policies in Africa have contributed to a heightened scholarly awareness of the close relationship between the phenomena of colonialism and genocide.

This insight is not as new as first apparent. From the 1950s, the struggle of anti-colonial resistance movements in Africa and Asia as well as the corresponding process of decolonization mobilized intellectuals and led to political debates about the exploitative nature of colonialism. Many activists, philosophers, and scholars like Frantz Fanon, Hannah Arendt, Jean-Paul Sartre, and Georges Balandier recognized and denounced the genocidal potential of colonialism, although most of them did not resort to the term 'genocide' coined by the Polish-Jewish international lawyer Raphael Lemkin in 1944.[2] Lemkin himself was well aware that genocide cannot be separated analytically from colonization when he stated:

Genocide has two phases: one, destruction of the national pattern of the oppressed group; the other, the imposition of the national pattern of the oppressor. This imposition, in turn, may be made upon the oppressed population which is allowed to remain or upon the territory alone, after removal of the population and the colonization of the area by the oppressor's own nationals.[3]

For all that, Lemkin was not an anti-imperial or anti-colonial thinker like Cesaire and Fanon. Although he regarded the German and Belgian excesses in Central and Southern Africa as genocidal, he considered colonialism and the European 'mission civilisatrice' an important step in overcoming the assumed backwardness of the 'dark continent'.[4]

Lemkin's ambivalence about colonial rule in Africa persists in the field of genocide studies. In much of the scholarly literature it is suggested that genocide is an exclusively modern phenomenon. The murder of the Ottoman Armenians by the Young Turks during World War I and the Holocaust are widely perceived as ideal types of genocide because of the perpetrators' alleged 'irrational' motives: nationalism and racism. The perpetrators of colonial mass violence, by contrast, are believed to be driven by 'rational' motives like greed and revenge. Such an

---

[1] Allan D. Cooper, 'Reparations for the Herero Genocide: Defining the Limits of International Litigation', African Affairs 106:422 (2007), 113–26 (113).

[2] A. Dirk Moses, 'Empire, Colony, Genocide: Keywords and the Philosophy of History', in idem (ed.), Empire, Colony, Genocide: Conquest, Occupation, and Subaltern Resistance in World History (New York: Berghahn, 2008), 3–54.

[3] Raphael Lemkin, Axis Rule in Occupied Europe (Washington DC: Carnegie Endowment for International Peace, 1944), 79.

[4] On this mission in Africa, see Alice L. Conklin, A Mission to Civilize: The Republican Idea of Empire in France and West Africa, 1895–1930 (Stanford: Stanford University Press, 1997); Dominik J. Schaller, 'Colonialism and Genocide: Raphael Lemkin's Concept of Genocide and Its Application to European Rule in Africa', Development Dialogue 50 (December 2008), 75–93; Moses, 'Empire, Colony, Genocide'.

artificially constructed distinction ignores the fact that génocidaires never rely on a single motive, and it leads to the distorted but widespread conclusion that the category 'colonial genocide' is analytically useless, and that no genocides occurred in colonial Africa. In traditional socio-scientific genocide studies, the history of European colonialism in Africa is often portrayed as a success story and a 'triumph of humanitarianism', as the following excerpt from a popular 'world history' of genocide demonstrates: 'The effect of the European presence was manifestly ameliorative, as were the long-term effects of the introduction of Western medicine, education and legal and customary practices, and the inclusion of these places in the modern global economic system.'[5]

Lemkin's own multifaceted conception of genocide shows that the spread of European civilization by colonial and imperial rule cannot be so easily enlisted in an optimistic narrative of progress. Brutal suppression of indigenous resistance, forced labour, and the expulsion of Africans from arable land were the norm rather than the exception. Violence was the essential element in the management of colonial empires.[6] Could the inclusion of Africans in a modern European-style capitalist economy be seen as a blessing when it was designed to lead to the deliberate destruction of indigenous social and political institutions as well as African customs and cultural heritage?[7] Lemkin had these policies (amongst others) in mind when he developed the concept of genocide. For these reason, the study of genocide in colonial Africa requires systematic methodological reflection. Five main issues need to be addressed before various aspects of colonial mass violence in Africa can be further explored.

Firstly, the legacy of colonial rule in Africa is highly controversial. Whereas Western apologists praise the supposed technological and cultural benefits of European colonialism, African voices claim the 'underdevelopment' and almost all current political and socio-economic problems from which their continent suffers can directly be traced back to both the transatlantic slave trade and imperial conquest. The most prominent adherent of this position was Walter Rodney whose 'How Europe Underdeveloped Africa' influenced a whole generation of Africanists.[8] Although the critical literature rightly highlighted how the roots of many African conflicts lie in the colonial period, it tended to ignore African agency. Too

---

[5] William D. Rubinstein, *Genocide: A History* (London: Longman, 2004), 102–3.

[6] John McCulloch, 'Empire and Violence, 1900–1939', in Philippa Levine (ed.), *Gender and Empire* (Oxford: Oxford University Press, 2004), 220–39.

[7] The Africanist Mahmood Mamdani opposes this view. He argues that the British abandoned the idea of 'civilizing' the Africans by the time of the 'scramble of Africa' and that they preferred to conserve the 'traditional' African societies in order to facilitate their rule over the continent. See Mahmood Mamdani, *Citizen and Subject: Contemporary Africa and the Legacy of Late Colonialism* (Kampala: Fountain, 1996).

[8] Walter Rodney, *How Europe Underdeveloped Africa* (London: Bougle-L'ouverture, 1972). Equally important were the early works of Immanuel Wallerstein on Africa and European-style capitalism. See Immanuel Wallerstein, 'Africa in a Capitalist World', *Issue: A Journal of Opinion* 3:3 (1973), 1–11.

often, Africans were portrayed as helpless victims of Western power and violence. Nor did historiography pay much attention to indigenous resistance and how the Africans' manifold reactions to European imperialism fuelled the dynamics of colonial violence. Colonial masters were far from omnipotent. There were limits to their power claims and many Africans succeeded in defying the colonial system.

These insights are important for our understanding of the excessive violence inherent to colonial wars in Africa: European settlers and colonial soldiers resorted to genocidal methods of warfare when they were afraid that they could lose the control over the situation. Even so, although African societies were deeply affected by genocidal violence and economic exploitation, they usually managed to recover and to remain living and innovative entities. African survival strategies and processes of societal reconstruction after foreign rule and genocide have not attracted the interest of historians until recently. Not only was disinterest responsible for the neglect of these important aspects, but also most Western historians' inability to deal with original African sources, i.e., oral testimonies.

Thirdly, the genocide concept can oversimplify the genocidal conjuncture. As an originally legal framework, it suggests a clear-cut distinction between perpetrators and victims that is difficult to reconcile with empirical evidence.[9] Africans were not only victims of colonialism. The Europeans could not have conquered the continent without indigenous collaboration. Colonial armies and administrations consisted mainly of African mercenaries and support staff, and some African groups benefited enormously from the advent of the colonizers and relied on the Europeans' help to climb to a position of power.[10] Consider the Tutsi of Rwanda: it was their rulers' readiness to collaborate with the German invaders that contributed decisively to the extension of their supremacy over the Hutu. The cases of the Zulu in Southern Africa and of the Ethiopian Empire also show intra-African conquest and even genocide. If both the Zulu and the Ethiopians fell victim to excessive violence unleashed by British and Italian forces in 1879 and 1936, respectively, the Zulu and Ethiopian Amharas had themselves used genocidal violence in order to build and extend their empires decades earlier.[11]

---

[9] For a fundamental and much debated criticism of the genocide concept, see Christian Gerlach, 'Extremely Violent Societies: An Alternative to the Concept of Genocide', *Journal of Genocide Research* 8:4 (2006), 455–71.

[10] Ronald Robinson, 'Non European Foundations of European Imperialism: Sketch for a Theory of Collaboration', in Roger Owen and Bob Sutcliffe (eds), *Studies in the Theory of Imperialism* (London: Longman, 1972), 117–41.

[11] Michael R. Mahoney, 'The Zulu Kingdom as a Genocidal and Post-Genocidal Society, c. 1810 to the Present', *Journal of Genocide Research* 5:2 (2003), 251–68. On the violent Amharization of the Oromo, see P. T. W. Baxter, 'Ethiopia's Unacknowledged Problem: The Oromo', *African Affairs* 77:308 (1978), 283–96. On the systematic suppression of Oromo culture and language in the Ethiopian Empire: Mekuria Bulcha, 'The Politics of Linguistic Homogenization in Ethiopia and the Conflict over the Status of "Afaan Oromoo" ', *African Affairs* 96:384 (1997), 325–52.

Fourthly, the study of colonial mass violence in Africa must resist generalizing conclusions. Seven European nations participated in the 'scramble for Africa' in the 1880s. Their motives, financial as well as infrastructural requirements, and colonial cultures differed considerably, as did their modes of governance and administration. Almost all of these empires lacked a coherent structure and were chaotic clusters of settler, trade, plantation, and military colonies that all entailed different forms of rule. The spectrum ranged from direct and almost totalitarian control to indirect rule where African elites enjoyed a great deal of autonomy. Some colonies were marked by a mosaic of diverse types of rule. In German East Africa (present-day Tanzania), for example, some territories were governed by civil administrations, others by military authorities. The treatment of the indigenous populations and the degree of violence used to establish and to maintain the colonial order depended decisively on the intended use of a colony and the administrative structures of its government. Colonial administrations dominated by the military usually resorted to extreme measures like genocidal violence in order to suppress African resistance. The complexity and polymorphy of imperial rule in Africa makes it difficult to formulate a grand theory of colonial mass violence of universal application.

Fifthly, only in recent years have historians realized the importance of colonial mass violence in the global history of collective violence.[12] Colonial genocide has even become a widely used distinct category. However, it is important to note that genocidal violence in most of colonial Africa differs in some considerable ways from genocides committed in North American and Australian settler colonies: European colonization of Africa did not inevitably lead to the expulsion and/or annihilation of the indigenous populations. There are two reasons for this difference: whereas colonization preceded the formation of bureaucratic colonial states in America and Australia, European settlement followed the establishment of colonial administration in Africa. As a result, the colonial states in the British New World territories were almost unlimitedly dominated by settlers' interests. In Africa, by contrast, the settlers' influence and ability to fight and expel the Africans on their own was more restricted because the colonial states were still weak and their power relied on the cooperation with indigenous chiefs.

A more important reason why Europeans normally did not envisage physically exterminating the Africans in large parts was their dependency on indigenous labour power.[13] Most parts of Africa were not attractive for European migrants

---

[12] On how European colonialism provided radical ideologies of the twentieth century with the idea of population economy and genocidal thinking, see Jürgen Zimmerer, 'Colonialism and the Holocaust: Towards an Archaeology of Genocide', in A. Dirk Moses (ed.), *Genocide and Settler Society. Frontier Violence and Stolen Indigenous Children in Australian History* (New York: Berghahn, 2004), 49–76.

[13] Patrick Wolfe, 'Land, Labor, and Difference: Elementary Structures of Race', *American Historical Review* 106:3 (2001), 866–905.

who could have replaced the Africans as indentured servants or contract workers. Even so, this does not mean that genocide did not occur in Africa. As will be shown, colonial wars often degenerated into genocidal slaughter. Southern Africa, which is a special case in the colonial history of Africa because of its appeal for European settlers, saw many of these genocidal wars.

SOUTHERN AFRICA AS A ZONE OF VIOLENCE

The strategic importance of the Cape of Good Hope for the sea route from Europe to India had a significant impact on the history of Southern Africa. This region experienced the beginnings of European colonization and settlement much earlier than other parts of sub-Saharan Africa. The relatively mild climate conditions and the absence of tropical diseases in the coastal areas made South Africa a favourable living space for European settlers. Another catalyst for European colonization was the availability of arable land and the region's diversity and richness of natural resources, which include most notably gold, copper, iron, and platinum. For these reasons, Southern Africa's colonial history is in many ways comparable to the European conquest of North America: the establishment of trading posts at the coast line, a lasting influx of settlers and constant extensions of the frontier, the permanence of colonial wars and the expulsion of the autochthonous populations from their ancestral lands, the import of slaves, and the formation of systems of strict racial segregation are key characteristics of the historical processes in these two regions.

This is not the only significant development which shaped the history of Southern Africa. The violent empire-building of the Zulu in the early nineteenth century in combination with environmental degradation and drought led to massive streams of migration and an ethnic reorganization in many areas. The nine Cape Frontier Wars in the nineteenth century and the constant movement of white settlers further east also contributed to the population migration and political disruption in the region. Thus, the *Mfecane*, the demographic and ethnic transformation of the 1820s and 1830s, cannot be traced back to the nation-building of the Zulu alone because of its interplay with European colonization.[14] What also sets South Africa apart from many other African regions under colonial control was the grave conflict between two emerging European settler communities. It should be noted, though, that hostilities between the Boers and the British 1899–1901 were

---

[14] Carolyn Hamilton (ed.), *The Mfecane Aftermath. Reconstructive Debates in Southern African History* (Johannesburg: Wits University Press, 1995).

not 'white man's war', because both parties relied to a great extent on African support troops.

Several interconnected clusters of conflicts thus raged in this region. Their origins lie in the mid-seventeenth century with the modest beginnings of European colonization. When the Dutch East India Company (Vereenigde Oostindische Compagnie, VOC) decided to establish a trading post at the Cape of Good Hope in 1651, there were no plans for extensive European settlement in the region. Nevertheless, the presence of the VOC attracted Dutch, German, and Huguenot immigrants in the following decades. At the end of the eighteenth century, a small European settler community consisting of about 15,000 members existed at the Cape. The indigenous peoples of the region were either pastoralists or hunter-gatherers. In the early years of colonization, the pastoralist Khoikhoi and the Europeans maintained a more or less cooperative relationship and traded goods. The Africans provided the Europeans with meat in exchange for iron, copper, and tobacco. But the relations between these two groups worsened when the VOC started to foster the colonization of the Cape region. Former employees of the company, the so-called free burghers, were encouraged to move to the interior of Southern Africa and to settle there to avoid the intermediate trade of the Khoikhoi. Regular attacks on these outposts by the Khoikhoi, and both the Boers' religious conviction that they were a 'chosen people' and that the Africans were 'Canaanites' doomed to be destroyed by God contributed to a radicalization of the European settlers' attitude and behaviour. For the Boers, the most imminent danger for a secure existence as independent and self-sustaining farmers was these 'Bushmen', traditional hunter-gatherer groups or impoverished and dispossessed Khoikhoi. Commandos of the Boers launched frequent attacks on the Bushmen and forced the hunter-gatherers to retreat to the Kalahari desert or to mountain areas where most of the refugees were hunted down by Europeans in the second half of the eighteenth century.[15] The primary goal of the assaults by the Boers was the extinction of the Bushmen as independent and viable groups. In 1774, for example, a raid by European settlers led to the killing of 500 Bushmen alone. Women and children were usually captured and pressed into slavery.[16]

Although Europeans perceived the vanishing of Southern Africa's indigenous populations as a natural and inevitable development, humanitarian and philanthropic

---

[15] Clifton C. Crais, *White Supremacy and Black Resistance in Pre-Industrial South-Africa: The Making of the Colonial Order in the Eastern Cape, 1770–1865* (Cambridge: Cambridge University Press, 1992).

[16] On the so-called General Commando of 1774, see Nigel Penn, 'Land, Labour, and Livestock in the Western Cape during the Eighteenth Century', in Wilmot G. James and Mary Simons (eds), *The Angry Divide. Social and Economic History of the Western Cape* (Cape Town: D. Philip, 1989), 2–19, especially 16–18; Jan-Bart Gewald, 'Untapped Sources: Slave Exports from Southern and Central Namibia up c.1850', in Carolyn Hamilton (ed.), *The Mfecane Aftermath: Reconstructive Debates in Southern African History* (Pietermaritzburg: Natal University Press, 1995), 412.

circles in Great Britain denounced the Boers' policy of extermination.[17] When the British annexed the Cape Colony in 1806, they soon aimed at the dismantling of slavery. Nevertheless, the British presence in Southern Africa did not lead to the pacification of the region, but to a further escalation of violence as British control expanded territorially. The British pushed the frontier eastwards and encouraged European settlement. In 1820 alone, up to 4,000 white colonists intruded into the eastern borderland of the Cape Colony. There had been several hostile encounters between the *trekboers* (Dutch settlers) and the Xhosa around the Great Fish River region of the Eastern Cape. The Xhosa were a Bantu-speaking people who relied mainly on cattle breeding. In the 1850s, about 100,000 Xhosa lived in Southern Africa. The British advance resulted in a significant intensification of violence. Both British troops and European settlers fought six major frontier wars (often referred to as 'Kaffir Wars') against the Xhosa in the nineteenth century. The Xhosa far outnumbered the European settlers and resisted the colonial conquest tenaciously. European farms were regularly attacked and in 1819 the city of Grahamstown was almost overrun by the Africans.[18] The persistence of the Xhosa contributed to a radicalization of the settlers and led them to ever more extreme measures. The following appeal, published in the *Grahamstown Journal* on 10 April 1847 is typical in that respect:

Let war be made against the Kaffir huts and gardens. Let all these be burned down and destroyed. Let there be no ploughing, sowing or reaping. Or, if you cannot conveniently, or without bloodshed prevent the cultivation of the ground, take care to destroy the enemy's crops before they are ripe, and shoot all who resist. Shoot their cattle too wherever you see any. Tell them the time has come for the white man to show his mastery over them.[19]

Scorched-earth tactics characterized European warfare in Africa and had disastrous effects on the indigenous societies. When the Xhosa were deprived of much of their land and pushed further east by the British, their desperation made them susceptible to millenarian fantasies. The visions of a teenage girl made the Xhosa slaughter about 400,000 of their cattle from April 1856 to February 1857. Although historians still debate the Xhosas' motivation, it is generally believed that the Xhosa

---

[17] Patrick Brantlinger, *Dark Vanishings: Discourse on the Extinction of Primitive Races, 1800–1930* (Ithaca: Cornell University Press, 2003), 73–4.

[18] On the frontier wars against the Xhosa, see Christopher Saunders, 'Political Processes in the Southern African Frontier', in Howard Lamar and Leonard Thompson (eds), *The Frontier in History: North America and Southern Africa Compared* (New Haven: Yale University Press, 1981), 149–71; Ben Maclennan, *A Proper Degree of Terror: John Graham and the Cape's Eastern Frontier* (Johannesburg: Ravan Press, 1986); Timothy Stapleton, *Maqoma: Xhosa Resistance to Colonial Advance, 1798–1873* (Johannesburg: Jonathan Ball, 1994); Christoph Marx, 'Kolonialkrieg und rassistische Dämonologie: Das südliche Afrika im 19. Jahrhundert', in Mihran Dabag, et al., *Kolonialismus. Kolonialdiskurs und Genozid* (Paderborn: Fink, 2004), 167–84.

[19] Cited in Allister Sparks, *The Mind of South Africa. The Story of the Rise and Fall of Apartheid* (London: Ballantine Books, 1990), 65.

thought the destruction of their herds would reawaken their ancestors who could defeat the foreign conquerors.[20] In the aftermath of this seemingly irrational event, almost 40,000 Xhosa starved to death. The survivors lost their lands to European settlers and were driven into the service of the Europeans. The cattle killing was a catalyst in the process of the obliteration of the Xhosas' traditional lifestyle and their identity as independent pastoralists.

Another group that suffered massively from European imperialism and the consequences of colonial warfare were the Zulu. Until 1800, the chiefdom of the Zulu was only one among many others in KwaZulu-Natal. Under the auspices of their king Shaka (c.1787–1828), the Zulu revolutionized their method of warfare, defeated their neighbours, and established hegemonic rule in the region. To maintain their authority, the Zulu relied on policies of mass violence, such that one scholar has called their kingdom a genocidal society.[21] Although the Zulu have been portrayed as courageous warriors and evenly matched adversaries in literature and film, the wars between the British colonial troops and the Africans were far from symmetrical, and non-combatants were gravely affected. The European settlers' fear of the Zulu were heightened by a painful defeat of the British army in Isandhlwana in 1879. Rumours of the Zulus' alleged habit of mutilating British soldiers contributed to a further radicalization of the Europeans and to their desire to annihilate the Africans. The demand for a radical solution of the Zulu problem was widespread in the Cape Colony, as a correspondent of the *Daily News* observed:

A desire for extermination is, I must confess, one of the most painful peculiarities of the present time. If the ideas at present prevailing in some circles were allowed to have free play, I do not think there would be many Zulus of any age or of either sex alive this day twelvemonth.[22]

Indeed, the British campaign against the Zulu was a war of extermination. The systematic destruction of the economic foundation of Zululand, the refusal to take prisoners, and deliberate attacks against villages and civilians brought the Zulu to their knees. They were only saved from a policy of outright genocide by their king's readiness to surrender unconditionally.[23]

It is interesting to note that the same radicalization and totalization of war marked the military conflict between the Boers and the British 1899–1902. The Boers did not accept British rule of the Cape that had begun in 1806 and they

[20] For a critical discussion of the event, see Jeffrey Brian Peires, *The Dead Will Arise: Nonqqawuse and the Great Xhosa Cattle-Killing of 1856–7* (Bloomington, IN: Indiana University Press, 1989); Timothy Stapleton, '"They No Longer Care For Their Chiefs": Another Look at the Xhosa Cattle-Killing of 1856–57', *International Journal of African Historical Studies* 24:2 (1991), 383–92.

[21] Mahoney, 'The Zulu Kingdom as a Genocidal and Post-Genocidal Society.'

[22] *The Illustrated London News*, 12 April 1879. Cited in Michael Lieven, '"Butchering the Brutes All Over the Place": Total War and Massacre in Zululand, 1879', *History* 84:276 (1999), 617.

[23] Lieven, '"Butchering the Brutes All Over the Place".'

regarded the abolition of slavery an illegitimate interference by the British authorities. Between 1835 and 1846, about 14,000 Boers left the Cape and migrated eastward and north-eastward, where they founded independent republics. When gold and diamonds were found in the interior, the British increased their interest in the Orange Free State and Transvaal regions and tried to regain control over the Boers. In the war from 1899 to 1902, both the Boers and the British relied on their experiences of warfare against the Khoikhoi, Bushmen, Xhosa, and Zulu. Because the Boers were organized in small commandos, the British resorted to a policy of scorched earth and violence against non-combatants. To cut the Boer commandos from their supply sources, British army commanders and authorities ordered the incarceration of the Boer civilian population in concentration camps. Hygienic conditions and food supply were completely insufficient in these camps and led to the deaths of about 28,000 detainees, mainly women and children.[24]

Although the British were fighting against Europeans, they understood the conflict as a traditional colonial war and used the same methods with which they had defeated the Xhosa and the Zulu. In this way, the Anglo-Boer war is an important precursor of modern total war, as experienced in Europe only a few years later. But what exactly are the key characteristics of colonial wars? And why did so many colonial wars in Africa reach genocidal proportions?

THE GENOCIDAL POTENTIAL OF COLONIAL WARFARE IN AFRICA

On 2 October 1904, the supreme commander of the German colonial troops in South West Africa, Lothar von Trotha (1848–1920), issued his infamous genocide order:

I the great General of the German troops send this letter to the Herero people. The Herero are no longer German subjects.... The Herero people must leave the country. If the nation doesn't do this I will force them with the *Groot Rohr* [cannon]. Within the German borders, every Herero, with or without gun, with or without cattle will be shot. I will no longer accept women and children, I will drive them back to their people or I will let them be shot at.[25]

---

[24] For a discussion of the origins and the course of the Anglo-Boer War, see the contributions in Donald Lowry (ed.), *The South African War Reappraised* (Manchester: Manchester University Press, 2000).

[25] Proclamation by Lothar von Trotha (copy), 2 October 1904, German Federal Archive, Berlin Lichterfelde (GAF), Bestand Reichskolonialamt (R1001), 2098, 7–8.

In a letter to the chief of the German general staff, Lothar von Trotha reaffirmed his genocidal intention by noting he would not be ready to accept women and children as prisoners and that he would drive them into the waterless Omaheke desert where they would face death from starvation and exhaustion:

> To accept women and children who are for the most part sick, poses a great risk to the force, and to feed them is out of the question. For this reason, I deem it wiser for the entire nation to perish than to infect our soldiers into the bargain and to make inroads into our water and food supplies.[26]

The German general's measures were—from a military standpoint—not necessary anymore. The rebelling Herero had already been defeated in the battle at Hamakari on 11 August 1904. Lothar von Trotha's motives for the annihilation of the Herero were racist and social-Darwinist, as the following excerpt from an article written by the general reveals: 'At the outset, we cannot do without the natives. But they finally have to melt away. Where the climate allows the white man to work, philanthropic views cannot banish Darwin's law "Survival of the Fittest".'[27] Lothar von Trotha's superiors in Berlin and even the Emperor shared the racist worldview of their general.

As might be expected, colonial soldiers' and officials' behaviour and actions during wars against Africans were deeply shaped by racist attitudes. Most Europeans did not perceive their African counterparts as human beings who deserved respect and fairness. According to a widespread and influential British handbook for colonial soldiers, 'small wars' were understood as 'expeditions against savages and semi-civilised races'.[28] Even so, ideological factors such as racism alone cannot sufficiently explain the genocidal outcome of so many colonial wars. The complete physical annihilation of Africans was generally perceived as counterproductive and irrational because the colonizers were heavily dependent on their labour power for the work on plantations, farms, and in mines. Von Trotha's genocidal campaign, for example, met with strong disapproval in Germany. Paul Rohrbach, the most influential German colonial propagandist at the time, denounced the general's policy and stated: 'It was a mistake . . . to send a general to Southwest [Africa] . . . who did not understand that it would not be the important thing to destroy the natives as

---

[26] Letter by Lothar von Trotha to the chief of the German general staff von Schlieffen, 4 October 1904, GFA, R 1001, 2089, 5. Horst Drechsler, *Let Us Die Fighting: The Struggle of the Herero and Nama against German Imperialism* (London: Zed Press, 1980), 161.

[27] Cited in Gesine Krüger, *Kriegsbewältigung und Geschichtsbewußtsein: Realität, Deutung und Verarbeitung des deutschen Kolonialkriegs in Namibia 1904–1907* (Göttingen: Vandenhoeck und Ruprecht, 1999), 66.

[28] Charles Edward Callwell, *Small Wars: Their Principles and Practice*, 3rd edn (London: His Majesty's Stationery Office, 1906), 21.

enemies. . . . Southwest-Africa with natives was of much more value for us than without.'[29] But why then did most colonial wars degenerate into genocidal slaughter?

The transition from war to genocide is a complex process that undergoes various phases of cumulative radicalization and depends on a range of situational factors. A very decisive factor was military setbacks suffered by European colonial armies. It was the humbling defeat at Isandhlwana in January 1879 and the loss of up to 1,200 soldiers that seemed to confirm British settlers' claim that the 'Zulu problem' ought to be solved once and for all. Another example of such a military setback is the fall of Khartoum and the death of Gen. Charles Gordon in January 1885 at the hands of the Mahdists, which was perceived as a national disgrace and led to a severe political crisis in London. This is the reason why the British reconquest of the Sudan in 1898 resulted in the carnage of the Mahdists. The French conquest of Algeria in the 1830s and 1840s reached genocidal dimensions when Arab tribes under Abd al-Qadir launched successful attacks against the invaders. Even Alexis de Tocqueville, who later became an ardent critic of French exterminationist policies in Algeria, had been in favour of radical means to defeat Abd al-Qadir:

We shall never destroy Abd-el-Kader's power unless we make the position of the tribes who support him so intolerable that they abandon him. . . . All means of desolating these tribes must be employed. . . . I believe that the right of war authorizes us to ravage the country and that we must do it, either by destroying harvests during the harvest season, or year-round by making those rapid incursions called razzias, whose purpose is to seize men or herds.[30]

A comparative analysis of colonial wars in Africa shows that colonial powers are ready to act against their economic interests and to use genocidal violence in order to avoid or avenge humiliating defeats against 'semi-civilized' adversaries. Europeans perceived indigenous resistance not only as a threat to their ambitions in the colonies but to their imperial project as such because a possible failure diminished their prestige in the eyes of imperial rivals.

The radicalization of military campaigns in the African colonies manifested itself in the use of methods of warfare that were morally and legally outlawed (at least theoretically) in the European theatres of war. In the following, five of these deadly methods will be outlined.

Most colonial conflicts were asymmetric wars because of the Africans' guerrilla tactics. As many of the examples and quotation above have shown, the burning of indigenous settlements and crops were integral elements of colonial warfare. *Scorched-earth tactics* usually resulted in famines and had disastrous effects on African societies. In German East Africa (Tanzania), the colonizers deliberately

[29] Paul Rohrbach, *Um des Teufels Handschrift. Zwei Menschenalter erlebter Weltgeschichte* (Hamburg,: Hans Dulk, 1953), 64.

[30] For a discussion of the genocidal dimension of the French conquest of Algeria 1830–75, see Ben Kiernan, *Blood and Soil. A World History of Genocide and Extermination from Sparta to Darfur* (New Haven, CT: Yale University Press, 2007), 364–74. Quote on pages 370–1.

used hunger as a weapon to suppress the Maji-Maji movement 1905–8, as the following quotation by the German captain Wangenheim reveals: 'In my view, only hunger and distress can bring about a final submission. Military actions alone will remain more or less a drop in the ocean.'[31] Fields and granaries were systematically destroyed by German troops who prevented cultivation and confiscated everything eatable. Hunger and consequent diseases led to the deaths of about 250,000 Africans. Entire areas in Southern Tanzania were depopulated.[32]

Although the Geneva Protocol of 17 June 1925 prohibited the use of gas and poison in war, European powers still resorted to chemical warfare in the colonies. Before the adoption of the international treaty, the British army used mustard gas against Arabs in Iraq in 1920 and against Afghans on the northwest frontier. Winston Churchill, Secretary of State for War at the time, made clear that he considered gas to be the ideal weapon for colonial wars: 'I do not understand this squeamishness about the use of gas. I am strongly in favour of using poison gas against uncivilised tribes.'[33] Between 1921 and 1927, the 'Spanish Army of Africa' launched gas attacks to put down the Riffian Berber rebellion led by Abdel Karim in Northern Morocco. The 'intensive and continuous bombing with the aid of the most harmful of all gases' did not only aim at defeating the Berber rebels. According to the Spanish King Alfonso XIII, the intention of the gas campaign was 'the extermination, like that of malicious beasts, of the Beni Urriaguels [a Berber tribe] and the tribes who are closest to Abdel Karim'.[34] The reason for this extremist position was the military disaster in Annual where 3,000 Berbers managed to kill more than 10,000 Spanish colonial soldiers in July 1921. This embarrassing defeat caused a political crisis in Madrid and put both the King and the military leadership under immense pressure. Italy faced similar problems in Libya and regularly bombed the oases of the resisting tribes with phosgene and mustard gas in the 1920s. The quality and quantity of chemical warfare reached a new dimension in Mussolini's imperial war against Ethiopa 1935–41. The Ethiopian Emperor Haile Selassie (1892–1975) made the Italian war crimes and their consequences public when he called for international support at the headquarters of the League of Nations on 30 June 1936:

Special sprayers were installed on board aircraft so that they could vaporize, over vast areas of territory, a fine, death-dealing rain. Groups of nine, fifteen, eighteen aircraft followed one another so that the fog issuing from them formed a continuous sheet. It was thus that, as

[31] Gustav Adolf Graf von Götzen, *Deutsch-Ostafrika im Aufstand 1905/06* (Berlin: Dietrich Reimer, 1909), 149.

[32] Felicitas Becker, 'Traders, "Big Men" and Prophets: Political Continuity and Crisis in the Maji Maji Rebellion in Southeast Tanzania', *Journal of African History* 45:1 (2004), 1–22.

[33] David E. Omissi, *Air Power and Colonial Control: The Royal Air Force 1919–1939* (Manchester: Manchester University Press, 1990), 160.

[34] Sebastian Balfour, *Deadly Embrace: Morocco and the Road to the Spanish Civil War* (Oxford: Oxford University Press, 2002), 135.

from the end of January 1936, soldiers, women, children, cattle, rivers, lakes and pastures were drenched continually with this deadly rain. In order to kill off systematically all living creatures, in order to more surely to poison waters and pastures, the Italian command made its aircraft pass over and over again. . . . These fearful tactics succeeded. Men and animals succumbed. The deadly rain that fell from the aircraft made all those whom it touched fly shrieking with pain. All those who drank the poisoned water or ate the infected food also succumbed in dreadful suffering.[35]

Although the Italian *Regia Aeronautica* did not drop gas bombs on the major cities, the Ethiopian population suffered for a long time from chemical pollution. There are no official figures but the Italian gas attacks likely killed tens of thousands of Africans.[36]

The persistence of many African guerrilla movements and their backing by the autochthonous society often allowed military leaders and colonial authorities to conclude that only *forced migration* or the *deportation* of the indigenous population could lead to sustainable 'pacification'. In June 1930, the Italian marshal Badoglio ordered the total evacuation of the Djebel al-Akhdar in Libyan Cyrenaica. Up to 100,000 Bedouins, half of the whole region's population, were driven away. The Italian marshal was well aware that this measure would in all likelihood result in mass death. In a letter to his superior, he stated:

As for overall strategy, it is necessary to create a significant and clear territorial separation between the controlled population and the rebel formations. I do not hide the significance and the seriousness of this measure, which might be the ruin of the so-called subdued population . . . But by now the course has been set and we must carry it out to the end, even if the entire population of Cyrenaica must perish.[37]

After the suppression of the Herero and Nama revolts in German South West Africa in 1908, colonial officials and settlers suffered from a paranoid fear of new indigenous unrest, and they considered the deportation of all surviving Herero to New Guinea. German authorities saw the deportation of about 200 Nama to Togo and Cameroon from 1904 to 1910 as a social engineering experiment about whether Namibians could survive in tropical regions. Only a handful of the deportees in fact survived and returned to South West Africa. The outbreak of World War I averted the further implementation of these ideas.[38]

---

[35] Speech of H.M. the Negus Haile Selassie (Ethiopia), in: League of Nations Official Journal, Special Supplement No. 151: Records of the 16th Ordinary Session of the Assembly. Plenary meetings of 30 June to 4 July 1936. Text of the debates, Part II, Geneva 1936, 25.

[36] Aram Mattioli, *Experimentierfeld der Gewalt. Der Abessinienkrieg und seine internationale Bedeutung 1935–1941* (Zürich: Orell Füssli, 2005), 109, 114–16; Giulia Brogini Künzi, *Italien und der Abessinienkrieg 1935/36. Kolonialkrieg oder Totaler Krieg* (Paderborn: Schöningh, 2006), 260–6.

[37] Alexander de Grand, 'Mussolini's Follies: Fascism in its Imperial and Racist Phase, 1935–1940', *Contemporary European History* 13:2 (2004), 131.

[38] Dominik J. Schaller, 'Kolonialkrieg, Völkermord und Zwangsarbeit in "Deutsch-Südwestafrika" ', in *idem* et al. (eds), *Enteignet, Vertrieben, Ermordet. Beiträge zur Genozidforschung* (Zürich: Chronos, 2004), 147–232. On the deportations in particular, 189–95.

Many colonial wars in Africa saw the confinement of expelled civilians or prisoners of war in concentration camps. Although these concentration camps cannot be equated to the Nazis' extermination camps like Auschwitz or Treblinka, they turned out to be death camps nonetheless. Malnutrition, insufficient hygienic conditions, forced labour, and the brutal behaviour of the guards caused the deaths of tens of thousands of Africans in European camps in the twentieth century alone. The mortality of African prisoners in German South West Africa during and immediately after the 1904–8 war was almost fifty per cent according to official German documentation.[39] To defeat the Mau Mau uprising led by the Kikuyu in Kenya 1952–60, the British colonial government incarcerated hundreds of thousands of Africans in concentration camps or in settlements ringed with barbed wire.[40] Although the British claimed that their goal was the 'pacification' of the region and the 'civilizing' of the alleged barbarian African rebels, it is more likely that their murderous campaign aimed at the elimination of the Kikuyu as decisive political actors in late colonial Kenya. The British understood the use of excessive mass violence as the only way to suppress the Kikuyu rebellion and to save their African empire.[41]

No colonial wars occurred without massacres and the systematic killings of prisoners. The young Churchill, who joined the British campaign against the Sudanese Mahdists in 1898, denounced the military leadership's deliberate policy of not taking prisoners and of killing wounded enemies: 'I shall merely say that the victory at Omdurman was disgraced by the inhuman slaughter of the wounded and that Kitchener was responsible for this.'[42] Churchill's statement suggests that the murder of prisoners was not just a spontaneous act. In the Ethiopian case, the murder of prisoners can directly be traced back to Benito Mussolini. When the Duce heard about the Amhara rebellion in 1937, he told the Italian Governor-General of Ethiopia: 'Prisoners and their accomplices and the uncertain will have to be executed.'[43]

[39] Ibid. 177.

[40] There is no consensus about the actual number of detainees in British concentration camps in Kenya. While Caroline Elkins speaks of up to one and a half million Kikuyu prisoners, David Anderson estimates that 'only' up to 70,000 Kikuyu were incarcerated. Caroline Elkins, *Britain's Gulag. The Brutal End of Empire in Kenya* (London: Pimlico, 2005), xii; David Anderson, *Histories of the Hanged: Britain's Dirty War in Kenya and the End of the Empire* (London: Weidenfeld and Nicolson, 2005).

[41] Thus, the British intentions were not genocidal as Caroline Elkins suggests in her work: 'Mau Mau became for many whites in Kenya . . . what the Armenians had been for the Turks, the Hutu for the Tutsi, the Bengalis to the Pakistanis, and the Jews to the Nazis' (*Britain's Gulag*, 49).

[42] Cited in Martin Daly, *Empire on the Nile: The Anglo-Egyptian Sudan, 1898–1934* (Cambridge: Cambridge University Press, 2004), 4.

[43] Cited in G. Bruce Strang, *On the Fiery March: Mussolini Prepares for War* (Westport, CT: Praeger, 2003), 22.

Although genocidal warfare may be ordered by the military command or the colonial authorities, massacres were committed by ordinary soldiers or settler militias. Therefore, it is important to focus on these 'men on the spot' to fully understand the dynamics of radicalization inherent to so many colonial wars. When colonial soldiers reported about atrocities in their memoirs or in letters home they explained the violence they committed against African civilians by referring to social Darwinist ideas. Thus, they claimed that their actions were part of an alleged natural process that would inevitably lead to the vanishing of 'inferior races'. These ideological explanations often merely served as retrospective justifications, however. As social-psychological literature on the development of soldiers' readiness to kill non-combatants has shown, overstraining, stress, and fear are decisive reasons for genocidal behaviour. This is especially true for the colonial situation in Africa where settlers on the frontier were living in a constant fear of the indigenous population and developed paranoid fantasies about African revolts. European soldiers who had been brought to Africa to suppress indigenous resistance were not at all familiar with the geography and topography of the region and had no idea about its inhabitants. Furthermore, many Europeans suffered from the harsh climate and from tropical diseases. All these situational factors shaped the Europeans' extremely violent behaviour towards Africans during colonial wars.

As the colonial period in Africa ranged from the sixteenth century up to the end of the cold war and the collapse of the apartheid regime in South Africa in 1994 it is difficult to estimate how many colonial wars exactly the Europeans waged and how many Africans fell victim to them. But as I have shown above, there is no doubt that most of these military campaigns reached genocidal dimensions because excessive violence was deliberately targeted against both combatants and women and children.

CULTURAL GENOCIDE AND FORCED LABOUR

Colonial mass violence should not be reduced to the physical killing of Africans alone. European colonizers deliberately used another form of violence in Africa: the dissolution of indigenous culture encompassing political and socio-economic institutions, religious beliefs, and historical heritage. For Lemkin, the intended annihilation of a group's culture and identity constitutes an act of genocide. Anthropologists usually call practices of cultural destruction 'ethnocide'.[44]

[44] Lemkin, *Axis Rule*, 82–91; Robert Jaulin, *La Paix Blanche: L'introduction à l'Ethnocide* (Paris: Seuil, 1970).

The driving force for the 'Scramble for Africa' since the 1880s was the European powers' wish to extend their spheres of economic and political influence so that they were able to compete with their imperialist rivals. Africa was perceived as an important reservoir for much desired raw materials, and its inhabitants were expected to plant, extract, and process these materials as cheap labourers. Unsurprisingly, Africans were generally not interested in abandoning their subsistence economies and tried to avoid work on European-owned plantations or mines. The consequence was a chronic shortage of indigenous labour power in most sub-Saharan colonies. To overcome the Africans' reluctance and to integrate them into a 'modern' European economic system, the imperial conquerors embarked on the strategy of eliminating the indigenous populations' economic independence. This objective effectively required the destruction of traditional cultures and ways of life. Thus the forced settlement of nomadic groups and the transformation of hunter-gatherer societies into proletarians was an important precondition for the establishment of a capitalist economy in Africa. Missionaries served as agents of this kind of cultural genocide by inculcating a colonial working morale among the Africans. Some extremists even claimed that Africans ought to be deprived of any 'tribal identity' and transformed into a helot class of workers. The German publicist Paul Rohrbach, who had himself served in the colonies, was an ardent advocate of these utopias of white supremacy in Africa:

Only the necessity of losing their free national barbarianism and of becoming a class of servants for the whites provides the natives—historically seen—with an internal right of existence. . . . The idea that the Bantus would have the right to live and die according to their own fashion is absurd. It is true for peoples as well as for individuals that their existence is only justified if they contribute to general progressive development.[45]

Surprisingly, literature on European colonial rule in Africa has not yet paid sufficient attention to the destruction and theft of indigenous cultural heritage by Europeans. Probably the best known case is the looting of Benin by a British army under the command of Harry Rawson in 1897. The invaders systematically destroyed a great amount of artefacts and seized the famous Benin Bronzes, many of which are still displayed in the British Museum. Another well-known example is the demolition of the Mahdi's tomb in Omdurman by Kitchener in 1898. The general's act caused a popular outrage in Great Britain. In his report on the Sudanese campaign, Winston Churchill attacked Kitchener's rudeness and denounced the destruction of this 'fine building which might attract the traveler and interest the historian' as 'an act of vandalism and folly'.[46]

[45] Paul Rohrbach, *Deutsche Kolonialwirtschaft: Südwest-Afrika* (Berlin: Buchverlag der Hilfe, 1907), 285.

[46] Winston S. Churchill, *The River War: An Historical Account of the Reconquest of the Soudan*, 2 vols (London: Longmans, 1899), ii.215.

Europeans established coercive systems all over the continent and exploited hundreds of thousands of Africans as slave labourers. Two of the most brutal and inhuman regimes of forced labour were practised in German South West Africa and in the Belgian Congo. Colonial authorities in Namibia proclaimed that all 'tribal organization' had come to an end and issued decrees that restricted the indigenous populations' freedom of movement. Furthermore, all Africans had to carry a tiny identity badge around the neck. In Leopold II's 'Congo Free State' the Africans paid a high price for the profitable rubber exploitation. The colonizers severely punished and burned the villages of the local population when it did not manage to provide the assigned rubber quotas. The Belgians resorted to hostage-taking, massacres, and flogging to make their African subjects collect the precious and much desired natural resource. It is estimated that the Belgian reign of terror in Central Africa resulted in a population decline of fifty per cent or, in absolute numbers, in the deaths of several million Congolese.[47]

The cases of German South West Africa and the Belgian Congo have become symbols for the exploitative character of European colonial rule in Africa. Raphael Lemkin understood them as genocides and emphasized that the extermination of the 'natives' was the official state policy of both the Germans and the Belgians. In his unpublished study on German rule in Africa, Lemkin described the German idea of colonization as such:

The Germans did not colonize Africa with the intention of ruling the country justly, living in peace with the true owners of the land and developing its resources for the mutual advantage of both races. Their idea was to settle some of the surplus German population in Africa and to turn it into a German white empire. Bismarck said, 'A German who can put off his Fatherland like an old coat is no longer a German for me,' and it was undoubtedly this idea which encouraged the policy of deliberate extermination.[48]

For Lemkin, forced labour in the Belgian Congo and in German South West Africa was thus more than mere economic exploitation of the indigenous population. He perceived it—particularly in the German case—as a form of annihilation through work. But Lemkin was off the mark when he praised British colonialism as a blessing and examplar for other European nations. Although British and French colonial authorities proclaimed the 'cultivation of the natives' and the promotion of the Africans' general welfare as their official aims, forced labour and excessive flogging were integral elements of colonial rule all over Africa. The weakness of many colonial states and the lack of authority of colonial officials over settlers fostered a culture of violence on farms and plantations. Colonial governments in

---

[47] Adam Hochschild, *King Leopold's Ghost: A Story of Greed and Heroism in Colonial Africa* (Boston: Houghton Mifflin, 1999).

[48] Raphael Lemkin, 'The Germans in Africa', unpublished typewritten manuscript (*c.*1950), Jacob Rader Marcus Center of the American Jewish Archives, Hebrew Union College, Cincinnati, Raphael Lemkin Papers, Box 6, Folder 9, 49–50, cited in Schaller, 'Colonialism and Genocide', 86.

Africa regularly issued decrees to advancing the security of African workers, although European farmers and entrepreneurs did not want to be subject to state regulations and successfully managed to evade state control.[49]

CONCLUDING REMARKS: NO SILENCE
OF THE GRAVEYARD

While European colonial rule lasted only several decades, it had a profound impact on Africa. The history of European colonialism in Africa is above all of unprecedented socio-economic, political, and cultural change, mass violence, and exploitation. Until recently, the historiography of colonialism and genocide has portrayed the Africans as passive and apathetic victims of European power and violence. The German historian Horst Drechsler's notion of 'the silence of the graveyard' regarding the situation of the Herero after the German campaign of genocide in 1904 is typical in that respect. But Africa did not degenerate into a graveyard because of the Europeans' attempt to transform the continent and its inhabitants according to their ideas. European colonialism did not succeed in completely destroying African cultures and identities. Africans always found ways to preserve their cultures and to reconstitute their social organizations, however totalitarian and coercive the colonizers' policies and fantasies about absolute power were. At the same time, the legacies of colonial rule, including policies of divide and rule and unequal treatment of different peoples, and the establishment of arbitrary interstate and intrastate boundaries that would remain contested after the departure of the Europeans, combined to influence future patterns of mass intergroup violence, as illustrated by the chapters by Alex De Waal and Omar McDoom elsewhere in this volume.

FURTHER READING

Balfour, Sebastian, *Deadly Embrace: Morocco and the Road to the Spanish Civil War* (Oxford: Oxford University Press, 2002).

Ben-Ghiat, Ruth and Mia Fuller (eds), *Italian Colonialism* (New York: Palgrave Macmillan, 2005).

---

[49] McCulloch, 'Empire and Violence', 227.

Elkins, Caroline, *Britain's Gulags. The Brutal End of Empire in Kenya* (London: Pimlico, 2005).

Hull, Isabel V., *Absolute Destruction. Military Culture and the Practices of War in Imperial Germany* (Ithaca, NY: Cornell University Press, 2005).

Klein, Thoralf, and Frank Schumacher (eds), *Kolonialkriege. Militärische Gewalt im Zeichen des Imperialismus* (Hamburg: Hamburger Edition, 2006).

Lieven, Michael, '"Butchering the Brutes All Over the Place": Total War and Massacre in Zululand, 1879', *History* 84:276 (1999), 614–33.

Lowry, Donal (ed.), *The South African War Reappraised* (Manchester: Manchester University Press, 2000).

Marchal, Jules, *Lord Leverhulme's Ghosts: Colonial Exploitation in the Congo* (London: Verso, 2008).

Schaller, Dominik J., 'Colonialism and Genocide: Raphael Lemkin's Concept of Genocide and its Application to European Rule in Africa', *Development Dialogue* 50 (December 2008), 75–93.

—— 'From Conquest to Genocide: Colonial Rule in German Southwest Africa and German East Africa', in A. Dirk Moses (ed.), *Empire, Colony, Genocide. Conquest, Occupation, and Subaltern Resistance in World History* (New York: Berghahn, 2008), 296–324.

Zimmerer, Jürgen, and Joachim Zeller (eds), *Genocide in German South-West Africa: The Colonial War of 1904–1908 and its Aftermath* (Monmouth: Merlin Press, 2008).

CHAPTER 18

....

GENOCIDE AT THE TWILIGHT OF THE OTTOMAN EMPIRE

....

HILMAR KAISER

WORLD WAR I saw the almost complete annihilation of the Ottoman Armenians. The destruction stands at the centre of an intense debate. Some historians claim that Armenians organized uprisings in the rear of the Ottoman army and comparably few Armenians were killed during an anti-insurrection campaign.[1] Others do not address the genocide directly, but provide insights into the functioning of the state military, the 'Special Organization' (TM—Teşkilat-ı Mahsusa),[2] an organization that had been founded by the ruling Committee of Union and Progress (CUP) for intelligence, counter-insurgency, and other tasks that the government did not want to be associated with, and Ottoman demographic policies.[3] These studies

[1] Yusuf Halaçoğlu, *Ermeni Tehciri ve Gerçekler (1914–1918)* (Ankara: Türk Tarih Kurumu, 2001); *idem, Sürgünden Soykırıma. Ermeni İddiaları* (Ankara: Babıali Yayıncılığı, 2006); Hilmar Kaiser, 'Dall'impero all repubblicca: le continuità del negazionismo turco', in Marcello Flores (ed.), *Storia, verità, guistizia. I crimini del XX secolo* (Milan: Bruno Mondadori, 2001), 89–113; *idem,* 'Le génocide arménien: négation 'à l'allemande', in Comité de Défense de la Cause Arménienne (ed.), *L'actualité du Génocide des Arméniens* (Paris: Edipol, 1999), 75–91.

[2] Erdal Aydoğan, 'Teşkilât-ı Mahsusa', in Hikmet Özdemir (ed.), *Türk–Ermeni İhtilafı. Makaleler, Turkish–Armenian Conflict. Articles* (Ankara: Türk Büyük Meclisi Kültür, Sanat ve Yayın Kurulu Yayınları, 2007), 399–427.

[3] Fuat Dündar, *İttihat ve Terakki'nin Müslümanları İskân Politikası (1913–1918)* (Istanbul: İletişim Yayınları, 2001); *idem, Modern Türkiye'nin Şifresi. İttihat ve Terakki'nin Etnisite Mühendisliği (1913–1918)* (Istanbul: İletişim Yayınları, 2008).

discuss Ottoman wartime policies and undermine claims of an Armenian uprising, as large-scale demographic programmes would have been unthinkable under such conditions: the deportation of over three million people (Armenians and non-Armenians) depended on the absence of substantial resistance.

Other authors assume that the genocide was part of a policy that used the 'opportunity' afforded by the war to realize a scheme that had been in the making for years. Such interpretations stress the role of the CUP. The party had supposedly used the TM to execute the genocide, but the organization was a part of the Ottoman military.[4] Critically, the approach suggests coherent planning ahead of the crime while fragmented evidence is seen as a proof for a conspiracy.

Recent case studies have avoided generalizations based on limited sources.[5] Accordingly, claims of long-term genocidal planning appear to be untenable. Instead, it has become evident that the development of the war determined the timing of deportations and massacres.[6] Moreover, the genocide cannot be separated from demographic policies that targeted other communities, like the Greeks, Nestorians, Syrian Orthodox Christians, Circassians, and Druzes, and depended on the extraction of Armenian assets. The CUP's goal was the establishment of total control over state and society.[7] This chapter will consider the development of the genocide in the context of wider Ottoman demographic policies and late Ottoman history.

THE OTTOMAN CONTEXT

Since the founding of the empire, deportations formed part of Ottoman policies by which unwanted groups were replaced with controllable populations. A solid tax base was crucial for the maintenance of bureaucracy and army.[8] A major divide in Ottoman society was that between Muslims and non-Muslims. While Muslim

[4] Vahakn N. Dadrian, *The History of the Armenian Genocide. Ethnic Conflict from the Balkans to Anatolia to the Caucasus* (Providence, RI/Oxford: Berghahn Books, 1995); Taner Akçam, *A Shameful Act: The Armenian Genocide and the Question of Turkish Responsibility*, trans. Paul Bessemer (New York: Metropolitan Books, 2006).

[5] Uğur Ü. Üngör, '"A Reign of Terror": CUP Rule in Diyarbekir Province, 1913–1913', MA Thesis, University of Amsterdam, 2005.

[6] Donald Bloxham, *The Great Game of Genocide: Imperialism, Nationalism, and the Destruction of the Ottoman Armenians* (Oxford, Oxford University Press, 2005).

[7] Fikret Adanır and Hilmar Kaiser, 'Migration, Deportation, and Nation-Building: The Case of the Ottoman Empire', in René Leboutte (ed.), *Migrations and Migrants in Historical Perspective. Permanencies and Innovations* (Brussels: Peter Lang, 2000), 273–92.

[8] Rudi Paul Lindner, *Nomads and Ottomans in Medieval Anatolia* (Bloomington, IN, Research Institute for Inner Asian Studies, 1983).

communities constituted a majority by 1914, Christian communities formed a sizeable part of the empire's population. Importantly, Greeks and Armenians played critical roles in the Ottoman economy. Non-Muslims had some autonomy in internal community affairs, while being subjected to discriminatory taxation and an inferior legal status.[9] Following a weakening of government control, local competitors for the tax revenue emerged from urban and rural elites in the seventeenth and eighteenth centuries.[10] Early in the nineteenth century, the central authorities began eliminating this competition.[11] This re-centralization policy, however, did not check the rise of nationalist movements and the founding of independent Balkan states. Increasingly, Ottoman governments depended on European support. In return, they granted concessions and other privileges to European nationals. The governments were further weakened by increasing foreign debt that led to bankruptcy and tightening European control over the tax basis.[12] The loss of territory to European powers and secessionist groups intensified tensions even more.

Following a defeat by Russia, in the 1878 Congress of Berlin the Sublime Porte accepted territorial losses and reforms, including improvements for Ottoman Armenians. For years, Ottoman authorities had increased taxation while local elites had not stopped levying their own duties. The government did, however, not stop this abuse nor provide security, allowing continued double taxation. Competition for land increased the insecurity of Armenian life and property. The central government was partly responsible. For years, the Sublime Porte had settled Muslim immigrants to strengthen control over areas feared to be threatened by foreign occupation or national movements like the Armenian highlands. Many newcomers had survived ethnic cleansing in the Balkans, Caucasus, and the Aegean.

Lacking funds, the government regularly abandoned settlers without supplies, tacitly supporting their occupation of non-Muslim property.[13] In the Armenian highlands, Kurdish leaders joined in the competition for land, registering

[9] Benjamin Braude and Bernard Lewis (eds), *Christians and Jews in the Ottoman Empire: The Functioning of a Plural Society* (New York: Holmes and Meyer, 1982).

[10] Bruce McGowan, 'The Age of the Ayans, 1699–1812', in Halil İnalcik and Donald Quataert (eds), *An Economic and Social History of the Ottoman Empire, 1300–1914* (New York: Cambridge University Press, 1994), 637–758.

[11] Andrew G. Gould, 'Pashas and Brigands: Ottoman Provincial Reform and Its Impact on the Nomadic Tribes of Southern Anatolia, 1840–1885', PhD Dissertation, University of California: Los Angeles, 1973.

[12] J. A. R. Marriott, *The Eastern Question: An Historical Inquiry in European Diplomacy*, 3rd edn (Oxford: Oxford University Press, 1924); Donald C. Blaisdell, *European Financial Control in the Ottoman Empire: A Study of the Establishment, Activities, and Significance of the Administration of the Ottoman Public Debt* (New York: Columbia University Press, 1929; rpt. New York: AMS, 1966).

[13] Abdullah Saydam, 'XIX. Yüzyılda Adana Eyaletinin Sosyo-Ekonomik Yapısı Hakkında Bir Rapor', *Belgelerle Türk Tarih Dergisi* 71 (1991), 27–33; Gould, *Pashas and Brigands*.

Armenian land in their names with the support of the authorities. Kurdish tribes used Armenian fields as pastures, demanded shelter for the winter, often taking possession by killing the owners and abducting women and children. The erosion of Armenian landholding was part of a policy to create a Muslim majority in Armenian districts. In the face of government indifference to Armenian protests, Armenians appealed to the Berlin Congress; thereby the 'Armenian Question' entered the agenda of European diplomacy.[14]

Reforms did not materialize. The Ottoman government continued its settlement programme, attracting as many Muslims to its territory as possible.[15] Increasing tensions between Armenians and Muslims favoured the rise of Armenian political organizations in the 1880s. These parties intended to protect villages. For its part, the government created the Kurdish 'Hamidieh' cavalry in 1890. The units were used against Armenian organizations and rewarded with tax relief. They enriched themselves openly at the cost of Armenians or other Kurds.[16] When in 1894 Armenian mountain dwellers in Sassun opposed double taxation, Ottoman troops and Kurds slaughtered them, starting a series of massacres. Throughout 1895 and 1896, Hamidiehs and Muslim villagers and townsmen massacred Armenians, plundering property, seizing land, and abducting women. The government furthered the weakening of Armenian communities by deporting survivors from Sassun, making room for more Muslim settlers.[17]

In the absence of foreign intervention, the Ottoman government organized the massacre of thousands of Armenians in Constantinople in 1896.[18] It survived the ensuing diplomatic crisis with a promise for reform. The Ottoman authorities continued to suppress political discontent as opposition remained weak and split along ethnic and ideological lines. By 1908, however, a severe economic crisis intensified social discontent.[19] An army mutiny forced the weakened government to accept parliamentary rule. The coup triggered intercommunal fraternizations

[14] Arshag O. Sarkissian, *History of the Armenian Question to 1885* (Urbana: University of Illinois Press, 1938).

[15] United Kingdom, National Archives, Kew Gardens, Foreign Office (hereafter: FO) 195/2073, Massy to Chargé d'Affaires, Adana, Dec. 31, 1900, no. 31; ibid. FO 195/2095, Jan. 16, 1901, no. 7; ibid. Massy to O'Conor, Adana, May 5, 1901, no. 24.

[16] Martin M. Van Bruinessen, *Agha, Scheich und Staat. Politik und Gesellschaft Kurdistans* (Berlin: Edition Parabolis, 1989), 248–9; Jelle Verheij, 'Die armenischen Massaker von 1894–1896: Anatomie und Hintergründe einer Krise', in Hans-Lukas Kieser (ed.), *Die armenische Frage und die Schweiz* (1896–1923) (Zürich: Chronos Verlag, 1999), 69–129. Louise Nalbandian, *The Armenian Revolutionary Movement: The Development of Armenian Political Parties through the Nineteenth Century* (Berkeley/ Los Angeles: University of California Press, 1963).

[17] Avedis Nakashian, *A Man Who Found a Country* (New York: Crowell, 1940), 135.

[18] Hugo Von Köller, *Von Pasewalk zum Bosporus. Ein abenteuerliches Junkerleben* (Berlin-Leipzig: Brunnen Verlag, 1927), 245–8.

[19] Donald Quataert, 'The Economic Climate of the "Young Turk Revolution" in 1908', *Journal of Modern History* 51 (1979), D1147–61; *idem*, 'Machine Breaking and the Changing Carpet Industry of Western Anatolia, 1860–1908', *Journal of Social History* 19 (1986), 473–89.

and Muslim and Armenian parties cooperated in parliament.[20] In April 1909, a counter-revolution caused a setback. Massacres had been prepared in many places as well but were prevented by CUP members. In Cilicia, 25,000 to 30,000 Armenians were slaughtered by reactionaries who took advantage of religious fervour, dire economic conditions, inflation, and the competition for land and jobs. Despite their defeat, the reactionaries' strength impressed the CUP, which decided to integrate the oppositional Muslim provincial elites. Accordingly, Armenian demands for reform and the restitution of property met with new resistance, giving fresh impetus to Kurdish outrages and occupation of Armenian land. Armenian communities lost their representatives through the killing of teachers, priests, party leaders, and village headmen. Disillusioned, the leading Armenian party, the Armenian Revolutionary Federation, broke with the CUP in 1912, on the eve, as it transpired, of another series of catastrophic events. British ambassador Gerard Lowther concluded that the 1890s massacres had been 'succeeded by fifteen years of draconian methods spelling even a worse extensive "elimination" of the Armenian element.'[21]

ETHNIC CLEANSING OF GREEKS AND BULGARIANS

During the Balkan Wars of 1912–13, a coalition of Balkan states defeated the Ottoman Empire, which lost Macedonia, Epirus, Kosovo, and Western Thrace. The consequences were felt far beyond the war zone. During the fighting all states had massacred and displaced civilians. The rationale was to eliminate competing claims to occupied or re-occupied regions. At least 339,074 Muslims fled to Ottoman-held territory, while 376,186 still had remained behind by January 1915. The government was unprepared for the influx of destitute refugees and many of them died of starvation or disease.[22]

In response, the Ministry of the Interior reorganized its settlement policies while the CUP unleashed a clandestine campaign against Ottoman Greeks and

---

[20] For an overview, see Erik Jan Zürcher, *Turkey: A Modern History* (London/New York: I. B. Tauris, 2004).

[21] FO 424/237/570, Lowther to Grey, Constantinople, Dec. 31, 1912, no. 1129.

[22] Carnegie Endowment for International Peace, *Report of the International Commission to Inquire into the Causes and Conduct of the Balkan Wars* (Washington, DC: Carnegie Endowment for International Peace, 1914); Murat Bardakçı, *Talât Paşa'nın Evrak-ı Metrûkesi. Sadrazam Talât Paşa'nın Özel Arşivinde Bulunan Ermeni Tehciri Konusundaki Belgeler ve Hususî Yazışmalar* (Istanbul: Everest Yayınları, 2008), 39, 45.

Bulgarians.[23] Party cadres and government officials coordinated attacks along the Aegean littoral.[24] The authorities' complicity became evident as criminals were allowed to continue their outrages and force thousands of Greeks to flee. Then they recorded displaced Greeks and their property. The state coordinated the displacements and the settlement of immigrants, thereby obstructing the return of the legal owners.[25] The campaign continued into World War I when Greek communities were officially deported and their property seized. A minimum of 163,975 Greeks were expelled or fled to Greece, while at least 93,088 were deported to interior provinces. As many as 58,039 Bulgarians were expelled to Bulgaria.[26]

THE ARMENIAN REFORM SCHEME

Another major challenge for the CUP following the Balkan Wars was the resurgence of the Armenian Reform question. Armenian leaders had brought up their grievances with European powers. The latter forced a new reform plan on the Ottoman government. The eastern provinces were divided into two regions, each under a European high commissioner overseeing reforms. The CUP opposed the scheme and stalled its implementation while threatening the Armenian leadership. The issue remained unresolved until the beginning of World War I provided the CUP with an opportunity to abandon the scheme.[27]

WORLD WAR I

A secret military alliance with Germany gave the CUP new political leverage. In October 1914, the Ottoman government abrogated the 'Capitulations' that had

[23] H. Yıldırım Ağanoğlu, *Osmanlı'dan Cumhuriyet'e Balkanlar'ın Makûs Talihi Göç* (Istanbul: Kum Saatı, 2001), 346–54.

[24] Midhat Şükrü Bleda, *İmparatorluğun Çöküşü* (Istanbul: Remzi Kitabevi, 1979), 54–6.

[25] Bundesrepublik Deutschland, Auswärtiges Amt, Berlin, Politisches Archiv (hereafter: AA-PA), Türkei 168/11, A 12811, Wangenheim to Bethmann Hollweg, Therapia, June 25, 1914, no. 175; ibid. A 13109, Humbert to Wangenheim, Smyrna, June 25, 1914, no. 2795; copy enclosure in Wangenheim to Bethmann Hollweg, Therapia, June 6, 1914, no. 179; ibid. A 13846, Schönberg to Mutius, Therapia, July 9, 1914; enclosure in Mutius to Bethmann Hollweg, Therapia, July 10, 1914, no. 187.

[26] Bardakçı, *Evrak-ı Metrûkesi*.39, 45, 79, 80–1.

[27] Armen Garo, *Bank Ottoman. Memoirs of Armen Garo*, trans. Haig T. Partizian, ed. and intro. Simon Vratzian (Detroit: Armen Topozian, 1990), 182–92.

granted foreign nationals some immunity from Ottoman law. The CUP also wanted to pre-empt foreign interventions in support of the non-Turkish communities.[28] Now the CUP targeted Zionist settlers in Palestine. The Ministry of Interior installed Manastirli Bahaeddin Bey, its expert for Zionist affairs and a member of the TM, as governor of Jafa. The official announced that he would destroy the Zionist movement; all foreign Jews would have to leave while new arrivals would not be permitted. Jewish settlers who had become Ottoman citizens were harassed and others discouraged from applying. On 5 November 1914, authorities searched Jewish houses for arms and documents, demanding the surrender of all guns legally owned by Zionists. The latter were forced to purchase guns to meet the number of guns demanded from them. At the same time, Bahaeddin promised Muslim villagers the Zionist settlers' land and women so that fear of massacre spread. On 17 December 1914, police rounded up and deported Jews to Egypt. Due to German and US opposition, however, the campaign slowed down until it gained new momentum in 1917.[29]

NESTORIANS

Throughout the summer of 1914, the Ottoman government was concerned about Russian advances towards the Kurdish and Nestorian population. On 26 October 1914, Talaat ordered the deportation of the Nestorians from Hakkari to western provinces where they should be dispersed among Muslims. Three days later, the scheme was, however, postponed for lack of forces and soon abandoned for the time being.[30] The deportation scheme was probably connected with the imminent Ottoman attack on Russia. Apparently, the CUP suspected that the Nestorians would join forces with Russians and tried to pre-empt that danger. Seeing that its suspicions did not materialize, the CUP shelved the project. Avoiding deportation did not, however, mean escaping massacre during Ottoman cross-border raids into

[28] Ulrich Trumpener, *Germany and the Ottoman Empire, 1914–1918* (Princeton: Princeton University Press, 1968), 38–9; AA-PA, Türkei 159, no. 2/14, A 32771, Neurath to Bethmann Hollweg, Pera, Nov. 5, 1915, no. 654.

[29] Israel, Central Zionist Archives, Jerusalem, Z 3/52, Ruppin to Lichtheim, Jaffa, Mar. 24, 1915, enclosure to Action–Committee to Members, Berlin, Apr. 4, 1915; Isaiah Friedman, *Germany, Turkey and Zionism, 1897–1918* (Oxford: Oxford University Press, 1977); Henry Morgenthau, *Ambassador Morgenthau's Story* (Garden City, NY: Doubleday, Page, 1918), 370.

[30] Türkiye Cumhuriyeti, Başbakanlık Osmanlı Arşivi, Istanbul, Dahiliye Nezareti (hereafter: DH) Şifre Kalemi (hereafter: ŞFR) 46–78, Talaat to Van province, Oct. 26, 1914, Emniyet-i Umumiye Müdiriyeti (hereafter: EUM) Spec. 104; ibid. 46–102, Minister to Van province, Oct. 29, 1914, EUM Spec. 107; ibid. 46–195, Talaat to Van province, Nov. 5, 1914, EUM Spec. 113.

Iran or following the collapse of the Ottoman front along the Iranian border in 1915. Further inland, Syrian Orthodox Christians were massacred alongside Armenians in Diarbekir province.[31] Their killing appears, however, not to have been part of a central government policy. The provincial authorities were repeatedly instructed to treat Syrian Orthodox differently than Armenians.[32]

ARMENIANS

In August 1914, Ottoman TM units started undercover cross-border operations into Russian territory. The goal was the softening of Russian border defences and to foment a rebellion among the Muslim population.[33] Following an Ottoman naval attack on Russian Black Sea ports on 29 October 1914, France, Britain, and Russia declared war on the Ottoman Empire. On 14 November 1914, the Ottoman Empire declared a 'Holy War'. In December 1914, the Ottoman Third Army launched an offensive, hoping to take the Russians by surprise. The attack failed, however, and the army was almost annihilated. During their retreat, irregular units and fleeing Muslim civilians began plundering and massacring Armenian villages. The atrocities were motivated by the lack of supplies and a desire for revenge.[34] By spring 1915, the Ottoman army suffered further defeats on Sinai and the Mesopotamian and Iranian fronts. On 18 March 1915, an allied fleet nearly forced the Dardanelles.[35] In view of this danger, the Ottoman government prepared to evacuate the government and the imperial court from Constantinople.

Following defeat in Iranian Azerbaijan, Ottoman troops turned the region before the advancing enemy into a wasteland. They annihilated local Armenians although the latter had remained loyal. The campaign's principal target was the Armenian community in Van. The city was the Armenian political centre of the eastern provinces. Here, Armenian leaders organized and coordinated political

---

[31] Precise information about these atrocities is still lacking, but it appears that almost all surviving Nestorians fled the area. David Gaunt, *Massacres, Resistance, Protectors: Muslim-Christian Relations in Eastern Anatolia During World War 1* (Piscataway, NJ: Gorgias Press, 2006); Üngör, *Reign of Terror*.

[32] See for instance: DH.ŞFR 57–102, Minister to Diarbekir, Bitlis, Harput, Aleppo provinces, Urfa district, Oct. 25, 1915, EUM Spec. 91, 51, 86, 113, 42; ibid. 70–79, Shukru to Diarbekir province, Nov. 23, 1916, Aşâir ve Muhâcirîn Müdiriyeti Umûmiyyesi, Settlement Dept. Gen. 1089.

[33] Arif Cemil, *I. Dünya Savaşı'nda Teşkilât-ı Mahsusa* (Istanbul: Arba Yayınları, 1997), 27–32.

[34] Hilmar Kaiser, ' "A Scene from the Inferno": The Armenians of Erzerum and the Genocide, 1915–1916', in Hans-Lukas Kieser and Dominik Schaller (eds), *Der Völkermord an den Armeniern und die Shoah / The Armenian Genocide and the Shoah* (Zürich: Chronos Verlag, 2002), 129–86.

[35] Carl Mühlmann, *Das deutsch-türkische Waffenbündnis im Weltkrieg*. Mit einem Geleitwort von W. Foerster (Leipzig: Koehler and Amelang, 1940), 43.

campaigns and, in case of need, the community's self-defence. Therefore, the Ottoman civilian and military authorities gave the elimination of this suspected internal foe priority over combating the Russians. The government forces attacked on 20 April 1915 and massacred surrounding Armenian villages with few exceptions. In the city, however, the government forces were defeated by Armenian defenders and withdrew on 17 May 1915 before Russian forces reached the city.[36]

Having received news about the defence at Van and expecting an imminent attack on the Dardanelles, Talaat ordered the arrest of Armenian community leaders empire-wide on 24 April 1915. In Constantinople, the police rounded up Armenian, among others, journalists, clerics, politicians, and teachers. The arrested were sent to the interior where the majority was killed. Armenian elites in the provinces suffered the same fate.[37]

INITIAL DEPORTATIONS

The April arrests were not the start of general deportations although Armenians from Zeitun were re-directed to Der Zor, the new main destination for deportees. On 2 May 1915, the Ministry of War suggested the deportation of all Armenians from the eastern border regions to the Russian lines or to interior provinces. As in the case of the Greeks, the Armenians should immediately be replaced by Muslim settlers.[38] Within a week, the governors of Erzerum, Bitlis, and Van provinces were ordered to deport, in cooperation with the army, Armenians towards the Syrian Desert and Mosul.[39] On 23 May 1915, the deportations were extended to districts in historic Cilicia and border areas of Mosul province. Armenians could keep their movable possessions. They were to be distributed in villages and small towns. New Armenian villages had to be at least twenty-five kilometres away from railway lines and could not exceed fifty households. Moreover, Armenians must never exceed

[36] Onnig Mukhitarian, *An Account of the Glorious Struggle of Van—Vasbouragan*, trans. Samuel S. Tarpinian ([Detroit, MI]: General Society of Vasbouragan, 1980).

[37] Hikmet Özdemir and Yusuf Sarınay (eds), *Türk-Ermeni İhtilafı. Belgeler (Turkish–Armenian Conflict: Documents)* (Ankara: Türk Büyük Meclisi Kültür, Sanat ve Yayın Kurulu Yayınları, 2007), 18–27. Yusuf Sarınay, 'What Happened on April 24, 1915?: The Circular of April 24, 1915, and the Arrest of the Armenian Committee Members in Istanbul', *International Journal of Turkish Studies* 14:1–2 (2008), 75–101.

[38] Özdemir and Sarınay, *İhtilâfı*, 33–7.

[39] DH.ŞFR 52–281, Minister to Tahsin Bey, May 7, 1915 EUM Spec. 4090; ibid. 52–282, Minister to Tahsin, Mustafa Abdülhalık, Djevdet, May 9, 1915, EUM Spec. Dept. 409[0?]; Türkiye Cumhuriyeti, Başbakanlık Devlet Arşivleri Genel Müdürlüğü, Osmanli Arşivi Daire Bakanlığı, *Osmanlı Belgelerinde Ermeniler (1915–1920)* (Ankara: Başbakanlık Basımevi, 1994), 28–9.

ten per cent of the Muslim population. Local authorities were responsible for the execution of the plan.[40]

On 24 May 1915, the Entente powers declared that they would hold all Ottoman citizens and officials personally accountable for their role in the persecution of the Armenians. The declaration defined the outrages that had occurred so far as crimes against humanity.[41] The Ottoman government responded on 27 May 1915 with a 'provisional law' that gave Ottoman military commanders the right to deport anyone they wished to. Three days later, the Ministry of the Interior issued a manual for its Department for the Settlement of Tribes and Immigrants, specifying the deportations' implementation.[42] Armenian immovable property was to be seized and used for the settlement of Muslims. Evidently, the deportations were not a temporary emergency measure but should permanently change the demographic map.[43]

ARMENIAN PROPERTY

On 10 June 1915, the Ministry of Interior regulated the liquidation of Armenian property. All property had to be registered while perishable goods and livestock were to be auctioned off immediately. The Muslim migrants were settled first, then nomads. The newcomers had to be capable of farming or operating the businesses they received. Non-distributed real estate was to be auctioned off. In sum, Armenian owners had lost their property rights and could not object.

On 26 September 1915, the government passed a provisional law concerning the property of Armenian deportees. Nominal attention was given to the rights of creditors who could present their claims, but obstacles rendered the pursuit of their interests impracticable. Even if claimants won their case, they could not obtain already liquidated properties. On 6 January 1916, Talaat stated that the Ottoman economy had to become an exclusively Muslim one. He decreed that Armenian property must fall into Muslim hands. On 23 November 1916, the government also sanctioned the seizure of property of Armenians who had not been deported.

---

[40] Özdemir and Sarınay, İhtilâfı, 46–9, 66–9; DH.ŞFR, 53–91, Minister to Mosul province, Urfa, Zor districts, May 23, 1915, EUM; ibid. 53–92, Minister to Adana, Aleppo provinces, Marash district, May 23, 1915, EUM; ibid. 53–93, Minister to Erzerum, Van, Bitlis provinces, May 23, 1915, EUM; Osmanlı Belgelerinde Ermeniler, 33–4; Bloxham, Great Game, 84–5. For an overview based largely on Armenian sources see Raymond Kévorkian, Le génocide des arméniens (Paris: Odile Jacob, 2006).
[41] Arthur Beylerian (ed.), Les grandes puissances, l'Empire ottoman et les Arméniens dans les archives françaises (1914–1918), Recueil de documents (Paris: Publications de la Sorbonne, 1983), 29.
[42] Özdemir and Sarınay, İhtilâfı, 64–5, 72–81; Kaiser, 'Négation', 81–3.
[43] Özdemir and Sarınay, İhtilâfı, 72–6, 78–81.

The Ottoman government faced strong competition for the loot throughout the expropriation. Local elites, government officials, common criminals, and Armenians themselves succeeded in obtaining or hiding parts of property that otherwise would have been transferred to the government.[44]

THE SECOND WAVE OF DEPORTATIONS

As with the expropriations, by the extension of deportations far beyond the war zone the Ottoman government demonstrated that military considerations were not the driving force behind the deportation programme. On 19 June 1915, the Third Army ordered the extension of deportations and the removal of all Armenians from the Erzerum, Trebizond, Van, Bitlis, Harput, Diarbekir, and Sivas provinces.[45] The vast extension of the deportation programme necessitated adjustments by the authorities. Given the massive number of deportees, recordkeeping emerged as a major task. Repeatedly, the Ministry of Interior demanded information on Armenian villages, their location and agricultural potential, number of deportees and the route along which they had been deported, Armenian real estate, and suggestions for settlement of prospective settlers.[46] On 22 June 1915, Armenians who had converted to Islam were allowed to stay behind for the time being and had to undergo special registration. The order was personally addressed to the provincial governors, who were all trusted CUP members. They had to keep it secret and destroy the evidence.[47]

Throughout July 1915, the central authorities requested population data and information on the progress of the deportations and their impact on the ethnic make-up of the areas in question. The region around Diarbekir had been earmarked for Turkification and the settlement of other Muslim nationalities prohibited.[48] As Armenians were not to exceed ten per cent of the population, the

[44] Hilmar Kaiser, 'Armenian Property, Ottoman Law, and Nationality Policies during the Armenian Genocide, 1915–1916', in Olaf Farschild, Manfred Kropp, and Stephan Dähne (eds), *The First World War as Remembered in the Countries of the Eastern Mediterranean* (Würzburg: Ergon Verlag, 2006), 49–71.

[45] Türkiye Cumhuriyeti and Genelkurmay Başkanlığı, *Arşiv Belgeleriyle Ermeni Faaliyetleri 1914–1918*, vol. i (Ankara: Genelkurmay Askeri Tarih ve Stratejik Etüt Başkanlığı Yayınları, 2005), 187–8.

[46] DH.ŞFR 54–15, Ali Munif to Adana, Aleppo, Erzurum, Bitlis, Van, Diarbekir provinces, Marash district, June 14, 1915, İskan-ı Aşair ve Muhacirin Müdiriyeti (hereafter: IAMM); ibid. 54–136, Ali Münif to Harput, Trebizond, Sivas provinces, Canik district, June 24, 1915, IAMM.

[47] DH.ŞFR 54–100, Minister to Governors of Van, Trebizond, Erzurum, Bitlis, Harput, Diarbekir, Sivas, Djanik, June 22, 1915, EUM Spec. 4531.

[48] DH.ŞFR 54–272, Minister to Diarbekir province, July 3, 1915, IAMM 54; ibid. 54/A-51, Minister to all provinces districts, July 20, 1915, EUM Spec. 397; ibid. 54/A-100, Minister to Erzerum, Adana, Bitlis, Aleppo, Diarbekir, Sivas, Trebizond, Harput, Van provinces, Urfa, Djanik, Marash districts, July 24, 1915, EUM Gen. 400.

government had to face an increasingly large 'surplus' population that survived the death marches from the eastern provinces. As a countermeasure the settlement zones were broadened within the Mosul and Aleppo provinces and extended to today's Southern Syria and Jordan.[49]

The unfolding human disaster soon reached such proportions that the authorities were faced with an unexpected problem. Thousands of Armenian children had been left behind along supply lines and in cities and villages. In many places, local Muslims had taken children in, be it for altruistic or other reasons. Now the government tried to regain control of the situation. The Ministry of Education was put in charge of the children. Those younger than ten years of age were to be admitted to government orphanages, but adequate facilities were lacking or non-existent.[50]

Many families had given up children in face of imminent massacre or because they could no longer provide for them. Massacres in villages and towns were mostly avoided to preclude loss of property by plundering and burning like in the 1890s and in 1909.[51] The killing of Armenians during the deportations took place in several stages. While most Armenian men had been drafted into the army, there were still many older men, teenagers, deserters, and those who had paid the military exemption tax among the deportees. The government escorts, mostly gendarmes or local militia, usually separated most of the men from the caravans during the first days of the deportation. The men and boys were then taken away and killed. Males who either succeeded in disguising themselves as women or managed to bribe the guards gained a temporary reprieve from massacre. The men usually did not resist their murderers, not wanting to endanger the lives of their families.[52]

At specific locations along the route the deportees were camped for some days while several convoys were merged. During this respite, the deportees were informed that a massacre was imminent and asked to give up their children and teenage girls or to buy their way out of the predicament by paying a ransom. In this way, the authorities induced the deportees to surrender large amounts of money and valuables that otherwise could be obtained only with difficulty and effort as the deportees often swallowed precious stones and coins. Similar to a modern turnpike system, the convoys passed successive notorious massacre sites; where those who could not longer pay were murdered. Following the massacres, the killer squads searched the corpses for valuable documents, like life insurance policies and financial documents that could be used by the state to claim the benefits as being the legal heir of the victims.

---

[49] Özdemir and Sarınay, İhtilâfı, 144–8.

[50] DH.ŞFR 54–163, Minister to Harput province, June 26, 1915, EUM Spec. 4573; ibid. 54–411, Ali Munif to provinces, July 12, 1915, IAMM 378; ibid. 54/A-54, Ali Munif to Sivas province, July 20, 1915, IAMM 66; Özdemir and Sarınay, İhtilâfı, 118–19.

[51] Kaiser, 'Armenian Property'.

[52] AA-PA Türkei 183/40, A 32613, Sarkis Manukian to Rössler, Aleppo, Nov. 25, 1915; enclosure 2 in Rössler to Bethmann Hollweg, Aleppo, Nov. 30, 1915, K. no. 110, no. 2725.

The killing squads operated under the command of trusted CUP members who were either administrators or officers, or had been assigned to the TM. The composition of these units varied from district to district. While TM units were responsible for massacres close to the combat zone, the gangs in the interior districts included local militiamen, gendarmes, Kurdish tribal groups, or cut-throats hired from the local population for the occasion. The convoys' escorts cooperated with the killing squads in coordinating the delivery of the victims at the assembly points so that comparably few men could murder large numbers of victims with swords and daggers within a short period of time. Major massacre sites, located near transit camps like the Kemah gorge near Erzindjan, Lake Khazar near Harput, and the valleys south of Firindjilar near Malatia, shared certain characteristics. The sites were mountainous but still close to overland roads. Thus, the deportees could be easily transported to the massacre sites while having relatively few escape routes. Rivers and deep gorges facilitated the hiding or disposal of corpses.

The killers were rewarded with a part of the stolen property and women and children, depending on availability or preferences. Armenian boys survived in Muslim villages and among tribes as slaves working as either shepherds or farm hands. Their survival was, nevertheless, uncertain as replacements were cheaper than adequate food rations. Girls were mostly used as house servants or sex slaves and, if lucky, as brides within the family. This way the family saved payment of a dowry, a major expense within the life cycle of a Muslim peasant family. Moreover, converted Armenian children who were raised by Muslims could keep the inheritance from their original families, thereby generating considerable new income. The absorption of Armenian women into Muslim families presented no problem as the women were forced to become Muslim and the nationality of the males defined the identity of the family. Some, however, objected to the CUP's extermination policy and wanted to save a person from abuse and almost certain death.[53]

Following the murder of most men and older boys during the initial phase of the deportations, the history of the Armenian genocide became by and large that of women and children. It marked a reversal of gender roles within the Armenian community where women were subjected to patriarchal structures that limited their independent decision-making and contacts with outsiders. Moreover, women from exclusively armenophone communities had to cope with situations where they could only communicate with other deportees. Mostly women and children became the target of random and systematic rape. The violence was targeted at destroying the Armenian individuals' and community's self-perception by inflicting lasting psychological harm. Rape meant an irreparable transgenerational loss of self-esteem, or 'honor', for Armenians, even if they lived beyond the reach of the Ottoman government. The women's counter-strategies included disguising their age, forms of physical

---

[53] Kaiser, 'A Scene'; Özdemir and Sarınay, İhtilâfı, 194–5.

individual or joint resistance, but often suicide was the only 'protection' from rape left.

Escape from the caravans was no common option as the deportations had eliminated places of refuge within whole provinces. Nevertheless, Armenian women developed strategies defying the CUP's genocidal logic. Elder women gave up their food ration for the children and girls were given up before the boys. Once only boys were left, the mother tried to protect at least one male descendant at the cost of her own life. Thus, women focused not on individual survival but that of the family as they understood it, and were willing to engage in activities that stood in extreme contrast to their social values.[54]

THE THIRD WAVE OF DEPORTATIONS

By early August 1915, the government extended the deportations to the central and western provinces. Areas with small Armenian communities were excluded as were some urban communities in part.[55] Now the government sanctioned the ongoing dispersion of young Armenian children among non-Turkish Muslim villages. The government's own assimilation efforts gained new momentum in 1916. It appears that the authorities relied on private and foreign institutions to keep the children alive until government institutions were put in place.

Unlike in the eastern provinces, large numbers of Armenians were deported by railway or along the railway lines. Again, the authorities tried to keep track of the deportees, their number, place of origin, and current location. Following protests from the US, German, and Austro-Hungarian embassies, Catholic and Protestant Armenians, who had so far not been deported, were exempted, unless they constituted a concern. Moreover, the number of remaining Armenians and their percentage of the total population had to be ascertained. Protests and production breakdowns secured the permanent or temporary exemption of Armenian

[54] Eliz Sanasarian, 'Gender Distinction in the Genocidal Process: A Preliminary Study of the Armenian Case', *Holocaust and Genocide Studies* 4:4 (1989), 449–61; Ara Sarafian, 'The Absorption of Armenian Women and Children into Muslim Households as a Structural Component of the Armenian Genocide', in Omer Bartov and Phyllis Mack (eds), *In God's Name. Genocide and Religion in the Twentieth Century* (New York/Oxford: Berghahn Books, 2001), 209–21. Armen Anush, *Passage Through Hell: A Memoir*, trans. Ishkhan Jinbashian (Studio City, CA: Hagop and Knar Manjikian, 2005). Donald E. Miller and Lorna Toryan Miller, *An Oral History of the Armenian Genocide* (Berkeley: University of California Press, 1993).

[55] DH.ŞFR 54/A-200, Minister to 4th Army command, July 31, 1915, IAMM Statistical Dept. 63. *Osmanlı Belgelerinde Ermeniler*, 81.

specialists and workers, while families of Armenian soldiers that still remained behind were distributed among Muslim villages.[56]

Already at the end of August 1915, Talaat was certain that the Armenian Question had been solved.[57] In the western provinces, however, the large number of deportees created considerable problems for operating the railways and increased the chaos in and around Aleppo, the cross-roads of the deportation. Streamlining the transfer of deportees and recordkeeping remained a major challenge. In response, Talaat dispatched a special envoy, Shukru Bey, to the railway and northern Syria. Increasingly, deportee convoys from central and eastern regions were re-directed towards Mosul.[58] The measure came in response to the rapid progression of deportations in the western and central provinces. By 18 September 1915, many districts had already been entirely emptied. Exempted Armenians had been dispersed among Muslim villages up to five per cent of the population. Two months later, Talaat decreed that those exempted had to become Muslims.[59]

On 7 October 1915, Shukru Bey issued new regulations for the deportations to the Syrian Desert. He had established new administrative offices along the lower Euphrates for the coordination of the deportations. Henceforth, the optimal size of a deportation caravan was 1,000 deportees. Rakka, Harran, and Der Zor were designated as settlement regions for hundreds of thousands who had to be individually registered. The extension of the deportations increased the government's expenses. In response, the authorities used proceeds from Armenian property for the financing of deportations.[60]

In spring 1916, the deportations from interior and eastern provinces came to a halt as relatively few Armenian women and children were left. These were to be dispersed in exclusively Muslim villages or taken into orphanages. Women of childbearing age had to marry Muslim men.[61]

---

[56] DH.ŞFR 55–206, Minister to Sivas province, Aug. 25, 1915, EUM Gen. 5256; ibid. 55–323, Talaat to Angora province, Aug. 30, 1915, EUM Spec. 67; ibid. 59–111, Hasan Shafi, Dept. IAMM Director, to provinces, Dec. 27, 1915, IAMM Gen. 790; Hilmar Kaiser, 'The Baghdad Railway and the Armenian Genocide, 1915–1916: A Case Study in German Resistance and Complicity', in Richard G. Hovannisian (ed.), *Remembrance and Denial: The Case of the Armenian Genocide* (Detroit: Wayne State University Press, 1998), 67–112; *idem, Cross-roads*; Özdemir and Sarınay, *İhtilâfı*, 174–5, 178–9, 208–9; DH.ŞFR 54/A-294, Minister to Izmid district, July 28, 1915, EUM Spec. 43; DH.ŞFR 55–211, Minister to Syria, Adana, Konia, Ankara, Aleppo provinces, Urfa, Zor Marash districts, Aug. 25, 1915, EUM Spec. 5258; ibid. 55–208, Minister to provinces, Aug. 25, 1915, EUM Spec. 5260; ibid. 55/A-230, Talaat to Adana province, Sunday Sept. 12, 1915, EUM Spec. 64.

[57] AA-PA Türkei 183/38, A 26474, Hohenlohe to Bethmann Hollweg, Pera, Sept. 4, 115, no. 549; Özdemir and Sarınay, *İhtilâfı*, 234–7.

[58] Özdemir and Sarınay, *İhtilâfı*, 262–3, 272–3; DH.ŞFR 55/A-145, Talaat to provinces, Sept. 18, 1915, EUM Gen. 568.

[59] *Osmanlı Belgelerinde Ermeniler*, 93–96; DH.ŞFR 57–281, Talaat to provinces, Nov. 4, 1915, EUM Spec. 6270.

[60] Özdemir and Sarınay, *İhtilâfı*, 300–15, 380–3.

[61] Ibid. 424–6, 438–9, 442–3.

THE LOWER EUPHRATES

Those deportees that survived the death march and reached the Syrian Desert found themselves trapped in a system of camps that stretched along the Euphrates to Der Zor. In the camps, the Ottoman authorities exposed them to contagious diseases like typhus which killed hundreds daily. Refusal to provide water and food increased the high mortality among the emaciated victims. Here as well, Muslims were eager to obtain Armenian women. Authorities registered such marriages but did not record the deaths of the former Armenian husbands.[62]

In January 1916, the route along the Euphrates was littered with human corpses and bones, bearing testimony to the ongoing killing of deportees and death by exhaustion, famine, and disease.[63] The government monitored the number and death of deportees but recordkeeping became more complicated when the authorities started emptying outlying camps and forced the Armenians into the desert camps around Der Zor. In June 1916, deportations to Mosul and Syria were stopped. Consequently, Armenians had to be distributed within the Der Zor region and adjoining districts of Aleppo province.[64]

The local economy could not support the tens of thousands of Armenians in the small desert settlements while the authorities watched the impact of a killing famine and ravaging pandemics. Nevertheless, Talaat accelerated the dispatch of Armenians into the disaster zone. The authorities reacted swiftly when they learned that bribed gendarmes were allowing deportees to escape from the desert and return to Aleppo.[65]

In July 1916, Talaat repeatedly ordered the dissolution of Armenian camps near the military supply lines along the Euphrates River. He declared that Armenians were a military threat and must be moved to appropriate locations. Accordingly,

---

[62] Raymond Kévorkian, 'Le sort des déportés dans les camps de concentration de Syrie et de Mésopotamie', in *Revue d'histoire arménienne contemporaine* 2 (1998), 7–61; idem, 'Témoignages sur les camps de concentration de Syrie et de Mésopotamie', ibid. 62–215; idem, 'Autres témoignages sur les déportations et les camps de concentration de Syrie et de Mésopotamie (1915–1916)', ibid. 219–44; Helmut Becker, *Äskulap zwischen Reichsadler und Halbmond. Sanitätswesen und Seuchenbekämpfung im türkischen Reich während des Ersten Weltkriegs* (Herzogenrath: Verlag Murken-Altrogge, 1990); DH. ŞFR 58–114, Talaat to Suad Bey, Oct. 24, 1915, EUM Spec. 47.

[63] AA-PA Türkei 183/41, A 5498, Rössler to Bethmann Hollweg, Aleppo, Feb. 9, 1916, no. 366 K, no. 18; Rahmi Apak, *Yetmişlik Bir Subayın Hatıraları* (Ankara, Türk Tarih Kurumu, 1988), 149.

[64] DH.ŞFR 62–199, Minister to Zor district, Apr. 1, 1916, EUM Spec. 6; ibid. 64–165, Talaat to Zor district, May 31, 1916, EUM 22; ibid. 64–175, Talaat to Zor district, June 1, 1916, EUM Gen. 47469; ibid. 64–239, Talaat to Aleppo province, June 7, 1916, EUM Gen. 47701 Spec. 79; ibid. 64–248, Talaat to Zor district, June 7, 1916, EUM Gen. 47702 Spec. 25; ibid. 65–51, Talaat to Aleppo province, June 18, 1916, IAMM, Settlement Dept. Spec. 85.

[65] DH.ŞFR 64–292, Minister to Zor district, June 13, 1916, IAMM 28; ibid. 66–21, Talaat to Diarbekir province, July 18, 1916, EUM Gen. 49557 Spec. 39; ibid. 66–43, Talaat to Aleppo province, July 20, 1916, EUM Spec. 72.

Armenians in the employ of military transport had to be replaced by Muslims, thereby depriving the deportees of their only income. On 8 August 1916, Talaat ordered a count of all Armenians in the region and inquired into their percentage of the population. By the time of this order, the governor of Der Zor organized large-scale massacres. Near Der Zor, the governor burned alive approximately one thousand Armenian children. At the Khabur River, Chechen killing squads that had already massacred the inhabitants of the Rasulain camp slaughtered under government supervision Armenians by the tens of thousands. Again, the concentration of Armenian deportees assured that comparably few perpetrators could kill huge numbers of victims with axes and knives within a relatively short time while the authorities secured the victims' remaining valuables.[66]

Following these major massacres, the Ottoman government geared down its extermination programme. Der Zor remained a destination for deportees, particularly political suspects. The Armenians were continuously registered. In October 1916, the settlement commission at Rakka forwarded a list to Constantinople identifying 373 deportees from Amasia, Marash, and Hadjin.[67] Tracking surviving Armenians remained a concern for Talaat. He continued to monitor the progress, assimilation, and annihilation through population surveys while ideas for new settlement projects continued to be developed.[68]

The annihilation of the Armenians provided the government with a material basis for a restructuring of the Ottoman demographic map. In 1916, the authorities used the Armenian real estate in western and central provinces for the settlement of Kurdish tribal confederations. Like the last remaining Armenians, the newcomers were settled in small groups among Turkish-speaking Muslims to assimilate them. Their leaders were detained in distant locations. The area around Diarbekir, Urfa, and Adiaman received Muslim migrants, especially Albanians, and was designated as a 'Turkification region'. Kurds, Druze, Greeks, Shiites, and a variety of smaller groups were subjected to the programme. By 'Turkifying' entire regions as well as other non-Turkish and non-Muslim communities, the CUP sought to remove competing claims to Ottoman territory. The Kurds of Dersim had become alarmed by the extermination of Armenians as early as July 1915, fearing that they would be

[66] DH.ŞFR 66–19, Talaat to Zor district, July 19, 1916, EUM; ibid. 66–94, Talaat to Zor district, July 29, 1916, EUM Gen. 43 Spec. 1676; ibid. 66–159, Talaat to Zor district, Aug. 6, 1915, EUM Spec. 46; ibid. 66–170, Talaat to Zor district, Aug. 8, 1916, EUM Spec. 47; Ara Sarafian, compiler, *United States Official Records on the Armenian Genocide 1915–1917* (Princeton/London: Gomidas Institute, 2004), 555–60; AA-PA Türkei 183/45, A 31831, Rössler to Radowitz, Aleppo, Nov. 5, 1916, K. no. 104; no. 3045; Anush, *Passage*; Kaiser, 'A Scene', 184–5.

[67] DH.ŞFR 69–261, Talaat to Marash district, Nov. 13, 1916, EUM Gen. 2942 Spec. 34; DH. EUM. Gen. 7–17/A, Rakka Settlement Commission to Ministry of Interior, Oct. 27, 1916.

[68] DH.,ŞFR 69–120, Talaat to provinces, Oct. 29, 1916, EUM KLU 53999 Spec. 559; Türkiye Cumhuriyeti, Genelkurmay Başkanlığı, *Arşiv Belgeleriyle Ermeni Faaliyetleri 1914–1918*, vol. vii (Ankara: Genelkurmay Askeri Tarih ve Stratejik Etüt Başkanlığı Yayınlari, 2007), 320.

killed next. In response they sheltered Armenian refugees and formed joint Kurdish–Armenian resistance groups.[69]

THE DEATH TOLL

The number of Armenian victims is unknown. Ottoman data filed in 1914 suggest an Armenian population of 1,281,173 or, adjusted for undercounting, at least 1,718,132.[70] Government data from 1915 shows that in Erzerum and Bitlis provinces 98,178 Armenians had been killed in clashes or had fled. The 67,792 Armenians of Van province were not deported, reflecting massacres and also Armenian resistance and flight. Of these 165,970 Armenians about 65,081 survived by escaping to Russian lines.[71] By April 1917, 284,157 Armenians remained, bringing the number of Armenians accounted for to 349,238. The statistics probably did not include Armenians in hiding and those who had converted. These formed, however, only a fraction of the 1,368,894 Armenians who had disappeared from Ottoman records. This suggests that over 1.1 million Armenians had lost their lives due to government policies. Possibly more than 150,000 Armenians had been forcibly assimilated. These low estimates are based on government data and do not cover Armenian losses in 1917 and 1918.[72] It must be emphasized that most survivors suffered from physical injuries, diseases, and psychological traumata. Many had been maimed. When these medical emergencies are taken together with the survivors' age and gender composition, and the annihilation of the secular and religious elites, the

---

[69] DH.ŞFR 54/A-128, Talaat to Erzerum, Diarbekir Bitlis provinces, July 25, 1915, Spec. Dept.; Adanır and Kaiser, 'Migration'. See also Dündar, *Türkiye'nin Şifresi.*

[70] This figure represents a low estimate. An Armenian census arrived in 1913 at 1,914,620 Armenians while leaving out some communities. Mutlu adjusted 1914 Ottoman data by 34% for undercounting. Ottoman statistics from the Turkish military archives gives a total of 1,219,323 Armenians, but omits at least 65,850 Armenians of Diarbekir province. Thus bringing the adjusted Armenian population to 1,718,132. Servet Mutlu, 'Son Dönem Osmanlı Nüfusu: Müslüman ve Ermeniler', in Şafak Ural, Feridun Emecen, and Mustafa Aydın (eds), *Türk-Ermeni İlişkilerinde Yeni Yaklaşımlar. Uluslararası Sempozyum 15–17 Mart 2006* (Istanbul: Istanbul Üniversitesi Yayınları, 2008), 57–77; Raymond H. Kévorkian and Paul B. Paboudjian, *Les Arméniens dans l'Empire ottoman a la veille du génocide* (Paris: Les Éditions d'Art et d'Histoire, 1992), 60; Genelkurmay Başkanlığı, *Ermeni Faaliyetler,* i, 607, 609.

[71] Genelkurmay Başkanlığı, *Ermeni Faaliyetler,* i, 159–70. I have estimated Armenian losses among those killed at 50% for Van and Erzerum provinces, and at 70% for Bitlis.

[72] Bardakçı, *Evrak-ı Metrûkesi,* 108–39. The document is undated; however, the data on Beirut were taken from a report compiled in March 1917. DH.EUM 2 Şb 74–55, Muhiddin to Ministry of Interior, Beirut, March 12, 1917, Chief Secretariat Gen. 374 Spec. 19 Secret.

remaining Armenians were a disintegrating fragment of their former community rather than resembling just a numerically reduced population.

THE AFTERMATH

After the Ottoman defeat, the victorious allies, Armenian survivors, and the Ottoman opposition tried to bring the CUP criminals to justice. Many of the key figures, among them Talaat, had, however, fled. Others were protected by post-war Ottoman administrations. Nevertheless, some perpetrators were condemned by Ottoman courts. The government had an interest in putting the blame for the killings on the TM and Kurds, thereby exculpating the state. The proceedings produced documents that provided insights into the organization of the massacres.[73] Within months, the CUP regrouped and began, under its new name, the National Movement, a successful campaign against Armenian survivors, Greeks, and the Western powers. The CUP overcame its internal opponents and competitors for territories within the Ottoman core provinces outside the Arab-speaking regions. In the aftermath of the 1921–2 Greco-Turkish war with its huge interethnic violence, the international community sanctioned with the Treaty of Lausanne in 1923 the realities created by the CUP during the Armenian genocide, and furthered the ethnic homogenization of Anatolia by sanctioning the Greco-Turkish 'population exchange'.[74]

CONCLUSION

The Armenian deportations were not the result of an Armenian rebellion. On the contrary, Armenians were deported when no danger of outside interference existed. Thus Armenians near front lines were often slaughtered on the spot and not deported. The deportations were not a security measure against rebellions but depended on their absence. The initial deportations resembled earlier measures against Greeks, Nestorians, and Zionists. The dramatic extension of deportations in May 1915 showed signs of improvisation. No detailed regulations for the

---

[73] Osman Selim Kocahanoglu, *Divân-ı Hârb-i Örfî Muhamekatı Zabıt Ceridesi. Tehcir Yargılanmaları (1919)* (Istanbul: Temel Yayınları, 2007); Kaiser, 'Dall'impero'.

[74] See Ben Lieberman's chapter in this volume.

administration of Armenian property or the assimilation of women and children existed. The execution of deportations was largely left to provincial administrators who had to find their own means for the task at hand. Nevertheless, the CUP understood that the deportations afforded it a unique opportunity to acquire the Armenian communities' assets and finance not only the government's budget but also an ambitious demographic engineering programme, the Turkification of the empire's core provinces. Talaat viewed the negative economic consequences of the deportations as a price the government had to pay.[75]

The assimilation of Armenian children and women overwhelmed the state's resources and local Muslim initiative became decisive. Thus, many Armenian children and women entered Kurdish and Arab households while the state intended the Turkification of Armenian children and young Armenian women. Local competition for Armenian property was another field where the Turkification programme encountered sustained competition from local circles.

The central authorities monitored the deportations and tried to keep precise counts of deportees. The loss of life caused by death marching, famine, diseases, and systematic massacres along the routes appears to have been part of the government's programme. The government assigned to the deportees settlement areas in thinly populated districts with very limited arable land. Here they were not to exceed ten per cent of the Muslim population. Thus, the Ottoman authorities were faced with an Armenian 'surplus' population that could not be accommodated or assimilated. Financing Armenian deportee camps for extended periods of time was out of the question already at the start of the deportations as the Ministry of Interior had declared that it was impossible to feed the comparably few Zeitun deportees. The deaths caused by starvation were therefore not unforeseen but appear systematic.[76] The same holds true for deaths caused by disease. By May 1915, the Ottoman authorities had adequate information about the prevention of infectious diseases, particularly typhus, but deliberately exposed Armenian deportees to infection. The employment of so-called natural causes for death and massacres at remote locations in the eastern provinces, hidden from foreign observers, caused hundreds of thousands of deaths.

Nevertheless, far too many Armenians still survived and reached the lower Euphrates. Armenian resilience and a series of survival strategies as well as undercover relief work made this survival possible. In response, in the summer of 1916, the central authorities coordinated the concentration of survivors in a few localities before they were slaughtered under government supervision. However, it seems that in 1915, the CUP had no coherent single plan for the extermination of the

---

[75] Hilmar Kaiser, 'Die deutsche Diplomatie und der armenische Völkermord', in Fikret Adanır and Bernd Bonwetsch (eds), *Osmanismus, Nationalismus und der Kaukasus: Muslime und Christen, Türken und Armenier im 19. und 20. Jahrhundert* (Wiesbaden: Ludwig Reichert Verlag, 2005), 226–7.

[76] DH.ŞFR 52–292, Minister to Konia province, May 9, 1915, EUM Spec. 22.

Armenians. It is more likely that Talaat and his associates accepted mass murder as a viable policy option to be employed in case problems arose. The CUP leadership habitually opted for genocide in the interest of Turkish nationalism.

FURTHER READING

Bryce, James, and Arnold Toynbee (eds), *The Treatment of Armenians in the Ottoman Empire, 1915–1916. Documents Presented to Viscount Grey of Fallodon by Viscount Bryce*, uncensored edition, ed. and intro. Ara Sarafian (Princeton: Gomidas Institute, 2000).

Bloxham, Donald, *The Great Game of Genocide: Imperialism, Nationalism, and the Destruction of the Ottoman Armenians* (Oxford, Oxford University Press, 2005).

Captanian, Pailadzo, *Mémoires d'une déportée* (Paris : Flinikowski, 1919).

Dadrian, Vahakn N., *The History of the Armenian Genocide: Ethnic Conflict from the Balkans to Anatolia to the Caucasus* (Providence, RI/Oxford: Berghahn Books, 1995).

Kaiser, Hilmar (in collaboration with Luther and Nancy Eskijian), *At the Crossroads of Der Zor: Death, Survival, and Humanitarian Resistance in Aleppo, 1915–1917* (Princeton, NJ: Gomidas Institute, 2001).

Kévorkian, Raymond, *Le génocide des arméniens* (Paris: Odile Jacob, 2006).

Kieser, Hans-Lukas, and Dominik Schaller (eds), *Der Völkermord an den Armeniern und die Shoah* (*The Armenian Genocide and the Shoah*) (Zürich: Chronos Verlag, 2002).

Miller, Donald E., and Lorna Toryan Miller, *An Oral History of the Armenian Genocide* (Berkeley: University of California Press, 1993).

Odian, Yervant, A*ccursed Years: My Exile and Return from Der Zor, 1914–1919*, trans. Ara Stepan Melkonian, intro. Krikor Beledian (London: Gomidas Institute, 2009).

Trumpener, Ulrich, *Germany and the Ottoman Empire, 1914–1918* (Princeton: Princeton University Press, 1968).

....

CHAPTER 19

MASS DEPORTATIONS, ETHNIC CLEANSING, AND GENOCIDAL POLITICS IN THE LATER RUSSIAN EMPIRE AND THE USSR

....

NICOLAS WERTH

BETWEEN the middle of the nineteenth century and the middle of the twentieth, the immense areas of the Russian Empire and then the Soviet Union were the scene of extreme forms of state violence, though of course in very different historical contexts. This violence included massive deportations, ethnic cleansing, and famines intentionally inflicted in order to end peasant and nationalist resistance to

Soviet policies. Can we discern continuities in the policies of state violence as they were conducted by the Czarist regime and by the Bolshevik regime that issued from the revolution of October 1917?

At first sight, the categories of the population targeted by the two regimes seem very different: the Czarist state's violence was directed chiefly against ethnic minority groups, and took place in areas of 'internal colonization' on the margins of the immense Russian Empire—the Caucasus and Central Asia. In contrast, Soviet state violence was aimed first at 'class enemies' ('kulaks', 'bourgeois', and 'people of the past') in the framework of a revolutionary struggle whose objective was the 'construction of socialism'. However, if we look more closely, this difference becomes less sharp in the mid-1930s. At that time we see a remarkable change in the criteria of discrimination: class criteria are replaced by ethnic discriminations that culminate in the great wave of deportations of vast numbers of 'punished peoples' from 1941 to 1944. This change must surely be seen as paralleling the change in the Soviet political system: once 'socialism' and the 'classless society' were constructed (which had been officially proclaimed 'completed' at the Party's Seventeenth Congress in early 1934), emphasis was henceforth placed on strengthening the cohesion of the enormous 'state of nations' that the USSR had become, a new type of empire. In a context of growing international tensions, and with another world war on the horizon, the question of minorities in diaspora (Soviet citizens of Polish, German, Baltic, Korean, Chinese, Iranian, Afghan, Turkish, etc. origin) suspected of being a 'hotbed of spies and saboteurs in the pay of hostile enemy powers' became increasingly crucial.

At the same time, the problem of national minorities that were still not very 'Sovietized' twenty years after the Revolution arose with a vengeance and those involved were for the most part the same mountain peoples of the Caucasus who had given the Czarist regime so much trouble. During the 'Great Patriotic War', the Soviet regime used alleged collaboration with the German occupying forces as a pretext for dealing 'definitively' with these peoples who were resisting Sovietization by 'punishing' them, that is, by deporting all of them 'in perpetuity'. The persistence of the imperial dimension, certain unintegrated groups' resistance to Russification or Sovietization, the context of armed conflicts (colonial conquest, the First and Second World Wars)—these three parameters of 'long duration' justify our comparison of different forms of state violence over the period of a century. Nonetheless, the extraordinary magnitude of the practices of mass deportation and ethnic cleansing as a way of managing populations and territories (not to mention genocidal policies making use of famines) are particularly distinctive of the Soviet experience between 1917 and 1953. Between these two dates, more than six million people were deported, of whom a million and a half (most of them children and elderly persons) died premature deaths; six million more died as a result of famines from 1931 to 1933—famines caused not by climate but by the predatory policies of the Stalinist state. These figures must be compared with the three million people who were forced to leave their homelands or displaced as a result of policies related to ethnic cleansing during the last fifty years of the Czarist regime.

This chapter addresses the main specificities of the great episodes of deportation and ethnic cleansing in the later Russian Empire and in the Soviet Union, as well as an immense event that remained completely hidden for more than half a century, the 'man-made famines' of the early 1930s.[1] It also incorporates discussion of the applicability or otherwise of the word 'genocide' to the Ukrainian famine of 1932–3 and the deportation of the 'punished peoples' from 1941–4.

Deportations and Ethnic Cleansing in the Russian Empire (1860–1914)

It was during the final phase of the wars of conquest in the Caucasus (from the late 1850s to the early 1860s) that the Czarist regime resorted for the first time to a policy of ethnic cleansing. The latter took place in the more general framework of a 'populations policy' that sought to catalogue and classify, according to their degree of 'reliability' and 'loyalty' to the regime, the diverse peoples of the Russian Empire.[2] In 1858, Alexander II approved a plan proposed by Prince Bariatinskii, Viceroy of the Caucasus, for 'cleansing' the western Caucasus of its 'autochthonous tribes' and settling Russian colonists there. During an important military council presided over by Prince Bariatinskii in late August 1860, it was clearly indicated that 'only a policy of terror could force the tribes to leave their *auls* [mountain villages] to make room for colonists.'[3] Over five years, half a million people were forced to leave under threat: their villages were burned and razed by the army, and civilians massacred in large numbers. It is estimated that nearly two million Caucasians were driven from their homes and lands between the end of the 1850s and the end of the 1870s.[4] At the same time, several hundred thousand colonizers (Russians, Ukrainians, Cossacks) received various subsidies from the army or the state in

---

[1] The expression 'man-made famine' is James Mace's. See his pioneering article, 'The Man-Made Famine of 1932–1933: What Happened and Why', in *The Great Man-Made Famine in Ukraine*, ed. *Ukrainian Weekly* (Jersey City: Svoboda Press, 1983).

[2] Peter Holquist, 'To Count, to Extract, and to Exterminate: Population Statistics and Population Politics in Late Imperial and Soviet Russia', in Ronald Grigor Suny and Terry Martin (eds), *A State of Nations: Empire and Nation-Making in the Age of Lenin and Stalin* (Oxford: Oxford University Press, 2001), 111–44. This view is challenged by Bob Geraci in A. Dirk Moses (ed.), *Empire Colony Genocide* (New York: Berghahn, 2008).

[3] Holquist, 'To Count', 117.

[4] Ibid. 119.

exchange for settling on part of the territories that had been emptied of their inhabitants. After the conquest of the Caucasus, Central Asia became a second area for experimenting with this new 'populations policy'.[5] In the event of a major European conflict involving Russia, a certain number of preventative measures were planned (hostage-taking, massive arrests, and deportations) to dissuade any revolt on the part of the native populations considered 'unreliable'. 'Muslim natives' were not the only targets. Among the 'suspect populations' that might help the enemy and betray Russia were not only the 'Caucasian peoples' but also, on the western fringes of the Empire, Jews and Russian subjects of German origin. The First World War was to give military men an opportunity to put these theories largely into practice.

FORCED DISPLACEMENTS AND 'PREVENTATIVE DEPORTATIONS' OF JEWS AND GERMANS DURING WAR (1914–16)

During the First World War, the military authorities, which were all-powerful in areas near the front, displaced or deported about a million persons solely because of their nationality or ethnic origin. They were for the most part German or Austro-Hungarian nationals,[6] but they also included Russian subjects of German or Jewish origin who were considered 'unreliable elements'. Nonetheless, it is not always easy to reconstitute the precise context of these forced displacements. They were part of a vast exodus of civilian populations from areas near the front, a movement that was partly spontaneous and partly brought about by the 'scorched earth' policy carried out by the Russian army as it retreated.[7] The expulsions and displacements were only occasionally transformed into organized, systematic deportations. Moreover, analysis of the forced displacements and deportations brings out the crucial role played in these operations by the military, whereas the government remained divided and powerless to control the actions of army commanders, and especially those of the head of the General Staff, General Yanushkevich, who was the main instigator of this policy.

---

[5] Holquist, 'To Count', 120.

[6] This point will not be developed here. Cf. S. G. Nelipovic, 'Nemeskuju pakost' uvolit'bez neznostej...Deportacii v Rossii 1914–1917' ('Getting Rid of the German Filth without Hesitations...Deportations in Russia, 1914–1917'), *Voenno-istoriceskii Zhurnal* 1 (1997), 35–49.

[7] A. N. Kurcev, 'Bezency pervoi mirovoi voiny v Rossii, 1914–1917' ('Refugees in the First World War in Russia, 1914–1917'), *Voprosy Istorii* 8 (1999), 98–112.

The Russian army's first expulsions of Jewish communities took place in Poland, during the first weeks of the war. On 5 September 1914, the whole Jewish population of the little town of Pulawy (pop. 3,000) was forced by troops to leave within twenty-four hours and to find its own means of transportation. During the following weeks, many similar events occurred: on 14 October, in Grodzin (Warsaw province), the military authorities gave the town's 4,000 Jews three hours to clear out.[8] The commander justified these 'preventative' expulsions, which were often accompanied by violence perpetrated by the troops, by pointing out that the Jews, who spoke Yiddish, a language 'close to German', were just so many potential spies and traitors.[9] Starting in late 1914, expulsions of Jews, aggravated by the practice of taking hostages chosen among the local notables, took on a massive character in Austrian Galicia, which was temporarily occupied by Russian troops after a successful military campaign.[10] With the setbacks and then the rout of the Russian army during the summer of 1915, the expulsions of Jewish communities in areas near the front increased and were transformed in some places into genuine organized deportations using special rail convoys. Thus in a few weeks (May–June 1915), ninety-eight per cent of the 30,000 Jews living in Curland were deported to the Ukrainian province of Ekaterinoslav.[11] The expulsions and deportations of Jews culminated in September and October 1915: during these two months, the military forced the departure of several hundred thousand Jews from the province of Minsk, as well as the whole of the Jewish community of Pskov.[12] These massive deportations were often accompanied by violence indeed, veritable pogroms, which aroused the reprobation of the Prime Minister, Goremykin. The discussions among high civilian and military officials concerning the 'Jewish question' revealed, in fact, two different forms of discrimination with regard to the Jewish community: among conservative bureaucrats, there was a traditional anti-Judaism that sought to confine Jews to precisely defined regions; among the military men, there was an anti-Semitism that had more to do with the effort to identify populations considered 'suspect' and to move them away from zones of military operations.

Among the other 'suspect populations' displaced by force were Russian subjects of German origin, notably German 'colonists', farmers who had long before settled in the Polish provinces of the Empire and in western Ukraine (the provinces of Volhynia, Podolia, Kherson, and Ekaterinoslav). On 5 January 1915, the Army Chief

---

[8] Peter Gatrell, *A Whole Empire Walking. Refugees in Russia during World War I* (Bloomington: Indiana University Press, 1999), 18–22.

[9] Quoted by Eric Lohr, *Enemy Alien Politics within the Russian Empire during World War I*, PhD dissertation, Harvard University, 1999, 123.

[10] The new military governor of Lvov, Count Bobrinski, was a notorious anti-Semite and played a major role in this systematic policy of expulsions, which were accompanied by numerous pogroms.

[11] Lohr, *Enemy*, 135.

[12] Gatrell, *A Whole Empire Walking*, 23–8.

of Staff, General Yanushkevich, ordered the expulsion of not just the colonists, but all Russian subjects of German origin living in the Polish provinces. Nonetheless, the implementation of this plan was hampered by the rapid advance of the German army in Poland, starting in April and May 1915. On the other hand, in the regions remaining under the control of the Russian army, about 400,000 German colonists in the provinces of Volhynia, Podolia, and Kiev were expelled and expropriated between the summer of 1915 and the beginning of 1917.[13]

In order to assess these repressive actions, we have to recall that they took place in a context of total war, in regions near the front where the boundaries between the civilian and military spheres were largely erased, and were connected with a massive flight of civilian populations who had been driven out of their homes by the scorched earth policy followed by the retreating Russian army starting in 1915. About five million civilians joined the exodus.[14] Moreover, within the confines of the Russian Empire, the Central Powers conducted an identical policy of expelling and deporting populations considered 'suspect' or 'hostile': thus the German *Ober Ost* administration ordered the departure of hundreds of thousands of 'Slavs' from areas conquered in Poland and the Baltic countries; similarly, Austro-Hungarian authorities drove out of reconquered Galicia large parts of the Ruthenian population, which was thought favourable to the Russians.[15]

Punitive Deportations during the Civil Wars: The Emblematic Episode of 'De-Cossackization' (1919–20)

The end of the 'imperialist war', made official by the Treaty of Brest-Litovsk in March 1918, went almost unnoticed by Russian society in the midst of revolution, the armed conflict being continued along shifting fronts via a civil war that had already begun. At that time, the boundaries between the front and the rear areas, between the civilian and the military spheres, had disappeared.[16] The civil war that began in the spring of 1918 was far more than a military conflict between two structured camps, that of the Revolution (the 'Reds') and that of the

---

[13] Lohr, *Enemy*, 140.
[14] Gatrell, *A Whole Empire Walking*, 145.
[15] Holquist, 'To Count', 124–6.
[16] On these processes, cf. Nicolas Werth, 'Les déserteurs en Russie: violence de guerre, violence révolutionnaire et violence paysanne (1916–1921)', in Stéphane Audoin-Rouzeau et al. (eds), *La violence de guerre, 1914–1945* (Bruxelles-Paris: Complexe/IHTP, 2002), 99–117.

Counter-Revolution (the 'Whites'). It was in reality an extraordinarily complex overlapping of various forms of conflict. If none of the camps involved had a monopoly on violence, only the Bolshevik revolutionary project, which was based on a theory of civil war, indeed, a 'scientific' vision of society and the cult of the strong state, provided the coherence necessary for conceiving certain planned operations of social engineering such as 'de-Cossackization'—an unprecedented attempt to eliminate, by means of 'mass terror' and deportation,[17] a social group that had a specific organization and its own status. This is not the place to recount the history of this project,[18] but rather to highlight a few striking characteristics that make de-Cossackization an important stage in the history of the practices of deportation.

Some of the Cossacks (particularly the Cossacks of Kuban) who had been stripped in December 1917 of the advantageous status they had enjoyed under the old regime,[19] and whom the Bolsheviks had classed as 'kulaks' and 'class enemies', joined the White forces that had been assembled in southern Russia during the spring of 1918. During the Red Army's advance towards Ukraine and southern Russia in early 1919, punitive detachments of special Cheka troops exterminated tens of thousands of Cossacks in the Don region. These operations were not measures of military retaliation taken in the heat of combat; they were a response to a political directive issued at the highest level of the Party (the Orgburo of the Central Committee) on 24 January 1919. This secret directive gave the order to 'implement mass terror against the rich Cossacks who will have to be exterminated and physically liquidated down to the last one, and in general, against all Cossacks who have participated directly or indirectly in the struggle against Soviet power'.[20] Confronted by this orgy of violence, the Cossacks along the Don rebelled. Operating behind the Red Army, which was fighting General Denikin's troops farther south, the insurgent Cossacks made a major contribution to the striking successes of the White armies during the summer of 1919. To weaken the Cossacks, Iosif Reingold, the chairman of the Revolutionary Committee of the Don,[21] proposed playing on the antagonism between the Cossacks and their non-Cossack neighbours and implementing, along with 'Red Terror', a policy of 'rearranging' Cossack territories and deportation. This policy was experimented with towards the end of 1920, after the final defeat of the White armed forces. In October and November 1920, five Cossack *stanitsy* (large towns) in the Terek region (North

---

[17] The expression 'mass terror' is used in the secret directive issued by the Orgburo of the Central Committee of the Bolshevik Party, 24 January 1919. Cf: *Izvestia TsK KPSS* 6 (1989), 177–8.

[18] On de-Cossackization, cf: Peter Holquist, 'Conduct merciless mass terror: decossackization on the Don, 1919', *Cahiers du monde russe* 28:1–2 (1997), 127–62; V. L. Genis, 'Raskazacivanie v Sovetskoi Rossii' ('The de-Cossackization in Soviet Russia'), *Voprosy Istorii* 1 (1994), 42–56; N. F. Bugaï and A. M. Gonov, *Kavkaz: narody v eselonax (The Caucasus: Deported Peoples)* (Moscow: Insan, 1998), 81–96.

[19] Having the privilege to bear arms, to self-organize, and receiving a considerable quantity of land.

[20] The text of this circular can be found in *Izvestia TsK KPSS* 6 (1989), 177–8.

[21] RGASPI, 5/2/106/7.

Caucasus) were entirely emptied of their inhabitants (9,000 families, or about 45,000 persons). All the men between the ages of eighteen and fifty were deported to the Donets Basin, where they were forced to work in the mines. As for the women, the elderly, and the children, they were expelled 'with authorization to settle in other towns further north'.[22] All the deportees' livestock was confiscated. Their houses and lands were redistributed to non-Cossacks, and especially to the neighbouring Chechens, 'who have always shown their deep attachment to the Soviet government', the responsible military officer noted.[23] In order to make the irreversible character of this deportation clear, the names of the Cossack *stanitsy* were changed. Finally, to make an example, the *stanitsa* Kalinovskaia, considered the most 'hostile' to Soviet power, was completely razed.

It will be noted, however, that given the size of the country and the extreme violence of the civil war, these punitive deportations remained relatively limited. Despite its successes, in 1920 the Bolshevik regime hesitated to engage in another test of strength with the Cossack community which had been weakened but was still ready to defend itself by force of arms. Moreover, as is shown by the field reports submitted by the head of the deportation operations in October and November 1920, the logistics were notoriously inadequate for carrying out large-scale deportations.[24] De-Cossackization remained a large project that was never fully carried out.

The 'Liquidation of the Kulaks as a Class' (1930–2)

'De-kulakization' or the 'liquidation of the kulaks as a class' was part of the Bolshevik government's offensive against part of the peasantry, which began during the civil war and was momentarily interrupted by the NEP 'truce' declared by the regime in 1921 when it was confronted by the magnitude of peasant resistance. However, the context was different: whereas in 1920–1 large segments of the peasantry were actively resisting Bolshevik policy, in 1929–30 it was a peasant society that had been pacified that was the target of the Stalinist Revolution 'from above'. To justify his attack, Stalin referred to the 'threat' that 'kulaks' posed to the very survival of the Soviet regime, which was being strangled by the

---

[22] The rest of the group was authorized to 'settle' in villages at least fifty kilometres away.

[23] Order issued on 23 October 1920 by General Medvedev, the officer responsible for the operation (RGASPI, 85/ 11/131/ 11).

[24] The slowness of the operations of deportations is explained by the lack of railway cars.

kulaks' deliberate refusal to sell their wheat to the state. Stalin and many Party leaders were still traumatized by the threat of starvation experienced by many town dwellers during the civil war and wanted to ensure that never again would such a possibility recur.

The de-kulakization campaign begun towards the end of 1929 had in reality a twofold objective: to 'extract' (the term used in official directives) the elements likely to resist the collectivization of the countryside being launched at the same time, and to 'colonize' the vast, inhospitable areas of Siberia, the Great North, the Urals, and Kazakhstan. The first objective corresponded to the view, clearly expressed by the Bolsheviks when they took power, that peasant society contained 'exploitative elements' that were irremediably hostile to the regime and that had to be 'liquidated'. The second objective was, in a more contextual manner and in connection with the launching of the first Five Year Plan, part of a vast project of using labour provided by prisoners or deportees to develop the country's inhospitable areas, which were rich in natural resources.[25] In this context, expropriation and deportation were chosen as the principal modalities for liquidating the kulaks as a class. In three years (1930–2), more than five million kulaks were expropriated, more than two and a half million men, women, and children deported, and several hundred thousand arrested and sent to camps. At the end of January 1930, each region received, from the Party's highest political authority, the Politburo, 'quotas for de-kulakization in the first and second categories'. The 'first-category kulaks', defined as 'activists engaged in counter-revolutionary actions', were to be arrested and transferred to camps after a 'rapid appearance before a *troika*' (a special court under the jurisdiction of the political police), or even 'shot, in the case of the most hardened among them, who are likely to resist'. The 'second-category kulaks', defined as 'rich peasants, but less actively engaged in counter-revolutionary activities', were to be arrested, expropriated, and deported, along with their families, to remote regions of the country.

To carry out these arrests and deportations, a veritable military logistics, unprecedented in peacetime and mobilizing hundreds of rail convoys and tens of thousands of special troops provided by the OGPU, was set up. However, the vast scale of this project led to immense problems in coordinating the militarized operations of deportation carried out by the OGPU and the settlement of the deportees, which was left to the initiative of local authorities who were overwhelmed or indifferent. Thus 'deportation-colonization' often became 'deportation-abandonment': hundreds of thousands of deportees were left to their fate on the steppes or in the taiga, along railway tracks, without regular food supplies or

---

[25] On de-kulakization, cf. in particular the collections of documents published under the direction of V. P. Danilov, *Tragedia sovetskoï derevni* (*The Tragedy of the Soviet Countryside*), vol iii: 1930–1933 (Moscow: Rosspen, 2002); idem, *Sovetskaia derevnia glazami VCK-OGPU-NKVD* (*The Soviet Countryside seen by the Cheka-OGPU-NKVD*), vol. iii: 1930–1931 (Moscow: Rosspen, 2003).

work. Epidemics and shortages (and even, in some cases, famine) decimated the deportees, first of all the children and the elderly. About fifteen per cent of the deportees died during the first year. In the following years, the deportees' conditions improved very little. They were given a 'special status' that made them veritable social pariahs, 'special displaced persons' (their official name); were stripped of their civil rights; were forbidden to leave 'special villages' that were generally isolated from everything in the most remote regions of Siberia, the Great North, or Kazakhstan; and were subjected to a veritable forced labour in agricultural or industrial structures controlled by the OGPU. The archives of the Department of Special Populations attached to the Gulag mention very heavy losses among the deportees: in 1930–1, more than 500,000 had disappeared, died, or escaped out of the two million peasants deported; in 1932, more than 200,000 escapees, nearly 100,000 deaths (or an annual mortality rate of eight per cent); in 1933, more than 200,000 escapees and more than 150,000 deaths (or a mortality rate of fourteen per cent)! Let us add that children, and especially infants, constituted the largest portion of the deaths. In 1933, for example, the annual rate of infant mortality in the special villages for deportees in Western Siberia reached sixty per cent![26] These few figures give some idea of this great operation of social engineering that was supposed to eliminate a social class, and beyond that, to subject the peasantry as a whole to an unprecedented expropriation.

THE GREAT FAMINES OF 1931–3

Between 1931 and 1933, more than six million people, the great majority of them peasants and livestock-raisers, died of hunger in the Soviet Union as a result of terrible famines. In 1931, the first famines struck Kazakhstan, the most important livestock-raising area in the USSR, where the collectivization of the herds resulted in a decline of eighty-five per cent in the number of animals in only three years.[27] Between 1930 and 1933, the population of Kazakhstan, estimated at six and half million at the end of the 1920s, dropped by two million (600,000 fled; 1,400,000 died of hunger or in epidemics). That is, the population decreased by thirty per cent—a proportion unequalled elsewhere, in any of the regions of the USSR struck by the shortages and famines following the forced collectivization of the countryside. Beginning in spring 1932, famine resulting from excessive State procurements

---

[26] Juri Poliakov (ed.), *Naselenie Rossii v XX veke* (*The Population of Russia in the Twentieth Century*), vol i (Moscow: Rosspen, 2000), 278–80.

[27] On the famine in Kazakhstan, cf. Isabelle Ohayon, *Du nomadisme au socialisme. Sédentarisation, collectivisation et acculturation des Kazakhs en URSS, 1928–1945* (Paris: Maisonneuve, 2006).

reached not only Western Siberia[28] and the regions of the lower and middle Volga (300,000 to 400,000 deaths in one year), but also the rich plains of Kuban, in the North Caucasus, which were administratively connected to Russia, but populated mainly by Ukrainians and Cossacks (400,000 to 500,000 deaths), and the Ukraine (3.5 million to 3.8 million deaths).

In 2006, the Parliament of the Republic of Ukraine officially recognized that the famine of 1932–3 was a genocide perpetrated by Stalin's regime against the Ukrainian people. The term used today in Ukraine to designate this famine, *Holodomor*, is explicit: it combines the words *holod* (hunger) and *moryty* (to kill by privations, to starve, to exhaust). Thus it clearly emphasizes the intentional aspect of the phenomenon. The description of the 1932–3 famine as a genocide is not, however, universally accepted among historians who have studied the question, whether they be Russians, Ukrainians, or Westerners. We can distinguish two main interpretive trends. In one camp are historians who see the famine as having been artificially organized by Stalin's regime in 1930 to break the back of the Ukrainian peasants' resistance, which was particularly strong, to the kolkhoz system and in addition, to destroy the Ukrainian nation in its 'peasant-national' specificity, which constituted a serious obstacle to the transformation of the Soviet Union into an imperial state of a new kind, dominated by Russia. These historians adhere to the genocide thesis. In the other camp are historians who, while recognizing the criminal nature of Stalin's policies, consider it necessary to study all the famines of the years 1930–3 (in Kazakhstan, Ukraine, part of Western Siberia, and the Volga regions) as a complex phenomenon in which several factors, ranging from the geopolitical situation to the imperatives of industrialization, played an important role alongside Stalin's 'imperial intentions'.[29] For these historians, the term 'genocide' is not appropriate to describe the famine of 1932–3 in Ukraine and Kuban.

A third position is emerging. As Andrea Graziosi rightly suggests, in light of the most recent research, it is possible to propose a way of moving beyond the two main existing lines of interpretation. According to Graziosi, who draws particularly on the work of the American historian Terry Martin[30] as well as on that of the Ukrainian historians Juri Shapoval and Vassili Vassiliev,[31] from the late summer of 1932 on, the Ukrainian famine is characterized by a high degree of specificity with regard to Soviet famines as a whole during the period from 1931 to 1933. The latter (including the terrible Kazakh famine) appear to be direct but unforeseen,

[28] On the famine in Western Siberia, cf. M. K. Malyseva and V. S. Poznansii, *Kazaki-bezentsy ot goloda v Zapadnoi Sibiri, 1931–1934* (Almaty: Iz. Terra, 1999).

[29] On the development of historical writing on the Ukrainian famine, Andrea Graziosi, 'Les famines soviétiques de 1931–1933 et le *Holodomor* ukrainien. Une nouvelle interprétation est-elle possible et quelles en seraient les conséquences?', *Cahiers du monde russe* 46:3 (2005), 453–72.

[30] Terry Martin, *The Affirmative Action Empire. Nations and Nationalism in the Soviet Union, 1923–1939* (Ithaca, NY/London: Cornell University Press, 2001).

[31] Yuri Shapoval and Valeri Vasiliev, *Komandiri velikogo golodu* (Kiiv: Geneza, 2001).

unprogrammed, *unintentional* consequences of policies inspired by ideology that had been implemented since the end of 1929: forced collectivization, de-kulakization, sedentarization of nomads and semi-nomads (in Kazakhstan), and the imposition of the kolkhoz system, which the peasants saw as a 'second form of serfdom', arbitrary or totally disproportionate levies on their harvests of cereals and on their herds.

Until the summer of 1932, the Ukrainian famine, which was already underway, was related to other famines that began earlier. But starting in August and September 1932, the Ukrainian famine changed in nature when Stalin developed his 'national interpretation of the famine' (Terry Martin). As is shown by the recently published correspondence between Stalin and his main aides during the summer of 1932,[32] Stalin then persuaded himself that a vast resistance front ranging from simple kolkhozians to Ukrainian communist leaders had been constituted in Ukraine in order to refuse to deliver to the state the agricultural products necessary to supply food for the cities and for export. In a letter sent to Lazar Kaganovitch on 11 August 1932, Stalin went so far as to write: 'We are in danger of losing the Ukraine—"the party, the state, and even the organs of the political police and the republic" are infested with nationalist agents and Polish spies.'[33] Henceforth, Stalin had made up his mind to use the weapon of hunger, to aggravate the famine that was beginning, to instrumentalize it, to *intentionally amplify it* in order to punish the peasants who, according to him, were 'carrying on a war of sabotage against the Soviet government . . . , a war to the death'.[34] His two closest collaborators, Vyacheslav Molotov and Lazar Kaganovitch, were sent to Ukraine and the North Caucasus as 'plenipotentiaries' charged with 'purging' and bringing into line the local communist organizations that were 'dragging their feet'—and sometimes even refusing to implement excessive plans for cereals deliveries. Reinforcements composed of 'activists' were sent from Russia, and armed detachments of the political police engaged in veritable punitive actions in the Ukrainian kolkhozes in order to requisition all the available wheat, including seed grain for the next harvest.[35] If the peasants were hardest hit—by hunger, leading to the death, under the most atrocious conditions, of millions of persons—repression also affected

[32] R. W. Davies, O. Khlevniuk, et al. (eds), *Stalin i Kaganovich. Perepiska, 1931–1936* (Moscow: Rosspen, 2001).

[33] Martin, *The Affirmative Action Empire*.

[34] Ibid. 273–4.

[35] In this respect, a document recently exhumed from the archives seems to be fundamental. This is a secret directive issued by Stalin on 22 January 1933, ordering 'an immediate end to the massive exodus of peasants fleeing Ukraine and Kuban on the pretext that they are looking for bread. The Central Committee and the Council of the People's Commissars', Stalin wrote, 'have proof that this exodus from Ukraine is being organized by enemies of the Soviet government, socialist-revolutionaries and Polish agents, for the purposes of propaganda intended to discredit, by means of the peasants fleeing toward regions of the USSR north of Ukraine, the kolkhoz system in particular and the Soviet system in general' (RGASPI, 558/11/45/109).

local officials and Ukrainian intellectuals who were arrested and imprisoned. In December 1932, two secret decrees issued by the Politburo put an end—in Ukraine and in Ukraine only—to the policy of 'indigenizing' managers that had been pursued since 1923 in all the federal republics; Ukrainian 'nationalism' was firmly condemned.

Recent research undoubtedly shows the strong specificity of the Ukrainian case, at least from the second half of 1932 on. On the basis of these new elements, how should we describe the whole of the measures Stalin's regime took to punish by hunger and terror the Ukrainian peasantry as an ethnically defined group, measures whose result was the death of more than four million people in Ukraine and the North Caucasus? The crucial point—so far as the use of the term genocide is concerned—on which historians, including Ukrainian historians, differ is this: Did Stalin target the peasants of Ukraine and Kuban qua peasants or qua Ukrainians? For some historians, the main objective of the famine was to break down peasant resistance, not national resistance. Other historians insist, on the contrary, that the peasants of Ukraine and Kuban were targeted first of all as Ukrainians; for Stalin the question of the Ukrainian peasantry was in fact 'essentially a national question, the peasantry constituting the main force behind the nationalist movement.'[36] Breaking the Ukrainian peasantry amounted to breaking the most powerful nationalist movement capable of opposing the process of constructing the Soviet Union.[37] This specifically anti-Ukrainian orientation, these historians conclude, allows us to describe as genocide the whole of the political actions Stalin's regime undertook intentionally, starting at the end of the summer of 1932, to punish by hunger and terror the Ukrainian peasantry, actions whose consequence was the death of more than four million persons in Ukraine and the North Caucasus.

DEPORTATIONS AS 'CLEANSING' AND 'MAKING SECURE' THE USSR'S BORDER AREAS (1935–9)

Beginning in 1935, the Soviet regime launched a number of deportations aimed at 'cleansing' the Soviet Union's border areas (which were increasingly seen as veritable front lines) of their 'ethnically and socially suspect elements'. Since 1923,

[36] On these divergent interpretations, cf. Roman Serbyn, 'The Ukrainian Famine of 1932–1933 as Genocide in the Light of the UN Convention of 1948', *Ukrainian Quarterly* 62:2 (2006), 87–106.

[37] According to the letter sent by Stalin to the writer Cholokhov on 6 May 1933, quoted in N. Werth, 'Un Etat contre son peuple', in S. Courtois and N. Werth et al. (eds), *Le Livre Noir du Communisme* (Paris: R. Laffont, 1997), 237–8.

the border areas—twenty-two kilometres deep—had been put under a special system of surveillance carried out by border guards connected with the political police. Starting in 1934, this system was further strengthened. In February and March 1935, several operations were begun to cleanse the borders considered most strategic (the region around Leningrad, the Soviet–Polish border). In the Leningrad region, an initial operation resulted in the deportation of some 3,500 families of Finnish, Latvian, or Estonian origin, who were sent to Kazakhstan, Siberia, and Tajikistan.[38] At the same time, 8,300 families (41,650 individuals) were deported from the border districts around Kiev and Vinnitsa to eastern Ukraine; citizens of Polish and German origin represented more than half the deportees, the others being classified as 'socially alien elements'.[39] In these first operations, which were still limited and selective, the ethnic criterion was 'blended' with class considerations, which were more accepted in communist political culture. Thus among the Soviet citizens of Finnish origin deported from the Leningrad region were first of all the 'individual' peasants who had not joined the kolkhozes, small craftsmen, individuals deprived of the vote, and other representatives of socially stigmatized groups. The cleansing operations in border areas were continued and expanded in 1936, encompassing 20,000 families from the Leningrad region and Western Ukraine.[40] Officially, 'administratively transferred' contingents—to use the NKVD's bureaucratic terminology—were not assimilated *stricto sensu* to the 'special displaced persons', expropriated and stripped of the civil rights. A few concessions were made to ease their resettlement. Nevertheless, the sole fact that they were under the administrative control of the office for 'special populations of the Gulag' and that they were required to stay put for an indefinite period, made their condition very similar to that of the special displaced persons.

The obsession with cleansing the border areas to prevent 'enemy agents' from infiltrating the country within the various diasporas (Polish, German, Finnish, Baltic, Romanian, Korean) grew still stronger in 1937–8, the years of the Great Terror. Several hundred thousand Soviet citizens of Polish, German, Baltic, Finnish, or Romanian origin, along with many other citizens who had (or had earlier had) any professional, familial, or simply geographic (inhabitants of border regions were particularly vulnerable) connection with countries identified as hostile, were arrested and executed.[41] In this repressive context of unprecedented violence (let us recall that in 1937–8, more than a million and a half individuals were arrested by the NKVD, about half of whom were executed), the collective deportation of some 200,000 persons expelled from border areas seems almost anodyne. In September

[38] Martin, *Affirmative Action Empire*, 333.
[39] Ibid. 330.
[40] GARF, 9479/1/36/12–16.
[41] Cf. Nicolas Werth, 'Repenser la Grande Terreur', *Le Débat* 122 (November–December 2002), 118–39.

and October 1937, the great programme of deportation struck the Korean community that had settled in the border districts on the Soviet Far East (the regions of Vladivostok, Khabarovsk, and Birobidzhan). In a secret resolution passed by the Central Committee on 21 August 1937, this massive deportation was justified by the fact that the Koreans constituted 'a hotbed of spies and diversionists' for the Japanese secret services, which were said to be 'particularly active since the occupation of Manchuria by Japanese troops'. For the first time, the totality of a national minority—no less than 172,000 individuals—was deported to Uzbekistan or Kazakhstan.[42] The Koreans were settled, under precarious conditions, in settlement villages and kolkhozes specially reserved for them.

Deportations of Populations to Territories Annexed Following the German–Soviet Non-Aggression Pact (1940–1)

In the instructions he gave in September 1939 to NKVD officers charged with Sovietizing the western Ukraine and Belarus, Vsevolod Merkulov, the head of State Security, emphasized the historical importance of the operations about to be undertaken: in a few months, the NKVD was going to complete a cleansing of the country's enemies that the USSR's 'organs' had worked on for twenty years. All the repressive measures that had been tried out since 1917 would have to be used. However, the political, operational, and logistic expertise that had been acquired over two decades made it possible to predict victory over the enemy.[43]

These instructions help us understand the exemplary shortcut represented by the deportations carried out in the territories annexed by the USSR after the German–Soviet Non-Aggression Pact. For the first time, the repressive practices that had been widely tested on Soviet society were exported. Their brutality profoundly traumatized Polish, Latvian, Lithuanian, and Estonian societies that were subjected to Sovietization; but for the occupation authorities, the policies implemented were only duplicating, in an almost routine way, measures already being applied to Soviet citizens, without crossing any additional threshold of violence.

[42] Martin, *Affirmative Action Empire*, 333.
[43] RGANI, 89/18/1/ 3–6.

In the wake of the mass killings committed by the NKVD two years earlier in the context of the 'secret repressive operations' of the Great Terror (within sixteen months, between 700,000 and 800,000 persons were executed in the USSR), about 25,000 Polish citizens belonging to Poland's military, political, and economic elites who had been incarcerated in three 'special camps' in Kozielsk, Ostachkov and Starobielsk, were executed in April 1940 as 'sworn enemies of the Soviet system'.[44] In addition, between September 1939 and June 1941, about 110,000 persons were arrested and sentenced by the NKVD's special courts. A detailed analysis of these sentences allows us to draw two main conclusions. If the Polish social and political elites were particularly affected in the first months of the Sovietization of Poland, during which the 'revolutionary criterion' ('crushing the dominant classes of the bourgeois state') was pushed all the way, the Jews, who were suspect as 'speculators', 'Bundists', or 'Zionists', were also widely repressed (contrary to a notion long put about, according to which a Jewish minority was supposed to have 'profited' from the Soviet occupation), as were Ukrainians and Belorussians, when they were classified as kulaks or 'nationalists'.[45] Moreover, a study of the distribution of the punishments inflicted by the NKVD's special courts and by military tribunals from 1939 to 1941 shows that sentences handed down were not more severe for foreign nationals in an occupied country than for Soviet citizens arrested at the same time.[46]

A third form of repression used in occupied Poland, the deportation of some 320,000 Poles (and 80,000 Balts and Moldavians in other territories annexed by the USSR in 1940) was also carried out in accord with a schema that had already been thoroughly tested over the preceding years. From February 1940 to June 1941, four major deportation operations were organized, each targeting specific categories of the population that had become suspect in the eyes of the authorities. The first operation, implemented on 10 February 1940, was supposed to concern primarily a particular group of 'colonists and military foresters' to whom the Polish government had granted lands in border districts as a reward for their services during the Soviet–Polish war of 1920. In reality, the 27,000 families (about 140,000 individuals) deported in February 1940 represented a much larger contingent of socially alien elements (landowners, industrialists, government officials, policemen). The sources used by A. Gurianov[47] enable us to follow with great precision the preparations for these deportations, the planning for the assignment of contingents

[44] Among the most complete studies on this period, see R. G. Pikhoia, V. P. Kozlov et al. (eds), *Katyn* (Moscow: Fond Demokratia, 1997).

[45] O. A. Gorlanov and A. B. Roginskii, 'Ob arestax v zapadnyx zonax Belorussii I Ukrainy v 1939–1941 g', in A. E. Gurianov (ed.), *Repressii protiv Poliakov I pol'skix grazdan* (Moscow: Zvenia, 1997), 77–113.

[46] Ibid. 105.

[47] A. Gurianov, 'Polskie specpereselentsy v SSSR v 1940–1941' ('Polish Special Displaced Persons in the USSR in 1940–1941'), in *Repressii*. 124.

to hundreds of 'colonization villages' distributed over twenty-four regions from Arkhangelsk to Irkutsk, and the setting up of logistics (convoys, police forces, lists of persons to be deported) that were intended to avoid a new 'deportation-abandonment' and to 'rationalize the economic management of the contingents'.[48] This rationalization, much vaunted in bureaucratic reports, should not lead us to forget the suffering endured by the deportees, both during the journey and when they arrived. From 1 March 1940 to 1 July 1941, the office of 'special settlements' registered, among the contingent deported in February 1940, 10,864 deaths, or 7.7 per cent of the total number of persons deported.[49]

A second operation provided for the deportation before 15 April of three new categories that were very different but each bore a stigma on the scale of exclusion: the stigma of class, for the families of Polish officers taken prisoner, the stigma of being high officials in the state apparatus, the stigma of being large landowners or industrialists who had been arrested (and on the point of being executed in the three camps where they had been regrouped);[50] for prostitutes, the stigma of being 'social parasites'; for refugees from western Poland who had moved into the zone of Soviet occupation and who had tried to return to the German zone but had been turned back, the stigma of being migrants.[51] This operation was implemented on 13 April; about 61,000 persons were deported. In contrast to the first contingent, which had been assigned to colonization villages with the status of special displaced persons, this second contingent, composed chiefly of women, the elderly, and children, was scattered over hundreds of kolkhozes and other small factory towns in Kazakhstan, which further increased the total isolation of these families of outcasts, impoverished and knowing nothing about what had happened to their loved ones. A third operation, implemented on 28 and 29 June 1940, targeted mainly Polish refugees, most of them of Jewish origin, who had sought refuge in the Soviet zone to escape Nazi persecution. These refugees were suspect in the eyes of the Soviet occupation authorities for several reasons: because of their social position, their vocations (many of them were merchants or professionals), their political past (Bundists and Zionists were rather numerous among the Jewish intelligentsia), and their refusal—which was frequent—to adopt Soviet nationality and to conform to 'Soviet legislation regarding passports' (which forbade them, among other things, residence in large cities). In the framework of this third great operation of deportation, about 75,000 refugees (eighty-four per cent of which

---

[48] Resolution of the Council of the People's Commissars no. 2122–617 ss, 29 December 1939 (GARF, 5446/1/510/ 163–165).

[49] Gurianov, 'Polskie specpereselentsy', 118–19; N. Bugaï, *L.Beria-I.Stalinu, Soglasno vasemu ukazaniju . . . (L. Beria to J. Stalin, 'In accord with your instructions . . .')* (Moscow: AIRO-XX, 1995), 12–13.

[50] Werth, 'Un Etat contre son peuple', 234–5.

[51] Gurianov, 'Polskie specpereselency', 116–17.

were Jews) were deported to various regions of northern Russian and Siberia, and confined to colonization villages.[52]

Finally, between 22 May and 20 June 1941, the NKVD implemented a fourth great operation of deportation that was particularly ambitious because it concerned not only the territories of Ukraine and Belarus that had been attached to Poland between 1920 and 1939, but also Moldavia (annexed from Romania in August 1940) and the three Baltic countries incorporated into the USSR in 1940. The deportation plan ratified by the Politburo on 16 May 1941 defines ten categories of individuals to be arrested, sent to a camp, or deported. Most of these categories had already been used in the earlier operations; the places where the deportees were to be assigned or interned varied depending on the categories defined. In all, between 22 May and 20 June 1941, between 105,000 and 110,000 persons—including about 45,000 Poles—were arrested. Of this number, about 20,000 were sent to a camp, and 85,000 to 90,000 deported to Siberia (the regions of Novossibirsk, the Altai, Omsk, and Krasnoiarsk) and Kazakhstan.[53] When the last convoys of deportees from western Belarus, which had been Polish territory, passed through Minsk on 22 June 1941, the German invasion of the USSR had already begun.

TOTAL ETHNIC DEPORTATIONS OF 'PUNISHED PEOPLES' DURING THE 'GREAT PATRIOTIC WAR'

In the course of the Great Patriotic War, more than two million Soviet citizens belonging to ethnic minorities accused of being a hotbed of potential agents for the Nazi invader (Soviet citizens of German origin),[54] or of having 'collaborated with the occupier' (Chechens, Ingushes, Kalmyks, Balkars, Karachays, Crimean Tatars) were deported and confined to special villages in one of the inhospitable regions of the country, thus joining the vast cohort of special displaced persons. In comparison with the deportations analysed up to this point, those carried out between 1941 and 1944 have a number of specific characteristics, the most remarkable of which is no doubt that they were aimed at destroying whole national minorities that had been declared to be 'enemies of the Soviet regime'. The goal was not to physically eliminate all the individuals belonging to these national groups, but rather to make

---

[52] See note 49.

[53] A. Gurianov, 'Masctaby deportatsii naselenija v glub' SSSR, mai-ijun' 1941' ('The Scope of the Deportation of Populations to Remote Regions of the USSR in May–June 1941'), in *Repressii*, 149–60.

[54] Werth, 'Un Etat contre son peuple', 241.

the 'punished' nation disappear as such, to exclude it from the 'great family of Soviet socialist nationalities'. The three waves of deportation took place between the summer of 1941 and the end of 1944. The first of these (September 1941 to March 1942) struck all Soviet citizens of German origin (more than a million persons), who were deported to Kazakhstan or Siberia. Since Soviets of German origin were relatively widely dispersed over a large area (about a third of them lived in the German autonomous region of the Volga, but the other two-thirds were distributed over a dozen regions), the NKVD, with the approval of the highest state authorities, began a whole series of targeted deportations, region by region, prepared several weeks in advance, and implemented on the basis of lists provided by various offices. In order to ensure that the cleansing would be as complete as possible, the NKVD went so far as to hunt up and arrest several tens of thousands of soldiers and officers of German origin serving in the Soviet army. Some of the deportees, those most capable of working were, in addition, put into the battalions of the 'labor army' in which living and working conditions were similar to those in the camps of the Gulag.[55]

From November 1943 to June 1944, a second wave of deportations (about 900,000 persons) struck six non-Slavic peoples (Kalmyks, Karachays, Balkars, Chechens, Ingush, Crimean Tatars) who were accused of 'collective collaboration' with the enemy during the brief period when their regions had been under partial German occupation. This was the pretext under which the government sought to 'definitively settle'[56] the question of these areas that were little Sovietized and poorly controlled, despite frequent police raids.

The third wave of deportations (July–November 1944) was more limited (it affected about 200,000 persons) and was part of the policy, already largely implemented during the second half of the 1930s, of 'securitizing border zones'. The deportees included notably the Bulgar, Greek, and Armenian communities along the coast of the Black Sea, as well as Turkish–Mezkheti, Khemshin, and Kurd minorities that had settled along the borders with Turkey and Iran.

In November 1948, a decree issued by the Presidium of the Supreme Soviet of the USSR stipulated that the 'peoples punished during the Great Patriotic War' would keep their defamatory status 'in perpetuity'. This decision implied that every member of the punished community transmitted, from one generation to the next, the 'collective crime' committed by his ancestors. But can we deduce from this that 'elements of racial politics had surreptitiously slipped into Stalinist ethnic cleansing'?[57] An analysis of Stalinist policy regarding nationalities indicates that the regime did not persecute this or that people because of alleged 'biological defects'.

---

[55] P. Polian, *Ne po svoiei vole. Istoria i geografija prinuditel'nyx migratsii v SSSR* (Moscow: OGI Memorial, 2001), 114–15.

[56] In the terms used by Bogdan Kobulov, Vice-Minister of the Interior, who was responsible for the deportation of the Chechens and the Ingushes in February 1944, among other things.

[57] Eric Weitz, 'Racial Politics without the Concept of Race', *Slavic Review* 61:1 (2002), 18.

Its goal was not to eliminate this or that race or ethnic group, but rather to eradicate any form or manifestation of ethnic or national particularism that might hamper the project of constructing a community of Soviet socialist nationalities and slow the realization of the communist utopia. Based on the conviction that nationalities, like social classes, were socio-historical formations and not racial or biological entities, the treatment inflicted on 'punished peoples' or 'enemy nations' was more closely related to a form of 'ethno-historical excision'.[58] The regime sought more to eradicate the national, cultural, and historical identities of a community than to physically eliminate every one of its members. This probably explains why a regime perfectly capable of implementing vast genocidal operations did not set up extermination camps on the Nazi model.

Nevertheless, a few historians think that the deportations and ethnic cleansing of the Soviet punished peoples, whose intentional nature is indubitably documented, along with all the planning stages and the implementation, constitute genocides in the sense defined by the UN Convention.[59] They argue that in these operations the Soviet regime was 'deliberately inflicting on the group conditions of life calculated to bring about its physical destruction in whole or in part', recalling, for example, that of the 600,000 persons deported from the Caucasus from late 1943 to early 1944, 147,000 (almost a quarter) were dead four years later (the highest death rate being that among children); whereas only 28,000 births were registered![60]

What these differing interpretations among historians show is both the weaknesses of the definition of genocide adopted in 1948—a definition at the same time too restrictive and too general—and the porous nature of the borderline between ethnic cleansing and genocide. As Norman Naimark has rightly noted, 'ethnic cleansing opens the way to genocide, mass crimes necessarily being involved in emptying a land of its people.'[61]

A rapidly drawn up inventory of the deportations, ethnic cleansings, and genocidal policies conducted by the Soviet regime is devastating. One observation is inescapable: the distinction between peacetime and wartime no longer appears pertinent when one is studying the specific form of mass violence constituted by massive deportations of groups considered to be socially or ethnically 'alien' to the national community. Over the years, deportations became a more or less permanent way of managing not only these groups, but also territories. In this respect, they differ radically from the forced displacements of populations implemented by the Czarist regime during its wars of colonial conquest (in the Caucasus, and to a lesser extent, in Central Asia) and from the preventative deportations organized by

---

[58] See Francine Hirsch, 'Race without the Practice of Racial Politics', ibid. 40.

[59] See, for example, J. Otto Pohl, *Ethnic Cleansing in the USSR, 1937–1939* (Westport CT: Greenwood, 1999).

[60] On these figures, cf. Werth, 'Un Etat contre son peuple', 244.

[61] Norman Naimark, *Fires of Hatred: Ethnic Cleansing in Twentieth-Century Europe* (Cambridge, MA: Harvard University Press, 2001), 87.

Russian military authorities during the First World War. Every repressive project whose genesis, degree of intentionality, preparation, execution, and consequences we can now reconstruct on the basis of archival documents that have recently been made available must naturally be situated in its specific historical context and analysed in its *continuum* and its duration. The Soviet example has in any event one great advantage: it shows the juridical frameworks and the definitions laboriously worked out by political scientists and historians in order to 'classify' crimes perpetrated by governments remain generally unsatisfactory when confronted by the extraordinary inventiveness of regimes seeking to persecute people.

FURTHER READING

Bugai, Nikolai, *The Deportation of Peoples in the Soviet Union* (Commack, NY: Nova Science, 1996).

Courtois, Stéphane, Nicolas Werth, et al., *Le Livre noir du communisme* (Paris: R. Laffont, 1997).

Gatrell, Peter, *A Whole Empire Walking: Refugees in Russia during World War I* (Bloomington: Indiana University Press, 1999).

Graziosi, Andrea, 'Les famines soviétiques de 1931–1933 et le *Holodomor* ukrainien. Une nouvelle interprétation est-elle possible et quelles en seraient les conséquences?', *Cahiers du monde russe* 46:3 (2005), 453–72.

Holquist, Peter, 'Conduct merciless mass terror: decossackization on the Don, 1919', *Cahiers du monde russe* 28:1–2 (1997), 127–62.

Mace, James, 'The Man-Made Famine of 1932–1933: What Happened and Why', in *The Great Man-Made Famine in Ukraine*, ed. *Ukrainian Weekly* (Jersey City: Svoboda Press, 1983).

Martin, Terry, *The Affirmative Action Empire. Nations and Nationalism in the Soviet Union, 1923–1939* (Ithaca, NY/London: Cornell University Press, 2001).

Polian, Pavel, *Against Their Will: The History and Geography of Forced Migrations in the USSR* (Budapest: Central European University Press, 2004).

Serbyn, Roman, 'The Ukrainian Famine of 1932–1933 as Genocide in the Light of the UN Convention of 1948', *Ukrainian Quarterly* 62:2 (2006), 87–106.

Suny, Ronald Grigor, and Terry Martin (eds), *A State of Nations: Empire and Nation-Making in the Age of Lenin and Stalin* (Oxford: Oxford University Press, 2001).

CHAPTER 20

THE NAZI EMPIRE

CHRISTOPHER R. BROWNING

GENOCIDE in the Nazi Empire issued from a confluence of traditions: anti-Semitism, racism, imperialism, and eugenics. None of these was unique to Germany, but they came together in a lethal combination in Germany under the Nazi dictatorship to provide the ideological underpinnings for three clusters of genocidal projects. The first was the 'purification' of the German race through the mass murder of the mentally and physically handicapped within the Third Reich and the expulsion and mass murder of 'Gypsies' from the Third Reich. The second was a demographic revolution or ethnic restructuring within the lands deemed to be Germany's future *Lebensraum* through the decimation, denationalization, and expulsion of the predominately Slavic populations living there. The third was the systematic and total mass murder of every Jew—man, woman, and child—caught within the German *Machtbereich* or 'sphere of power'. It was this genocidal project that the Nazi regime called the 'Final Solution to the Jewish Question', and it is the total historical experience of the Nazi persecution of the Jews, culminating in the 'Final Solution', that I refer to as the 'Holocaust'.

IDEOLOGICAL UNDERPINNINGS OF NAZI GENOCIDE

Anti-Semitism, with its origins in the Christian–Jewish adversarial relationship dating back two millennia, was the oldest of these fateful traditions. What had begun as one of many dissident or reform movements within Judaism during the ministry of Jesus became a rival monotheistic sect with incompatible theological claims concerning his identity following his death. This theologically driven conflict became immensely asymmetrical in the fourth century, when Christianity became the official religion of the Roman Empire. Judaism—unlike various pagan sects—was not outlawed and destroyed, but Jews were left in the precarious status of a permitted albeit despised religious minority.

At the beginning of the second millennium, the position of the Jewish minority in Western Europe became more precarious, as theological anti-Judaism transformed into anti-Semitism. After centuries of contraction and decline, Western Europe experienced an explosive growth and change in the eleventh–thirteenth centuries. The underside of this first great European modernization was disorientation and embitterment on the part of many. The Jews were not only the most obvious symbol of religious anxiety and doubt in a new era of rational challenge to religious orthodoxy but also became the symbol of usury and debt in a new monetary, commercial economy, of clannishness amidst unsettling social change. In short, the Jews became the subject of a broad, multifaceted negative stereotype. Normal human individuality was denied them while negative traits were both generalized to all Jews and predicated upon an essential inferiority, of which stubborn religious unbelief was now just one among many indicators.[1]

This broad negative stereotype remained deeply embedded in European culture, even though growing secularization diminished the centrality of religious difference. The 'Dual Revolution' of the nineteenth century—democracy and nationalism on the one hand and urbanization and industrialization on the other—brought legal equality, economic opportunity, and social mobility to the newly emancipated Jews, but Europe's second great modernization also inflamed its 'social losers' against its most visible beneficiaries. European anti-Semitism experienced a major revival, with Jews now portrayed in an updated negative stereotype as exploitive capitalists, subversive revolutionaries, avant garde destroyers of traditional values and cultural standards, and aliens to the national community.

If the Dual Revolution had complex repercussions in European society, so did the Scientific Revolution. Confidence in the capacity of human rationality to master nature bred confidence that human behaviour could be understood with similar scientific certainty, and hence explaining the past and prescribing solutions to current political problems was possible through knowing the 'laws of history'. Marxism, based on class struggle as the law of history, was the most coherent ideological product of this intellectual development. More diffuse but even more widespread was the belief that race, not class, was the fundamental explanatory category of human behaviour, and Social Darwinism—applying selective

---

[1] Gavin Langmuir, *History, Religion, and Antisemitism* (Berkeley: University of California Press, 1990), 275–305.

catchphrases and metaphors such as 'struggle for survival' and 'survival of the fittest' to human relations—provided the appearance of scientific legitimacy to racial theories of history.

European expansion and conquest (with especially lethal consequences for the native populations of the western hemisphere) had been proceeding for centuries, but reached its apogee in the nineteenth, due to Europe's exponential growth in power owing to the mobilizing capacities of the modern nation-state and the economic and technological capacities of the Industrial Revolution. Europe's easy domination of other peoples and territories was accepted as the natural and inevitable historical culmination of European superiority and native inferiority, explained by race, rather than the result of a temporary and historically contingent imbalance of power. A competitive nation-state system and a competitive capitalist economy drove Europeans to maximize the exploitation of their imperial domains, in which coercion and repression of the native populations were only partially curtailed by notions of the 'white man's burden' to bring the blessings of higher civilization to those deemed inferior and primitive. Europeans became accustomed to treating dominated populations abroad in ways no longer thinkable in Europe itself, with perhaps German South West Africa and the Belgian Congo the most extreme cases but still symptomatic of a much broader pattern of attitudes and behaviour.

The temptation to enlist racial theorizing, seemingly legitimized by science and validated by European expansion, in support of anti-Semitism was too great to resist, and Wilhelm Marr articulated the conceptual marriage in 1873. Jews, he argued, were not a group defined by religious belief or ethnic custom but rather by immutable racial characteristics impervious to conversion or assimilation. The accumulated traits of the centuries-old but now updated negative anti-Semitic stereotype—formerly perceived as a mysterious affliction—were now explained as the inescapable Jewish racial inheritance.

If racial anti-Semitism was one unfortunate fruit of enlisting seeming scientific legitimacy in the service of politics, eugenics was another. Underlying the eugenics movement was the belief in fundamental human inequality based on heredity and thus the conviction that limiting the procreation of inferior people and maximizing that of superior people would improve mankind. By the early twentieth century advocates of eugenics were pushing for laws authorizing the sterilization of individuals deemed to be carriers of hereditary defects, but several potentially lethal 'slippages' in the rhetoric of eugenics were apparent. Some of the allegedly hereditary defects were behaviours that frequently were conditioned by both heredity and environment. And not just individuals but entire groups—often categorized by class or race—were ranked as hereditarily inferior (on the grounds of such subjective qualities as feeble-mindedness, shiftlessness, and lack of sobriety) and were perceived collectively as threatening to cause society-wide degeneration.

All of these traditions were present throughout Europe and North America by the early twentieth century. But did they have a particular prominence or resonance in Germany? The clearest case seems to be eugenics. Though the USA was home to eugenics-driven laws authorizing the sterilization of individuals that unequally impacted poor people, non-whites, and recent emigrants, in Germany eugenics enjoyed widespread respectability in the universities and medical profession. Called 'race hygiene' by some, eugenics was seen not just as a defence of society from the perceived threat of individual deficiencies but a defence of the superior German, Nordic, or Aryan race. And it was in Germany that Binding and Hoche went beyond the typical advocacy of sterilization and openly argued for laws permitting the killing of those deemed 'unworthy of life' in order to relieve both families and society of the 'burden' of caring for incurable and degenerate people whose lives had no purpose or value.

The fate of the Herero and Nama in German South West Africa certainly likewise suggests a particular genocidal continuity between Germany's colonial practices in its Wilhelmine empire in Africa and Nazi empire in Europe. Isabel Hull has made a strong case that one element of continuity from genocide in South West Africa to Germany's fateful defeat in World War I was the institutional culture of the German military obsessed with a doctrine of 'absolute destruction'.[2] But Hull does not argue for a simple, straight line from South West Africa to Auschwitz. Indeed, the example of South West Africa must be qualified in several ways. In quantitative terms of loss of life, for instance, the Belgians in the Congo outdid the Germans in South West Africa many fold. And South West Africa was not the sole template of German colonial practices. In East Africa they waged brutal 'wars of destruction' to repress native resistance, but the goal was unconditional surrender and total submission, not genocide. Tribes that submitted were immediately enlisted and armed as auxiliaries to combat those still resisting. In short, German colonial practices in Africa were not distinct from those of other imperial powers.

Vejas Liulevicius has suggested an important link between German colonial practices in Eastern Europe during World War I and subsequent Nazi practices there. The German military established a model colony called *Ober Ost* (in terms of current boundaries: northeast Poland, Lithuania, southern Latvia, and western Belarus). They aimed to impose total control but also to carry out *Kulturpolitik*, lifting up the native populations from filth, disease, and ignorance to become disciplined, productive, and grateful subjects. Instead, hyperexploitation and degrading controls caused growing resentment, and the presence of a foreign conqueror awakened national consciousness. Having hoped to manipulate and cultivate 'lands and peoples', the Germans increasingly surrendered to a mindset of managing 'space and race'. Deprived of what they perceived as their rightfully

[2] Isabel Hull, *Absolute Destruction: Military Culture and the Practice of War in Imperial Germany* (Ithaca, NY: Cornell University Press, 2005).

earned conquest of the East, they longed to return to these hated lands and despised populations but next time without any illusion of a cultural mission. Indeed, the post-war depredations of the *Freikorps* foreshadowed the destructive potential of rage over defeat, unlimited imperial appetite, and fanatical anti-Bolshevism.[3]

Ironically, continuity between nineteenth-century anti-Semitism in Germany and the Holocaust is more tenuous. Less than one per cent of the population, highly assimilated German Jews had achieved a degree of prominence in economic, professional, and cultural life, accompanied by a deep attachment to their country, unequalled elsewhere in Europe. Unlike German Catholics and Socialists, they were not subjected to outright discriminatory legislation, even if more subtle forms of exclusion limited their role in the officer corps and civil service. Noisy, single-issue anti-Semitic parties failed conspicuously. Anti-Semitism as a political platform was co-opted by the Conservative Party in the 1890s, and—as Shulamit Volkov has argued—became a 'cultural code' or political buzzword for all that conservatives opposed: liberal democracy, socialism, unfettered capitalism, internationalism, and cultural experimentation.[4] But anti-Semitism among the traditional conservatives did not obtain the intensity and priority that it would in the burgeoning German Right of the 1920s. And the behaviour of German troops in Eastern Europe during the First World War confirmed among the local Jewish populations Germany's image as the land of decency and opportunity for Europe's Jews.

HITLER AND NATIONAL SOCIALISM

Between 1914 and 1933, Germans experienced a staggering accumulation of disasters: a prolonged war of attrition and starvation blockade, unexpected military defeat, revolution, a humiliating treaty settlement, hyperinflation, and finally the unprecedented unemployment of the Great Depression. The tenuous democratic majority that had emerged in the 1912 elections and established the Weimar Republic in 1919 rapidly withered away thereafter. Neither an authoritarian traditional Right nor a revolutionary Left could fill the void in an increasingly fragmented and polarized German society. Longing for economic recovery and prosperity, the restoration of great power status and national pride, the end of political gridlock, and a return to the mythical social unity of the spirit of 1914,

---

[3] Vejas Liulevicius, *War Land on the Eastern Front: Culture, National Identity, and German Occupation in World War I* (New York: Cambridge University Press).

[4] Shulamit Volkov, 'Antisemitism as a Cultural Code', *Leo Baeck Institute Yearbook* 23 (1978), 25–46.

Germans provided the National Socialists with a degree of broad cross-class support unattainable by any other party and hence the decisive electoral plurality that—in alliance with the traditional conservatives and key elites—brought Hitler to power.

The Nazi dictatorship was certainly sensitive and catered to the longings and illusions of German society, but how Hitler perceived reality now also mattered. As German historians like Eberhard Jäckel established in the 1960s, Hitler was not simply a power-hungry and opportunistic demagogue.[5] He had a coherent ideological vision or *Weltanschauung*. Moreover, his was an ideological vision shared by an 'uninhibited generation' of committed young men whose formative years were the two decades of German disasters and who would provide the fanatical and energetic leadership of key components of the Nazi regime.[6] Also important, many aspects of this ideological vision at least partially 'overlapped' with broadly held sentiments in German society, providing a common vocabulary, the comfort of seeming familiarity, and a shared emotional resonance between regime and society on key issues.

Hitler's ideological vision has been aptly summed up under the terms 'race and space'. For Hitler, history was the outcome of the natural and unfettered struggle between races for the 'living space' or *Lebensraum* that underpinned each race's relative strength to compete and capacity to reproduce. In this struggle, the various European races had emerged as the superior 'culture-creating' races of the world, and the hardy German/Aryan race—shaped and winnowed by the harsh environment of northern Europe—had the potential to triumph over its rivals. However, Germany's deserved victory in World War I had been thwarted and now its very viability and continued existence were threatened by the suffocating terms of the Versailles Treaty and the debilitating effects of Weimar democracy.

German defeat and democratic revolution had a common source in an alleged betrayal or 'stab in the back' by Jewish revolutionaries who subverted the German war effort by undermining unity and continued willingness to sacrifice on the home front. For Hitler, the Jews were not just another race in the natural competition for space, but an unnatural and subhuman element that could not hold its own land and establish its own state and therefore could exist only as a parasite living off other races. Jews destroyed their host races in two ways. First, they destroyed the 'purity' of the host race by race-mixing. As 'pure blood' was axiomatically assumed to be vital to the strength of a race, such race-mixing was deemed fatal to a race's capacity to wage the unceasing struggle for *Lebensraum*

---

[5] Eberhard Jäckel, *Hitler's Weltanschuung: A Blueprint for Power* (Middleton, CT: Wesleyan University Press, 1972).

[6] Michael Wildt, *Generation des Unbedingten. Das Führerkorps des Reichssicherheitshauptamtes* (Hamburg: Hamburger Edition, 2002); and Ulrich Herbert, *Best. Biographische Studien über Radikalismus, Weltanschauung und Vernuft, 1903–1989* (Bonn: Dietz, 1996).

(witness the decline of Rome when its hardy peasant-soldier stock mixed with its conquered subjects). Second, Jews were the carriers and disseminators of insidious ideas that weakened a people's will to wage a no-holds-barred struggle for survival. In this regard, the subversive effects of three supposed Jewish conspiracies were held to provide ample historical evidence: Christianity, with its pacifistic doctrine of turn the other cheek and love thy neighbour; liberalism, with its belief in fundamental human equality; and Marxism, with its proclamation of proletarian solidarity above national loyalty.

If Hitler's obsession with and hostility towards Jews was an implacable element of his ideological outlook, and if the destruction of Weimar democracy and the Versailles Treaty settlement were inherent preliminary goals, the territorial site of Germany's *Lebensraum* was theoretically open. Here the attraction of the East—as the site of successful German expansion in World War I (framed as the continuation and culmination of Germany's historic *Drang nach Osten*), inhabited by primitive Slavs undeserving of and incapable of developing such vast spaces, the demographic centre of Jewish reproduction, and now the headquarters of the 'Jewish Bolshevik' conspiracy for world revolution—proved irresistible. That the Hitler regime would culminate in an attack on the Soviet Union—characterized as a military campaign for *Lebensraum* at the expense of Slavs, an ideological crusade against Bolshevism, and a race war against the Jews—was the logical implication of a shared ideological vision. The march towards this destiny in turn spawned a series of genocidal projects that drew upon past legacies and were consistent with Nazi ideology but which were nonetheless historically contingent. They fell into three categories: those implemented within the Third Reich, those implemented within German *Lebensraum*, and those implemented throughout the German sphere of power.

GENOCIDAL PROJECTS WITHIN THE THIRD REICH

Upon coming to power in January 1933, Hitler and the National Socialists set about establishing their dictatorship and 'coordinating' German society with frightening speed. In addition to crushing their political enemies and demolishing pluralism, they also set out to purify the German people of those they deemed to be biologically defective or 'degenerate' members. Their reproduction would 'dilute' and 'weaken' the vitality, strength, and purity of the German racial community and thereby undermine its capacity to wage relentless and unending struggle successfully, and their continued existence also would be an economic 'burden' that drained resources from rather than contributed to that struggle. Hence, the regime pursued quite literally the surgical exclusion of those deemed hereditarily defective through compulsory sterilization, as decreed in the 'Law for the Prevention of Hereditarily Diseased Offspring' in July 1933.[7]

However, those Germans considered biologically or hereditarily defective could not be neatly and easily categorized in mass by legal definition. The categories of affliction justifying compulsory sterilization included hereditary physical defects and illnesses as well as nebulous mental and behavioural categories considered hereditary, such as feeblemindedness, manic-depression, schizophrenia, and severe alcoholism. 'Applications' for compulsory sterilization could be made by doctors, institution directors, and public health officials, and were adjudicated on an individual basis by 'hereditary health courts', whose verdicts (routinely around ninety per cent in favour of sterilization) were enforced by the police. Congenital feeblemindedness was both the most imprecise diagnosis and most frequently invoked justification (roughly fifty per cent followed by schizophrenia at twenty-five per cent). In the pre-war years, over three hundred thousand Germans were sterilized.[8]

The transformation of the *Volksgemeinschaft* from the mythic inclusive national community of August 1914 to the Nazi ideal of an exclusive biological-racial community was intensified by a number of additional measures. A whole battery of anti-natal and pro-natal measures supplemented the 1933 law. Moreover, compulsory sterilization was fatefully expanded in 1937 to include strictly racial characteristics. The offspring of German mothers and African fathers, who were among the French army troops that took part in the postwar occupation in Germany, were pejoratively referred to as the 'Rhineland bastards'. As the oldest of these African-German children approached maturity, the Nazi regime took action. In the summer of 1937, hundreds of these children were summarily sterilized.[9]

Between political opponents to the regime, who could be recovered for the racial community through altering behaviour by punishment, coercion, and re-education on the one hand, and the biologically defective who were barred from reproducing through sterilization on the other, was a murky borderland inhabited by people identified and stigmatized as 'asocials'. These people were seen not only as aesthetic blemishes on the Nazi image of the racial community, but also as stubborn non-conformists who constituted a dissident threat to the Nazis' capacity to impose both uniform and productive behaviour.[10] The tendency was always to subsume

[7] Gisela Bock, *Zwangssterilisation im Naizionalsozialismus: Studien zur Rassenpolitik und Frauenpolitik* (Opladen: Westdeutscher Verlag, 1986).

[8] Henry Friedlander, *The Origins of Nazi Genocide: From Euthansia to the Final Solution* (Chapel Hill: University of North Carolina Press, 1995).

[9] Rainer Pommerin, *'Sterilisierung der Rheinlandbastarde': Das Schicksal einer farbigen deustchen Minderheit 1918–1927* (Düsseldorf: Droste, 1979).

[10] Klaus Scherer, *'Asozial' im Dritten Reich: Die vergessenen Verfolgen* (Munich: VOTUM Verlag, 1990).

asocial behaviour, when judged irremediable, within the biologically defective. Two groups in particular within the Third Reich increasingly fell victim to this tendency to treat asocial behaviour as a racial-biological threat: homosexuals and 'Gypsies' (Sinti and Roma). Homosexuals were perceived as offensive to public morality, symbolic of the sexual licence of Weimar, subversive of Nazi notions of manly camaraderie, and treasonously withholding their procreative powers from the community. Over time, those deemed incorrigible homosexuals (the 'seducers' who were allegedly the real source of the problem) were subjected not only to incarceration but also to sterilization, castration, or execution.[11]

Nowhere can the tendency of the Nazi regime to merge its categories of habitual criminal, feebleminded, asocial, and racial alien be seen more clearly than in its treatment of Sinti and Roma, pejoratively referred to as *Zigeuner*.[12] The victims of widespread prejudice and discrimination before 1933, the Sinti and Roma were stereotypically characterized as parasitical, criminal, lazy, and rootless. After 1933 in Germany they were disproportionately subjected to the Nazi regime's measures against asocial habitual criminals, vagrants, and beggars. In fact, one category of asocial behaviour subject to 'preventive detention' was simply exhibiting a 'Gypsy-like' lifestyle, even when those involved were not Gypsies. After 1935, Sinti and Roma were increasingly confined to Gypsy camps. The Sinti and Roma were likewise disproportionately subjected to compulsory sterilization on the grounds of feeblemindedness. The Nürnberg Laws did not mention *Zigeuner*, but subsequent commentaries declared them to be of 'alien blood' and subject to the same prohibitions that affected Jews. Himmler in turn set up a Central Office for the Fight against the Gypsy Nuisance and declared the 'Gypsy problem' to be a 'matter of race'.

In the war years persecution, incarceration, and sterilization gave way to widespread killing in the case of two groups whose very existence within the boundaries of the Third Reich was now to come to an end: the mentally and physically handicapped on the one hand and Sinti and Roma on the other. In the summer of 1939, Hitler set in motion planning for the 'euthanasia' of both severely deformed newborns and institutionalized mentally ill adults deemed both incurable and incapable of productive work. With the outbreak of war, institutionalized Polish mental patients in the territories of the Polish corridor quickly annexed to

[11] Geoffrey Giles, 'The Institutionalization of Homosexual Panic in the Third Reich', in Robert Gallately and Nathan Stoltzfuss (eds), *Social Outsiders in Nazi Germany* (Princeton, NJ: Princeton University Press, 2001), 233–55; and *idem*, 'Männerbund mit Homo-Panik: Die Angst der Nazis vor der Rolle der Erotik', in Burkhard Jellonnek and Rüdiger Lautmann (eds), *Nationalsozialistischer Terror gegen Homosexuelle: Verdrängt und Ungesühnt* (Paderborn: Ferdinand Schönigh, 2002), 105–18.

[12] Michael Zimmerman, *Rassenutopie und Genozid: Die nationalsozialistische 'Lösung der Zigeunerfrage'* (Hamburg: Christians, 1996). Guenter Lewy, *The Nazi Persecution of the Gypsies* (New York: Oxford University Press, 2000) contains much valuable information but argues for a very restricted notion of genocide that excludes the Sinti and Roma as genocidal victims.

the Third Reich were killed by firing squad. This particular killing action inaugu-
rated in the fall of 1939 expanded to include Polish patients in the Warthegau as
well as German patients in Pomerania and East Prussia. It also undertook the initial
experiments in using carbon monoxide to poison rather than shoot its victims,
both in prototype gas chambers in Posen and in a prototype itinerant gas van.[13]
The nationwide programmes then got underway. Deformed newborns were sent to
special wards in select hospitals and killed by drug overdose. The centralized killing
programme of adults, designated as T 4, coordinated the inventory of patients in
institutions throughout Germany, after which the selected victims were sent to one
of six killing centres equipped with gas chambers utilizing bottled carbon monoxide. This centralized programme was halted by Hitler in August 1941, when its
operations became too public and evoked too much unease and protest. Nonetheless, decentralized killing of targeted adults continued in selected hospitals, usually
through lethal injection or medication, to the end of the war. All Jewish patients
were killed without selection, either in the euthanasia centres in Germany or
following deportation to Poland. And finally, in a programme designated Operation 14f13, touring teams of T 4 doctors conducted selections in the concentration
camps, after which the victims were sent to one of the euthanasia killing centres.
Altogether, by the end of the Nazi regime, some 150,000 people had been subjected
to 'medicalized' killing in these various operations aimed at ridding Germany of
those deemed 'unworthy of life' due to mental or physical handicaps as well as
some 20,000 concentration camp prisoners who were deemed medically 'unfit'.[14]

In contrast to Hitler's direct instigation of and involvement in the killing of the
German handicapped, he exhibited virtually no interest in the fate of the Sinti and
Roma. The fact that the Nazi regime nonetheless carried out a genocidal assault
against them demonstrates how lethal can be the combination of pervasive popular
prejudice, institutionalized racism, empowered local authorities, and a bureaucratic police state that develops the habit of solving problems through repression and
mass murder. The Sinti and Roma were subjected to vacillating, contested, and
sometimes contradictory policies, which provided some loopholes for survival. But
ultimately more than two-thirds of the Sinti and Roma in the Third Reich and
Protectorate perished in Nazi camps, and many of those spared death were
sterilized and thus subjected to a form of 'delayed genocide'. In 1938–9, some
3,000 Austrian Gypsies from the Burgenland were sent to German concentration
camps as part of several actions against the 'work shy' and asocials, and few
survived the high mortality rates of prolonged incarceration. Plans in the fall of
1939 to deport all Sinti and Roma, along with all Jews, into the General Government failed, but in May 1940 2,800 were deported from western Germany (at the

---

[13] Volker Riess, *Die Anfänge der Vernichtung 'lebensunwerten Lebens' in dem Reichsgauen
Danzig-Westpreussen und Wartheland 1939/40* (Frankfurt: Peter Lang, 1995).
[14] Friedlander, *The Origins of Nazi Genocide*.

instigation of the military, who pronounced them a security risk) into the General Government, from where few ever returned.[15] In November 1941, 5,000 Gypsies were deported from Austria to the Lodz ghetto and then killed in the gas vans of the Chelmno death camp the following January. In February 1942 some 2,000 Gypsies were expelled from East Prussia to Bialystok, some of whom were then expelled yet further east to Brest the following fall. In both places they suffered high mortality under terrible conditions. In December 1942, Himmler ordered the deportation of more than 20,000 Sinti and Roma from the Third Reich and the Protectorate to Auschwitz-Birkenau. Most perished from the terrible living conditions in the 'Gypsy family camp' there or after re-assignment to other camps. Three contingents—1,700 from Bialystok in March 1943, 1,000 sick prisoners in May 1943, and the final remnant of some 3,000 with the closing of the Gypsy family camp in August 1944—were sent to the Birkenau gas chambers.[16]

The killing of the Sinti and Roma from the Third Reich was not total, however, for at least 6,000 were exempted from the deportations Himmler ordered in December 1942. One exempted category was 'racially pure Gypsies', reflecting Himmler's idiosyncratic views (contested by Martin Bormann among others) that the Gypsies—in distinct contrast to Jews—were 'Aryans' whose worst traits resulted from all-too-frequent race-mixing. Also exempted were *Zigeuner-mischlinge*, who had been accepted by 'pure' groups, 'socially adjusted Gypsies' with regular jobs and residences, Gypsies married to Germans, and Gypsies either in military service or working in war-important jobs. Eligibility for exemption was decided by the local criminal police, and many *Zigeunermischlinge* were threatened with loss of their exemption from deportation if they did not submit to sterilization. Such exceptions combined with the lack of a clear programme and premeditated 'intent' to kill all Gypsies has led at least one scholar, Guenther Lewy, to argue that Nazi mass killing in this case did not constitute genocide—a view not widely shared by others.[17]

While Germans deemed 'unworthy of life' as well as the vast majority of Sinti and Roma were no longer to exist within the boundaries of the Third Reich, similar genocidal projects targeting these specific groups did not extend beyond those boundaries. Institutionalized patients elsewhere in occupied Europe suffered grievously and died in large numbers from lack of care and starvation. In places where the German occupiers wanted the buildings they occupied or to subject them to experiments (as in Belarus), they were massacred. But there was no plan or programme to kill all institutionalized, handicapped people throughout German-occupied Europe. Likewise, Gypsies beyond the boundaries of the Third Reich were

[15] Zimmermann, *Rassenutopie und Genozid*, 172.

[16] Ibid. Lewy, *The Nazi Persecution of the Gypsies*.

[17] Lewy, *The Nazi Persecution of the Gypsies*, 221–4. In contrast, see: Zimmermann, *Rassenutopie und Genozid*, 369–81.

often killed on local initiative but not as part of a continent-wide programme mandated from Berlin. On Soviet territory itinerant or 'wandering Gyspies' were killed in large numbers as alleged spies, partisans, and disease carriers, but 'sedentary Gyspies' were generally spared. However, in certain areas—such as Estonia[18] and the Crimea—local German authorities killed all Gypsies. In Serbia, a distinction was made by gender and age. The German military was short of victims to fill its self-imposed reprisal quotas and shot adult male Gypsies alongside adult male Jews. But Gypsy women and children were released from the Semlin camp outside Belgrade before the Jewish women and children interned there were gassed. The same distinction of different treatment between victims within the Third Reich and beyond can be made for the persecution of homosexuals. Himmler, who was phobic about German homosexuals, had no desire to discourage or repress homosexuality in the occupied territories, for he viewed non-procreative sex among non-Germans as beneficial to Germany.

GENOCIDAL PROJECTS WITHIN GERMAN *LEBENSRAUM*

As the German path to seizing *Lebensraum* in the Soviet Union led through other East European countries of mixed populations, the Nazi regime had to negotiate an unpredictable diplomatic and military course as well as experiment in the demographic reconstruction of the populations that came under its control. Hitler had hoped to ally with Poland against the Soviet Union, but when no agreement was reached with the Poles, he instead invaded and partitioned that country in cooperation with the Soviet Union. The German-occupied half of partitioned Poland then became the first real 'laboratory' for transforming non-German lands into German *Lebensraum* through engineering a demographic revolution. The outlines were sketched in late September and early October 1939. The German share of Poland was to be split yet again in two, with the western regions 'incorporated' directly into the Third Reich while the remainder was reduced to the status of a German colony designated as the General Government. Heinrich Himmler was adamant that 'one only possesses a land when even the last inhabitant of this territory belongs to his own people.'[19] Thus making the 'incorporated territories' truly part of the Third Reich was to be achieved by expelling all eight million

[18] Anton Weiss-Wendt, 'Extermination of the Gypsies in Estonia during World War II: Popular Images and Official Policies', *Holocaust and Genocide Studies* 17/1 (spring 2003), 31–61.
[19] National Archives microfilm, T175/122/266598ff: Himmler Memorandum, 25 June 1940.

non-German inhabitants into the General Government—a policy later dubbed 'ethnic cleansing' by Slobodan Milošević, but one that Hitler then referred to as *Flurbereinigung* or 'basic cleansing'. These lands, emptied of all but the 'ethnic Germans' already living there, were to be repopulated by 'calling back home to the Reich' all the ethnic Germans living in the lands of Eastern Europe ceded to Stalin in the Nazi-Soviet Non-Aggression Pact (namely the Baltic states, eastern Poland, and Bessarabia).[20] The initial uprooting and dissolution of ethnic German communities in much of Eastern Europe was not, therefore, the result of German defeat and Red Army revenge at the end of the war, but rather the calculated policy of Heinrich Himmler and his SS demographic engineers in 1939–41.

The genocidal implications for Poles under German occupation were twofold. Not only were millions of Poles in the incorporated territories to be expelled into the General Government, with total loss of property and regardless of loss of life, but within the General Government the Poles were to be reduced to a denationalized mass of slave labourers. Polish leadership classes and carriers of Polish national identity and culture were targeted for elimination. The rest of the Polish population was to be deprived of meaningful education, held to minimum food rations, and subjected to forced labour either at home or, increasingly, in Germany. The sheer logistical magnitude of the Nazi expulsion plans and the reality of wartime economic needs for continued production prevented complete ethnic cleansing from the incorporated territories, but the decimation of the Polish intelligentsia and exploitation of Polish forced labour continued unfettered.[21]

Until the unforeseeably quick victory over France in the west, the time frame for continued expansion of German *Lebensraum* in the east had to remain uncertain. Thus the German occupiers were constructing a defensive wall along the Nazi-Soviet demarcation line into the summer of 1940, after which German planning shifted from the defensive to the offensive. When Hitler decided to abandon the Non-Aggression Pact and invade the Soviet Union, he also exhorted and proclaimed that this campaign would take the form not of a conventional war bur rather of a 'war of destruction'. The once distant vision but now immediate prospect of territorial conquest of vast *Lebensraum* in the east, an ideological crusade against communism, and the ultimate confrontation with the demographic centre of world Jewry found resonance and produced feverish planning throughout the Nazi regime.[22] The military removed Soviet civilians from the protection of martial law, mandated the execution of captured communist 'commissars' and the

---

[20] Götz Aly, *'Final Solution': Nazi Population Policy and the Murder of the European Jews* (London: Arnold, 1999); and Phillip Rutherford, *Prelude to the Final Solution: The Nazi Program for Deporting Ethnic Poles, 1939–1941* (Lawrence: Kansas University Press, 2007).

[21] Czeslaw Madajczyk, *Die Okkupationspolitik Deutschlands in Polen 1939–1945* (Berlin: Akademie Verlag, 1987).

[22] Alex Kay, *Exploitation, Resettlement, Mass Murder. Political and Economic Planning for German Occupation Policy in the Soviet Union, 1940–1941* (New York: Berghahn Books, 2006).

infliction of collective reprisal against any manifestation of resistance behind the lines, and arranged for military cooperation with and logistical support for mobile SS killing squads or *Einsatzgruppen*. The economic planners envisaged a systematic exploitation and looting of Soviet territory and accepted as self-evident that 'umpteen million people will doubtless starve to death, if we extract everything necessary for us from the country.'[23] Meeting with his SS leaders on 12–15 June 1941, Himmler confided that the coming conflict 'will be a racial struggle of pitiless severity, in the course of which 20 to 30 million Slavs and Jews will perish through military action and crisis of food supply'.[24] When victory seemed imminent in mid-July 1941, Hitler proclaimed that the newly conquered territories would be transformed into a German 'Garden of Eden'. Over the next year Himmler's planners worked on various versions of a *Generalplan Ost*, which envisaged both the settlement of Germans in the conquered *Lebensraum* and the reduction of the native population from 45 to 14 million through death or expulsion into Siberia.[25] The death—mostly from starvation and exposure—of more than two million Soviet soldiers in German POW camps in the first nine months of the war,[26] the calculated starvation blockade of Leningrad, and the escalating death of Soviet civilians from starvation and massacre behind German lines indicate clearly that the even vaster decimation of the Soviet population envisaged by Nazi planners was no idle speculation. Only German defeat precluded full realization of the genocidal intentions of *Generalplan Ost* and even vaster loss of life.

THE GENOCIDE OF THE JEWS

Nazi persecution of the Jews was initially one component of the other two evolving genocidal projects: first, the biological-racial purification within the Third Reich, and second the massive population decimation and ethnic cleansing within German *Lebensraum*. In 1941–2, however, the Final Solution gained an autonomy, priority, and singularity apart from all other persecutory and genocidal policies of the Nazi regime. Its goal was the total and systematic elimination of every last

---

[23] Nürnberg Document 2718-PS: note on conference of state secretaries, 2 May 1941.

[24] The testimony of Erich von dem Bach-Zelewski in *Trials of the Major War Criminals before the International Military Tribunal*, iv.482–8, and in Justiz und NS-Verbrechen, xx.413.

[25] Helmut Heiber (ed.), 'Der Generalplan Ost', *Vierteljahrshefte für Zeitgeschichte* 6 (1958), 281–325; and Mechtild Rössler and Sabine Schleiermacher (eds), *Der 'Generalplan Ost': Hauptlinien der nationalsozialistischen Planungs- und Vernichtungspolitik* (Berlin: Akademie Verlag, 1993).

[26] Christian Streit, *Keine Kameraden. DieWehrmacht und die sowietischen Kriegsgefangenen 1941–1945* (Stuttgart: DVA, 1978).

Jew—man, woman, and child—within the Nazi sphere of power, and was therefore a genocidal project that ultimately had no geographical limit or boundary other than the reach of the German military.

During the pre-war years of the Nazi regime, the persecution of the Jews aimed at excluding them from both the German *Volksgemeinschaft* and German soil. The anti-Jewish legislation of 1933 constituted the 'civic death' of German Jews. It ended Jewish emancipation by denying them equality before the law and expelling them from the civil service as well as cultural and associational life and sharply curtailing their activities in the professions. The Nürnberg Laws of 1935 completed the 'social death' of German Jews, outlawing marriage and sexual relations between Jews and 'Aryans' and rendering any continuing social ties vulnerable to denunciation and criminal prosecution. Numerous laws in 1938 resulted in the 'economic death' of Germans Jews through completing the transfer (euphemistically dubbed 'aryaniza-tion') and expropriation of Jewish property and eliminated the last free participa-tion of Jews in the German economy—a process that had been steadily underway since 1933. By the mid-1930s, SS specialists on Jewish policy had clearly articulated the goal of this escalating persecution—to create a Third Reich 'pure of Jews' (*judenrein*). Life was to be made so intolerable that all German Jews would voluntarily emigrate despite the near total loss of property entailed in leaving Germany and the ever rising barriers to immigration elsewhere. When Germany annexed Austria in March 1938, SS experts (Adolf Eichmann in particular) could move from theory to practice, devising measures to compel the departure of Jews from Austria at a rate far exceeding Jewish emigration from the Old Reich.

Despite the effort to create a German Third Reich pure of Jews through ever intensifying persecution and expulsion, nearly half the German Jews remained trapped in the Old Reich (as defined by 1937 boundaries) when war broke out in 1939. And the addition of Austrian and Czech Jews in 1938 and 1939 underlined the paradoxical dilemma facing the Nazis, namely that every diplomatic and military success that added territory was simultaneously a step backwards in achieving a Third Reich pure of Jews. With the outbreak of war and the prospect of even greater territorial gain (as well as ever greater numbers of Jews) imminent, Hitler sought to cut the Gordian knot by signalling his followers through his January 1939 Reichstag speech about his expectations. If the Jews caused another world war, he prophesied, it would result in the destruction of the Jewish race in Europe.

Hitler's followers, especially Heinrich Himmler, understood the signal and acted accordingly. They included all Jews within the German sphere in three successive plans for ethnic cleansing and population decimation. Thus, in the fall of 1939, all Jews—beginning with the Jews of the incorporated territories but then encom-passing all Jews of pre-war Germany—were to be expelled to a Lublin Reservation in the furthest corner of the German empire. This territory was deemed especially suitable since its marshy character would ensure a decimation of the Jewish population. With victory over France and its overseas empire at German disposal in June 1940, SS and Foreign Office experts devised the Madagascar Plan, in which all Jews of the German sphere were to be sent to that French colony in the Indian Ocean as soon as Britain dropped out of the war and its merchant marine could be seized for that purpose. Finally, with the decision for Barbarossa, the Nazis planned that following victory all European Jews would be expelled to 'a territory yet to be determined'—code language for the Siberian and Arctic wastelands of a defeated Soviet Union. With each successive plan the scope and murderous implications intensified, as did the frustrations of the planners when the first two proved impractical in turn.

Preceding Barbarossa, Himmler had noted that 20 to 30 million 'Jews and Slavs' would perish. Military guidelines for troop behaviour called for ruthless measures against 'bolshevist agitators, guerrillas, saboteurs, Jews', and military propaganda identified the commissars and party functionaries targeted for summary execution as 'mostly filthy Jews'.[27] Heydrich likewise targeted 'Jews in party and state positions' for summary execution. And the planners of mass starvation surely knew from the experience of the Polish ghettos that when food was scarce, Jews were always the first to starve. In short, genocide of the Soviet Jews, through some unspecified combination of execution, expulsion, and starvation and according to some unspecified timetable, was implied in Nazi plans for the war of destruction.

The implicit became explicit over the summer of 1941. Following Hitler's proclamation in mid-July that the conquered Soviet territories should be transformed into a German Garden of Eden, Himmler reinforced the 3,000 men of the *Einsatzgruppen* with nearly 20,000 Order Police and *Waffen*-SS for behind-the-lines killing operations. And following Himmler's various tours of the eastern front to visit such units, targeting shifted from the selective mass murder of Jewish leadership and more broadly Jewish men of military age to the mass murder of all Jews but especially women and children. By late August 1941 the systematic 'liquidation' of Soviet Jewry was underway.

Concerning the fate of the European Jews west of the Soviet Union, the fundamental change in vision—from 'solving the Jewish question' through a combination of expulsion and decimation to solving it through systematic and total mass murder—occurred in the fall of 1941. Between mid-September and mid-October, three key decisions were taken. Himmler's role in all three can be documented, though a surviving paper trail leads to Hitler only in the first. These three decisions were as follows: to begin deporting Jews from the Third Reich to intermediate stops in the eastern ghettos of Lodz, Minsk, and Riga before sending them 'yet further to the east' the following spring; to construct camps equipped with gassing facilities in Belzec, Chelmno, and elsewhere; and to ban all further Jewish emigration since,

---

[27] Helmut Krausnick and Hans-Heinrich Wilhelm, *Die Truppe des Weltanschauungskrieges: Die Einsatzgruppen des Sicherheitspolizei und des SD, 1938–1942* (Stuttgart: DVA, 1981), 125, 136.

according to Heydrich, such Jews 'would be too much out of the direct reach of the measures for a basic solution to the Jewish question to be enacted after the war'.[28]

The Final Solution was to be implemented throughout the German sphere of power, not just within German *Lebensraum*. Eichmann's preparatory document for Heydrich at the Wannsee Conference (20 January 1942) listed all 11 million European Jews, including those of Portugal, England, Ireland, Finland, and the European areas of Turkey. But Europe was not the limit. As Hitler informed the Grand Mufti of Jerusalem in a meeting on 28 November 1941: 'Germany has resolved, step by step, to ask one European nation after the other to solve its Jewish problem, and at the proper time, direct a similar appeal to non-European nations as well.' When German troops broke through the Caucasus into the Middle East, he had no imperial goals, he assured the Grand Mufti. 'Germany's objective would then be solely the destruction of the Jewish element residing in the Arab sphere.'[29] While Hitler's sincerity in renouncing territorial gains in the Middle East is doubtful, his commitment to killing Jews there is not. When Rommel's troops invaded Egypt and threatened Palestine in the summer of 1942, plans were made to dispatch an *Einsatzgruppe*.[30]

Though the Third Reich lasted for twelve years and the Second World War for six, most of the killing of the Final Solution was in fact compressed into a very short period. As of March 1942, some twenty to twenty-five per cent of all victims of the Holocaust had already perished. Just eleven months later, by February 1943, some seventy-five to eighty per cent of all victims had been killed. This massive genocidal assault was accomplished through three distinct but occasionally overlapping sets of killing operations. East of the old Nazi–Soviet demarcation line, numerous mobile firing squads—usually organized by the Higher SS and Police Leaders or Security Police successors to the *Einsatzgruppen* but comprising a bewildering array of available manpower, including local militias—conducted regional sweeps and liquidated the Jewish communities in one city, town, and village after another. In Poland, repeated *Aktionen* emptied one ghetto after another, with the bulk of the Jews put on trains and sent to their immediate death in the gas chambers of Chelmno, Belzec, Sobibor, and Treblinka, and a small minority granted a brief stay of execution in various slave labour camps.

In the other countries of Europe, Germany approached various puppet and satellite governments on the one hand or its own occupation regimes on the other

[28] Political Archives of the German Foreign Office, Pol. Abt. III 246, Luther memorandum, 17 October 1941.

[29] *Akten zur deutschen auswärtigen Politik*, Series D, vol. 13/2, 718–21 (Schmidt memorandum, 30 November 1941).

[30] Klaus-Michael Mallmann and Martin Cüppers. ' "Beseitigung der jüdisch-nationalen Heimstätte in Palästina": Das Einsatzkommando bie der Panzerarmee Afrika 1942', in Jürgen Mathäus and Klaus-Michael Mallmann (eds), *Deutsche, Juden, Völkermord: Der Holocaust als Geschichte und Gegenwart* (Darmstadt: WBG, 2006). 153–76.

to round up and turn over their Jews for deportation. This was usually done with the help of local collaborators, and the most common destination of these deportation trains was Auschwitz-Birkenau. Major deportation programmes began from Slovakia, France, Belgium, and the Netherlands in 1942, and from Bulgaria and Greece in the spring of 1943. In the wake of defeat in Stalingrad in February 1943, however, German leverage on collaborating regimes declined, and the pace of deportations slackened from those countries in which Germany was dependent upon the cooperation of others. The key exception in this regard was the tragic deportation of nearly one-half million Hungarian Jews in May/June 1944, immediately following the German installation of a more compliant satellite government there. The last phase in the genocide of the European Jews then resulted from the 'death marches', as the Germans continually forced surviving Jewish camp inmates to withdraw before the Allied advance under the most lethal conditions in the last months of the war.

Ultimately, the Nazi Revolution was to be a racial revolution that reconfigured the demographic make-up of the Nazi empire. The destruction of the Jews was the most comprehensive and far-reaching component of this racial revolution and has become the paradigmatic historical example of total genocide. The further the genocide of the Jews progressed while the chances of German victory simultaneously diminished, the more obsessed and paranoid Hitler and other leading Nazis became about their imagined Jewish threat as a 'world Jewish conspiracy'.[31] While no other group targeted by the Nazis took on such mythical and threatening proportions, numerous other groups perceived as either constituting a danger to German racial purity and strength within the Third Reich or occupying 'space' claimed as vital German *Lebensraum* were also targeted for decimation or elimination through various programmes of expulsion, starvation, and mass murder. However imprecise the notion of destruction 'in part' of the genocide convention may be, the actual fate of the handicapped and Sinti and Roma within the Third Reich and the intended fate of the Slavs of Eastern Europe pass this threshold.

FURTHER READING

Aly, Götz, *'Final Solution.' Nazi Population Policy and the Murder of the European Jews* (London: Arnold, 1999).
Browning, Christopher, and Jürgen Matthäus, *The Origins of the Final Solution: The Evolution of Nazi Jewish Policy, September 1939-March 1942* (Lincoln: University of Nebraska Press, 2004).

[31] Saul Friedländer, *Nazi Germany and the Jews*, vol ii: *The Years of Extermination* (New York: HarperCollins, 2007). Jeffrey Herf, *The Jewish Enemy: Nazi Propaganda during World War II and the Holocaust* (Cambridge, MA: Harvard University Press, 2006).

Burleigh, Michael, and Wolfgang Wippermann, *The Racial State: Germany 1933–1945* (New York: Cambridge University Press, 1991).

Friedlander, Henry, *The Origins of Nazi Genocide: From Euthanasia to the Final Solution* (Chapel Hill: University of North Carolina Press, 1995).

Friedländer, Saul, *Nazi German and the Jews*, vol i: *The Years of Persecution*, and vol ii: *The Years of Extermination* (New York: HarperCollins, 1996, 2007).

Gerlach, Christian, *Krieg, Ernährung, Völkermord. Forschungen zur deutschen Vernichtungspolitik im Zweiten Weltkrieg* (Hamburg: Hamburger Edition, 1998).

Hilberg, Raul, *The Destruction of the European Jews*, 3rd edn (New Haven, CT: Yale University Press, 2003).

Kay, Alex, *Exploitation, Resettlement, Mass Murder. Political and Economic Planning for German Occupation Policy in the Soviet Union, 1940–1941* (New York: Berghahn Books, 2007).

Lewy, Guenther, *The Nazi Persecution of the Gypsies* (New York: Oxford University Press, 2000).

Longerich, Peter, *Politik der Vernichtung. Eine Gesamtdarstellung der nationalsozialistischen Judenverfolgung* (Munich: Piper, 1998).

Madajczyk, Czeslaw, *Die Okkupationspolitik Deutschlands in Polen 1939–1945* (Berlin: Akademie Verlag, 1987).

Rutherford, Phillip, *Prelude to the Final Solution: The Nazi Program for Deporting Ethnic Poles, 1939–1941* (Lawrence: Kansas University Press, 2007).

Schleunes, Karl, *The Twisted Road to Auschwitz: Nazi Policy toward German Jews 1933–1939* (Urbana: University of Illinois Press, 1970).

Wendling, Paul, *Health, Race and German Politics between National Unification and Nazism, 1870–1945* (Cambridge: Cambridge University Press, 1989).

Zimmerman, Michael, *Rassenutopie und Genozid: Die nationalsozialistische 'Lösung der Zigeunerfrage'* (Hamburg: Christians, 1996).

CHAPTER 21

....

TWENTIETH-CENTURY CHINA

ETHNIC ASSIMILATION AND INTERGROUP VIOLENCE

....

URADYN E. BULAG

GENOCIDE AND ITS DISCONTENTS

....

DISSIDENT nationalists of the Mongol, Tibetan, and Uyghur minorities in the People's Republic of China (PRC) now contend that China has committed physical and cultural genocide against their nationalities. The Inner Mongolian People's Party, an exiled Mongolian dissident group, claims that genocide was carried out by the Chinese against the Mongols during the Cultural Revolution, and some insist that 'it is proper to state that the so-called policy of "improving Mongolian people's traditional way of production" is a type of cultural genocide.' Uyghur nationalists also maintain that they have been suffering from the twin genocides. Indeed, for Tibetan nationalists, Inner Mongolians and Uyghurs have already been culturally genocided as they have been outnumbered by Chinese settlers in their own homelands, so their fates now serve as handy mirrors for what will become of Tibet. A Tibetan in exile opined on the eve of the railway connection to Lhasa in 2006 thus: 'When the railway will be fully operational, Chinese migration to Tibet will likely accelerate and crush the last hopes of Tibetan cultural survival as similar projects have done in Eastern Turkestan [Xinjiang] and Inner Mongolia.'[1]

Cultural genocide has now become a staple of the Dalai Lama's criticism of Chinese treatment of Tibetans. As early as October 1996, in an interview in *Le Monde*, the Dalai Lama remarked: 'A kind of cultural genocide is in progress in Tibet. And even if losing her independence is acceptable, then still the destruction of our spirituality, of Tibetan Buddhism, is unthinkable. Protecting the Tibetan heritage has become my primary occupation.'[2] On 16 March 2008, two days after the Chinese suppression of riots in Lhasa which triggered a month-long pro-Tibetan protest against the worldwide Beijing Olympic torch relay, the Dalai Lama again accused the Chinese government of carrying out 'cultural genocide' by promoting the influx of Chinese migrants into Tibet and by means of restrictions on Buddhist practices: 'Whether intentionally or unintentionally, some kind of cultural genocide is taking place.'[3]

Genocide, a neologism introduced in the 1940s characterizing a state's or a dominant group's mass killings of a culturally, ethnically, or religiously different minority group, carries legal, moral, and political consequences for the accused. The term has empowered victimized groups to redress wrongs, often becoming a basis for demanding increased autonomy or independence. Fearing secession and state disintegration, the Chinese government, like all national governments, has rejected categorically all such allegations, calling them 'nothing but lies', insisting that the Tibetans, and all ethnic minorities in the PRC for that matter, enjoy full political rights of autonomy and have prospered under the Chinese rule; their population has multiplied, and the Chinese state has been investing heavily to maintain and promote their cultural heritage.[4]

Some Western scholars seem to concur. Donald Lopez Jr. has criticized the Dalai Lama and the Tibetans in exile for desiring national independence of Tibet based on a claim to protect Tibetan 'national culture and nature' even while Tibetan Buddhism has become phenomenally successful only after it has been removed

---

[1] Wu Yunna, 'Another High Tactic of the Cultural Genocide by the CCP', [online] (2002), available at http://web.radicalparty.org/pressreview/print_right.php?func=detail&par=3685; 'China's Occupation of East Turkistan, Genocide of Uyghurs', [online] (21 July 2008), available at http://www.ireport.com/docs/DOC-48003; Tenzin Dargyal, 'Bombardier and the Tibetan Cultural Genocide', Op-Ed, International Campaign for Tibet, [online] (30 May 2006), available at http://www.savetibet.org/media-center/tibet-news/bombardier-and-tibetan-cultural-genocide (accessed 29 July 2008).

[2] Quoted in Donald S. Lopez, Jr., *Prisoners of Shangri-La: Tibetan Buddhism and the West* (Chicago/London: University of Chicago Press, 1998), 199.

[3] 'Dalai Lama accuses China of "cultural genocide" ', *USA Today*, 16 March 2008, available at http://www.usatoday.com/news/world/2008-03-16-china-tibet_N.htm (accessed 29 July 2008).

[4] Information Office of the State Council of the People's Republic of China, 'Regional Ethnic Autonomy in Tibet' (May 2004), available at: http://english.peopledaily.com.cn/200405/23/eng20040523_144150.html

from its native soil.[5] Barry Sautman has launched a vehement attack on the Tibetan accusations of cultural genocide, insisting that Tibetans, instead of being extinguished either as a culture or as a population, have thrived during the Chinese communist rule.[6] He denies that Tibet is an internal colony of China; rather Tibetans enjoy equal rights as citizens, and he buttresses his claim by quoting the Dalai Lama, who has expressed willingness to accept the Chinese rule, and has acknowledged that Tibetan culture is part of Chinese culture. Tom Grunfeld went further by discrediting the foundational text of the genocide case—the findings of the International Commission of Jurists in the wake of the 1959 Tibetan uprising which made the original allegation that the Chinese had committed cultural genocide—as a product of cold war anti-communism.[7]

These open rebuttals of the Tibetan genocide charge are significant, not just for their high-profile defence of the Chinese record in Tibet, but for the fact that theirs are not isolated voices. It is notable that the Western academic community has been by and large reluctant to use the term genocide for China's treatment of ethnic minorities, except perhaps for describing the Manchu destruction of the Dzungar Mongols in the early period of the Qing dynasty (1644–1911),[8] even if they are sympathetic with the minorities and concerned with the human rights situation in Inner Mongolia, Tibet, and Xinjiang. To be sure, before the 1990s, Western studies of China's nationalities were much more inclined to talk of China's *assimilation* of nationalities, though they never denounced China as a 'prison of nationalities' as they did the Soviet Union, Yugoslavia, and many other communist multinational countries. Since the late 1980s, scholars have rejected the theories of assimilation, moving instead to emphasize the Chinese state's 'creation' of fifty-six *minzu* or nationalities and allotment of autonomies to all but the Han, the majority.[9] In the post-structural theorization about majority and minority relationship as being intersubjective, minority differences are said to have been accentuated or reified for the very purpose of constructing and sustaining the Han Chinese majority.[10] The paradigm shift in conceptualizing the 'nationality question' in China as ethnic

---

[5] Lopez, *Prisoners of Shangri-La*.

[6] Barry Sautman, 'Colonialism, Genocide, and Tibet', *Asian Ethnicity* 7:3. (2006), 243–65. *Idem*, 'Tibet and the (Mis-)Representation of Cultural Genocide', in *idem* (ed.), *Cultural Genocide and Asian State Peripheries* (New York: Palgrave Macmillan, 2006), 165–279.

[7] Tom Grunfeld, *The Making of Modern Tibet* (Armonk, NY: M. E. Sharpe, 1996), 146–9.

[8] Peter Perdue, *China Marches West: The Qing Conquest of Central Eurasia* (Cambridge, MA: Harvard University Press, 2005). Mark Levene, *Genocide in Age of Nation State*, vol ii: *Rise of the West and the Coming of Genocide* (London: I. B. Tauris, 2005).

[9] Dru C. Gladney, *Muslim Chinese: Ethnic Nationalism in the People's Republic* (Cambridge, MA: Harvard University Press, 1991); Katherine Palmer Kaup, *Creating the Zhuang: Ethnic Politics in China* (Boulder, CO: Lynne Rienner, 2000).

[10] Dru C. Gladney (ed.), *Making Majorities: Constituting the Nation in Japan, Korea, China, Malaysia, Fiji, Turkey, and the United States* (Stanford: Stanford University Press, 1998).

relationship poses a significant challenge to minority nationalists' perception of their fates.

How do we reconcile these two diametrically opposed views of the Chinese state behaviour to ethnic minorities? Has it 'created' minorities or 'destroyed' them? We have now come to an impasse largely caused by disagreement not only over the meaning of 'genocide' but more importantly over how even to conceptualize ethnicity in China.

In this chapter, I invoke a Chinese political concept of 'sinicization' (*hanhua*, literally becoming Han Chinese), with a hope to capture the nature of ethnic relations in China historically, and the political fate of ethnic groups in contemporary China. As will be clear, sinicization has powerful genealogical and governmental dimensions; it is not primarily an 'acculturation' process as it is understood generally.[11] Sinicization may not kill people directly, but it murders the non-Chinese sense of genealogical differences and their polities.

SINICIZATION AND POLITICIDE

To focus on sinicization is to take up a theme indigenous to China and key to understanding China's treatment of non-Chinese people historically. It is not an uncontroversial concept in Chinese studies circles, however. In the Western academia, sinicization is at the centre of assessing what are called 'conquest dynasties', such as the Mongol Yuan (1271–1368) and the Manchu Qing (1644–1911), especially the latter. Promoted by Mary Wright and Ping-ti Ho, sinicization was a major paradigm from the 1950s to the 1980s to explain the Manchu success in conquering and ruling China for more than two and half centuries.[12] The paradigm held that the Manchu adopted a policy of 'systematic sinicization' by sponsoring neo-Confucian norms of government, so much so that in the second half of the dynasty, the Manchu became largely sinicized, losing their own language and ethnic identity and becoming simply a ruling class.

The sinicization thesis has recently received powerful head-on challenges from historians of the Qing period. Evelyn Rawski, in a major polemic against Ping-ti Ho in 1996, argued that the key to Qing success in empire building lay in its ability

---

[11] Cf. Lemkin's objection to using terms like 'Germanization', 'Magyarization', 'Italianization'. Raphael Lemkin, *Axis Rule in Occupied Europe: Laws of Occupation, Analysis of Government, Proposals for Redress* (Washington DC: Carnegie Endowment for International Peace, 1944), 80.

[12] Mary Wright, *The Last Stand of Chinese Conservatism: The T'ung-Chih Restoration, 1862–1874* (Stanford: Stanford University Press, 1957); Ping-Ti Ho, 'The Significance of the Ch'ing Period in Chinese History', *Journal of Asian Studies* 26:2 (1967), 189–95.

to use its cultural links with the non-Han peoples of Inner Asia and to differentiate the administration of the non-Han region from the administration of the former Ming realm. She further argued that sinicization was nothing but twentieth-century Chinese nationalist ideology. More recently, Pamela Crossley and Mark Elliot countered the sinicization thesis by insisting that the Manchu rulers were deeply concerned with maintaining what Elliot called Manchu 'ethnic sovereignty'.[13]

Should we then abandon sinicization as an analytical concept as we have genocide? Surely sinicization also refers to the fate of the Yueh and of Nanzhao—originally non-Chinese areas in the south that were indeed submerged into Chinese culture. In fact, the Manchu embarked on systematic sinicization of themselves and the non-Chinese polities towards the end of the Qing even though trying to maintain their own sovereign domination. Moreover, the theoretical recognition of our common intersubjective ground hasn't abrogated the genealogical and political problems of sinicization in China.

The genealogical underpinning of sinicization is imbedded in the Confucian order of *xia-yi zhibian* (Chinese-barbarian distinction), and its avowed goal of *yixia bianyi* (using Chinese to transform barbarians) as preordained law of the world. It is most eloquently embodied in the famous ancient adage *fei wo zu lei, qi xin bi yi* (if he is not of our lineage, he is sure to have a different heart), suggesting that even if, as a non-Chinese, one speaks Chinese and behaves like a Chinese in every way, one is bound to be perfidious. Thus, for those who have been culturally sinicized to pass as Chinese must invent new genealogies to prove their Chineseness through patrilineal descent.[14] It follows that sinicization is inherently 'geneacidal', not so much in the sense of killing physically a non-Chinese people (though killing was often rampant and mutual), nor necessarily forcing them to speak Chinese, but in the sense of altering or obliterating their collective genealogical descent. Once the sense of foreign descent is eliminated, a non-Chinese group is deemed Chinese and is allowed to retain some of their ethnic customs. This explains the regional differences of the Chinese communities.

Sinicization subscribes to the Confucian political ideology whereby the civilized or Chinese be administered separately from the barbarians, and it has a mission to

---

[13] Evelyn S. Rawski, 'Presidential Address: Reenvisioning the Qing: The Significance of the Qing Period in Chinese History', *Journal of Asian Studies* 55:4 (1996), 831; Pamela K. Crossley, *A Translucent Mirror: History and Identity in Qing Imperial Ideology* (Berkeley: University of California Press, 1999); Mark C. Elliot, *The Manchu Way: The Eight Banners and Ethnic Identity in Late Imperial China* (Stanford: Stanford University Press, 2001).

[14] For the dialectics of Chinese culturalism and racism, see Patricia B. Ebrey, 'Surnames and Han Chinese Identity', in Melissa J. Brown (ed.), *Negotiating Ethnicities in China and Taiwan* (Berkeley: Institute of East Asian Studies, University of California, 1996), 19–36; Frank Dikötter, *The Discourse of Race in Modern China* (Stanford: Stanford University Press, 1992); Prasenjit Duara, *Rescuing History from the Nation: Questioning Narratives of Modern China* (Chicago: University of Chicago Press, 1995).

bring the barbarians under the same political administration for the Chinese. It is in carrying out this mission that we can find the negation and intended destruction of the non-Chinese peoples' organizational structure and their ethnic sovereignty. Thus, I suggest that essentially sinicization constitutes 'politicide' whose purpose is the destruction of the capacity to produce or reproduce a polity with the eventual aim of eliminating the 'political identity' of an ethnic group.[15]

Sinicization as a Confucian political programme should be located in the unification of China under the Qin dynasty (221–206 BCE), which established a *junxian* or centralized bureaucracy to govern Chinese local regions under an autocratic emperorship, and banished the former *fengjian* or feudal system. The *fengjian* system did not die out, but was allowed to persist amongst 'barbarians' at the margins of Chinese dynasties, granting them a certain amount of autonomy. Barbarians were seen by the Chinese as genealogically different as they were removed from the Chinese civilization. They were imagined to have bestial origins, hence dangerous to the Chinese, a conviction borne out by repeated wars. This difference warranted separate administrations under the *fengjian* system, but the difference did not have an intrinsic value as it had to be destroyed through changing the *benxing* (nature) of the barbarians by means of both altering their genealogy and bringing them under the centralized *junxian* administrative system. This was best manifest in a policy called *gaitu guiliu*, meaning replacing the *tusi* (native) officials with the court-appointed civilian officials (see below). One might argue that the *fengjian* was a concession to peoples beyond the reach of the Chinese power, and *junxian* system was the political arm of sinicization, predicated as it was on transformation of so-called barbarians, serving as a mechanism to expand Chinese polity, limited only by its military power.

The *fengjian* system had a different fate in 'conquest dynasties' established by Inner Asians, whom the Chinese call barbarians. In a conquest dynasty, the Chinese Confucian civilization would often be deprived of its hegemonic status, made equal to, if not lower than, other value systems brought into the dynasty. Buddhism, for instance, was powerfully promoted by the non-Chinese rulers in Northern Wei, Tang, Liao, Jin, Yuan, and Qing dynasties. Of course, not all conquest dynasties were the same. The Mongol Yuan and Manchu Qing statecrafts, closely reflecting their original confederate structure, were predicated on divide and rule, rather than centralization. The Mongol Yuan recognized four major ethnic groups—Mongol, Semu (coloured-eyed people, referring to the Turks, Arabs, and Europeans),

---

[15] Politicide as I use here does not refer to mass killings for political reasons as originally proposed by Barbara Harff. It is used in the sense defined by Baruch Kimmerling as 'a process that covers a wide range of social, political, and military activities whose goal is to destroy the political and national existence of a whole community of people and thus deny it the possibility of self-determination'. Barbara Harff, 'Recognizing Genocides and Politicides', in Helen Fein (ed.), *Genocide Watch* (New Haven, CT: Yale University Press, 1992), 28; Baruch Kimmerling, *Politicide: Sharon's War against the Palestinians* (London: Verso, 2003), 4.

Hanren (Han people, including Khitan, Jurchen, and Han subjects of the northern Song) and Nanren (southern people, referring to the subjects of the southern Song), and the Manchu Qing five ethnic groups—Manchu, Mongol, Tibetan, Hui (Muslims), and Chinese. Neither the Mongols nor the Manchu tried to Mongolize or Manchuize the populations. The primary concern of these two conquest dynasties was to maintain the ethnic sovereignty of the ruling groups by means of largely separate administrations for the different components of their empires, with 'China' ruled in a Chinese way and the other parts ruled according to their own local political cultures. Sinicization would have defeated the very purpose of their conquest.

However, non-Chinese conquest dynasties were not always immune from adopting the sinicizational model. When a conquest dynasty adopted the sinicizational model, it would often have more devastating effect on their non-Chinese allies in the empire than a Chinese dynasty would. This was because the policy came from 'the inside' rather than from the outside. The Northern Wei dynasty (386–534 CE) is a case in point. Of Särbi (Chinese: Xianbei) or Inner Asian nomadic origin, after moving the capital to Luoyang in 494, Emperor Xiaowen (467–499 CE) adopted a policy of systematic sinicization, issuing edicts to ban Särbi clothing, language, and surnames, all to be replaced by those of the Chinese. Sinicization marginalized the Särbi's own martial tradition, ultimately exposing them to both internal rebellion and external invasions.[16] Similarly, the Manchu attempt to destroy non-Chinese polities towards the end of the empire was symptomatic of sinicization, and it led to the loss of the support of their allies.

The *tusi* office was an indirect rule institution established by the Mongols during the Yuan dynasty—in the place of the Han, Tang, and Song institution of *jimi fu* (haltered-and-bridled prefecture), a concessionary administration for frontier peoples—to rule non-Chinese groups in today's Yunnan, Guizhou, and Sichuan. The institution was taken over by the Chinese Ming dynasty, which, however, repeatedly tried to eliminate it by establishing prefectures, departments, and counties, a policy called *gaitu guiliu*. The Qing initially maintained the *tusi* system, but it embarked on *gaitu guiliu* around 1700. The rationale was not so much 'the logic of the expanding empire demanded it,' as John Herman suggested,[17] but rather because the Manchu rulers had never been able to identify with the non-Chinese peoples such as the Lolo, Miao, and Turen, as they had with the Mongols,

---

[16] For a dissenting view, see Dorothy C. Wong, 'Ethnicity and Identity: Northern Nomads as Buddhist Art Patrons during the Period of Northern and Southern Dynasties', in Nicola Di Cosmo and Don J. Wyatt (eds), *Political Frontiers, Ethnic Boundaries and Human Geographies in Chinese History* (London: RoutledgeCurzon, 2003), 80–118.

[17] John E. Herman, 'The Cant of Conquest: Tusi Offices and China's Incorporation of the Southwest Frontier', in Pamela Kyle Crossley, Helen F. Siu, and Donald S. Sutton (eds), *Empire at the Margins: Culture, Ethnicity, and Frontier in Early Modern China* (Berkeley: University of California Press, 2006), 161.

Turkic Muslims, and Tibetans. In this region, the Chinese were deemed more useful to the Manchu conquerors, so the direct rule took on the Chinese institutional structure, establishing prefectures and counties.

The Manchu controlled the Inner Asians through a variety of means such as military conquest, marital alliance, religious patronization, and conferring titles.[18] The Manchu administration of various Inner Asian groups was extremely variegated, at times brutal, even genocidal to some less compliant groups, but most groups enjoyed some degrees of autonomy vis-à-vis the Qing court, and they were not subject to cultural assimilation to the Manchu or the Chinese. In fact, for the greater part of the Qing dynasty, the Mongols, Muslims, and Tibetans enjoyed higher status than the Chinese, and their lands were protected from Chinese migration.

The Manchu alliance with the Inner Asians was awkward from early on, due largely to the perennial Russian threat. After the first Opium War in 1840, as European powers and Japan encroached on Qing territories, native rules, originally designed to rally the Inner Asian peoples or to pacify them, now became a menace, transforming Inner Asia from the rear base to the perilous frontier, constituting a 'problem'. 'China proper' (*zhongguo benbu/bentu*), on the other hand, changed from a target of conquest to heartland.

The Qing suppression of the Muslim rebellions in the mid-nineteenth century heralded a sinicizational transition in the Qing empire, turning against its erstwhile Inner Asian allies. For the first time in Qing history, a Chinese army under the command of a Chinese general was deployed in Inner Asia. In 1884, on crushing the rebellion in Huijiang (Muslim regions), the native rules were abrogated, and the lands were renamed *Xinjiang sheng* (New Dominion province) with officials directly appointed by the Qing court.[19] The key to understanding the provincial (*xingsheng*) system in the frontier was that it was not just an establishment of a direct rule from the centre following the Confucian administrative system of *junxian*. Rather it was settler-colonialist in character, intended to make the Chinese population the bulwark of the new frontier regime.

Settler-colonization became an official Qing policy in 1902 when *xinzheng* (New Policy) was introduced in the wake of the Boxer Rebellion. It was a typical case of 'official nationalism', viz., the Manchus almost totally identified with the Chinese interest, and tried to extend the Chinese skin over the gigantic imperial body.

---

[18] See Chia Ning, 'The Li-fan Yuan of the Early Qing Dynasty', PhD dissertation, Johns Hopkins University, 1992. Joseph Fletcher, 'Ch'ing Inner Asia c. 1800', and 'The Heyday of the Ch'ing Order in Mongolia, Sinkiang and Tibet', in John K. Fairbank (ed.), *The Cambridge History of China*, vol x: *Late Ch'ing, 1800–1911, Part I* (Cambridge: Cambridge University Press, 1978), 35–106; 351–408. Nicola Di Cosmo, 'Qing Colonial Administration in Inner Asia', *International History Review* 20:2 (1998), 287–309.

[19] James A. Millward, '"Coming onto the Map": "Western Regions" Geography and Cartographic Nomenclature in the Making of Chinese Empire in Xinjiang', *Late Imperial China* 20:2 (1999), 61–98.

Mongolia was now turned into a frontier, subjected to a new policy of 'open up'—
fangkeng mengdi—in which Mongolian land was slated for cultivation by bringing
in Chinese farmers. Of course, there had already been significant Chinese settlement in the Mongol regions, especially in Josotu league, and in 1891 the Chinese
farmers massacred tens of thousands of Mongols in a rebellion called Jindandao.
Under this new official programme, large areas of fertile Mongol land, instead of
being rented from greedy or needy princes as had happened previously, were
forcefully confiscated and sold to Chinese settlers, a measure bringing tens of
thousands of Chinese peasants within a short period of time, and provoking
open resistance from Mongol princes. The same open-up policy had been carried
out unofficially much earlier in Manchuria, the Manchu's own homeland, so that
in 1907 Manchuria was seamlessly turned into three provinces—Heilongjiang, Jilin,
and Fengtian (changed to Liaoning in 1954), making it unmistakably Chinese. Less
than half a century later, Manchuria lost its name, and began to be known as
Dongbei (the Northeast) or *Dongsansheng* (the Eastern Three Provinces).[20]

If the provincialization of Manchuria went unopposed thanks to the Manchu's
own initiative and perhaps more importantly because Manchuria was largely
emptied of the Manchu who had been scattered in garrison towns throughout
the empire, their Inner Asian allies were less compliant. The threat of the New
Policy to the autonomy of the Mongol princes and the wide-scale violence between
Mongols and Chinese settlers in Inner Mongolia prompted Outer Mongolia to
declare independence in December 1911 with overwhelming response from Inner
Mongolia. Tibet soon followed suit. It is ironic that the Manchu sinicization and
their official nationalist programme in the Inner Asian frontier did not save them,
for Chinese nationalists, subscribing to the orthodox Confucian *xia-yi* distinction,
treated Manchu as alien barbarians unfit to rule China, holding them accountable
not only for humiliating the Chinese by conquering and ruling them, but for failing
to defend China against European and Japanese encroachments.[21] The Qing

---

[20] Burensain Borjigin, 'The Complex Structure of Ethnic Conflict in the Frontier: Through the
Debates around the "Jindandao Incident" in 1891', *Inner Asia* 6:1 (2004), 41–60. Tsai Sheng Luen,
'Chinese Settlement of Mongolian Lands: Manchu policy in Inner Mongolia/A Case Study of Chinese
Migration in Jerim League', PhD dissertation, Brigham Young University, 1983; Thomas. R.
Gottschang and Diana Lary, *Swallows and Settlers: The Great Migration from North China to
Manchuria* (Ann Arbor, MI: Center for Chinese Studies, University of Michigan, 2000); Mark C.
Elliot, 'The Limits of Tartary: Manchuria in Imperial and National Geographies', *Journal of Asian
Studies* 59:3 (2000), 603–646; Li Narangoa, 'The Power of Imagination: Whose Northeast and Whose
Manchuria?', *Inner Asia* 4:1 (2002), 3–25.

[21] Peter C. Perdue, 'Erasing the Empire, Re-racing the Nation: Racialism and Culturalism in
Imperial China', in Ann Laura Stoler, Carole McGranaham, and Peter C. Perdue (eds), *Imperial
Formations* (Santa Fe: School for Advanced Research Press, 2007), 141–69; Peter Zarrow, 'Historical
Trauma: Anti-Manchuism and Memories of Atrocity in Late Qing China', *History and Memory* 16:2
(2004), 67–107.

empire crumbled in 1911, and with it the integrity of the Manchu as an organized political entity.

The new Republic of China founded in 1912 was thoroughly sino-centric even though it proclaimed a 'union of five races' (*wuzu gonghe*)—Chinese, Manchu, Mongol, Tibetan, and Muslims.[22] The multinational veneer was soon replaced by a new concept—*zhonghua minzu*, the Chinese nation, in which the four non-Chinese races were not recognized as having separate ethnic identities; instead, they were to be treated as lineages (*zongzu*) of the Chinese nation stemming from the same ancestors of the Chinese—Yan and Huang emperors.[23] This genealogical nationalism was unprecedented in Chinese history, not only in imagination, but also in scope. The denial of different genealogical descent lines of the non-Chinese peoples was accompanied by efforts to destroy their native polities implemented during the Qing and bring them under the provincial system, a sinicizational policy carried out in full force in Mongolia first.

Outer Mongolia's independence was lost when it was forced to participate in a tripartite conference with Russia and China, resulting in an autonomous state in 1915, recognizing China's suzerainty. The autonomy was annulled by a Chinese invasion in 1919 only to provoke another Mongol rebellion, eventually resulting in a Mongolian People's Republic (MPR) proclaimed in 1924 under the Soviet aegis. The 'loss' of Outer Mongolia further strengthened the Chinese determination to eliminate native administrations.

Inner Mongolia bore the brunt of the Chinese attacks. As early as 1915, the Republic of China established three *tebie xinzheng qu* (special administrative regions)—Suiyuan, Chaha'er, and Rehe—in the territory of Inner Mongolia over the Mongolian leagues and banners. In 1928, as the Chinese Nationalist Party (the Nationalists) won the civil war and built a Nationalist government, further pushing for an exclusively Chinese nationalist agenda, these special administrative zones were formally turned into provinces. 'Inner Mongolia' thence disappeared from the map of the Republic of China. Several more provinces were built in China's Inner Asian frontiers in the same year: Ningxia in the Muslim-inhabited areas to the north of the Gansu corridor, Qinghai in the Mongol–Tibetan–Muslim area of Kokonuur, and Xikang in the Khamba region of eastern Tibet.

Sinicization, as we have seen, became first and foremost a nationalist project in the Republican China. The vehemence the project took points to the extreme anxiety of the Chinese Nationalists to build both a strong unitary state and a homogeneous nation to stand up to challenges by other nations in the age of

---

[22] Joseph W. Esherick, 'How the Qing Became China', in Joseph W. Esherick, Hasan Kayali, Eric Van Young (eds), *Empire to Nation: Historical Perspectives on the Making of the Modern World* (Lanham: Rowman AND Littlefield, 2006), 229–59.

[23] James Patrick Leibold, 'Constructing the Zhonghua Minzu: The Frontier and National Questions in Early 20th Century China'. PhD dissertation, University of Southern California, 2002.

imperial nationalism. In this anxiety, the Chinese nationalists tolerated not even Chinese local autonomy, still less frontier non-Chinese autonomy. In declaring the Manchu, Mongols, Muslims, and Tibetans as genealogically Chinese, ethnicity took the form of *bianzheng* (frontier governance). Since there was no ethnic question as there were no officially recognized ethnic groups, the nationalist project was declared accomplished upon destroying frontier administrations and establishing provinces and counties settled by Han Chinese 'lineage' of the Chinese nation. After 1928, only the MPR and the 'Tibet proper' ruled by the Dalai Lama were beyond the reach of the Chinese power, but their demolition and provincialization remained the undying dream of the Chinese Nationalists until their own demise in 1949.

SINICIZATION THROUGH NATIONALITY REGIONAL AUTONOMY

The Republican China's politicidal programme of sinicization provoked intense resistance from the non-Chinese peoples who now began to fight for autonomy and some even for independence. Some turned to external powers as the only hope for their survival as a collective group, appealing to the principles of national self-determination and colonial liberation. In the 1930s, an Inner Mongolian autonomous government emerged with Japanese help. Like the Japanese, the Chinese Communist Party (CCP), as a militant opposition party aspiring to take over the government from the ruling Nationalists, found in the non-Chinese nationalism a useful energy to tap, hoping to use minorities as useful allies to fight a common enemy. It was in the CCP's effort to win the confidence of minorities that the party's harshest and most effective denunciation of the Nationalists' sinicization programme was heard.

In 1935, when the beleaguered CCP settled in Yan'an of north China, facing pressure from the Nationalists and a looming war with Japan, Mao Zedong made a solemn declaration to the Mongols of Inner Mongolia, in which he denounced the Nationalists' non-recognition of 'minority nationalities' and their 'sinicization' policy for the suffering it caused to the Mongolian people. He vowed that his Soviet government would restore the original Mongol league and banner system, pledging, 'Under no circumstances should other nationalities be allowed to occupy the land of the Inner Mongolian nation or expropriate it under various excuses.' In 1945, poised to challenge the Nationalists in the post-WWII settlement, Mao condemned the Nationalists for denying the existence of nationalities in China and particularly for the crime of 'the massacre of Mongolians of the Ikhchao

[Yekejuu] League in 1943, the armed suppression of the minority nationalities in Sinkiang [Xinjiang] since 1944 and the massacres of the Hui people in Kansu Province in recent years'.[24]

'Promise', 'recognition', 'sympathy' were, as we have seen, the strategies of the CCP used to intervene on behalf of the beleaguered minorities, but these concepts are as illocutionary as governmental. Inner Mongolian communists-cum-nationalists were the first to respond to the CCP and established an Inner Mongolia Autonomous Government in May 1947 with the CCP support. Since the founding of the People's Republic of China (PRC) in 1949, an autonomous system called *Minzu quyu zizhi* (Nationality Regional Autonomy) has been implemented for newly classified minority nationalities—55 as of today—each organized under a territorial administrative unit. By the end of 2002, in addition to the five province-level autonomous regions, there were 76 autonomous prefectures, 28 prefecture-level autonomous cities, 699 autonomous counties, and 68 county-level autonomous counties. These autonomous areas cover 63.72 per cent of China's territories, and officially recognized minorities constitute 8.41 per cent of China's total population with a substantial number living in non-autonomous areas of China.[25]

The post-revolutionary official storyline of the CCP nationality policy is that it has 'saved' the minorities from 'extinction' under the imperialists and the Nationalists, and the minorities have been living happily and gaily in a great family of nationalities since 1949. But why do minority nationalists by and large decry CCP's nationality policy as genocidal, and nothing short of genuine autonomy would guarantee their continued survival as mentioned at the beginning of this chapter? The answer requires a closer look at the kind of autonomy the CCP instituted to minorities.

Autonomy, for the CCP, is a tool of political expediency, and is granted according to the power relations in a given situation. It is above all a mechanism for integrating a politically organized group into the Chinese sovereignty, rather than an institution in recognition of their intrinsic difference. Autonomous power is reduced and even rescinded according to the degree of integration. This is a systemic issue having its foundation in the 'unitary' national structure of the PRC rejecting the federal system.[26] Below are some features of the Nationality Regional Autonomy (NRA) as implemented for minority nationalities.

First, a non-Chinese group is not 'granted' an NRA, but 'brought into' NRA only when a new native leadership is ideologically and organizationally incorporated or

---

[24] Stuart R. Schram (ed.), *Mao's Road to Power: Revolutionary Writings 1912–1949* (Armonk, NY: M. E. Sharpe, 1999), v.71. Mao Zedong, 'On Coalition Government', in *Selected Works of Mao Tse-tung* (Peking: Foreign Languages Press, 1967), 256.

[25] National Bureau of Statistics of China, *China Statistical Yearbook* (Beijing: China Statistics Press, 2003), 43.

[26] Baogang He, 'Minority Rights with Chinese Characteristics', in Will Kymlicka and Baogang He (eds), *Multiculturalism in Asia* (Oxford: Oxford University Press, 2005), 56–79.

subordinated to the CCP which practises 'democratic centralism'. The founding of the Inner Mongolia Autonomous Government in 1947 was initially mired in a bitter struggle about whether it should be led by the Inner Mongolia People's Revolutionary Party or the CCP. With the CCP leadership firmly established, the autonomous government was seamlessly changed to the Inner Mongolia Autonomous Region, an integral part of the PRC in October 1949. Similarly, it took the destruction of the semi-independent Tibetan Government in 1951, flight of the Dalai Lama to India in 1959, and the removal of the Panchen Lama from Tibet in 1964, to prepare a condition to establish a Tibet Autonomous Region in 1965. Bringing into NRA is therefore not recognition of native polity, but its reorganization into a system little different from the Chinese provincial and county administrative system, with the leadership directly appointed by the CCP. In fact, although the executive leaders of the NRA areas have been from titular nationalities (except during the Cultural Revolution), the main power—the posts of Party secretary and chairmanship of the People's Congress—has been in the hands of the Han, with very few exceptions.

Second, the NRA is a combination of nationality autonomy and regional autonomy; it is institutionally designed to use the regional principle to trump the nationality principle. It is characteristic of all autonomous places to include substantial number of Han Chinese, and in many cases, the Chinese outnumber the titular minorities in their own autonomous locality. Indeed, the NRA was justified on an 'objective' reality of *da sanju, xiao juju*—implying that minorities lived in small compact communities, and scattered amidst other groups, especially the Han Chinese. The insistence on the Han incorporation was justified also on the ground of evolutionism and Confucian ethics. In this logic, since socialist modernity required economic and political advancement, Han, as an advanced people by default, had to be there, with the ostensible altruistic purpose to 'help' minorities to 'progress'. A more practical concern was national security, seeing minority nationalities as secessionist and subversive. Thus, with the Han as the indispensable component of NRA, this autonomy has attained key features of settler-colonialism.

The imbrication of nationality autonomy and regional autonomy, buttressed by ideological and national security imperatives, pit the minorities and the Han against each other. The PRC established a large Chinese colony called Xinjiang Production and Construction Corp created in 1954, a year before the founding of the Xinjiang Uyghur Autonomous Region, and the Corp has 2.5 million Han Chinese working there now. In addition, Han settlers gradually built up their presence throughout Xinjiang, increasing from six per cent in 1949 to over forty per cent of the region's entire population at present. In Tibet, the number of Han settlers is the most serious contention between the Tibetans and the Chinese, constituting the core basis for the Tibetan independence movement and the Dalai Lama's demand for 'genuine' autonomy. Tibetans contend that they have already become a minority in their own homeland; the Chinese government and some academics insist, however, either that this phenomenon is confined to Lhasa or that Chinese residents there are largely seasonal migrants, but not settlers.[27]

In Inner Mongolia, the issue of Chinese settlement has equally exasperated ethnic tension, forcing even Mongol cadres to rebel. The issue was not so much about the Chinese becoming the majority—by 1949, the Chinese had already outnumbered the Mongols by seven to one. Rather, it was about the Chinese settlers challenging the nominal Mongol autonomous rights, thus prompting Ulanhu, the most prominent Mongol CCP cadre, to reissue Mao's 1935 declaration to the Inner Mongols in 1965, using Mao's promise as the source of Mongolian autonomy. In the subsequent struggle, the entire Mongol cadre corps became the target of a witch-hunt as they were suspected of being underground nationalists conspiring with the Soviet Union and the Mongolian People's Republic to tear away Inner Mongolia from China. Between 1968 and 1969, an Inner Mongolia-wide campaign against Mongol nationalists was carried out, in which 16,222 people were killed by official Chinese acknowledgement. Between 1969 and 1979, the Inner Mongolia Autonomous Region was territorially dissected, with the western part divided up by Gansu province and Ningxia Hui Autonomous Region, and the eastern part by Heilongjiang, Jilin, and Liaoning provinces, leaving only the central part under the direct Chinese military regime. This destruction is the very source of a new wave of Mongolian nationalism. The high death toll has been characterized as genocidal.[28]

Third, the NRA regions follow the same socialist modernization path as in China proper, but development is characterized by explicit ethnic division of labour. The developmentalist state prioritized developing heavy industry and natural resource extraction industry in Inner Mongolia from the first Five-Year Plan in the early 1950s. In 1964, fearing a war with the Soviet Union and the United States, the Chinese government launched a large-scale programme called the Third Front, transferring many military and heavy machinery plants in the coastal cities and Manchuria to the western and south-western mountainous regions inhabited by

---

[27] Yan Hao, 'Tibetan Population in China: Myths and Facts Re-examined', *Asian Ethnicity* 1:1 (March 2000), 11–36. Barry Sautman, ' "Demographic Annihilation" and Tibet', in Barry Sautman and June Teufel Dreyer (eds), *Contemporary Tibet: Politics, Development, and Society in a Disputed Region* (Armonk, NY: M. E. Sharpe, 2005), 230–57.

[28] Uradyn E. Bulag, 'Inner Mongolia: The Dialectics of Colonization and Ethnicity Building', in Morris Rossabi (ed.), *Governing China's Multiethnic Frontiers* (Washington, DC: University of Washington Press, 2004), 84–116; Tumen and Zhu Dongli, *Kang Sheng yu Neirendang Yuan'an* (*Kang Sheng and the Wrongful Case of the Inner Mongolia People's Revolutionary Party*) (Beijing: Zhonggong Zhongyang Dangxiao Chubanshe, 1995); Wu Di, ' "Neirendang" Da Xue'an Shimo' ('The Beginning and the End of the "Neirendang" Massacre Case'), in Song Yongyi (ed.), *Massacres during the Cultural Revolution* (Hong Kong: Kaifang Zazhi She, 2002), 59–109; Altandelekei, *Mongolian Genocide during the Cultural Revolution in Inner Mongolia*, trans. Yang Haiying (in (Shizuoka University Departmental Bulletin Paper, 2008). [in Japanese] Available at: http://ir.lib.shizuoka.ac. jp/bitstream/10297/2552/1/080716001.pdf

minorities such as the Yi and Tibetans. More than thirty new industrial cities have developed over the decades with their population being largely Chinese settlers. In 2000, as China's coastal industries began to shift from assembling to manufacturing, thereby requiring increasing amount of natural resources which the western region has in abundance, China launched a new national programme called Develop the West, *xibu dakaifa*, in imitation of the American westward expansion model. In all these programmes, minority participation is minimum.

Fourth, the NRA purports to enjoy one of the world's most favourable affirmative action policies, but it proves to have cynical outcome for minorities. Minorities are allowed to speak their languages, if they still can.[29] They are also exempted from the one-child policy. Although individually minorities have benefited from such favourable policies, so have the majority individuals, many of whom have adopted minority identity to accrue personal benefits. These individuals do not need to satisfy any criteria for being a minority, nor do they need to demonstrate any traits associated with a minority, except wearing minority dresses on ceremonial occasions. They do not enrich minority cultures and languages, but 'water down' or 'hollow out' them, in Juha Janhunen's terms, resulting in what he calls an 'ethnic inflation', whereby populations of many minority groups have multiplied dramatically. 'Altogether, ethnic inflation is best seen as a government tool for the rapid assimilation of the minorities under a minimal danger of ethnic conflict.'[30] One may add that such inflation can happen only when an ethnic group is deprived of any internal mechanism to control its internal boundary.

As is clear, although the CCP recognized the existence of nationalities, nonetheless solving the 'nationality question' has been an integral part of the CCP's overall plan to 'reconstruct' China. This has been carried out by means of the NRA. Rogers Brubaker's characterization of the early Soviet nationality policies was equally applicable to China:

first, to harness, contain, channel, and control the potentially disruptive political expression of nationality by creating national-territorial administrative structures and by cultivating, co-opting, and (when they threatened to get out of line) repressing national elites; and second, to drain nationality of its content even while legitimizing it as a form, and thereby to promote the long-term withering away of nationality as a vital component of social life.[31]

---

[29] A major exception appears to be Xinjiang, where the government has intervened to discourage Uyghur language. Many Uyghur language schools have been merged with Chinese language schools beginning in the mid-1990s, which has been characterized as 'linguicide—the forced extinction of minority languages'. Arienne M. Dwyer, *The Xinjiang Conflict: Uyghur Identity, Language Policy, and Political Discourse* (Washington, DC: East-West Center Washington, 2005), 39.

[30] Juha Janhunen, 'Tungusic: An Endangered Language Family in Northeast Asia', *International Journal of the Sociology of Language* 173 (May 2005), 43.

[31] Rogers Brubaker, *Nationalism Reframed: Nationhood and the National Question in the New Europe* (Cambridge: Cambridge University Press, 1996), 25.

We thus have in NRA a unique paradox of nationality-building for the purpose of nationality-destruction; politicide was a built-in feature of China's nationality building.

RECTIFICATION OF NAMES: THE FINAL SOLUTION?

The rapidly changing ethnoscape and administrative landscape in China's ethnic minority frontier are unmistakably the success story of sinicization, aided by a number of techniques, including but not limited to corporatism, developmentalism, nationalism, and the NRA system. This new 'reality' has to be reconceptualized, renamed.

Recall that the Dalai Lama's demand for 'genuine autonomy' is based on his conviction that the NRA does not serve as an institution to protect Tibetan cultural identity, quite the reverse. Ironically, the Chinese government and the Chinese settlers are not happy with this 'form' of autonomy either, even though it is defended as the best possible measure for fully guaranteeing minority identity. In the remainder of this chapter, I focus on *zheng ming* (rectification of names), the quintessential Confucian technique of governance—'to govern is to rectify'—now used by the Chinese government and some academics to 'name away' the political identities of minorities and to fuse them into a revamped Chinese nation in the recent two and half decades.

We can now identify a distinct governmental measure to rectify names in many areas of ethnicity in China. There have been increasing calls to change the name 'autonomous *regions*' to 'autonomous *provinces*'. In Inner Mongolia, the rectification of place names is explicitly linked to a new mode of governance, for many prefecture level leagues (Mongolian: *aimag*; Chinese: *meng*) have been changed to *zhixiashi* (municipality) under a programme called *che meng she shi*—revoking the league to establish municipality, some even losing their Mongol names to Chinese ones. In 1981, barely two years after Jo'uda League was returned to the Inner Mongolia Autonomous Region, it was renamed Chifeng Municipality. This was followed by Jerim League, which was changed to Tongliao Municipality in 1999. As of 2008, four more leagues have been turned to municipalities, though their Mongol names have survived. The rationale for this rectification of names was given by the party secretary and the mayor of Tongliao Municipality, both ethnic Chinese, who wrote in a glowing piece published in *People's Daily* on 6 October 1999: 'This is the result of deepening reform, expanding opening-up, and accelerating development undertaken by the people of Tongliao under the leadership of the Party . . . By replacing league with municipality (*che meng she shi*), history once again gives Tongliao people a development opportunity that comes only once in a thousand years.'[32] What this suggests is that development opportunities for ethnic Chinese require changing an NRA area into a cosmopolitan, and better an explicitly Chinese, space marked by a Chinese name.

The rectification of names are already taking place in many NRA places where some native toponyms, even ethnonyms, have been distorted or rendered only in Chinese, sometimes with an explicit aim of domesticating a transnational people. For instance, the Kirghiz inside China is rendered Ke'erkezi, whereas outside China it is Ji'erjisi; the Evenki inside China is called Ewenke, but Aiwenji for those in Russia.[33] Place names are not just names reflecting the topographical features of the NRA regions; they reflect the cultural, physical, and social environments of the name-givers. In changing the names of the places, these places are expropriated from their native residents, making them unable to culturally associate with their own land. A new ethno-archaeology is now on the rise whereby minority scholars collect toponyms as a way of keeping memory of their homeland alive.

The most fundamental rectification pertains to renaming 'the Chinese People' (*zhongguo renmin*) as 'the Chinese Nation/Nationality' (*zhonghua minzu*) since the late 1980s. This is a move away from the communist statehood to embrace the principle of national state whose subject is not class-based 'people of various nationalities' but nation. In this new move, the term *minzu* (nation/nationality) has come to refer to the entire citizens of China, thereby creating a question of how to call minority nationalities (*shaoshu minzu*). Since the mid-1990s, the English translation of *minzu* has been officially changed from 'nationality' to 'ethnic group' or simply 'ethnic'. Although the Chinese term *minzu* for minorities is retained in official usage, the academic community has opted for a neologism, *zuqun*, literally meaning ethnic group, in an effort both to follow the Euroamerican academic norm and to 'depoliticize *minzu*'. In this rendering, nationality is understood as a political and territorial concept, and the designation of minorities as 'nationalities' is deemed detrimental to 'national unity', conducive to secessionism.

In the cacophony of depoliticizing *minzu*, some scholars have even suggested changing the very term of *zizhi* (autonomy; literally self-rule) to *gongzhi* (literally joint rule), translating the latter as 'jointnomy'. The key purpose of this putative innovation is to render the Chinese settlers as legitimate residents of autonomous areas, making them indigenous to the land, thereby breaking the *zhuti* (titular)

---

[32] Uradyn E. Bulag, 'From Yeke-juu League to Ordos Municipality: Settler Colonialism and Alter/Native Urbanization in Inner Mongolia', *Provincial China* 7:2 (2002), 207.

[33] Naran Bilik, 'Names Have Memories: History, Semantic Identity and Conflict in Mongolian and Chinese Language Use'. *Inner Asia* 9:1 (2007), 23–39. See also Magnus Fiskesjö, 'The Autonomy of Naming: Kinship, Power and Ethnonymy in the Wa Lands of the Southeast Asia-China Frontier', in Yangwen Zheng and Charles MacDonald (eds), *Personal Names in Asia: History, Culture and Identity* (Singapore: University of Singapore Press, 2008).

principle in the current system that endorses minorities as the sole proprietors of their respective autonomous areas.[34]

Most of the new grand conceptual narratives have made inroads among Chinese officials, the population at large, including so-called liberal intellectuals and Chinese students or new immigrants living in Western countries. They now see the Tibetan and Uyghur 'questions' partly as a result of a semiotic concession to minorities. For instance, the most common claim today is that the Tibetan demand for genuine autonomy harms 'the people of all ethnics in Tibet' (*Xizang gezu renmin*, or for short *Xizang ren*). We may say that many new conglomerate 'jointnomous' peoples have been created: *Xizang Ren* for the Tibet Autonomous Region, *Xinjiang Ren* for the Xinjiang Uyghur Autonomous Region, and of course *Neimeng Ren* for the Inner Mongolia Autonomous Region, and so on. These new peoples are all 'indigenous'!

Depoliticized, ethnic minorities can now be safely embraced and appropriated as constituting the property of the reconstituted Chinese nation and culture. Today, minorities are once again genealogically modified and secured as *Yanhuang zisun* (children of Yan and Huang emperors) sharing the same ancestors with the Han Chinese. It is not surprising that despite the demise of their native polities or autonomies, or perhaps precisely because of it, minority cultures, especially their ceremonial parts, have been 'revitalized'. Minorities sing and dance, and ethnic tourism is booming. The kind of ethnic cultures that exist in China today can only be described as 'spectacular', forming a dazzling new ethnoscape.

It may now be concluded that sinicization has made a remarkable success in the PRC more than any other time in Chinese history. Chinese policies have been directed at destroying the possibility that non-Chinese national identity might have any political meaning, at destroying the minorities' capacity to think and do politics independently as sovereign ethnic groups. In the PRC, the power of sinicization has derived from several major sources: the nationalizing imperative of the Chinese state that has not only domesticated non-Chinese peoples as Chinese minorities, but subtly redefining minority identity to be an aspect of Chineseness, rather than different from Chinese; the hegemonic representation of sinicization as modernization which renders the Chinese culture as superior a priori, and which imposes the Chinese culture as a gesture of benevolence that cannot be rejected; large-scale Han Chinese settlement in minority areas and repression of minority dissent; and most crucially the penetration into and tearing apart the inner fabric of the minorities through the CCP's organizational restructuring. What results is a unique complex of both politicide and simulacrum of cultural efflorescence.

[34] Ma Rong, 'Lijie Minzu Guanxi de Xin Silu: Shaoshu Zuqun Wenti de "Qu Zhengzhi Hua"' ('New Perspective to Understand Ethnic Relations: De-politicization of Ethnicity'), *Bejing Daxue Xuebao* 41:6 (2004), 122–33; Zhu Lun, 'Minzu Gongzhi Lun: Dui Dangdai Duo Minzu Guojia Zuji Zhengzhi Shishi de Renshi' ('On Ethno-national Jointnomy: A Study of the Political Realities in Ethno-national Communities in Contemporary States with Multiple Ethnic Groups'), *Zhongguo Shehui Kexue* 4 (2001), 95–105.

FURTHER READING

Blondeau, Anne-Marie and Katia Buffetrille (eds), *Authenticating Tibet: Answers to China's 100 Questions* (Berkeley: University of California Press, 2008).

Bovingdon, Gardner, *Autonomy in Xinjiang: Han Nationalist Imperatives and Uyghur Discontent* (Washington, DC: East-West Center Washington, 2005).

Brown, Kerry, *The Purge of the Inner Mongolian People's Party in the Chinese Cultural Revolution, 1967–69: A Function of Language, Power and Violence* (Folkestone: Global Oriental, 2006).

Bulag, Uradyn E., *The Mongols at China's Edge: History and the Politics of National Unity* (Lanham: Rowman and Littlefield, 2002).

Gladney, Dru C., *Dislocating China: Reflections on Muslims, Minorities, and Other Subaltern Subjects* (London: C. Hurst, 2004).

Herman, John E., *Amid the Clouds and Mist: China's Colonization of Guizhou, 1200–1700* (Cambridge, MA: Harvard University Press, 2007).

Liu, Xiaoyuan, *Reins of Liberation: An Entangled History of Mongolian Independence, Chinese Territoriality, and Great Power Hegemony, 1911–1950* (Stanford: Stanford University Press, 2006).

Margolin, Jean-Louis, 'Mao's China: The Worst Non-Genocidal Regime?', in Dan Stone (ed.), *The Historiography of Genocide* (Houndmills: Palgrave Macmillan, 2008), 438–67.

Millward, James, *Eurasian Crossroads: A History of Xinjiang* (New York: Columbia University Press, 2007).

Shakya, Tsering, *The Dragon in the Land of Snow: A History of Modern Tibet since 1947* (London: Pimlico, 1999).

Smith, Warren W., Jr., *China's Tibet?: Autonomy or Assimilation* (Lanham: Rowman and Littlefield, 2008).

Starr, S. Frederick (ed.), *Xinjiang: China's Muslim Borderland* (Armonk: M. E. Sharpe, 2004).

CHAPTER 22

....

POLITICAL
GENOCIDES IN
POSTCOLONIAL
ASIA

....

ROBERT CRIBB

ETHNIC AND POLITICAL GROUP IDENTITY

....

MASS political killing presents a special analytical problem in genocide studies. The slaughter of human beings because of the political beliefs and attitudes they held, or were presumed to hold, cost millions of lives during the twentieth century. In terms of the number of victims, the most extensive such killings—in the Soviet Union, Indonesia, China, and Cambodia—match events unambiguously regarded as genocide. Yet mass political killing is not prima facie covered by the 1948 UN Convention that makes genocide a crime in international law. In identifying genocide as acts intended to destroy a 'national, ethnical, racial or religious' group, the definition seems almost pointed in its exclusion of political killing. Nor does mass political killing match the broader perception that genocide is primarily a phenomenon of interethnic relations. Raphael Lemkin, who coined the term, succinctly characterized genocide in 1945 as 'deliberately wiping out whole peoples'.[1] His broader work, too, emphasized the character of genocide as an act of cultural and social destruction, which compounded the crime of mass murder. Generations of genocide scholars since Lemkin have invested great energy into refining this characterization, but this refinement has worked mainly to identify more complex processes of ethnic extermination. There remains a persistent reluctance in the field of genocide studies to allow mass political murder to qualify as genocide. Schabas put this position forcefully: 'Confusing mass killing of the members of the perpetrators' own group with genocide is inconsistent with the purposes of the Convention, which was to protect national minorities from crimes based on ethnic hatred.'[2] Even though the Holocaust against the Jews was accompanied by a savage persecution of German socialists and other political enemies of the Nazis, there is a powerful inclination to see the ethnic dimension of the persecution as raising the Holocaust to a different level of turpitude from that of the political murders. This inclination crystallized in the 1988 coining of a new word, 'politicide', by Harff and Gurr to designate mass killings in which the victims were targeted for their political affiliation, rather than their ethnicity.[3] The term, now two decades old, has had a mixed academic career. Although it has been used by those who, like Harff and Gurr, are reluctant to regard political killings as genocide, its form suggests that it applies to any kind of political killing, including perhaps assassinations. Other scholars, Schabas amongst them, prefer to use the term 'crimes against humanity' when discussing mass killing with political motives.

Every definition is suspended in a web of explicit and implicit understandings of the world. The definition of genocide that separates it from mass political killings is located within a deep-seated perception in Western intellectual life that ethnic identity is primordial, or at least historical, whereas political identity is a matter of choice. Only a minority of scholars today see national identity as arising from the deep cultural identity of a distinct people, but the mainstream of scholarly writing on nationalism nonetheless emphasizes that the national identity of each individual is a product of powerful, even inescapable, forces of socialization. One is not Indonesian, or Iranian, or Italian, or Icelander by choice, but rather by virtue of the circumstances in which one grows up. By contrast, political identity is understood to be malleable. One is left or right or centrist as a consequence of reflection on the problems of the world. Even if the circumstances in which one grows up are influential, they are not decisive—a conservative upbringing can and often does produce a radical; a political career can shift from right to left and back again.

[1] Raphael Lemkin, 'Genocide: a Modern Crime', *Free World* 9:4 (1945), 39.
[2] William Schabas, *Genocide in International Law: The Crimes of Crimes* (Cambridge: Cambridge University Press, 2000), 119.
[3] Barbara Harff and T. R. Gurr, 'Toward Empirical Theory of Genocides and Politicides: Identification and Measurement of Cases since 1945', *International Studies Quarterly* 37:3 (1988), 359–71.

This distinction between primordial ethnic identity and acquired political identity leads to a significant difference in moral judgement. Aside from our condemnation of any atrocity or injustice, we feel especial indignation when people are punished for what they are, rather than what they have done. This indignation appears when we suspect, for instance, that members of minority communities receive harsher treatment in the legal system than do members of the majority. Indignation is most acute, however, in that quintessential genocidal image of the massacre of women and children, the aged and infirm, for no other reason than the ethnic group that they belong to. In the case of political killings, by contrast, indignation is often tempered by the rationalization that the victims had chosen to engage in politics and that their doom, even if unjust, was a consequence of their own fatal decisions. This moral contrast between the innocent and the defiant—the moral distinction between those who are made victims for what they are and those who are made victims for what they have done, or failed to do—in fact reaches into the heart of genocide studies itself. Although the UN Convention definition identifies four straightforward categories of victim ('national, ethnical, racial, or religious'), genocide scholars have often not been inclined to explore religious victimization as a distinct form of genocide unless it is linked with ethnicity, as in the persecution of Jews.

The broader human consequences of ethnic destruction and political killing also appear to be different. Ethnic identity is often perceived as part of the cultural heritage of humankind, an irreplaceable human resource which, if lost, can no more be recovered than can an animal or plant species that has been driven to extinction. Genocide, Lemkin stressed, is a crime against humanity not just because the mode of killing repudiates basic human values but also because the destruction of human cultural diversity is a crime against all of us, not just the immediate victims. By contrast, again, the dominant image of the victims of political and religious persecution is that they go to their deaths confident that their beliefs will live on after them and that their deaths may even hasten progress towards eventual victory. Tertullian's epigram, 'The blood of martyrs is the seed of the church,' has been echoed in countless variants across the centuries. A host of political rationalizations exists moreover for the destruction of political enemies. Wading through a sea of blood pouring from slain political enemies in order to achieve a glittering future for humankind may be a repellent image, but in the modern world it has been far less repellent than the genocidal slaughter of children.

In the decades since the term genocide was coined and its official definition was set, however, important reasons have emerged for regarding the distinctions between ethnic and political mass killing as rather less significant than they appeared to be in the 1940s. First, trends in scholarship have challenged the presumption that ethnic identity is simply primordial or historically determined. In 1983, Eric Hobsbawm and Terence Ranger coined the term 'invention of tradition', which drew attention to the fact that many of those elements that constitute the most visible and most appealing features of cultural identity were in fact created con-sciously or half-consciously and rather recently as cultural symbols, rather than being deeply embedded in a cultural-historical past.[4] This insight implies a mallea-bility of culture that sits uneasily with primordialist and historical assumptions of the deep roots of ethnic identity. It implies that cultural identity can be acquired in similar way to political identity. The cultural studies turn in scholarship has reinforced this insight. Cultural studies scholars have deconstructed the notion of cultural authenticity, showing that the privileging of some essentialized cultural form, on the basis of its antiquity and or some other marker of validity, is itself a cultural construction.[5] Cultural studies scholars have also celebrated cultural innovation, especially hybridity.[6] This new understanding of culture as something constantly in flux, constantly reinvented, constantly created, has eroded the notion that cultural heritage is a fragile treasure to be preserved by interventionist protec-tive measures. None of these insights devalued culture in moral terms; on the contrary, cultural studies celebrated cultural diversity and heterogeneity in a way that the older canonical approach did not. But they cast profound doubt over the presumption that any culture could define a 'whole group' in the way specified by the UN Convention. By asserting that culture, as a living, changing phenomenon, could not be preserved without destroying it, cultural studies eroded the broad philosophical underpinning of ethnic identity as a special category in social affairs. With this erosion, the argument for restricting the term genocide to ethnically directed killing was also diminished.

Second, other analytical trends in social science began to highlight similarities between political and ethnic identity. Some of these similarities are especially marked in the so-called pillarization (*verzuiling, pilarization*) of Dutch and Belgian society. For much of the nineteenth and twentieth centuries—the period following the emergence of mass politics—Dutch and Belgian societies were vertically seg-mented into pillars (*zuilen*) according to religion and political ideology. Dutch society was marked by four pillars, Protestant, Catholic, socialist, and liberal, each of them with its own political parties, trade unions, newspapers, schools, univer-sities, hospitals, sporting and cultural associations, and building societies. Even large private firms were often strongly associated with a single *zuil* and would hire staff only from that segment of the population. The *zuilen* were defined by belief, including political belief, and they constituted whole social worlds within which people were born, raised, trained, matched, employed, entertained, cared for, and eventually buried. Political differences gave rise to cultural differences, including

---

[4] Eric Hobsbawm and Terence Ranger (eds), *The Invention of Tradition* (Cambridge: Cambridge University Press, 1983).

[5] Chris Barker and Paul Willis, *Cultural Studies: Theory and Practice*, 2nd edn (London: Sage, 2003), 392.

[6] Ibid. 23–4.

differences in language use, which gave them a quasi-ethnic character.[7] In Belgium, in fact, ethnicity was part of the pillarization structure, with *zuilen* defined also by the ethnic distinction between Dutch-speaking Flemings and French-speaking Walloons. The Dutch–Belgian case in other words shows that ideological identity can be expressed in public life in ways very close to the public expression of ethnicity.

During the nineteenth and twentieth centuries, moreover, we also saw from time to time a close association between national and political identities. This association is encapsulated in the term 'un-American', used at the highest levels of the United States in the 1950s in an attempt to align national identity with a conservative ideological approach to the world. A similar strong overlap between ideology and nationality has been apparent at times in the identification of Nazism with Germany, Communism with the Soviet Union and China, liberal internationalism with Sweden, and Islam with Iran.

Of course, none of the considerations outlined above means that national and ethnic identities are the same as ideological identities. Nonetheless, they blur the boundary between these forms of identity in a way that removes the obvious distinction between 'acts committed with intent to destroy, in whole or in part, a national, ethnical, racial or religious group' and acts committed with similar intent to destroy a political group. The ethnic genocides that dominate the discussion in this volume had a variety of overlapping motives. In some cases, the aim was dispossession—the displacement of original occupants from land so that others could use it, or the removal of a category of people from powerful positions in society so that others could take those positions. In some cases, the aim was to prevent secession or alliance with an external power. In other cases, the genocide was driven by a doctrinaire belief that members of the targeted group contaminated the national polity, polluting society in a moral sense and blocking policies that would have been in the interests of those to whom the nation properly belonged.

The four great mass political killings that took place in the twentieth century shared this complex of motives, but in all cases that third motive was the most salient. These mass killings were attempts to rid the body politic of a vast group of people whose very existence seemed inimical to the nation as the perpetrators conceived it. The mass killings arose from fundamental conflicts over the national character of the Soviet Union, Indonesia, China, and Cambodia. The protagonists in each case agreed on the physical framework provided by national borders, but they were engaged in a struggle to reshape the fundamentals of national character within those borders. The destruction of political enemies in these cases was not just a grab for factional power or economic interest but the extermination of an alternative nation within the state. In this respect, the victims indeed constituted a

---

[7] Arend Lijphart, *Verzuiling, Pacificatie en Kentering in de Nederlandse Politiek* (Amsterdam: J. H. de Bussy, 1968).

'national' group in the terms of the UN Convention. The mass political killings, moreover, did not simply target political protagonists but rather victimized whole families. Unlike the punishment of the families of political enemies in earlier times, when it was intended to enhance the savagery of punishment and to diminish the possibility that vengeful survivors might form a renewed threat to the regime, this destruction was rationalized at the time by claims that the individual victims were themselves culpable. Sometimes on the general basis of class, sometimes on the more specific basis of family connections, the perpetrators of these killings turned their enemies into quasi-ethnic groups and committed genocide upon them.

The political genocide in the Soviet Union is analysed in this volume by Nicolas Werth, and therefore will be discussed here only in passing. Of the other three, the Indonesian killings targeted communists whereas the Chinese and Cambodian killings were carried out by communists. All three took place in the course of little more than a decade (1965–1979) at the height of the cold war. Intense global political antagonisms were thus acted out on three national stages, as was also the case in the genocides of secessionist movements discussed in this volume by Geoffrey Robinson. Although we know that the main protagonists in the cold war were capable of immense direct brutality against their enemies—the United States in Indochina, the Soviet Union in Afghanistan—and although we know that the United States had some complicity in the Indonesian killings, the roots of all three political genocides lay primarily in the national histories of the countries concerned and in the vastly different futures which communism and its alternatives appeared to map out for modernizing societies.

INDONESIA

Between October 1965 and March 1966, the Indonesian army and its political allies carried out the murder of approximately half a million members and associates of the Indonesian Communist Party (*Partai Komunis Indonesia*, PKI). The killings were part of a seizure of power by anti-communist sections of the army led by General Suharto, who went on to become Indonesia's longest-serving president, removing from office his predecessor President Sukarno, who had declared the country's independence from the Dutch in 1945. Suharto's long regime was marked by the brutal repression of other opponents, including secessionists in Aceh, East Timor, and Papua, and by deep-seated corruption, but it also delivered impressive economic growth and a dramatic reduction in poverty.

The killing of the communists was presented as a response to an ambiguous coup launched in Jakarta early on the morning of 1 October 1965 by a group calling itself the 30th September Movement. Much controversy has existed over this coup. Mid-ranking army officers were involved in the kidnapping and killing of six senior anti-communist generals (a seventh narrowly escaped). The plotters claimed to have acted to forestall a coup that they claimed had been planned by the anti-communist generals for 5 October. After their bold initial strike, however, the plotters appeared confused and were easily suppressed by Suharto as head of the army's Strategic Reserve (KOSTRAD). The controversy over the coup relates to the question of who may have been involved aside from the immediate organizers. Responsibility for devising the coup has been attributed variously (and in various combinations) to the PKI, to Sukarno, to the air force (which was generally sympathetic to the Left), and to Chinese intelligence operatives. It has also been identified as a 'black' operation carried out by variously Suharto, the CIA, and MI6, designed to provide a pretext for the suppression of the Left in Indonesia. Recent research has indicated that the coup was most likely a joint endeavour by the army officers directly involved and a small group around the communist party chairman, D. N. Aidit, and that it was intended both to forestall an anti-communist coup and to push Indonesia decisively to the Left.[8]

The PKI was at that time the third largest communist party in the world, the largest in the non-communist world. It had risen from the ashes of an unsuccessful rebellion in 1948 during Indonesia's War of Independence to run fourth in the 1955 general elections. It had publicly eschewed armed revolution and was pursuing the strategy, later identified with Euro-communism, of aiming to win power by electoral means.[9] It was a strong advocate for social justice and was considered unusual amongst Indonesian political parties for its efficiency and freedom from corruption. The party, however, had enemies, including those who remembered the brutality of its 1948 uprising, religious groups apprehensive about the party's atheism, landowners fearful of the party's base amongst landless peasants, and establishment members of the bureaucratic, political, and military elites who recognized in the party a hungry new elite that would displace them if it had the chance. Fear that the PKI would win enough seats in the planned 1959 elections to guarantee it a place in government was an important element in anti-communist support for President Sukarno when he dismantled the democratic system between 1957 and 1959, replacing it with what he called 'Guided Democracy', a semi-authoritarian system under his own direction.[10]

Although anti-communists initially saw Guided Democracy as a freezing of existing political strengths, the PKI appeared to thrive. It continued to win support

---

[8] John Roosa, *Pretext for Mass Murder: The September 30th Movement and Suharto's Coup d'Etat in Indonesia* (Madison: University of Wisconsin Press, 2006).

[9] Robert Cribb, 'The Indonesian Marxist Tradition', in Colin Mackerras and Nick Knight (eds), *Marxism in Asia* (London: Croom Helm, 1985), 251–72.

[10] Herbert Feith, 'Dynamics of Guided Democracy', in Ruth McVey (ed.), *Indonesia* (New Haven: Human Relations Area Files, 1963), 309–409.

in the countryside, the bureaucracy, and even sections of the armed forces. It also developed a community of affiliated organizations, covering peasants, women, trade unions, artists, and so on with an even larger membership.[11] President Sukarno, moreover, increasingly saw the PKI as a political counterweight to the power of the army. He wove the PKI into a new national ideology, NASAKOM (nationalism, religion, communism), giving it a formal place at the centre of the Indonesian national identity, and his public rhetoric increasingly adopted the terminology of the party.[12] The party gave vehement support to Sukarno's campaign against the creation of the new state of Malaysia out of British colonies in maritime Southeast Asia, and urged that the armed forces pursue an armed struggle against the new state, a struggle that would take them far away from the centre of power in Java. The party began to argue (though unsuccessfully) for the arming of workers and peasants, and began to launch direct actions in the countryside to implement a 1960 law on redistribution of land.[13] As President Sukarno aged and showed signs of illness, it appeared increasingly possible that the party might slip effortlessly into political power, despite the fact that it held no senior cabinet posts and despite its lack of access to weapons. These circumstances created a perception in Indonesia that the country was approaching a decisive moment in its history, in which either the PKI would come to power or the army would move decisively to eliminate the party as a political force.

Research on the killings that followed the 1965 coup is still meagre, but at least three patterns of killing are evident.[14] In some regions, army units, especially the para-commando RPKAD, moved systematically from village to village, using lists obtained from ransacked PKI offices or from local informers to identify party members and leftist activists, who were then summarily shot. This was the pattern in places where the PKI had been a prominent and not necessarily antagonistic part of the local landscape, so that it had relatively few enemies and its support base included many people who were attracted by its general social activism and reputation for incorruptibility. In other regions, the killings were carried out

[11] Donald Hindley, *The Communist Party of Indonesia 1951–1963* (Berkeley: University of California Press, 1964).

[12] Donald E. Weatherbee, *Ideology in Indonesia: Sukarno's Indonesian Revolution* (New Haven, CT: Yale University Press, 1966).

[13] Rex Mortimer, *The Indonesian Communist Party and Land Reform, 1959–1965* (Clayton, Vic.: Centre of Southeast Asian Studies, Monash University, 1972).

[14] Robert Cribb (ed.), *The Indonesian Killings of 1965: Studies from Java and Bali* (Clayton, Vic.: Monash University Centre of Southeast Asian Studies, 1990); Geoffrey Robinson, *The Dark Side of Paradise: Political Violence in Bali* (Ithaca, NY: Cornell University Press, 1995); John Roosa, Ayu Ratih, and Hilmar Farid (eds), *Tahun Yang Tak Pernah Berakhir: Memahami Pengalaman Korban 65: Esai-Esai Sejarah Lisan* (Jakarta: Lembaga Studi dan Advokasi Masyarakat, 2004); Hermawan Sulistyo, 'The Forgotten Years: The Missing History of Indonesia's Mass Slaughters Jombang-Kediri 1965–1966', PhD thesis, Arizona State University, 1997; R. A. F. Paul Webb, 'The Sickle and the Cross: Christian and Communist in Bali, Flores, Sumba and Timor, 1965–1967', *Journal of Southeast Asian Studies* 17:1 (1986), 94–112.

primarily by local militias drawn from amongst the PKI's enemies. These killers had often been engaged in earlier conflicts with the party over issues such as land reform and they responded to clear signals from the army that violent action against communists would not be punished. In still other regions, the army actively sought to engage other sections of society in the killing. Party members were ordered to report to the authorities. When they did so, or if they were caught on the run, they were detained in makeshift jails, before being handed over in batches to execution teams assembled from local communities. The enthusiasm of these teams seems to have varied widely. Some participants were recruited unwittingly and suddenly found themselves in a forest clearing, expected to cut the throats of a handful of hooded, anonymous victims. Others took part to establish their own anti-communist credentials. Others had been moved by lurid propaganda stories about communist excesses put about to stoke popular hostility to the party. The rightwing generals who died in the October coup were said to have been sexually mutilated by communist women before they were killed; communists all over the country were accused of preparing pits for the bodies of the anti-communist victims they allegedly planned to slaughter on party orders.

There is no evidence of systematic records being kept of the killings. Most were carried out clandestinely, often at night. Graves were unmarked and recorded only in the memories of perpetrators and occasional bystanders. Memoirs by witnesses to the killings are exceedingly sparse and an unknown number of victims, including a few relatively senior party members, survived by fleeing and changing their identities. Nonetheless, circumstantial evidence suggests that around half a million people were killed, one-sixth of the party's claimed membership.[15] Members of the women's organization Gerwani, affiliated with the PKI and accused of involvement in torture of the generals, were especially targeted, but a large majority of the victims were men. Although it has often been suggested that Indonesians used the opportunity presented by the purge to settle private scores, there is very little evidence of the killing of people who were not believed to be communist. Nor is there evidence that Indonesia's Chinese minority was targeted for killing, though there was some lesser violence in the form of burning of shops and expulsion from small towns.

In the aftermath of the killing, more than a million people passed at least briefly through military detention camps.[16] Some prisoners spent ten years in detention on the remote island of Buru in eastern Indonesia. Only a few dozen senior figures from the party and the left wing of the army were brought to trial; the rest were

---

[15] Robert Cribb, 'How Many Deaths? Problems in the Statistics of Massacre in Indonesia (1965–1966) and East Timor (1975–1980)', in Ingrid Wessel and Georgia Wimhöfer (eds), *Violence in Indonesia* (Hamburg: Abera, 2001), 82–98.

[16] Greg Fealy, The Release of Indonesia's Political Prisoners: Domestic Versus Foreign Policy, 1975–1979 (Melbourne: Monash Asia Institute, 1995).

detained on the basis of military fiat. Even after they were released, their identity cards were marked with the letters ET (for *eks-tahanan*, ex-prisoner) and they were forbidden to vote or to work in a wide range of supposedly sensitive jobs, including education and the oil industry. The alleged sins of the party members, moreover, were visited upon their families for decades thereafter. Thirty years after the 1965 coup, Indonesians wishing to work in sensitive areas or even, in some circumstances, to complete their education, were required to show that they were 'environmentally clean', meaning that they had no close family connections with anyone who had been 'involved', according to the government's flexible sense of the term, with the PKI.[17]

Since soon after the emergence of the idea of Indonesia in the early twentieth century, communism had presented a distinctive set of ideas about the fundamental character of the nation. The extermination of the party in 1965–6 thus represented not just the exclusion of a political ideology from national legitimacy but also the genocidal destruction of the people who bore a certain idea of the nature of the Indonesian nation.

CHINA

The Chinese Communist Party (CCP) came to power in 1949, defeating the anti-communist Nationalist government of Chiang Kaishek. Once in power, the Party embarked on a thoroughgoing restructuring of Chinese society, collectivizing agriculture, placing businesses under Party supervision, and promoting rapid industrial development. Within the Party itself, however, there was a wide range of opinion about the extent of change that was needed and about the pace that should be maintained. The Party Chairman, Mao Zedong, favoured more radical and more rapid change, and on his initiative the Party pursued what proved to be a disastrous programme of rapid industrialization in 1958–61, known as the Great Leap Forward. Under the programme, peasant labour was redirected into industrial production. Along with unfavourable weather, these policies led to a collapse in harvests and a famine in which millions died of starvation. The death toll is officially stated to have been 14 million, but some observers have suggested substantially higher numbers.[18] In contrast with the famine genocide in Ukraine

---

[17] Ariel Heryanto, *State Terrorism and Political Identity in Indonesia: Fatally Belonging* (London: Routledge, 2006).

[18] Peng Xizhe, 'Demographic Consequences of the Great Leap Forward in China's Provinces', *Population and Development Review* 13:4 (1987), 639–70; Judith Banister, 'Population Policy and Trends in China, 1978–83', *China Quarterly* 100 (1984), 717–41.

in 1932–3, there is no reason to believe that the Great Leap Forward Famine was deliberately engineered to destroy or weaken any social group. Rather, it was the consequence of the blind confidence of Party leaders in the capacity of human will to achieve official goals and the unwillingness of officials to report anything except abundant fulfilment of those goals.

From the start, the CCP was fearful of forces in Chinese society that might block or hamper its policies and which might even seek to remove it from power. Although the Party had come to power with a formidable reputation for patriotism and efficiency, it was well aware that vast numbers of Chinese were unconvinced of the need for its radical programmes. Remnants of the Nationalist government, moreover, remained in power on the island of Taiwan, and publicly affirmed their intention to reconquer the mainland. From October 1950, too, Communist Chinese troops were in direct conflict with US forces in the Korean War. The CCP responded to this sense of threat with a series of savage purges intended to remove various kinds of 'dangerous' element from Chinese society. The targets of these purges in the 1950s and early 1960s included those defined as class enemies (land-lords and business owners), people politically associated with the previous regime, alleged spies for outside powers, dissident intellectuals, followers of organized religion, and party members suspected of the abuse of power. The fate of those purged varied from public executions to beating, to jailing or exile in the country-side, to public humiliation, confiscation of possessions, and loss of career pro-spects. Estimates of the number of executions in this period range from 400,000 to 2 million,[19] but very little empirical work has been done to test these estimates. These purges were marked by the Party's recruitment of a new generation of young revolutionaries who had not participated directly in the earlier struggle against the Nationalists but who now became engaged in internal revolution.

The fears of Party chairman Mao Zedong that the revolution might be reversed grew more acute after the death of Stalin and the rise of more moderate leaders in the Soviet Union. Because the Soviet Union had been the CCP's most important ally and had provided its basic development model, Mao was particularly alert to the risk that moderate forces would arise, as they had in the Soviet Union, within the Communist Party itself. Whereas the purges of the 1950s had mainly targeted categories of people who were demonstrably not of the Party, in the 1960s Mao began to search for a way of purifying the Party itself, along with society as a whole. The mass killing of communists in Indonesia in 1965–6 added to Mao's

---

[19] Maurice Meisner, *Mao's China and After: a History of the People's Republic* (New York: Free Press, 1986), 81; Benedict Stavis, *The Politics of Agricultural Mechanization in China* (Ithaca, NY: Cornell University Press, 1978), 29. Jean-Louis Margolin, 'China: A Long March into Night', in Stéphane Courtois (ed.), *The Black Book of Communism: Crimes, Terror, Repression* (Cambridge MA: Harvard University Press, 1999), 79.

apprehension. Here was a communist party that had allowed itself to be defeated by resurgent rightists. He was determined that no such fate would befall the CCP.

To counter these supposed threats, Mao formally launched the so-called Great Proletarian Cultural Revolution in May 1966.[20] The action was characterized as 'cultural' because it demanded a fundamental change in attitudes, rather than what was portrayed as lip-service to the ideals of the revolution. In August 1966, the Party's Central Committee summed up the issues as follows:

> Although the bourgeoisie has been overthrown, it is still trying to use the old ideas, culture, customs, and habits of the exploiting classes to corrupt the masses, capture their minds, and endeavor to stage a comeback. The proletariat must do just the opposite: It must meet head-on every challenge of the bourgeoisie in the ideological field and use the new ideas, culture, customs, and habits of the proletariat to change the mental outlook of the whole of society. At present, our objective is to struggle against and crush those persons in authority who are taking the capitalist road, to criticize and repudiate the reactionary bourgeois academic 'authorities' and the ideology of the bourgeoisie and all other exploiting classes and to transform education, literature and art, and all other parts of the superstructure that do not correspond to the socialist economic base, so as to facilitate the consolidation and development of the socialist system.[21]

A small group of ultra-radical party leaders, later derogatorily known as the 'Gang of Four', systematically purged the upper echelons of the Party of those considered to be potentially revisionist.

Because the heart of the problem, in Mao's view, lay within the Party itself, the principal agents of the Cultural Revolution were young, radicalized Chinese, male and female, who were described collectively as Red Guards. Their movement emphasized intense loyalty to Mao and his teachings, summarized in the celebrated *Little Red Book*, and an implacable hostility to individuals, institutions, and forms of behaviour that were not unambiguously embedded in the Maoist view of the world. The Red Guards surged through Chinese society to root out all traces of what were called the 'Four Olds'—old customs, old habits, old culture, and old thinking. Included in these vices were any sign of affection for or interest in China's traditional culture, the culture of any of the country's ethnic minorities, or Western thought and culture. Anyone who possessed suspect books or works of art, who listened to Western or traditional music, who had Western education or connections with Western businesses, or who seemed hesitant to embrace the full exuberance of the Maoist revolution was a likely target. Victims were routinely removed from their jobs and their unacceptable possessions were burnt or smashed. They

---

[20] On the Cultural Revolution in Chinese politics, see Harry Harding, 'The Chinese State in Crisis, 1966–9', in Roderick MacFarquhar (ed.), *The Politics of China: The Eras of Mao and Deng*, 2nd edn (Cambridge: Cambridge University Press, 1997), 148–247; and Roderick MacFarquhar and Michael Schoenhals, *Mao's Last Revolution* (Cambridge, MA: Harvard University Press, 2006).

[21] Central Committee of the CCP, 'Decision Concerning the Great Proletarian Cultural Revolution', 8 August 1966.

themselves would be dragged into the street, self-incriminating placards placed around their necks or dunce's caps placed on their heads. They were forced to confess publicly to their shortcomings while crowds jeered at them. The beating of victims was widespread and as the campaign grew in intensity, increasing numbers were beaten to death or were permanently crippled. A remarkable number of Party leaders committed suicide.

This early phase of the Cultural Revolution attracted much attention because of the character of the Red Guards. Energy and enthusiasm with which the Red Guards celebrated violence and sought to smash every vestige of the old order seemed to be the world's most extreme manifestation of a general revolt of the young that later found expression in the anti-establishment movements of 1968 in the West. The Cultural Revolution was also remarkable for the destruction it caused to China's physical heritage, the distrust it created between family members, the disruption it caused to the lives and careers of members of the middle levels of Chinese society, and the chaos it brought within the Party. Mao as chairman of the Party appeared to be orchestrating the destruction of the central political institution that he had helped to create.

By early 1967, not only had the education system been laid waste and the system of local government largely dismantled by the Red Guards, but workers' communes had begun to seize control of factories and businesses. In many parts of the country rival factions—Red Guard, worker, military—competed for practical control in what was close to civil war. Under these conditions, Mao began to engineer a reversal of the extreme devolution of power, calling for the establishment of 'revolutionary committees' that included both Party cadres with demonstrated 'revolutionary' qualities and, crucially, representatives of the People's Liberation Army. The creation of these committees intensified the conflict in China's provinces, as rival factions tested each other's power and struggled for inclusion in the emerging elites.[22] At the same time, the Gang of Four widened the purge of the Party under the slogan 'Campaign to Purify Class Ranks'. In the purge, a secret committee investigated the backgrounds of all party cadres and removed anyone with previous links to Westerners or the Nationalists or whose family background included bourgeois elements. As part of the attempt to purge counter-revolutionary attitudes, millions of students, bureaucrats, and intellectuals were sent to the countryside to learn peasant values through intense indoctrination and the discipline of hard physical labour and difficult conditions.[23] About 12 million 'educated

[22] Wang Shaoguang, *Failure of Charisma: The Cultural Revolution in Wuhan* (Hong Kong: Oxford University Press, 1995).

[23] In a provocative essay, Jin Qiu discusses the preference of former Red Guards for remembering their own suffering in this period while ignoring the suffering they inflicted on others; see 'Victim or Victimizer: The Reconstruction of the Cultural Revolution through Personal Stories', in Kenneth Christie and Robert Cribb (eds), *Historical Injustice and Democratic Transition in Eastern Asia and Northern Europe: Ghosts at the Table of Democracy* (London: Routledge, 2002), 13–23. A particularly powerful memoir of this period is Rae Yang, *Spider Eaters* (Berkeley: University of California Press, 1997).

youth' were caught up in this process. Although the transfer to the countryside was couched as a measure against counter-revolutionaries, in fact a large number of Red Guards were removed in this way from the cities and from all opportunities to continue agitating. Something close to normal rule began to be restored only in 1971.

Early accounts of the Cultural Revolution emphasized the violence of the Red Guards and implied that the revolutionary committees had been Mao's way of putting back into the bottle the genie of youth radicalism that he had released in 1966 once it had served the purpose of removing his enemies within the Party.[24] Recent research, however, has shown that this period of revolutionary committees was a time of intense political killings, in addition to the broader phenomenon of civil war between rival armed groups. The evidence lies in official government publications that record massacres for the years 1966–71.[25] The deaths are recorded in county almanacs, sometimes simply referring to 'many killings' or reporting that they took place 'frequently', sometimes giving specific numbers, as in the following report from Quanzhou County in Guangxi:

October 3, [1967]. In Sanjiang Brigade, Dongshan Commune, the militia commander Huang Tianhui led [the brigade militia] to geng-sha [push into a cliff to kill] 76 individuals of the brigade—former landlords, rich peasants and their children—in the snake-shaped Huanguaneng canyon.... From July to October, [other] 850 individuals [in the county]— the four-type elements (Landlords, Rich Peasants, Counterrevolutionaries, and Bad Elements) and their children—were executed with firearms.[26]

The killing of children was particularly marked in the Cultural Revolution massacres, probably because they were believed to share their parents' inappropriate class background.[27] The pattern of killings was different from county to county and province to province, with the Inner Mongolian Autonomous Region apparently suffering most heavily.[28] Walder and Su, who have investigated these records most closely, conclude that between 750,000 and 1.5 million people were

[24] Juliana Pennington Heaslet, 'The Red Guards: Instruments of Destruction in the Cultural Revolution', Asian Survey 12:12 (1972), 1032–47; Harding, 'The Chinese State in Crisis', 243–44 (Harding cites an official death toll of 34,800 and a 'not ... unreasonable' estimate of half a million).

[25] For a discussion of the circumstances in which these reports were compiled, see Andrew G. Walder and Yang Su, 'The Cultural Revolution in the Countryside: Scope, Timing and Human Impact', China Quarterly 173 (2003), 79.

[26] Quoted in Yang Su, State Sponsorship or State Failure? Mass Killings in Rural China, 1967–68, Paper 03–06 (Irvine, CA: Center for the Study of Democracy, University of California, 2003), 5.

[27] See Yang Su, 'Mass Killings in the Cultural Revolution: a Study of Three Provinces', in Joseph Esherick, Paul Pickowicz, and Andrew George Walder (eds), The Chinese Cultural Revolution as History (Stanford: Stanford University Press, 2006), 107–8.

[28] See Uradyn Bulag's chapter in this volume, and Wu Di, 'The Aftermath of the Cultural Revolution in Inner Mongolia', in Kenneth Christie and Robert Cribb (eds), Historical Injustice and Democratic Transition in Eastern Asia and Northern Europe (London: Routledge, 2002), 24–37.

killed in rural areas during these years, with a similar number being maimed by beatings.[29]

Much is still uncertain about the circumstances of most of the killings and of the identities of the victims. As in Indonesia, however, the mass political killings of the Cultural Revolution were marked by a sense that the future of the country was at stake, meaning that extreme measures were justified to suppress the enemies of the newly consolidating order. In both cases, the characterization of these enemies was both casual and precise: in China, the victims were defined as 'class enemies', in Indonesia as 'communists', both categories representing a kind of person, rather than a culpable act. Whereas the perpetrators of the Indonesian killings have been almost entirely silent on their actions, detailed records exist of the revolutionary committee meetings at which executions were planned and the names of the victims were decided. Although the committees recruited militias to assist on the task of extermination, the actions took place under clear official mandate.[30] And although the Chinese government has since rehabilitated most of the surviving victims of the Cultural Revolution (unlike Indonesia's government, which continues a range of discriminatory practices against those linked with the Communist Party), there has been no attempt to rehabilitate or to memorialize the dead. Those who took part in the killings were often promoted within the Party in subsequent years.[31]

The Chinese killings, like those in Indonesia, were aimed at the elimination of a whole group of people believed to embody a different idea of Chinese nationhood. Whereas the victims in Indonesia were defined principally by their formal affiliation with the Communist Party or one of its affiliates, the victims in China were defined more broadly by class, so that the slaughter often encompassed whole families.

CAMBODIA

The Communist Party of Kampuchea (CPK), better known as the Khmer Rouge (Red Khmers, or Cambodians), came to power in Cambodia in the final phase of the Second Indochina War (1954–75). Little was known about the party in the rest of the world and most observers were surprised, sometimes disbelieving, when news emerged that the party had launched a massive re-engineering of society to

[29] Walder and Yang Su, 'The Cultural Revolution in the Countryside', 74–99.
[30] Yang Su, 'Mass Killings in the Cultural Revolution', 108.
[31] Ibid.

create a pristine communist state and had killed its political and class enemies on a massive scale. The regime was removed in 1979 by a Vietnamese invasion, following Khmer Rouge attacks on Vietnam that aimed to recover former Cambodian territory in the Mekong Delta. The Khmer Rouge resumed guerrilla resistance in the countryside and, with the support of China and the United States (which regarded Vietnam as an ally of the Soviet Union), retained Cambodia's United Nations seat until 1982. From 1982 until 1991, it remained the strongest element within the Coalition Government of Democratic Kampuchea which, though internationally recognized, controlled only a small part of the country.

In early historical times, what is now Cambodia had been the centre of a series of powerful kingdoms, whose splendour is still reflected in the vast monuments of Angkor. In later centuries, however, the Khmer had been unable to prevent the inroads of neighbouring Siamese and Vietnamese states. By the end of the seventeenth century, Cambodia had lost to Vietnam control of its sea access through the Mekong Delta, and it ceased to be a major power. During the nineteenth century, France incorporated Cambodia, along with neighbouring Vietnam and Laos, into French Indochina but Cambodia experienced few of the direct consequences of colonialism that were visited on Vietnam. The Cambodian monarchy remained in place under the French protectorate, bolstered by French power and in turn conferring legitimacy on French domination. The modern sector of the economy and the bureaucracy was dominated by French, Vietnamese, and other outsiders.

Cambodia became independent in 1953 as a constitutional monarchy in the context of the closing phases of the First Indochina War, whose most important outcome was the partition of Vietnam between rival northern (communist) and southern (anti-communist) states in 1954. This partition set the framework for the Second Indochina War, in which the United States and its southern allies fought the north, which had backing from the communist bloc. Although the Cambodian leader, Prince Norodom Sihanouk, asserted Cambodia's neutrality and was one of the pioneers of the Non-Aligned Movement, the country was increasingly drawn into the conflict by the fact that Vietnamese communist forces used it as a sanctuary and by the heavy-handed US response, which included massive bombing of communist-dominated regions. In 1970, Sihanouk was overthrown in a pro-Western military coup by Gen. Lon Nol, who created the Khmer Republic.

The bombing and the consequent hardship in the countryside caused, for instance, by the death of an estimated seventy-five per cent of the draught animals needed to cultivate the fields appear to have generated increasing support for the CPK. Although the party had depended on Vietnamese military support and protection in its early days, it increasingly pursued its own line and defended the separate priorities of the Cambodian revolution against the 'Indochina' imperatives of the Vietnamese. Khmer Rouge forces captured the capital, Phnom Penh, on

17 April 1975, two weeks before the fall of Saigon to Vietnamese communist forces, and the CPK renamed the country 'Democratic Kampuchea'.[32]

CPK doctrine demanded the rapid creation of a fully communist society. The party believed that communism could be established within a single country and that industrialization and urbanization, conventionally seen as essential in the Marxist historical sequence, could and should be bypassed. 'We will be the first nation to create a completely communist society without wasting time on intermediate steps,' one of their leaders is reported to have said.[33] Party ideologues argued that a just, prosperous, and entirely self-reliant society could be created by 'unleashing the productive power of the masses' in a programme of vast irrigation works designed to allow rice to be grown all year round. This programme required that the energies of the Khmer people be redirected from commerce (money and banking was abolished and replaced with barter), from religion (religious observance was punished and places of worship were destroyed),[34] and from the corruption and distractions of urban life and foreign values in general. Accordingly, nearly all inhabitants of the cities were shifted to rural areas, where they were set to work on infrastructure projects. Private property was abolished and work was collectivized to varying degrees from region to region. In some places, collectivization included communal dining. The party had previously implemented many aspects of this programme in 'liberated' areas in the countryside before the fall of Phnom Penh.

Whereas many communist parties allowed a respected but subordinate role to 'progressive' elements from enemy classes, the CPK expressed a doctrinaire hostility to these classes from the start. In theory, the party permitted people who had held official positions or possessed some wealth under the old order to accept re-education and to immerse themselves in the peasant values of the new order. In practice, however, the party was vigilant for any sign amongst these old elements of failure to conform to the new order. The strongest social division in Cambodia under the Khmer Rouge was thus between the 'old people'—those who had been under effective communist government in the 'liberated' areas before 1975—and the 'new people' (perhaps numbering two million or more), most of them displaced from the cities. It was made clear to these people that their survival depended on utter compliance with Khmer Rouge norms. Many survivors reported that they were told words to the effect, 'To spare you brings no benefit; to destroy

---

[32] Ben Kiernan, *How Pol Pot Came to Power: A History of Communism in Kampuchea, 1930–1975* (London: Verso, 1985).

[33] Karl D. Jackson, 'The Ideology of Total Revolution', in *idem* (ed.), *Cambodia, 1975–1978: Rendezvous with Death* (Princeton: Princeton University Press, 1992), 63.

[34] Some 40,000–60,000 Buddhist monks were defrocked and forced into labour brigades; Christians and Muslims, including the indigenous Muslim Cham minority, were targeted as followers of foreign beliefs. Temples, mosques, and churches were destroyed, along with sacred objects such as Buddha images and copies of the Bible and the Qur'an.

you brings no loss.'[35] New people were subject to intense re-education, and they were set to hard physical labour under difficult, often unhealthy conditions, generally with meagre food rations. Families were often split up and sent to different parts of the country. They were closely monitored by Khmer Rouge cadres and trivial infringements of rules or signs of persisting bourgeois or foreign values, such as expressions of nostalgia for pre-revolutionary times, could be punished by summary execution. It was reported that people were executed for wearing glasses (a sign of pre-revolutionary wealth and intellectualism) or for having soft hands that betrayed a lack of experience in hard work. Survivors reported that Khmer Rouge children were particularly vigilant in identifying and punishing signs of un-revolutionary attitudes amongst the new people.[36] Members of Cambodia's ethnic minorities—indigenous Muslim Chams and immigrant Chinese and Vietnamese, as well as CPK cadres in the east of the country who had been in contact with Vietnamese communists—were especially suspect because of their presumed foreign sympathies and suffered an even higher death rate than the general population.[37]

In the period 1975–9, some 17,000 people passed through the Tuol Sleng (S-21) interrogation centre in Phnom Penh. Victims of the regime's growing paranoia, these people included both alleged foreign spies and growing numbers of party cadres who were interrogated and tortured. They were forced both to confess to complex conspiracies against the regime and to reveal the names of their supposed co-conspirators who were then called in for interrogation in a widening circle of victimization, which also included small children.[38]

There are significant difficulties in estimating both the total number of victims of the Khmer Rouge and the precise causes of death. Researchers have used demographic data, sample surveys amongst survivors, and forensic evidence from grave sites, as well as comparative evidence concerning the practicalities of mass killings from other contexts. Although much uncertainty remains, there are strong indications that the death toll was a little over two million out of a 1975

---

[35] See, for instance, Ben Kiernan, *The Pol Pot Regime: Race, Power, and Genocide in Cambodia under the Khmer Rouge, 1975–1979*, 2nd edn (New Haven, CT: Yale University Press, 2002), 4.

[36] François Ponchaud, *Cambodia Year Zero* (London: Allen Lane, 1978); Michael Vickery, *Cambodia 1975–1982* (Sydney: Allen and Unwin, 1984); Elizabeth Becker, *When the War Was Over: The Voices of Cambodia's Revolution and Its People* (New York: Simon and Schuster, 1986); Jackson (ed.), *Cambodia, 1975–1978*; David P. Chandler, *The Tragedy of Cambodian History: Politics, War, and Revolution since 1945* (New Haven, CT: Yale University Press, 1991); Alexander Laban Hinton, *Why Did They Kill: Cambodia in the Shadow of Genocide* (Berkeley: University of California Press, 2005) discusses the motivation for the killings using insights from psychology. There is now a substantial literature of survivor accounts of the Khmer Rouge period in Cambodia. Two powerful memoirs are Loung Ung, *First They Killed My Father: A Daughter of Cambodia Remembers* (Pymble, NSW: HarperCollins, 2000), and Pin Yathay, *Stay Alive, My Son* (Chiang Mai: Silkworm Books, 2000).

[37] Kiernan, *The Pol Pot Regime*, 251–309.

[38] David P. Chandler, *Voices from S-21: Terror and History in Pol Pot's Secret Prison* (Berkeley: University of California Press, 2000).

population of around 8 million. Of these victims, it seems plausible that forty to fifty per cent were executed, with the remainder dying of disease and starvation under conditions created deliberately or carelessly by the Khmer Rouge authorities.[39] The deaths were unevenly distributed across the population of Cambodia. Vietnamese, Cham, and other ethnic minorities suffered the most; new people suffered much more than old people.

CONCLUSION

The Indonesian killings of 1965–6 cost half a million lives. The killings during the Cultural Revolution in China claimed a million. Although these are massive death tolls, both episodes involved only a relatively small proportion of the total populations of those two countries. The political killings in the Soviet Union took place on a much larger scale, but they proceeded as a multitude of separate episodes, some involving ethnically defined victims, some in which hardship played a greater role in the death toll than did execution. As a result, the Soviet killings are difficult to comprehend as a single event. The Cambodian killings, by contrast, claimed twenty-five per cent of a population of eight million in little more than three years. Even though the perpetrators shared the ethnicity of most of their victims, it seemed immediately unreasonable to many genocide scholars to treat the Cambodian killings as anything other than genocide. A UN rapporteur is said to have coined the term 'auto-genocide' as an uncomfortable acknowledgement of the fact that the events in Cambodia seemed to match the enormity of ethnic genocide, yet did not fit the conventional interpretation of the UN definition.[40] Since the 1980s, however, the term auto-genocide has largely disappeared and the experience of Cambodia continues to sit uncomfortably on the sharp frontier of genocide studies, bringing other mass political killings such as Indonesia and China in its wake.

Whether these cases can properly be considered as genocide depends above all on the changing scholarly understanding of the nation, as it influences the meaning of the term 'national' in the UN Convention. The political killings in Indonesia, China, and Cambodia here and there crossed ethnic boundaries—the Khmer Rouge's treatment of the Cham was genocidal under any definition of the term— but at their core they were political conflicts within a single ethnic group. They

---

[39] Bruce Sharp, 'Counting Hell: the Death Toll of the Khmer Rouge Regime in Cambodia', [online]. Available at http:// www.mekong.net/cambodia/deaths.htm

[40] Martin Shaw, *What is Genocide?* (London: Polity Press, 2007), 76.

were not, however, mere expressions of a culture of political violence in which disputes were routinely resolved with the gun, the knife, or the crowbar. Rather they were the outcome of fundamental struggles over national character. In each case, the perpetrators were not simply eliminating a political enemy. They saw themselves as shaping the character of their nation by removing a category of people who could never be a legitimate part of it. This category was defined by membership of the communist party in Indonesia and by imputed class membership in China and Cambodia, but the rationale for purging was similar in all three cases. The nation as it was envisaged by those in charge could not survive the presence of masses of people with different national conceptions. The mode of purging, too, involved the persecution of whole communities of people, not just leaders or cadres.

The fact, however, that these three political genocides took place within little more than a decade also demands explanation. They occurred in the context of the cold war, a time of acute polarization between secular ideologies that is probably unprecedented in world history. The fate, not just of individual nations but also of the world as a whole, seemed to be at stake. This polarization almost certainly strengthened the inclination of both sides in these conflicts to demonize their enemies. It also gave an international dimension to all three political genocides: the perpetrators believed themselves to be eliminating enemies who were all the more dangerous for the powerful allies that they were believed to have on the other side of the cold war divide. In the case of Indonesia, the awareness of the Indonesian military that they had the backing of the United States played a role in the confidence with which they acted.[41] In the early twenty-first century, the ideological polarization that marked the twentieth century appears distinctly muted, replaced by a religious polarization that few in the middle of the twentieth century would have considered possible. Political genocides may turn out to be a phenomenon of a rather specific phase in human history, but it would be distressing if the twenty-first century turns out to be one in which the religious dimension of genocide needs urgent attention.

FURTHER READING

Becker, Elizabeth, *When the War was Over: The Voices of Cambodia's Revolution and its People* (New York: Simon and Schuster, 1986).
Chandler, David P., *The Tragedy of Cambodian History: Politics, War, and Revolution since 1945* (New Haven, CT: Yale University Press, 1991).

[41] Bradley R. Simpson, *Economists with Guns: Authoritarian Development and U.S.-Indonesian Relations, 1960–1968* (Stanford: Stanford University Press, 2008).

Cribb, Robert (ed.), *The Indonesian killings of 1965–1966: Studies from Java and Bali* (Clayton, Vic.: Monash University Centre of Southeast Asian Studies, Monash Papers on Southeast Asia 21, 1990).

—— 'Genocide in Indonesia, 1965–1966', *Journal of Genocide Research* 3:2 (2001), 219–39.

Harding, Harry, 'The Chinese State in Crisis, 1966–9', in Roderick MacFarquhar (ed.), *The Politics of China: The Eras of Mao and Deng*, 2nd edn (Cambridge: Cambridge University Press, 1997), 148–247.

Kiernan, Ben, *The Pol Pot Regime: Race, Power, and Genocide in Cambodia under the Khmer Rouge, 1975–1979*, 2nd edn (New Haven, CT: Yale University Press, 2002).

MacFarquhar, Roderick, and Michael Schoenhals, *Mao's Last Revolution* (Cambridge, MA: Harvard University Press, 2006).

Robinson, Geoffrey, *The Dark Side of Paradise: Political Violence in Bali* (Ithaca, NY: Cornell University Press, 1995).

Roosa, John, *Pretext for Mass Murder: The September 30th Movement and Suharto's Coup d'Etat in Indonesia* (Madison: University of Wisconsin Press, 2006).

Walder, Andrew G., and Yang Su, 'The Cultural Revolution in the Countryside: Scope, Timing and Human Impact', *China Quarterly* 173 (2003), 75–99.

Yang Su, 'Mass Killings in the Cultural Revolution: A Study of Three Provinces', in Joseph Esherick, Paul Pickowicz, and Andrew George Walder (eds), *The Chinese Cultural Revolution as History* (Stanford: Stanford University Press, 2006), 96–123.

....

CHAPTER 23

STATE-SPONSORED VIOLENCE AND SECESSIONIST REBELLIONS IN ASIA

....

GEOFFREY ROBINSON

INTRODUCTION

....

THE second half of the twentieth century was marked by the phenomenon of state-sponsored violence against secessionist rebellions. That was certainly true in Asia where newly independent states, including India, Sri Lanka, Pakistan, Burma (Myanmar), Thailand, Indonesia, and the Philippines, all sought to quell one or more armed movements for autonomy or independence by resort to violence. In most of those places, moreover, state-sponsored violence against armed secessionist movements has continued with only slight interruption into the twenty-first century.

This chapter examines comparatively four instances of such violence. Focusing on East Pakistan, the Karen areas of Burma, West Papua in Indonesia, and East Timor, it begins with an empirical account of each case, asking: what were the origins and dynamics of the violence, who were the perpetrators, and who were the victims? In addressing these questions, it also considers how these events have been analysed. What terms and concepts have been used to describe the violence, how consistently have they been applied, and how useful are they in understanding what happened? Building upon these accounts, the chapter considers whether there are discernible patterns in these four cases and, if so, what they might signify. What can they tell us, for example, about broader theories of genocide and violence, about the role of states, of ideology, and of 'underlying' cultural, social, and economic tensions in genocide?

In its simplest form, the argument here is that the violence against secessionist movements in all of these places was shaped by the confluence of powerful historical trends in the post-war period, including the reification of ethnicity as a political category during and immediately after the colonial period; the legitimacy accorded the use of violence both as a tool of liberation and as a means to maintain political order; the rise of military-dominated authoritarian states in the decades after the Second World War; the support of those regimes, and their use of violence, by powerful Western states; the generally permissive normative legal and political environment particularly in the context of the cold war; and the hegemonic discourse and practice of 'development' and 'modernization' that have characterized the entire post-war period.

At the same time, I argue that state violence in these cases did not flow inevitably from such broader historical trends, but was invariably shaped by the specific attitudes, policies, and practices of both secessionist movements and state authorities, and by the historical dynamic of the conflict between them. After all, there were places where these broad structural conditions did not give rise to secessionist movements, or where states responded to them in different ways. The violence that might reasonably be called 'genocidal', moreover, generally did not begin with genocidal intentions. Rather, it was the result of a process of escalation, and of the development over time of distinctive repertoires and institutional cultures among states and secessionist movements that together made extreme violence and genocide more likely. Finally, I argue that, with some exceptions, accounts of the violence in these cases—and in particular their designation as genocide or not—have been shaped less by an objective accounting or analysis of the facts of each case, than by considerations of their political significance to major world powers, and by their fit with prevailing, but always shifting, political and scholarly agendas.

EAST PAKISTAN

Over several months in 1971, East Pakistan became the site of widespread, targeted violence that some scholars and other observers have described as genocide.[1] The violence left an estimated one million people dead, and resulted in the mass exodus of between eight and ten million others to neighbouring India.[2] In addition, tens of thousands of women are said to have been raped in the course of the conflict, though exact numbers have been impossible to establish, in part because of the systematic silencing of women's voices since 1971.[3] The violence ended abruptly in December 1971, with the surrender of Pakistani forces in the face of Indian military intervention. Shortly thereafter, East Pakistan became the independent state of Bangladesh.

The vast majority of the victims of this violence were Bengalis, the majority ethnic group in East Pakistan, with real or alleged supporters of independence among the principal targets. While many of those killed and displaced were Bengali Muslims, substantial numbers were Hindus.[4] The perpetrators were overwhelmingly members of the Pakistani Army and local militia groups mobilized for the purpose. That neat picture was complicated, however, by the fact that Bengalis, including members of the pro-independence Awami League and its armed supporters, the Mukti Bahini, also engaged in acts of violence, including murder and rape, against those they perceived to be their enemies. The latter group included the Biharis, an Urdu-speaking ethnic minority group in East Pakistan, and Bengalis who had sided with Pakistan during the conflict.

As this brief portrait suggests, the violence of 1971 was related to long-standing cultural and linguistic differences between the peoples of East and West Pakistan. Geographically separated by some 1,200 miles, the majority of Punjabis in the West and Bengalis in the East spoke different languages and embraced different cultural practices, and these differences had helped to generate tensions between East and West within years of Pakistan's formation in 1947. But these differences did not automatically give rise to—and cannot on their own explain—the extreme violence of 1971. Rather, the violence stemmed from the wider political context of the post-independence period.

---

[1] See, for example, Rounaq Jahan, 'Genocide in Bangladesh', in Samuel Totten et al. (eds), *Century of Genocide: Eyewitness Accounts and Critical Views* (New York: Routledge, 2004), Chap. 9. It was also called genocide at the time. See, for example, Sydney H. Schanberg, 'Kennedy, in India, Terms Pakistani Drive Genocide', *New York Times*, 18 August 1971.

[2] Estimates of the number killed vary widely, from 300,000 to 3 million, but there is now general agreement that the total was about one million, roughly half of whom died as refugees fleeing the Pakistani Army. See Mathew White, 'Death Tolls for the Major Wars and Atrocities of the Twentieth Century', [online]. Available at http://users.erols.com/mwhite28/warstat2.htm#Bangladesh.

[3] See Nayanika Mookherjee, '"Remembering to Forget": Public Secrecy and Memory of Sexual Violence in the Bangladesh War of 1971', *Journal of the Royal Anthropological Institute* 12 (2006), 433–50.

[4] See International Commission of Jurists, *The Events in East Pakistan, 1971*, [online]. Available at http://www.globalwebpost.com/genocide1971/docs/jurists/1_preface.htm

A vitally important element of that context was the rising political power of the Pakistani Army. Although Pakistan remained a parliamentary democracy in form, by the late 1950s the Army had come to play a central role in national politics. In 1970–1, when the crisis came to a head, the country was led by a former Army Chief of Staff, Gen. Yahya Khan, the Army was the pre-eminent political power in the country, and its extreme nationalist ethos of Punjabi supremacy permeated the state. The dominance of the military at that juncture was critically important in generating the violence of 1971, primarily because it facilitated and made more likely the use of excessive force to solve a complex political problem.

The violence of 1971 also stemmed from the conscious articulation of ethnic and regional differences for political ends after independence in 1947. Political mobilization on the basis of ethnic identity served to entrench differences, and set in motion the cycle of hostility that led to violence. Very soon after independence, cultural and linguistic differences became the focus of intense political contestation, with Bengalis complaining that, despite their numerical superiority in the country, political and economic power were concentrated in the West, and that Bengalis were being treated as second-class citizens. These perceptions had a strong basis in fact, and were the foundation for growing Bengali demands for autonomy or independence, articulated by the Awami League under the leadership of Sheikh Mujibur Rahman. The party's demands, summarized in the latter's 'Six Points', amounted to a form of confederalism which would have ended West Pakistan's dominance of the country. Pressure from the Awami League coincided with mounting unrest in West Pakistan and insistent demands from other opposition parties for an end to military rule. In the face of this opposition, Gen. Yahya Khan promised direct elections. The elections, held in December 1970, resulted in what would have been an absolute majority for the Awami League in parliament. Unwilling to countenance such an outcome, in late February 1971 political leaders in Islamabad indefinitely postponed the convening of parliament.

It was against this backdrop that the violence of 1971 unfolded. The postponement led quickly to angry demonstrations in East Pakistan, and to some acts of violence. Then, on the night of 25 March 1971 Pakistani Army forces launched an unusually heavy-handed crackdown in the East, known as Operation Searchlight. Using artillery and thousands of ground troops, the initial assault targeted university student dormitories and Hindu villages in and around the capital, Dhaka, leaving hundreds dead. The extreme brutality of that operation prompted Mujibur Rahman of the Awami League to declare the independence of 'Bangladesh' the following day. Over the next several months, the behaviour of Pakistani forces aided the rebels in garnering support from the local population, in mobilizing their own armed force, the Mukti Bahini, and in winning the backing of neighbouring India.

A central element in the strategy of the Pakistani forces, and one that led inevitably to the killing of a great many non-combatants, was the classic counter-insurgency tactic of separating rebel forces from the civilian population. In practice, that approach led to sweeping assaults on villages suspected of supporting the rebels. In the course of those operations, entire villages were burned to the ground, civilians were summarily executed, and women were raped. The violence was also fuelled by problems of command and control. Pakistan Army soldiers quickly came to view all Bengalis as the enemy, and acted in anger at reports that their comrades had been killed or captured by enemy forces. Official Pakistani inquiries and victims alike concurred that resulting atrocities were partly the result of a failure by officers to constrain or limit the unlawful actions of soldiers—and indeed of their encouragement of such actions.[5] Beyond these general patterns, it is clear that particular groups were deliberately targeted by the Army, on the grounds that they constituted enemies of the state. These included, most notably, members of the Awami League, students, and Hindus, a great many of whom were killed as they fled the violence to India.[6]

Finally, the violence was shaped by the prevailing international context and by the actions of key states in 1971.[7] That environment was broadly conducive to the exercise of power by military regimes, and to the use of extreme violence against secessionist movements. This was, after all, the height of the cold war and a time when President Nixon and Henry Kissinger were engaged in the most cynical use of military force and secret diplomacy to achieve US political and strategic objectives. As a US ally, and a crucial interlocutor in the US search for rapprochement with China, Pakistan had good reason to believe that its harsh repression of the rebels in East Pakistan would be met with either silence or support by the United States. And so it was. Despite the internal assessment of US officials in Dhaka (East Pakistan) that the events constituted 'genocide', the Nixon administration publicly denied any knowledge of atrocities, and provided Pakistan with assurances of its diplomatic and military support.[8] Pakistan's leaders were less astute in their assessment of the likely posture of neighbouring India, which they deemed unlikely to intervene. In fact, after the Pakistani Army crackdown of March 1971, India provided substantial political, economic, and military support to the rebels and a place of refuge for millions of Bengalis, and eventually launched a major military assault both in the East and the West, forcing Pakistan to surrender in December 1971 and bringing a swift end to the violence.

[5] For an official Pakistani account of the atrocities, see *The Report of the Hamoodur Rehman Commission of Inquiry into the 1971 War* (Vanguard: Lahore, 2000).

[6] See International Commission of Jurists, *The Events in East Pakistan*, esp. Part II.

[7] On the international dimensions of the conflict, see Robert Victor Jackson, *South Asian Crisis: India, Pakistan, and Bangla Desh; A Political and Historical Analysis of the 1971 War* (New York: Praeger, 1975); and O. Marwah, 'India's Military-Intervention in East Pakistan, 1971–1972', *Modern Asian Studies* 13 (1979), 549–80.

[8] See National Security Archive, 'The Tilt: the U.S. and the South Asian Crisis of 1971', [online]. Available at http://www.gwu.edu/~nsarchiv/NSAEBB/NSAEBB79/.

Given the extent and severity of the violence in East Pakistan, and the evidence that it was part of a planned military operation by government forces, it is perhaps not surprising that most Bangladeshis, as well as contemporary observers and some foreign scholars, have used the term genocide to describe it. And yet, when compared to some other instances of state-sponsored killing—such as those by the Khmer Rouge in 1975–9—it is striking how little serious scholarly work has been devoted to this case since the 1970s. Beachler has argued that this curious silence stems from two important conditions that have little to do with the violence itself.[9] First, in contrast to the Khmer Rouge killings of 1975–9 which were initially condemned as genocide by major Western powers,[10] the United States in particular had no interest in drawing critical attention to the violence committed by its ally Pakistan, and certainly no interest in describing it publicly as genocide. As a consequence, the idea that this was a genocide simply did not gain traction among key states or within intergovernmental bodies like the UN. Second, in contrast to other instances of state-sponsored killing, in which major powers were known to have been directly complicit, the evidence of direct Western involvement in the violence in East Pakistan was neither compelling nor well known.[11] As such, after a brief flurry of criticism, the case fell off the intellectual and political agendas of scholars and activists on the Left. In contrast to some other cases, moreover, the case was not embraced by the community of genocide scholars until quite recently. One possible explanation for that lapse is that the field of genocide studies has been slow to describe as genocide instances of violence that differ significantly from the Holocaust.[12] A final reason for the lack of serious attention paid to the events of 1971 may be that the secessionists themselves were armed, and were responsible for acts of violence against minority groups. At least in public perception, and probably for some scholars, that rendered the attribution of blame, and the use of the term genocide, more problematic. In short, because the violence did not resonate in obvious way with the political agendas of Western states, or with the interests and propensities of scholars, and because it lacked a simple narrative of good versus evil, it has received far less attention than might seem warranted.

[9] Donald Beachler, 'The Politics of Genocide Scholarship: The Case of Bangladesh', *Patterns of Prejudice* 41 (2007), 467–92.

[10] US characterizations of the killings shifted significantly after the Vietnamese invasion of Cambodia in 1979. For many years thereafter, the United States worked with China and Thailand to minimize the Khmer Rouge brutality in order to blacken Vietnam's reputation.

[11] Some evidence of US complicity was revealed by Seymour Hersh in the early 1980s, but his work was an exception to the rule. Seymour M. Hersh, *The Price of Power: Kissinger in the Nixon White House* (New York: Summit Books, 1983).

[12] I am grateful to Robert Cribb for this insight.

THE KAREN IN BURMA

Whereas the state violence in Pakistan in 1971 targeted a single opponent, and the conflict was resolved quickly in favour of the secessionists, in neighbouring Burma (Myanmar) the state has battled dozens of different armed secessionist movements since independence in 1948, and none of those conflicts have been resolved in favour of a rebel group. Among the many ethno-linguistic groups that have taken up arms against the government, the largest and most tenacious has been the Karen, who currently number some five to seven million (among Burma's total population of 47 million), most of whom live in the hilly eastern areas of the country bordering Thailand.[13] Under the leadership of the Karen National Union (KNU), and its armed wing, now called the Karen National Liberation Army (KNLA), they have been fighting for autonomy or independence in some form since 1948.[14] Although exact figures have not been established, human rights organizations and scholars have estimated that tens of thousands of Karen civilians have died as a consequence of government military campaigns since then, and more than one million others have been forcibly displaced, or subjected to torture, forced labour, and sexual violence.[15]

In a superficial sense, the conflict and violence have their roots in the ethnic and cultural differences that exist between the Karen minority and the Burman majority that has controlled the state since 1948.[16] As in the case of Pakistan, however, Karen ethnic identity has been at least as much the product of a history of political contestation—and of violence itself—as a 'natural' or primordial fact of life. As in Pakistan, for example, the violence in Burma has stemmed in part from the imposition of colonial and post-colonial boundaries that sought to incorporate territories and peoples never previously governed as one citizenry.[17] Before the British established full colonial rule in Burma in 1886, the Karen had seldom been

---

[13] Human Rights Watch, 'They Came and Destroyed Our Village Again': The Plight of Internally Displaced Persons in Karen State (New York, 2005), 16.

[14] See Martin J. Smith, Burma: Insurgency and the Politics of Ethnicity (London: Zed Books, 1999), and Hazel J. Lang, Fear and Sanctuary: Burmese Refugees in Thailand (Ithaca, NY: Cornell Southeast Asia Program Publications, 2002).

[15] For eyewitness accounts and analysis of the killings and other abuses, and for casualty estimates, see Human Rights Watch, 'They Came and Destroyed Our Village Again'; Amnesty International, Burma: Extrajudicial Execution and Torture of Members of Ethnic Minorities (London, 2001); and Martin Smith and Annie Allsebrook, Ethnic Groups in Burma: Development, Democracy and Human Rights (London: Anti-Slavery International, 1994).

[16] On Karen culture, see Charles F. Keyes, Ethnic Adaptation and Identity: The Karen on the Thai Frontier with Burma (Philadelphia: Institute for the Study of Human Issues, 1979).

[17] Ananda Rajah, 'A "Nation of Intent" in Burma: Karen Ethno-nationalism, Nationalism and Narrations of Nation', Pacific Review 15:4 (2002), 517–37.

part of a political entity called 'Burma'.[18] Quite the contrary, like many ethnic groups now located inside Burma's modern border—such as the Shan, Chin, Kachin, Mon, Kayah, and Karenni—the Karen had for many years belonged to relatively autonomous political power centres, as often as not hostile to the rulers of various Burman kingdoms based in the lowlands.[19] Indeed, their political distance from those kingdoms led many Karen to welcome the British conquest of Burma, to embrace the message of Protestant missionaries, and to become loyal supporters of British rule. The British repaid Karen loyalty by recruiting them into the colonial army, and granting them a significant measure of self-rule. Their close ties to British authority rendered the Karen objects of suspicion and hatred by pre-war Burman nationalists. That enmity was exacerbated during the Second World War as the nationalists fought on the side of the invading Japanese armies, ruthlessly attacking Karen who had remained loyal to the British.[20] This longer history of conflict helped to cement a sense of Karen identity while giving rise to anxiety about the position of Karens in an independent Burma. It was also one of the key reasons, when autonomy was not granted by the new regime, the Karen took up arms against the state.

Nevertheless, on their own, the existence of a distinct identity and a history of enmity cannot explain the violence that has characterized the state response to Karen demands since independence. As in the case of Pakistan, the explanation lies at least in part in the character of the post-colonial Burmese state, and the central role of the Army in the process of state formation.[21] Like Pakistan, Burma gained its independence in 1948 through negotiation with the British, and for the next decade or so, it was governed by a civilian political elite that had embraced parliamentary democracy. By the late 1950s, however, growing dissatisfaction with civilian rule—and particularly its inability to handle various rebel movements—encouraged the Burmese Army to intervene in political life, and in 1962 to seize power outright in the name of national unity and order. Notwithstanding some changes in the name of the regime, the military has remained in power ever since. Certain general features of Burma's military state—including its extreme intolerance of dissent, its insistence on national unity, and its reliance on force to answer any challenge to its authority—have made violence against the Karen (and other rebel groups) virtually inevitable.

---

[18] On the colonial history of Burma, see Hugh Tinker, *The Union of Burma* (London: Oxford University Press, 1967), 1–33; and Lang, *Fear and Sanctuary*, 26–31.

[19] On this point, see Keyes, *Ethnic Adaptation and Identity*; and Lang, *Fear and Sanctuary*, 26–9.

[20] Tinker, *Union of Burma*, 9–10.

[21] Callahan has argued, for example, that Burma's state has acted as it has, in part, because it has been dominated by 'war fighters' who have adopted coercion-intensive institutions in the process of state formation. Mary P. Callahan, *Making Enemies: War and State Building in Burma* (Ithaca, NY: Cornell University Press, 2003).

The particular character of state violence against the Karen has also been shaped by specific aspects of Burmese military doctrine, policy, and practice. Against the Karen, and other armed insurgents, the Burmese Army (the *Tatmadaw*) has employed a counter-insurgency strategy known as the 'four-cuts', formally adopted in 1968. Aimed at separating guerrillas from their civilian support base by 'cutting' their access to food, intelligence, recruits, and finances, in practice this strategy has resulted in the subjection of civilians to systematic violence, terror, and forcible displacement.[22] The violence has also been fuelled by the government's heavy-handed approach to economic 'development' in Karen and other minority areas. In the name of development projects aimed primarily at extracting oil and other natural resources—and with the acquiescence of large transnational corporations like Unocal and Total—the authorities have forcibly displaced the populations of entire Karen villages. They have also conscripted tens of thousands of Karen villagers to work without compensation and under appalling conditions on infra-structure projects, such as road and pipeline construction, or as porters for military units.[23] These tendencies have been further compounded by a culture of impunity that has developed within the *Tatmadaw* over more than half a century. Recogniz-ing that they are completely beyond the reach of the law, and seeing that officers condone and even encourage brutal behaviour, ordinary soldiers have little incen-tive to act in a humane way.

As in East Pakistan, it is widely accepted that the extreme brutality of the *Tatmadaw* has served to heighten the antagonism of Karen and other minorities towards Burmans and the Burmese state.[24] That hostility has helped to reinforce demands for independence, and to sustain recruitment efforts, despite what appear to be very dim prospects for victory. The resilience of the resistance has also been sustained by the economic resources controlled by the Karen and some other minority groups. Most important, by virtue of their geographical position along the border between Burma and Thailand, for long periods they have been able to control a black market cross-border trade in valuable products including timber, gems, arms, and drugs.[25]

Finally, the contours and trajectory of violence against the Karen have been shaped significantly by the wider regional and international political context within which they have occurred. In contrast to their resort to partition to address competing

---

[22] On the four-cuts strategy and its consequences for civilian populations, see Lang, *Fear and Sanctuary*, 37–43; and Smith and Allsebrook, *Ethnic Groups in Burma*, 78–84.

[23] On the problems of development and forced labour, see Human Rights Watch, *'They Came and Destroyed our Village Again'*; and Karen Human Rights Group, *Forced Labour Orders since the Ban: A Compendium of SPDC Order Documents Demanding Forced Labour since November 2000* (Bangkok, 2002).

[24] Lang, *Fear and Sanctuary*, 42–3.

[25] Mary P. Callahan, *Political Authority in Burma's Ethnic Minority States: Devolution, Occupation and Coexistence* (Washington, DC: East-West Center, 1997); Lang, *Fear and Sanctuary*, 41.

political demands in the subcontinent, in Burma the British managed to deflect calls for the creation of separate ethnic or religious states. Like virtually all post-colonial political elites, moreover, Burma's new leaders accepted the colonial boundaries as the basis for the new nation-state, and sought to maintain those boundaries at all costs. That task was rendered more difficult not only by the emergence of armed ethnic rebel groups throughout the country, but also by the arrival on Burmese soil of hundreds of thousands of Kuomintang (KMT) troops from China in 1949. Supported by the United States and its allies, those troops soon became involved in the illicit trade of weapons and drugs, not only helping to destabilize the civilian regime in Rangoon, but also militarizing the largely minority areas bordering China and Thailand.

More broadly, from the 1940s to the early years of the twenty-first century, the actions of key powers encouraged the resort to arms both by rebels and by the state, and facilitated a pattern of extreme brutality against civilian populations on the part of Burmese forces. During the cold war, for example, key Western states either encouraged or acquiesced in the establishment of military regimes, and turned a blind eye to the abuses they committed in the name of security and order. Beginning in the late 1980s, Western governments began to criticize Burma's rulers for their systematic violations of human rights, but their acquiescence in those abuses over almost three decades had already led to the deep militarization of ethnic minority areas, both through the presence of Burmese troops there and through the routine resort to military means by the ethnic groups themselves. Meanwhile, major transnational corporations continued to do business with the regime, thereby facilitating the continuation of state violence. The violence against the Karen and other minorities has also continued because some key Asian states, most conspicuously China, but also the regional grouping known as ASEAN, have preferred to maintain cordial ties with the regime, and have consequently remained largely silent on the question.[26]

Discussion of state violence against the Karen has been largely excluded from more general studies of genocide. Apart from Karen partisans, moreover, those most familiar with the case have not generally described the violence as genocidal. More commonly, it has been portrayed as part of a general problem of militarization and systematic human rights abuse in Burma. The reluctance to use the term genocide in this instance is in some respects understandable. For one thing, the numbers of Karen killed, even if large in proportion to the group's population, appear relatively small in comparison with some of the better known genocides of the twentieth century. Moreover, international human rights organizations, like Human Rights Watch and Amnesty International, which have been at the forefront of efforts to document the violence against Burma's ethnic minorities, have generally adopted a very strict, legalistic, definition of the term, and consequently seldom apply it even in cases of widespread and systematic violence.

[26] Lang, *Fear and Sanctuary*, 45.

At the same time, it is difficult to avoid the conclusion that other factors have played a role. One problem is that for much of the past fifty years, powerful Western states have had no compelling political interest in the Karen that would warrant calling the attacks upon them a genocide. Their near silence has undoubtedly served to limit public interest in the matter, and may also have kept scholarly attention to a minimum. The few scholars who have examined the case, moreover, have quickly found that it is a very complicated story. The Karen, after all, are only one of many ethnic groups that have been targeted by the state of Burma, and like the secessionists in East Pakistan, they are not entirely blameless in the cycle of violence. Further complicating matters, there have been serious conflicts among Karen over matters of strategy and leadership. In short, the evidence does not lend itself to an easy designation of good and bad actors.

WEST PAPUA

State violence against secessionist groups has also been a recurring theme in Indonesia, an archipelagic state comprising scores of ethno-linguistic groups, and considerable religious diversity. That pattern has been especially clear in West Papua where, in a population of just over two million, between 10,000 and 30,000 civilians have been killed and countless others displaced by Indonesian military campaigns and 'development' efforts over the past fifty years.[27] Since the 1960s, West Papua (also known as West New Guinea, West Irian, and Irian Jaya) has also been the site of heavy-handed state initiatives of cultural assimilation and 'Indonesianization'.

As in Pakistan and Burma, Papuan secessionists have typically justified their demands for independence on the basis of claimed ethnic and cultural distinctiveness from the rest of Indonesia, and especially its dominant ethnic group, the Javanese. As elsewhere, however, contemporary Papuan identity is, at least in part, the product of European colonial rule, and of Indonesian state policy and practice.[28] In the final negotiations over Indonesian independence in 1949, the Dutch insisted that Papua should remain under their control, arguing that the Papuans

[27] On the violence in West Papua, see Robin Osborne, *Indonesia's Secret War: The Guerilla Struggle in Irian Jaya* (Sydney/Boston: Allen and Unwin, 1985). For estimates of numbers killed, see Mathew White, 'The Lesser Unpleasantries of the Twentieth Century', [online]. Available at: http://users.erols.com/mwhite28/warstat5.htm#Irian62.

[28] On the historical development of Papuan identity, and the *Organisasi Papua Merdeka*, see David Webster, '"Already Sovereign as a People": A Foundational Moment in West Papuan Nationalism', *Pacific Affairs* 74:4 (2001–2), 507–28.

were entitled to develop towards a separate independence by virtue of their very different appearance from most Indonesians. Over the next decade or so, Dutch authorities encouraged a sense of Papuan cultural distinctiveness and contributed to the emergence of a fledgling Papuan political identity.[29] Nevertheless, by the early 1960s that shared identity was still limited to a rather small group of educated Papuans. Dispersed through some of the least accessible terrain in the world, with little in the way of communications or common historical experience to bind them, most of the population did not yet share that vision.

That pattern began to change significantly through the 1960s as the Dutch, facing considerable international pressure, relinquished control of Papua to Indonesia. The de facto transfer was effected under UN auspices in 1962–3, and then formalized through a deeply flawed, but UN-approved, plebiscite in 1969.[30] The 1960s saw the start of the first serious demands for independence and the emergence of an armed rebel movement, officially named the *Organisasi Papua Merdeka* (OPM) in 1969. The OPM emerged largely in response to the Indonesian takeover, and with the recognition that peaceful strategies had failed. Significantly, the 1960s also saw the consolidation of the power of the Indonesian Army, and with it the formation of a state, known as the New Order, whose leadership was notoriously intolerant of dissent, and obsessed with national unity, stability, and security. It adopted the mantra of 'development' as its central rationale, and routinely used force to deal with its real or perceived enemies.[31] Needless to say, the OPM—officially described as a 'security disruptors movement'—was among those deemed to represent an unacceptable threat to national stability and unity, and on those grounds subjected to concerted campaigns of violence by state forces over the next three decades.

The persistence and the appeal of the OPM since then has stemmed, in large part, from the harshness of the measures taken by the central state to repress the rebels. Beginning in the late 1960s, Indonesian military forces deployed in Papua adopted a repertoire of counter-insurgency tactics that had been developed in other operations—most notably against the Darul Islam movement in the 1950s, and the Indonesian Communist Party (PKI) in 1965–6. These included the mobilization of local militia forces as Army proxies, the systematic use of torture and harsh interrogation against suspected OPM supporters, and attacks on settlements thought to be supporting or protecting rebel fighters.[32] Over time, the negative

---

[29] On the colonial period, see C. L. M. Penders, *The West New Guinea Debacle: Dutch Decolonisation and Indonesia, 1945–1962* (Honolulu: University of Hawai'i Press, 2002).

[30] On the Act of Free Choice and the role of the UN, see John Saltford, *The United Nations and the Indonesian Takeover of West Papua, 1962–1969* (London/New York: Routledge, 2003).

[31] On the history of the Indonesian Army, see Harold Crouch, *The Army and Politics in Indonesia* (Ithaca, NY: Cornell University Press, 1978).

[32] For accounts of these military campaigns and their consequences, see Osborne, *Indonesia's Secret War*; and Amnesty International, *Indonesia: Continuing Human Rights Violations in Irian Jaya* (London, 1991).

effects of these tactics have been exacerbated by what I have called the 'institutional cultures' of impunity and terror that have become deeply embedded in the Indonesian Army and its proxies.[33] Like the *Tatmadaw* in Burma, then, through its systematic brutality the Indonesian military has actually helped to create in Papua the enemy it seeks to crush.

Indonesia's presence has been rendered even more odious to Papuans by the routine cultural arrogance of government officials, as evidenced in state efforts to 'Indonesianize' the population. Describing Papuans as backward or stone-age peoples in need of civilization, Indonesian authorities have adopted both the language and the policies of a colonial authority.[34] In the early 1960s, for example, Indonesia's foreign minister explained that the government's policy towards the people of West Papua was 'to get them down out of the trees, even if we have to pull them down'.[35] To that end, campaigns have been launched since that time to compel local people to wear Western-style clothing, to teach them the Indonesian language, and to settle nomadic populations in villages and towns.[36] In the name of development, moreover, Indonesian authorities have energetically pursued the colonial-era project of 'transmigration' under which people from the more densely populated islands of Java and Bali have been transferred to Papua, ostensibly to make it more productive, but also to instruct local people in wet-rice agricultural techniques of those regions.[37] Finally, in search of tax and other revenue to fill state coffers, the state has parcelled out to transnational corporations the rights to Papua's vast mineral resources, which include some of the richest gold and copper deposits in the world. The huge mining operations undertaken by Freeport have become the focus of intense criticism by Papuans and others, who have complained that they have sullied the natural habitat, and provided a pretext for local officials and soldiers to run protection rackets and other illicit schemes, while offering little in the way of jobs or other economic benefit to the local community.[38]

As in the case of East Pakistan and of the Karen in Burma, the dynamic of violence in Papua has also been influenced by the wider international context. As noted earlier, the emergence of a Papuan identity and demands for independence were to some extent the result of Dutch colonial policy. UN acquiescence in the plebiscite of 1969, for example, arguably made the OPM's resort to violence much more likely, while depriving the movement of a strong international legal basis for

---

[33] See Geoffrey Robinson, *'If You Leave Us Here, We Will Die': How Genocide Was Stopped in East Timor* (Princeton: Princeton University Press, 2010), ch. 3.

[34] J. Pouwer, 'The Colonisation, Decolonisation and Recolonisation of West New Guinea', *Journal of Pacific History* 34 (1999), 157–79.

[35] Cited in Osborne, *Indonesia's Secret War*, 136.

[36] See D. Gietzelt, 'The Indonesianization of West Papua', *Oceania* 59 (1989), 201–21.

[37] On transmigration and its critics, see Osborne, *Indonesia's Secret War*, 125–36.

[38] See, for example, D. Leith, 'Freeport and the Suharto regime, 1965–1998', *Contemporary Pacific* 14 (2002), 69–100.

its independence struggle. Although some small regional states like Vanuatu have shown a measure of sympathy for rebel demands, their influence has been over-shadowed by key Western states whose silence in the face of Indonesian violence has virtually guaranteed its continuation. Viewing the New Order regime as an important bulwark against communism at the height of the cold war, as a vital economic prize and, after 2001, as a valuable ally in the so-called war on terror, those states have been reluctant to do or say anything that might upset good relations with Indonesian authorities. In this regard, Australia has played an especially dubious role, denying virtually all claims for political asylum by Papuans, and doing little else to constrain Indonesian violence.[39]

Given its long duration and its dire consequences for the population, it is striking that the violence in West Papua has seldom been described as genocidal or included in general studies of genocide. States, scholars, and international human rights organizations have tended instead to portray the violence as a problem of the violation of human rights, as a denial of the right to self-determi-nation, or as forced cultural assimilation. As in the case of the Karen, the reluctance to use the term genocide may simply reflect the fact that the absolute numbers of people killed in West Papua has been small in comparison to other cases. But, if East Pakistan and Burma are any guide, it is probably also because major Western powers have had no compelling political interest in highlighting the plight of Papuans. On the contrary, as noted above, it has been in their interest to maintain cordial relations with Indonesia, and so to remain silent on the subject of Papua. That silence has gone largely unchallenged by genocide scholars who appear to be only dimly aware of the existence of West Papua, or of the state-sponsored violence that has been committed there for more than 40 years. International church and NGO networks have campaigned energetically to draw attention to the problem of human rights abuse and forced cultural assimilation in the territory, but they have been unable to generate the kind of political pressure that alone might bring a real change in the posture of major powers.

EAST TIMOR

Among the cases reviewed here, East Timor stands out as perhaps the most notorious instance of state-sponsored violence against an independence

---

[39] R. R. Premdas, 'The Organisasi Papua Merdeka in Irian Jaya—Continuity and Change in Papua New Guinea's Relations with Indonesia', *Asian Survey* 25 (1985), 1055–74. Also see F. K. Kalidjernih, 'Australian Indonesia-Specialists and Debates on West Papua: Implications for Australia-Indonesia Relations', *Australian Journal of International Affairs* 62 (2008), 72–93.

movement. A Portuguese colony for more than 300 years, East Timor was invaded by neighbouring Indonesia in December 1975, and occupied until 1999 when some eighty per cent of the population voted in favour of independence in a UN-supervised referendum. In the course of the twenty-four-year occupation, at least 100,000 people died, most of them as a result of hunger and disease brought about by Indonesian policies.[40] Indonesian authorities have insisted that the figures have been inflated and that any casualties were the unavoidable consequence of war. By contrast, most independent observers have concluded that the deaths were the direct and predictable consequence of Indonesian policy and practice, and some have described the outcome as genocide.[41]

As in the other cases examined here, the conflict and violence in East Timor were in important respects a legacy of European colonial rule. Although the population spoke, and still speaks, at least a dozen different languages and had some history of internal political division, by the time the Portuguese announced their plans to leave in 1974, a small but influential elite had come to view East Timor as having a distinct political identity which justified its designation as an independent nation-state.[42] Yet that sense of national identity was not by itself a reason for conflict with Indonesia, or for the appalling violence that followed. Nor did the conflict stem from the fact that East Timor's population was predominantly Catholic or animist while Indonesia's was mainly Muslim. In fact, before 1975 there was no indication of any serious religious or cultural hostility between the peoples of East Timor and Indonesia. It was only after the December 1975 invasion, and the direct experience of Indonesian rule, that a consciousness of such differences spread widely among the population. In other words, the idea of an East Timorese national identity was reinforced, and the will to resist was deepened, not by the prior existence of 'primordial' differences, but by the experience of Indonesian rule itself.[43]

The dynamic of violence in East Timor from 1975 to 1999 was in many respects very similar to the pattern observed in other areas under Indonesian rule. As in West Papua, for example, the Indonesian military described the independence movement as 'security disruptors' or terrorists, and sought to cut them off from the civilian population. Similarly, the tactics employed to achieve that end entailed the forced displacement and relocation of the civilian population, the deliberate

[40] See Amnesty International, *East Timor–Violations of Human Rights.* (London, 1985); and East Timor Commission for Reception, Truth, and Reconciliation (CAVR), *Chega!* (Dili, 2006), [online]. Available at: http://www.cavr-timorleste.org/en/chegaReport.htm.

[41] See, for example, James Dunn, *Timor: A People Betrayed* (Sydney: ABC Books, 1996); and Ben Kiernan, *Genocide and Resistance in Southeast Asia: Documentation, Denial and Justice in Cambodia and East Timor* (New Brunswick: Transaction Publishers, 2008).

[42] On the colonial period and the origins of the nationalist movement in East Timor, see John Taylor, *Indonesia's Forgotten War: The Hidden History of East Timor* (London: Zed Books, 1991); and José Ramos-Horta, *Funu: The Unfinished Saga of East Timor* (Trenton, NJ: Red Sea Press, 1986).

[43] On this point, see Robinson, *'If You Leave Us Here, We Will Die'.*

destruction of villages, crops, and livestock, and the torture, rape, arbitrary imprisonment, and summary execution of suspected supporters of independence. The victims of these campaigns were overwhelmingly civilians living in rural areas. Most died of starvation and disease in the first five years of the occupation, but a considerable number were killed, or died following torture or arbitrary detention, by Indonesian forces and their proxies.[44]

As in the other cases discussed here, the violence was fuelled by the distinctive doctrines, practices, and attitudes of military authorities. The Army's doctrine of 'total peoples' defense', for example, was the basis for the mobilization of local militia forces, which spread violence more widely among the population.[45] Meanwhile, the deeply rooted pattern of impunity, and the 'institutional culture of terror' within the Indonesian Army and its proxies, ensured the continued use of torture, rape, and other forms of terror against presumed supporters of independence. The clearest manifestation of that pattern, but hardly the only one, was the Santa Cruz massacre of 12 November 1991, in which some 270 young people were killed by Indonesian Army troops who opened fire on a peaceful pro-independence demonstration at a cemetery in Dili. The cycle of violence was further accelerated by the arrogant attitudes and policies of Indonesian government authorities, who tended to look upon the East Timorese as backward and in need of civilization. To that end, they imposed a variety of schemes aimed at Indonesianizing the population—including birth control, Indonesian language education, and transmigration—which East Timorese regarded with deep suspicion and hostility, and which had the effect of deepening their sense of identity and grievance.

Finally, as in the other cases discussed here, the violence in East Timor was shaped in significant ways by the international context in which it occurred. Most obviously, it was facilitated, even encouraged, by the support New Order authorities received from key states, notably the United States, the UK, and Australia.[46] The 1975 invasion, for example, took place less than 24 hours after Indonesian President Suharto met US President Ford and Secretary of State Kissinger, and received from them an unequivocal green light to proceed.[47] After the invasion, the United States and other states provided vital diplomatic, economic, and military

[44] The most complete account of these tactics and their consequences is in CAVR, *Chega!*

[45] On the history of this doctrine, and of the militias, see Geoffrey Robinson, 'People's War: Militias in East Timor and Indonesia', *South East Asia Research* 9:3 (2001), 271–318.

[46] The best analysis of the role of the international community in aiding and abetting the violence in East Timor is Joseph Nevins, *A Not-So-Distant Horror: Mass Violence in East Timor* (Ithaca, NY: Cornell University Press, 2005).

[47] The memorandum of that conversation and other US government documents related to the Indonesian invasion can be found at National Security Archive, 'East Timor Revisited: Ford, Kissinger and the Indonesian Invasion, 1975–76', [online]. Available at: http://www.gwu.edu/~nsarchiv/NSAEBB/NSAEBB62/. On Australia's role, see Wendy Way (ed.), *Documents on Australian Foreign Policy: Australia and the Indonesian Incorporation of Portuguese Timor, 1974–1976* (Canberra: Department of Foreign Affairs and Trade, 2000).

assistance to Indonesia, and played an active role in silencing the evidence of violence that made its way out of the territory. Some of that assistance was provided at precisely the time that Indonesian forces were committing their most egregious acts of violence against the civilian population. The devastating military campaigns of the late 1970s, for instance, entailed the use of sophisticated weapons systems, including counter-insurgency aircraft (OV-10 Broncos), napalm, and high-powered weapons, provided by the United States and other Western allies. It is safe to say that without such support neither the invasion nor the genocide would have happened.

If in these ways East Timor's experience was similar to the other cases considered here, there were some respects in which it was very different. For example, whereas secessionist movements elsewhere stuck steadfastly to the use of violent means in pursuit of their objectives, from the mid-1980s East Timor's resistance gradually shifted towards a strategy that emphasized diplomacy, clandestine organization, and non-violent demonstrations. And where others continued to use the language and symbolism of 'national liberation', East Timor's leaders began increasingly to speak the language of universal human rights.[48] Together, these shifts helped to win the movement significant international support, and to ensure that East Timor's cause received a sympathetic hearing, not only among human rights NGOs and solidarity groups, but also within the Catholic Church, at the UN, and among legislators and policy-makers in major states. The cause received a further boost in 1996 when two East Timorese were awarded the Nobel Prize for Peace. Despite its small size, by the late 1990s these developments had made the problem of East Timor an issue powerful Western states could no longer ignore.

East Timor's contested international legal status also helped to disrupt the cycle of violence, and eventually to end it. In contrast to West Papua, where the UN ratified the 1969 plebiscite transferring formal sovereignty to Indonesia, East Timor's 'incorporation' as an Indonesian province was never recognized by the UN. That important legal issue ensured that East Timor remained a matter of international dispute throughout the period of the occupation, providing a strong basis for those demanding independence, and highlighting the violence there. The singular importance of this wider context became evident in 1998–9, when mounting international pressure at a time of domestic economic and political crisis in Indonesia prompted the country's new President to propose a UN-supervised referendum on East Timor's political status. It became even clearer in September 1999, when escalating violence in the aftermath of the vote led some to predict a second genocide. At that critical juncture, major powers that had for years turned a blind eye to Indonesian violence in East Timor chose instead to authorize an armed

[48] On these shifts see Robinson, 'If You Leave Us Here, We Will Die', esp. ch. 4.

intervention to end it. That move, in turn, paved the way for the withdrawal of Indonesian forces, and for East Timor's formal independence in 2002.[49]

Finally, East Timor differs from the other cases discussed here in the way it has been portrayed by outside observers and scholars. Like the Pakistani Army's campaign in East Pakistan, Indonesia's war in East Timor in the late 1970s was quickly described by nationalists and a handful of sympathetic scholars and human rights activists as genocidal. These outside observers, for the most part on the Left, saw in East Timor a perfect example of what they considered to be the general political and moral failings of Western governments. Yet, whereas scholars soon lost interest in the case of East Pakistan (or began to question the applicability of the term genocide in that case), interest in East Timor grew steadily, and it began to be included in general studies of genocide.[50] The shift was due, in part, to a growing public awareness of conditions in the territory, particularly after the Santa Cruz massacre of 1991, and the wealth of credible information that became available for scholarly examination. But it also stemmed from the fact that by the 1990s—in marked contrast to all of the other cases discussed here—the East Timor issue had become a subject of serious political concern among major powers and within the UN. In large part, that was because of the unusual success of the resistance and of international solidarity groups in highlighting the direct complicity of those states in the violence in East Timor; nothing even remotely similar had been achieved in East Pakistan or the other two cases. Finally, it seems likely that Indonesia's campaign of violence in East Timor has come to be described as genocide because, over the years, the resistance movement and its sympathizers abroad managed to develop and disseminate a compelling narrative of the conflict, in which East Timorese were portrayed entirely as courageous victims, and the Indonesian state as wholly evil. It is now clear that that portrait was an oversimplification, but the narrative is well established, and will not easily be rewritten.

DISCUSSION

At first glance, the experiences of state-sponsored violence in East Pakistan, Burma, West Papua, and East Timor seem to display a bewildering diversity. There were marked differences, for example, in the ethnic and cultural character of the secessionist movements, in the duration and extent of the violence, in the numbers killed

---

[49] For a detailed account of the violence surrounding the 1999 referendum, and the reasons for international intervention, see ibid.

[50] See, for example, Totten et al. (eds), *Century of Genocide*; and Kiernan, *Genocide and Resistance in Southeast Asia*.

and otherwise affected, and in the ways in which the violence has been portrayed. A closer examination, however, reveals what appear to be significant similarities among these cases, most notably in the historical conditions that shaped the secessionist movements and the states that sought to crush them, in the character of the states committing the violence, in the broader international environment within which the violence occurred, and in the processes through which political conflict turned to violence, and violence itself escalated. It also reveals some intriguing patterns in the ways that scholars and others have portrayed the violence. While recognizing that these cases are in many respects unique, my sense is that, viewed together, they may offer insights into the study of state-sponsored violence and genocide more generally.

First, they highlight important caveats about the relevance of cultural and ethnic identity in the dynamic of secessionist and state violence. Notwithstanding the claims of state authorities, secessionists, and many outside observers, it is clear that the violence in each of these places was not primarily an expression of pre-existing or primordial cultural or ethnic difference. Indeed, the political objectives of those who challenged state authority—the secessionist movements—were rooted in, or justified by reference to, ethnic or racial identities either created by or reified under colonial rule. Likewise, in all of these cases, the 'nation' whose unity and security state authorities sought to maintain was, to a very significant degree, the legacy of colonial rule. Political conflict and violence, moreover, was clearly not the product of pre-existing or primordial ethnic identities but, in contrast, actually helped to create and to solidify those identities.

The wider implication of these observations is that history itself has a defining importance in the dynamic of genocide and other forms of political violence. Most obviously, past violence significantly increases the likelihood of future violence. In part, that is because the experience or memory of violence can help to create or deepen a sense of group identity and enmity. In part too it is because history, including memories of past violence, provides the essential raw material for political leaders seeking to mobilize populations to take part or at least acquiesce in mass violence.[51] Importantly, historical experience and memory also provide the organizational and behavioural models, as well as the rhetorical tool kit, that are the foundation of future violence, and that shape its character. These observations certainly appear to make sense for the cases considered here, which all involve long histories of violence, where political leaders on all sides have appealed to that history in mobilizing their followers, and where both identities and enmities appear to have stiffened through the experience of violence.

---

[51] For variations on this argument, see Paul R. Brass, *Theft of an Idol: Text and Context in the Representation of Collective Violence* (Princeton: Princeton University Press, 1997); and Stanley Tambiah, *Levelling Crowds: Ethnonationalist Conflicts and Collective Violence in South Asia* (Berkeley: University of California Press, 1996).

Second, these cases suggest that state-sponsored violence is shaped in significant ways by the character of state institutions, and more specifically by the attitudes, policies, and practices of state authorities. It is especially noteworthy that all of these cases involved violence committed by states dominated by the military, and obsessed by national unity, security, and order. All invoked the absolute right to maintain their territorial integrity, and to meet any attempt to breach national unity with unlimited force. More specifically, in their effort to maintain national unity, security, and order each of these states developed and employed repertoires of violence that entailed the massive use of force against civilians. The counter-insurgency strategies employed in each case, moreover, typically strengthened the resolve of the secessionists, primarily because of their brutality and because they targeted civilians thought to be supporting resistance movements.

These observations are pertinent to a common theme in much genocide litera-ture, which points to the importance of state ideology in fuelling genocide and mass violence. Weitz, for example, has highlighted the centrality of a utopian or revolu-tionary vision in some of the twentieth century's best known genocides.[52] The evidence from the four cases considered here lends some support to that view, but also suggests the need for its refinement.[53] For while the state ideologies of Pakistan, Burma, and Indonesia evinced a strident nationalism, and contained a powerful undercurrent of racism, they could hardly be characterized as utopian or revolu-tionary. Indeed, if any ideology can be said to have driven the state-sponsored violence in these cases, it was the ideology of an arrogant, bellicose militarism, wrapped in the guise of legitimate nationalism and benign 'developmentalism'.[54] These four cases also highlight the need to look beyond the conventional state ideologies envisioned by Weitz and others, to consider the conditioning effects on genocide of broader 'systemic' factors including geopolitical competition and 'development'.[55]

Third, in all four cases discussed here the international environment was critical in shaping both the strategies and language of secessionist movements and the state violence against them. Most obviously, violence against secessionists was

[52] Eric D. Weitz, *A Century of Genocide: Utopias of Race and Nation* (Princeton: Princeton University Press, 2003), 237.

[53] A number of authors have taken issue with this argument. Straus, for example, has noted that the leaders who instigated the genocide in Rwanda 'did so primarily to win a civil war, not to radically restructure society'. Scott Straus, *The Order of Genocide: Race, Power, and War in Rwanda* (Ithaca, NY: Cornell University Press, 2006), 11. Also see Dirk Moses, 'Toward a Theory of Critical Genocide Studies', *On-line Encyclopedia of Mass Violence* [online]. Available at: http://www.massviolence.org/Toward-a-Theory-of-Critical-Genocide-Studies.

[54] That conclusion is broadly consistent with a wider scholarship suggesting a close link between nationalism and mass killing. See, for example, Michael Mann, *The Dark Side of Democracy: Explaining Ethnic Cleansing* (New York: Cambridge University Press, 2005).

[55] Notable proponents of this approach to genocide studies include Donald Bloxham, Dirk Moses, Mark Levene, and Christian Gerlach.

conditioned by the provision of military, diplomatic, and economic assistance by key states, or simply through their silence and acquiescence. These observations are broadly consistent with a substantial body of literature that has highlighted the role of powerful states in conditioning mass violence and genocide.[56] And yet, this simple portrait of national self-interest tells only a part of the story. The case of East Timor, in particular, suggests the potentially critical importance of the wider geopolitical context, and within it the role of non-state actors of international norms and legal regimes, and of individual acts of courage, in shaping—even stopping—state violence.

That observation is not entirely new. A number of scholars have highlighted the ways in which geopolitical context can shape state violence. Others have pointed to the possibility that acts of conscience on the part of non-state actors—including the media, religious groups, and NGOs—might prevent, stop, or at least slow the dynamic of mass violence.[57] In addition, some scholars have drawn attention to the ways in which shifts in international norms and legal regimes might affect the prospects for intervention to stop mass killing and genocide.[58] What is needed is a framework that draws these elements together. Apart from adding a new dimension to the analysis of state violence, it would serve to highlight the essentially contingent quality of genocide and mass violence, and thereby reject any notion that they are inevitable or unstoppable.

Finally, given the broad similarities among these cases, it is striking that some have very commonly been described as genocide while others have not. In this respect, East Timor and, to a lesser extent, East Pakistan stand out. The violence in those places has been described as genocide, and has been included in general comparative studies of the subject while, with some rare exceptions, the egregious violence in Burma and West Papua has not. It is fair to ask why this is the case. The answer does not appear to lie in any obvious sense in the nature of the violence itself, in the intentions of the perpetrators, or in the religious or ethnic composition of the population affected. On all of these dimensions, the differences among the four cases are not especially significant. That leads inevitably to the conclusion that other factors were at work.

The discussion of the four cases above suggests at least two possibilities. First, it would appear that the term genocide has been selectively applied to those cases of state-sponsored violence that have entailed substantial political costs for Western powers, while the rest have typically been described as instances of civil war, ethnic cleansing, cultural assimilation, or human rights abuse. Here the case of East

---

[56] See, for example, Samantha Power, 'A Problem from Hell': America and the Age of Genocide (New York: Basic Books, 2002).

[57] See, for example, David Webster, 'Non-State Diplomacy: East Timor 1975–99', Portuguese Studies Review 11:1 (2003), 1–28.

[58] See, for example, Geoffrey Robertson, Crimes against Humanity: The Struggle for Global Justice (New York: New Press, 2000).

Timor is especially instructive. In the first fifteen years of the Indonesian occupation, Western states were able to deny or obscure the extent and nature of the violence. With the rise of powerful religious and secular solidarity groups after 1991, however, and a growing public awareness of the violence, the political costs of acquiescence and complicity for those states grew exponentially, and transformed the conflict into an international issue of considerable importance for those states. Only then did the case of East Timor come to be widely regarded as an instance of genocide.

A second possibility is that scholars, political actors, and the general public are less likely to describe as genocide a case in which the narrative is too complicated—and particularly where both sides have engaged in violence. Secessionists used violence in all of the cases discussed here, but East Timor was again something of an exception. As long as the resistance was engaged primarily in armed resistance, only a handful of solidarity groups and scholars were prepared to describe the Indonesian state violence as genocide. However, as the resistance began to shift away from armed struggle in the mid-1980s, and to focus instead on a diplomatic approach that adopted the language of universal human rights rather than national liberation, international sympathy grew, and the term genocide came to be more widely accepted.

To sum up, these cases suggest the need for a reconsideration of some of the more widely accepted approaches to the study of state violence and genocide, and further reflection on the use and utility of the term itself. More specifically, greater attention needs to be paid to the dynamic historical interaction between the broad structural forces that condition state violence and the specific intentions, policies, and practices of both states and secessionist movements. In that regard, approaches attentive to the effects of historical experience and memory, to processes of state formation, to the impact of international norms and legal regimes, to geopolitical context, and to the role of a wide range of non-state actors would be especially helpful. Finally, there is a need for continued introspection on the part of scholars and others with respect to the use of the term genocide. If the term is to have any analytical value at all—and if it is to be useful as something more than a moral and political epithet—we must adopt a far more rigorous understanding of its meaning, and examine our own motivations in choosing, or declining, to invoke it.

FURTHER READING

Amnesty International, *Indonesia: Continuing Human Rights Violations in Irian Jaya* (London, 1991).

Callahan, Mary P., *Making Enemies: War and State Building in Burma* (Ithaca, NY: Cornell University Press, 2003).

East Timor Commission for Reception, Truth, and Reconciliation (CAVR). *Chega!* (Dili, 2006); available at http://www.cavr-timorleste.org/en/chegaReport.htm

Human Rights Watch, *'They Came and Destroyed Our Village Again': The Plight of Internally Displaced Persons in Karen State* (New York, 2005).

Imama, Jahanara, *Of Blood and Fire: The Untold Story of Bangladesh's War of Independence* (New Delhi/New York: Sterling, 1989).

Osborne, Robin, *Indonesia's Secret War: The Guerilla Struggle in Irian Jaya* (Sydney/Boston: Allen and Unwin, 1985).

The Report of the Hamoodur Rehman Commission of Inquiry into the 1971 War (Lahore: Vanguard, 2000).

Robinson, Geoffrey, *'If You Leave Us Here, We Will Die': How Genocide Was Stopped in East Timor* (Princeton: Princeton University Press, 2010).

Smith, Martin J., *Burma: Insurgency and the Politics of Ethnicity* (London: Zed Books, 1999).

Taylor, John, *East Timor: The Price of Freedom* (London: Zed Books, 1999).

....

CHAPTER 24

NATIONAL SECURITY DOCTRINE IN LATIN AMERICA

THE GENOCIDE QUESTION

....

DANIEL FEIERSTEIN

DURING the second half of the twentieth century, large sections of the population were exterminated in various parts of Latin America. Most of these events followed a similar pattern and were the result of what became known as the National Security Doctrine. Developed primarily by the United States, this policy widened the sphere of international conflict to Latin America in the belief that the region could play a strategic role in the fight against communism, an ideological struggle that had no territorial boundaries.

The National Security Doctrine was inspired by the cold war but also by the methods developed by Western powers in various counter-insurgency struggles. In particular, the methods applied by the 'French school' in Indochina and Algeria and adopted by the Americans during the Vietnam War were later taught at numerous military and ideological training centres in Latin America. The most important of these was the School of the Americas, first established in the Panama Canal Zone in 1946 to train Central American forces. Following the success of the

Cuban Revolution in 1959, another branch of the School was opened at Fort Benning, Georgia, in 1963 to teach 'French' counter-insurgency tactics. Thus, the practice of systematic annihilation of political enemies in Latin America, which began as early as 1954 with the military coup in Guatemala, continued almost until the beginning of the twenty-first century, spreading throughout practically all of Latin America.

This chapter analyses the general characteristics of these developments, their similarities and differences, and the possible connections between civil wars in the region and processes of mass extermination, taking into account that there were no real wars in many of the territories in which these practices were applied. It also examines the controversial question of whether some of these events—particularly the cases of Guatemala and Argentina, as they have been analysed in court sentences and academic research—could be understood through the genocide concept, bearing in mind especially what the concept of genocide can contribute to a better understanding of the differences among these events and the strategic purpose of the political repression in some of the Latin American societies.

EARLY ANNIHILATION PROCESSES
IN LATIN AMERICA

During the nineteenth century, most of the newly independent Latin American states annihilated various indigenous populations that inhabited their territories. This was done to secure borders, establish a state monopoly on violence, and change the juridical status of Indian communities that had formed separate 'republics' during the colonial period. Argentina and Chile are good examples of nation-states founded on the annihilation of indigenous groups. Elsewhere, like Bolivia and Peru, however, these goals were achieved by forcing indigenous populations into submission rather than annihilating them completely.[1]

Indigenous populations were also attacked and sometimes deliberately annihilated in wars between these newly independent states. For example, Argentina, Brazil, and Uruguay all but destroyed isolationist Paraguay and annexed large tracts of its land in the War of the Triple Alliance (1864–70). However, instances can be

---

[1] In Argentina more than 13,000 Mapuches and thousands of Wichi, Pilagá, and Guarani were annihilated during 1850–90. In Chile, thousands of Mapuches were also annihilated at the end of the nineteenth century.

found well into the twentieth century, such as the massacres of Haitians in the Dominican Republic in 1937.[2]

In fact, during the twentieth century, the indigenous populations of Latin America were often slaughtered by private companies. In order to open up new territories, the national governments of the region gave entrepreneurs a free hand in areas historically occupied by indigenous groups. Territories where this policy was applied during the twentieth century include Southern and Western Mexico, where indigenous groups were repeatedly attacked by paramilitary forces; various parts of the Amazon forest in Brazil; Eastern Paraguay, where the Ache Indians and other groups were enslaved or starved to death from the nineteenth to the end of the twentieth century; Southern Paraguay and Northern Argentina; where the Wichís, Tufas, and other groups were annihilated; Southern Chile and Argentina; where the Mapuches were permanently harassed; and numerous parts of Central America.

After this necessarily brief account of the annihilation of indigenous peoples during the nineteenth and early twentieth centuries, we shall now consider the role played by the so-called Doctrine of National Security in unifying existing processes of political repression and extermination throughout Latin America. This doctrine also marked a shift from the targeting of indigenous groups as such to a situation in which ethnicity played only a secondary role, if any, in the choice of victims.

POLITICAL REPRESSION UNDER THE NATIONAL SECURITY DOCTRINE

Although the National Security Doctrine was promoted throughout the region by the United States during the cold war, its first true antecedent was the Argentine Conintes Plan (Plan for Civil Insurrection against the State), which appeared soon after the visit of a French military mission to Argentina in 1957. The Conintes Plan spoke of a 'national menace' from an 'internal political enemy', defined clearly as a 'political identity' and not from an 'ethnic viewpoint'. This doctrine, which was already being used by a democratic government to repress political opponents in Argentina at the end of the 1950s, was to be applied even more harshly by military governments in the following decades in Latin America.

From the late 1950s onwards, the so-called Meetings of American Armies became a regular institution and an ideal channel for spreading the National Security

---

[2] Richard Lee Turtis, 'A World Destroyed, A Nation Imposed: The 1937 Haitian Massacre in the Dominican Republic', *Hispanic American Historical Review* 82:3 (2002), 589–635.

Doctrine among the military all over Latin America. US involvement in the overthrow of Jacobo Arbenz in Guatemala in 1954, Stroessner's dictatorship in Paraguay from 1954 onwards and Duvalier's dictatorship in Haiti from 1957, together with a unanimous concern among right-wing Americans about the 'communist threat' after the Cuban Revolution in 1959, all helped to spread the new American vision of conflict in Latin America, a vision focused on the 'war against the Communism' in which Latin America was seen as a key battleground in a cold war—and sometimes even a Third World War—of global dimensions. The 'enemy' was not only revolutionary movements but any populist, religious, or indigenous movements with progressive ideas aimed at bringing about social change.[3]

The concept of 'dirty war', originating in French counter-insurgency doctrines, was soon applied to all situations of conflict in Latin America whether these involved guerrilla movements waging civil war against dictatorial regimes (as in Colombia, El Salvador, or Nicaragua), or military-political opposition groups too small to spark a civil war or even to control sizeable portions of territory (as in Guatemala or Peru). In most countries, including Argentina, Bolivia, Brazil, Chile, Paraguay, and Uruguay, armed opposition groups were not even professional insurgents and so to describe these conflicts as 'wars' was exaggerated, to say the least.

Nevertheless, the concept of 'dirty war', 'counter-insurgent war', or 'anti-subversive war' became the ideological justification for turning Latin America's armed forces into armies of occupation on their own territories. Generally, a military regime took control of government and/or paramilitary forces operating in conjunction with the armed forces. The regime then proceeded to transform society through the institutionalization of terror at every level of daily life. To do so, it resorted to a whole arsenal of terror, including concentration camps, systematic murder of entire groups (families, villages, ethnic and religious communities), and extensive use of torture and rape as weapons of physical and psychological destruction.

A Brief Outline of Cases

This section describes briefly the main developments in the region country by country before going on to examine their shared characteristics and consequences.

---

[3] During the 1970s many of the Argentinean military believed that they were fighting a Third World War, as can be seen in conference papers and other writings from this period. The inspiration for this idea came especially from André Beaufre's *Introduction to Strategy* and the works of other French counter-insurgents. For an analysis of this way of perceiving conflict, see Horacio Verbitsky, *La última batalla de la Tercera Guerra Mundial* (Buenos Aires: Sudamericana, 2002).

In 1954, a US-sponsored military coup in Guatemala toppled Jacobo Arbenz's democratic government after it began to introduce land reforms. In the twelve months following the coup there were around 3,000 political murders. After a revolt by junior military officers in 1960, which led to armed insurrection in the countryside, repression intensified and it was not until 1996 that the government signed peace accords, ending the internal conflict.

During this thirty-six-year period, the military and paramilitary Guatemalan forces assassinated and/or disappeared more than 200,000 people. This was a deliberate attempt at political and social engineering involving indigenous communities, villages, groups, and whole regions, with terror reaching its peak roughly between 1978 and 1990. The methods used in the Guatemalan case were copied, in a limited range, all over Latin America.

Most experts agree about the appropriateness of the term 'genocide' to describe the atrocities committed in Guatemala, not only because of the sheer number of victims (almost ten per cent of the total population was killed) but also because of the targeting of ethnic groups and nations, including different Mayan populations.[4] The term genocide is justified in this case—but not solely for the reasons just mentioned. Rather, it was the systematic nature of the annihilation that made it genocide, as the groups were defined by the perpetrators. Groups were killed in Guatemala under the National Security Doctrine for exactly the same political reasons that they were killed in some of the other Latin American countries, the only difference being that in Argentina, Bolivia, Chile, and Haití the number of victims was much smaller. However, in countries like Brazil, Uruguay, and Honduras, the killing was neither systematic nor clearly defined as groups. Maybe the genocide concept could clarify the differences and similarities among different processes.

In 1954, the year of the military coup in Guatemala, Gen. Alfredo Stroessner seized power in Paraguay from another military dictator, Federico Chávez. Stroessner's regime, which lasted until 1989, immediately aligned itself with American policies and anti-communism in the region, and later with the National Security Doctrine. From the mid-1970s, Paraguay participated actively in Operation Condor, a clandestine programme for political repression drawn up by South America's right-wing dictatorships under which Argentina, Brazil, Bolivia, Chile, Ecuador, Paraguay, Peru, and Uruguay exchanged intelligence and prisoners, and cooperated in carrying out repressive measures, including joint operations. The Association of Relatives of the Detained and Disappeared in Paraguay estimates that under Stroessner there were between 3,000 and 4,000 political murders, with

---

[4] Among them, for example, we could include Frank Chalk and Barbara Harff. Concerning this kind of analysis see, particularly, the work of Marc Drouin, 'Atrocity Crimes and the Genocide Continuum in Guatemala, 1978–1984', Paper presented at the *Second International Meeting on Genocidal Social Practices: From Europe to Latin America and Beyond: The Continuity of the Genocidal Social Practices, Buenos Aires, November 20–22.*

many thousands more imprisoned and tortured. In fact, a large number of documents relating to Operation Condor were found in Paraguay in 1992 and although Stroessner was overthrown by his own party in a military coup in 1989, Paraguay remains one of the few countries in the region where democracy still has not been restored.

Haiti, on the Caribbean island of Hispaniola, had remained within the American sphere of influence ever since it was invaded and occupied by the United States in 1915. Thus, when François Duvalier (Papa Doc) became president in 1957, he was quick to implement the National Security Doctrine, a policy continued by his son, Jean Claude Duvalier (Baby Doc), who succeeded him in 1971. The paramilitary groups known as the 'tonton macoutes' that Papa Doc set up to exert repression continued to operate after the overthrow of Baby Doc in 1986 and are still active. Haitian paramilitary forces are reckoned to have claimed around 30,000 victims, with up to 500,000 people driven into exile during the Duvalier family's dictatorship.[5]

The Dominican Republic, which shares the island of Hispaniola with Haiti, was ruled by the pro-American dictator Trujillo from 1930 until his assassination in 1961. Thus, when Juan Bosch became president in 1963 after the first free elections in over thirty years, his government lasted less than a year. An expeditionary force of US Marines was sent 'to prevent Communism taking hold of the Republic', and Bosch was replaced by Joaquin Balaguer, who had acted as interim president after Trujillo died. The exact number of people killed during the invasion and the repression that followed is unknown but it is estimated at several thousands.[6]

In March 1964, another military-led coup ousted the populist President of Brazil, João Goulart. Again, the coup was allegedly 'to frustrate the communist plan to seize power'.[7] The dictatorship that followed lasted until 1989, and although there was a gradual transition to democracy after 1985, the first ten years of military government were marked by harsh repression which went under the name of 'Operação Limpeza' or 'Operation Clean-Up'. Although the Brazilian State passed a law in 1995 admitting responsibility for the murder of 136 people between 1961 and 1979, new cases came to light the following year. In a book called 'The Right to Memory and Truth' published by the Special Commission on the Political Dead

---

[5] María Paz Fiumara; *Exitos y fracasos: las fuerzas armadas y de seguridad en El Salvador y Haití* (Bibliotecas CLACSO (http://www.clacso.org.ar), 2004); Elizabeth Abbott, *Haiti: The Duvaliers and Their Legacy,* (New York: McGraw-Hill, 1988).

[6] Bosch was one of the first to emphasize the paradoxically systematic role that paramilitary forces would play in annihilation processes in Latin America. See Juan Bosch, *El pentagonismo, sustituto del imperialismo,* cited in Verbitsky, *La última batalla de la Tercera Guerra Mundial,* 19. See also G. Pope Atkins, *Arms and Politics in the Dominican Republic* (Boulder, CO: Westview Press, 1981).

[7] 'Ato Institucional I, 9, Government of Brazil, April 1964', cited in Marcelo Raffin, *La experiencia del horror* (Buenos Aires: Editores del Puerto, 2006), 132.

and Disappeared of Brazil at the end of 2007, the government officially admitted responsibility for the murder of 479 people.

In November 1964, a military coup also put an end to the government of the Nationalist Revolutionary Movement (NRM) in Bolivia. It is true that the NRM itself had resorted to political repression during the 1950s, setting up concentration camps after it came to power in 1952. However, the military junta that replaced it was quick to align its policies with US interests and extend the repression to include political assassination and frequent periods of martial law. It is estimated that from 1966 to 1986 between 3,000 and 8,000 people were executed by 'death squads' under the orders of various military governments. During this period, Ernesto 'Che' Guevara, who had gone to Bolivia to spread his own brand of revolution, was captured with the help of US Army Special Forces and executed.

For a brief period in 1971, Bolivia was ruled by an anti-imperialist revolutionary government, with Gen. Juan Jose Torres as president. But Torres was overthrown in the same year by another military coup led by Gen. Hugo Banzer. Banzer's regime became increasingly repressive, especially after the military coup in Chile in 1974 and the subsequent alignment of Bolivia and Chile with the National Security Doctrine. Torres himself was murdered in Buenos Aires in 1976 under 'Operation Condor'.

Finally, Banzer was replaced by a new military junta in 1978, the first of many between 1978 and 1982. In 1980, democracy triumphed briefly after a popular uprising forced general elections. But the president-elect, Socialist Hernán Siles Suazo, was so unacceptable to both the military dictatorships of the region and the United States that he was deposed before he could take office. In the same year, 1980, Luis García Meza Tejada seized power in the so-called 'cocaine coup', coordinated from Buenos Aires by an Argentinean army intelligence unit and financed largely by drug trafficking. García Meza was one of the most brutal dictators of the period and during his one year in office he had more than 500 political opponents murdered or 'disappeared'. However, international isolation eventually forced his resignation on 3 August 1981 and the Bolivian military remained in power for only another year. Siles Suazo was finally sworn in as president in 1982.

To implement repression, a succession of military governments hired many international perpetrators of genocide such as former SS officer Mario Busch and his team of pro-Nazi Croatian Ustaschas/Ustaše, and former Gestapo officer Klaus Barbie, known as the Butcher of Lyon, who was finally sentenced to life imprisonment in 1987 for the deaths of 4,000 people during World War II.[8]

In 1972, the president of Uruguay's Colorado Party, Juan Maria Bordaberry, came to power during an institutional crisis and placed the Uruguayan Armed

---

[8] See Jorge Gallardo Lozada; *De Torres a Banzer : diez años de emergencia en Bolivia* (Buenos Aires: Ediciones Perisferia, 1972) and, particularly, Gregorio Selser, *Bolivia : el cuartelazo de los cocadólares* (México: Mexsur, 1982).

Forces in charge of the campaign against the urban guerrilla of the Tupamaros movement.[9] The following year, he dissolved Congress, banned trade unions, and outlawed the Communist Party and other left-wing organizations. Although the governments of Bordaberry (1972–6) and later Aparicio Méndez (1976–81) were headed by civilians, effective power remained in the hands of the Armed Forces. However, in 1980, a change in the constitution proposed by the Uruguayan military was rejected in a referendum. In 1984, the so-called 'Naval Club Agreement' between the military and the main Uruguayan political parties led to general elections, which were won by the Colorado Party. The newly elected democratic government finally took power in 1985.

It is reckoned that between 1972 and 1985 the Uruguayan military forces murdered about 100 political prisoners and a further 160 people disappeared. In addition, thousands more were arrested and tortured and tens or even hundreds of thousands were forced into exile. Indeed, around 300,000 Uruguayans emigrated during this period—just over ten per cent of the country's population—many of whom were surely forced to leave for political reasons.[10]

On 11 September 1973, Salvador Allende's democratic socialist government in Chile was overthrown in a bloody military coup strongly backed by the US Department of State. Allende himself was killed or committed suicide during the bombing of the presidential palace. General Augusto Pinochet took control of the country and, although his regime became more permissive in the late 1980s, he did not step down until March 1990 after losing a plebiscite in 1988.

In February 1991, after examining some 3,000 cases of alleged human rights abuses, the National Commission for Truth and Reconciliation determined (in the so-called Rettig Report) that during the Pinochet era more than 1,000 people had been murdered and another 1,000 political detainees had disappeared, also presumably murdered.[11] The Commission concluded that the real number of victims was probably greater and that many cases will never be reported.

In addition, an unspecified number of people were interned in concentration camps. Different researchers have calculated the number of detainees at between several thousand and several tens of thousands but—as with the numbers of murdered and/or missing persons—it is likely that the true figures exceed these

---

[9] For declarations by the Uruguayan governments of the period and a clear analysis of the process, see Luis Roniger and Mario Sznajder, *El legado de las violaciones a los derechos humanos en el Cono Sur: Argentina, Chile y Uruguay* (La Plata: Ediciones al Margen, 2005). The document cited above can be found on p. 32.

[10] See Marcelo Raffin, *La experiencia del horror* (Buenos Aires: Editores del Puerto, 2006) and Luis Roniger and Mario Sznajder, *El legado de las violaciones a los derechos humanos en el Cono Sur: Argentina, Chile y Uruguay* (La Plata: Ediciones al Margen, 2005).

[11] See Elías Padilla Ballesteros, *La memoria y el olvido. Detenidos Desaparecidos en Chile* (Santiago de Chile: Ediciones Orígenes, 1995). Ongoing judicial inquiries in Spain have since brought to light more victims and have helped to clarify the choice of victims.

estimates, given that most of the perpetrators remain at large and that there is no protection for victims or witnesses in Chile.

As mentioned earlier, a forerunner of the National Security Doctrine was implemented in Argentina in the late 1950s. In 1966, Gen. Juan Carlos Organia imposed a hard-line military regime to exclude the Peronists from power. Numerous popular uprisings followed until Perón (in exile since 1955) finally returned to Argentina and formed a democratic government in 1973. However, following Perón's death in July 1974, a systematic campaign of terror known as 'Operation Independence' began in the province of Tucumán. This model was repeated throughout the country after Gen. Jorge Rafael Videla seized power in 1976 and until the military dictatorship collapsed in 1983.

Officially, over 13,000 people disappeared or were murdered between 1974 and 1983 although Argentinean human rights organizations put the total at between 20,000 and 30,000. The systematic nature of the repression was unique in Latin America. A complex network of over 500 concentration camps was set up across the country and numerous political organizations, trades unions, student unions, and neighbourhood associations were ruthlessly dismantled and suppressed. That is why some researchers and Argentine courts have applied the genocide concept to understand the Argentinean experience.

Moreover, the Argentine 'success' was exported to Central America in the late 1970s and early 1980s, when the Argentinean military trained 'special' forces in Honduras, El Salvador, and Nicaragua, in torture and mass murder, as well as how to dispose of the bodies. As mentioned earlier, the Argentinean army also played a key role in the military coup in Bolivia in 1980.

In 1980, after more than twenty years of uninterrupted rule, the military government in Honduras created counter-insurgency units, specialized military intelligence groups and 'death squads', based on the French counter-insurgency model used in the Latin American Southern Cone, concerning the decision to annihilate the 'political enemies'. The Argentinean and US governments both played a key role in training these repressive forces. Despite the election of a civilian president in Honduras in 1981, political kidnappings and murders actually increased, persisting until the end of the decade.

The Committee of Relatives of Disappeared Prisoners in Honduras places the number of disappeared and murdered at more than 200. The victims were mostly political leaders, lawyers, and members of trades unions, student movements, groups expressing solidarity with the victims of other conflicts in Central America, or members of religious groups. During the 1980s, this pattern was repeated in Ecuador, Mexico, Venezuela, and Panama.

All the instances of repression considered so far occurred in peacetime. However, civil wars in Colombia, Nicaragua, El Salvador, and Peru have also claimed tens of thousands of victims, many of them civilians. Again, the pattern is similar to that found in other Latin American countries: devastation of towns and villages, executions of rural indigenous communities, disappearances, and political murders. In Colombia and Peru (and more recently in Mexico), political repression became intertwined with the fight against the drug trafficking, generating a confused layering of conflicts. Even more recently, attempts to brand organizations like the Revolutionary Armed Forces of Colombia (FARC) and the National Liberation Army (ELN) as 'terrorist organizations' and to include them in the new global strategies of the 'war on terror' have led to a further endorsement of repressive policies.

CHARACTERISTICS OF THE REPRESSION IN LATIN AMERICA

As this brief summary of events has shown, terror was used systematically in different Latin American countries in the second half of the twentieth century in order to transform whole societies and so destroy any possibility of political opposition to pro-US policies. Intelligence was gathered and state and paramilitary forces were established to intimidate, kidnap, torture, and murder political opponents. The widespread practice of disappearing the victims served to eliminate evidence, as well as instilling terror in the communities to which the victims belonged and denying relatives and friends the chance to grieve for their loved ones.

Although similar methods were used throughout the region, the scale and the systematic character of the repression varied from country to country. In some cases, violence was ferocious but limited to small, clearly defined people, as in Brazil, Ecuador, Uruguay, and Honduras, where the number of political murders is estimated in hundreds. By contrast, thousands or tens of thousands of people from all walks of life were murdered in Chile, Argentina, Paraguay, and Bolivia. Here, the sheer extent of the repression shows a deliberate policy of social transformation involving the systematic destruction of trades unions, political parties, student groups, and so on. In short, the aim was not the political persecution of specific individuals but the devastation of social groups as such.

Guatemala has become the archetype of this modus operandi because of the scale and duration of the repression and its impact on the population, with whole communities being wiped out, as happened during the civil war in El Salvador. However, in the late 1970s and early 1980s it was Argentina that had the dubious distinction of organizing repression and political intervention throughout the rest of Latin America. The Argentinean army not only trained Latin America's military—particularly in Honduras and El Salvador in counter-insurgency tactics, torture and the art of disappearing people, but also designed and participated in the military coup in Bolivia in 1980.

THE CONCEPT OF WAR

Many analysts and international observers, as well as the perpetrators themselves, have used the term 'war' (counter-insurgency war, civil war, anti-subversive war, dirty war, etc.) to describe the terror implemented by some of Latin America's dictators. The concept of war is inappropriate because it suggests that the victims were mostly armed combatants, rather than the unarmed civilians that the vast majority really was. It also tends to gloss over the true nature and purpose of the atrocities committed against them.

Although modern warfare has blurred the distinction between combatants and non-combatants, producing ever growing numbers of civilian victims, even many *armed* conflicts of Latin America lacked the basic conditions that military theorists consider necessary to speak of war. Minimally, these consist of a confrontation between professional armies; control of territory; and, in the case of civil war, the alignment of most of the population with the different parties in conflict.[12] If we accept these three prerequisites for war, only Colombia, Peru, Nicaragua, and El Salvador were ever actually at war. In Argentina, the Ejército Revolucionario del Pueblo (People's Revolutionary Army)—which had little to do with most of the victims in Argentina—never managed to control even the mountainous region in the province of Tucumán where it had set up its headquarters, while guerrilla forces in Guatemala were unable to liberate any area of the country, their only support coming from indigenous and peasant farming villages. In other countries, the insurgents did not have the backing or the resources to control any territory. Moreover, none of the insurgent forces in these countries—with the exception of the Unión Revolucionaria Nacional Guatemalteca (Guatemalan Revolutionary National Union) during the 1980s—commanded professional troops. Instead, military–political groups divided their time between political and military activities, without ever becoming professional armies.

The concept of war, then, has proved more useful for legitimizing the actions of the perpetrators than for constructing a theoretically principled understanding of the specific nature of these conflicts. Attempts to describe such conflicts only in terms of 'repression' are also problematic, because they tend to look at individual cases in isolation, treating them as 'excesses' committed by Latin American dictators, rather than as a set of common policies based on a shared ideology of

---

[12] For an analysis of two different theories of war and their possible application to events in Latin America, see Juan Carlos Marín, *Los hechos armados. Argentina, 1973–1976. La acumulación primitiva del genocidio* (Buenos Aires: PICASO/La Rosa Blindada, 1996), which describes the events in Argentina as a 'civil war'; and Eduardo Luis Duhalde, *El Estado Terrorista Argentino. Quince años después, una mirada crítica* (Buenos Aires: EUDEBA, 1999) or Carlos Flaskamp, *Organizaciones político-militares. Testimonio de la lucha armada en Argentina (1968–1976)* (Buenos Aires: Ediciones Nuevos Tiempos, 2002), which take a different view.

'national identity' and 'security' and aimed at transforming and 'purifying' the societies of Latin America, in their own words.

ARGENTINA: A DEBATABLE EXAMPLE OF THE USE OF THE GENOCIDE CONCEPT

The term genocide has been widely used to describe the extermination of indigenous communities in Guatemala. It has generally been avoided when referring to similar developments in other Latin American countries, because the destruction of political groups was excluded—at the request of Great Britain and the Soviet Union (among others)—from the definition of genocide adopted by the UN General Assembly in the Convention on the Prevention and Punishment of the Crime of Genocide in 1948.

This exclusion focuses narrowly on ethnicity rather than a wider vision of the political objectives of genocide. This restriction occurred not only at the drafting stage of the Convention with regard to the strategy of annihilation pursued by the Third Reich, but also in analyses of subsequent conflicts in Indonesia, Cambodia, the Balkans, and Africa.

The military repression in Argentina is a good testing ground for the notion that in modern times—except in wartime and during colonial occupation—genocide has been perpetrated 'from within'. Firstly, there are some legal sentences concerning that genocide happened in Argentina.[13] Secondly, unlike what happened in Guatemala, ethnicity and religion played an almost negligible role in the choice of victims with the exception of the 'non-systematic' anti-Semitism of the perpetrators in Argentina, a fact that has forced many genocide scholars to go beyond the analysis about which specific groups were annihilated and reconsider the strategic purpose of genocide in Argentina as a whole, as a practice directed against the whole Argentinian group.

Let us look first at the legal position on the Argentine genocide. In 1999, following extensive enquiries, Judge Baltazar Garzón of the Fifth Central Court of Instruction in Madrid indicted ninety-eight members of the Argentinean military for crimes of genocide and terrorism. Although Spain's Audiencia Nacional later altered the charges to crimes against humanity (Adolfo Scilingo was finally

---

[13] See, particularly, the sentences against Miguel Osvaldo Etchecolatz, 2006, and Christian Von Wernich, 2007, by the Federal Criminal Oral Court No. 1 of La Plata, Buenos Aires Province, Argentina, available in Spanish at http://www.ladhlaplata.org.ar/juicios.htm. More than likely other sentences will follow, as the trials in Argentina continue.

convicted on this count in 2005), the Federal Criminal Oral Court No. 1 of La Plata, Argentina, has since sentenced Miguel Osvaldo Etchecolatz (former Director General of Investigations for the Buenos Aires Police) and Christian Von Wernich (a police chaplain), for 'crimes against humanity within the framework of the genocide that occurred in Argentina between 1976 and 1983'.

In the case of Etchecolatz, the Court recognized that the charge of genocide had been rejected on a technicality known as the 'principle of congruity' (the charge had not been included in the original investigations) but went on to give a lengthy justification of why the genocide label should be applied to the Argentinean experience.

The grounds of the sentence included the following points:

1) Political groups were included in all drafts of the Convention on Genocide following UN Resolution 96/1 of the General Assembly, December 11, 1946. Political groups were not excluded for legal reasons from the Convention but because of 'the prevailing political circumstances at the time', a reason not supported by the philosophy of law.

2) Even though the Convention excludes political groups, the Court considered that 'there is no impediment to the use of the term genocide' in describing what happened in Argentina, namely, the 'partial annihilation of a national group', since Argentina's Supreme Court ruled (in Causa 13/84 against the Argentine Military juntas) that 'we consider as proven the practices of mass destruction implemented by those calling themselves the Process of National Reorganization . . . , a process that was practically identical throughout the country and prolonged in time'.

3) The Court also deemed that 'the plural and pluripersonal acts alleged were acts against a group of Argentineans or residents of Argentina that could be differentiated, and which no doubt were differentiated by those who organized the persecution and harassment' and these actions 'consisted of deaths, prolonged illegal detentions . . . , tortures, confinements in clandestine detention centers . . . , removing detained children and giving them to other families— forcibly transferring children of the group to another group—so that the idea is clearly present of the extermination of a group of the Argentinean population. This was not done in a random or indiscriminate fashion, but with the intention of destroying a section of the population . . . composed of those citizens who did not fit the type pre-established by the promoters of the repression as necessary for the new order to be installed in the country.'

4) Developing this argument, the Court further considered that those targeted for extermination were not specific individuals; rather 'thousands were disappeared or killed for no political or ideological reason other than the fact that they belonged to certain communities, sectors or groups of the Argentinean nation

(national group) which [the perpetrators] considered, in their inconceivable criminal logic, to be incompatible with the Process.'

5) Finally, the Court considered that 'the term "national group" is absolutely valid for analyzing what happened in Argentina since the perpetrators set out to destroy part of the social fabric in order to produce a sufficiently substantial change so as to affect the State in its entirety. Given the inclusion of the term "total or partial" in the definition of the 1948 Convention, it is evident that the Argentinean national group has been annihilated "partially" and to a sufficiently substantial extent as to alter the social relations within the nation . . . the annihilation in Argentina was not spontaneous, was not fortuitous, was not irrational: this was the systematic destruction of a "substantial part" of the Argentine national group, with the intention of transforming it as such, redefining its way of life, its social relations, its destiny, its future.'

For this reason, the sentence concludes that 'from all that has gone before it is indisputable that we are not dealing as we previously expected with a mere succession of crimes, but rather with something significantly greater than deserves the name of genocide.'[14]

At the time of writing, preliminary investigations have begun into the repression in the Argentinean province of Tucumán in 1974–5, which is now being treated as a crime of genocide from the very beginning.

The specific charge presented in all these cases has been the partial destruction of the Argentinean national group, in accordance with article II of the Convention on the Prevention and Punishment of the Crime of Genocide.

However, labelling the Argentine experience as genocide has been controversial, particularly outside Argentina. One of the main arguments of the lawyers and international organizations that rejected Garzón's and Argentina's sentences has been that

[T]he victims were individually chosen for their political beliefs and not because they belonged to a group, which would imply that those responsible for their disappearance and/ or murder did not have the necessary criminal intent as they did not intend to destroy a group but only to eliminate political dissidents.[15]

That is the reason human rights organization Nizkor has presented an amicus curiae under Spain's courts to modify the sentence from genocide to crimes against

[14] All the quotes were extracted to the sentence against Echetcolatz by the Federal Oral Criminal Court No. 1 of La Plata, September 2006, available in Spanish at http://www.ladhlaplata.org.ar/juicios.htm

[15] The amicus curiae presented by the human rights organization Nizkor in the trial against Adolfo Scilingo requested he be sentenced for 'crimes against humanity', but not under the concept of 'genocide'. For the complete amicus curiae and the sentence of Spain's Audiencia Nacional, see http://www.nizkor.org

humanity. At the moment, national and international lawyers and human rights organizations are discussing these two ways of understanding the facts: genocide or crimes against humanity. The question continues to be controversial.

The researchers and lawyers that supported the idea that genocide occurred in Argentina says that there is ample evidence that the vast majority of the victims were social activists belonging to trades unions, student organizations, or neighbourhood associations, and so the notion of 'individual political dissidence' has proved difficult to sustain, because there was a group dimension. Also, there are more than 500 cases in which the children of activists were kidnapped and, in some cases, tortured, murdered, or disappeared—children that by no stretch of the imagination could be classed as 'political dissidents'.

Nevertheless, it is insufficient to prove that political activists and their children were systematically persecuted and murdered or even that a network of over 500 concentration camps was set up all over Argentina for this purpose. Indeed, the defenders of the genocide position, says that focusing too narrowly on the fact that the victims belonged to certain groups distracts attention away from the real intentions of the perpetrators—the transformation of the rest of Argentinean society by eliminating these groups and what they represented.

For a better understanding of the debate, we turn now to public declarations made by some of the perpetrators themselves and which are widely quoted in the academic literature and, particularly, as a 'genocide proof' in the Argentine Court sentences.[16]

The Voice of the Perpetrators

Nine months after the military coup, Gen. Jorge Rafael Videla, who headed the military government between 1976 and 1980, the worst years of repression, declared in an interview in the magazine *Gente* that

Argentina is a Western and Christian country, not because a notice at Ezeiza Airport says so, but because of its history. It was born Christian under Spanish rule; it inherited its Western culture from Spain and it has never renounced this condition; on the contrary, it has defended it. It is to defend this Western and Christian condition as a way of life that this

---

[16] This is just a small sample of the declarations that have been collected. A much larger sample can be found in the grounds of the accusations and sentences against Miguel Osvaldo Etchecolatz and Christian Von Wernich at http://www.ladhlaplata.org.ar/juicios.htm. For an analysis of these declarations see Daniel Feierstein, *El genocidio como práctica social* (Buenos Aires: Fondo de Cultura Económica, 2007).

struggle has begun against those who have not accepted this way of life and have tried to impose a different one.[17]

A year later, in a newspaper interview published in *La Prensa*, Videla added that it was not the fact that some individuals might 'think differently' that was being persecuted by the military dictatorship, but the effects this might have on the way other members of society behaved. In Videla's own words:

Within our way of life, nobody is deprived of freedom just because they think differently; but we consider it a serious crime to attack the Western and Christian way of life and try to change it for one that is completely alien to us. The aggressor in this type of struggle is not just the bomber, the gunman or the kidnapper. At the intellectual level, it is anyone that tries to change our way of life by promoting subversive ideas; in other words, who tries to subvert, change or disrupt [our] values... A terrorist is not just someone who kills with a gun or a bomb, but anyone who spreads ideas that are contrary to Western and Christian civilization.[18]

It was not just Videla who thought in this way. One of the main promoters of French counter-insurgency methods, Gen. Alcides Lopez Aufranc, who had attended courses at the École de Guerre in Paris in 1957, argued that 'The Argentinean political spectrum must be modified. Otherwise, we will have to call elections sooner or later and the alternatives are Peronists, radicals and Marxists.'[19]

Many similar declarations by the repressors are on record. But perhaps the clearest indication of the military dictatorship's intention to systematically reorganize Argentinean society is to be found in the name the regime gave itself—'Proceso de Reorganización Nacional' ('Process of National Reorganization'). The process was worked out in detail by Gen. Diaz Bessone, the Minister of Planning, in his 'National Project', which argued that 'the real objective is to organize a new and viable political system and to make the achievements of [our] armed intervention irreversible.'

Going on to analyze what he calls 'the foundational stage' of the Process of National Reorganization, Diaz Bessone emphasized the following:

Founding a new republic is no easy matter... The armed forces must be sufficiently alert, determined and resourceful to act simultaneously as an efficient fighting force against guerrillas and terrorists; an efficient surgeon that will remove the evil from all social classes and walks of life; an efficient government that will steer the ship of the state skillfully and prudently; and last but not least, parents of the new republic, strong, united, just, free, supportive of others, clean, exemplary... But it is only fair to point out that since no national project was outlined beforehand, little has been achieved so far to accomplish the remaining objectives, which are to defeat not only the guerrillas but subversion 'in totum,'

[17] Jorge Rafael Videla, in *Gente*, 22 December 1976.
[18] Jorge Rafael Videla, in *La Prensa*, 18 December 1977.
[19] Declarations cited in Enrique Vázquez, *La última. Origen, apogeo y caída de la dictadura militar* (Buenos Aires: EUDEBA, 1985), 115.

so laying strong foundations for the birth of the new republic . . . This national project, the political project, the creative project of life in common, will have no meaning, nor will it illuminate Argentina's path ahead, unless it is applied now. Otherwise, we run the risk of going astray or falling behind those nations that actively determine the course of history. Moreover, our failure so far to solve the basic problems may give our opponents the chance to regroup as long as those who create and sustain subversion remain alive.[20]

In short, Diaz Bessone is arguing that this regime, which defines itself as a 'Process of National Reorganization', must supplement military action against guerrilla forces with 'surgery' to 'remove the evil' from every part of society and so make way for a 'New Republic'. In other words, a series of individuals and groups must be annihilated to achieve the transformation—or to guarantee security and purity—of society. The enemy is not just armed guerrilla forces, nor is this an exercise in indiscriminate terror against the population as a whole. Instead, it is a clearly defined 'surgical operation' on previously defined sections of the population whose disappearance is meant to have an 'irreversible' effect on Argentinean society.

Although state repression in Argentina is better documented than that in Chile, Bolivia, or Guatemala, the logic applied by the perpetrators in these countries was similar, although the Argentine systematic nature of the concentration-camps structure was not present in almost any other experience.

On the other hand, in the Guatemalan case, the other Latin American experience analysed as genocide by many researchers into the genocide studies field, the annihilation of indigenous communities had less to do with ethnicity or religion per se than with the perpetrators' perception of these communities as natural allies of the guerrillas. Thus, the Guatemalan genocide was motivated *primarily* by a decision to politically transform Guatemalan society rather than by racism. The same is true of the many so-called ethnic killings in Bolivia and El Salvador, where racism among the 'rank and file' was manipulated instrumentally for strategic political ends.

By contrast, Brazil is a clear example of state repression that targeted specific individuals, but not necessarily whole groups. Rather, terror was imposed through imprisonment, mistreatment, and sporadic, selective killings. While these crimes clearly fit the category of crimes against humanity, it is difficult to classify them as genocide in the absence of any clearly identifiable cases of systematic annihilation against any group.

Most researchers have refused to consider the possibility of genocide unless it involves the persecution of ethnic groups. It is one of the controversial points in the analysis about Latin American experiences.

---

[20] A fundamental part of the 'National Project'—including the passage cited above—is reproduced as an annex in Vázquez, *La última*, 299–327.

However, one of the risks of this kind of approach could be the distortion of the strategic purpose of the annihilation processes, that in any case was directed to ethnic groups 'as such' but was directed against different groups (many of them, ethnic groups) by 'political reasons'. This viewpoint also blurs the distinction between cases like Argentina, where society 'transformation' or 'purification' was brought about by the systematic annihilation of whole groups, and other cases like Brazil, where the state pursued the same goal by different means.

On the contrary, some researchers are convinced that to extend the genocide concept to those crimes committed under 'political reasons' could trivialize the genocide concept and turn it into a non-precise legal tool.

The debate continues openly, not only in courts, but also in academic research.

THE CONSTRUCTION OF COLLECTIVE MEMORY

This chapter has argued that state repression carried out in various Latin American countries under National Security Doctrine constituted attempts to transform whole societies. Although repression in some countries was limited in scope, in others—particularly in Guatemala, Bolivia, Chile, Argentina, Paraguay, and El Salvador—the policy chosen was the systematic annihilation of some groups of the population.

It has also argued that the notion of genocide as the partial destruction of a national group *by members of the same group* highlights the strategic nature of acts committed by agents of the state in some Latin American countries. This view of genocide may, in turn, provide us with a broader and deeper understanding of other instances of mass destruction in the twentieth century, from Nazi Germany to Indonesia, Cambodia, and the former Yugoslavia. These cases are often misunderstood because of a refusal by scholars to examine the deeper political nature of almost all the modern genocides.

Many Nazis are on record as saying that their objective was to transform German society (and then the whole of Central Europe) and that the eradication of the Jewish, Sinti, Roma, and Slav populations from the Reich was aimed at achieving a Reich free from 'ideological infections'. This is not to deny the racist philosophy of National Socialism—simply to emphasize its predominantly political nature, although it could be debatable.

Similarly, the policy of the Khmer Rouge between 1975 and 1979 of forcibly depopulating cities and relocating people on collective farms, killing any that resisted, was aimed at a global transformation of Cambodian society. Again, the first victims were political groups and intellectuals. More recently, the policies of 'ethnic cleansing' carried out in Bosnia during the late 1980s and early 1990s were intended to break up the Yugoslav federation and transform Bosnia into a homogeneous Serbian society or, if this were not possible, to transform the Yugoslav federation into territorially independent nations that no longer considered themselves to be members of a Yugoslav society. In fact, the first victims were people of mixed race in Bosnia-Herzegovina, especially in the cosmopolitan city of Sarajevo, together with Serbian, Croatian, and Bosnian politicians and intellectuals who argued for the need to preserve a Yugoslavian identity.

CONCLUSION

The history of Latin America in the second half of the twentieth century illustrates with unusual forcefulness what lies at the heart of modern genocide processes. It demonstrates clearly how, in some cases, the systematic annihilation of certain groups serves as a tool for the partial destruction and transformation of society from within. The fact that in Latin America these groups were clearly chosen for political rather than ethnic or religious reasons facilitates the understanding of similar processes where the ethnic or religious elements are more intertwined. Although discussion of the appropriateness of the genocide concept to analyse some of these facts continues to be controversial, the mere debate could produce a better understanding of the mass annihilation processes all over the world, through the Latin American peculiarities.

On the other hand, maybe if the collective memory of genocide is one of definitively differentiated groups annihilating one other, the strategic aims of genocide will be fulfilled. Jews and Sinti and Roma will never be seen again as Germans; Serbs, Croatians, and Bosnians will never again be Yugoslavs; 'Communist Indians' will never again be Guatemalans; and 'subversive delinquents' will never be Argentineans.[21]

And so these 'alienated' ways of constructing memory gradually force those who survive to align themselves on one side or another. The survivors are *either* Germans *or* Jews, *either* Serbs *or* Bosnians—until they can no longer see how the processes of annihilation have transformed their societies and the ways they construct their own identities. The trials currently taking place in different countries into what happened in Latin America in the second half of the twentieth

[21] One of the best and most readable analyses of the modes of construction and possible deconstruction of the processes of identity is Benedict Anderson, *Imagined Communities: Reflections on the Origin and Spread of Nationalism* (London/New York: Verso, 1991), which questions the so-called 'eternal' or 'essential' nature of 'national identities'.

century may be an opportunity for us all to reframe these ways of constructing memory.

Alternatively, we can forget that these processes of annihilation ever occurred and accept the fragmentation of our societies, as well as the dissolution of our identities that has resulted from them. We can also forget that the concept of 'national identity'—the recurrent justification for genocide in our modern world—is no more than a social construction dating back some two hundred years. During this time, our ability to kill one another has increased almost daily because we have failed to understand that 'national identity' is no more than a pretext to annihilate 'others' as well as the 'other' hidden within ourselves.[22]

FURTHER READING

Armony, Ariel, *Argentina, the United States and the Anti-Communist Crusade in Central America, 1977–1984* (Athens: Ohio University Press, 1997).

Corradi Juan, et al., *Fear at the Edge: State Terror and Resistance in Latin America* (Berkeley: University of California Press, 1992).

Feierstein, Daniel, 'Political Violence in Argentina and Its Genocidal Characteristics', *Journal of Genocide Research* 8:2 (2006), 149–68.

—— *El genocidio como práctica social. Entre el nazismo y la experiencia argentina* (Buenos Aires: FCE, 2007).

Feitlowitz, Marguerite, *A Lexicon of Terror* (Oxford: Oxford University Press, 1998).

Ibarra, Carlos Figueroa, 'The Culture of Terror and Cold War in Guatemala', *Journal of Genocide Research* 8:2 (2006), 191–208.

Grandin, Greg, *The Last Colonial Massacre: Latin America in the Cold War* (Chicago: University of Chicago Press, 2004).

McSherry, Patrice J., *Predatory States: Operation Condor and Covert War in Latin America* (Lanham: Rowman and Littlefield, 2005).

Menjivar, Cecilia, and Néstor Rodríguez, *When States Kill: Latin America, the U.S. and Technologies of Terror* (Austin: University of Texas Press, 2005).

Roniger, Luis, and Mario Sznajder, *The Legacy of Human Rights Violations in the Southern Cone* (Oxford: Oxford University Press, 1999).

[22] I thank Dirk A. Moses, Donald Bloxham, and Douglas Town, whose detailed suggestions greatly improved the final manuscript.

CHAPTER 25

GENOCIDE AND POPULATION DISPLACEMENT IN POST-COMMUNIST EASTERN EUROPE

CATHIE CARMICHAEL

INTRODUCTION

BETWEEN 1990 and 2010, the political map of the Balkans and Caucasus changed as Communist regimes collapsed and border disputes escalated. Some of the most bitter conflicts were in areas where there were mixed populations with large 'minority' populations that did not recognize potential changes in borders (Russians in Chechnya or Serbs in Croatia, Bosnia, and Kosovo). Not all ethnically mixed regions did experience conflict: the Baltic and other mixed regions such as Transylvania avoided significant bloodshed. For conflict to take place there must be sufficient ideological mobilization to allow the politics of violence to flourish. Religious identities, heavily repressed during the Communist era, became a defining part of the rejection of that system. Orthodoxy and Catholicism were revitalized as a political alternative after years of official atheism. A revival of militant

Islamism after the success of Ayatollah Khomeini in Iran in 1979 radicalized politics in both the Balkans and the Caucasus. This religious revival exacerbated tensions between ethnic communities in contested regions, giving politicians an apparently 'traditional' pretext for augmenting their power within narrow ethnically based constituencies.

The decline of Soviet power in the Transcaucasian region precipitated fighting in the Azerbaijani autonomous *oblast* of Nagorno-Karabakh between the Azeri minority and Armenians, with the exodus of the former in the 1990s. Conflict between the former *oblast* of South Ossetia and the Georgian government erupted in both 1991 and 2008, with military intervention by the Russians against the Tbilisi government. The dissolution of the Chechen-Ingush Autonomous Soviet Socialist Republic in 1991 into the republics of Chechnya and Ingushetia sparked two brutal wars between the Russian Federation and those Chechens who wanted full sovereign independence. In the former Communist state of Yugoslavia, over 120,000 people died in a series of local wars (*mali ratovi*) triggered by organized Serb resistance to the independence of Bosnia and Croatia where many ethnic Serbs were living. Both conflicts were settled in 1995, with significant territorial revisions in Bosnia. In 1999, conflict over the status of the Serbian region of Kosovo, largely populated by pro-independence Muslim Albanians, led to NATO intervention, ethnic cleansing spearheaded by the government troops of Slobodan Milošević, and the subsequent rout of the Serbs.

The 'unmixing' of populations before the 1990s also followed historical trends. The long collapse of the Ottoman Empire in the Balkans had led to a dispersal of populations, particularly Muslims and Orthodox Serbs. When the Serbs were unified in the first Yugoslavia after 1918, the other nationalities resented their dominance. In the Caucasus, the rejection of Russian hegemony and the embrace of a wider Islamic identity had its origins in the colonial expansion of the Tsarist state in the region over the previous two hundred years. Recent violence dramatically simplified the ethnic composition of many areas and millions became permanent refugees. During the 1990s, about sixty per cent of Bosnia's population was either temporarily or permanently displaced. At the time of the declaration of Bosnian independence in 1992, approximately seventeen per cent of the republic's population were Croats; now the number is about fourteen per cent. This pattern was repeated elsewhere. The Serb minority in Krajina, Slavonija, and more recently Kosovo shrank considerably, but in Bosnia, their percentage of the overall population actually rose from thirty-one per cent in 1991 to thirty-seven per cent in 2006. Bosnian Muslims now live in confined areas of the Western Federation territory rather than in the towns of the eastern part of the republic, where once they formed a majority, and they have also moved to other former Yugoslavian republics.

THE 'NATIONAL QUESTION' AND COMMUNISM

Marxist views on national self-determination evolved in the years immediately before the First World War.[1] Somewhat reacting against classic dialectical materialism, which tended to view national identity as part of the 'superstructure', Josef Stalin argued that national identity was unlikely to wither away and was therefore infrastructural: 'a historically evolved, *stable* community of language, territory, economic life and psychological make-up manifested in a community of culture.'[2] When the Soviet Union was founded in 1922, it was supposed to be a union of equal nation-states, but some nations were more equal than others. It initially contained four republics, subsequently dividing into fifteen discrete republics, albeit under the leaden influence of Moscow. More problematically, the Russian Republic included sixteen 'autonomous republics' (including the Chechen-Ingush republic) and numerous administrative units or *oblasti*. The Communist states created borders that in some cases could only be maintained by their firm political control.

For the most part, the internal 'republican' borders that Communist authorities fashioned in Europe and Eurasia were to prove durable. The USSR's 1922 boundaries largely survived the collapse of the country in 1991, creating new independent states 'from within'. The estimated 35 million Communist-era ethnic Russian or Russian-speaking migrants in the 'near abroad' did not generally aspire to join the new Russian Federation, preferring to gain citizenship in Lithuania, Latvia, Estonia, Belarus, Ukraine, or Kazakhstan wherever possible.[3] In Europe, the status of Transdniester (a small unrecognized territory between Moldova and Ukraine with a mixed Moldovan, Russian, and Ukrianian population) has sparked tensions, but as the peaceful situation in the Baltic indicates, ethnic nationalism is not always an overwhelming political force.[4] The Czech and Slovak Socialist Republics, created in 1969 (from the one reform to survive the crackdown after the Prague Spring), separated fairly amicably in 1992. The controversial establishment of the People's Republic of Poland in 1952 had involved a dramatic push to the West and incorporation of former German territory and the expulsion of German speakers as well as bitter disputes between Ukrainians and Poles in the late 1940s. Nevertheless, with no will to contest these borders or reverse the ethnic cleansing of the previous

[1] Erik van Ree, 'Stalin and the National Question', *Revolutionary Russia* 7:2 (1994), 214–38.

[2] Eric Hobsbawm, *Nations and Nationalism since 1780: Programme, Myth, Reality* (Cambridge: Cambridge University Press, 1992), 5.

[3] Vera Tolz, 'Conflicting "Homeland Myths" and Nation-State Building in Postcommunist Russia', *Slavic Review* 57:2 (1998), 267–94.

[4] Henry E. Hale, *Foundations of Ethnic Politics: Separatism of States and Nations in Eurasia and the World* (Cambridge : Cambridge University Press, 2008).

generations, Poland evolved peacefully into a modern democratic state from 1989 onwards. The German Democratic Republic founded in 1949 was fairly easily absorbed by the former West Germany in 1990 without bloodshed, territorial revisions, or major protest. The contrast between violent and peaceful transition to post-Communism is instructive, suggesting that without individuals willing to spark protest and lead territorial revisionist movements, borders can attain legitimacy over time, whatever their actual ethnic or religious composition. Despite the relative lack of violent political unrest associated with the break-up of these Communist states, there proved to be major unresolved problems linked primarily to unresolved border questions. It was these areas in which the most serious and genocidal conflicts developed after the 1990s. It is also likely that (often unacknowledged) prejudice against Islam hampered the creation of stable Muslim nations in both the Soviet Union and Yugoslavia.

THE STATUS OF NAGORNO-KARABAKH

The war in Nagorno-Karabakh from 1988 until 1994 was a direct consequence of the collapse of Communist authority and unresolved border questions from the pre-Communist period. In 1922 a 'Transcaucasian Federal Republic' had been created, consisting of Georgia, Azerbaijan, and Armenia, which was to last until 1936. This region had seen intense fighting during the First World War between Imperial Russia and the Ottomans and the early 1920s and bitter divisions already existed between the region's Christian Armenian and Muslim Azeri populations.[5] After 1936, the individual republics enjoyed full national status within the USSR, which did not itself solve the status of minorities. Although Nagorno-Karabakh was in Azerbaijan, over ninety per cent of the *oblast* population was Armenian. In February 1988, the Armenian political authorities in Nagorno-Karabakh, emboldened by Mikhail Gorbachev's promises of restructuring (*perestroika*), voted to unify the *oblast* with the Armenian Republic; the event is generally seen as precipitating the crisis as it is likely that they remained deeply inimical to Muslim neighbours and were no longer forced to share power in the absence of Soviet pressure. In March 1988, the Armenian authorities began to expel Azeris from the mountainous region after an Azeri pogrom in the city of Sumqayit/Sumgait on the Caspian Sea resulted in the deaths of 26 local

---

[5] Donald Bloxham, *The Great Game of Genocide: Imperialism, Nationalism, and the Destruction of the Ottoman Armenians* (Oxford: Oxford University Press, 2005), 232–3.

Armenians and destructive riots which led to thousands more being injured, including Azeris. Although the Soviet media tried to repress news of the tragedy for several weeks, the pogrom was a signal that Soviet authority had dwindled and that restructuring would bring problems. Both the Soviet Union and Yugoslavia had low homicide rates before the breakdown of authority.[6] Fear of state reprisal against manifestations of 'divisive' nationalism had helped to minimize public disorder in Communist societies. So great a shock was the news of the Sumgait pogrom that the Dagestani poet Razul Gamzatov called it a 'Chernobyl of the spirit'.[7]

In the following six years, Armenia and Azerbaijan fought over the issue, with peace finally brokered by the Russians in 1994. Historical prejudices had enflamed relations between the two states. The Azerbaijani capital, Baku, had been the site of bitter pogroms between Muslims and Armenians in 1905.[8] The latter were often more prosperous and some anti-Armenian actions took on the character of 'class' warfare. The Armenians, still collectively traumatized by the genocide of 1915, saw the (generally Shi'ite) Azeris as a Muslim 'menace' to a Christian identity under threat in the entire region. The Soviet invasion of Afghanistan in December 1979 under the terms of the Brezhnev Doctrine, which promised to prop up troubled Communist regimes, led directly to a revival in Islamic fundamentalist politics, which spilled over the Soviet border. Anti-Soviet sentiment had already been inspired by the dramatic surge of radical religious politics during the Iranian revolution earlier that year. Muslim volunteers or Mujahideen joined the pro-Azerbaijan forces during the Afghan war, just as they were to help the Bosnian government in the early 1990s. The long-term result of the war was the exodus of non-Armenians from Nagorno-Karabakh and the deaths of up to 30,000 people and displacement of thousands. Armenians now constitute over ninety-five per cent of the population. Although now the region is now de facto independent of Azerbaijan and enjoys the status of a 'quasi-state', it has been heavily dependent on Armenia for trade and most other forms of support, in the way that Republika Srpska has been reliant on Serbia.[9] Like Bosnia it remains one of the most heavily land-mined parts of the world with several hundred deaths and injuries reported since the conflict began.[10]

---

[6] John B. Allcock, *Explaining Yugoslavia* (London: Hurst, 2000), 383.

[7] Roy Medvedev and Giulietto Chiesa, *Time of Change: An Insider's View of Russia's Transformation* (London: I. B. Tauris, 1991), 224.

[8] The events of that year were dramatically described in Luigi Villari, *Fire and Sword in the Caucasus* (London: Unwin, 1906).

[9] Pål Kolstø, 'The Sustainability and Future of Unrecognized Quasi-States', *Journal of Peace Research* 43:6 (2006), 733.

[10] Physicians for Human Rights, *Landmines: A Deadly Legacy* (New York: Human Rights Watch, 1993), 144.

The Chechen Crisis and
the Russian Federation

Although largely Sunni Muslim Chechens were a clear majority in Chechnya, the capital, Grozny, had a large number of Russians living there before 1991, perhaps fifty per cent of the population. Relations between the two groups, difficult since Russian expansion in the late eighteenth century, were badly enflamed by the deportation of Chechens to Kazakhstan and Siberia in 1944 on the grounds that the whole nation was deemed to have collaborated with the Nazis. Many were also executed before deportation or died en route, a tragedy that played an important part in the repudiation of the Soviet legacy.[11] Effectively barred from political participation until the mid-1980s, the All-National Congress of the Chechen People (NCCHP) sensed the weakness of the authorities in turmoil in Moscow in September 1991 and killed the local Soviet representative, moving towards de facto independence. The Russian President Boris Yeltsin opposed these moves, sending in troops in November 1991. The Chechens resisted, declaring independence in 1993. Unlike the other new states that sprung from the ruins of the Soviet Union, defined as 'union republics' in the Soviet Constitution, Chechnya did not have the legal 'right' to succeed, a status not recognized by the NCCHP, but crucial to our understanding of why Moscow opposed this independence so bitterly, when it had accepted the departure of Ukraine and the other former republics.[12] Many Muslim states recognized Chechnya, creating further regional polarization. The situation between ethnic groups began to deteriorate. Russians and other non-Chechens living there were subjected to intimidation and began to leave. The government of Dzhokhar Dudayev, who like Tudjman and Mladić had been a Communist general, faced internal opposition, which Yeltsin exploited. In December 1994, the Russians invaded Chechnya and came under heavy international criticism for their intense bombing of the capital, Grozny, and use of special troops from the interior ministry who hunted down and slaughtered Chechen fighters in a so-called *zachistke* or 'cleansings'. As the Chechen troops retreated from their lost capital, they killed as many Russian soldiers as they could and were joined by Mujahideen from other parts of the Muslim world. Dudayev, who had grown up as the child of exiles in Kazakhstan and imbibed their resentment,[13] was killed by the Russian military in

---

[11] Brian Glyn Williams 'Commemorating "The Deportation" in Post-Soviet Chechnya: The Role of Memorialization and Collective Memory in the 1994–96 and 1999–2000 Russo-Chechen Wars', *History and Memory*, 12:1 (2000), 101–34.

[12] Brian Stormo, 'The Unsuccessful Secession of Chechnya', *International Relations Journal* 1 (2004), 22.

[13] Mike Bowker, 'Conflict in Chechnya', in Cameron Ross (ed.), *Russian Politics under Putin: Normality, Normalcy or Normalisation* (Manchester: Manchester University Press, 2004), 256.

1996. His successor, Zelimkhan Yandarbijev, signed a peace agreement later that year, sensing the Russian public's lack of support for the war and Yeltsin's declining authority. Over half a million civilians were displaced between 1994 and 1996 and many went to neighbouring Ingushetia.

In the late summer of 1999, the Russians started bombing Chechnya again in retaliation for terrorist activities in Moscow and Chechen support for the ongoing war in Dagestan, which had radicalized Russian public opinion. By the winter they retook Grozny, committing atrocities in the village of Alkhan-Yurt and the suburbs of the capital.[14] Russian President Vladimir Putin introduced a new constitution in May 2000, but still effectively faced guerrilla insurgency in the mountains and a sharp rise in Islamic militancy. Action against the Chechens may have raised the profile and popularity of Putin, as he deployed increasingly tough language and military tactics, but also led to terrible 'retribution' in the form of bombings in Moscow and Beslan in 2004. Over 200,000 Russians and 20,000 Armenians left Chechnya in the 1990s, and non-Muslims now number less than five per cent of the total population. At least 4,000 Russian soldiers died during the two wars and the number of Chechen fighters killed may well be higher. The number of Russian and Chechen non-combatants who died probably was at least twice this number.[15]

WAR AND ETHNIC CLEANSING IN SOUTH OSSETIA AND ABKHAZIA

Like Nagorno-Karabakh, South Ossetia had also been granted *oblast* status within the Georgian SSR. Prior to Soviet disintegration, just under thirty per cent of the South Ossetian population was Georgian and Christian, the rest being largely Muslim Ossetians (who also lived across the border in the Russian *oblast* of North Ossetia). The new Georgian government wanted to dissolve the *oblast* status and integrate the region into their state, although the Ossetian population had already voted for pro-independence candidates in elections in October 1990. In January 1991, the Georgian Army entered the capital Tskhinvali and were reported to have killed over 1,000 people before a ceasefire was announced the following year, backed by Moscow.[16] About 100,000 also fled to North Ossetia during the

[14] James Hughes, *Chechnya: From Nationalism to Jihad* (Philadelphia: Pennsylvania University Press, 2007), 120.

[15] Matthew Evangelista, *The Chechen Wars: Will Russia Go the Way of the Soviet Union?* (Washington, DC: Brookings Institution, 2002), 84.

[16] Mike Bowker, *Russia, America and the Islamic World* (Dartmouth: Ashgate, 2007), 143.

fighting. Distance from the Georgian government increased and a referendum on independence was passed in 2006, supported by ninety-nine per cent of those who voted. This was boycotted by ethnic Georgians, just as Serbs boycotted referenda in Kosovo and Bosnia in the 1990s. On 8 August 2008, Georgian troops re-entered Tskhinvali, provoking an armed response from the Russian Federation. 'Volunteers', many of whom were from outside South Ossetia, had already begun to attack Georgians living there and the government of Mikheil Saakashvili reacted to documented reports of ethnic cleansing. After Russian troops invaded Georgian territory proper the following week, bombing the town of Gori, Saakashvili agreed to a ceasefire. According to the terms drawn up by French President Nicolas Sarkozy, the International Community would open 'international discussions' on the regions stability and security. The rhetoric of genocide, self-defence, and humanitarian intervention was used by both sides.

The Black Sea region of Abkhazia, which had been an autonomous republic within Soviet Georgia, resisted incorporation into Georgia in 1992. After Georgia lost a war against the Abkhaz and their Russian allies in 1993, at least half of the Georgian population and most of the other ethnic groups numbering about 250,000 fled or were forced to leave (in some cases by Muslim Chechens who had joined the Abkhaz). As political divisions have hardened, this is likely to be a permanent displacement. In late August 2008, the Russian Federation recognized the independence of both Abkhazia and South Ossetia. Earlier that month they also had backed the Abkhaz militarily and moved into Georgian territory around the town of Poti before the Saakashvili government capitulated. Arguably the recognition of Kosovo in 2008 gave considerable impetus in both cases of secession and has 'unfrozen' conflicts which had been previously thought to have stagnated.[17] Forgetting Chechnya, Putin had already declared in 2007 that 'if we decide . . . that the principle of self-determination is more important . . . than territorial integrity, then we must apply this principle to all parts of the world and not only to regions where it suits our partners.'[18]

CRISIS AND GENOCIDE IN YUGOSLAVIA

When the Communist partisans began to establish a new government during the War in Yugoslavia (1941–5), they realized their ultimate success lay in balancing the interests of the different nationalities that had been the subjects of the Karadjordjević

---

[17] Rick Fawn, 'The Kosovo—and Montenegro—effect', *International Affairs* 84:2 (2008), 269.
[18] Ibid. 286.

monarchy before the war. Fanatically loyal to their charismatic leader Josip Broz Tito, Yugoslavs remained united by the policy of 'brotherhood and unity' until the 1970s or even later in some republics, notably Bosnia. The internal boundaries drawn up in 1946 by the Stalin-influenced Edvard Kardelj, and revised again by him in 1974, were dramatically unstable after the demise of Communism. Although the new Yugoslavian state had been 'largely manned by the Serbs of Bosnia and Croatia',[19] it had also been specifically designed to keep Serbia weak in a confederation in which they represented forty-two per cent of the overall population. By the death of Tito in 1980, cracks in the system began to emerge, especially as the 1974 Constitution designated the Serbian regions of Kosovo and Vojvodina as 'autonomous', a status they had been denied in 1946.[20]

The legacies of previous wars and genocide remained part of the lived experience of the subsequent generations. More than one million Yugoslavs had died in the 1940s, most the victims of other Yugoslavs rather than the occupying Germans and Italians. Many were 'possessed', as the historian Milorad Ekmečić put it, by their memories of the 1940s.[21] Ivan Čolović argued that the 'discourse of warlike ethnic nationalism places contemporary events . . . outside the co-ordinates of historical time . . . (offering) a mythic, anti-historical perception of time.'[22] Certainly during the 1990s, past grievances frequently seemed more important to extremists than the human rights of the living.

Some Serbs also feared that increasing population growth amongst the largely Muslim Kosovo Albanians (Kosovars) threatened the status of Serbs living there. Ethnic Serbs had begun to drift out of the region attracted by jobs in industrial centres and their numerical share of the population dwindled to just over ten per cent (it had been more than twenty-five per cent when Serbia annexed Kosovo from the Ottomans in 1912). Although few were inclined to actually live there, Serbs felt attached to their medieval legacy, particularly splendid Orthodox monasteries, and regarded it as a fault line between Christian and Islamic civilization. The Communists had dithered over the status of Kosovo in 1945, ultimately preferring to keep it rather than hand it over to Enver Hoxha in Albania. This decision was made to avoid ethnic violence and a Serb backlash, but perhaps merely prolonged the controversial question of the region's status.

After the death of Tito, nationalist Serbs became less restrained about criticizing the new status of Kosovo. They claimed, without much empirical foundation, that

[19] Stevan K. Pavlovitch, 'Serbia and Yugoslavia—The Relationship', *Southeast European and Black Sea Studies* 4:1 (2004), 102.

[20] Daniele Conversi, 'Central Secession: Towards a New Analytical Concept? The Case of Former Yugoslavia', *Journal of Ethnic and Migration Studies* 26:2 (2000), 340–1.

[21] Tim Judah, *The Serbs: History, Myth and Destruction of Yugoslavia* (New Haven, CT: Yale University Press, 1997), 132–3.

[22] Ivan Čolović, *The Politics of Symbol in Serbia: Essays in Political Anthropology* (London: Hurst, 2002), 13.

they were subject to 'genocide' in the region,[23] that women were frequently raped, and that the whole population felt intimidated by Kosovars. Popular fears were stirred up by the media, the church, and the Serbian Academy's memorandum of 1986, which addressed the 'tortured' question of Kosovo.[24] In this atmosphere of frenzy and a sharp rise in publically expressed nationalism across the country, an apparatchik Slobodan Milošević was able to manoeuvre and intimidate his way into power. He brought a new rhetoric to the masses by promising to defend the rights of Serbs everywhere and by surrounding himself with a retinue of Kosovo Serb *squadristi*. Serb nationalists simultaneously revived plans set out by the extremist Četnici,[25] who had murdered Bosnian Muslims and Kosovo Albanians during the 1940s.[26] At the same time, these nationalists accused the Croatians, led by dissident historian Franjo Tudjman, of being descended from the Ustaša, who had run a Nazi-puppet state from 1941 to 1945 and committed genocide against the Serbs.

Shortly after the outbreak of fighting in Bosnia, the British newspaper *The Daily Mirror* ran a headline that reverberated around the world: 'Belsen 92: The picture that shames the world'. The picture was of emaciated prisoners in an ad hoc detention centre that had been set up by the Serbs in their breakaway republic. At the time, comparisons between the terrible predicament of the Bosnian Muslims (and the Croatians in the previous year) and Third Reich victims seemed apt as propaganda, particularly as international intervention to stop the fighting during the first post-Communist Balkan crisis was deemed to be so ineffective. The Croatian sociologist Stjepan Meštrović insisted that the war in Croatia was 'genocide', as did his colleague Norman Cigar in relation to Bosnia.[27] In 2007, Serbia as a state was cleared of genocide at The Hague Tribunal (ICTY). The international court did rule, however, that the slaughter of an estimated 8,000 men and boys as 'combatants' at Srebrenica in July 1995 was genocide. In 1999, Milošević became the first serving head of state to be indicted for war crimes. Many regarded him as the primary instigator of the crisis because of the support he gave to Serb nationalists

[23] The use of the word genocide when referring to the declining position of Serbs in Kosovo was popularized by Dimitrije Bogdanović, *Knjiga o Kosovu* (Belgrade: SANU, 1985), 7.
[24] Bože Čović (ed.), *Izvori velikosrpske agresije* (Zagreb: August Cesarec and Skolska knjiga, 1991), 296–300.
[25] Safet Bandžović, 'Koncepcije Srpskog kulturnog kluba o preuređenju Jugoslavije 1937–1941', *Prilozi* 30 (2001), 163–93.
[26] On Bosnia see, Tomislav Dulić, *Utopias of Nation: Local Mass Killing in Bosnia and Herzegovina, 1941–42* (Uppsala: Acta Universitatis Upsaliensis, Studia Historica Upsaliensia, 2005); and Vladimir Dedijer, *Genocid nad muslimanima 1941–45, Zbornik documenta i svjedočenja* (Sarajevo: Svjetlost, 1990). On Kosovo, see Jozo Tomasevich, *War and Revolution in Yugoslavia: Occupation and Collaboration* (Stanford: Stanford University Press, 2001).
[27] Stjepan G. Meštrović, *Genocide after Emotion: The Post-Emotional Balkan War* (London: Routledge, 1996); Norman Cigar, *Genocide in Bosnia: The Policy of 'Ethnic Cleansing'* (College Station: Texas A&M University Press, 1995).

between 1987 and 1999. The judgement against him would have been an important landmark in legal history, but his death while on trial in 2006 prevented his case from being concluded.[28]

WAR IN CROATIA 1990–5

Milošević and his supporters precipitated the break-up of the League of Communists in January 1990. The Yugoslavian republics, now with increasing autonomy and acting like nations-states in waiting, moved towards free elections, choosing from a range of non-Communists, many of whom were nationalists. In Croatia, a government was formed by Tudjman, notorious for his 1990 revisions of the estimated numbers killed in fascist Croatia, especially the Jasenovac death camp.[29] His government made further provocative gestures towards the minority Serbs, banning Cyrillic road signs and rehabilitating Ustaša fascists such as Mile Budak.[30] In his role as a propagandist, Budak had revived the Habsburg anti-Serb 1914 slogan 'Srbe na vrbe' ('Hang Serbs on the willows'),[31] and the significance of the attempt to restore his reputation in 1990 was not lost on local Serbs. During the Second World War, the Ustaša government had perpetrated what Tomislav Dulić has called an 'attempted genocide', which led to the deaths of sixteen to seventeen per cent of the total Serb population.[32] The element of trauma amongst Serbs should not be underestimated. They had also suffered huge losses during the First World War due to aggressive military actions by the Habsburg Army and a terrible typhus epidemic.[33] With their fear of Islamic encroachment, which stemmed from the years of Ottoman oppression and the legacy of earlier genocides,[34] ordinary

[28] For a discussion of the trial see William A. Schabas, 'International Justice for International Crimes: An Idea whose Time Has Come', European Review 14 (2006), 421–39.

[29] Franjo Tudjman, Bespuća povijesne zbiljnosti: rasprava o povijesti i filozofiji zlosilja (Zagreb: Nakladni zavod Matice hrvatske), 1990.

[30] Dubravka Ugrešić, The Culture of Lies: Antipolitical Essays (University Park, PA: Penn State Press, 1998), 228.

[31] Milan Bašta, Rat je završen sedam dana kasnije (Belgrade: OOUR, 1986), 151.

[32] Tomislav Dulić, 'Mass Killing in the Independent State of Croatia, 1941–1945: A Case for Comparative Research', Journal of Genocide Research 8:3 (2006), 274.

[33] Mark Levene, Genocide in the Age of the Nation State, vol ii: The Rise of the West and the Coming of Genocide (London: I. B. Tauris, 2005), 323; Andrej Mitrović, Serbia's Great War 1914–1918 (London: Hurst, 2007).

[34] Cathie Carmichael, '"Neither Water, nor Wine, Neither Turks nor Slavs, But Odious Renegades": Anti-Islam and Ideologies of Ethnic Cleansing in the Balkans', in Steven Vardy and Hunt Tooley (eds), Ethnic Cleansing in Twentieth Century Europe (New York: Columbia University Press, 2003), 113–32.

Serbs were highly vulnerable to cynical nationalist politicians particularly in areas such as Krajina, where bodies had been hastily disposed of in the limestone ravines in the 1940s and were only then being uncovered and reburied.[35]

Croatian independence triggered a Serb reaction at a time when many across Yugoslavia had been radicalized by the Kosovo issue. By the time of full independence, Tudjman faced an open insurrection led by the Serbian Democratic Party (SDS), which attempted to form a breakaway 'autonomous region' within Croatia. Terrible fratricidal violence took place in the Krajina region, Slavonija, and the Adriatic hinterland in late 1991. 'Ethnic cleansing' (a term first introduced by the Serbs themselves to describe their putative fate in Kosovo) was widespread and horrific. The Danubian town of Vukovar was reduced to a pile of rubble by Serb paramilitaries backed by remnants of the Yugoslavian National Army (JNA), who were better armed and trained, although individual soldiers were often demoralized by the crimes they witnessed.[36] A paramilitary group led by Arkan (the gangster Željko Ražnatović) killed about 250 Croats in a nearby abattoir.[37] Landmines were planted in the Dinaric coastal region, accompanied by the gratuitous destruction of hotels, buildings, orchards, and farms to deter Croats from returning or to 'punish' them. At the same time, the Croatian government tolerated abuses towards Serbs remaining within their territory, most of whom left the capital, Zagreb, between 1991 and 1995.[38] More than 10,000 civilians were killed in Croatia and by 1995 as many as 300,000 people had been displaced. The United Nations moved in during January 1992 to supervise the borders between the autonomous regions and government-held territory, which restored a semblance of peace, but at the price of dividing and separating the two communities. In August 1995, after substantial US-backed rearmament the Croatian government took Krajina in 'Operation Storm' and most of the Serb population left, fearing for their safety. The Croatian Ambassador to France described the actions of the Serbs as 'auto-nettoyage ethnique' (self ethnic-cleansing),[39] but Gen. Ante Gotovina who led the campaign has been accused of crimes against humanity with respect to the remaining Serbs and is currently on trial in the Hague. As in Nagorno-Karabakh from whence most Azeris fled, Croatia effectively lost most of its historic Serb minority in 1995 and since then very few have returned with those remaining in ghettos. For a triumphant President Tudjman, the exodus was the solution to

---

[35] Bette Denich, 'Dismembering Yugoslavia: Nationalist Ideologies and the Symbolic Revival of Genocide', *American Ethnologist* 21:1 (May 1991), 367–90.

[36] *Vukovar. Poslednji Rez* (Belgrade: B92 2006), documentary written and produced by Janko Baljak and Drago Hedl.

[37] Marcus Tanner, *Croatia: A Nation Forged in War* (New Haven, CT: Yale University Press, 1997), 266–7.

[38] Brad K. Blitz, 'Refugee Returns, Civic Differentiation, and Minority Rights in Croatia 1991–2004', *Journal of Refugee Studies* 18:3 (2005), 362–86.

[39] Smiljan Simac, 'Croatie, Serbie: les fausses symétries', *Le Monde* (25 May 1999), 13–14.

Croatia's 'centuries-old problem'.[40] Denying any responsibility for the act, he stated: 'We didn't ask the Serbs to leave. And it's their problem if 90% of them packed their bags.'[41]

WAR AND GENOCIDE IN BOSNIA-HERCEGOVINA

In many respects, events in Bosnia resembled the deteriorating circumstances in Croatia in 1991. In parliament, the SDS led by Radovan Karadžić threatened the government of President Alija Izetbegović with 'hell' if Bosnia-Hercegovina left Yugoslavia.[42] Despite this threat, the government called a referendum on independence in April 1992, which was boycotted by almost one-third of the population of the republic, largely on the instruction of the SDS (much as the December 1991 referendum in Nagorno-Karabakh had been boycotted by the Azeri minority of more than twenty per cent of the population). Of those who did vote, over ninety-nine per cent opted for full independence from what remained of Yugoslavia. Karadžić argued that independence was illegal without the support of all three of the 'constituent' Bosnian nationalities and that they would be in the majority had they not been subjected to genocide in the past. The referendum revealed just how deep the chasm between those who wanted to leave Yugoslavia and those who wanted to be in a Serb-dominated state had become.

From this inauspicious foundation, the government declared independence and promptly faced widespread and highly organized Serb resistance. The armed Serbs rapidly took over the northern and eastern parts of the country. Just as Zagreb had remained with the government during the Croatian war, the capital, Sarajevo, remained a stronghold of the Bosnian government. Muslims fled into the towns such as Goražde, Srebrenica, and Žepa, which became virtual ghettos, often without transport links, medical supplies, or basic foodstuffs. In the first weeks Serb paramilitaries, effectively protected by the JNA, murdered civilians, especially the vulnerable elderly and left their mutilated bodies on display. The British journalist Michael Nicholson described their tactics as 'elitocide' when it became clear that the Serbs had also attacked Muslim and Croat political activists and prominent community leaders.[43] Paramilitaries also killed dozens of foreign

---

[40] James Gow, *Triumph of the Lack of Will: International Diplomacy and the Yugoslav War* (London: Hurst, 1997), 43.

[41] Florence Hartmann, *Milošević: La Diagonale du Fou* (Paris: Denoël, 1999), 244.

[42] Ibid. 247.

[43] David Rieff, *Slaughterhouse: Bosnia and the Failure of the West* (New York: Simon and Schuster, 1995), 113.

journalists that summer. Backed by an armed wing of the SDS, the Bosnian Serb Army (VRS) was quickly formed in 1992 and commanded by former Communist general Radko Mladić, making Bosnia a country under occupation. The Serb forces set up prison camps at Manjača, Prijedor, and Omarska, inviting 'weekend warriors' or war tourists to torture their former neighbours,[44] thus spreading guilt and complicity beyond the SDS, the VRS, and the ranks of paramilitaries. The alarming incidence of crimes against humanity led to the establishment of the International Criminal Tribunal for the former Yugoslavia (ICTY) to punish breaches of international law, which was convoked in The Hague in 1993 and has subsequently sentenced over 100 of those indicted.[45]

President Izetbegović, a Muslim dissident imprisoned for his views by the Communists, appealed to the International Community to help him defend the newly recognized state. During the early stages of the war, a UN embargo on importing armaments had crippled his government's ability to defend itself, as the remnants of JNA armaments were in the hands of the Serb rebels. International ineptitude made the fate of Bosnia worse, delaying government military successes.[46] Peace treaties such as the one set forward by Cyrus Vance and David Owen in 1993, which proposed dividing Bosnia into ethnic 'cantons', may have speeded up the ethnic cleansing of some regions to make Serb and Croat claims stronger. Emboldened by plans to divide the Bosnian state, Croat Defence Council paramilitaries (HVO) began targeting Bosnian Muslims in Hercegovina in 1993, particularly in the town of Ahmići, in which they killed over 100 civilians. International human rights lawyer Payam Akhavan arrived there soon afterwards, describing the 'all-embracing form of the destruction of this village and its inhabitants'.[47] The Croatian officer Tihomir Blaškić was deemed by the ICTY in 1997 to have had some 'command responsibility' for the massacre and has since served a nine-year sentence.

After UN Protection Force intervention in June 1992, the fighting stagnated somewhat, except for an ongoing siege of the capital, Sarajevo, designed to lower government morale, and the dramatic battle for the crucial city of Bihać, which would have linked Serb gains in Northern and Eastern Bosnia with Krajina. Many Bosnian Muslims were confined to so-called 'safe havens' in the Eastern towns supervised by the UN, but lacked supplies and were in effect trapped. Under the terms imposed by the UN they were also disarmed, which left them completely dependent on the international community for defence. By 1995, the Bosnian government had begun to reverse the military stagnation of the previous three

---

[44] One of the best accounts of Bosnian camp atrocities is Roy Gutman's, *A Witness to Genocide: The First Inside Account of the Horrors of Ethnic Cleansing in Bosnia* (Shaftesbury: Element, 1993).

[45] http://www.un.org/icty/

[46] There are several astute criticisms of international ineptitude, including Brendan Simms, *Unfinest Hour: How Britain Helped to Destroy Bosnia* (Harmondsworth: Penguin Press, 2001).

[47] http://www.un.org/icty/kupreskic/trialc2/judgement/kup-tj000114e-3.htm, accessed on 27 January 2008.

years. As the rebel Serbs were pushed out of Krajina by Croatian rearmament and military action and they had failed to take the UN 'safe haven' Bihać despite huge losses, their military tactics became more desperate and the VRS more demoralized.[48] Inadequate protection from Dutch UN troops in July 1995 led to the surrender of the 'safe haven' of Srebrenica to Mladić and the slaughter of almost the entire Muslim male population of about 8,000. Over 100,000 people including soldiers and civilians died as a result of the war, most either in the summer of 1992 by paramilitaries or during the sieges of Sarajevo and Bihać. By far the highest number of individuals killed were an estimated 65,000 Muslims, although 25,000 Serbs and 8,000 Croats also died. Bosnia's Muslims and Serbs were also heavily displaced and an estimated two million left either temporarily or to rebuild their lives elsewhere.

In late 1995, Bosnian politicians eventually signed the Dayton Peace Treaty, brokered primarily by the USA. The treaty created an odd administrative arrangement, with Serb-controlled territory ('Republika Srpska') to the east and the Bosnian Muslims and Croats in control of the south-west and capital. The treaty may have created the precondition for future separate states. It did allow for the return of some refugees; most towns have not recovered their previous status.[49] The communities remain effectively divided with the past being kept alive by successive administrations. Bomb craters in the capital have since been painted red and are known as 'Sarajevo roses'.[50] In 2005, a poster commemorating the tenth anniversary of the genocide at Srebrenica was defaced with 'it will happen again'.[51] Extremism remained in evidence in neighbouring republics. In the second round of the 2008 presidential elections in Serbia, the candidate Tomislav Nikolić for the Radical Party, heavily linked to the paramilitaries in the 1990s, won 47.97 per cent of the popular vote.

THE KOSOVO CRISIS

The issue of Kosovo, which remained untouched at Dayton, entered Serbian politics in the mid-1970s and has remained there ever since, fuelling a growth in

---

[48] Phillip Corwin, *Dubious Mandate: A Memoir of the UN in Bosnia, Summer 1995* (Durham, NC: Duke University Press, 1999), 202.

[49] Francine Friedman, *Bosnia and Herzegovina: A Polity on the Brink* (New York, Routledge, 2004), 80.

[50] Fran Markowitz, 'Census and Sensibilities in Sarajevo', *Comparative Studies in Society and History* 49:1 (2007), 49.

[51] Paul B. Miller, 'Contested Memories: The Bosnian Genocide in Serb and Muslim Minds', *Journal of Genocide Research* 8:3 (2006), 313.

extremist political groups, especially the Serbian Radical Party (SRS). The 1983 funeral of Aleksandar Ranković, former Minister of the Interior who had favoured Serb domination in the region, was an ominous sign of popular discontent as people lined the streets to pay their respects.[52] More than any other Communist politician, he had been associated with Belgrade centralization and therefore seen as a foil to Kardelj, architect of the loathed 1974 Constitution. The 1974 rights of Kosovo were effectively revoked by Milošević in 1989. Thereafter until 1999, the region was effectively run from Belgrade without significant cooperation with the vast majority of Kosovars, a situation as 'separate worlds'[53] or even 'Apartheid'.[54] Led by Gandhi-inspired Ibrahim Rugova, eighty per cent of the region's population voted for independence in 1992 by a margin of ninety-eight per cent. This vote, which had been boycotted by the region's Serbs, was also ignored internationally.

Rugova kept the door open to dialogue with Milošević, even during the NATO bombing of the Federal Republic of Yugoslavia (FRY) in 1999. While his strategy kept a semblance of peace, a whole generation of Kosovo's young people were deprived of any participation in the state. A large male diaspora working abroad from 1981 onwards contributed to the formation of a guerrilla Kosovo Liberation Army (KLA). Ironically its strategy of armed resistance had certain similarities with the uprising in the 'Serbian Autonomous Regions' (SARs) in 1990–2, but this time with the cautious support of the many UN countries, who saw the Serbs as the primary villains of the piece. The similarity may not be entirely coincidental. Kosovars had also been JNA conscripts, imbibing Tito's philosophy of preparedness for defence. The KLA, which also drew on local Kaçak bandit traditions in areas like Drenica,[55] deliberately provoked clashes with the Serb authorities and increasingly found support within their community. In 1998, one of their founders, Adem Jashari, and his entire family were killed by the police, a massacre that led to an international backlash. The Belgrade government received a number of ultimatums from an international community led by the NATO countries in Rambouillet in 1999, which were primarily designed to avoid another Bosnia.

Milošević found himself caught between internal nationalism and international disapproval at Rambouillet. Unable to abandon Kosovo and agree to the stipulated referendum due to the wrath of his own nationalists, and definitely unable to withstand NATO airpower in the long run, he allowed the Yugoslavian Army (VJ)

---

[52] Mitja Velikonja, *Religious Separation and Political Intolerance in Bosnia and Herzegovina* (College Station, Texas: Texas A&M Press, 2003), 223.

[53] Shkëlzen Maliqi, *Kosova: Separate Worlds: Reflections and Analyses 1989–1998* (Priština: Dukagjini, 1998).

[54] Sevdie Ahmeti, 'Forms of Apartheid in Kosovo', in Dušan Janjić and Shkëlzen Maliqi (eds), in *Conflict or Dialogue: Serbian-Albanian Relations and the Integration of the Balkans* (Subotica: Open University, 1994), 205–25.

[55] Michel Roux, *Les Albanais en Yougoslavie: Minorité nationale, territoire et développement* (Paris: Foundation de la maison des sciences de l'homme, 1992), 214–15.

to pursue a desperate policy of ethnic cleansing, possibly believing that terrible acts of violence would depopulate Kosovo as it had done in Bosnia and parts of Croatia, and refugees would have to remain in neighbouring Macedonia and Albania where they had fled. The VJ killed over 10,000 Kosovars during a campaign of air strikes upon Serbia and Montenegro in 1999 that did not see a single NATO fatality. Up to 500 non-Kosovar citizens of the FRY were also killed by NATO as it started to drop cluster bombs in an attempt to break morale, especially in some of the larger cities. Individuals associated with the opposition, such as the journalist Slavko Čuruvija, were assassinated and an atmosphere of panic and recrimination against the Milošević regime developed, which resulted in his dramatic downfall the following year. The Kosovars, emboldened by NATO support, returned to their shattered homes in the summer of 1999 after the surrender of the FRY. They then began a process of revenge against local Serbs and Roma (whom they felt had supported the regime) and as many as 700 were killed that year.

After the war, the region was administered by the UN. More Serbs left over the following years, leading to a further decline in their numbers. In 2005, the UN appointed a special envoy, Martti Ahtisaari, to negotiate a situation, which led to full independence for Kosovo in 2008. The declaration precipitated a Serb backlash in areas in the north of the country, particularly in the town of Mitrovica, which has effectively resisted the authority of the new state just as the Serbs had done in Krajina from 1990 to 1995.

VIOLENCE, CYNICISM, AND POST-COMMUNIST IDENTITIES

The break up of Yugoslavia cost well over 120,000 lives and led to the displacement of millions. The root cause of violence was Serb discontent with the borders of the successor states, which they rejected in order to establish their own quasi-states before the new administrations had a chance to oppress them as a minority. Extreme elements revived fascist plans for ethnic cleansing from the Second World War, during which time Kosovars and Bosnian Muslims had been attacked by Serb nationalists and Serbs by the Croatian Ustaša and Kosovars. Serb extremists aroused international opposition primarily because they took up violence *as their first resort*. Undoubtedly distrust of Muslim Kosovars and Bosnians as well as a hatred of Croatian nationalism existed at the level of Serb popular culture, but these emotions were not the primary cause of the fighting. The war was one of intricate strategy to gain as much territory and people for any future Serbian state(s) as possible and frequently coordinated by nationalists from within Serbia itself (or 'joint criminal enterprise' around Milošević as it was called at The Hague). This strategy failed in Kosovo, Krajina, and Croatia but worked in Bosnia, where violence was 'rewarded' by the Dayton Treaty. But this was a pyrrhic victory indeed, as in 2006 Serbia lost its long-term ally Montenegro when the latter voted for complete independence, severing it from the Adriatic coast. A considerable number of Montenegrins who voted for independence were displaced Albanians and Bosnians who had taken up residence there.

There was very little evidence of interethnic 'hatred', although the international media frequently discussed 'violent' Balkan mentalities. Stjepan Meštrović and his colleagues, for instance, stated that 'the Yugoslav civil war exhibited barbaric acts of cruelty, massacres and the mutilation of the living as well as corpses that they beg for an explanation. Our explanation is that when one examines the history of the Balkans, such savagery appears to be fairly typical.'[56] This view was common and pronouncements by academics appear to have encouraged policy makers. Speaking in February 1993, primarily to prevent the implementation of the UN Genocide Convention, US Secretary of State Warren Christopher thought that 'the end of communist domination of the former Yugoslavia raised the lid on the cauldron of ancient ethnic hatreds . . . It has long been the cradle of European conflict and remains so today.'[57] But there were certainly more plausible and less essentialist explanations. For the sociologist Bojan Baskar the 'cynical' nature of post-Communist politicians and their readiness to use liminal elements within society such as convicted prisoners, hooligans, and gangsters to break the Hague Conventions is a more plausible explanation for violence, which was hardly universal through the former Yugoslavia.[58] Muslims living in Serbia were generally left alone during the entire Bosnian war, as were over 100,000 Kosovars living in Belgrade in 1999. Those atrocities that did take place were carried out to remove populations from land during a period of the breakdown of authority, not primarily because of 'ancient hatreds'.

To what extent can it be stated that the wars in Yugoslavia in the 1990s constitute a clear case of genocide? The nationalist Serbs wanted to remove non-Serbs from regions that they claimed and they were prepared to kill them en masse in the process, a strategy revealed most starkly in Eastern Bosnia in the summer of 1995 and Kosovo in 1999. Ethnic cleansing 'bled', as Norman Naimark suggested, into genocide.[59] Unlike the apocalyptic Nazis, they did not consider it their 'fundamental

---

[56] Stjepan Meštrović, Slaven Letica, and Miroslav Goreta, *Habits of the Balkan Heart: Social Character and the Fall of Communism* (College Station: Texas A&M University Press, 1993), 61.

[57] Tim Allen and Jean Seaton, *The Media of Conflict: War Reporting and Representations of Ethnic Violence* (London: Zed Books, 1999), 1.

[58] Bojan Baskar, *Dvoumni Mediteran. Študije o regionalnem prekrivanju na vzhodnojadranskem območju* (Koper, Knjižnica Annales, 2000), 156.

[59] Norman M. Naimark, *Fires of Hatred: Ethnic Cleansing in Twentieth Century Europe* (Cambridge, MA: Harvard University Press, 2001), 3.

duty' to kill all of their perceived enemies, but as many as necessary to gain what they wanted.[60] In doing so they destroyed ancient populations and civilizations as well as much of their material culture. In their attempts to control regions they claimed, armed Serb extremists committed acts designed not only to kill individuals, but also to destroy morale and break community cohesion such as gang rape and torture.[61] In 1993, the European Commission estimated conservatively that 20,000 Bosnian women had been raped, which was 'among the largest documented cases of this kind in recent history'.[62]

One of the major problems that these wars raised was the integrity of state borders, the autonomy of individual states, and consistency of political principles. The international community chose to recognize the Izetbegović government despite the fact that a third of the citizens of Bosnia did not. It chose to recognize Tudjman even with open rebellion in Krajina. By ignoring Kosovo for years, regardless of the wish of eighty per cent of its population for independence as reflected in the 1992 referendum, Serb nationalists received a clear message that the international community did not care what happened within the borders of the FRY so long as they did not have to deal with it. This pattern appears to have continued in international relations. In 2007, US Secretary of State Condoleeza Rice declared that South Ossetia was 'part of Georgia . . . we believe in Georgia's territorial integrity,' thus ignoring the referendum of the previous year in which ninety-nine per cent of those who took part opted for full independence.[63] Only after direct Russian military intervention did her government recognize the need for 'discussions' on the region's status.

The conflicts in the Caucasus and Balkans were primarily caused by the collapse of Communist authority, unresolved border questions in contested areas often with large minorities, and the frequent willingness of post-Communist leaders to break international laws with respect to the treatment of both captured soldiers and non-combatants. With the exception of Croatia, the majority of violence in this period was concentrated in regions that lay on the border between Islamic and non-Islamic cultures. The Serb insurrection in Croatia created a violence exemplar that ricocheted across the Balkans. The collapse of Soviet power coincided with or even triggered a rise in Islamic militancy in the Caucasus and Middle East and inspired guerrilla groups to form. When the Afghan Taliban entered the capital, Kabul, in 1996, they mutilated the body of the former president Mohammad Najibullah, whose government had previously committed atrocities against them,

---

[60] Aleksa Djilas, *The Contested Country: Yugoslav Unity and Communist Revolution 1919–1953* (Cambridge, MA: Harvard University Press, 1991), 123.

[61] Caroline Kennedy-Pipe and Penny Stanley, 'Rape in War: Lessons of the Balkan Conflicts in the 1990s', in Ken Booth (ed), *The Kosovo Tragedy: The Human Rights Dimension* (London: Frank Cass, 2001), 67–84.

[62] Stefan Wolff, *Ethnic Conflict: A Global Perspective* (Oxford: Oxford University Press, 2007), 103.

[63] Fawn, 'The Kosovo—and Montenegro—Effect', 285.

and hanged him from a traffic light to symbolize the complete defeat of pro-Soviet civilization. Chechen and Azeri militants have often viewed their fighting in terms of restoring an Islamic moral order.[64] In the former Yugoslavia, Serb nationalists claimed that they were fighting against Islamic encroachment, which became effectively a self-fulfilling prophecy after 11 September 2001. Although a rise in religious consciousness may not wholly explain the occurrence of violence in these regions, successionists and politicians eager to redraw boundaries cynically exploited the idea of an ideological purpose and traditional identities under threat to motivate and legitimize armed resistance.

FURTHER READING

Bracewell, Wendy, 'Rape in Kosovo: Masculinity and Serbian Nationalism', *Nations and Nationalism* 6:4 (2000), 563–90.

Broz, Svetlana, and Laurie Kain Hart (eds), *Good People in an Evil Time: Portraits of Complicity and Resistance in the Bosnian War* (New York: Other Press, 2004).

Chufrin, Gennadi, *The Security of the Caspian Sea Region* (Oxford: Oxford University Press, 2001).

Greene, Thomas, 'Internal Displacement in the North Caucasus, Azerbaijan, Armenia and Georgia', in Roberta Cohen and Francis Mading Deng (eds), *The Forsaken People: Case Studies of the Internally Displaced* (Washington DC: Brookings Institution, 1998), 233–312.

Gow, James, *The Serbian Project and its Adversaries: A Strategy of War Crimes* (London: Hurst, 2003).

Hoare, Marko Attila, *How Bosnia Armed: The Birth and Rise of the Bosnian Army* (London: Saqi Books, 2004).

Mertus, Julie, *Kosovo: How Myths and Truths Started a War* (Berkeley: University of California Press, 1999).

Politkovskaya, Anna, *A Small Corner of Hell: Dispatches from Chechnya* (Chicago: University of Chicago Press, 2003).

Ramet, Sabrina P., *Nationalism and Federalism in Yugoslavia 1962–1991*, 2nd edn (Bloomington: Indiana University Press, 1994).

Sells, Michael, *The Bridge Betrayed: Religion and Genocide in Bosnia*, 2nd edn (Berkeley: University of California Press, 1998).

Thompson, Mark, *Forging War: The Media in Serbia, Croatia, Bosnia and Hercegovina* (Luton: University of Luton Press/Article 19, International Centre against Censorship, 1999).

Williams, Brian Glyn, 'Caucasus Belli: New Perspectives on Russia's Quagmire', *Russian Review* 4:4 (2005), 680–8.

[64] Brian Glyn Williams, 'The Russo-Chechen War: A Threat to Stability in the Middle East and Eurasia?', *Middle East Policy* 8, no. 1 (March 2001), 128–48.

CHAPTER 26

....

GENOCIDAL WARFARE IN NORTH-EAST AFRICA

....

ALEX DE WAAL

INTRODUCTION

....

THE modern history of the Horn of Africa is marked by protracted violence. The two powerful states of the region, Ethiopia and Sudan, are hybrid imperial creations, each one an amalgam of African and European colonialisms. For centuries, the dominant states of the Ethiopian highlands and the Nile Valley have been predators on the peoples of their peripheries, inflicting slavery, subjugation, and massacre upon them. The other states of the Horn, Eritrea and Somalia (and the entities that replaced the latter), were forged out of resistance to the two dominant centres of state power, and each exists insofar as it can dispense violence.[1] Revolutionary elites in both Ethiopia and Sudan have sought radical transformation of their states, but ended up replicating and intensifying the patterns of violence they inherited.

---

[1] Djibouti, as a quasi-imperial military-commercial outpost, will not be discussed in this chapter.

The categories 'war' and 'genocide' do not adequately describe the nature of violence in the Horn. Mass killing in the region has not been dealt with adequately by genocide scholars and has yet to develop its own comparative and analytical literature. Armed conflict is so protracted that peace is the exception. Normal is a low level of conflict and insecurity, most of it perpetrated by states and state-associated elites, but also involving armed formations contending for state power, resisting state power, or pursuing other agendas. These persistent conflicts intermittently erupt into episodes of extreme brutality in which thousands or tens of thousands of non-combatants are killed. Massacres, subjugation of identity, forced removals, and violent destruction of autonomous governance have all occurred. The term 'genocide' has been indiscriminately used by local dissidents and foreign critics to the extent that its political currency has been devalued. The US government designated the events in Darfur, Sudan, during 2003–4 as genocide. Sadly, the scale and nature of the killing, displacement, and famine in Darfur during that period was not exceptional in the modern history of the Horn of Africa. In contrast, good arguments could be made that half a dozen or so other episodes in the previous fifteen years have as strong a claim to that label. The central argument advanced in this chapter is that isolating individual episodes of killing and displacement and labelling them as genocide is not a useful exercise. The tasks before us are to explain the ubiquity of violence and the recurrence of massacre and displacement of genocidal dimensions.

This chapter consists of four substantive sections. The first outlines the key themes. A second part briefly surveys the position of the Horn of Africa within scholarly and legal approaches to genocide. The major part outlines twenty-two episodes of extreme violence, including mass killing and group-targeted repression, over the past half century. The final section extracts some key themes and draws some general conclusions.

VIOLENCE, IDENTITY, AND STATEHOOD

Violence is inscribed in the political formations of the Horn. Ethiopia and Sudan are both conquest states, their modern boundaries carved out of myriad pre-existing socio-political formations almost always through military suppression, commonly followed by the imposition of garrison settlements or mercenary-commercial entrepôts. They have common features and important differences. Independent African states in the Ethiopian highlands, the Nile Valley, and the Sudanic belt all consisted of an agrarian core that was settled and taxed and a periphery from which tribute, slaves, and other resources were extracted.

Ethiopia was the classic African empire, ruled by a sovereign claiming descent from the biblical King Solomon. Observers described the king as a despot whose writ scarcely extended beyond the gates of his capital city[2]—a nice encapsulation of the paradox of absolute rulers commanding weak structures of governance. Ethiopia retained its independence during the 'scramble for Africa' from the 1880s, its Emperor Menelik II finding it possible to participate as a (junior) partner in that imperial carve-up, extending his frontiers into areas where his predecessors had only sent their most audacious raiding parties. By such means, the subjugation of the Oromo and other peoples of the empire was accomplished.[3] In the newly conquered territories of the empire, the characteristic face of government was the military governor and the armed settler, the latter known as *neftegna*, 'rifleman'. A racial-religious hierarchy existed among the Emperor's subjects. A small minority ruled. The aristocracy, clergy, and settlers applied the pejorative 'Galla' to the Oromo serfs and the even more derogatory 'Shankila' to the enslaveable peoples of the southern and western marchlands. Territorial conquest, the reduction of subjugated peoples to commodities, and the infliction of legitimized violence without recourse by the rulers characterized this imperial system.

Sudan was a variant. The states of the eighteenth- and nineteenth-century Nile Valley and eastern Sahel, including the Funj Kingdom and the Fur Sultanate, differed only in degree. They were smaller in scale and their rulers sought legitimacy through Islam. In the nineteenth century they were overthrown by the ambitious rulers of Ottoman Egypt and replaced by a hybrid empire on the Nile. Rather than the government having its own military servants and financial structures, the state was itself a tool of merchants and mercenaries. Outside the 'metropolitan provinces' along the river itself north of Khartoum, the characteristic face of governance was the raiding party—the *ghazwa* or state-licensed freebooting expedition to acquire ivory and slaves. The combination of Islam and colour differences created a deep imprint of racism.[4] Sudanese resistance to the conquest took the form of millenarian Mahdism, a revolution that expelled the Egyptians and their European mercenary generals and ushered in a messianic and also profoundly violent state that lasted until its warriors were machine-gunned by the British army in 1898.

Colonial invasion was extremely violent in all parts of the Horn of Africa. The British march up the Nile Valley from 1896 to the 1920s was marked by blood; the Italian occupation of Eritrea and Somalia in the 1880s and finally Ethiopia itself in 1935 was accompanied by massacre, chemical weapons, and the murder of much of

---

[2] Dame Margery Perham, *The Government of Ethiopia* (London: Faber and Faber, 1969).

[3] Mohamed Hassan, *The Oromo of Ethiopia: A History 1570–1860* (Cambridge: Cambridge University Press, 1860); Bonnie K. Holcombe and Sisai Ibssa, *The Invention of Ethiopia: The Making of a Dependent Colonial State in Northeast Africa* (Trenton, NJ: Red Sea Press, 1990).

[4] Stephanie Beswick, *Sudan's Blood Memory: The Legacy of War, Ethnicity and Slavery in South Sudan* (Rochester, NY: University of Rochester Press, 2006).

Ethiopia's educated class in a prison that gained the name 'Alem Bekagn', 'farewell to the world'.

Decolonization in the 1950s and 1960s was marked by more violence and the beginnings of a series of insurrections that have continued, in one form or another, for half a century. The creation and sustaining of the post-colonial entities of Eritrea and Somalia involved both protracted violence against Ethiopia and internal violence. The intermittent emergence of South Sudan as an autonomous entity, in opposition to Khartoum, displays similar patterns.

Minority groups—Ethiopia's Amhara aristocracy and Sudan's riverain Arabized elite—kept power in both states through control of administration, commerce, and the military. They co-opted and repressed provincial elites. A succession of revolutionary counter-elites in Ethiopia and Sudan—mostly from the same social strata as those they overthrew—sought to transform their states under slogans of socialism, nationalism, and Islamism, but usually succeeded only in adding new layers of violence to those that already existed. With its long tradition of statecraft, Ethiopia has been better able to mobilize big armies and maintain effective administrative structures. But at moments of crisis, peasant revolts spring up across the country and the fundamental weakness of the state is revealed.[5] The Sudanese state has been chronically weak and unstable, reproducing the historic pattern whereby it was a tool in the hands of mercantile–military partnerships.[6] The result has been long-term reliance on purchasing loyalty from provincial elites who command militia, creating cycles of peripheral violence that both generate endless war and prevent insurgents from coalescing into forces that can overrun the centre. These long-running conflicts and struggles for state power form the backdrop to the intermittent but predictable instances of mass killing and displacement that constitute the third section of this chapter. The ruling groups sustain themselves despite disorder on their peripheries. Despite generating instability, these states persist. The secondary states of the Horn— Eritrea, Somalia and its successors, and the putative South Sudan—reproduce the same violent political pathologies, but without the remarkable ability of those deeper rooted states to bounce back from the brink of autodestruction.

There are three main types of peaks of violence that recur within this political matrix. The first and commonest is *ethnically targeted rural massacre*. This typically occurs within counter-insurgency or frontier policing operations. Noting that the region is characterized by ethnic mobilization for civil politics, armed conflict, or peripheral control, it is unsurprising that insurgents, counter-insurgents, and frontier warlords alike tend to target ethnic groups. Given the toolkit for low-cost

---

[5] Gebru Tareke, *Ethiopia: Power and Protest: Peasant Revolts in the Twentieth Century* (Cambridge: Cambridge University Press, 1991).

[6] Peter Woodward, *Sudan 1989–1989: The Unstable State* (London: Croom Helm, 1990); Abdullahi Gallab, *The First Islamic Republic: Development and Disintegration of Islamism in the Sudan* (London: Ashgate, 2008).

counter-insurgency that involves intimidating a civilian population, forcible relocation, control of food and livelihoods, and using local proxies which are paid in loot, it is unsurprising that most casualties in these operations are civilian. Nor is it surprising that famine is a typical outcome that causes more deaths than violence itself.

The second is the *repression of political opposition* through mass detention, torture, and execution in the urban centre of state power. Ethiopia's Red Terror is the supreme exemplar of this though there are smaller scale instances in every state in the region.

The third paradigm of extreme violence we may call *the 'blow-around' of violent conflict*. This occurs when the perpetrator of violence is not acting at the direct behest of a state, though the group may initially have been armed or even created by a state. The massacres in Somalia after the collapse of the Siad Barre government are examples of this. One may fairly point the finger of blame at Siad Barre for having deliberately fostered militarized tribalism as a stratagem for either remaining in power or creating mayhem should he be removed. Much of the violence in Darfur since the 1980s is similarly attributable to the high price of loyalty extracted from patrons in Khartoum, Libya, and Chad by military-tribal entrepreneurs on the frontier, who then pursue their local ambitions through violence.

THE HORN OF AFRICA AND THE STUDY OF GENOCIDE

Before 2004, an essay on genocide in the Horn of Africa would have been, by definition, an exercise in contentious labelling. Despite the numerous cases of mass killing in the Horn over the past two centuries, unabated in recent decades, most scholars of genocide dealt with the region in passing or not at all. Cases of cursory treatment include Totten,[7] Harff and Gurr,[8] Fein,[9] Kiernan,[10] and Jones.[11]

---

[7] Samuel Totten, *Teaching about Genocide: Issues, Approaches and Resources* (Greenwich CT: Information Age, 2004).

[8] Barbara Harff and Ted Robert Gurr, 'Towards Empirical Theory of Genocides and Politicides: Identification and Measurement of Cases since 1945', *International Studies Quarterly* 32:3, 1988, 359–71, at 364–5; Barbara Harff, 'No Lessons Learned from the Holocaust? Assessing Risks of Genocide and Political Mass Murder since 1955', *American Political Science Review* 97:1 (2003), 57–73, at 60.

[9] Helen Fein, 'Accounting for Genocide after 1945: Theories and Some Findings', *International Journal on Group Rights* 1 (1993), 79–106, at 87.

[10] Ben Kiernan, *Blood and Soil: A World History of Genocide and Extermination from Sparta to Darfur* (New Haven, CT: Yale University Press, 2007), 594–7.

[11] Adam Jones, *Genocide: A Comprehensive Introduction* (London: Routledge, 2006).

However, the Horn of Africa is also the locus of two important innovations in the use of the label genocide to apply to instances of mass killing. One case is the Ethiopian designation of the 1977–8 Red Terror as genocide, in conformity with the country's penal code.[12] In this case, the guerrilla movement that took power in 1991 prosecuted officials of its predecessor, including the former head of state, Mengistu Haile Mariam, who was convicted of genocide in absentia on 13 December 2006.

The second case in which the label genocide has been used by a state with the power to act on its words was on 9 September 2004 when the US Secretary of State determined that the conflict in Darfur, Sudan, constituted genocide. Following an investigation sponsored by the State Department and carried out by the Coalition for International Justice,[13] Colin Powell told the US Senate Committee on Foreign Relations that 'genocide has been committed in Darfur and that the government of Sudan and the Jingaweit[sic] bear responsibility—and genocide may still be occurring.'[14] In his next sentence, he said that no change in policy followed from this determination. If we were to apply Powell's criteria more widely, then we would identify genocides very widely in the region. Equally, we could attempt to apply more restrictive definitions and find no cases at all.

Comparable though less remarked difficulties arise with identifying wars. The beginnings and ends of wars are typically defined by the belligerents to suit their own political purposes. Insurgents create heroic myths of origin around their first military actions, not mentioning their rivals who may have started fighting earlier, or glossing over the fact that their first actions were criminal raids. The parties to a peace treaty—both belligerents and mediators—concur that the signing of an agreement marks the end of a war, even though the immediate post-war period may actually be just as violent, as 'other armed groups' (to use recent Sudanese terminology) are removed from the scene. Thus, Sudan's first civil war is commonly dated 1955–72—from the Torit Mutiny to the Addis Ababa Agreement—though in fact there was little organized violence during 1957–60. About 1,000 people were violently killed in Darfur in the year after January 2005 (when major hostilities ended), while larger numbers died in 'peaceful' South Sudan over the same period, many of them in disarmament exercises. Most wars are defined by an act of political collusion between the adversaries. An interesting exception is the thirty-year 'shifta war' in the Somali regions of Kenya—shifta means 'bandit' and it suited both colonial and post-colonial authorities to dismiss the Somali insurgents as

[12] In an important anomaly, Ethiopian law (Penal Code of the Empire of Ethiopia of 1957, Proclamation 158 of 1967, Articles 281–6) contains a definition of genocide that includes 'political groups' as a category, in line with Lemkin's earlier formulation, allowing for charges of genocide to be brought against those who ordered mass killings of political opponents.

[13] Samuel Totten and Eric Markusen, *Genocide in Darfur: Investigating the Atrocities in the Sudan* (New York: Routledge, 2006).

[14] Colin L. Powell, 'The Crisis in Darfur', written remarks before the Senate Foreign Relations Committee, Washington DC, 9 September 2004.

bandits while also maintaining military rule in the district. This exception illustrates how coercive rule in frontier regions can be as violent in 'peacetime' as in 'war'—the distinction may have little relevance to the experience of life and death of the local inhabitants.

What drives the recurrent massacres and forced removals in the Horn is the attempt of state leaders to sustain their dominance in a turbulent system. How does a centre of state power with limited legitimacy and severe resource constraints control its far-flung peripheries? And how does a minority elite sustain itself in power in the metropolis? It is by exemplary violence and by purchasing the loyalty of local leaders with supplies of guns and a licence to pillage their neighbours.

EPISODES OF MASSACRE AND FORCED REMOVAL IN THE HORN

As the discussion above will have indicated, studying lethal violence against civilians in the Horn of Africa can present major problems of definition. One concept that does travel well is 'massacre', as utilized by Semelin: 'a generally collective form of action, involving the destruction of non-combatants.'[15] This section provides twenty-two illustrative cases of either individual or recurrent massacre and forced removal, which form the sharp peaks of violence and violation amid a broken landscape of conflict, frontier governance, and struggles for power.

Ethiopia and Eritrea

Seven episodes of mass killing and one of mass expulsion demand consideration in Ethiopia and Eritrea.

Massacres in Eritrea and the Ogaden, 1960s

The extension of imperial rule into the newly acquired territories of Eritrea and the Ogaden (the latter inhabited by ethnic Somalis) was marked by military campaigns that involved the widespread burning of villages and killing of civilians. These were akin to colonial pacification campaigns, intended to demonstrate the power of the

---

[15] Jacques Semelin, *Purify and Destroy: The Political Uses of Massacre and Genocide* (London: Hurst, 2007), 323.

state and to punish those who dared resist. The biggest of these campaigns was mounted in lowland Eritrea in 1966–7.[16]

The Red Terror, Addis Ababa, 1977–8

The Ethiopian revolution was a bloody affair almost from the outset. While the deposition of Emperor Haile Selassie in September 1974 was bloodless—the army controlled the city with just half a dozen tanks and the ageing monarch offered no resistance when he was taken away into detention and ultimately to his death—it was rapidly followed by a peasant jacquerie against aristocrats and landlords, the summary execution of sixty ministers from the previous government, a crackdown in the Eritrea city of Asmara, and shootouts among the revolutionaries themselves.[17]

Beginning in February 1977, the military junta that had taken power repressed an urban insurrection with exceptional brutality. The challenge was mounted by the Ethiopian People's Revolutionary Party (EPRP), a leftist militant group with a strong following among students, that had helped initiate the revolution but felt that it had been hijacked by the soldiers. The EPRP began a campaign of assassinating government officials. At the same moment, an internal power struggle within the ruling Provisional Military Administrative Committee (known as the Dergue) was resolved in favour of Col. Mengistu Haile Mariam. Mengistu set about the systematic destruction of the urban opposition, which entailed giving power and impunity to neighbourhood leaders to arrest and execute individuals on the merest suspicion of opposition sympathies. Estimates of the number killed in Addis Ababa alone are in excess of 10,000,[18] plus many others elsewhere in the country. An entire generation of educated Ethiopians was either killed or driven from the country. In a second wave of killing, the Dergue turned on its own civilian supporters, eradicating the All-Ethiopia Socialist Movement (known by its Amhara acronym, MEISON).

The two rival leftist parties, EPRP and MEISON, had developed ethnic profiles during the early 1970s. The EPRP was identified as mostly Amhara and Tigrayan while MEISON was chiefly Oromo. However, ethnicity was not the dominant characteristic of either party and neither was it the reason for the repression. The struggle was political and military. The aim was to cow the opposition into complete acquiescence. The Dergue called its campaign the 'Red Terror', consciously evoking precedents in Revolutionary France and Bolshevik Russia. The term 'genocide' only became current later, especially after 1991 when the incoming government set up the Special Prosecutor's Office to bring charges against the individuals responsible for many instances of killing and torture.

---

[16] Africa Watch, *Evil Days: Thirty Years of War and Famine in Ethiopia* (London: Africa Watch, 1991), ch. 2.

[17] Rene LeFort, *Ethiopia: An Heretical Revolution?* (London: Zed Books, 1983).

[18] Babile Tola, *To Kill a Generation: The Red Terror in Ethiopia* (Free Ethiopia Press, 1989).

War in the North, 1977–91

The Emperor Haile Selassie's failure to resolve peacefully Eritreans' grievances about the loss of their status as partners in a federation was a major reason for his downfall in 1974. His army's military campaigns in rural Eritrea involved burning villages, confiscating livestock, and killing civilians. His successors did no better and by 1977 were resolved on a military solution to the Eritrean nationalist rebellion. Over the subsequent fourteen years, a succession of immense offensives were mounted against the positions of the Eritrean People's Liberation Front (EPLF), which quickly developed from a classic guerrilla movement into a conventional army with mechanized brigades, lacking only an air force. Meanwhile, insurrection also erupted immediately to the south in Tigray, where the Tigray People's Liberation Front (TPLF) mounted a mobile guerrilla war. Most of the time the EPLF and TPLF were in alliance and their combined forces ultimately defeated the Mengistu government in 1991.

During the 1980s, Ethiopia fielded the largest conventional army in sub-Saharan Africa, with more than 300,000 regular soldiers in addition to militia. It was a mechanized force equipped by the Soviet Union, with thousands of tanks and scores of aircraft. By the final campaign, the EPLF and TPLF (the latter now the leading member of the Ethiopian People's Revolutionary Democratic Front) each fielded armies of more than 80,000. Estimates of battlefield fatalities ran into hundreds of thousands for the course of the war.

The Ethiopian government counter-insurgency sought to destroy the social and economic base of the rebels. The aim was not extermination but victory and control, but the partial destruction or removal of ethnic groups was employed as an instrument in pursuit of those goals. Killing of civilians was routine during military operations and patrols and at checkpoints. The air force was used against civilian targets. In the worst single incident, an estimated 1,800 market-goers were killed during a day's aerial bombardment in Hausien in Tigray on 22 June 1988.[19] Hausien was not a military target but the government was trying to destroy the morale and economic base of the insurrection. The counter-insurgency also created famine, partly deliberately and partly as the inevitable outcome of a military strategy that included offensives aimed at the agriculturally productive areas of northern Ethiopia and Eritrea, restrictions on trade and movement in government-controlled areas, bombing of markets in rebel-controlled areas, and efforts to stop relief aid going to rebel areas while assistance in government areas was used to further military aims, including feeding militia (reserves and auxiliaries to the army).[20] A final element in the counter-insurgency was forcible relocation of

[19] Africa Watch, *Evil Days: Thirty Years of War and Famine in Ethiopia* (London, 1991), 258–64.
[20] Alex de Waal, *Famine Crimes: Politics and the Disaster Relief Industry in Africa* (London: James Currey, 1997), ch. 6.

populations, targeting especially those thought to be sympathetic to the rebellions, to southern Ethiopia.[21]

The Ethiopian government of the time was a Marxist-Leninist military dictatorship imposed upon a centuries-old tradition of statehood.[22] The army and state institutions, rather than local proxies, were the main instrument of violence.

War in the South, 1977–84

The conduct of the war in Eritrea and Tigray was foreshadowed by the Ethiopian government's counter-insurgency in the south, targeting Somalis and Oromos. This overlapped with the war to expel the invading Somali army in 1977–8. This war was almost entirely unreported.[23] Among the methods used were coordinated ground and air offensives against rebel strongholds, scorched earth operations through areas in which civilians were supporting the rebels, closing of markets and withholding of relief, forced relocation to planned villages ('villagization'), and (towards the end of the period) the resettlement of people from the north in areas that remained rebellious. Journalists estimated 25,000 civilian fatalities in 1978–9 alone.[24] A smaller rebellion in the adjoining district of Sidamo in 1981 saw some of the largest single massacres, possibly because the area is thickly populated and it is difficult for people to flee. For example, more than 1,000 were reported killed when the air force used a fuel-air explosion in the valley of Gata Warrancha in March that year.

The Lower Omo Valley

By the late 1980s, the south-western corner of Ethiopia, bordering Kenya and Sudan, had become a lawless and militarized area beyond the control of the three governments and indeed rebel forces too. This area has a history as a violent frontier plundered by states and freebooters.[25] Local cattle herders' social structures also came to function as military formations, both as resisters and as collaborators in this depredation, and also for local raiding. Emblematic of violent transformation is the fact that one group in the far south of Ethiopia, the Nyam-Atom tribe (whose name means 'Elephant Eaters') renamed themselves Nyang-Atom ('Carriers of New Guns').[26] Warfare in this remote region became far more deadly when automatic

---

[21] Jason Clay, Sandra Steingraber, and Peter Niggli, *The Spoils of Famine: Ethiopian Famine Policy and Peasant Agriculture* (Cambridge, MA: Survival International, 1985).

[22] Christopher Clapham, *Continuity and Change in Revolutionary Ethiopia* (Cambridge: Cambridge University Press, 1988).

[23] Africa Watch, *Evil Days*, ch. 5.

[24] Ibid. 86.

[25] Donald Donham and Wendy James, *The Southern Marches of Imperial Ethiopia: Essays in History and Social Anthropology* (Athens: Ohio University Press, 2002).

[26] Jan-Åke Alversson, *Starvation and Peace or Food and War: Aspects of Armed Conflict in the Lower Omo Valley, Ethiopia* (Uppsala: Scandinavian Institute for African Studies, 1989), 87 (quoting Serge Tornay).

weapons became readily available.[27] Feuding and raiding, including reciprocal cases of homicide, were common between a host of groups, among them the Nyangatom and their smaller and less well-armed neighbours, the Mursi.[28] One cycle of killing occurred in 1987, culminating in the slaughter of 600–800 Mursi—over ten per cent of the entire Mursi population. The next year, in reprisal for the killing of 15 policemen, Kenyan forces killed 200 Nyangatom raiders and 500 civilians and burned five villages inside Ethiopia as well as others in Kenya. Similar reprisals against the Toposa, who live inside Sudan, were reported.

The Expulsions of 1998

In 1991, the EPLF-PRDF overthrew the Mengistu government. A new government was formed in Ethiopia and a new independent state in Eritrea. Rarely had partition gone so smoothly. It did not last. In 1998, a border incident in an otherwise insignificant village called Badme quickly escalated into a two-year conventional war. This was fought by well-disciplined regular armies along a well-defined frontline. There were an estimated 70,000 fatalities among the troops on both sides. Civilian casualties were few. The principal exception to civilian immunity was the expulsion of 75,000 Ethiopians of Eritrean origin beginning a month after the war began. There was a smaller reciprocal expulsion of Ethiopians from Eritrea. Many of those initially arrested were members of Eritrea's ruling party, former Eritrean soldiers, or prominent in Eritrean organizations in Ethiopia (all of them entirely legal at the time). Round-ups and expulsions continued for well over a year, broadening to include anyone of Eritrean origin.

Gambella 2003–4

In December 2003, an estimated 400 civilians belonging to the Anuak ethnic group were killed by mobs that included soldiers in the town of Gambella, state capital of the western Ethiopian region of the same name.[29] Further reports of killings and the destruction of villages continued. The violence was rooted in political tensions consequent on political decentralization, in which different ethnic groups, which took on political personalities during the resistance to Mengistu and the subsequent ethnic federalism of the EPRDF, contested for control of regions. In Gambella, tensions over voting and land rights among the indigenous Anuak and Nuer and highland settlers led to violence. The central government was at first reluctant to intervene and failed to contain the crisis, and then after the 2003 massacre sealed off the area and dispatched the army to crush the incipient rebellion.

---

[27] The Kenyan government did not distribute automatic weapons and instead tried to rely on its police and army to control its borderlands. Regularly, livestock raiders win military encounters with the state forces.

[28] David Turton, 'Warfare, Vulnerability and Survival: A Case from Southwestern Ethiopia', *Cambridge Anthropology* 13:2 (1988–9).

[29] Human Rights Watch, 'Targeting the Anuak: Human Rights Violations and Crimes against Humanity in Ethiopia's Gambella Region' (New York, March 2005).

Coda: Eritrea

After 2001, the Eritrean government led by President Isseyas Afewerki has regressed into a peculiarly nasty form of dictatorship. Challenged by many of his colleagues in government over his failures to deliver on promises of democratization and the blunders that had led to a lost war, Isseyas responded by arresting eleven leading party members. None has been seen since. Subsequently all civil society and independent media were repressed. Eritrea is a small country with an efficient party and the President has exercised total personal control of political life even as the country has spiralled into economic collapse. It has been efficient politicide. Eritrea has not witnessed genocidal massacre but few believe that Isseyas will hand over power willingly or liberalize. The dangers of mass murder are considerable.

Somalia

Four episodes of mass killing and forced displacement in the Somali wars warrant our attention.

War in the North 1988–9

Following its defeat by Ethiopia in 1978, the Somali government of Siad Barre became discredited. The Somali National Movement (SNM) headed armed opposition, with core support among the Isaaq clan family of north-west Somalia. In May 1988 the SNM nearly captured Hargaisa, the main city of the north-west, and another town, Burao. Siad Barre responded by reportedly declaring that the Isaaq should be wiped out. His son-in-law and commander of the operation, Gen. Mohamed Said Hersi Morgan, reportedly answered that the order couldn't be fulfilled because there were too many of them to kill. This is the closest case of attempted extermination of a group in north-east Africa, thwarted by the intrinsic difficulty of carrying out such a task when faced with fierce armed resistance and the ability of the population to flee across a nearby border.

The city of Hargaisa was destroyed in the government's counter-attack. (No other city in contemporary Africa has suffered comparable destruction.) Tens of thousands of people were killed. Virtually the entire populations of Hargaisa and other towns fled the country. The livelihoods of the people of north-west Somalia were all but destroyed by looting, the collapse of markets, the destruction of infrastructure, and the dissemination of landmines which meant that camel herds were unable to move safely to many areas of pasture. Testimonies from the war are extraordinarily harrowing, comparable in the intensity of fear and violence to the depths of the Rwanda genocide.[30]

---

[30] Africa Watch, *Somalia: A Government at War with Its Own People: Testimonies about the Killings and the Conflict in the North* (New York, 1990).

Wars in the South 1990–3

President Siad Barre reportedly promised that he would take Somalia to hell with him if he were driven from power. He made good on that promise. In the last year of Siad Barre's rule and the two years immediately following his overthrow, a number of overlapping wars of extreme brutality unfolded with much of the violence directed at the uprooting of ethnic groups. Among them was the dispossession, massacre, and expulsion of the farming minorities of southern Somalia. The two river valleys of Jubba and Shebelle and the rainlands in between were inhabited by two minority Somali clans, the Digil and Rahanweyn, clusters of Cushitic peoples distantly related to the Somalis, including the Shebelle and the Gabwing (also known as Gabaweyn), and Somali Bantus. These people occupied the most valuable farmland in the country and as the economy shifted to irrigated schemes, merchants and government officials acquired land leases and dispossessed the minority farmers. The land grab reached its arbitrary and violent peak as the state imploded.[31] The Somali Bantus were the worst hit. Almost all the surviving members of this community were refugees in Kenya by the mid-1990s and substantial numbers have been resettled in the United States.[32] This is the most complete case of ethnic cleansing in the Horn.

A second component was the ethnic cleansing of Mogadishu as the rebel militias took control of the city in 1991, culminating in urban warfare that cost an estimated 10,000 lives between November 1991 and February 1992. A third component was the war and famine that unfolded across a swathe of territory in 1992 as Siad Barre's loyalist militias attempted a comeback and were repulsed. A campaign of terror, looting, and revenge killing caused hunger and disease which claimed an estimated 250,000 lives.[33]

The War of 2006–9

Somalia gained a modicum of stability in the years between 1994 and 2006. The north-west (target of Siad Barre's war of 1988) seceded to create the unrecognized but stable state of Somaliland. In the south, there were fourteen failed attempts to put together a government. These didn't succeed, but by 2006 Mogadishu itself achieved recognizable municipal governance through a network of Islamic courts. The Islamists' overreached, sparking a fightback from their adversaries and an Ethiopian invasion. Fighting intensified in October 2007, after which 300,000 people fled the city and thousands were killed. The killings and expulsions were

---

[31] Catherine Besteman and Lee Cassanelli (eds), *The Struggle for Land in Southern Somalia: The War behind the War* (Brighton: Haan, 2003).

[32] Catherine Besteman, 'Genocide in Somalia's Jubba Valley and Somali Bantu Refugees in the U.S.', SSRC Webforum, *How Genocides End*, 9 April 2007, available at http://howgenocidesend.ssrc.org/Besteman/

[33] de Waal, *Famine Crimes*, ch. 8.

targeted politically, with both sides assassinating clan elders and civil society leaders deemed unsympathetic.

This war has also involved the Somali region of Ethiopia in another conflict, with the collapse of local government and the conduct of wide-ranging and violent counter-insurgency and frontier policing.

The Wajir Massacre

North-east Kenya is inhabited by ethnic Somalis. In 1963, as Kenya's independence approached, it became clear to the British that the majority wanted to join Somalia. Rather than accede to this demand, the British placed the Northern Frontier District under military rule. Irredentist insurrection was defeated but emergency powers were exercised for thirty years. Somalis were treated as second-class citizens.[34] The largest single massacre was perpetrated against the Degodia clan at the Wagalla airstrip near the town of Wajir, in February 1984.[35] Over a four-day period the Kenyan army systematically killed many hundred, probably well over one thousand, men.

Sudan

Sudan has been in a state of armed conflict for the majority of the fifty-plus years since it achieved independence in 1956. Since the outbreak of the second north-south war in 1983, armed conflict has been continuous in the country, until 2004 in the south and intermittently in several regions of the north.

There have been few attempts to quantify the death toll in southern Sudan, but one analytical compilation estimated the death toll at 1.9 million up to 1998.[36] The data are better for Darfur though the figures remain controversial, with best estimates at 200,000 excess deaths or more.[37] In both cases, hunger and disease killed many more than violence. Nine episodes of mass killing are examined here.

The First Civil War

Sudan's first civil war (1955–72) opened with a massacre of northern traders and government officials in the town of Torit and witnessed a number of massacres of southerners by government soldiers and policemen over the subsequent years, notably in the town of Wau in 1965.

---

[34] Africa Watch, *Kenya, Taking Liberties* (London, 1991).

[35] S. Abdi Sheikh, *Blood on the Runway: The Wagalla Massacre of 1984* (Nairobi: Northern Publishing House, 2007), available at http://www.scribd.com/doc/2551019/BLOOD-ON-THE-RUNWAY-The-Wagalla-Massacre-of-1984

[36] Millard Burr and Robert Collins, 'Quantifying Genocide in Southern Sudan and the Nuba Mountains, 1983–1998' (Washington, DC: US Committee on Refugees, 1998).

[37] Centre for Research on the Epidemiology of Disasters, 'Darfur: Counting the Deaths' (Brussels, May 2005); John Hagan and Alberto Polloni, 'Death in Darfur' *Science* 313 (2006), 1578–9.

The Massacre of the Mahdists and the Elimination of the Communists

A year after seizing power in 1969, the leftist government of Jaafar Nimeiri faced rebellion from the armed followers of the Mahdi's grandson in Omdurman, the twin city of the capital, Khartoum, and at their headquarters at Abba Island on the Nile. Resistance was crushed with overwhelming force including sorties flown by the air force, resulting in more than one thousand fatalities, including civilians.

The following year, Nimeiri's allies in government, the Sudan Communist Party, tried to seize power in a coup. After three days, the coup failed and Nimeiri turned on his erstwhile comrades with a level of savagery rarely seen among the Sudanese elite. Dozens were hanged and hundreds imprisoned in a wide-ranging crackdown.

Slaughter in Bahr al Ghazal 1985–9

The second civil war of 1983–2005 was larger in scale than the first and marked by the use of tribal militia from the earliest days. In July 1985, the transitional government of Gen. Abdel Rahman Suwar al Dahab took the decision to arm Baggara Arab tribes in south Kordofan and south Darfur to fight against the insurrection of the SPLA. This was a fateful decision, taken partly because of lack of money and partly because the regime feared that a stronger army might overthrow the government itself. In the early days, the militiamen were not paid, simply encouraged to reward themselves with looted cattle. It set a pattern for plunder and impunity and local partnerships between traders, military intelligence officers, and militia commanders to profit from the violence.

In 1987, two Sudanese academics documented ethnically targeted mass killings in the war zone of Bahr el Ghazal and the town of ed Da'ien, the latter outside the war zone.[38] The following year, an anonymous report, 'Sudan's Secret Slaughter', documented mass killings in Wau, carried out by the army and a proxy militia, targeting Dinka. In 1989, a report by Amnesty International on militia killings in Bahr el Ghazal detailed a similar pattern.[39] Relief aid to the displaced population was obstructed.[40] Exceptionally high death rates were recorded in several displaced camps during 1988.[41] In the 1990s, the militia raids abated as the leaders of the Baggara tribes recognized that participating in the war on these terms was no longer in their interests.

The Juba Massacres 1992

In June and July 1992, the SPLA carried out military attacks on the southern capital of Juba and nearly captured the city. One of the reasons for the near success was the

---

[38] Ushari Ahmad Mahmud and Suleyman Ali Baldo, 'Al Diein Massacre: Slavery in the Sudan' (Khartoum: University of Khartoum, 1987).

[39] Amnesty International, 'Sudan: Human Rights Violations in the Context of Civil War' (London, 1989).

[40] David Keen, *The Benefits of Famine: A Political Economy of Famine and Relief in Southwestern Sudan* (Princeton: Princeton University Press, 1994); African Rights, *Food and Power in Sudan: A Critique of Humanitarianism* (London, 1997).

[41] de Waal, *Famine Crimes*.

simultaneous mutiny of the southern army units inside the city. In response to the attacks and the mutiny, Sudanese security implemented a thorough and brutal crackdown. This was done having first ensured that there was no international scrutiny, by expelling foreign diplomats and aid workers. The details of the arrests, detentions, and executions have never come to light. However, they are reliably reported to include thousands of extrajudicial executions.

The Nuba Mountains Jihad 1988–93

The Sudan government's assault on the Nuba Mountains culminated in 1992–3 with the most ambitious campaign of the entire war. The SPLA began operations in the area in 1987, sparking a vicious counter-insurgency that included the execution of hundreds of community leaders and educated people, and the use of militia to burn villages and punish groups suspected of supporting the rebels. The campaign of 1992 was officially declared a jihad.[42] The aim of the campaign extended beyond crushing the SPLA rebellion to include forcibly relocating the entire Nuba population out of their homeland into 'peace camps' where they would take on a new identity.[43] The systematic use of rape was documented in the Nuba, as a means of destroying communities and creating a generation with a new identity. Unlike most other cases in which the use of rape as weapon is inferred rather than directly documented, Sudanese security officers went on the record saying that it was policy.[44] This campaign, mounted by a revolutionary government at the height of its ideological hubris, represented a more far-reaching attempt at violent social re-engineering than anything attempted before or since. At its head were civilian Islamist ideologues who did not conceal their contempt for the Nuba way of life with its traditions of music, wrestling, and body-painting, and the Nuba's tolerant mix of Islam, Christianity, and traditional religions. Had the campaign succeeded, the Nuba would have ceased to exist as an identifiable society. As it was, the plan was defeated by a combination of Nuba resistance and divisions within the Sudan government, with the army preferring to restrict the aims of the campaign to military victory rather than Islamist transformation as well.[45]

SPLA Factional Infighting 1991–4

In August 1991, three senior SPLA commanders launched a coup against the leadership of John Garang. They succeeded only in splitting the movement and setting in motion a bloody internecine war. The 'Nasir Faction' consisted of the would-be putschists, while the 'Torit Faction' was the mainstream SPLA led by

---

[42] Alex de Waal and A. H. Abdelsalam, 'Islamism, State Power and Jihad in Sudan', in Alex de Waal (ed.), *Islamism and Its Enemies in the Horn of Africa* (London: Hurst, 2004).

[43] African Rights, *Facing Genocide: The Nuba of Sudan* (London, 1995).

[44] *Sudan's Secret War*, BBC Television, July 1995.

[45] Alex de Waal, 'Averting Genocide in the Nuba Mountains of Sudan', SSRC Webforum, *How Genocides End*, December 2006, available at: http://howgenocidesend.ssrc.org/de_Waal2/

Garang, which ultimately prevailed. Khartoum security became actively involved in deepening the split and furthering the fragmentation of the SPLA.

The split became an ethnic war. Its nadir was in September–November 1991 when Nuer forces of the Nasir Faction attacked the Dinka heartland of Bor and massacred many hundreds, probably thousands, of civilians in a series of raids. Many women were raped or abducted. The countryside was stripped of cattle and other property, and more people died of hunger and disease as a direct result.[46] Witnesses to the immediate aftermath describe a scene of complete devastation with corpses scattered throughout villages and along roads. The following two years saw reprisal raids and counter-attacks as the SPLA split degenerated into a Nuer–Dinka tribal war which created what became known as the 'hunger triangle' in the heart of southern Sudan.

Clearing the Oilfields, 1997–2000

Subsequent counter-insurgency campaigns in the Southern Sudanese oilfields[47] and in Bahr el Ghazal[48] were also mounted with a combination of extreme violence and scorched earth tactics. In these cases, the Sudan army operated alongside southern militia leaders and rebel defectors who opposed the SPLA. The objective of the oilfields campaigns was straightforward: the government wanted to exploit oilfields that lay in the middle of the war zone. It was a bold plan that succeeded through the support of China and a handful of foreign companies, the disarray of the SPLA, and because the government was prepared to remove virtually the entire civilian population from the key areas. As the transport, security, and oil infrastructure went in, the population was cleared out. It was the largest scale of successfully forced relocation of the entire war.

Islamist slogans often accompanied government mobilization for the oilfields campaigns. However, the country's leading Islamists disparaged these as 'jihad for oil'. By the end of the 1990s, Sudan's Islamist experiment had clearly failed and the Islamist movement itself was split, with calls for jihad sounding increasingly hollow.

Darfur 2003–4

Significant conflicts occurred in Darfur in 1987–9, 1991, 1995–7, 1999, and 2001–3 prior to the recognized outbreak of insurrection in February 2003.[49] These conflicts included different configurations of the following factors: local ethnic disputes, spillover of the Chadian civil war, SPLA incursion, and government overreaction to local insurgency, especially by mobilizing proxy militia forces. The 2003 rebellion was more significant than its predecessors because of the large-scale involvement of Chadian army officers, the extensive military supplies provided by the SPLA

---

[46] African Rights, *Food and Power in Sudan*, 289–90.
[47] Human Rights Watch, *Sudan: Oil and Human Rights* (New York, 2003).
[48] Human Rights Watch, *Famine in Sudan: The Human Rights Causes* (New York, 1999).
[49] Julie Flint and Alex de Waal, *Darfur: A New History of a Long War* (London: Zed, 2008).

(which was at the time negotiating a peace agreement with Khartoum) to the Sudan Liberation Army (SLA), the emergence of the Justice and Equality Movement (JEM) drawn from former Darfurian Islamists suspected of having ties to would-be putschists in Khartoum, and the extent to which local state officials had been backing and arming Arab militia. After the rebels overran Darfur's main airbase in April 2003, the government decided on a military response at scale. True to form, it used proxy militia in the frontline of its offensives, in this case drawn principally from camel-herding Arab tribes, and popularly known as *janjawiid*.

From June 2003 to March 2004, the Sudan army, militia, and air force mounted a series of vast scorched earth offensives in northern and western Darfur. The main method of the forces was targeting civilian communities, especially Fur, Masalit, and Zaghawa, the groups that formed the mainstay of the SLA and JEM. Estimates for the numbers of civilians killed are in the scores of thousands. The scorched earth tactics combined with obstruction of relief created a humanitarian disaster that caused a further 150,000 deaths. More than two million people were forcibly displaced.

Between January and March 2004 the government inflicted crushing military defeats on the SLA and JEM, and in April they signed a ceasefire. This was violated by both sides, with the rebels responding to their calamitous setbacks by taking the offensive in eastern and southern Darfur, where the government deployed the same tactics, albeit on a smaller scale, over the succeeding nine months. Data on attacks and fatalities indicate that the number of civilian casualties dropped away sharply after the ceasefire and dropped further with the end of major hostilities in January 2005. The situation thereafter was one of a low-intensity conflict, with the rebel groups fragmenting and occasionally fighting one another, and the government's erstwhile proxies losing their enthusiasm for the war and becoming freelance, turning on one another, or turning their guns on the government. The conflict during 2005–9 consisted of a mixture of banditry, interethnic conflict, harassment of civilians including displaced persons, and occasional offensives and counter-offensives by government and rebels. The pattern was a familiar one from the protracted wars in the south and elsewhere, of a background level of killing (in this case, perhaps 100 people per month) with occasional sharp spikes with several hundred being killed. By 2006, Darfur's war was intermingled with the conflict in Chad, with many of the belligerent forces fighting on both sides of the border.

Islamist ideology played no role in the Darfur war, with former Islamists on both sides. However, a number of the Arab leaders involved were associated with an Arab supremacist organization known as the Arab Gathering. Originally created in Libya, with adherents in Chad as well as Sudan, this took many forms over the years, and consists more of a flexible and ad hoc network than a disciplined organization. Nonetheless, Arab extremist and supremacist slogans were commonly heard during the campaigns of 2003–4. Some of those militants subsequently reconsidered their positions, reaching out to the rebels or even switching sides, and deploying similar rhetoric against the government.[50] By 2007, Arab supremacist calls were hollow, and the government's overriding interest was simply holding onto power.

CONCLUSION

Across the Horn of Africa over recent decades, massacres, forced displacement, and famine are the common occurrences during organized warfare and in the frontierlands of states. Lethal violence against rival elites is also the ultimate resort of those in power when under threat. Cases lie on a spectrum between modestly effective and centralized state authority and the complete absence of state authority. Ethiopia's military campaigns in the 1980s are an instance of a centrally planned counter-insurgency that failed only because the EPLF and TPLF were comparably efficient as military–administrative entities. The fragmentation that marked the demise of Siad Barre's government in 1991 stands at the other extreme. The Sudanese cases and the destruction of north-west Somalia lie in-between, where governments have sufficient power to unleash the forces of destruction, but not enough to control those forces once unleashed. Gambella is an interesting anomaly, where a relatively capable central government initially remained distant from a growing crisis, but then intervened to stop it, albeit brutally. Possibly, what we can draw from this is that the principal difference between a stronger state (Ethiopia) and a weaker one (Somalia, Sudan) is the differential capacity to stop violence when its immediate goal has been achieved. Urban intra-elite killing was prominent in the 1970s, notably in Ethiopia, but has not disappeared.

Ideologies have been pressed into service for state-building and war-making in the Horn, including communism, nationalism, and Islamism. Militant rhetoric accompanies every military mobilization but should rarely be taken at face value. At particular instances in Ethiopia and Sudan, extremist ideology has gone beyond cynical deployment as a tool of popular agitation, to determine the actual objectives and methods of a military–political campaign. This was the case at the height of the Ethiopian revolution, during and after the Red Terror, and at the zenith of the Islamist hubris in Sudan in the early 1990s. The failures of the Ethiopian programmes for coercive socialist transformation and the Sudanese jihad against the Nuba have much to do with the internal contradictions of ambitious extremist plans in complex societies, where governments possess limited financial and political resources.

---

[50] 'Meet the Janjaweed', *Channel 4 News*, UK, 13 March 2008.

If we look further back in history, we see important continuities with the comparable episodes of violence in the nineteenth and early twentieth centuries. These historic parallels are often alive in the minds of contemporary actors, for example the southern Sudanese leaders who dwell on their people's experience of slavery. Over a century's time span, political ideologies including Islamism and Arabism appear ancillary to these ongoing struggles for power at the centre and control at the periphery. The continuities emerge stronger than the transformations, and the regimes in each country tend to revert to type.

Sudan demands a special case in the study of massacre and displacement. Its wars and massacres have many similarities with those of its neighbours but it also possesses its own distinctive way of war. Sudan is a country of paradoxes. Its government is too weak to build truly effective mechanisms for repression and military control, but despite international ostracism, the ruling elite is strong enough to remain secure.[51] The persistence of conflicts in the peripheries reflects the facts that the central government can survive regardless, but also that it uses local proxies that it cannot control. Khartoum can start wars but very rarely can it stop them. Racism persists in Sudan and is thoughtfully analysed by Sudanese from all quarters,[52] but exhortations to racial violence are usually opportunistic. This is true of both central ruling elites which control states and the provincial elites which use violence to assert their claims on the centre. For example, the same Darfurian Arab militia leaders who called for the 'eradication' of African tribes have at other moments made political deals with those tribes and called for war against Khartoum. As noted by the historians of the triangular Sudan–Libya–Chad wars, with reference to the political about-turn of the most ideologically Arab supremacist of Chad's factional leaders, 'Ideology, principle and even honor were no substitute for self-preservation by the chieftains of the Sahara.'[53]

One important conclusion to be drawn from this survey of massacre and related events in the Horn of Africa is that selecting the Red Terror and the Darfur war for the label 'genocide' is arbitrary. They are two exemplars of patterns of violence that have recurred in the region for decades. If scholars of genocide, lawyers, and policymakers are resolved that one or either of these cases is indeed genocide, then numerous other instances warrant the same consideration. Such a reclassification of the Horn of Africa as the location of recurrent genocide would have important implications for the field of genocide studies and international law and policy.

---

[51] Alex de Waal, 'Sudan: The Turbulent State', in *idem* (ed.), *War in Darfur and the Search for Peace* (Cambridge MA: Harvard University Press, 2007).

[52] Francis M. Deng, *War of Visions: Conflict of Identities in Sudan* (Washington, DC: Brookings Institute, 1995); A. H. Abdel Salam, 'Race Relations, Ethnicity and Human Rights', in A. H. Abdel Salam and Alex de Waal (eds), *The Phoenix State: Civil Society and the Future of Sudan* (Trenton, NJ: Red Sea Press, 2001); Alex de Waal, 'Who are the Darfurians?', *African Affairs* 104 (2005), 181–205.

[53] Millard Burr and Robert Collins, *Darfur: The Long Road to Disaster* (Markus Weiner, 2006), 236.

FURTHER READING

African Rights, *Facing Genocide: The Nuba of Sudan* (London, 1995).

Africa Watch, *Somalia: A Government at War with Its Own People: Testimonies about the Killings and the Conflict in the North* (New York, 1990).

Besteman, Catherine, and Lee Cassanelli (eds), *The Struggle for Land in Southern Somalia: The War Behind the War* (Brighton: Haan, 2003).

Clay, Jason, Sandra Steingraber, and Peter Niggli, *The Spoils of Famine: Ethiopian Famine Policy and Peasant Agriculture* (Cambridge, MA: Survival International, 1985).

Deng, Francis M., *War of Visions: Conflict of Identities in Sudan* (Washington DC: Brookings Institute, 1995).

Flint, Julie, and Alex de Waal, *Darfur: A New History of a Long War* (London: Zed Books, 2008).

Keen, David, *The Benefits of Famine: A Political Economy of Famine and Relief in Southwestern Sudan* (Princeton: Princeton University Press, 1994).

LeFort, Rene, *Ethiopia: An Heretical Revolution?* (London: Zed Books, 1983).

Tareke, Gebru, *The Ethiopian Revolution: War in the Horn of Africa* (Princeton: Yale University Press, 2009).

Turton, David, 'Warfare, Vulnerability and Survival: A Case from Southwestern Ethiopia', *Cambridge Anthropology* 13:2 (1988–9).

CHAPTER 27

....

WAR AND GENOCIDE IN AFRICA'S GREAT LAKES SINCE INDEPENDENCE

....

OMAR MCDOOM

IT is a sad fact that every generation born since independence in Uganda, the Democratic Republic of Congo (DRC), Rwanda, and Burundi has lived through either a war or genocide.[1] No single figure exists for the overall death toll in this troubled subset of countries in the Great Lakes. A low-end estimate would stand at 1.4 million while 2.6 million would be at the high end.[2] Moreover, these numbers reflect violent deaths only. They would increase considerably if the indirect effects of war and genocide, notably disease and hunger, were also counted. These

---

[1] A generation is assumed to be twenty-five years.

[2] This range of estimates was calculated by aggregating scholarly estimates for all individual episodes of violence across all four countries. The low and high estimates respectively are Uganda (270,000, 821,500), DRC (204,000, 354,000), Rwanda (509,500, 871,000), and Burundi (450,000, 620,000). See the Appendix for a list of these individual episodes.

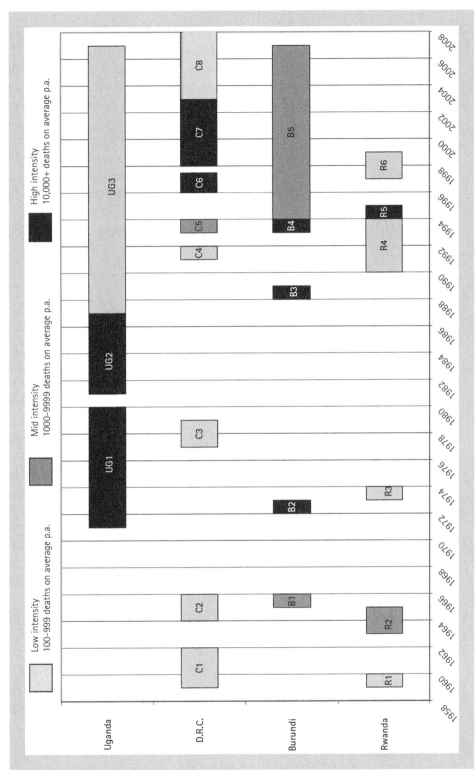

Fig. 1. Timeline comparing the duration and estimated intensity of violence against civilians in the Great Lakes since Indepedence (author's compilation)

numbers have also reinforced clichéd perceptions of the region as Africa's heart of darkness. But what accounts for the Great Lakes' terrible civilian death toll? The web of violence that has entangled the region is complex and individual episodes are often interconnected. This chapter has been written with the first-time observer of the region in mind. It has two main goals: first, it aims to summarize the post-colonial record. It describes all the principal episodes of violence against civilians in each country since independence. Figure 1 illustrates the chronology of this vio-lence in a comparative timeline. Second, the chapter provides a critical overview of the violence. It identifies the characteristics that define the regional context in which these numerous episodes of violence occurred. Readers will find it helpful to refer to the individual cases of violence described in the Appendix before they read on. The analysis that follows frequently draws on them to illustrate its main points.

HISTORICAL SYNOPSIS

As Figure 1 illustrates, the Great Lakes do not constitute a single zone of continuous violence.[3] While the period 1990 to 2007 marks a major intensification in violence across all four countries, until that time each country followed a distinct trajectory in which the violence varied in its origins, frequency, and intensity.

Uganda has experienced one of the longest periods of prolonged violence against civilians. It begins in 1971 with Gen. Idi Amin Dada whose brutal police state is responsible for killing an estimated 50–300,000 Ugandans until he was himself forcibly deposed in 1979 (event UG1). His eventual successor, Milton Obote (1980–6), seized power in a coup and then engaged in a brutal counter-insurgency to retain it, claiming another 200–500,000 lives (event UG2). Yet the 1986 victory of Yoweri Museveni's rebel group over Obote still did not bring peace to the country. Insurgencies flared again, concentrated in the north of the country. The rebel Lord's Resistance Army emerged in 1987 to destabilize northern Uganda for much of the next two decades until peace talks began in 2006 (event UG3).

The Congolese post-colonial experience with violence began with independence in 1960. Secession attempts by two renegade provinces were bloodily suppressed by government forces (event C1). At the same time, the country's first Prime Minister, Patrice Lumumba, was deposed after only 82 days in office and assassinated shortly thereafter. Discontent with the new regime inspired a pro-Lumumbist rebellion in 1964 (event C2). While the rebellion was quashed in 1965, the country's

---

[3] Figure 1 counts only deaths attributable to acts of violence. The figures would be considerably higher if the deaths caused indirectly as a result of disease and hunger for example were also counted.

commander-in-chief, Joseph-Désiré Mobutu, exploited the political opportunity to seize power. For the next thirty-two years, he used repression and patronage to rule the country until his grip on power began to weaken from a combination of gross economic mismanagement and pressure for political liberalization in the early 1990s (events C4 and C5). In 1996, as the Mobutist regime faltered, Rwanda and Uganda initiated the first Congo War (event C6). They led a military alliance that definitively toppled Mobutu. However, the man installed as the country's new President, Laurent Kabila, turned against his former sponsors. This was in part the motivation for the Second Congo War in 1998 (event C7). The war was complex, involving numerous domestic rebel groups and external actors with varying agendas. Although many of the key actors finally reached a peace settlement in 2002, several spoiler groups chose not to participate. Their continued activities in the east of the country leave it a lawless and insecure region for ordinary Congolese at the end of 2007 (event C8).

Rwanda and Burundi, each tiny, land-locked countries composed of ethnic Hutu majorities and Tutsi minorities, followed different paths to violence after their independence in 1962. Burundi quickly became a Tutsi ethnocracy. Hutu uprisings in 1965, 1972, 1988, and 1993 drew brutal responses from its Tutsi-controlled government and army (events B1–B4). The Hutu civilian population was the primary victim. The 1972 insurrection infamously resulted in a selective genocide of Burundi's Hutu elite. The Tutsi army, militia, and elements of the civilian population killed an estimated 100–200,000 Hutu. The 1993 uprising was triggered by the election and subsequent assassination of the country's first Hutu President, Melchior Ndadaye. The Tutsi army's harsh reaction to the uprising marked Burundi's descent into a civil war that, at the end of 2007, had still not been definitively resolved (event B5).

Rwanda's post-colonial experience is almost the converse of its neighbouring cousin. Even before independence, in 1959 a revolution began (event R1) that ultimately overthrew the country's Tutsi monarchy and instead ushered in two successive Hutu-dominated republics (1962–73 and 1973–94). The revolution and ensuing marginalization of the Tutsi population caused tens of thousands to go into exile. On several occasions, this Tutsi refugee community attempted to return to Rwanda by force of arms (events R2 and R4). Its most determined effort in 1990 provoked a four-year civil war (event R4) that culminated in the Rwandan President's assassination and the 1994 genocide. A newly-installed extremist government unleashed the army and militia groups and, with the participation of elements of the Hutu civilian population, they killed an estimated 500–850,000 individuals, overwhelmingly Tutsi (event R5). It is only through the victory of the largely Tutsi rebel group that the slaughter ended. The Hutu génocidaires were pushed out of Rwanda, mostly into the DRC, where elements continued a low-grade insurgency against Rwanda's new government (event R6).

REGIME TRANSITIONS

What, if any, then is the underlying feature behind many of the individual episodes of violence summarized above? The region's numerous wars and occasional genocides have most often occurred in the context of extra-constitutional regime changes. In fact, there have been very few legal and peaceful transfers of power from one individual or group to another in the post-colonial history of the Great Lakes.[4] Instead, regime transitions have tended to occur in one of three ways:

1) military coup;
2) victory in civil wars; and
3) assassination of the head of state.

Often some combination of these events has occurred to install a new regime. Most have been accompanied by violence.

Military coups have been the most common method. On occasion, these have been 'palace revolutions': a bloodless change in leadership, often originating from within the ranks of the ruling elite. Burundi exemplifies this pattern with coups in 1966, 1976, and 1987, all led by ethnic Tutsi men, who were all from the same ethnic subgroup (Hima), and all from the same region of the country (Bururi). However, more often than not, military takeovers of moribund civilian administrations have been accompanied by violence. These have usually occurred for one of two reasons. First, military men have either fomented or taken advantage of violence to seize power. In Rwanda in 1973, a young Gen. Juvénal Habyarimana in collaboration with other military officers astutely exploited the instability created by popular anti-Tutsi violence to assume power (event R3). Habyarimana became Rwanda's second head of state since independence and presided over its Second Republic until his assassination triggered Rwanda's genocide in 1994. Second, in order to consolidate newly established positions, military autocrats have then engaged in purges to eliminate their opponents. In Uganda, Gen. Idi Amin Dada ruthlessly eliminated real and imagined enemies after ousting Milton Obote from power in 1971 (event UG1). By one estimate his paranoia resulted in the deaths of 300,000 individuals over the course of his eight-year rule.[5]

Armed rebellion has been the second method for toppling governments in the Great Lakes. These have, unsurprisingly, proved to be the most violent form of regime transition. Massive violence and genocide has been most likely to occur when a rebellion has ended through outright military victory instead of negotiated settlement.

---

[4] When peaceful transitions have occurred, they have almost always been the result of flawed elections in which incumbents who originally came to power through force have been successful in legitimizing their position *ex post*.

[5] See A. B. K. Kasozi, N. Musisi, et al., *The Social Origins of Violence in Uganda, 1964–1985* (Montreal/Buffalo: McGill-Queen's University Press, 1994), 104.

As the state has usually had a superior military capability, the asymmetry has compelled challengers to engage in guerrilla warfare. In response the government has often resorted to counter-insurgency strategies designed to 'drain the seas'.

A first common tactic in such strategies has been to target civilians systematically to punish and deter them from supporting the insurgents. Civilians have found themselves caught between the insurgents and the government troops. In Uganda's Bush War the main theatre for war was the infamous Luwero triangle in which the rebel National Resistance Army established itself (event UG2). Ethnic Bagandan civilians who inhabited the region became the victims of government orders to destroy villages as well as atrocities committed by rank-and-file soldiers to which their superiors turned a blind eye. Similarly, Burundi's Tutsi-controlled army consistently punished civilians for Hutu uprisings. Rebellions in 1965, 1972, 1988, and 1993 each resulted in massacres of Hutu civilians (events B1–B4). The Rwandan government has also punished civilians for rebel actions. It sponsored massacres of Tutsi civilians during the country's civil war in reprisal for rebel attacks (event R4). In the four years leading up to the genocide in 1994, between two and three thousand Tutsi civilians were killed.

A second popular tactic used in the region's counter-insurgency campaigns has been the quasi-internment of civilians. In these cases, the rural population has been forced to leave their homes and instead to live in so-called displacement camps. The tactic is designed to deprive rebels of the opportunity to recruit fighters as well as to deny them food and intelligence. Individuals found outside of the camps could be assumed to be rebels. Thus in northern Uganda, locked in a protracted civil war since 1986, the government interned civilians on a massive scale in its counter-insurgency campaign against the rebel Lord's Resistance Army (event UG3). At the peak, over 1.6 million northern Ugandans lived in these camps, ostensibly for their own protection, emptying the countryside of people. However, a survey in 2005 found that appalling camp conditions had created an alarming mortality rate. Disease, hunger, and violence had resulted in an estimated one thousand excess deaths per week, mostly among children under the age of five.[6] The Burundian army has also employed this tactic, more forcefully, in the multifronted civil war that has beset the country since 1993 (event B5). Government soldiers looted, raped, and burned homes in order to drive civilians into 're-groupment camps' where humanitarian conditions were dire. An unknown number of Burundians died in this way.

Assassinations of heads of state have been the third way in which regime change has often occurred. Aspiring to the highest public office has been a dangerous ambition in the Great Lakes. Burundi has experienced the highest number of assassinations: Louis Rwagasore in 1961; Pierre Ngendandumwe and Léopold Biha (attempted assassination) in 1965; Charles Ndizeye in 1972; and Melchior

---

[6] See Ministry of Health, Government of Uganda, *Health and Mortality Survey among Internally Displaced Persons in Gulu, Kitgum, and Pader Districts in Northern Uganda. Kampala, Uganda* (2005).

Ndadaye in 1993. The last three each preceded massive violence against civilians (events B2, B3, and B4). However, the most infamous case has been Rwanda's President in 1994. Unknown assassins shot down the plane carrying Juvénal Habyarimana as it was coming in to land at Kigali airport on 6 April 1994. The sudden gap created by Habyarimana's death created an opportunity for Hutu extremists to seize power. They went on to implement the world's swiftest genocide that claimed, according to one estimate, up to 850,000 lives in little over one hundred days (event R5).[7] Similarly in Zaire, a young Joseph Mobutu, the country's military commander, led a coup in 1960 that culminated in the execution of Patrice Lumumba, the country's first post-independence leader. His assassination inspired his supporters to launch a violent rebellion in 1964 to challenge those complicit in his assassination (event C1). Finally, it is worth noting that these assassinations and coups that have become part of the historical record represent probably only a fraction of the true number. Unsuccessful attempts to overthrow governments have usually gone unreported, especially those that originated from within the ruling elite itself. Incumbents have preferred to avoid the exposure of such serious internal divisions.

However, it is not only during extra-constitutional regime transitions that violence has occurred. Conflict has also accompanied sanctioned transitions, in particular the shift from authoritarian to democratic rule. Incumbent elites, reluctant to surrender power, have resorted to violence in the run-up to elections to intimidate the opposition and to assure their own political survival. The democratization wave across Africa in the 1990s was no exception. In Zaire Mobutu deployed the state's security apparatus to suppress student protests in the early 1990s (event C4). In Rwanda, the sudden switch to a multiparty system in 1991 under international pressure created a new political space. It quickly led to the creation of opposition parties with youth wings which violently clashed among themselves and with the ruling party and that also allowed for the organization of an extremist minority (event RS).

The post-election period has also been susceptible to conflict. Electoral losers have resorted to violence to contest democratic outcomes. In Burundi, the Tutsi military elite would not accept the result of the 1993 election in which a Hutu President, Melchior Ndadaye, was victorious. His assassination a mere four months into office precipitated the onset of a bloody and chronic civil war (event B4). Yet violence is not an inevitable by-product of democratization. For example, contrary to many fears, the DRC held relatively peaceful elections in 2007. The 2002 peace settlement that had brought many former warlords into a transitional government held. Jean-Pierre Bemba, the former rebel leader who lost in the second round of the 2007 Presidential elections, did not resort to arms in large part because of strong external pressure to keep the peace.

---

[7] See G. Prunier, *The Rwanda Crisis: History of a Genocide* (Kampala, Uganda: Fountain, 1999), 265.

Thus regime transitions, both sanctioned and unsanctioned, in the Great Lakes have often been accompanied by violence. In the remainder of the chapter, I suggest seven important characteristics that define the regional context in which these transitions occurred.

CHARACTERISTIC ONE: AUTHORITARIAN REGIMES

Poor governance is the first contextual characteristic behind violent regime transitions in the region. Authoritarian states run by autocrats have been the norm in the Great Lakes and democratic states led by elected leaders the exception.

The region's authoritarian regimes have typically relied on two instruments to govern: repression and patronage. When autocrats have possessed the means to reward their security forces richly and to bribe their potential opponents adequately, authoritarian regimes have in fact been supportive of peace and order. Indeed, as Figure 1 indicates, the period of least violence was the 1970s when single-party, authoritarian rule was solidly in place across all four countries. However, when autocrats have lost these means, their ability to govern has been compromised, which has encouraged challengers willing to use violence to topple them. It has been the transition between regimes, a period of disorder, in which wars and genocides have most often occurred. Violence arises when control of the centre is contested and power is in flux.

In Uganda Idi Amin exemplified the first method—coercive rule—in his bid to assure a position for which he enjoyed little natural legitimacy (event UG1). The numerous institutions of the state security apparatus that flourished under Amin held the power of life and death over ordinary Ugandans. Like their patron, they remained largely unaccountable for their actions. The second method—neo-patrimonial rule—has also generated grievances. Privileging a few often meant excluding the many. Autocrats established clientele networks based on ethnic, clan, and/or regional allegiances to assure their influence in the absence of popular legitimacy. Within these networks, a small minority monopolized power and allocated the state's wealth among their own. This form of patronage, while effective in buying loyalty, was inherently exclusionary and accentuated social cleavages. Thus, for example, small, elite groups of Hutu and Tutsi each dominated post-independence power at the expense of the other ethnic group in Rwanda and Burundi respectively.

The inner circles of power within neo-patrimonial regimes in fact have often gone beyond simple ethnic or tribal markers. In Burundi, two Tutsi subgroups initially vied for power after independence: the high-status Banyaruguru and the low-status Hima. Ultimately, Tutsi-Hima came to rule the country from 1965 to

2003. In Rwanda, the intra-ethnic contest was regional: a north–south split. A southern Hutu elite under Gregoire Kayibanda controlled the state during Rwanda's First Republic (1962–73) while a group of northern Hutu under Juvénal Habyarimana dominated during the Second Republic (1973–1994).

In short, the authoritarian nature of governance in the Great Lakes is an important characteristic of violent regime transition. The reluctance of ruling elites to pass on the baton of power has compelled opponents to use force to wrest it from them when the opportunity has presented itself. The vast clientele networks which/underpinned these regimes have strongly resisted efforts to take away the personal, material benefits of power that they enjoyed.

CHARACTERISTIC TWO: NATURAL RESOURCE ENDOWMENT DIFFERENCES

The asymmetry in resource endowments between resource-rich DRC and comparatively resource-poor Rwanda, Burundi, and Uganda is the second important characteristic of the context for violence in the region. The immense natural wealth of the DRC has long attracted the attention of outsiders willing to use force to obtain them and has been likened to a curse.[8] The actors—and the resources they extracted—have varied over the country's history. Belgium's King Léopold II, when the Congo was his private territory, began by squeezing rubber from its population. The Belgian government, after seizing the territory, diversified into mining and palm oil. The postcolonial era saw further expansion of this extraction: coltan, gold, diamonds, copper, cobalt, oil, gas, and timber have all been extracted and sold to benefit a small minority. With the weakening of Mobutu's grip on the country in the 1990s, the DRC's resource-poor neighbours, Rwanda, Burundi, and Uganda, seized the opportunity to share in the wealth. Local warlords and foreign corporations have also been complicit in the exploitation. In all these cases, there has been very little distribution of the country's natural wealth to its people. Ordinary Congolese have, to the contrary, been the victims of violent conflict motivated and sustained by the DRC's massive resource endowment as exemplified by the second Congo War (event C7). Rwanda and Uganda invaded the DRC in 1998 in part to preserve the economic interests they had each secured during the first Congo War two years earlier (event C6). Even with the formal conclusion of the war in 2002 Rwandan forces continued covert incursions into the east to protect Rwandan material interests there. At the end of 2007, warlords

---

[8] See for example Human Rights Watch, *Democratic Republic of Congo: The Curse of Gold* (New York, 2005).

and rebel militia continued to operate in the east financed in part by the sale of these plundered resources (event C8).

CHARACTERISTIC THREE: DIFFERENCES IN PHYSICAL GEOGRAPHY

Differences in both borders and terrain have also helped violence to persist in the region. Looted resources, arms, rebels, and refugees have all moved easily across the region's porous and multiple borders. With nine countries surrounding it, the DRC has suffered the most from illicit cross-border movements, especially from Rwanda, Burundi, and Uganda. These flows have contributed to the tangled web of violence in the region and conflicts have rarely remained purely internal affairs. Policing the DRC's borders is a massive task. It has exceeded the capacities of its capital, Kinshasa, and also taxed those of the international community. MONUC, a 17,000-strong UN peacekeeping mission deployed following the second Congo war (event C7), has been unable to enforce an arms embargo effectively.[9] The flow of small arms has been an important factor in keeping the flames of conflict in the region alive.

The contrast in physical terrain between countries in the Great Lakes has also aided insurgencies. The tiny, densely-populated, and highly-cultivated territories of Rwanda and Burundi have made it difficult for rebel groups to operate un-detected. In contrast, the expansive territory of the DRC has provided superb con-ditions for insurgents. Its dense rainforests, volcanic mountain range, and limited road network have made it an ideal environment in which to wage a guerrilla war. With the capital, Kinshasa, far away both physically and mentally, numerous rebel groups have indeed emerged in the distant east of the country. Rwanda, Burundi, and Uganda in contrast have been comparatively close to the mineral-rich east. Their influence in the east has often rivalled or surpassed that of the Congolese state. In addition to home-grown groups, rebels from other countries have also been drawn to the region. Rwanda's former military and militia responsible for its genocide, Burundi's Hutu rebel group, the Palipehutu-FNL, and Uganda's Lord's Resistance Army have all operated from the DRC's lawless east, for example. Its terrain has provided an attractive cover for many of the region's insurgents.

---

[9] MONUC: 'Mission Des Nations Unies en République Démocratique du Congo'.

CHARACTERISTIC FOUR: PREDATORY ARMIES

Soldiers—both government and rebel—have been responsible for much of the violence committed against civilians in the region. A shortage of modern, professional armies trained in international humanitarian norms of warfare is another defining characteristic of the region. Indeed, civilian deaths outnumber those of armed combatants. In wartime, rape and pillage continue to be seen as legitimate rewards. Even in peacetime soldiers 'tax' civilians with impunity, a problem exacerbated when they are poorly paid. The Zairean Armed Forces under Mobutu, particularly towards the end of his regime (event C4), and rebel forces in the post-Mobutu eastern Congo have both exemplified this predatory military behaviour.

Military establishments have enjoyed unusual influence within each country, mainly because many of the region's authoritarian regimes emerged from coups led by military elites. The lack of legitimacy of military-headed regimes led their leaders to rely on and to privilege their armed forces in order to protect their positions, and to recruit on the basis of ethnic and regional loyalties. In Uganda, Milton Obote made the northern ethnic groups, the Acholi and Langi, the backbone of his army between 1980 and 1986. Yoweri Museveni subsequently purged them from the national army, replacing them with groups that had been loyal to him during the Bush War (event UG2). Ethnic affiliation has been important in rebel recruitment as well, as exemplified by the numerous ethnically based militia that emerged in the second Congo war (event C7): Lendu, Hema, Hutu, and Tutsi have all formed the backbone of rebel groups in eastern Congo.

CHARACTERISTIC FIVE: AN UNSTABLE REGIONAL BALANCE-OF-POWER

Many of the internal conflicts in the region have been connected to broader geopolitical rivalries. Proxy wars have been an important means through which the regional balance-of-power has been altered. The potential profit from natural resource exploitation in the DRC—especially since the fall of Mobutu—has been an added incentive for neighbouring countries to sponsor proxy rebel groups. Often, this has happened covertly. Rwanda and Uganda, for example, have denied their alliances with various rebel groups in eastern Congo despite reports that they have advised and armed them since the late 1990s. Alternatively, neighbours have allowed rebels to use their territories as rear bases from which to launch attacks. In the 1960s, Burundi allowed Tutsi exiles from Rwanda to make repeated incursions over its border in their bid to return home (event R2). Similarly, since the early 1990s Hutu rebel groups have initiated military campaigns from Tanzania and the DRC into Burundi in their bid to topple the Tutsi-dominant regime (event B5).

Rwanda's genocide in 1994 dramatically shifted the regional balance-of-power. Rebel victory ended the genocide, overthrew Rwanda's extremist Hutu government, and put a Tutsi-dominant government into power. The genocidal Hutu army and militia went into exile in eastern Congo. The ensuing instability, and the insecurity that accompanied it, has become an important rationale and driver of military action in the region. The former Hutu army and militia continued their attacks on Rwanda and also targeted Congolese Tutsi in eastern Congo. In response, Rwanda has made numerous incursions into eastern Congo in the name of self-defence. It points to the regrouping of the Rwandan Hutu army and militia first as the ALIR (Armée pour la Libération du Rwanda) and then as part of the FDLR (Forces Démocratiques pour la Libération du Rwanda) as proof of the threat at its borders (event C8). It also claims it is acting to prevent another genocide, this time of Congolese Tutsi. This unstable balance-of-power persisted at the end of 2007 and has been at the heart of much of the region's most recent period of violence.

CHARACTERISTIC SIX: REFUGEE COMMUNITIES AND THE CYCLE OF VIOLENCE

The scale of the refugee problem in the Great Lakes is the sixth defining contextual characteristic for violence in the region. The official number of recognized refugees in the DRC, Burundi, Uganda, and Rwanda stood at 542,746 at the end of 2006.[10] There were an additional 2,675,321 internally displaced persons (IDPs) receiving assistance from UNHCR. Refugees have been an important mechanism in the cycle of violence. They have been both the product of conflict and the source of further conflict in the region. The role of refugee camps in perpetuating violence in the region has played out in two main ways. First, they have acted as a sanctuary for rebel fighters. As war has approached civilians invariably have fled en masse, usually across the nearest border. Rebel soldiers have often fled with them and distinguishing combatants from civilians has been problematic. Located just over the border, out of reach of government forces, rebel combatants regroup and

---

[10] See UNHCR, *Statistical Yearbook, Trends in Displacement, Protection, and Solutions 2006* (Geneva). In addition there are just over 393,000 Burundian refugees in Tanzania, mainly the product of Burundi's 1972 genocide.

recover. In addition refugee and IDP camps have attracted the humanitarian industry. The food and medical supplies relief workers have brought have made easy pickings for both government and rebel combatants. Rwanda's genocide in 1994 resulted in an estimated two million Hutu civilians fleeing the advance of the rebel group, the Rwandan Patriotic Front (RPF) (event R5). The majority sought sanctuary in eastern Congo along with government soldiers and militia implicated in the genocide. The international community, in contrast to its intransigence during the genocide, rapidly deployed massive humanitarian resources to the region to assist the refugees. As a result, it stood accused of also assisting many of Rwanda's génocidaires.

The second refugee–conflict linkage has been through armed return. Caught between unwelcoming hosts and repressive home countries, refugee communities have often mobilized to fight their way back to the old country. Tutsi refugees from Rwanda's 1959 Hutu revolution (event R1) established the Rwandan Alliance for National Unity in 1979, the antecedent to the Rwandan Patriotic Front. The RPF went on to launch Rwanda's civil war in 1990 that culminated in its genocide. Similarly, Burundi's 1972 Hutu genocide resulted in Hutu refugee camps established just over the border in Tanzania (event B2). These camps gave birth to the radical Hutu rebel group, the Palipehutu, in 1972 and subsequently to the more moderate FRODEBU in 1980. Each was determined to break the Tutsi grip on power in Burundi and started a chronic and bloody rebellion to do so (event B5). Yet it is not just through their support of rebel activity that refugee camps have made casualties of civilians. The camps established have often been death traps in themselves. Disease, usually malaria, has been the chief killer. Bodies weakened from hunger and fatigue have easily succumbed and led to mortality rates far in excess of those under peacetime conditions. Internal displacement camps created during Uganda's and Burundi's civil wars have been major sources of death. In both cases, civilians were forced into these camps as part of a government counter-insurgency strategy. Displacement camps strongly resembled internment camps.

CHARACTERISTIC SEVEN: ETHNICITY AND EXCLUSIONARY IDEOLOGIES

Although tribalism is too simple a lens through which to view violence in the region, the importance of ethnic identity should not be dismissed altogether. Most importantly, ethnic differences have served as useful narratives or become the basis of exclusionary ideologies. As such, they have aided in the mobilization of public support, bolstered recruitment during wartime, and provided cohesion among rebel and government soldiers. At times, these narratives have also provided the rationale for violence. One of the most well-established ethnic narratives has been that of minority Tutsi domination and manipulation in the region. In Rwanda, both before and during the genocide, extremists played on collective Hutu memory of historical subjugation by Tutsi to mobilize popular anti-Tutsi sentiment. A Tutsi ruling elite had indeed governed Rwanda's socio-political order prior to Rwanda's Hutu revolution in 1959. In Congo, the Tutsi minority in its eastern territories has historically also been the target of popular resentment and state exclusion. In 1981, Zaire passed a law that called into question the citizenship of its Kinyarwandaphone Tutsi community. In South Kivu province, a subset of Congolese Tutsi, the Banyamulenge, has been the target of deep-seated animosity from other ethnic groups. This animosity has provided Rwanda, controlled by the Tutsi-dominant RPF, with the rationale for repeated incursions into eastern Congo following the end of the second Congo war in 2002 (event C7). The Tutsi-controlled RPF claimed that its ethnic kin were likely to become victims of another genocide. This same rationale has also provided eastern Congo's infamous renegade general, Laurent Nkunda, with the justification for not integrating his forces into Congo's new national army following the end of the second Congo war. He cited the threat to his Tutsi brethren posed by the FDLR, the armed rebel group composed in part of Rwandan Hutu génocidaires that continues to operate in the East.

Yet the violence cannot be reduced to the mere existence or multiplicity of ethnic or tribal differences. First of all, the region's ethnic conflicts have usually involved only a small number of the myriad ethnic groups within it. Rwanda and Burundi are highly unusual demographically in sub-Saharan Africa in that they are essentially bi-ethnic societies, each composed of a Hutu majority and a Tutsi minority. Violence has indeed followed ethnic lines in these countries. Yet Uganda and the DRC are multiethnic societies and only a small handful of their ethnic groups have been drawn into violent conflict. The vast majority have coexisted without bloodshed. Secondly, violence has been as much the product of intra-ethnic power struggles as it has interethnic rivalries. In the run-up to Rwanda's genocide, the principal tension was between Hutu moderates and extremists. The newly-created political parties split along these lines as hardliners rejected a peaceful settlement of Rwanda's ongoing civil war (event R4). In Burundi, the numerous Hutu rebel groups in its civil war factionalized along similar lines as rival leaders emerged (event B5). The net effect has been to prolong the fighting.

In short, it is not the mere existence or diversity of ethnic groups that is a defining characteristic of the region. Rather, it is the degree to which myths and narratives about certain ethnic groups have become entrenched in societies and are utilized in wars and genocides that is important.

CONCLUSION

The focus of this chapter has been violence against civilians. The chapter has suggested some of the important characteristics which have defined the context in which the wars and genocides responsible for the region's very high civilian death toll have occurred. Yet it should be acknowledged that the estimates are problematic. The estimate in this chapter was aggregated from secondary sources. However, the component figures are sometimes given without an explanation of the methodology, if any, used to establish them. We need more reliable estimates. Reports based on nationally representative surveys have started to appear. Moreover, these have revealed that violence has not been the most important cause of death in wars and genocide. Disease and malnutrition have been the chief culprits. Damage to the state's health and sanitation systems has killed indirectly. In the DRC alone an estimated 5.4 million people died between August 1998 and April 2007 in excess of the norm.[11] As many as 2.1 million deaths occurred *after* the formal conclusion of the Second Congo War in 2002. Moreover, the overwhelming majority were not victims of violence but instead individuals who had succumbed to illness and undernourishment, usually children under the age of five. Thus, while the region's wars and genocides evoke images of AK-47s and machetes, we should not forget the less visible but much more deadly and chronic effects of these forms of violence on civilian populations.

Appendix

SUMMARIES OF INDIVIDUAL EPISODES OF VIOLENCE IN REGION

I. UGANDA

Event UG1: 1971–9: State terror under Idi Amin

Idi Amin presided over a highly authoritarian regime that used violence to maintain control of the state and to repress its civilian population. Following his military coup bringing him to power in 1971, Amin purged the various security institutions of individuals seen as favourable to his ousted predecessor, Milton Obote. His new state

---

[11] See International Rescue Committee, *Mortality in the Democratic Republic of Congo: An Ongoing Crisis* (New York: International Rescue Committee, 2007).

security apparatus institutionalized violence as the basis of authority. Influential elites and ordinary civilians alike were imprisoned, tortured, and murdered, sometimes for their perceived opposition to Amin but sometimes arbitrarily. In addition, between 1977 and 1978, Amin authorized death squads to target ethnic Acholi and Langi elites in response to sabotage activities by Obote agents. Between 1978 and 1979, conspiracies and mutinies to topple Amin resulted in further purges. Amin's policies resulted in the estimated killing of between 50,000 and 300,000 civilians.[12]

Event UG2: 1981–5: Civil War

A multipronged rebellion begins following contested national elections. After Idi Amin was forcibly removed in 1979 by an alliance of forces led by Tanzania, weak transitional government motivated Milton Obote to seize power a second time in 1980. National elections to legitimize Obote's coup were rigged in his favour and this precipitated an armed challenge to his authority. The most significant rebel group, the National Resistance Movement under Yoweri Museveni, came to control an area known as the Luwero triangle, leading to a brutal counter-insurgency campaign by Obote's Ugandan National Liberation Army (UNLA). The UNLA committed many atrocities against mainly ethnic Bagandan civilians in this area. In addition, the UNLA also perpetrated atrocities in the West Nile region where the rebel group, the Ugandan National Rescue Front, operated and also preyed on the civilian population. The West Nile region was the homeland of Idi Amin and the UNLA was composed of mainly ethnic Acholi and Langi who had been previously targeted by Amin. Altogether it is estimated between 200,000 and 500,000 civilians were killed in this period.[13]

Event UG3: 1986–2006: Northern Ugandan Insurgencies

Following the 1986 victory of the National Resistance Movement (NRM) in the civil war, several insurgent groups emerged in northern Uganda to challenge Yoweri Museveni's new government. The most violent and persistent of these, the Lord's Resistance Army (LRA), began in 1987 led by Joseph Kony. Claiming a spiritual motivation based on the Ten Commandments, the LRA began a twenty-year guerrilla campaign in northern Uganda. The violence against civilians waxed and waned in this period. The main victims of the violence were the ethnic Acholi population, from which the LRA also abducted children to serve in the rebel organization. However, the insurgency spread to affect ethnically Teso and Langi regions. As part of its counter-insurgency campaign the government forced the civilian population into

---

12 Kasozi, Musisi, et al., *The Social Origins of Violence in Uganda*, 104.
13 Ibid. 145.

displacement camps. At its peak in 2002, over 1.6 million lived in these camps. According to a 2005 World Health Organization survey, mortality rates reached 1,000 excess deaths per week, mostly from illness. The LRA raided these camps and conducted ambushes on the roads, killing civilians until peace talks began in southern Sudan in 2006. As these continued, the security situation remained fragile.

II. Democratic Republic of Congo

Event C1: 1959–61: Transition to Independence and Secessionist Wars

Almost immediately following independence in 1960 two provinces, Katanga and S. Kasai, seceded. The national army was ordered to suppress the two rebellions. In South Kasai, where conflict between ethnic Luba and Lulua had ignited in 1959, the army killed mostly Luba civilians as it headed to end the Katangan secession. At the request of Congo's new Prime Minister, Patrice Lumumba, the UN fielded a 20,000-strong mission to the region. The secessions were brought to an end in 1962. No figure exists for civilians killed in South Kasai though the UN Secretary-General, Dag Hammarskjold, characterized it as genocide.

Event C2: 1964–5: Lumumbist Rebellion

Supporters of the assassinated former Prime Minister Patrice Lumumba launched a rebellion on four fronts in 1964 to topple the government of his rival, President Joseph Kasa-Vubu. The commander-in-chief of the army, Joseph-Désiré Mobutu, contracted foreign mercenaries to assist the national army in quashing the rebellion. In September 1964 one rebel group succeeded in capturing Kisangani, in North Congo, where it declared a separate government. In a combined offensive Belgian paratroopers dropped by US planes, foreign mercenaries, and elite units of the national army destroyed the rebel government. Seventy Europeans and nearly 1,000 Congolese were killed during this operation, code-named Red Dragon. The involvement of foreign troops made Kasa-Vubu unpopular with other African Heads of State. Mobutu exploited his unpopularity to seize power in a military coup in 1965.

Event C3: 1977–8: Shaba Secessionist Wars

In 1977 Katangan secessionists, the Front for the National Liberation of Congo (FNLC), attacked the province of Shaba (aka Katanga) from across the border in Angola. As their advance captured towns, Mobutu sent in the national army assisted by Moroccan troops who successfully repelled the invaders. With the rebels routed, the national army launched a 'pacification' campaign against the Katangan civilian population. The casualty count is unknown but the campaign generated an estimated 200,000 refugees. The FNLC launched a second attack in 1978 and this time captured Kolwezi town in South Katanga. This time French and Belgian troops were sent in to expel the FNLC. The International Red Cross found the bodies of 95 Europeans and 111 Zairean civilians. Reports conflicted as to whether they were deliberately massacred by rebels, caught in crossfire, or killed by Congolese government soldiers.

Event C4: 1991: Decline of Mobutu's Regime

Civilians were the victims of violence committed by and against a weakening Mobutu regime. Under internal and international pressure to democratize, Mobutu permitted the creation of multiple political parties and a Sovereign National Congress. Aid donors also dramatically cut their support to Zaire. As a result Mobutu began to lose control of the state. Student protests in Lubumbashi in 1991 were suppressed, resulting in a massacre of fifty to a hundred. Unpaid soldiers rioted in Kinshasa in 1991 and again in 1993 that left altogether 145 civilians dead. Further protests in Kinshasa in 1992 were quashed by the army, resulting in 30 dead.

Event C5: 1993: Decline of Mobutu's Regime continued

In North Kivu, eastern Congo, violent conflict over land following ethnic lines broke out. Mobutu sent the Presidential Guard and Civil Guard to quell the fighting. Without means to sustain themselves, the soldiers instead preyed on the civilian population. The arrival of the Rwandan Hutu military and militia following Rwanda's genocide in 1994 turned the focus of the violence against the Congolese Tutsi community. No body count was done but newspapers reported thousands of civilians were killed and 200,000 displaced.

Event C6: 1996–7: First Congo War

As Mobutu's regime weakened, in October 1996 neighbouring Rwanda and Uganda co-sponsored an alliance of four rebel groups in eastern Congo, the Alliance of Democratic Forces for the Liberation of Congo (AFDLC) led by Laurent Kabila, to capture Kinshasa. The war began when Rwanda, claiming its security was threatened by Hutu soldiers and militia responsible for Rwanda's genocide in 1994, crossed into *eastern* Congo to dismantle forcibly the refugee camps within which the fugitive génocidaires were operating. Rwandan soldiers massacred Hutu refugees in the camps. The death toll is unknown as the UN was forced to stop before completing its investigation. AFDLC troops then moved west and captured Kasai and Katanga provinces, and with the aid of Angolan troops, finally took Kinshasa in May 1997. Mobutu fled the country and Kabila was installed as the new President.

Event C7: 1998–2002: Second Congo War

Civilians were the principal victims of a second proxy war between the DRC and its neighbours. In order to improve his domestic popularity, DRC's new President, Laurent Kabila, distanced himself from his sponsors by expelling Rwandan and Ugandan advisors from the country. He instead attacked the unpopular Congolese Tutsi minority in the east with the aid of the fugitive Hutu army and militia responsible for Rwanda's genocide. As a result his former allies, along with Burundi, invaded again in 1998, with their own troops and through two new proxy rebel groups. Rwanda sponsored the Congolese Rally for Democracy (RCD) and Uganda supported the Movement for the Liberation of Congo (MLC). On the other side Kabila received support from Angola, Zimbabwe, and Namibia initially and Sudan, Chad, and Libya later. As the war progressed, it became more complex. Rwanda and Uganda turned from allies into enemies and the rebel groups splintered into factions. Kinshasa did not fall but the country instead divided into three de facto regions. Broadly, Uganda and aligned rebel groups controlled the north, Rwanda and its aligned rebel groups controlled the east, and Kabila and his allies controlled a southern strip running from Kinshasa to Katanga. Each plundered their territory, taxing civilians and extracting its natural wealth. Hundreds of thousands were displaced by the violence. The state apparatus, including vital healthcare, water, and sanitation services, collapsed. An International Rescue Committee survey estimates that by 2002 3.3 million people had died, mostly of disease and hunger. As much as 1.6 per cent had died of violence in the survey period. In 1999 the Lusaka Agreement led to the deployment of an eventually 17,000-strong UN mission (MONUC) but the ceasefire was ignored. In 2001 Laurent Kabila was assassinated by one of his bodyguards and his son, Joseph Kabila, was installed in his stead. Finally in December 2002 a 'Global All Inclusive Agreement' was signed under which a transitional power-sharing government was to be installed and a new constitution and national elections were to be prepared. Although the violence diminishes, it does not stop, least of all in the east.

Event C8: 2002 onwards: Warlordism in Eastern Congo

Civilians continued to be caught between various rebel groups and government forces in eastern Congo. Following the signing of the Global All Inclusive Agreement in 2002 to end the war, the principal armed rebel groups agreed either to demobilize or to integrate into the new national army. However, rebel factions that refused to join emerged in the east and chose to remain warlords. The most important of these was the North Kivu group led by Laurent Nkunda and aided by Rwanda. It stated it would not disarm while the fugitive and mainly Hutu rebel group, the Democratic Forces for the Liberation of Rwanda (FDLR), remained at large and continued to threaten Congolese Tutsi, in particular an ethnic Tutsi subset, the Banyamulenge of South Kivu. The national army, FARDC, continued to battle Nkunda and was widely believed to collaborate with the FDLR against him. At the same time the integrated FARDC continued to suffer both from defections such as those of Mai Mai militia units and from ill-discipline with reports of its involvement in looting and rape. All of these groups continue to clash and Nkunda remains at large at the end of 2007. In another region, Ituri in north-eastern DRC, conflict ignited in 1999 between ethnic Lendu and Hema rebel groups over land. Uganda, whose troops controlled the territory played the role of both 'arsonist' and 'fireman'. The fighting quickly devolved into criminal predation on the civilian population. It is believed several thousand civilians from both groups were killed during this period. At the end of 2007, the Ituri-based rebel groups agreed to integrate into the national army. Amid these various conflicts, the UN mission, MONUC, attempted to remain neutral but its peacekeepers became targets themselves. Elections in 2006, which passed with little pre- or post-electoral violence, resulted in victory for Joseph Kabila over former MLC rebel leader Jean-Pierre Bemba. However, this has had only a marginal impact on violence in the east. Rebel groups, and their foreign sponsors, continue to prey on the population and extract the natural wealth of the territories they control. At the end of 2007, Ituri, North and South Kivu, and Katanga provinces remain insecure and massive displacement, in the order of hundreds of thousands of people, continues. An International Rescue Committee survey in 2004 estimated 3.9 million have perished since 1998. Two per cent of all deaths in the survey period were the result of violence.

III. BURUNDI

Event B1: 1965: Transition to Independence: Political Assassinations

A failed Hutu coup and Hutu attacks on Tutsi civilians led to reprisal attacks against Hutu civilians by Tutsi elements of the army and a youth militia. In the run-up to independence in 1962, Burundi held national elections in September 1961 contested between two rival groups of traditional princes (ganwa): the Bezi, represented by the UPRONA party, and the Batare, represented by the Christian Democrat Party (PDC). Louis Rwagasore, leader of the UPRONA party, won only to be murdered a few weeks later by a PDC-hired assassin. In the ensuing leadership crisis the main political cleavage evolved from a Bezi–Batare ganwa rivalry into a Hutu–Tutsi ethnic antipathy within the UPRONA party. Burundi's traditional monarch, Mwami Mwambutsa—historically popular among both Hutu and Tutsi—resumed a governing role and called for legislative elections in May 1965 after the Hutu Prime Minister he appointed, Pierre Ngendandumwe, was also assassinated three days into his office. Although Hutu won a majority, the Mwami instead appointed a ganwa, Léopold Biha, as Prime Minister. As a result a small group of Hutu army officers and gendarmes shot Biha (albeit not fatally) in the Mwami's Royal compound only to be stopped by Tutsi army officers led by Captain Micombero. At the same time Hutu mobs in the northern province of Muramvya mistakenly believed the Tutsi had turned against the Mwami and attacked Tutsi civilians. This resulted in reprisals by the army and radical UPRONA youth wing, the Jeunesse Révolutionnaire Rwagasore (JRR), in which an estimated 5,000 Hutu civilians were killed.[14] The Biha attack also resulted in a purge of Hutu soldiers, gendarmes, and politicians, leaving the security forces exclusively within Tutsi control. The Mwami left the country and in November 1966 the young Tutsi Hima military officer Michel Micombero seized power from the Mwami's appointed regent, Ndizeye, to become the President of Burundi's First Republic.

Event B2: 1972: Selective Genocide of Hutu Elite

A Hutu insurrection resulted in the army and youth militia committing reprisal genocidal violence against Hutu elites across the country. Following his coup, President Micombero moved to make Burundi's First Republic a Tutsi ethnocracy. Claiming a conspiracy to overthrow the government, Micombero purged senior Hutu politicians and army officers in 1969. Then in 1971 a rival Tutsi group, the high-status Banyaruguru from Muramvya province, was politically neutralized in a series of show trials. It was in this context that on 29 April 1972 an organized Hutu insurrection arose to challenge Micombero's authoritarian and ethnocentric regime. The insurgents orchestrated a simultaneous attack in the capital Bujumbura and in Rumonge, southern Burundi. The Tutsi-dominant army quickly suppressed the Bujumbura attack—which involved only 40–60 insurgents—but the Rumonge attack, comprising 300–500 rebels, killed 1000–2000 Tutsi civilians before it was stopped on 5 May. The army massacred tens of thousands of Hutu in its counterinsurgency in the rebellious region. In the first week in the capital senior Hutu

---

[14] R. Lemarchand, *Burundi: Ethnic Conflict and Genocide* (Washington, DC/Cambridge: Woodrow Wilson Center Press, Cambridge University Press, 1996), 72.

politicians, civil servants, and army officers were arrested on suspicion of collaboration and then executed. Then after 5 May, the army with the radical UPRONA youth wing, the JRR, escalated the violence and began to massacre systematically Hutu elites across the country. State employees, teachers, businessmen, professionals, university students, and high school students all became victims. The Tutsi civilian population was mobilized to kill as well, though the extent of its participation and the degree to which it was willingly complicit are unclear. The total number of Hutu killed remains uncertain but one estimate places the casualty count at between 100,000 and 200,000 in the space of three months.[15] Having eliminated the Hutu counter-elite, Tutsi hegemony was assured for some time. This 'selective' genocide also led to a massive exodus of several hundred thousand Hutu refugees, most of whom sought safety in neighbouring Tanzania. The international community, while aware of the violence, did nothing to intervene and stop it.

Event B3: 1988: Hutu Insurrection

A spontaneous Hutu uprising led once again to reprisal violence from the Tutsi army against Hutu civilians. Although there had been two palace coups since the 1972 genocide, Tutsi control of the State continued. As with his two ousted predecessors, the President of the Third Republic, Pierre Buyoya, belonged to the Tutsi Hima subgroup and originated from Bururi in southern Burundi. After he seized power in 1987, however, Buyoya stated he wished to improve 'national unity'. In practice little altered to redress the Hutu–Tutsi power imbalance. In 1988 two communes in northern Burundi became the flashpoint for renewed ethnic violence. In response to rising ethnic tensions the gendarmerie was deployed to the region. However, this escalated tensions as Hutu feared a recurrence of 1972 and organized self-defence groups, manned barriers, and destroyed bridges. Hutu then attacked a local Tutsi businessman known for his role in 1972, which triggered a wave of violence leaving several hundred Tutsi dead. The army responded using helicopters and armoured cars to crush the uprising and killed an estimated 15,000 Hutu, causing about 50,000 Hutu to flee into Rwanda.[16]

Event B4: 1993: Assassination of Hutu President Ndadaye

The assassination of Burundi's first democratically elected Hutu Head of State resulted in localized Hutu attacks on Tutsi civilians that were in turn brutally

---

[15] R. Lemarchand, *Burundi: Ethnic Conflict and genocide* (Washington, DC/Cambridge: Woodrow Wilson Center Press, Cambridge University Press, 1996), 100.

[16] See R. Lemarchand, 'Burundi at a Crossroads', in G. M. Khadiagala (ed.), *Security Dynamics in Africa's Great Lakes Region* (Boulder, CO: Lynne Rienner, 2006), 126.

suppressed by the Tutsi army. In the aftermath of the 1988 violence, President Buyoya, a Tutsi, continued his quest for 'national unity'. In March 1993 a new constitution was adopted that permitted multipartyism. National elections held in June 1993 resulted in victory for the mainly Hutu FRODEBU party. In a historic moment Melchior Ndadaye, a Hutu, became Burundi's new President. However, on 21 October 1993 low-ranking Tutsi soldiers assassinated Ndadaye (though a UN Commission suggested the army's senior command was complicit). In response FRODEBU Hutu activists took hostage Tutsi men, executed them, and then went on to massacre Tutsi women and children. On the same day the army moved out to rescue the Tutsi survivors and killed Hutu civilians wherever it encountered them. An estimated 30–100,000 Hutu and Tutsi civilians were killed in this way. Several hundred thousand Hutu fled into Rwanda.

Event B5: 1993–2006: Burundian Civil War

Ndadaye's assassination led to a multifronted civil war between various Hutu rebel groups and the Tutsi army in which both Hutu and Tutsi civilians were targeted. Following the short-lived coup in 1993, Hutu rebel attacks gradually increased and Burundi slid into civil war. The sudden influx of Hutu refugees in 1994 from Rwanda's genocide aggravated this. In 1996 Pierre Buyoya seized power a second time in order to restore order but the violence continued to escalate. The army, acting increasingly independently of the civilian government, implemented brutal counter-insurgency measures. Notably it forcibly moved civilians into displacement camps where harsh conditions caused a humanitarian crisis. Hutu rebel groups engaged in a guerrilla war with the Tutsi army. They rarely confronted each other directly and instead civilians were the main victims of the violence. The Tutsi army commited multiple atrocities against Hutu civilians and Hutu rebels targeted civilians, both Tutsi and Hutu collaborators. The second Congo war in 1998 interweaves itself with the violence in Burundi. It caused rebel groups to factionalize and encouraged cross-border alliances. A peace process for Burundi eventually led to the Arusha Accord in 2000. It stipulated a ceasefire and a three-year transition. Although many parties signed on, the two main rebel groups, the CNDD-FDD and the Palipehutu-FNL, refused to do so and the war continued. Nonetheless in a historic moment at the end of the transition in 2003, Buyoya, a Tutsi, stepped down as President in favour of Ndayizeye, a Hutu. Continued peace talks with the two outstanding rebel groups eventually brought the CNDD-FDD into the government in 2005. The Palipehutu-FNL agreed to lay down its weapons in 2006. To date a very rough estimate is that 300,000 Hutu and Tutsi have been killed as a result of violence in the civil war.[17]

---

[17] Ibid. 41.

IV. RWANDA

Event R1: 1959–62: Hutu Revolution

Before independence, a short burst of mainly anti-Tutsi violence set in motion a series of events that led to a revolution overthrowing the Tutsi monarchy. Colonial Belgium had ruled Rwanda indirectly by reinforcing the rule of a Tutsi minority elite over the country's Hutu majority. As independence approached, however, Belgium co-sponsored with the Church a Hutu counter-elite. Ethnic tensions arose for control of the post-independence state. The trigger for violence was an attack on a Hutu political leader that provoked a rapid backlash against Tutsi across the country, leaving 200 dead. It also started a Tutsi exodus into Tanzania, Burundi, the DRC, and Uganda that reached 600,000 by 1973. In 1962 Rwanda officially became a Republic and Gregoire Kayibanda its first Hutu head of state.

Event R2: 1962–4: Tutsi Insurgent Attacks and Massacres

Tutsi exiled in Burundi by the Hutu revolution launched two attacks on Rwanda in 1962 and 1963–4 that resulted in government-sponsored massacres of Tutsi civilians. These were part of a wider series of insurgent attacks made between 1962 and 1967 to overthrow the fledgling Hutu Republic, and they left an estimated 6–13,000 dead.[18] The 1963–4 attack nearly reached the capital, Kigali, before it was repulsed by the Rwandan army. The government then organized local self-defence committees to defend against the enemy but in practice they targeted Tutsi civilians in reprisal.

Event R3: 1973: Ethnic Purges and Transition to Second Hutu Republic

The over-representation of Tutsi in educational establishments became the rationale for popular ethnic purges. Ethnic tensions were high in the wake of the Hutu genocide in Burundi the year earlier. They crystallized in January 1973 when Hutu students marched and demanded the expulsion of Tutsi students from secondary schools and the university to redress the ethnic imbalance. The purges spread to the public and private sectors and several dozen Tutsi were killed. Hutu army officers from northern Rwanda exploited the instability to overthrow the regime

---

[18] R. Lemarchand, *Rwanda and Burundi* (London: Pall Mall Press, 1970), 216, 219. See also S. Straus, *The Order of Genocide: Race, Power, and War in Rwanda* (Ithaca/London: Cornell University Press, 2006), 186.

dominated by Hutu from the centre and south of the country. General Juvénal Habyarimana became president of the Second Republic.

Event R4: 1990–4: Rwandan Civil War

Tutsi civilians were massacred in response to attacks by the mainly Tutsi rebel group, the RPF. In October 1990 the RPF, composed mostly of descendants of Tutsi exiles from the 1959 Hutu revolution, invaded Rwanda from across the Ugandan border. A guerrilla war ensued. The Rwandan government targeted its own Tutsi civilians in reprisal, accusing them of collaboration with the rebels. It arrested 13,000 Tutsi immediately after the initial attack in 1990 and tortured and killed several dozen. An estimated 2,000 more were killed in several massacres in northern and central Rwanda in which local authorities incited Hutu mobs to attack Tutsi civilians in response to alleged enemy threats.

Event R5: 1994: Rwandan Genocide

The assassination of Rwanda's Hutu president, Juvénal Habyarimana, triggered a nationwide extermination campaign that principally targeted the Tutsi ethnic group in its entirety. Since 1973 Habyarimana and a small Hutu elite from the north of the country had monopolized power to the exclusion of Tutsi and Hutu from other regions. The confluence of the start of a civil war in 1990 and the advent of multipartyism in 1991 together seriously threatened the power of the regime. The rebel RPF was able to capture and hold ground and the newly-created political parties were able to mobilize popular support against the Habyarimana government. In 1993 peace talks in Arusha yielded a power-sharing agreement between President Habyarimana, the mainly Tutsi rebel RPF, and the mainly south-central Hutu opposition parties. However, this arrangement divided the ruling Hutu elite and a hardliner group opposed to sharing power emerged. When Habyarimana's plane was shot down on 6 April 1994, it was widely assumed within Rwanda that the rebel RPF was responsible. The hardliner minority immediately took the opportunity to seize control of the state. It unleashed the Hutu-dominant army and youth militia against Tutsi civilians and moderate Hutu. In rural areas local authorities followed the lead of the new extremist central government and mobilized the Hutu civilian population to 'defend itself' against the Tutsi enemy. Those local authorities that resisted either were replaced or eventually gave in to the genocidal project. Many ordinary civilians faced the same choice. Over the next 101 days attack groups composed in the main of Hutu civilians hunted down Tutsi civilians—men, women, and children often known to them personally. The slaughter continued until the rebel RPF finally won the war and pushed the extremist government and armed forces over the border into the DRC. About two million ordinary Hutu followed them, creating a massive humanitarian crisis in the refugee camps established in Eastern Congo.

Event R6: 1997–8: North-west Insurgency

In the course of this insurgency rebels killed both Tutsi civilians and Hutu who did not cooperate while government forces in turn targeted Hutu civilians who collaborated with the insurgents. Following their defeat in the civil war in 1994 the Hutu army and militia regrouped in Eastern Congo and continued low-intensity attacks against RPF-controlled Rwanda. In 1997 they escalated their insurgency in the north-west and directly engaged RPF forces. They continued attacks on Tutsi civilians and initially enjoyed the support of the Hutu population—especially as certain RPF commanders punished Hutu civilians in reprisal for insurgent attacks. However, as RPF counter-propaganda took effect, the insurgents began to target uncooperative Hutu as well. The start of the Second Congo War in 1998 dampened the insurgency as Rwanda pushed its troops west in the DRC towards Kinshasa.

FURTHER READING

Amnesty International, *Human rights in Uganda: Report* (London: Amnesty International, 1978).

Hesselbein, G., *The Rise and Decline of the Congolese State: An Analytic Narrative on State-Making*, Crisis States Working Papers, DESTIN (London: London School of Economics, 2007).

International Crisis Group, *Congo at War: A Briefing on the Internal and External Players in the Central African Conflict* (Nairobi/Brussels: International Crisis Group, 1998).

Kasozi, A. B. K., N. Musisi, et al., *The Social Origins of Violence in Uganda, 1964–1985* (Montreal/Buffalo: McGill-Queen's University Press, 1994).

Lemarchand, R., *Burundi: Ethnic Conflict and Genocide* (Washington, DC/Cambridge: Woodrow Wilson Center Press/Cambridge University Press, 1996).

Mamdani, M., *When Victims Become Killers: Colonialism, Nativism, and the Genocide in Rwanda* (Princeton, NJ: Princeton University Press, 2001).

Nzongola-Ntalaja, G., *The Congo from Leopold to Kabila : A People's History* (London: Zed Books, 2002).

Prunier, G., *The Rwanda Crisis: History of a Genocide* (Kampala, Uganda: Fountain, 1999).

Straus, S., *The Order of Genocide: Race, Power, and War in Rwanda* (Ithaca, NY/London: Cornell University Press, 2006).

Turner, T., *The Congo Wars: Conflict, Myth, and Reality* (London: Zed, 2007).

Young, C., and T. Turner, *The Rise and Decline of the Zairian State* (Madison/London: University of Wisconsin Press, 1985).

PART V

THE CONTEMPORARY WORLD: RULES AND RESPONSES

CHAPTER 28

···

THE UNITED NATIONS, THE COLD WAR, AND ITS LEGACY

···

GERD HANKEL

ACCORDING to the Preamble of the Charter of the United Nations, the member states of this organization resolved 'to save succeeding generations from the scourge of war' as well as to act in a way that demonstrates 'faith in fundamental human rights, in the dignity and worth of the human person'. This was the spirit in which the UN General Assembly passed the Convention on the Prevention and Punishment of the Crime of Genocide on 9 December 1948 and adopted and proclaimed the Universal Declaration of Human Rights on 10 December 1948.

As demonstrated by the emergence and consolidation of the cold war, the reality of the situation was very different. The two superpowers pursued their own agendas based on their respective power politics (*Machtpolitik*) and the other states became trapped in block thinking. War and mass crime were only perceived and condemned as such within the relevant camps if their members could hold their ideological opponents responsible. For the most part, the United Nations watched helplessly from the sidelines. The states were meticulous in their efforts to ensure that the United Nations was not allocated any powers that could have led to any appreciable infringement of their sovereignty. The significant extent to which this broad understanding of sovereignty had taken hold is demonstrated by the difficulties faced by the United Nations since the end of the cold war when it has tried to adopt an active peace and security policy and enforce basic human rights.

INSTITUTIONAL HISTORY AND ARRANGEMENTS

The Second World War had a far greater influence on the world order established in its aftermath than its predecessor, i.e. the First World War. The avoidance of mass crimes, genocide, and violent imperial expansionism necessitated the adoption of measures that, in the interests of humanity, would eliminate threats even remotely comparable to those that Germany and its allies posed at the time. As in the case of the First World War, the initiative was once again taken by the USA. Initially, it only had plans for an alliance between the two leading 'English-speaking' democracies, i.e., the USA and Great Britain, which would be solely responsible for an international police force for world peace to be deployed in the case of an emergency. Following the German attack on the Soviet Union on 22 June 1941 and the Japanese attack on Pearl Harbor on 7 December 1941, however, they both aspired to establish a wider coalition of states. The Soviet Union and China were included in the alliance and they, in turn, brought their own proposals to the table. By the Yalta Conference in spring 1945, the preparations for the establishment of the new alliance, for which the USA still held overall responsibility, had already reached a stage where they could be presented as a concrete plan: 'We are resolved upon the earliest possible establishment with our allies of a general international organization to maintain peace and security. We believe that this is essential both to prevent aggression and to remove the political, economic, and social causes of war through the close and continuing collaboration of all peace-loving peoples.'[1]

The founding conference of the United Nations took place in San Francisco from 25 April to 26 June 1945. The Charter of the United Nations came into force on 24 October 1945. With its 111 articles, it is around four times longer than the Covenant of the League of Nations, the influence of which is clearly evident in a number of points. Nation-states were at the centre of the new international system, as had been the case at the time of the League of Nations. The notion of cooperation was still relatively novel and was repeatedly trumped by power politics; in the event of an external threat, the states—either individually or as an alliance—were clearly the main actors in the international system. This had already been demonstrated in the

---

[1] Quoted in Wilhelm G. Grewe and Daniel Erasmus Khan, 'History', in Bruno Simma (ed.), *The Charter of the United Nations: A Commentary*, 2nd edn, vol. i (Munich: C. H. Beck, 2002), 7.

aftermath of the First World War and would be confirmed again after the Second, but with two additional developments. First, the victors' alliance would outlast the war. It was to become the guarantor of a future peace, hence the name of the new organization, the United Nations, which refers to a declaration made by nations in early 1942[2] and commemorates the united front adopted in the fight against military aggression. Second, as already announced in Yalta, the new organization would help to eliminate the causes of the threat to peace and war, i.e., poverty, injustice, and oppression.

According to the wording of the Charter of the United Nations, the responsibility for world peace lies with the Security Council. Article 24, subsection 1 of the Charter states that 'In order to ensure prompt and effective action by the United Nations, its Members confer on the Security Council primary responsibility for the maintenance of international peace and security, and agree that in carrying out its duties under this responsibility the Security Council acts on their behalf.' Compared with the complicated procedure that prevailed between the Council and Assembly during the League of Nations era, this stipulation amounts to a clear allocation of powers. However, it does not yet explain how this 'international peace and security' should actually function. The only certainty was that intervention in the area of state sovereignty had to be allowed for this purpose. Without the limitation of state freedom of action, which was understood as an expression of sovereignty, there could be no international peace plan based on the principle of mutual accommodation. For this reason, Article 25 of the United Nations Charter states that the decisions of the Security Council are binding on all UN Member States. For the same reason, two articles later there is another provision that initially appears to contradict the above statement, but ultimately constitutes the precondition for its implementation. For, as demonstrated by the League of Nations, without the involvement of the great powers an international peace system is doomed to failure. Thus Article 27, subsection 3 of the Charter states that decisions of the Security Council on matters that are not merely procedural, i.e., questions concerning peace and international security in general, require the agreement of all five permanent members of the Security Council—France was included in this group at the San Francisco conference. In other words, it should not be possible for any decision to be taken that is incapable of gaining the support of the permanent members of the Security Council or, based on the less rigid variant now in force, not acceptable enough to enable them to abstain from voting, i.e., to waive their right of veto.

Thus the great powers established a privileged position for themselves. If this may be seen as the expression of a general balancing of power, it should not be forgotten that the main burden in the fight against the Axis powers was borne by

---

[2] The 'Declaration by United Nations' of 1.1.1942, ibid. 7.

Great Britain, her Dominions, the Soviet Union, and the USA, and that the political realities of the time were such that they only made long-term stability achievable through the establishment of a militarily strong centre of power.

What Article 2 of the UN Charter has to say in relation to the traditional rights of states and the idea of the new international order can be explained on the same predictable basis. It begins with a commitment to the 'sovereign equality' of the states (subsection 1), then refers to the obligation to engage in the peaceful settlement of disputes (subsection 3) and the prohibition on the use of interstate force (subsection 4), and ends with the prohibition on intervention in the essentially internal affairs of another state (subsection 7). It goes on to state that, based on its superior position, the Security Council alone is authorized to breach this principle of non-intervention. In accordance with Chapter VII of the Charter, it alone has the right to impose enforcement measures against a state in the event of a threat to or breach of the peace, or in the context of negotiations in association with an attack.

Given that they are not included in the list provided in Article 2, the elimination of poverty, injustice, and repression as the possible causes of new conflicts are not specified as principles of the UN. According to Article 1, subsection 3, the espousal of these causes is merely among the purposes of the organization; the use of the qualification 'merely' here may be explained by the lack of legal quality of these purposes. Unlike the principles listed in Article 2, they do not stipulate any rights and obligations but an outcome that should—but does not have to—be achieved. According to Article 1, subsection 3, the UN aims 'to achieve international cooper-ation in solving international problems of an economic, social, or humanitarian character and in promoting and encouraging respect for human rights and for fundamental freedoms for all without distinction as to race, sex, language, or religion'. This is referred to again and formulated in partly identical terms in Article 55 where it is also expressly stated that such conditions should give rise to 'peaceful and friendly relations among nations based on respect for the principle of equal rights and self-determination of peoples'.

Thus, it may be observed that human rights—if we adopt this term as a general concept denoting a minimum level of social and economic participation—were not allocated a particularly prominent position in the UN Charter. The Soviet Union saw no link between human rights and international security, Great Britain feared detrimental impacts on the stability of the Commonwealth because rhetoric about human rights conflicted with its racist colonialism, and the attitudes of many other states were also characterized by cautious reticence in this regard. Values relating to states, such as equality and non-intervention, took priority, and consid-eration of the basic rights that affect the lives of human beings was relegated to a secondary position; moreover, because these rights were not based on any legal obligation, compliance was dependent on the voluntary action of the individual states. The peace, for which the UN stood, was, therefore, primarily a negative peace, characterized by the absence of war. The additional task of establishing a positive peace, understood as the establishment of the preconditions that would make the outbreak of wars less likely due to their ethical unacceptability or unreasonableness, came second and by some distance.

THE COLLAPSE OF THE WAR COALITION, THE BIPOLAR DIVISION OF THE WORLD, AND THE RECENT ACCEPTANCE OF MILITARY FORCE

The gap between the initial aspirations of the UN and subsequent reality was a sizeable one. The signs indicating the collapse of the war coalition were already apparent at the foundation of the United Nations. They hinged on the USA's nuclear weapons project, which initially stood for the West's distrust of Soviet occupation policy in Central and Eastern Europe. The Soviet Union responded with a 'two-camp theory', i.e., involving the 'imperialistic-antidemocratic' Western camp and the 'anti-imperialistic-democratic' Eastern camp. The two camps stood in irreconcilable opposition. Predicting subsequent developments, George Kennan, the 'inventor' of containment policy, remarked in 1946 that, for Moscow, the UN was not a mechanism for establishing a stable world order but merely an arena in which states could pursue their own objectives for the maximum possible success. The fact that the USA adopted a very similar policy can be seen in its voting behaviour in the UN Security Council. While the Soviet Union used its veto on 115 occasions up to 1989, the USA did so in 69 cases (Great Britain in 30 cases, France in 18, and China in 3). Security policy was mainly practised outside of the UN. Just three years after the foundation of the UN, the Western powers formed an alliance in NATO that curtailed the security thinking of the original collective to its own sphere of influence. This development was mirrored a short time later on the East-bloc side with the establishment of the Warsaw Pact. Instead of one new global security system, there were now two, a situation that prevailed until the end of the military-political bipolarity. The Security Council imposed military sanctions on a state on just one occasion—i.e., Korea in 1950, at the beginning of the war there, and even this was not a real exception; the legality of this move was constantly contested by the Soviet Union and may be seen as a component of the American campaign against communism rather than an expression of a collective feeling of responsibility.

What subsequently happened in the relevant spheres of influence was far more fatal than the collapse of the collective security system. War after war was fought: wars of independence, wars of aggression and defence, proxy wars, civil wars, in which both civilians and combatants were the target of the most heinous of war crimes and crimes against humanity. Dictatorships were overthrown and replaced by new ones. The principles of the sovereign equality of states and non-intervention in the internal affairs of a state proved extremely useful instruments, particularly in cases involving the arbitrary extension of the borders of the internal *domaine réservé* of a state.

The number of war victims from the cold war period is estimated at over 20 million, with just one per cent, i.e., 200,000, originating from the northern hemisphere. All of the others died in the numerous armed conflicts that shook the southern hemisphere. Beyond the direct triggers of unresolved border issues, regional power ambitions, and ethnic and religious tension, in almost all of these conflicts the interests of the superpowers had a catalytic effect by creating or restricting action space for local actors, by intensifying, extending, and internationalizing existing conflicts, and even by curtailing them and establishing diplomatic solutions. The conflicts resembled those in Korea, Hungary, Vietnam, and Afghanistan, in which the Soviet Union or the USA intervened, those in the Congo and Angola where they aimed to consolidate or develop their positions through local warring parties—in other words, allowed the latter to fight on their behalf—or, finally in particular, those in the Latin American states, in which, in accordance with the Monroe Doctrine, suspicious governments were destabilized and replaced with regimes which complied with the wishes of the USA.[3]

A typical but less well known case in this regard is that of Guatemala where the democratically elected president, Jacobo Arbenz Guzmán, was overthrown in 1954. Guzmán had come to the attention of the USA through reforms that proposed inter alia the expropriation of the American United Fruit Company and through the purchase of weapons in the East bloc. The USA reacted with a typical CIA counter-insurgency operation called 'Operation Success' and replaced the Guzmán government with a politically palatable military dictatorship. This coup marked the beginning of a development that culminated in the rule of an increasingly oppressive regime which suspected the country's Indian majority of general support for a guerrilla movement that had emerged in response to the political repression and economic exploitation in the country. The war, which involved the repeated and targeted massacre of the Maya people, lasted a good three decades (1954–86). The dictatorial regime only managed to stay in power with the help of intensive US support. Military aid to the tune of hundreds of millions of dollars was paid and 'experts' sent to the country to train and arm the Guatemalan army and police. By the time the violence had subsided in the late 1980s and a peace agreement between the army commanders and guerrilla leadership was signed in 1996, over 200,000 people had lost their lives. According to the report compiled by the truth

---

[3] Noam Chomsky, *World Orders, Old and New* (London: Pluto Press, 1997), 37–44.

commission (*Comisión para el Esclarecimiento Histórico*) established in 1999, the military was responsible for ninety-three per cent of the approximately 42,000 deaths investigated. Moreover, genocidal acts were perpetrated against the Maya in at least four of the country's regions. The USA bore particular responsibility for this development. It and a series of private American companies exerted pressure to ensure the perpetuation of the country's archaic and unjust socio-economic order. It is known to have been informed about the massacres and atrocities but did nothing to prevent them.[4]

From this perspective, and considering the situation in other Latin American countries at the time of the cold war, the fact that 'violence [was] exacerbated by external factors', and that action motivated by a simplistic friend or foe philosophy on the part of the self-appointed democratic force for order in the north led to something 'known in Latin America as the National Security Doctrine', which actually means 'not defense against an external enemy, but a way to make the military establishment the masters of the game'.[5] Because the policy adopted by the Soviet Union at the time in its sphere of influence can be characterized in very similar terms—all that must be done is substitute 'communist' for 'capitalist' or 'imperialist', 'social worker' and 'trade unionist' for 'human rights activist' and 'dissident'—it is all the more astonishing that the blocs and their protagonists were able to reach something approaching a joint policy in the context of the UN.

In 1948, the Security Council decided for the first time to send an observer mission to monitor the ceasefire between Israel and its neighbours. Even if all that lay behind this action was a minimum common denominator, an emergency solution, so to speak (for there was and is no express legal basis for this action in the Charter), an attempt could be made to stabilize the situation and thus contribute to the establishment of a political solution through the demonstration of international presence. Because the conflicting parties had to agree to the mission and the use of violence on the part of the interveners was only authorized in the case of self defence,[6] this decision was less than a collectively borne—necessarily—armed attempt at conflict resolution from the outside. However, it was also more than idle fence-sitting and spectating as a result of the self-blockade in the Security Council. This was what mattered and was also the reason why other missions, to become known as 'blue helmet operations', were carried out and continue to be carried out to the present day.

---

[4] William A. Schabas, *Genocide in International Law* (Cambridge: Cambridge University Press, 2000), 168–9; on the report of the Guatemalan Truth Commission, http://www.juridicas.unam.mx/publica/librev/rev/boletin/cont/106/art/art6.pdf

[5] According to a report of the Colombian Human Rights Committee, quoted by Chomsky, *World Orders, Old and New*, 61.

[6] Moreover, the intervention troop had to be neutral and its deployment implemented on a voluntary basis.

Likewise in 1948, on 9 December, the UN General Assembly adopted the Convention on the Prevention and Punishment of the Crime of Genocide and, a day later on 10 December, it adopted the Universal Declaration of Human Rights. The lessons of the Second World War were to be drawn in both the Convention with its legally binding basis and the non-legally binding Declaration. Based on their normative requirements, the two instruments were also intended to represent the starting point and objective of the task set out for the General Assembly in accordance with Article 13 of the Charter. This task, i.e., 'promoting international cooperation' and the codification of international law, only assumed its true significance with the enlargement of the UN to include states in the southern hemisphere. While it had only 51 Member States in 1945, by 1960 this number had increased to 100 and in 1975 it reached 145, most of which were Asian and African.

The extent to which the different economic interests of the new members and their demands for the fair distribution of goods and better development opportunities could be instrumentalized again for the purpose of the cold war emerged when it came to casting the requirements of the Declaration of Human Rights in legally binding form. The General Assembly only succeeded in passing the two corresponding covenants, i.e., the International Covenant on Civil and Political Rights and the International Covenant on Economic, Social and Cultural Rights, eighteen years after the adoption of the Declaration. And it would take another ten years for the two human rights covenants to come into force in 1976. A few years earlier, in a resolution passed in October 1970,[7] the General Assembly supported individual provisions of the UN Charter and interpreted them in the light of past experience and desirable future developments. In this declaration, it named seven basic principles, including the duty of cooperation (for example, in the promotion of human rights and basic freedoms and in the abolition of all forms of racial discrimination and religious intolerance) and the principle of equal rights and self-determination of peoples. Finally, in 1984, the General Assembly adopted a Convention on the elimination of torture, i.e., the Convention against Torture and Other Cruel, Inhuman or Degrading Treatment or Punishment.

In order to protect against the violation of basic human rights, such as the right to life and bodily integrity, in addition to their binding prohibition, the General Assembly was also involved in making a universally observed obligation of the legal institution of the *jus cogens* through one of its ancillary bodies, the International Law Commission.[8] No state is to be allowed to violate 'compelling law'. It protected values that, in the view of the international community, were so essential that all of

---

[7] Resolution 2625 (XXV) of 24 October 1970 is called the 'Declaration on Principles of International Law Concerning Friendly Relations and Co-operation among States in Accordance with the Charter of the United Nations'.

[8] Through the inclusion of a *jus cogens* regulation in the Vienna Convention on the Law of Treaties between States (Article 53) of 1969, which came into force in 1980 and enjoys almost universal acceptance today.

their members were obliged to observe them. This purpose was also served by a second obligation, the *erga omnes* obligation.[9] According to this principle, legally accepted rights must be protected 'towards all', the idea behind it being that the normative aggregation of international law could no longer permit the serious violation of the latter, as otherwise the entire structure of international law would be permanently devastated, ultimately to the disadvantage of all states. For any body of law that can be violated without consequence corrodes and clears the way for the lethal political voluntarism of the states.

All in all, this sounds very positive and the UN, under whose auspices the task of codification proceeded, clearly made a considerable contribution in this regard. However, even an optimistic view of these developments cannot ignore the gap that existed between aspirations and reality in those years. There is no doubt that the Soviet Union and the USA attempted to impose their own conflict resolution rather than rely on the public institutions of the UN and other international institutions. The law of the UN Charter was all too often an ephemeral and negligible force in the face of the considerations of power politics.

THE LEGACY OF THE COLD WAR IN RELATION TO THE PROTECTION OF HUMAN RIGHTS

The cold war is now history. The Soviet Union collapsed and the political-military bipolarity disappeared along with it. As the only remaining superpower, the USA stressed the power of multilateralism and spoke of a new world order to be achieved with the participation of as many states as possible.

As we know—and not just since the second Iraq War—this is not quite how things have unfolded. However, the outcome of this development is contradictory. The fact that human rights has penetrated far onto the international political agenda cannot be ignored. The discourse surrounding human rights intensified after the end of the East–West conflict, in particular and, indeed, to the extent that apart from a few almost grotesque exceptions, such as North Korea and Myanmar (Burma), no state now adopts an anti-human rights position. The era in which the universal validity of human rights and basic freedom was disputed and their— entirely extant—Western form was held up against an Asiatic or Arab value system appeared to be over. Thus, the heads of state and government joyously declared at

---

[9] Developed in 1970 by the International Court of Justice in the *Barcelona Traction* case, cf. ICJ Reports 1970, here at 32, No. 33.

the UN Summit in 2005: 'We reaffirm that all human rights are universal, indivisible, interrelated, interdependent and mutually reinforcing'.[10]

Even if its semantic content were stretched to the limit, nobody who reads this sentence could conceive that a single leader or senior politician exists in the world who is unable to recite the list of main human rights. The participants of the World Summit 'corroborate' their validity; there is virtually no UN report in which they are not mentioned; working groups on the most wide-ranging topics refer to them; numerous UN projects, backed by non-governmental organizations, have been supporting them expressly in their local activity reports and brochures for years.

Yet the scale of the alternative reality, which can be accessed very quickly by perusing the annual reports of Amnesty International or Human Rights Watch, astounds. Amnesty International regularly reports of human rights violations in dozens of countries, of the most heinous of crimes ranging from murder, kidnapping, and torture to the restriction of freedom of opinion and the freedom of the press, which are also frequently accompanied by random imprisonment and the use of physical force. Human Rights Watch also lists numerous countries in which the worst cases of massive and systematic repression are recorded every year.

All of this takes place, moreover, in the presence of a series of complaint and notification procedures and sanctions, with which human rights violations can be censured and even prosecuted under criminal law. Enforcement procedures specified in the relevant conventions or their associated optional protocols exist. These include, first, the European Court of Human Rights, the Inter-American Court of Human Rights, and the African Court on Human and Peoples' Rights. In addition, the International Convention on Civil and Political Rights and its First Optional Protocol institute a Human Rights Committee and the Convention against Torture led to the establishment of a Committee against Torture (Articles 28 and 17). Finally, the mechanisms known as 1503 and 1235 procedures based on resolutions of the UN Economic and Social Council, for which the UN Human Rights Council is responsible, can also be mentioned here. None of these institutions can, however, resort to coercive means, their only option being persuasion or diplomatic pressure, which, however, are not easy to exercise. For although the violations are often fundamental in nature, they are not always part of a large-scale or systematic process; thus the international attention they attract is smaller in scope or more fleeting. Therefore, the efficiency of these procedures is largely dependent on the discernment capacity and willingness to cooperate of the states; it is not just their detractors who describe them as the 'world's biggest wastepaper basket'.[11]

---

[10] Cf. 2005 World Summit Outcome, http://www.un-ngls.org/un-summit-FINAL-DOC.pdf, section 121.

[11] On this point, see Norman Paech and Gerhard Stuby, *Völkerrecht und Machtpolitik in den internationalen Beziehungen* (Hamburg: VSA-Verlag, 2001), 676.

The so-called principle of universal jurisdiction offers a far more promising approach. What this ultimately amounts to is that no state that violates fundamental human rights can invoke its sovereignty, because it does not protect people who have acted on the mandate of such a state against being held to account by the legal system of a different country. Such a situation arose with perpetrators of the Rwandan genocide in Belgium and members of the Argentinean military in Spain. Although the history of the principle of universal jurisdiction—it began with the fight against piracy, whose perpetrators were seen as 'enemies of humanity' (*hostes humani generis*)—shows that serious crimes based on a plan were also mainly thought of in this case, national law enforcement is often more flexible and quicker than international jurisdiction. On the other hand, as the examples show,[12] it is more susceptible to opportunistic considerations.

That leaves the International Criminal Court, which has been at work since 1 July 2002 and is responsible for the prosecution of the most serious crimes 'of international concern'.[13] According to the list provided by the Rome Statute, these crimes are genocide, crimes against humanity, war crimes, and the crime of aggression (which, however, remains to be defined). Although the Court has carried out investigations of four countries (Democratic Republic of the Congo, Darfur/Sudan, Uganda, Central African Republic) and issued arrest warrants against twelve suspects, the implementation of both of these measures is proving very difficult. States fear excessive intervention in their internal affairs and powerful states such as the USA, China, and Russia actually do almost everything in their power to sabotage or ignore the Court.[14]

Therefore, it is possible to see that, even in the case of extensive human rights violations, the existing instruments of complaint and sanction are limited in their effect. Without the willingness to cooperate on the part of the states and their actual partial renunciation of sovereignty, they run dry. Against this background in particular, it sends out a fatal signal when democracies that describe themselves as liberal fabricate highly sophisticated exceptions from basic human rights protection for the purpose of boosting their fights against the real or supposed enemies of their country or value system. Memories are triggered of the times when political reality forced all protestation to the sidelines in defiance of the UN. Power politics superceded international law and, as part of this process, nothing was subject to closer scrutiny as long as the direction was right and the political alliance was not at risk.

---

[12] See http://www.hrw.org/press/2003/08/belgium080103.htm; German authorities provided a particularly shameful example in recent years when they allowed the Uzbekistan interior minister, who allegedly bore prime responsibility for a massacre resulting in several hundred fatalities carried out in the Uzbek city of Andischan, to leave the country unchallenged despite the fact that charges had been filed against him. It may be assumed that the continued use of a Luftwaffe airbase in Uzbekistan was more important.

[13] According to the Preamble to the Rome Statute of the International Criminal Court. Cf. http://www.icc-cpi.int.

[14] See the chapter of Donald Bloxham and Devin Pendas in this volume.

THE LEGACY OF THE COLD WAR IN TERMS OF COLLECTIVE INTERNATIONAL SECURITY

The understanding of collective security at international level has undergone enormous change since the end of the cold war. For a long time, Article 39 of the UN Charter, which states 'The Security Council shall determine the existence of any threat to the peace, breach of the peace, or act of aggression' and decides the measures to be taken 'to maintain or restore international peace and security', was understood as though it only concerned relations between states and did not involve situations within states. As a result, in the resolutions on Rhodesia and South Africa in the 1960s and 1970s, the Security Council was at pains to avoid the vocabulary of Article 39 and to avoid mobilizing other aggravating factors. The internal situation of a state only came into the focus of the Security Council with the end of the East–West conflict when the number of interstate conflicts decreased and intrastate conflicts increased. This arose in a way reminiscent of the original perceived threat of interstate conflict. Thus, for example, the resolution of 1991 on the creation of an exclusion zone in north Iraq still stressed the risk that the large numbers of fleeing Kurds could represent for the stability of the neighbouring countries of Turkey and Iran, thus enabling China, which usually reacts extremely sensitively to sovereignty-based interventions, to abstain.[15]

This changed in the subsequent resolutions. The risk of transnational impacts was no longer seen as a necessary justification for sovereignty-based intervention; irrespective of whether it was caused by a despotic regime or civil war, it was sufficient that violence and terror prevailed against the population in a country. The development went even further. The re-classification of human rights violations or breaches of humanitarian international law to threats to international peace in the sense of Chapter VII of the Charter was often accompanied by the decision to adopt measures that should counteract the emergence of conflicts and thus actually come under Chapter VI of the Charter, which, however, does not grant any corresponding power of enforcement. As a result, it may be said that the Security Council extended its authority considerably in recent years and drove back state sovereignty in the same measure.

In concrete terms, this extension of authority is evidenced, first, in the increasing imposition of peaceful sanctions against states in accordance with Article 41 of the Charter as, in this way, targeted pressure can be exerted against both groups and individuals. The catalogue of measures imposed here ranges from the imposition of travel bans, the seizure of assets deposited abroad, and the imposition of economic sanctions—the effect of which is, however, highly

---

[15] See the Resolution of the UN Security Council S/RES/0688 (1991) of 5 April 1991.

questionable[16]—against aggressive regimes that are hostile to human rights to the establishment of criminal courts. Second, it is also evidenced by the increasing debate surrounding the threat and use of military force in accordance with Article 42 of the UN Charter, i.e., surrounding the risking of human life and—what often appears to assume greater importance—the provision of considerable financial resources. The fact that the UN peace missions have changed is reflected in this debate. Blue helmets are no longer blue helmets. The deployments of international contingents of soldiers, who are strictly neutral and armed only for self-defence, with the agreement of the conflicting parties were followed by a series of additional missions which differed considerably in terms of their purpose and scope. Today, these are divided into four generations or categories. The first two represent peace-keeping measures while third and fourth generation blue helmet deployments also incorporate peace-making measures, which do not exclude the use of military force for purposes other than self-defence (so-called 'robust peace-keeping') and can also involve the assumption of executive tasks. The consensus of the conflicting parties is not essential; crucial alone is the objective of the operation as formulated in the Security Council resolution. In most cases, e.g., the mission in the Democratic Republic of the Congo, it is specified with a general reference to Chapter VII of the UN Charter (restoration of world peace and security) and substantiated with intermediary objectives to be achieved using 'all necessary means'.[17] The example of the UN deployment in the Congo also shows, however, that the adoption of a Security Council resolution is one thing and its implementation another. The UN does not have its own armed forces, although this was actually planned according to the Charter (Article 43 refers to special agreements in which the states make armed forces available to the United Nations). It depends on its member states' willingness to make troops available to it. This is not easy as the latter's interests are often not driven by humanitarian urgency but by a logic of their own, in which humanitarian concern is merely one factor among many. The Permanent Members of the Security Council constitute no exception here—in contrast. Out of the 34,000 blue helmet soldiers originally requested by the UN Secretary-General, around 7,000 are authorized by the Security Council, of which only 4,000 are gradually sent to the war zone by the member states.[18]

[16] For example, Iraq was subject to trade sanctions for over ten years. The regime itself was not bothered by them; the victims were the many Iraqis, above all Iraqi children, who showed increasing signs of malnutrition and illness and died in their thousands due to the unavailability of suitable medicines. Cf. Ramsey Clark, 'Letter to the Security Council', in Adam Jones (ed.), *Genocide, War Crimes and The West: History and Complicity* (London/New York: ZED Books, 2004), 273–5.

[17] Cf. S/Res/1565 (2004), 1.10.2004 or, more recently, S/Res/1807 (2008), 31 March 2008.

[18] According to the former German General and Assistant UN Secretary-General Manfred Eisele in relation to the example of the protection zones in Bosnia-Herzegovina. Cf. *idem*, 'Blauhelme als Krisenmanager', in Sabine von Schorlemer (ed.), *Praxishandbuch UNO. Die Vereinten Nationen im Lichte globaler Herausforderungen* (Berlin/Heidelberg: Springer, 2003), 34.

How far the disinterest of individual states, political-diplomatic cowardice, or simply excessive need can go was demonstrated in April to June 1994 in Rwanda and in July 1995 in Srebrenica. Not only was the United Nations Assistance Mission for Rwanda not reinforced, soldiers were actually withdrawn from the mission in response to pressure from the sending states. A few hundred soldiers were supposed to be able to contribute to the 'immediate cessation of hostilities'[19] in a state that was in the process of descending into a delirium of violence. Despite all the evidence, the UN Security Council was still avoiding any reference to genocide a good three weeks after the beginning of the massacre as this would have obliged the states to intervene in accordance with Article I and VIII of the Convention on the Prevention and Punishment of the Crime of Genocide.[20] Operation Turquoise, which finally took place under French command and by UN mandate,[21] came too late (it began on 23 June). Moreover, it was tainted from the outset by the suspicion that France's involvement was not motivated purely by humanitarian concerns but also by its desire to salvage its African policy in the region.

When the international community failed again a year later in Srebrenica and did nothing to prevent the genocide of the Bosnian Muslims who had fled to the UN-designated 'safe zone', demands for a general admissibility of humanitarian intervention increased, i.e., including that implemented by a state or alliance of states without the authorization of the Security Council, based on the justification that speed is of the essence in such emergency situations. The discussion surrounding this interpretation of humanitarian intervention is not new. It took place as far back as the nineteenth century when Europe's great powers intervened in areas of the Ottoman Empire, claiming to want to assist persecuted Christians there.[22] This approach was also successful; at least in part, however, the interventions carried out using military means were volatile in terms of power politics and therefore usually regarded with scepticism or openly condemned by states not involved in the action. For this reason, in the League of Nations era, such intervention was supposed to be rendered impossible by a system established for the protection of minorities and the collective security provisions of the Covenant, albeit with limited success which, again, was the reason for the stricter regulation applied in the UN Charter, which, with the exception of self-defence (Article 51 of the UN Charter), grants the right of intervention exclusively to the Security Council. This left no scope for the admissibility of humanitarian intervention in the sense referred to above. Thus, in the past, states that took military

---

[19] See, for example, UN Security Council Resolution 912 of 21 April 1994.

[20] For the discussion of this obligation, see Schabas, *Genocide in International Law*, 447–52; Samatha Power, *'A Problem from Hell': America and the Age of Genocide* (London: Flamingo, 2003), 358–64.

[21] See UN Security Council Resolution 929 of 22 June 1994.

[22] See Donald Bloxham, *The Great Game of Genocide: Imperialism, Nationalism, and the Destruction of the Ottoman Armenians* (Oxford: Oxford University Press, 2005), 31–8.

action against other states—Vietnam against Pol Pot's Cambodia in 1978, Tanzania against Idi Amin's Uganda in 1979— did not refer to the appalling human rights situation in these countries in justification of their action but gave precedence to territorial conflicts (Vietnam) and the right of reprisal as retribution for illegal attacks (Tanzania). The same applies to East Pakistan (Bangladesh) where India justified its intervention in 1971 with the desire to alleviate the extensive suffering endured by the civil population as a result of the war with West Pakistan (Pakistan), although strategic reasons (military weakening of West Pakistan) also played an important role in its decision to intervene. Military action was not recognized as legal in any of these cases. As the International Court of Justice noted in its ruling on Nicaragua in 1986: 'In any event, while the United States might form its own appraisal of the situation as to the respect for human rights in Nicaragua, the use of force could not be the appropriate method to monitor or ensure such respect.'[23]

This was the legal situation when NATO started to bomb Serbia in the spring of 1999 without a corresponding Security Council resolution. Due to the certain imposition of the Russian veto, such a resolution could not be expected to be forthcoming and the intervention was self-mandated on the basis of the humanitarian aim of saving the Kosovo Albanians from expulsion and annihilation.

The threat later emerged as having been highly exaggerated and part of a strategy to make the war along with its one-sided support unavoidable and to achieve independence for Kosovo through the military and economic weakening of Serbia. However, the law of the Charter had been contravened and the UN had been manoeuvred into a position of inability to preserve the peace through carefully orchestrated pressure and the forceful assistance of interested states. In response, it did with due professionalism what tends to be done in such situations involving confrontation with failure: it commissioned an inventory to obtain information on the status of the UN peace missions, the ways in which they need to be improved, and, with express reference to the controversy surrounding the war in Kosovo, how the law of humanitarian intervention should be shaped using the existing instruments of international law.

The first report was published in summer 2000.[24] It clearly lists the weaknesses of previous and ongoing blue-helmet missions, first and foremost their inadequate personnel and financial resources, their frequently erroneous analysis and convoluted chain of command, and, finally, the unclear question of what would happen 'afterwards', i.e., the consolidation of the 'secured' or 'built' peace. The second report

---

[23] Cf. ICJ Reports 1986, p. 14–150 (p. 134). As stated in Article 59 of its Statute, the rulings of the ICJ are only binding on the parties involved and in respect of the particular case in question; however, its decisions and non-binding advisory opinions are viewed as highly significant statements on existing (or non-existing) law, in particular customary international law.

[24] Report of the Panel on United Nations Peace Operations (Brahimi-Report), A/55/305-S/2000/809.

appeared around a year later.[25] Entitled *The Responsibility to Protect*, it stresses, first, the role of state sovereignty as a factor in the international order and thus as a cornerstone of the UN Charter. It then lists criteria that should facilitate international reaction to severe and systematic human rights violations in a country—the examples provided include ethnic cleansing, genocide, and other forms of mass murder.

The first of the four criteria is the 'right intention'. This demands that the main objective of intervention must consist in the termination of human suffering. According to the second criterion, the intervention must be the 'last resort': sufficient reasons must support the assumption that other non-military measures have no prospect of success. Third, the military action must not exceed the scope required to re-establish human safety; thus actions must be based on 'proportional means'. Moreover, they must, fourth, support sufficient expectation that the consequences of the intervention will not be worse than non-intervention, i.e., 'reasonable prospects'.

The report stated that the Security Council should remain responsible for decisions concerning intervention. To ensure that its decision-making capacity is not crippled by the right of veto, the authors proposed a code of conduct, on which the five Permanent Members of the Security Council were to agree. The most important point in this code of conduct was that none of the permanent members would be allowed to adopt an anti-humanitarian position in a situation that directly involved the self-conception of humanity (as expressed in recognition of a minimum human rights standard). The use of the veto should not be admissible in this case. An exception would only be made—and this is where the concession to realpolitik comes into play—for cases in which a Permanent Member would see its own vital concerns as coming under threat if it refrained from using the veto.[26]

As already mentioned, the report was compiled in 2001. Two events then occurred that brought this expertly formulated conception of international collective responsibility back down to earth with a bang. First, the Iraq war, which was justified by the USA and the 'coalition of the willing' with the supposedly imminent threat to peace posed by the Iraqi regime and other factors, including the intolerable human rights situation in the country, began in 2003. A Security Council resolution empowering the USA and its coalition partners to undertake this action did not exist. Second, in early 2006, the UN Secretary-General's Special

---

[25] *The Responsibility to Protect* (Report of the International Commission on Intervention and State Sovereignty, December 2001). The report is based on a Canadian initiative which, however, saw itself as a contribution to the inventory desired by the UN.

[26] Section 6.21 of the report refers to 'constructive abstention'. If this cannot be reached, the Member States would be called on, as already occurred in 1950 in the case of the *Uniting for Peace* Resolution, to provide recommendations for the taking of action and thus increase the pressure on the Security Council. And if this also fails, regional organizations, which, according to Chapter VIII of the Charter, are responsible for the settlement of 'local disputes'. Cf. ibid. sections 6.28–6.35.

Envoy for Sudan finally reported that the situation in the province of Darfur remained critical. The UN's sanctions, which were far too weak anyway, had not even been implemented. The powers that be in Khartoum were making fun of the UN while the expulsions and mass slaughter continued.[27]

Thus, here it was again, the gap between aspiration and reality. On the one hand, proposals for a more efficient peace security system are formulated and acknowledged and supported by the UN bodies, and, on the other hand, reasons or, to be more accurate, pretexts are found which reveal the responsibility of the states arising from the UN Charter to be nothing more than rhetoric. Intervention is instigated when it reflects economic and power-state interests; otherwise, it is not. In the latter case, the crimes perpetrated are merely, and only occasionally, deemed 'genocidal acts' and not crimes of genocide which, as everybody knows, make the call for intervention impossible to ignore.[28] However, the states appear to be able to live with 'genocidal acts', as though, depending on the label attached to the murder of some 300,000 people, the crime assumes a different dimension and the otherwise much invoked criterion of collective responsibility or security evaporates.

CONCLUSION: THE DUAL NATURE OF THE COLD WAR LEGACY

It could be said that no progress worth mentioning has been made in international law since the end of the cold war. It remains contradictory and subordinate to state interests, in particular where the prevention and punishment of mass crimes is concerned.

However, this is just one side of the story. A look back at the past can also reveal the progress made despite all of the surviving structures. Admittedly they are more theoretical in nature and, as repeatedly established here, they form the basis of claims not borne out by reality. But they are in the world, they exist, and there is hope that, even in practice, if promoted by international public opinion and the impatience of a globalized world, they will emerge from the long shadow of the past—albeit without, at the same time, in the name of an allegedly good central principle, unilaterally doing away with the Charter of the United Nations.

---

[27] 'Sudan: UN envoy says Security Council must enforce sanctions', available at: http://www.un.org/apps/news/story.asp?NewsID=17158&Cr=sudan&Crl=. Kofi Annan had published a report as far back as December 2004 entitled 'A More Secure World: Our Shared Responsibility' (A/59/565) and repeated almost word for word the list of criteria contained in the 2001 report.

[28] The Report of the International Commission of Inquiry on Darfur to the United Nations Secretary-General, 25.1.2005, section 518–20.

FURTHER READING

Cassese, Antonio, *International Law in a Divided World* (Oxford: Clarendon Press, 1992).

Dallaire, Roméo, *Shake Hands with the Devil: The Failure of Humanity in Rwanda* (Toronto: Random House Canada, 2003).

Gaddis, John Lewis, *The Cold War: A New History* (London: Penguin, 2006).

Goldsmith, Jack L., and Eric A. Posner, *The Limits of International Law* (Oxford: Oxford University Press, 2005).

Jones, Adam (ed.), *Genocide, War Crimes and the West: History and Complicity* (London/New York: Zed Books, 2004).

Schabas, William A., *Genocide in International Law* (Cambridge: Cambridge University Press, 2000).

Weiss, Thomas C., and Sam Daws (eds), *The Oxford Handbook on the United Nations* (Oxford: Oxford University Press, 2008).

CHAPTER 29

MILITARY
INTERVENTION

ALEX J. BELLAMY

THE commission of genocide and mass atrocities has provoked calls for military intervention by external actors since the nineteenth century.[1] From the 1820s to the 1870s, groups of activists collectively known as 'atrocitarians' agitated for armed intervention to protect Christians in the Greek, Syrian, and Bulgarian lands of the Ottoman Empire. At century's end, the USA invaded Cuba partly in response to calls from notable figures, including former President Theodore Roosevelt, that it should act to put an end to Spanish atrocities there.[2] In the twentieth century, the Armenian genocide, Holocaust, and more recent genocides in Bosnia and Rwanda all elicited widespread agitation in favour of armed intervention. The present century is no different, with activists in various parts of the world maintaining that those with the power to do so should intervene in Darfur to protect the civilian population there from its tormentors. In 2005, two centuries of political agitation produced a land-mark commitment from the world's governments when they unanimously declared their responsibility to protect populations from genocide and to take 'timely and decisive' action in cases where a state manifestly fails in its responsibility to protect.[3]

Historically, once started, genocides tend to end with either the military defeat of the perpetrators or the suppression (though not necessarily the annihilation) of the

[1] See Gary J. Bass, *Freedom's Battle: The Origins of Humanitarian Intervention* (London: Knopf, 2008).
[2] Ernest R. May, *Imperial Democracy: The Emergence of America as a Great Power* (New York: Imprint, 1961), 127.
[3] For accounts of the emergence of the Responsibility to Protect principle see Gareth Evans, *The Responsibility to Protect: Ending Mass Atrocity Crimes Once and for All* (Washington, DC: Brookings Institute, 2008), and Alex J. Bellamy, *Responsibility to Protect: The Global Effort to End Mass Atrocities* (Cambridge: Polity Press, 2009).

victim groups.[4] Only military force can directly prevent genocidal killing, stand between perpetrators and their intended victims, and protect the delivery of life-saving aid. But its use entails risks for all parties and does not necessarily resolve the underlying conflict. Its impact is difficult to predict and force might sometimes inflame rather than improve situations. Properly used, force can offer physical protection to populations in immediate danger. But it cannot compel the parties to build sustainable peace; rebuild shattered governments, economies, and societies; protect populations in the long term; or provide comprehensive security. Moreover, there is a real danger that a generalized right to intervene for humanitarian purposes could be abused, such as Russia's use of the 'Responsibility to Protect' as justification for its 2008 invasion of Georgia, and the use of humanitarian rhetoric to justify the 2003 invasion of Iraq.[5] Then there is the additional hazard that promises of intervention might encourage acts of rebellion that provoke genocidal responses.[6]

What is more, by the time external military forces can be deployed and the agents of genocide defeated, the death toll amongst the victim group is likely to be staggeringly high. Although his analysis may be considered overly pessimistic, Alan Kuperman's sober assessment of what intervention could have achieved in Rwanda provides a cautionary tale for would-be humanitarian warriors. Kuperman maintained that, had the USA speedily and successfully deployed forces to Rwanda in 1994 once it became known that genocide was under way, the total number of lives saved would have been around 'only' 125,000 of the approximately 500,000–800,000 victims of the genocide.[7]

In short, military intervention does not address why genocides happen in the first place and provides only a short-term palliative at best. Finally, it is important that we not allow a preoccupation with intervention to obscure the manner in which hegemomic powers, conceptions of statehood, and neo-liberal economics sustain the preconditions for genocide—a point ably demonstrated by Mark Levene in this volume.[8]

---

[4] The question of how genocides end remains relatively understudied. In 2006, the Social Science Research Council organized an insightful forum on this question. Available at http://howgenocidesend.ssrc.org/ (accessed 10 December 2008).

[5] I have detailed the misuse of humanitarian arguments in the Georgia case in Alex J. Bellamy 'Humanitarian Intervention', in Alan Collins (ed.), Security Studies (Oxford: Oxford University Press, forthcoming) and in the Iraq case in idem, 'Ethics and Intervention: The "Humanitarian Exception", and the Problem of Abuse in the Case of Iraq', Journal of Peace Research 41:2 (2004), 131–47.

[6] A 'moral hazard' documented by Alan J. Kuperman, 'Humanitarian Hazard: Revising the Doctrine of Intervention', Harvard International Review 26:1 (2004), 64–8, and idem, 'The Moral Hazard of Humanitarian Intervention: Lessons from the Balkans', International Studies Quarterly 52:1 (2008), 49–80.

[7] The precise death toll of the genocide is contested and estimates vary according to the data sources, time scales, and method of counting used. Although some analysts—Kuperman included—estimate the death toll to be significantly lower than 800,000, most studies put the toll somewhere around that figure. See Linda Melvern, Conspiracy to Murder: The Rwandan Genocide (London: Verso, 2006).

[8] Also see Mark Levene, 'A Dissenting Voice: Or, How Current Assumptions of Deterring and Preventing Genocide May be Looking at the Problem through the Wrong End of the Telescope, Part I',

The purpose of this chapter is to examine the role that military intervention can play in ending genocide and the political, moral, and legal debates that surround it. It proceeds in three parts. The first section briefly examines how genocides have ended since the beginning of the twentieth century, and explores the place of military intervention by external powers. The second section examines whether there is a moral and/or legal duty to intervene to end genocide. In the third section, I consider the reasons why states intervene only infrequently to put an end to genocide despite their rhetorical commitments.

Intervention and the Ending of Genocide

To what extent has military intervention brought genocide to an end? Table 1 sets out—in necessarily rudimentary form—how some of the most commonly accepted cases of genocide since 1900 have come to an end and reveals three important insights. First, with only two partial exceptions, once begun, genocidal killing ends in only one of two ways—by perpetrators deciding that they have achieved their objectives or with their military defeat. The partial exceptions are the Nuba Mountains and Bosnia cases. In the Nuba Mountains case, local resistance slowed the pace of killing and forced relocation, and divisions within the government brought about its end.[9] In the Bosnia case, a political settlement (the 'Dayton Accords') rather than the military defeat of the Bosnian Serbs ended the violence, although the Bosnian Serb leadership was coerced into accepting the accords by a combination of NATO air strikes and ground attacks (Operation 'Deliberate Force') and, more importantly, military advances by the Bosnian–Croat alliance forged and armed by the USA. The single largest act of genocide—the 1995 killing of 7,600 men and boys sheltering in Srebrenica—succeeded in its immediate aim of eradicating the Muslim males of that town.[10] To this day, Srebrenica remains an exclusively Serb town, an ethnic reality forged by genocide.

Journal of Genocide Research 6:2 (2004), 156. I have argued elsewhere that armed intervention needs to be seen as one part of a pattern of interaction between powerful and less powerful states and that much of that interaction contributes to the causes of genocide and mass killing in the first place. A first step to dealing with this would be to identify those patterns of interaction and encourage powerful states to engage first in the 'do no harm' principle. See Alex J. Bellamy, 'Humanitarian Responsibilities and Interventionist Claims in International Society', *Review of International Studies* 29:3 (2003), 320–41; and *idem*, 'Conflict Prevention and the Responsibility to Protect', *Global Governance* 14:2 (2008), 135–57.

[9] De Waal and Conley-Zilkic, 'Reflections', 5.

[10] Jan Willem Honig and Norbert Both, *Srebrenica: Record of a War Crime* (London: Penguin, 1996).

Table 1 Commonly Accepted Genocides since 1900 and How They Ended[11]

Date	Where	Ending
1904–5	German South West Africa (killing of Herero)	Decimation and 'pacification' of targeted group
1915–18	Ottoman Empire (forced deportation and killing of Armenians)	Largely successful 'cleansing' of Anatolia. Ottoman defeat in the First World War
1935–9	Ethiopia (Italy annihilation of Ethiopians as reprisal—envisaged 'Ethiopia without Ethiopians')	Decimation and pacification of targeted groups
1937–9	USSR (great purge of *kulaks* and others)	Decimation and pacification of targeted groups
1937–45	East Asia (Japanese destruction of Chinese in Manchuria, 'rape of Nanking', and genocidal atrocities in the Philippines and elsewhere)	Defeat of Japanese in the Second World War
1941–5	Nazi-occupied Europe (Jewish Holocaust)	Defeat of Nazis in the Second World War
1965–6	Indonesia (massacre of suspected communists)	Suppression of ethnic Chinese and elimination of communists as a political force
1967–70	Nigeria (Biafra) (genocidal killing in support of Federal forces in civil war)	Suppression of Biafran rebels and government victory in civil war
1971	Bangladesh ('cleansing' of Hindus by West Pakistan government)	Intervention by India
1972	Burundi (elimination of Hutus)	Suppression of Hutus, especially educated class.
1975–9	Cambodia (Khmer Rouge)	Intervention by Vietnam
1981–3	Guatemala (killing of 'communists' especially targeting five Maya groups)	Decimation and pacification of targeted group
1992	Sudan (Nuba mountains) (Jihad, mass killing, and forced relocation of Nuba people with genocidal intent)	Local resistance and disagreement within government of Sudan
1992–5	Bosnia ((i) general—mass killing of Bosnian Muslims mainly by Bosnian Serbs but also by Bosnian Croats; (ii) genocide at Srebrenica—killing of males by Bosnian Serbs)	(i) Peace settlement coerced by combination of NATO and Croat–Muslim forces; (ii) male population largely exterminated
1994	Rwanda (killing of Tutsi and Hutu moderates by Hutu militia supported by government)	Defeat of militia and government forces by Rwandan Patriotic Front (RPF)
2003–	Sudan—Darfur (killing and forced displacement of various African groups by government backed militias)	Decimation and forced removal of targeted group lead to reduction of violence

[11] Based on information in de Waal and Conley-Zilkic, 'Reflections'; Adam Jones, *Genocide: A Comprehensive Introduction* (London: Routledge, 2006); Ben Kiernan, *Blood and Soil: A World History of Genocide and Extermination from Sparta to Darfur* (New Haven, CT: Yale University Press, 2008).

However appealing, non-military measures such as economic and political sanctions, arms embargoes, inducements, 'naming and shaming', diplomacy, and threat of legal punishment have not, historically, sufficed to bring genocide to an end.

Despite the outpouring of academic literature on the subject and much political angst at the UN and elsewhere, external intervention to end genocide remains the exception rather than the norm. Of the fifteen cases identified in Table 1, seven ended more or less successfully for the perpetrators and a further two (Armenia and Bosnia-Srebrenica) ended badly for the perpetrators but not before they had achieved core goals ('cleansing' of Anatolia and Srebrenica). Of the genocides that did not end on the perpetrators' own terms, three endings were related to their military defeat in campaigns not directly related to the genocides (the defeat of the Ottoman Empire, Germany, and Japan in the First and Second World Wars), one was brought to an end by the perpetrators' defeat by local actors (Rwanda), and another by a combination of local and external actors (Bosnia). Across all the cases, local resistance played a significant part in ending three episodes (Nuba, Rwanda, Bosnia). Only two episodes were ended by external military intervention specifically aimed at defeating the perpetrators of genocide (Bangladesh and Cambodia). Somewhat counter-intuitively, both of these interventions were conducted unilaterally by post-colonial (not Western) states not primarily motivated by humanitarian concerns.[12] Although the West is commonly identified as the principal advocate of humanitarian intervention, there is scant evidence of Western military activism to end genocide since the start of the twentieth century. In short, there has been much less actual external military intervention to end genocide than there has been talk about such intervention.

Finally, although the broader literature on humanitarian intervention often suggests that interventions are not tantamount to war and involve a variety of different military tasks—sometimes labelled 'military expedients', such as protecting safe areas, humanitarian convoys, no-fly zones, etc.[13]—it seems clear that, on the whole, external intervention to end genocide requires the military defeat of the perpetrators. In other words, whatever may be required by other forms of external engagement in armed conflict, such as peace operations, military intervention to end genocide is identical in form to warfare and has the same objective, namely the military suppression of the enemy.

[12] As Wheeler points out, both interventions were primarily conceived and justified in terms of self-defence. See Nicholas J. Wheeler, *Saving Strangers: Humanitarian Intervention in International Society* (Oxford: Oxford University Press, 2000), 55–110.

[13] John G. Heidenrich, *How to Prevent Genocide: A Guide for Policymakers, Scholars and Concerned Citizens* (Westport, CT: Praeger, 2001), 163. Also see Bass, *Freedom's Battle*.

A Duty to Intervene?

....

Is there a duty to intervene to 'save strangers' from genocide?[14] I argue that there is a clear moral duty to intervene in circumstances where intervention is thought likely to do more good than harm. There is also evidence of an emerging—but much less well-established—legal duty. Both ideas, however, remain deeply controversial principally because armed intervention by external actors is rarely disinterested, leading some to fear that the duty to intervene can be a thinly veiled justification for a coercive form of Western hegemony or neo-imperialism that supports the very global system that nourishes the preconditions for genocide.

Usually associated with liberalism, cosmopolitanism, and the Christian Just War tradition, the case for intervention is typically premised on the idea that external actors have a *duty* as well as a *right* to intervene to halt genocide. For advocates of this position, all humans have certain fundamental rights—chief among them being the right not to be arbitrarily killed—and sovereign rights are conditional on the fulfilment of the state's responsibility to protect populations under its care. When states fail in their duties towards their citizens, they lose their right to non-interference.[15] There are a variety of ways of arriving at this conclusion. Some liberal cosmopolitans draw on the work of the German philosopher Immanuel Kant to insist that all individuals have certain fundamental rights that deserve protection.[16] Other advocates of the Just War tradition ground their arguments in Christian theology.[17] Still others argue that today's globalized world is so integrated that massive human rights violations in one part of the world have an effect on every other part. This social interconnectedness, they maintain, creates moral obligations.[18] One of the leading contemporary proponents of this view is former British Prime Minister Tony Blair. Shortly after NATO began its 1999 intervention in Kosovo, he gave a landmark speech setting out his 'doctrine of the international community'. Blair maintained that globalization was changing the world in ways that rendered traditional views of sovereignty anachronistic.[19]

---

[14] To use the phrase coined by Nicholas J. Wheeler.

[15] Fernando R. Tesón, 'The Liberal Case for Humanitarian Intervention', in J. L. Holzgrefe and Robert O. Keohane (eds), *Humanitarian Intervention: Ethical, Legal and Political Dilemmas* (Cambridge: Cambridge University Press, 2003), 93. The principle of non-interference is discussed in more detail below.

[16] Simon Caney, 'Human Rights and the Rights of States: Terry Nardin on Non-Intervention', *International Political Science Review* 18:1 (1997), 34.

[17] Paul Ramsey, *The Just War: Force and Political Responsibility* (Lanham, MD: Rowman and Littlefield, 2002), 20.

[18] The idea that interconnectedness creates *moral* responsibilities is eloquently set out by Thomas Pogge. See Thomas Pogge, *World Poverty and Human Rights*, 2nd edn (Cambridge: Polity Press, 2008).

[19] Tony Blair, 'Doctrine of the International Community', speech to the Economic Club of Chicago, Hilton Hotel, Chicago, 22 April 1999.

A further line of argument is to point to the fact that states have already agreed to certain minimum standards of behaviour and that military intervention to end genocide is not about imposing the will of a few Western states upon the many, but about protecting and enforcing the collective will of international society. Advocates of this position argue that there is a customary right (but not duty) of intervention to put an end to genocide and mass atrocities.[20] They maintain that there is agreement in international society that genocide constitutes a grave wrong warranting external intervention.[21] From this perspective, state practice since the end of the cold war suggests the emergence of a customary right of humanitarian intervention.[22] In particular, they point to the justifications offered to defend the American, French, and British-led intervention in Northern Iraq in 1991 to support their case. In that instance, the British argued that they were upholding customary international law, France invoked a customary 'right' of intervention, and the USA noted a 're-balancing of the claims of sovereignty and those of extreme humanitarian need'.[23]

According to this perspective, the movement towards acceptance of a customary right of humanitarian intervention was reinforced by state practice after Northern Iraq. Thus throughout the UN Security Council's deliberations about how to respond to Rwanda in 1994, no state argued that either the ban on the use of force (Article 2[4] of the UN Charter) or the non-interference rule (Article 2[7] of the Charter) should prohibit armed intervention to halt the bloodshed, suggesting that such intervention would have been legitimate in that case. What stood in the way of intervention in Rwanda was the fact that no government wanted to risk the lives of its own soldiers to save Africans (see below). Throughout the 1990s, the Security Council expanded its interpretation of 'international peace and security' and authorized interventions to protect civilians in safe areas (Bosnia), maintain law and order and protect aid supplies (Somalia), and restore an elected government toppled by a coup (Haiti). These cases prompted Thomas Weiss to argue that 'the notion that human beings matter more than sovereignty radiated brightly, albeit briefly, across the international political horizon of the 1990s.'[24] Progress did not stop at the turn of the century. Since 2000, the Security Council has mandated peacekeepers to protect civilians under threat in the Democratic Republic of

[20] Wheeler, *Saving Strangers*, 14.

[21] See A. C. Arend and R. J. Beck, *International Law and the Use of Force: Beyond the UN Charter Paradigm* (London: Routledge, 1993); Jack Donnelly, *International Human Rights*, 2nd edn (Boulder, CO: Westview Press, 1988); and Tesón, 'The Liberal Case'.

[22] See Wheeler, *Saving Strangers*, and Martha Finnemore, *The Purpose of Intervention: Changing Beliefs about the Use of Force* (Ithaca, NY: Cornell University Press, 2003).

[23] Adam Roberts, 'Humanitarian War: Military Intervention and Human Rights', *International Affairs* 69:3 (1993), 436–7.

[24] Weiss, 'The Sunset of Humanitarian Intervention', 135.

Congo, Burundi, Côte d'Ivoire, Liberia, and Darfur though it has usually insisted on receiving the consent of the host government.[25]

All this suggests that there is a growing international consensus around a moral duty to intervene to put an end to massive human suffering. However, there are also grounds for thinking that there is an emerging legal responsibility to do so as well, derived from a combination of the Responsibility to Protect principle and a recent ruling of the International Court of Justice (ICJ). Although it might be premature to speak of a specific legal obligation to intervene militarily, the emergence of such a duty is important because it places legal obligations on states and creates the potential for redress if those obligations are not satisfied.

In 2000 the Canadian government created the International Commission on Intervention and State Sovereignty (ICISS) to develop a way of reconciling sovereignty and human rights. The Commission's report, released in late 2001, was premised on the notion that the principle of non-interference 'yields to the responsibility to protect' when states are unwilling or unable to protect their citizens from grave harm.[26] The ICISS argued that the Responsibility to Protect entailed responsibilities to prevent and react to massive human suffering and help rebuild states and societies afterwards. Of the three responsibilities, the Commission identified the 'responsibility to prevent' as the single most important. In relation to the use of force for humanitarian purposes, the Commission proposed the adoption of criteria to guide decision-makers. Drawing from the Just War tradition, the Commission's proposed criteria included 'just cause thresholds' (large-scale loss of life or ethnic cleansing, actual or apprehended) and 'precautionary principles' (right intention, last resort, proportional means, and reasonable prospects).[27]

In 2005, the Responsibility to Protect was transformed from a concept advanced by a Commission of high-profile figures to an international principle unanimously endorsed by world leaders. At the 2005 World Summit summoned to consider a UN reform package, world leaders adopted a declaration affirming the Responsibility to Protect, which was subsequently reaffirmed by the UN Security Council in 2006. According to the UN Secretary-General Ban Ki-moon, the Responsibility to Protect principle agreed to by world leaders rests on three pillars:

---

[25] See Alex J. Bellamy and Paul D. Williams, *Understanding Peacekeeping*, 2nd edn (Cambridge: Polity Press, 2009), esp. chs. 5 and 14; Victoria K. Holt and Tobias C. Berkman, *The Impossible Mandate? Military Preparedness, the Responsibility to Protect and Modern Peace Operations* (Washington, DC: Henry L. Stimson Centre, 2006); and Lise Morje Howard, *UN Peacekeeping in Civil Wars* (Cambridge: Cambridge University Press, 2008).

[26] International Commission on Intervention and State Sovereignty (ICISS), *The Responsibility to Protect* (Ottawa: IDRC, 2001), p. xi.

[27] Ibid.

1) The responsibility of the state to protect its own populations from genocide, war crimes, ethnic cleansing, and crimes against humanity;
2) The international community's duty to assist states in meeting these obligations; and
3) The international community's responsibility to respond in a timely and decisive manner when a state is manifestly failing to protect its population, using Chapters VI (peaceful means), VII (coercive means authorized by the UN Security Council), and VIII (regional arrangements) of the UN Charter.[28]

Although much more work needs to be done to translate the Responsibility to Protect from words to deeds, the 2005 declaration is important because it is a politically potent principle based on unanimous consensus produced by one of the largest gatherings of heads of state ever seen.[29] It is important to stress the unanimity of consensus among Member States. Indeed, two traditional sceptics about this line of thinking, China and Russia, actually reaffirmed their commitment to the Responsibility to Protect principle in Security Council Resolution 1674 (2006).[30] Moreover, by referring to Chapter VII of the UN Charter, world leaders specifically recognized the need to consider the use of force to protect populations from genocide. This of course does not mean that governments will agree about the most appropriate and effective form of engagement with specific crises, but the principle helps define the parameters and at least means that they can no longer avoid public consideration of engagement.

It is well known that the 1948 Genocide Convention not only prohibits genocide but establishes a duty to prevent and punish it (Article 1). This duty to prevent genocide is widely understood to be a principle of customary international law.[31] However, it was never clear whether this general duty amounted to a legal obligation to intervene to halt specific genocides. Although some legal scholars have argued that Article I imposes a duty on the UN and its member states to act (including through military intervention) wherever a genocide takes place,[32] the majority view seemed to support US Secretary of State Colin Powell's assertion that the Convention's language did not impose such a wide-ranging obligation.[33]

[28] Ban Ki-moon, 'Responsible Sovereigns', address of the Secretary-General, SG/SM/11701, 15 July 2008; and Edward C. Luck, 'The United Nations and the Responsibility to Protect'; *Stanley Foundation Policy Analysis Brief*, August 2008.
[29] Luck, 'The United Nations', 3.
[30] On China's position on the Responsibility to Protect see Sarah Teitt, 'China and the Responsibility to Protect', *Global Responsibility to Protect* 1:2 (2009), 208–36.
[31] William Schabas, *Genocide in International Law: The Crime of Crimes* (Cambridge: Cambridge University Press, 2000), 500.
[32] Stephen J. Toope, 'Does International Law Impose a Duty upon the UN to Prevent Genocide?', *McGill Law Journal* 46:1 (2000), 187–94.
[33] Jerry Fowler, for example, argued that 'the language of the [Genocide] Convention does not provide any indication that such an extensive obligation was contemplated. Indeed it would be quite bizarre to think that the drafters intended in 1948 to make intervention in the internal affairs of other

However, important new light was shed on this issue by the ICJ's 2007 ruling in the *Bosnia and Herzegovina v. Serbia and Montenegro* case.

The Court found that Serbia was not guilty of genocide but had violated its Article 1 obligation to prevent and punish the crime of genocide. The ICJ found that, whilst states are not obliged to succeed in their efforts to prevent genocide, they 'must employ all means which are reasonably available to them to do so'.[34] Of course, it remains to be seen what measures may be thought to be 'reasonably available' to states in given situations. It is unlikely that each individual state now has a responsibility to intervene militarily to end genocide, and it should be remembered that measures to end genocide must be consistent with international law, which prohibits the use of force except in self-defence or with the express authorization of the UN Security Council.[35] However, it has been argued by the former UN High Commissioner for Human Rights, Louise Arbour, that the ruling—especially when taken in conjunction with the Responsibility to Protect principle—imposes specific responsibilities on the members of the UN Security Council, and the permanent members especially.[36] The UN Security Council has the legal authority to authorize armed intervention whenever it identifies a threat to international peace and security. Moreover, as the world's leading military powers, permanent members of the Security Council almost always have the military capacity to intervene to halt genocide. Thus armed with both the collective authority to intervene and—between them—the capacity to do so, it could be argued that armed intervention to halt genocide falls well within the scope of 'reasonably available' measures for permanent members of the Security Council.

This is not to say, of course, that armed intervention will be the most appropriate course of action in every case. And it should be noted that this line of argument depends on a very liberal interpretation of the law. Furthermore, whilst the Responsibility to Protect principle enjoys the unanimous support of the UN General Assembly, it does not resolve difficult questions about the most appropriate and effective response to specific cases of genocide and mass atrocities. Moreover, even with these caveats the idea that there might be a right or duty to intervene is controversial.

Opponents—including many Third World states—maintain that international order and the preservation of core values such as the right to self-determination requires something approximating an absolute ban on the use of force outside

states obligatory' ('A New Chapter of Irony: The Legal Definition of Genocide and the Implications of Powell's Determination', in Samuel Totten and Eric Markusen (eds), *Genocide in Darfur: Investigating the Atrocities in the Sudan* (London: Routledge, 2006), 131).

[34] In Marko Milanovic, 'State Responsibility for Genocide: A Follow-Up', *European Journal of International Law* 18:4 (2007), 686.

[35] Mark Gibney, 'Genocide and State Responsibility', *Human Rights Law Review* 7:4 (2007), 767.

[36] Louise Arbour, 'The Responsibility to Protect as a Duty of Care in International Law and Practice', *Review of International Studies* 34:3 (2008), 445–58.

the two parameters set out by the UN Charter—Security Council authorization (Chapter VII) and self-defence (Article 51)—and that the Security Council should interpret its remit narrowly.[37] The starting point for this position is the assumption that international society comprises a plurality of diverse communities each with different ideas about the best way to live. According to this view, international society is based on rules—the UN Charter's rules on the use of force first among them—that permit these communities to coexist relatively peacefully.[38] In a world characterized by radical disagreements about how societies should govern themselves, proponents of this view hold that a right and duty of humanitarian intervention would create disorder, as states would wage wars to protect and violently export their own cultural preferences. What is more, a right of intervention would open the door to potential abuse. Historically, states have shown a distinct predilection towards 'abusing' humanitarian justifications to legitimize wars that were anything but humanitarian. Most notoriously, Hitler insisted that the 1939 invasion of Czechoslovakia was inspired by a desire to protect Czechoslovak citizens of German ethnicity whose 'life and liberty' were threatened by their own government.[39] It was precisely because of the fear that states would exploit any loophole in the ban on the use of force that the delegates who wrote the UN Charter issued a comprehensive ban with only the two limited exceptions: force used in self-defence and under the authority of the Security Council.[40] In addition to the problem of abuse, many post-colonial states continue to oppose humanitarian intervention because they consider it a dangerous affront to another core principle, self-determination. They worry that a duty to intervene would grant a licence for the great powers to interfere in their domestic affairs, undermining their right to self-government.[41]

Although these are powerful arguments which should temper enthusiasm for and analysis of armed intervention, it is important to avoid the belief that the duty to intervene is an agenda exclusively, or even primarily, concerned with imposing Western values on the rest. On the one hand, those who caution against intervention as a matter of principle should be mindful of the evidence about how genocides end. On the other hand, it is important to not assume that the post-colonial world speaks as one on this issue. There are good grounds for thinking that there is genuine consensus that intervention, properly authorized, is a legitimate response to

[37] For a good exposition of this position, linking it to the views of several Third World governments see Mohammed Ayoob, 'Third World Perspectives on Humanitarian Intervention and International Administration', *Global Governance* 10:1 (2004), 99–118.

[38] A position set out and defended at length by Richard H. Jackson, *The Global Covenant: Human Conduct in a World of States* (Oxford: Oxford University Press, 2002).

[39] Ian Brownlie, 'Humanitarian Intervention', in John N. Moore (ed.), *Law and Civil War in the Modern World* (Baltimore: Johns Hopkins University Press, 1974), 217–21.

[40] An argument put forth in detail by Simon Chesterman, *Just War or Just Peace? Humanitarian Intervention in International Law* (Oxford: Oxford University Press, 2001).

[41] A position set out by Ayoob, 'Third World Perspectives'.

genocide and mass atrocities. Nine years before NATO intervened in Kosovo without the authority of the Security Council, a group of West African states (ECOWAS) did likewise in Liberia. Five years before the adoption of the Responsibility to Protect principle by world leaders, members of the African Union gave the regional institution a right to intervene in response to serious humanitarian emergencies.[42]

Another concern is that military interventions are always tainted by power politics because an intervener's motives are never wholly humanitarian.[43] Wil Verwey defined humanitarian intervention as 'the threat or use of force ... *for the sole purpose* of preventing or putting a halt to a serious violation of human rights.' He argued that there never had been genuine humanitarian interventions because prior interventions had almost always been motivated by non-humanitarian concerns. Such interventions could not be considered humanitarian or 'disinterested' and were therefore illegitimate.[44]

Although this line of thinking points to some important concerns, there are at least three problems. First, there are good reasons to suggest that states will not risk the lives of their own citizens in order to save the lives of others. As Donald Bloxham has persuasively argued, 'humanitarian intervention tends to occur only when the cause overlaps with the material interests of those intervening.'[45] By insisting that interveners be guided by purely humanitarian motives, the bar is placed so high that no military action could realistically pass the test, even though in some cases only military measures will remedy human suffering. From this perspective, it was entirely correct for the West not to intervene in Armenia, Rwanda, Srebrenica, and Darfur because they could not have done so in a disinterested fashion.

Second, motives and purposes are subjective and can be easily disguised by clever political leaders. Making motives the sole criterion of legitimacy is problematic, therefore, because it is very difficult for them to be properly assessed, especially without the help of considerable hindsight. Finally, focusing solely on what motivates an action tells us little about its consequences. Contra those that demand purely humanitarian motives, a self-interested intervention that ends a genocide (e.g. Vietnam in Cambodia) is surely preferable to a disinterested intervention that ultimately fails (e.g. USA in Somalia). Indeed, it is usually the presence of a degree

---

[42] See Paul D. Williams, 'From Non-Interference to Non-Indifference: The Origins and Development of the African Union's Security Culture', *African Affairs* 106:423 (2007), 253–79.

[43] See Bernard Williams, 'Humanitarianism and the Right to Intervene', in Geoffrey Hawthorn (ed.), *In the Beginning Was the Deed: Realism and Moralism in Political Argument* (Princeton, NJ: Princeton University Press 2005), 145–53.

[44] Wil Verwey, 'The Legality of Humanitarian Intervention after the Cold War', in E. Ferris (ed.), *A Challenge to Intervene: A New Role for the United Nations?* (Uppsala: Life and Peace Institute, 1992), 12–36; and Bhikhu Parekh, 'Rethinking Humanitarian Intervention', *International Political Science Review* 18:1 (1997), 55–74.

[45] Donald Bloxham, 'Genocide: Can We Learn from History?', *BBC History Magazine* (January 2007), 48.

of self-interest that makes states prepared to sacrifice the lives of their citizens to save foreigners from peril.

A more sophisticated position is put forward by Nicholas Wheeler. The starting point is the idea that humans, much less states, are never prompted to act by a single motive. Wheeler therefore argues that whilst motives are important they should not be the 'threshold' consideration. That is, actions that produce humanitarian good should not be condemned because they are not inspired by humanitarian motives. The key test should be that the means chosen by the intervener must not undermine the positive humanitarian outcome.[46] Thus, Vietnam's self-interested intervention in Cambodia should be applauded because the non-humanitarian motives did not undermine the humanitarian goal of removing the Khmer Rouge from power. By contrast, because the French government was primarily motivated by a concern to protect Hutu allies and Francophones in Rwanda, rather than a desire to end the Rwandan genocide, it chose a strategy that did relatively little to protect the genocide's victims. In that case, non-humanitarian motives undermined potential humanitarian outcomes. According to Wheeler's schema this should render the French intervention (*Operation Turquoise*) illegitimate.[47] This more sophisticated approach allows us to factor the important concerns expressed by Verwey into our assessment of intervention while acknowledging that states usually have mixed motives.

INHIBITORS TO INTERVENTION

Why, when there is so much agreement about the necessity of preventing and ending genocide, are states so reluctant to intervene militarily? This section examines three of the most often cited reasons for the failure to intervene—international law, political will, and prudential considerations.

International law

Questions about intervention tend to be framed around an enduring struggle between sovereignty and human rights. By this account, sovereignty refers to the rights that states enjoy to territorial integrity, political independence, and non-intervention. Where sovereign states are either unwilling or unable to protect the fundamental freedoms of their citizens, sovereignty and human rights come into

[46] Wheeler, *Saving Strangers*, 33–4.
[47] See ibid. chs 3 and 7.

conflict. This tension is evident in the UN Charter. Whilst calling for cooperation to reaffirm faith in fundamental human rights, the Charter (Article 2(4)) outlaws war as an instrument of policy with only two exceptions (each state's inherent right to self-defence [Article 51] and collective measures authorized by the UN Security Council [Chapter VII]) and affirms the principle of non-interference [Article 2 (7)]) by prohibiting the UN from interfering 'in matters essentially within the domestic jurisdiction of states'. These legal rights, it is often argued, constitute a powerful barrier to intervention, and it has proven very difficult to build sufficient consensus in the UN Security Council to persuade it to authorize intervention against a full-functioning state guilty of perpetrating genocide or mass atrocities. For example, in a March 2005 Security Council debate on whether to refer alleged crimes in Darfur to the International Criminal Court (ICC), the US representative explained that country's abstention by arguing that the Court 'strikes at the essence of the nature of sovereignty.'[48]

States that act without the authority of the Security Council can pay a very high price. For example, in 1979, when Vietnam invaded Cambodia and ousted the murderous Khmer Rouge regime, responsible for the death of some two million Cambodians, it was condemned for violating Cambodian sovereignty. China's representative at the UN described Vietnam's act as a 'great mockery of and insult to the United Nations and its member states' and sponsored a resolution condemning Vietnam's 'aggression'. The USA agreed.[49] France argued that 'the notion that because a regime is detestable foreign intervention is justified and forcible overthrow is legitimate is extremely dangerous. That could ultimately jeopardize the very maintenance of law and order.'[50]

However, there are grounds for doubting the extent to which international law actually is a barrier to intervention. Simon Chesterman has demonstrated that sovereignty has not in fact inhibited unilateral or collective intervention to uphold human rights in other countries. In response to arguments that intervention could be promoted by relaxing the prohibition on the use of force, Chesterman argued that 'implicit in many of the arguments for a right of humanitarian intervention is the suggestion that the present normative order is preventing interventions that should take place. This is simply not true. Interventions do not take place because states do not want them to take place.'[51] Ultimately, it was not primarily concerns about sovereignty that prevented timely intervention in Rwanda, but rather the basic political fact that no state wanted to risk its own troops to save strangers from genocide (see below).

---

[48] S/PV.5158, 31 March 2005, 12.
[49] Cited in Wheeler, *Saving Strangers*, 90–91.
[50] Cited in Chesterman, *Just War or Just Peace?*, 80.
[51] Ibid. 231.

What, though, of Vietnam's invasion of Cambodia? Was it not the case that Vietnam paid a heavy political and economic price because it was seen as violating Cambodia's sovereignty? This position certainly has merit but needs to be viewed alongside two other considerations. First, Vietnam was not principally motivated by humanitarian concerns nor did it justify its invasion as a humanitarian intervention. Second, and perhaps more importantly, we need to take the arguments levelled against Vietnam with a pinch of cold war salt. Whilst not denying the fact that many states, particularly some members of the Non-Aligned Movement, opposed Vietnam on principled grounds, political considerations played an important part in shaping the way that international society reacted to the intervention.[52] In the same year as Vietnam's invasion of Cambodia, Tanzania—a highly regarded state with a well-respected president, Julius Nyerere—invaded Uganda and deposed Idi Amin with barely a ripple of condemnation.[53]

Either way, it is clear that contemporary international law does not enable the forging of consensus on collective action to end genocide beyond provisions on Security Council authorization. This is where recent developments such as the Responsibility to Protect principle and *Bosnia v. Serbia* ruling, which seek to change the relationship between sovereignty, the responsibilities of states, and the place of non-interference, might have a positive effect.

Political Will

Following on from Chesterman's insight that interventions do not happen primarily because states do not want them to happen, the second major inhibitor of armed intervention is political will. Political will works in two ways to inhibit the chances of intervention to end genocide. The first, and least discussed, is the presence of prevailing interest. In other words, it is not just that powerful states lack the will to take risks to save strangers, but that their pursuit of their own interests leads them to support or shield the perpetrators. The link between China's (and to a lesser extent, Russia's) obstinate support for the government of Sudan and its interest in Sudanese oil and arms sales is well known.[54] But the West has also often put its own interests ahead of the protection of populations from genocide. As part of its long war against communism, it supplied arms to the Indonesian government as alleged communists were slaughtered and East Timor brutally repressed and helped fund, arm, and train the Khmer Rouge after its defeat by Vietnam. For

---

[52] Wheeler, *Saving Strangers*, 78–110.

[53] On this see Grant Evans and Kelvin Rowley, *Red Brotherhood at War: Vietnam, Cambodia and Laos since 1975*, 2nd edn (London: Verso, 1990).

[54] For instance, 'China and Darfur: The Genocide Olympics?', *Washington Post*, 14 December 2006, A30.

similar reasons, in the early 1980s the USA supported, funded, and armed the genocidal regime in Guatemala. Motivated mainly by its interest in preserving its influence in former colonial territories, France funded and armed the Hutu government in Rwanda and supplied a substantial portion of the guns and machetes that made genocide possible.[55] All of the permanent members of the Security Council, which has a special responsibility to protect populations from genocide, have therefore been implicated in genocide through their support for the perpetrators in the past half-century. Sometimes, therefore, political will prompts great powers to actively protect or assist perpetrators, presenting a major obstacle to the goal of ending genocide. The permanent members of the Security Council would therefore do well to begin their engagement with the ending of genocide by desisting from actively supporting its perpetrators.

The second, and more commonly discussed, aspect of political will relates to the idea that states consider themselves to be responsible first and foremost for the well being of their own citizens and are reluctant to spend tax money and risk the lives of their soldiers in order to save strangers from genocide in other countries. The effects of this lack of will were demonstrated in detail by the 1999 Report of the Independent Inquiry into the UN's failure to prevent and then halt the Rwanda genocide of 1994.[56] The report opened with a damning but general criticism, insisting that the Rwandan genocide resulted from the failure of the whole UN system.[57] The lack of resources and will was manifested in the UN mission deployed in Rwanda (UNAMIR) not being adequately 'planned, dimensioned, deployed or instructed' in a way that would have 'provided for a proactive and assertive role' in the face of the deteriorating situation in Rwanda.[58] The mission was smaller than recommended by the UN secretariat, slow to deploy owing to the reluctance of states to contribute troops, debilitated by administrative difficulties, and when troops did arrive they were generally inadequately trained and equipped.[59]

[55] On USA and Indonesia see Yves Beigbeder, *International Justice against Impunity: Progress and New Challenges* (The Hague: Martinus Nijhoff, 2005), 17–18; on US support for Guatemala's genocidal regime see the report of the UN-administered Historical Clarification Commission, *Memory of Silence: Report of the Commission for Historical Clarification: Conclusions and Recommendations* at http://shr.aaas.org/guatemala/ceh/report/english/toc.html (accessed 14 December 2008); on British support for the Khmer Rouge, see Tom Fawthrop and Helen Jarvis, *Getting Away with Genocide: Elusive Justice and the Khmer Rouge Tribunal* (Sydney: University of New South Wales Press, 2005), 68–9. On France and Rwanda see Daniela Kroslak, *The French Betrayal of Rwanda* (London: Hurst, 2007).

[56] This discussion draws on Bellamy and Williams, *Understanding Peacekeeping*, ch. 5.

[57] Independent Commission, *Report of the Independent Inquiry into the Actions of the United Nations during the 1994 Genocide in Rwanda*, 12 December 1999, 1.

[58] Ibid. 2.

[59] Ibid.

The Inquiry concluded, therefore, that the UN's failure in Rwanda was largely created by a critical disjuncture—endemic in many UN operations at the time[60]—between the tasks given to peacekeepers and their conceptual and material tools. For largely political reasons UNAMIR was conceived as a small, cheap, and consent-dependent operation despite evidence at the time that this would be inadequate. In a tragic coincidence of history, UNAMIR's mandate came onto the Security Council's agenda just one week after the killing of American peacekeepers in Somalia in the infamous 'Black Hawks down' incident. The USA was understandably in no mood to consider supporting the dispatch of more peacekeepers to Africa and insisted that any force sent to Rwanda be limited in size and dependent on the consent of the parties.

Prudential Considerations

Even when states have genuine moral concerns about the commission of genocide in foreign countries, prudential considerations or competing priorities may augur against armed intervention. The first prudential inhibitor to intervention is the calculation that intervention might do more harm than good. Prominent human rights NGO, the International Crisis Group, and individuals such as Gareth Evans and Francis Deng all argued against military intervention in Darfur on the grounds that it would be counterproductive, and indeed exacerbate the violence. They were supported in this view by a leading commentator on African affairs, Alex de Waal, whose own position on intervention changed between 2004 and 2006. Initially, de Waal argued that foreign troops could make a 'formidable difference' to the lives of Darfuri civilians.[61] Soon after, de Waal was invited to help the African Union in its efforts to broker a political settlement but the negotiators failed to persuade all but one of the rebel groups to sign the Darfur Peace Agreement. The experience of coming 'agonisingly close' to a political settlement and the further complication of the situation on the ground no doubt contributed to de Waal's change of heart on the potential for military intervention to make a 'formidable difference'. In 2006, he wrote:

The knock-down argument against humanitarian invasion is that it won't work. The idea of foreign troops fighting their way into Darfur and disarming the Janjaweed militia by force is sheer fantasy. Practicality dictates that a peacekeeping force in Darfur cannot enforce its will on any resisting armed groups without entering into a protracted and unwinnable counter-insurgency in which casualties are inevitable. The only way peacekeeping works is with

---

[60] See Part 3 of Bellamy and Williams, *Understanding Peacekeeping.*

[61] Alex de Waal, 'Darfur's Deep Grievances Defy All Hopes for an Easy Solution', *The Observer*, 25 July 2004, available at http://www.guardian.co.uk/society/2004/jul/25/internationalaidanddevelopment.voluntarysector (accessed 15 December 2008).

consent: the agreement of the Sudan government and the support of the majority of the Darfurian populace ... Without this, UN troops will not only fail but will make the plight of Darfurians even worse.[62]

Which version is more accurate—that foreign forces could make a 'formidable difference' to Darfuri civilians or that this position was 'sheer fantasy'? These are the sort of difficult questions that well-intentioned policy-makers must find answers to in the midst of the genocidal storm. Francis Deng, a well-respected diplomat and the UN's Special Representative on Internal Displacement for over a decade, supported de Waal's 2006 opinion. Non-consensual intervention, he concluded, would 'complicate and aggravate' the crisis by increasing the level of violence and undermining the potential for cooperation with the Sudanese government.[63]

There are clearly difficult choices that policy-makers confront when weighing up whether to commit troops to an intervention. When coupled with either countervailing interests or an absence of national interests and the danger of sustaining casualties, it is not hard to see why the uncertainty of success in any complex operation to combat genocide tends to produce scepticism about the merits of intervention. In addition to these considerations, we need to bear in mind that policy-makers often must balance competing priorities. For example, in relation to Darfur, the USA was required to balance its concern for the victims of genocide with the pursuit of its national security objectives in the War on Terror. The imperatives of the War on Terror made it difficult for the USA to seriously contemplate armed intervention in Darfur for three primary reasons. First, its military commitments in Iraq and Afghanistan meant that there was little spare capacity to intervene in Darfur. Intervention in Darfur would have required scaling back of the other major commitments and US policy-makers prioritized the War on Terror, stability in Iraq, and support for the Afghan government over stopping the genocide in Darfur. Second, the government of Sudan made itself an important source of intelligence information on Islamic extremism. Thus, American intelligence required a working relationship with the government of Sudan. Third, given the public relations disaster that accompanied the US intervention in Iraq, the last thing the USA needed was to antagonize the Arab world further by intervening against Sudan's Arab government on behalf of Darfur's African population.[64]

---

[62] Alex de Waal, 'The Book Was Closed Too Soon on Peace in Darfur', *The Guardian*, 29 September 2006, available at http://www.guardian.co.uk/commentisfree/2006/sep/29/comment.sudan (accessed 15 December 2008).

[63] E/CN.4/2005/8, 27 September 2004, paras. 22, 26, and 36.

[64] These points are documented in greater length in Paul D. Williams and Alex J. Bellamy, 'The Responsibility to Protect and the Crisis in Darfur', *Security Dialogue* 36:1 (2005), 27–47.

None of this is meant to justify inaction in the face of genocide but it goes some way towards explaining why it is that governments usually choose to stand aside when there is such a clear moral imperative to intervene to put an end to genocides once begun. It also helps illuminate the difficult choices that policy-makers confront.

CONCLUSION

Typically, genocide ends either with the suppression and/or destruction of the victim group or with the military defeat of the perpetrators. Only very rarely are those military defeats affected by the intervention of external powers spurred primarily by the intention to put an end to genocide. Indeed, only twice in the past century have states intervened to put an end to genocide, and in both cases the interveners had decidedly mixed motives. The problem, then, is not that there is too much humanitarian intervention in times of putative genocide, but that there is far too little. International society's default response to genocide is to stand aside and hope that the blood-letting comes to an end incidentally. This is despite the emergence of a clear moral, political—and some would say legal—responsibility to take timely and decisive action to put an end to genocide. It is, of course, correct to argue that the responsibility to protect populations from genocide does not create a duty of armed intervention in every case but we know that once genocide has begun, only the choice of the perpetrators or their military defeat is likely to bring it to an end. We should acknowledge, however, that decisions to intervene are fraught with difficulties. Military intervention is legally problematic, especially when there is no consensus in the Security Council. States, especially democratic states, are understandably reluctant to sacrifice their citizens in order to save foreigners in peril. Policy-makers therefore need to make difficult calculations about the prospective costs and benefits of armed intervention in a context of radical uncertainty. And, of course, there is no guarantee that intervention will succeed in saving lives.

No amount of institutional reform and rhetorical finessing can get around the fact that armed intervention to end genocide requires leaders who are prepared to pay the political costs of failure. These decisions will always be taken on an ad hoc and case-by-case basis and will always involve mixed motives, and require difficult judgments and a degree of risk taking. Because intervention to end genocide is so necessary and yet so rare, we commentators might help by worrying less about the damage done to international order by armed intervention against tyrants and more about the damage done to really existing human beings when international society stands aside. Clearly, non-violent prevention is much better than violent cure but, ultimately, we must face the fact that once genocide has begun only war on the perpetrators will bring it to a premature end. Leaders in democratic countries would find it easier to fulfil their moral commitments if their domestic constituents demanded that they do what was necessary to put an end to genocide. This could start, of course, with a commitment not to assist the perpetrators, even when material or strategic interests would seem to demand such support.

ACKNOWLEDGEMENTS

The author thanks Dirk Moses and Donald Bloxham for their insightful and comprehensive comments on an earlier draft of this chapter and assistance with redrafting. Thanks also to Ruben Reike, Paul D. Williams, and Sara E. Davies.

FURTHER READING

Bass, Gary J., *Freedom's Battle: The Origins of Humanitarian Intervention* (London: Knopf, 2008).

Bellamy, Alex J., *Responsibility to Protect: The Global Effort to End Mass Atrocities* (Cambridge: Polity Press, 2009).

Chesterman, Simon, *Just War or Just Peace? Humanitarian Intervention in International Law* (Oxford: Oxford University Press, 2001).

Evans, Gareth, *The Responsibility to Protect: Ending Mass Atrocity Crimes Once and for All* (Washington, DC: Brookings Institute, 2008).

Heidenrich, John G., *How to Prevent Genocide: A Guide for Policymakers, Scholars and Concerned Citizens* (Westport, CT: Praeger, 2001).

Holzgrefe, J. L., and Robert O. Keohane (eds), *Humanitarian Intervention: Ethical, Legal and Political Dilemmas* (Cambridge: Cambridge University Press, 2003).

Jones, Adam, *Genocide: A Comprehensive Introduction* (London: Routledge, 2006).

Kiernan, Ben, *Blood and Soil: A World History of Genocide and Extermination from Sparta to Darfur* (New Haven, CT: Yale University Press, 2008).

Melvern, Linda, *Conspiracy to Murder: The Rwandan Genocide* (London: Verso, 2006).

Wheeler, Nicholas J., *Saving Strangers: Humanitarian Intervention in International Society* (Oxford: Oxford University Press, 2000).

....

CHAPTER 30

PUNISHMENT AS PREVENTION?

THE POLITICS OF PUNISHING GÉNOCIDAIRES

....

DONALD BLOXHAM

DEVIN O. PENDAS

ALONGSIDE military and diplomatic intervention, as well as economic sanctions, criminal trials have become the international community's instrument of choice for reckoning with genocide and crimes against humanity. While the other responses tend in one way or another to be interventionist, seeking to halt genocide as it is occurring, what we term the legalist approach to of genocide is generally retrospective in orientation, seeking to punish acts that have already taken place. Although the initiation of legal proceedings has recently developed problematic interventionist aspects, the basic fact remains that law punishes past acts, rather than intervening in ongoing ones. Why has this preference for punishment arisen, what is it intended to achieve, and does it achieve it?

The preference does not arise, as some of the advocates of international legalism would maintain, as a way of depoliticizing the response to genocide. Quite the opposite: international criminal law remains a political instrument and a particularly inexpensive one at that. In both economic and political terms, international criminal trials require only limited expenditures of capital. Accordingly, trials tend to be highly disposable—all the more so because they take place after the fact. As for what international criminal law is intended to achieve, there are four justifications: retribution, special prevention (preventing the perpetrator from reoffending), general prevention (deterring other potential offenders), and moral pedagogy. This chapter will argue that none of these are achieved by international criminal law.

Law's crucial contribution is, instead, articulating a normative consensus that mobilizes *political* pressure for compliance. As a mechanism for articulating norms and forging consensus, the new international legalism offers a chance—albeit a modest one—to shift patterns of behaviour and place limited checks on the free hand of international power. But this is an ongoing political battle, one that can never be resolved by the simple establishment of international courts, conventions, and case-law, nor any of the other trappings of law. Whatever the aspirations of its jurist cheerleaders, international law will never be analogous to domestic law, and the two share little save the outward form. *International legalism remains a form of politics.*

Law's role as a continuation of politics by other means brings with it a downside. Precisely because legal responses to genocide are a form of politics, they are both readily manipulable for strategic ends and highly dependent upon the constellation of global political forces at any given moment. Often, for instance, allegations of human rights violations or genocide are instrumentalized to stigmatize political opponents, as exemplified by Colombia's recent attempt to have Hugo Chavez indicted at the International Criminal Court (ICC) for genocide for his support of the FARC guerilla movement in Colombia. Alternatively, international legalism can be used to validate military interventions where politically convenient, and in other cases to substitute for intervention when such action would not be politically convenient. Equally often, international trials simply provide a venue for the articulation of competing accounts of mass atrocities which cannot themselves be fully resolved in the courtroom, what Gerry Simpson has referred to as the 'proceduralized clash of competing ideologies'.[1]

This chapter will be divided into three roughly chronological sections, each dealing with an important stage in the chequered history of the legalist paradigm. Despite the real innovations of the nineteenth century, we take the Nuremberg trials as our starting point because the legal developments of the immediate post-war period served as the crucible for most subsequent developments in international legalism. Almost as soon as the Nuremberg model was developed and implemented in new legal instruments like the 1948 UN Convention on the Prevention and Punishment of Genocide, its efficacy was undermined by the global cold war, which thus marks the second phase of our analysis. The third phase deals with the re-emergence of the legalist paradigm in the first decade after the end of the cold war. International legal codes saw significant growth in this period, new international

---

[1] Gerry Simpson, *Law, War and Crime* (Cambridge: Cambridge University Press, 2007), 13.

criminal courts, both ad hoc and, from 2002, permanent, came into being and major trials for genocide and other crimes against humanity were conducted. The New World Order proclaimed by the first president Bush was implicitly a juridified one, in which legal norms would be universally applied through international institutions. The wave of utopian expectations surrounding these developments obscured the ongoing reality of power politics. The USA's reaction to 11 September 2001, its mounting opposition to the ICC, and its unilateral invasion of Iraq demonstrated that the limits of the legalist paradigm had not by any means been overcome. Indeed, the problems besetting the paradigm are intrinsic to the nature of an international political system based on nation-state sovereignty and influenced by 'great power' agendas. The cold war was only a particularly pointed illustration of the primacy of the political order over the legal.

THE PARADIGM ESTABLISHED:
THE POSTWAR MOMENT

In January 1942, the governments in exile of the occupied countries of Europe declared that among the principal aims of the Second World War should be 'the punishment, through the channel of organized justice, of those guilty and responsible for these crimes [by Nazi Germany], whether they have ordered them, or in any way participated in them.'[2] In October 1943, the Big Three Allies followed suit, proclaiming that any German soldiers or Nazi party members guilty of 'atrocities, massacres and executions' would be 'sent back to the countries in which their abominable deeds were done in order that they may be judged and punished according to the laws of these liberated countries.'[3] Those perpetrators whose crimes were without clear 'geographical localization' were to be punished by a subsequent 'joint decisions of the government of the Allies'.

With this, the Allies declared that justice, as much as peace or renewed international stability, would be an essential goal of post-war policy. There had of course been similar declarations in the First World War, culminating in the disastrous trials of German war criminals at Leipzig and of Turkish ones at Constantinople. What distinguished the declarations of the Second World War from their counterparts in the First was that this time, the Allies actually implemented their promises.

---

[2] Arieh J. Kochavi, *Prelude to Nuremberg: Allied War Crimes Policy and the Question of Punishment* (Chapel Hill: University of North Carolina Press, 1998), 20.

[3] *A Decade of American Foreign Policy: Basic Documents, 1941–49* (Washington, DC: Government Printing Office, 1950), 13.

Indeed, the chief lesson of the First World War for the architects of the post-Second World War international legal regime was that it was unwise to leave the punishment of war criminals to their own states. There were two distinct and not entirely consonant principles at work in the Allied response to this insight. First, there was the territoriality principle articulated in the Moscow Declaration, under which Nazi criminals would be punished by their victims. The second, not yet clear in the Moscow Declaration, was an internationalist principle, according to which some wartime criminals, the political leadership in particular, were in effect too big to be left to national courts. It was the Americans in particular who in the closing stages of the war came to embrace the idea of an international trial for the major war criminals.[4] The reasons for this were those of both principle, a moral opposition to the major alternative of summary executions, and political. Roosevelt's advisors wanted to ensure broad public backing for their post-war policy.

Consequently, the International Military Tribunal (IMT) at Nuremberg and its sister Tribunal in Tokyo were intended from the start to be only one element in a much broader effort at legal prosecution. Indeed, although Nuremberg's fame, both at the time and subsequently, has overshadowed the other trials for Nazi atrocities, the IMT was truly a drop in the ocean, quantitatively speaking. According to the latest estimates, more than 95,000 Germans and Austrians were convicted for wartime crimes throughout Europe.[5] Of these, 19 were convicted by the IMT.

Nonetheless, it is the IMT and to a less extent, the twelve so-called successor trials conducted by the American Military Tribunal, likewise at Nuremberg, that form the model for the subsequent development of the international legalist approach to genocide. In part, this is for statutory reasons. The London Charter, authorizing the IMT, criminalized three categories of offences. The least innovative of these, and hence the least controversial, was war crimes, namely, 'violations of the laws or customs of war'.[6] 'Crimes against peace' criminalized wars of aggression or in violation of international treaties. Although this was the crucial charge in the minds of the Americans at the time, it has been the one with the least subsequent international legal resonance. Finally, and in this context most importantly, the London Charter criminalized 'crimes against humanity'. These included the mass murder and persecution of civilians, as well as 'persecutions on political, racial, or religious grounds'.[7] War crimes and crimes against humanity both penalized the killing of civilians, the crucial difference being whether the victims and the perpetrators were of the same or different nationalities, and the connection to

[4] For the full story, see Kochavi, *Prelude*.

[5] Norbert Frei, 'Nach der Tat: Die Ahndung deutscher Kriegs- und NS-Verbrechen in Europa— eine Bilanz', in *idem* (ed.), *Transnationale Vergangenheitspolitik* (Göttingen: Wallstein, 2006), 32. The figures here only include convictions in Germany (East and West) through 1959.

[6] International Military Tribunal, *Trial of the Major War Criminals before the International Military Tribunal* (Nuremberg: IMT, 1947), i.11.

[7] Ibid.

military operations and military occupation. Crimes against humanity, unlike war crimes, could be perpetrated against a state's own citizens. Furthermore, persecutions were criminalized, 'whether or not in violation of domestic law of the country where perpetrated'. Thus, the London Charter for the first time prioritized international over domestic law and the sanctity of national sovereignty was, in principle at least, subordinated to international jurisdiction.

While the term genocide was used in the IMT indictment and in those of several of the successor trials to describe the criminal acts in question, it was not one of the criminal charges articulated in the London Charter. No Nazi criminals were ever convicted of genocide as such. Although war crimes and crimes against humanity between them cover most of the actions constituting genocide, the specificity of that crime as it was articulated by Raphael Lemkin and subsequently codified in the Genocide Convention was not formally part of the Nuremberg model. Lemkin's central insight was that certain atrocities targeted individuals as bearers of largely non-negotiable identities, that it was the groups themselves, rather than the individual victims, who were the real targets of the perpetrators. This view was to a degree implicit in the concept of persecution contained in crimes against humanity but Lemkin, who disliked the concept of crimes against humanity, wanted to go further and provide protection, not just to an amorphous humanity, but to the identifiable groups actually persecuted in the world. This notion, that certain kinds of human groups—those based on presumably 'fixed' identities—required special legal protection in a dangerous world, led to the first and most dramatic expansion of the Nuremberg model with the UN Genocide Convention of 1948.

In December 1946, the first session of the UN General Assembly passed a genocide resolution, GA Resolution 96 (I), at the behest of Cuba, India, and Panama.[8] It affirmed the criminal character of genocide and urged states to criminalize it under domestic law. As a non-binding resolution, it also called on the UN to study the feasibility of a more potent genocide convention. The Economic and Social Council of the UN and the Sixth (Legal) Committee wrote and debated various drafts of a genocide convention throughout 1947 and 1948, before finally passing the convention in December 1948. There was a good deal of bureaucratic back-and-forth in the legislative history of the genocide convention. This had little to do with bureaucratic inertia. It was easy (and cheap) to morally abhor genocide, as in the genocide resolution. Doing something about it invariably came with political costs attached. The most obvious and important of these was that formally criminalizing genocide in an international convention would inevitably entail at least nominal restrictions on the behaviour of states and potentially provide a pretext for international interference in domestic affairs. The potential for such intervention was deliberately and tightly limited by the UN Charter (the foundation stone of post-war political

---

[8] William A. Schabas, *Genocide in International Law: The Crime of Crimes* (Cambridge: Cambridge University Press, 2000), 42–7, 51–81.

order), which was a 'Westphalian document par excellence', stressing the central significance of the sovereign state as the fundamental building block of the international system.[9] Rhetoric aside, the architecture of that system as a whole was primarily structured towards prohibiting interstate warfare and the transgression of interstate boundaries, much less so with crimes committed within established state borders. Indeed, as had been the case in the interwar period and the nineteenth century, it was in certain circumstances simply preferable for internal population groups like Turkey's Kurds, or other potential secessionists, to be violently repressed in the interests of maintaining borders arrived at through earlier warfare.[10] A genocide convention threatened to undermine this carefully constructed edifice of post-war stability by introducing a countervailing principle of humanitarian intervention.

There was also the related question of jurisdiction. If genocide was a crime of state, who could prosecute it? As many would argue in the subsequent debates, only an international criminal court was likely to have the independence necessary to sit in judgment on such crimes. Yet a permanent court laying claim to a superordinate international jurisdiction proved to be an intolerable threat to national sovereignty for a great many delegates. Nuremberg was one thing, since it was an ad hoc tribunal with jurisdiction exclusively over Nazi crimes. A standing court was a different matter entirely. Finally, there was the simple fact that a convention would require a careful and authoritative definition of genocide. This could either narrow or expand the meaning of what was already becoming a particularly potent term of moral and political opprobrium.

In order to get the genocide convention passed at all, several compromises, which rendered the document virtually inert from the very start, were necessary.[11] The first and most important of these concerned jurisdiction. The initial secretariat draft of the genocide convention contained as an appendix two draft statutes for a permanent international criminal court, one with restricted jurisdiction over genocide alone, another with expansive jurisdiction over international crimes to be defined by the International Law Commission. The guiding assumption, even if it was not made explicit in the Convention, was that genocide was generally a state crime and therefore required international jurisdiction if there was to be any hope of prosecution. The French delegate to the Sixth (Legal) Committee strongly supported this notion. 'Genocide was committed only through the criminal intervention of public authorities; that was what distinguished it from murder pure and

---

[9] Kalevi J. Holsti, *The State, War, and the State of War* (Cambridge: Cambridge University Press, 1996).

[10] Donald Bloxham, *The Great Game of Genocide* (Oxford: Oxford University Press, 2005), ch. 1 and the second 'interlude'.

[11] Devin O. Pendas, 'Towards World Law?: The Failure of the Legalist Paradigm of War, 1945–1980', in Stefan-Ludwig Hoffmann (ed.), *Human Rights in the Twentieth Century: Concepts and Conflicts* (Cambridge: Cambridge University Press, forthcoming).

simple. The purpose of the convention which the Committee was drawing up was not to punish individual murders, but to ensure the prevention and punishment of crimes committed by rulers.'[12] Hence, it was imperative, he concluded, to establish an International Criminal Court forthwith. The French support for linking the genocide convention to the formation of an international court proved to be the minority position, however. The Venezuelan representative on the Sixth Committee, for instance, warned that

the institution of international criminal jurisdiction could only lead to unfortunate results, in view of the existing world situation. Friction might be created which could disturb the peace among nations. The establishment of international penal jurisdiction should be reserved for the future when international relations would be more favorable to such an institution.[13]

The Polish delegate concurred, saying that he could on no account 'sacrifice questions of principle' concerning the sanctity of national sovereignty. The Americans and the British, meanwhile, crafted a compromise that prevented the issue of an international court from torpedoing the negotiations altogether. At US initiative, Article VI of the final convention left open the possibility that in future, an International Criminal Court might have jurisdiction over genocide, while the British inserted into Article IX an option to have the existing International Court of Justice adjudicate interstate disputes over the interpretation of the convention. This was enough to satisfy supporters of international jurisdiction without alienating the advocates of national sovereignty.

The price was rather high, though. Article VI of the final convention states that perpetrators of genocide 'shall be tried by a competent tribunal of the state in the territory of which the act was committed'.[14] In other words, as long as the genocidal regime remains in place, there is no possibility whatsoever of an actual prosecution for genocide. Regime change would be a prerequisite for the prosecution of genocide. Given regime change, the trial would not threaten the interstate order because the perpetrators would already have been deposed and the erstwhile perpetrator state would remain under a new regime; absent regime change, both state and regime would remain untouched—all of this is the obverse side of the achievement of individualizing responsibility for state atrocity under international law (the state itself remains unprosecuted). The genocide convention was therefore effectively stillborn. It is hardly surprising that the first successful prosecution of genocide did not occur until the Akayesu case before the International Criminal Tribunal for Rwanda (ICTR) in 1998, and then not under the Genocide Convention

---

[12] UN Doc. A/C.6/SR 97, p. 373.
[13] UN Doc A/C.6/SR 130.
[14] Schabas, *Genocide*, 566.

but under the Statute for the ICTR. The Nuremberg breakthrough, according to which international law would trump domestic law, proved to be less a general principle than a short-term expedient.

THE DISAPPEARANCE OF THE PARADIGM:
THE COLD WAR

Nothing better illustrated the transitory nature of 'Nuremberg' than the collapse of the Nuremberg edifice in the 1950s. A growing German opposition to the Allied trial and occupation regimes found a conducive environment with the onset of the cold war. The need to placate German national sentiment amid the burgeoning political conflict with the USSR led first to the ending of the war crimes trials programmes in all western occupation zones in the late 1940s, in the context of a general easing of occupation policy. Later it resulted in a series of increasingly politicized 'sentence reviews' which ultimately developed the simple aim of releasing all war criminals, most of them prematurely.[15] The final four war criminals in US custody were released by 1958: the number incarcerated at the beginning of 1955 had been forty-one. Jails in the erstwhile British zone of Germany were empty by 1957.[16] Among those released after serving only a few years of life sentences and commuted death sentences were some of the worst Nazi offenders, including commanders of the *Einsatzgruppen* (SS killing squads) and senior members of the concentration camp hierarchy. Rejection of the legal validity of the trials was subtly built into articles 6 and 7 of the 1952 Bonn Treaty ending the Allied occupation statute.[17]

Treatments of the Nuremberg trials by legal scholars have generally been silent on the collapse of the legal machinery, focusing instead on the achievements of the courtroom itself, and the legacies created in law. Yet divorcing the German trials from any broader political context is to undermine one of the most important rationales for trial in the first place. That rationale, to paraphrase US chief prosecutor Robert Jackson's opening address before the IMT, was to impose the rule of law on naked power relations. In other words, the collapse of Nuremberg in the 1950s (along with that of the International Military Tribunal for the Far East)

---

[15] Donald Bloxham, *Genocide on Trial: War Crimes Trials and the Formation of Holocaust History and Memory* (Oxford: Oxford University Press, 2001), Chap. 4; Peter Maguire, *Law and War: An American Story* (New York: Columbia University Press, 2001).

[16] Maguire, *Law and War*, 256.

[17] Ibid. 229.

illustrates that law may influence the exercise of might but the process also works in reverse. The particular problem with the Nuremberg case is that much of its importance rested on the fact that it brought a major world power to book, but the enduring geopolitical significance of Germany (and Japan) effectively placed a limit on the extent of this reckoning.

Scholarly silence on the releases of the 1950s may be legitimate for a narrow legal approach that is only interested in legal instruments, institutions, and precedents, and can leap across time, like a frog jumping from one water lily to the next, landing selectively on those moments where the law does seem to come into its own.[18] According to that depiction, which mirrors some of the more teleological scholarship on the emergence of human rights, the cold war can be seen as a simple hiatus, an aberration in the development of worldwide democracy and international law; with the end of the cold war, the time of genuine sovereign accountability has now arrived, and we can just pick up where Nuremberg left off. As Geoffrey Robertson puts it on the concluding page of what is otherwise a measured assessment of the progress of humanitarian law: 'although the twenty-first century will have its share of despots, they will be fewer and in the absence of the Cold War, they will not have superpower support. There will no longer be any need to say, as FDR said of Grandfather Somoza, "he may be a son of a bitch, but he's our son of a bitch."'[19]

The alternative view, grounded in an appreciation of the political context so often missing from the work of legal scholars, is to see the cold war as a pointed illustration of some of the potentialities of 'our' (Western) political-ethical system. The cold war also illustrated how far legal and humanitarian language could be abused by strategic interest. Atrocities and aggressive wars were perpetrated by both sides and their proxies, while the rhetoric of international law and human rights was frequently used as a weapon to stigmatize the other side for things that one's own side was also doing, in a manner that disillusioned both former Nuremberg lawyers and historians of the trial.[20] Invocation of the genocide convention in the third quarter of the twentieth century over cases like Nigeria (Biafra) and East Pakistan (Bangladesh) only served to underline the irrelevance of the document as a concrete ground for political action, much like the rights declarations of the same period.[21] The UN Security Council was divided among its permanent members into capitalists and communists (neither

---

[18] See, e.g., Gary Jonathan Bass, *Stay the Hand of Vengeance: The Politics of War Crimes Tribunals* (Princeton, NJ: Princeton University Press, 2000).

[19] Geoffrey Robertson, *Crimes against Humanity: The Struggle for Global Justice* (New York: New Press, 1999), 387.

[20] Telford Taylor, *Nuremberg and Vietnam: An American Tragedy* (New York: Bantam, 1971); Eugene Davidson, *The Nuremberg Fallacy* (Columbia: University of Missouri Press, 1973).

[21] On Pakistan, A. Dirk Moses, 'The United Nations and the Failure to Prosecute: The Case of East Pakistan, 1971–1974', in Hoffman (ed.), *Human Rights in the Twentieth Century*, forthcoming.

'side' internally harmonious) while, in the General Assembly and among the temporary members of the Security Council, the situation was complicated by the representatives of a growing number of 'Third World' states as UN membership nearly tripled from 1945 to 1975. Some of these states provided the battlegrounds for the indirect warfare of the First and Second Worlds, and provided most of the death toll of the cold war. Other states were courted by the major protagonists in the economic-political-cultural contest, and thus gained temporary influence. Still others even succeeded in limited ways in using the UN to press their own agendas against Security Council states, as Algeria did with France. Almost none were prepared to compromise their hard-won post-colonial independence by supporting potentially intrusive human rights regimes or general principles of 'humanitarian intervention'. Indeed, one could with some justification view this as the major achievement of the Non-Aligned Movement.

The record of the cold war shows how dangerous it is to extrapolate to general trends from brief moments of 'legalist' triumph such as the year 1945. The legal optimism greeting the end of the Second World War was repeated at the end of the cold war; with the benefit of historical perspective we should be equally wary of succumbing to the temptations of that optimism. The end of the cold war left the most important 'vanquished' protagonist—what became Russia—untouchable in terms of accountability for crimes committed by the Soviet regime. Even in its weakened state, Russia remained too powerful for foreign powers to contemplate even retroactive interference in its 'domestic' affairs. There was no question in any circumstances of bringing the cold war victor to book for its earlier crimes—and insofar as any of the USA's former Latin American allies addressed the abuses of their former right-wing dictatorships, this was generally done outside the courtroom through truth and reconciliation processes, and in ways that could not threaten the socio-economic order that the dictators had put in place.[22] When criminal law was used in post-authoritarian Latin America, as in for instance Argentina, it was carefully calibrated so as to not disturb the fragile balance of domestic power and risk renewed violence.[23]

In the sense of taming power, therefore, the legal developments after the cold war are actually less impressive than the temporary achievements of Nuremberg. Yet it was precisely Nuremberg, alongside the Genocide Convention, that was invoked in the 1990s. With the end of communism in Eastern Europe, it became possible to talk more realistically—however temporarily—about a single world order with a single set of governing frameworks. Alongside firstly the vanguard organizations of free market capitalism and secondly the apostles of parliamentary democracies,

---

[22] Lawrence Weschler, *A Miracle, a Universe: Settling Accounts with Torturers* (Chicago: University of Chicago Press, 1998), and more generally, Robert I. Rotberg and Dennis Thompson (eds), *Truth v. Justice: The Morality of Truth Commissions* (Princeton, NJ: Princeton University Press, 2000).

[23] Carlos Santiago Nino, *Radical Evil on Trial* (New Haven, CT: Yale University Press 1996).

Western jurists could make their mark on shaping the norms of that order, and they were hurried into action by the ethnic cleansing and murder attendant on the dissolution of the former Yugoslavia.

THE PARADIGM REASSERTED

The unanticipated collapse of the Soviet Empire in 1989 and the ensuing end to the cold war brought with it sweeping, if short-lived, hopes for a peaceful, stable 'New World Order', in which the entire world increasingly came to resemble the United States and history itself came to an end as the great ideological struggles of the past gave way to a universal consumer democracy. Of course history did not end in 1989. Nor did the New World Order prove to be anything like as peaceful and stable as its proponents anticipated. Indeed, the collapse of the cold war order brought with it outbreaks of large-scale violence in unanticipated places, including Europe itself with the dissolution of Yugoslavia in the 1990s. In the absence of great power rivalries, much of the violence of the post-cold war period operated below the level of geopolitical concern for the major international actors. Secretary of State James Baker's notorious comment that the United States had no dog in the fight between Croatia and Serbia can be taken as indicative. Baker was only more blunt, not more callous than his many counterparts in the United States and Europe.

Given the lack of traditional great power 'interests' in many of the world's new conflict zones, interventions, even of the cynical proxy war variety typical of the cold war, were hard to justify.[24] At the same time, however, the near universal mediatization of the world meant that these conflicts were often difficult for politicians to simply ignore. If action was not necessarily called for, pseudo-action was. It is in this context that one must understand how the return of history after 1989 brought with it what Norbert Frei has called the 'return of law'.[25] International criminal tribunals, with their promise of retrospective punishment for mass atrocity, were ideally suited to providing the semblance of action while diffusing pressure to undertake more substantive interventionist measures. The initial impetus for the formation of the International Criminal Tribunal for the Former Yugoslavia (ICTY) came, after all, not from the members

---

[24] David Rieff, *Slaughterhouse: Bosnia and the Failure of the West* (New York: Touchstone, 1995); Philip Gourevitch, *We Wish to Inform you That Tomorrow We Will Be Killed with Our Families: Stories from Rwanda* (New York: Picador, 1998).

[25] Norbert Frei, 'Die Rückkehr des Rechts: Justiz und Zeitgeschichte nach dem Holocaust—eine Zwischenbilanz', in Arnd Bauerkämper, Martin Sabrow, and Bernd Stöver (eds), *Doppelte Zeitgeschichte: Deutsch-deutsche Beziehungen, 1945–1990* (Bonn: Dietz, 1998).

of the UN Security Council but from Human Rights Watch.[26] In the face of such pressure from below, it was largely what Pierre Hazan called the 'opportunistic steeplechase between France and the United States' that eventually led to the creation of the ICTY, as each tried to claim moral leadership while avoiding military action. That the ICTY was intended to be impotent is apparent in the complete lack of resources placed at its disposal initially. That in the end the tribunal was not quite so impotent as its creators initially planned was due largely to the political skills of its first two chief prosecutors, Richard Goldstone and Louise Arbour.[27] Goldstone, though not so effective as a prosecutor as his successors, was politically skilled and was able to mobilize private resources to get the tribunal up and running. Arbour forged an effective prosecutorial strategy that led to actual trials and, by indicting Slobodan Milošević in May 1999 for his ongoing crimes in Kosovo, interjected the tribunal directly into the political process in the Balkans and thereby made it more directly relevant than it would otherwise have been.

Nonetheless, two points are worth stressing about the two ad hoc UN tribunals of the 1990s, the ICTY and its sister tribunal for Rwanda, the ICTR. The first is that neither ever stopped anyone from committing a single crime. Arbour's indictment of Milošević during the Kosovo war may have made the tribunal an indispensible actor in the political process; it did not, however, prevent the atrocities in Kosovo from continuing. The second point concerns the independence of the courts. Obviously, as ad hoc tribunals, the ICTY and the ICTR were created with deliberately restricted jurisdictions. This in itself limited their remit considerably and kept them to a degree under the political control of their sponsors on the UN Security Council. If the tribunals, especially the ICTY, nonetheless achieved greater independence than their sponsors envisaged, this ought not to blind us to the ultimate limits the tribunals faced. After all, they remained dependent on state actors, the Americans in particular, for intelligence resources, as well, obviously, as on UN troops for the enforcement of their warrants and indictments. The real boundaries of this independence revealed themselves in the ICTY's investigation of NATO for war crimes during the air war in Kosovo. The simple fact that the ICTY investigated these was, in Louise Arbour's words, 'staggering' for the NATO powers.[28] Whatever the merits of the case, though, it can hardly be surprising that the ICTY found that NATO had committed no war crimes. NATO spokesperson Jamie Shea had reminded the prosecutor's office,

---

[26] Pierre Hazan, *Justice in a Time of War: The True Story behind the International Criminal Tribunal for the Former Yugoslavia* (College Station: Texas A&M, 2004), 14.

[27] John Hagan, *Justice in the Balkans: Prosecuting War Crimes in the Hague Tribunal* (Chicago: University of Chicago Press, 2003).

[28] Hazan, *Justice in a Time of War*, 130.

Don't bite the hand that feeds you . . . The people of NATO are the ones who apprehend the war criminals indicted by the Tribunal . . . We all want to see war criminals judged and I am certain that, when Prosecutor Arbour returns to Kosovo and sees the facts, she will indict the Yugoslav nationals, and no other nationality.[29]

This was exactly what happened under Arbour's successor, Carla Del Ponte.

The ad hoc tribunals of the 1990s thus must be seen as at best ambiguous institutions. On the one hand, there can be no doubt that many of the men and women working for these tribunals were passionate in their pursuit of justice. Nor can there be much doubt that those convicted by the ICTY and the ICTR richly deserved their punishment and that it is preferable to see such criminals punished rather than left free. However, the inflated promises made on behalf of these tribunals that, henceforth, war criminals and génocidaires would, in the words of Boutros Boutros-Ghali, 'know the sanction of international law' proved to be hyperbolic. Moreover, the fiasco of the Milošević trial, which dragged on for years before terminating with the former dictator's death in prison, has revealed an unavoidable tension between the hyper-careful concern for due process embodied in the ad hoc tribunals and the moral and political requirements of swift and efficacious justice.

The changed atmosphere of the 1990s also gave a renewed impulse to an older idea: the establishment of an International Criminal Court to go alongside the International Court of Justice established in 1945. The ICC came into effect in 2002, and its jurisdiction and functions are based on the Rome Statute of 1998. The ICC operates on the principle of complementarity with domestic courts: it will only concern itself with the prosecution of cases in which the state concerned is unable or unwilling to prosecute its citizens for breaches of international law. Like the ad hoc tribunals, the ICC's mandate is to consider genocide, crimes against humanity, and war crimes. It can also consider aggressive warfare, which, in the eyes of the Nuremberg lawgivers, was their most important legacy to international law.[30] But it cannot do so until a definition of aggressive war is internationally agreed, which is no insignificant obstacle, given the past difficulties in framing that concept.[31] Enforceability is another thing again, given the age-old use of aggressive warfare for the most powerful states, and the equally venerable tradition of states finding 'self-defensive' pretexts for warmongering.

A particularly important aspect of the ICC, like the ad hoc tribunals, is its genuinely international constitution. It is no longer possible to talk about

[29] Ibid. 132.

[30] On the institutional background, M. Cherif Bassiouni, 'The Permanent International Criminal Court', in Mark Lattimer and Philippe Sands (eds), *Justice for Crimes against Humanity* (Oxford: Hart, 2007), 173–211.

[31] Jonathan Bush, '"The Supreme . . . Crime" and Its Origins: The Lost Legislative History of the Crime of Aggressive War', *Columbia Law Review* 102 (December 2002), 2324–401.

'victor's justice' in prosecution in the way that it was in the Nuremberg era. Important elements implicit in the accusation of victor's justice persist, however. In particular, genuinely neutral enforcement will be difficult to achieve. The ICC by definition will depend on the cooperation of powerful states to enforce its decisions, making it difficult to imagine how it could ever enforce its will upon those states. This problem, already foreshadowed in the ICTY's ruling on the NATO bombing of Kosovo, is unlikely to go away any time soon.

The ICC cannot escape its subordination to the existing global power structure. The ICC's remit is constrained to states that have ratified and acceded to the Rome Statute. The only exceptions are for cases brought to the court's attention by the UN Security Council under Article VII of the UN Charter, concerning acts likely to disturb the peace internationally. Yet the three most politically and militarily powerful states with crucial permanent membership of the Security Council—the USA, China, and Russia—are not Rome signatories. (The USA has also signed bilateral immunity agreements with around one hundred states, including Rome signatories, to keep American nationals from the court's jurisdiction.) The three states are exempt from the court's scrutiny, and are in the best imaginable position to keep their allies, whether or not they are Rome signatories, out of the court's reach. Given that the Security Council's approval will often be necessary to enforce arrest warrants against ICC indictees, there is yet further scope for the Security Council to undermine the ICC. The extent to which the ICC, more specifically the office of the prosecutor (OTP), can enforce its will in the pursuit of politically significant suspects will in turn influence the seriousness with which the court is taken by the many signatory states, states which might also have to lend their troops to Security Council-mandated operations in pursuit of suspects.[32]

The practical constraints on the ICC help explain why the cases it is pursuing all stem from a part of the world of relatively low geostrategic significance for the major powers: Africa. It has been suggested, against a backdrop of long-standing self-interested Western interventionism in Africa, that the cases pursued in the Central African Republic, the Democratic Republic of Congo (DRC), Uganda, and Sudan are illustrations of neo-imperial victimization. This interpretation does not fit the facts. The first three cases were referred to the ICC by the states themselves, each of which is party to the Rome Statute—indeed, at least two of the referrals were partly motivated by the desire to delegitimize domestic political enemies for the sorts of crimes of which the referring state authorities were themselves not innocent. The Sudanese case was a Security Council referral

---

[32] On the credibility problems for the ICC, see Phil Clark, 'Ocampo's Darfur Strategy Depends on Congo', *Oxford Transitional Justice Research Working Paper Series*, 20 August 2008, available at http://www.csls.ox.ac.uk/otjr.php.

against a non-signatory state.[33] The African *marginality* that accounts for the heavy concentration of ICC effort there also helps explain why no greater international political investment was made to halt the crimes now under investigation while they were in progress.

It is at the nexus of punishment and intervention that the ICC has arguably exceeded the boundaries of legitimate behaviour for a legal institution. With some of the indictments in the case of Sudan, we see a potential conflation of the different preserves of intervention and legal redress. This is one step further along a road taken over Rwanda and, in the first instance, Yugoslavia, when legal proceedings were instituted in the midst of ongoing atrocity, not as a complement to interventionist action during it, but as a substitute for such action.[34] In the Sudanese case, the indictment of, inter alia, President Omar al-Bashir may prove an obstacle to negotiations over Darfur (and a destabilizing factor in southern Sudan) if the OTP pursues him irrespective of political consequences, or it may result in investigations being suspended as part of the bargaining process. In the first instance justice will come at the cost of possibly prolonging conflict (though in any case the OTP would be reliant in arresting Bashir and other military or political forces over which it itself has no direct influence). In the second instance justice will itself come to be seen as a disposable and explicitly political tool, thus undermining the universalistic claims of the jurists and threatening the legitimacy of the ICC.[35]

CONCLUSION: A BALANCE

Criminal trials are intended to punish crime. Such punishment has classically been justified in one of three ways, as retribution, as a means for preventing the

[33] For a defence of the ICC against the neo-imperialism charges, but one that does not address the concerns raised in this chapter, see Max du Plessis, 'The International Criminal Court and Its Work in Africa: Confronting the Myths', Institute for Strategic Studies paper 173 (November 2008). See p. 11 on DRC's and Uganda's attempt to use the court for political ends. See also Louisa Lombard, 'Justice for Whom? The ICC in the Central African Republic', on the SSRC Blogs: http://www.ssrc.org/blogs/darfur.

[34] Rachel Kerr, 'The Road from Dayton to Brussels? The International Criminal Tribunal for the Former Yugoslavia and the Politics of War Crimes in Bosnia', *European Security* 14:3 (2005), 319–37, here 325, and the material cited there in note 41.

[35] Chidi Odinkalu, 'What if Ocampo Indicts Bashir? 2'; Alex de Waal, 'Africa's Challenge to the ICC'; Heather Adams, 'Putting the Cart before the Horse', all on SSRC Blogs: http://www.ssrc.org/blogs/darfur; Stephen Oola, 'Bashir and the ICC: The Aura or Audition of International Justice in Africa', *Oxford Transitional Justice Research Working Paper Series*, 15 October 2008 at http://www.csls.ox.ac.uk/otjr.php. On the issue generally, Steven R. Ratner and Jason S. Abrams, *Accountability for Human Rights Atrocities in International Law* (Oxford: Oxford University Press, 2001), 224–5.

perpetrator from committing similar crimes again in future, and as a way of deterring other potential offenders from engaging in similar crimes themselves. In addition, trials for genocide and crimes against humanity have often been justified as forms of political and moral pedagogy.[36] In the end, though, none of these justifications make much sense when applied to genocide.

Retribution, as articulated most clearly by Immanuel Kant, argues that one punishes the criminal in order to restore the moral balance his or her crime has upset. Punishment is retribution, meted out by a court, according to a 'principle of equality' so that 'whatever undeserved evil you inflict upon another within the people, that you inflict upon yourself.'[37] Proportionality is the key element in this analysis. There are two problems with retributive justice as applied to genocide. First, retribution is an inherently individualizing approach to punishment. Yet genocide and crimes against humanity are, by their nature, systematic, mass crimes in which individual perpetrators operate within broad institutional or social frameworks. Consequently, the individualized moral claim at the heart of retributive justice tends to miss its mark. Second, it is difficult to conceive of a proportional retribution for genocide. After all, the most one can do is execute an individual perpetrator, which is hardly proportional to the thousands of murders for which he may be responsible. Indeed, pushed to its logical conclusion, proportionality would seem to require reciprocal genocide, which would clearly violate the principle of individual guilt at the heart of retributive justice, rendering such an approach internally incoherent.

Special prevention assumes that one punishes a criminal in order to prevent recidivism. Given that genocide and crimes against humanity are invariably political crimes, the risk of recidivism by individual perpetrators would depend entirely on political circumstances. Eliminate the conditions (the perpetrator state, for example, or the context of civil war) and one eliminates the chance of recidivism. In such circumstances, there would be no need to punish individual perpetrators at all. It might be claimed, as a variant of the special prevention argument, that indicting leaders for crimes still in progress might deter them from continuing to commit such offences. At best, the jury is still out on this claim, as in some of the African cases considered here. It is so far unclear whether indictments have had any impact on the behaviour of the political leadership of perpetrator states and, to the extent it has had an impact, whether that impact has been at all beneficial. It might, in fact, prove to be counterproductive, spurring leaders to greater efforts to complete their genocide, since they no longer have anything to lose, as was arguably the case with Milošević.

---

[36] Mark Osiel, *Mass Atrocity, Collective Memory, and the Law* (New Brunswick, NJ: Transaction, 1997).

[37] Immanuel Kant, *The Metaphysics of Morals* (Cambridge: Cambridge University Press, 1996), 105.

General prevention seems in many ways to be the most plausible explanation for why we should punish génocidaires. The claim is that punishing perpetrators deters future genocides. To begin with, there is no empirical evidence that this works and good reason to assume that it does not. The Serbian state, for instance, committed crimes against humanity in Kosovo long after the establishment of the ICTY; the existence of the ICTR in Tanzania did nothing to deter mass criminality in neighbouring DRC. It is not hard to see why this should be the case. Deterrence works, to the extent that it does, by raising the potential cost to the criminal of his or her crime, such that the anticipated benefit is no longer worth the risk involved.[38] Yet in some cases, genocide is, in Weberian terms, a value rational act, not an instrumentally rational one.[39] This means that questions of costs and benefits are explicitly excluded from consideration. What matters is the normative consistency of the act, not its anticipated success or failure. Consequently, raising the costs of acting in the given manner can have no impact whatsoever. In other cases, genocide can be triggered by a heightened sense of crisis and a paranoid evaluation of the threat posed by the victim group. In this situation, the cost of the failure to act, i.e., to commit genocide, is perceived by the perpetrating regime to be infinitely higher than any punishment that might be imposed in the event of failure and defeat. Besides, the sheer historical inconsistency of punishment for genocide removes the most important precondition for deterrence: relative certainty of punishment.[40] In any given genocide, perpetrators often number in the tens or even hundreds of thousands, while the numbers convicted remain at best in the hundreds or thousands; and, of course there are many genocides none of whose perpetrators ever reach trial.

The determination of which genocides or cases of large-scale crimes against humanity are prosecuted and which are ignored is largely a geopolitical one, as the proliferation of ICC cases against politically relatively marginal states in Africa shows. Elsewhere, given great power support for many genocidal regimes over the past 50 years, there can be a direct continuity between the political context which led to genocide and the subsequent impunity for génocidaires themselves, as for instance in Cambodia. It seems highly unlikely that there will be any indictments brought against perpetrators from close strategic allies of the United States as the

[38] John J. Donohue and Justin Wolfers, 'Uses and Abuses of Empirical Evidence in the Death Penalty Debate', *Stanford Law Review* 58 (December 2005), 791–846; and Richard Berk, 'New Claims about Execution and General Deterrence: Déjà vu All over Again', *Journal of Empirical Legal Studies* 2 (July 2005), 303–30.

[39] Max Weber, *Economy and Society: An Outline of Interpretive Sociology* (Berkeley: University of California Press, 1968), i.24–6.

[40] William C. Bailey, J. David Martin, and Louis N. Gray, 'Crime and Deterrence: A Correlation Analysis', *Journal of Research in Crime and Deliquency* 11 (1974), 124–43. Erling Eide in cooperation with Jorgen Aasness and Terje Skjerp, *Economics of Crime: Deterrence and the Rational Offender* (Amsterdam: North-Holland, 1994).

world's sole superpower. And even if such indictments were brought, the chances of them resulting in trials would be even slimmer. Absurd as it may be, the American president has congressional authorization to invade the Netherlands to rescue any Americans charged at The Hague should this become necessary.

Ours is not a purely materialist interpretation of international law. The very force of the label 'genocide' as mobilization slogan and condemnation illustrates, if only in the vigorous efforts of states like Turkey and Sudan to avoid its application, that the language of values can have real currency in the global arena. Underlying structural factors of the international political economy and geopolitical strategy do obviously come strongly into play in decisions as to who reaches trial, but the constitutions of internationally mandated courts, and the procedures in individual court cases, are generally not functions of those structural factors. Otherwise, as in the case of the American-dominated trial of Saddam Hussein, assiduously hived-off from the control of the United Nations, legal legitimacy would be totally lost. That legitimacy has been maintained is a credit to the committed individuals and organizations involved in such institutions as the ICTY, the ICTR, and the ICC, and a testament to the existence of an organized international *value community* of some sort beyond the international *power system* constituted by the world's most powerful states and multinational corporations. To what extent this legal community can prevail over the system in cases where their interests are antipathetic remains—to take the most optimistic assessment—an open question.

Even in conflicts which have been subject to adjudication, the problems of equitable prosecution have been enormous, in particular as a result of the post-genocidal power relations, both domestic and international. Cases where atrocities have been committed by all sides to a conflict, however unevenly, are particularly difficult in this regard. There may be prosecutions in which not all parties to a conflict involving multilateral atrocities are prosecuted, as in Rwanda or Uganda, and even—despite the extensive efforts of the ICC—the DRC.[41] Alternatively, different problems may arise as for instance with the ICTY's genuine efforts at proportionality in prosecution. The evidence seems to indicate that the ICTY's efforts have succeeded mainly in generating broad resentment against the court, with all ethnic parties feeling that the court is biased against them and overly lenient towards their adversaries.[42]

---

[41] Lombard, 'Justice for Whom?'; Lisa Clifford, 'ICC Risks Losing the Plot in Congo', *Institute for War and Peace Reporting Comment*, 21 November 2008, at http://www.iwpr.net

[42] Eric Stover and Harvey M. Weinstein (eds), *My Neighbor, My Enemy: Justice and Community in the Aftermath of Mass Atrocity* (Cambridge: Cambridge University Press. 2004); A. Uzelac, 'Hague Prosecutors Rest Their Case', *Institute for War and Peace Reporting* (27 December 2004); relatedly, Human Rights Watch, 'Justice at Risk: War Crimes Trials in Croatia, Bosnia and Herzegovina, and Serbia and Montenegro', *Human Rights Watch* 16:7 (2004), 1–31.

Finally, trials have been justified for their purported value as sites of moral and political pedagogy, particularly in the context of so-called democratic transitions. Unlike the other three justifications, which amalgamate trials for mass atrocity to ordinary criminal law, this argument highlights the specificity of such trials as elements in transitional justice.

The argument is that such trials can be effective means for establishing the history of past atrocities and thereby delegitimizing the perpetrator regime. While it is true that criminal prosecution can be highly effective at gathering evidence, it is less effective at marshalling this evidence to construct a coherent and accurate narrative. All too often the history lessons taught by criminal trials are distorted and misleading.[43] This is not due to any malice or incompetence on the part of the court but rather a result of the quite distinct methods and objectives of judges and historians.[44] Trials are not designed so much to ascertain what happened and why, as to determine who is to blame. By definition, trials are less interested in historical processes than they are in concrete manifestations of criminal intent; their goal is to establish individual guilt, not historical causation. As a consequence of this necessary focus on the individual in the dock, the remainder of the perpetrator polity can, with some justification, feel themselves exculpated. Unintentionally, then, such trials frequently end up serving as alibis for that majority of perpetrators and bystanders not prosecuted. Trials thus manifest an irreconcilable tension between any general pedagogical impulse and the individuating character of criminal justice.

However, even if trials unavoidably tend to teach inadequate history lessons, this in itself does not mean that they could not contribute to transitional justice. The form may be more important than the content. Mark Osiel contends that criminal trials are especially effective venues for 'stimulat[ing] public discussion in ways that foster the liberal virtues of toleration, moderation, and civil respect'.[45] Because such trials operate under the ground rules of liberal legalism (individual culpability, due process, fair defence, etc.), they perforce validate a pluralistic debate about the meaning of past atrocities, what Osiel terms 'civil dissensus'. According to this view, the benefit of the politico-legal system facilitating such a pluralism of views and the testing of one against the other, without imposing either in an authoritarian or unquestioning fashion, would become increasingly self-evident. As a consequence, the population will then come to embrace a liberal democratic polity.

---

[43] Devin O. Pendas, *The Frankfurt Auschwitz Trial, 1963–1965: Genocide, History and the Limits of the Law* (Cambridge: Cambridge University Press, 2005); Bloxham, *Genocide on Trial*.

[44] Carlo Ginzburg, *The Judge and the Historian: Marginal Notes on a Late-Twentieth-Century Miscarriage of Justice* (London: Verso, 1999); and Norbert Frei, Dirk van Laak, and Michael Stolleis (eds), *Geschichte vor Gericht: Historiker, Richter und die Suche nach Gerechtigkeit* (Munich: Beck, 2000).

[45] Osiel, *Mass Atrocity*, 2.

While theoretically appealing, the empirical evidence hardly supports this hypothesis, as the highly partisan responses to the ICTY show. Osiel's problem is ultimately one of scale. Such trials are unlikely to have this kind of liberalizing impact within post-conflict societies themselves, where they will if anything tend to harden, rather than ameliorate, the boundaries between conflicting parties. The exculpatory capacity of such trials for the unindicted can reinforce the sense of victimization, even among perpetrator groups (as, e.g., in Serbia or post-war Japan).

If trials are unlikely to deter genocide or democratize post-conflict societies, this does not mean that they can do no good in the world whatsoever. Above all, prosecuting genocide and crimes against humanity is a statement of principle, an act of symbolic disapproval on the part of the international community. This may have limited significance for the parties to specific conflicts, and can even be counterproductive for democratization, but it is important to the international community itself. It is an aspirational statement about what we hope the international community can become. To remain silent in the face of genocide would be to tacitly approve it, as is all too often the case at the moment. By extension, prosecuting genocide can be a useful instrument for forging an emerging consensus regarding international norms. Such trials pose in insistent terms the question of what is right and they offer answers, however modest, which can be incorporated into international political conversations. Such an emergent consensus can be discerned, again in a modest way, in the relatively wide adoption of the Rome Statute of the ICC, keeping in mind again that the most important international powers have thus far refused to join the court. Still, that so many countries are now ready to adopt a standing international court, when a few short decades ago almost none were, is a sign of at least limited progress. Of course, the legalist paradigm is all too easily subject to manipulation. This is why it is important for genuinely independent NGOs, media outlets, and ordinary citizens to monitor the use and abuse of international legal norms. International criminal law is too important to be left to lawyers alone, whose claims to embody a universal class of disinterested humanitarians evinces an all too evident partiality. Likewise, if international criminal law is to function at all, even in an aspirational vein, it must not be left to the sole discretion of politicians, who are the very incarnation of sectional and sectarian interest. The norms of international criminal law must be incorporated into an emerging global civil society, the inchoate and fragile international *value community* that nevertheless offers the most realistic hope we have for a somewhat more humane future.

If supporting the *norms* embodied in international law is important, expecting too much from the *institutions* of international law is a potentially dangerous self-deceit, and one encouraged by the bold claims made by prominent observers of and participants in the ad hoc tribunals and the ICC. When the institutions of law trespass into the domain of active intervention in ongoing conflicts involving genocide or crimes against humanity, they can, on one hand, introduce an inflexible element into a situation in which diplomatic flexibility is of the essence, or they can, on the other hand, become overtly politicized and thus delegitimized. Law courts should only serve as *part* of the means of negotiating the *aftermath* of crises. Law talk should not claim more than it can achieve in the very messy and quintessentially political world of conflict resolution and regime transition.

FURTHER READING

Bloxham, Donald, *Genocide on Trial: War Crimes Trials and the Formation of Holocaust History and Memory* (Oxford: Oxford University Press, 2001).

Cooper, John, *Raphael Lemkin and the Struggle for the Genocide Convention* (Basingstoke: Palgrave MacMillan, 2008).

Earl, Hilary, *The Nuremberg SS-Einsatzgruppen Trial, 1945–1958: Atrocity, Law, and History* (Cambridge: Cambridge University Press, 2009).

Hagan, John, *Justice in the Balkans: Prosecuting War Crimes in the Hague Tribunal* (Chicago: University of Chicago Press, 2003).

Hazan, Pierre, *Justice in a Time of War: The True Story behind the International Criminal Tribunal for the Former Yugoslavia* (College Station: Texas A&M, 2004).

Maguire, Peter, *Law and War: An American Story* (New York: Columbia University Press, 2001).

Osiel, Mark, *Mass Atrocity, Collective Memory, and the Law* (New Brunswick, NJ: Transaction, 1997).

Pendas, Devin, *The Frankfurt Auschwitz Trial, 1963–1965: Genocide, History and the Limits of the Law* (Cambridge: Cambridge University Press, 2005).

Schabas, William A., *Genocide in International Law: The Crime of Crimes* (Cambridge: Cambridge University Press, 2000).

Simpson, Gerry, *Law, War and Crime* (Cambridge: Cambridge University Press, 2007).

CHAPTER 31

....

FROM PAST TO FUTURE*

PROSPECTS FOR GENOCIDE AND ITS AVOIDANCE IN THE TWENTY-FIRST CENTURY

....

MARK LEVENE

INTRODUCTION
....

> Severe problems of overpopulation, environmental impact, and climate change cannot persist indefinitely: sooner or later they are likely to resolve themselves, whether in the manner of Rwanda or in some other manner not of our devising, if we don't succeed in solving them by our own actions.[1]

How should we understand the wellsprings of genocide? The above statement could be read as either a list of potential ingredients or a line of explanatory inquiry at marked variance with nearly all standard treatments of our subject. Indeed, from

---

* A longer version of this piece entitled 'Predicting Genocide in an Age of Anthropogenic Climate Change: An Interim Report,' can be found on the Crisis Forum website at http://www.crisis-forum. org.uk/events/workshop1_resources.php.

[1] Jared Diamond, *Collapse: How Societies Choose to Fail or Survive* (London: Penguin, 2005), 328.

Lemkin onwards, most genocide scholars have been at pains to distance the phenomenon, at least in its contemporary guise, from any explanation of a generalizing kind. To travel down that road would be to diffuse 'genocide' into something wholly more amorphous. Even in so far as it is clearly a matter of violence, inclusion of any particular case history *as* genocide rests on the fulfilment of criteria that mark it as *only* belonging to that special category of violence. Thus to speak of an event as genocide is almost *ipso facto* to repudiate the possibility that it might have been shaped or determined by factors or circumstances associated with the politics, economics, or social or cultural behaviour of dominant international society. In contrast, genocide is almost always assumed to mark a radical rupture with, or from its norms. It is aberrant; abnormal; the outcome of sad, malfunctioning polities, usually led by seriously mad or bad leaders.

Here I propose an alternative approach, briefly stated, as dependent on underlying but systemic *preconditions* broadly common to crises of state and out of which genocide has regularly emanated. Their historical roots are in some respects quite straightforward. The avant-garde model of the coherent nation-state developed in a limited number of early modern polities in Western Europe and then North America in tandem with efforts to achieve the maximization of their resource potential—human, biotic, and material—as determined by the needs of an almost perpetual military competition or actual warfare between these polities. It was no accident that the states that were most successful in this competition were not only the most technologically innovative but also the most predatory in their efforts to develop and utilize their respective resource bases for the capital accumulation necessary in turn to feed that technological advance. Asset-stripping corporate capitalism, state formation—or reformulation—and military revolution, though coming through various, often unrelated pathways, thus coalesced in the late-eighteenth-century West as a potent nexus of all three. The paradigm also necessarily carried its own dynamic logic, the shorthand for which we might read in social Darwinian terms not so much as the survival of the fittest but rather the survival of the *fastest*.

Thus, we have the protean beginnings of what one historian has dubbed the 'Great Acceleration' towards the contemporary globalized political economy.[2] To make good, or perhaps more soberly put, simply to stay afloat in a world as determined by the new Western dispensation, required emulation of its practice. The alternative was to go under, that is, to be colonized. Even with the later shift after 1945, to the post-colonial framework in which all formerly Western colonized zones nominally became sovereign and independent entities, the urge to hothouse, preferably industrial development became the *sine qua non* of each and every one, to the point where 'advocacy of anything short of maximum economic growth

---

[2] J. R. McNeill, 'Social, Economic and Political Forces in Environmental Change: Decadal Scale (1900 to 2000)', in Robert Constanza et al. (eds), *Sustainability or Collapse: An Integrated History and Future of People on Earth* (Cambridge, MA: Dahlem University Press, 2007), 301–29.

came to seem a form of lunacy or treason.'[3] This did not fundamentally shift the balance of geopolitical and economic power away from the metropoli, at least not until quite recently. In contrast, it simply intensified the urge of more self-consciously aware and resentful latecomer states within the periphery and semi-periphery to seek their own short cuts to catch-up.

In an earlier piece exploring the likely contours of violence in the near-future of our contemporary world, I proposed a three-tier schema with some passing reference to this model as proffered by Immanuel Wallerstein.[4] A first tier consisted of wealthy First World countries (the 'liberal West') closely approximating what under the era of bipolarity was also referred to as the 'free world'. A second tier was made up of the vast majority of modern nation-states, not only those in the former Soviet bloc but polities in all hemispheres who continued to see themselves as bona fide players in the international system competition for position and power. A third tier was posited as more notional than real. Nevertheless, it was based on the argument that some of the very poorest, weakest, and most underdeveloped countries who had entered into forced-pace, usually state-driven modernization to meet the institutional demands of the system were already so broken by the challenge that it was only a matter of time and/or the termination of tier one ('international') aid before they ceased to operate as *effective*, infrastructurally cohesive states altogether. Suggested candidates for this unfortunate grouping included 'much, if not all, of sub-Saharan Africa, as well as possibly large chunks of Central Asia'.[5]

The further implication of this schema was that potential trajectories, patterns, and ultimately forms of violence were specific to each tier. In tier one, for instance, it was posited that while these state-societies were directly or indirectly responsible, or at least complicit for much of the conflict or threat of conflict, including genocide in the world at large, they were largely insulated themselves from suffering extreme, mass violence within their own domestic contexts. In tier three, by contrast, the actuality or likelihood of violence was endemic and rampant, yet, paradoxically, was insufficient in the way of state authority to scotch or at least put a brake on its widespread but diffused prevalence and persistence.

---

[3] J. R. McNeill, 'Social, Economic and Political Forces in Environmental Change: Decadal Scale (1900 to 2000)', in Robert Constanza et al. (eds), *Sustainability or Collapse: An Integrated History and Future of People on Earth* (Cambridge, MA: Dahlem University Press, 2007), 302.

[4] See Immanuel Wallerstein, *The Capitalist World-Economy* (Cambridge: Cambridge University Press, 1979), and *The Modern World System*, 3 vols (San Diego/New York: Academic Press, 1974–88), for the Wallersteinian system. Also Mark Levene, *Genocide in the Age of the Nation State*, vol. i: *The Meaning of Genocide* (London/New York: I. B. Tauris, 2005), ch. 3, for a fuller rendition of the argument herein.

[5] Mark Levene, 'Connecting Threads: Rwanda, the Holocaust and the Pattern of Contemporary Genocide', in Roger W. Smith (ed.), *Genocide: Essays toward Understanding, Early Warning and Prevention* (Williamsburg, VA: Association of Genocide Scholars, 1999), especially 46–9.

It was thus in tier two that the *preconditions* of modern genocide were at their greatest: on the grounds that it was precisely in these states that the driving forces associated with the developmentalist imperatives of the system were at their most intense and urgent. However, as this tier two grouping ranged from large, relatively strong states such as China or Russia at one end, to small, relatively weak ones such as Rwanda and Burundi, at the other, Wallerstein's distinction between semi-periphery and periphery proved ultimately less apposite to the argument than understanding the crises of states out of which the actual *conditions* for genocide emanated. If, however, the overriding implication of the 1999 article was that both the preconditions and conditions of modern genocide remained closely inter-twined with the very driving forces, not to say building blocks of our contemporary global system, some ten years on, the purpose of this chapter is to reconsider the argument in the light of environmental evidence which now puts the long-term sustainability of the entirety of the international system in serious doubt.

It has been known for some decades that the scope, scale, and relentlessly accelerating pace of developmentalism is entirely out of synch with the carrying capacity of the planet.[6] Now, with the full effects of that developmentalism self-evident in terms of the knock-on consequences of greenhouse gas emissions (GHG) on the biosphere, one might even propose that the appropriate question is not so much about whether there will be future genocide but whether there will be future generations of *Homo sapiens* upon this planet at all.[7]

If this of its own might be grounds for deciding that the study of our subject is facing redundancy we have already hinted at why ongoing predictive analysis could be of value to the greater cause of humanity's survival. If the growing scope, scale, and frequency of genocidal events in the most recent centennial sequence is itself an indicator of the cul-de-sac nature of systemic drives towards the unattainable, we might expect the acceleration of those drives set against increasing environmental blockages—not least global warming—to be an equally strong indicator of where we are more generally heading. By the same token, if the scale of biospheric breakdown actually begins to unravel the statist project, then we might expect to see the specific path of genocide radically diffuse or possibly metamorphose into *other* forms of violence.

To be sure, making prognostications about the future is to enter onto dangerous terrain. That said, developing scenarios for future climate change impacts as set against different levels of GHG emissions has become practically a staple of climate

---

[6] Donatella Meadows et al., *The Limits to Growth* (New York: Universe, 1972), for the classic study.

[7] See WWF report, *Climate Change, Faster, Stronger, Sooner* (London: WWF, 2008), available at http://assets.wwf.org.uk/downloads/cc_science_paper_october_2008_1.pdf. Also David Wasdell, 'Radiative Forcing and Climate Sensitivity', initially prepared for the Tällberg Consensus Project, 'The Tipping Points We Cannot Cross: Defining the Boundary Conditions for Planetary Sustainability', 25–26 June 2008, revised and expanded 10 December 2008. Available at http://www.jimhadams.com/eco/RadiativeForcingEd3.doc

and earth science modelling. What is needed now, however, is a broader contextualization of genocidal potentialities that take into account the genuine environmental, including climatic factors.

We have sought to develop this analysis—albeit only in the most sparse outline—by offering two new routes into the future. Both are necessarily grounded in realities of the present. Both hold fast to the three-tier approach. However, if the earlier exposition might be characterized as one of 'business as usual', that is, in which genocide continues to be a symptom of systemic dysfunctionality but in which political and economic factors are assumed to be paramount, what we seek to do in our additional Scenario 1 is work up the argument by suggesting how resource scarcity (linked to the ongoing demands of the global economic system) plus population pressures are creating a matrix of destabilizing forces in their own right. Our forecast, as previously, implies that genocide could be one of *several* possible outcomes in terms of extreme, mass violence. Indeed, our focus on the Great Lakes region of Central Africa, more especially the eastern Congo, contains within it the proposition that tier-three conditions are particularly indicative of what we describe as post-genocidal conflict.

Does this mean paradoxically, that genocide *qua* genocide could be on the wane? As a prelude to Scenario 2—in which we introduce the true elephant into the room: anthropogenic climate change—we offer the briefest of commentaries on the case of the Chittagong Hill Tracts (CHT). This is a region where environmental breakdown, while intermeshed with other more standard factors, can already be seen to be symptomatic of a descent into genocidal conflict. The key point about the pursuit of this theme in Scenario 2, however, is that the disruptive potential of climate change, whether writ small in terms of the single state, or writ large in terms of the international system, is entirely exponential. All the more reason why it cannot be ignored by genocide scholars, nor anybody else. Whether climate change will simply be a 'threat multiplier' to already existing conflicts—as security analysts now repeatedly tout[8]—or *the* key factor in a civilizational collapse, only time will tell. In our concluding remarks, we briefly iterate the current direction of flow towards ever greater violence, as a consequence of the perpetuation and/or intensification of present conditions. Gazing into this crystal ball, however, will not clarify whether genocide will be a major facet of this ravaged landscape. It will simply confirm the urgent necessity for a paradigmatic shift in our relationship not only to each other but to our precious planet if we are to avoid not simply genocide but *omnicide.*

---

[8] CNA, *National Security and the Threat of Climate Change* (VA: CNA Corporation, 2007), http://www.securityandclimate.cna.org/

SCENARIO 1: BUSINESS AS USUAL AS SET AGAINST THE CARRYING CAPACITY OF THE PLANET

Back in 1972, a small team of far-sighted, US-based systems analysts produced a report for the Club of Rome on future prospects for humanity. They did so by extrapolating available data, particularly on industrialization, food production, pollution, and demographic patterns, as set against the carrying resource capacity of the planet. Their conclusion was stark: exponential growth would lead to ecological overshoot, the consequence of which would be 'a rather sudden and uncontrollable decline' within a time frame of one hundred years. *Limits to Growth* was a landmark event and so duly received a barrage of criticism from mainstream policy-makers and academics.[9] More than thirty years on, however, leading scientific report after report corroborates the fundamental contours of the team's findings. The Millennium Ecosystem Assessment in 2005, for instance, concluded:

Over the past fifty years, human beings have changed ecosystems more rapidly and extensively than in any comparable period of time in human history, primarily to meet rapidly growing demands for freshwater, timber, fiber, and fuel. This has resulted in a substantial and largely irreversible loss in the diversity of life on Earth.[10]

More recently, in late 2007, a report from the UN Environment Program represented simply one more authoritative voice iterating that the planet's water, land, air, plants, animals, and fish stocks were all in 'inexorable decline'.[11] Meanwhile, a new generation of 'ecological footprint' scientists are setting out, with a degree of mathematical precision, the gap between the current demands of the human *Oikumene* and the limits of planetary supply. One leading figure, for instance, calculates that while in practice the Earth can offer 1.8 hectares of cropland, pasture, forest, and fishing ground to each of us, what we are on average consuming amounts to 2.2. hectares. More sobering still, the Earth's ability to regenerate its resources is taking some fifteen months against what we are using up in twelve. Again, the picture is abundantly clear: our current globalized political economy as it developed out of a particular but relatively recent historical

---

[9] See Dennis L. Meadows, 'Evaluating Past Forecasts, Reflections on One Critique of The Limits to Growth', in Constanza et al., *Sustainability*, 399–415, for a more recent assessment.

[10] Millennium Ecosystem Assessment (MEA) 2005, extract reprinted in Nathan J. Mantua, 'A Decadal Chronology of 20th Century Changes in Earth's Natural Systems', in Constanza et al., *Sustainability*, 292.

[11] See John Vidal, 'Global Food Crisis Looms as Climate Change and Fuel Shortages Bite', *Guardian*, 3 November 2007.

trajectory is radically at odds with nature's bounty with the consequence that 'overshoot will ultimately liquidate the planet's ecological assets'.[12]

The $64,000 question for us is what does all this mean in terms of human, more exactly social and political consequences? It should not be rocket science to deduce that as environmental stress on the human condition sets in and, with it, loss of control over what previously had been assumed to be normal and predictable, something—or *things*—will have to give, with likely violent repercussions. But that still poses the questions where, when, and how? This, however, hardly needs to be a matter of future forecasting. If the scientific pronouncements are correct, then there should be enough evidence in the recent or present-day record to confirm the relationship between environmental pressures and forms of conflict.

However, while the relationship between Third World population increase and environmental stress is the standard point of access into this subject the greatest destroyers of planetary resource in overall global terms are not the poor at all, but the rich. The average Briton burns up more fossil fuels in a day than a Tanzanian family uses in an entire year. Indeed, if we were to make further striking comparisons, if everyone's ecological footprint were European we would need 2.1 planet Earths to sustain us, while if we all followed the US lead, we would need nearly five.[13] But if more needs to be said below about the *localized* causes of extreme violence, including genocide in the Third World—again both poor tier two and tier three—countries, let us just for one moment run with the implications of still hegemonic tier one efforts to continue a maximized control of Third World mineral and energy supply against the backdrop of an increasingly undisputed resource scarcity. Here, for instance, is a report extract from defence analysts working under the British Ministry of Defence on a possible near-future scenario for Africa:

Climate change and HIV/AIDS, scarcity of food and water and regional conflict could lead to Africa becoming a failed continent, where even large, currently self-sustaining states become chaotic. Outside engagement and intervention would effectively be limited to a small-number of well-defended entry points and corridors, which would provide access to raw materials essential to the global economy. Nations or corporations wishing to trade with Africa would increasingly be required to provide security for their nationals and the necessary support to sustain critical areas of access and security.[14]

---

[12] Mathis Wackernagel, quoted in Fred Pearce, *Confessions of an Eco-Sinner: Travels to Find Where My Stuff Comes From* (London: Eden Project Books, 2008), 315.

[13] Johann Hari, 'Don't Call It Climate Change—It's Chaos', *Independent*, 15 November 2005; 'World Economy Giving Less to Poorest in Spite of Global Poverty Campaign Says New Research', 23 January 2006; http://www.neweconomics,org/gen/news.growthisntworking.aspx

[14] From DCDC (Development, Concepts, and Doctrines Centre, MOD), 'Strategic Trends, 2030', quoted in Nick Mabey, *Delivering Climate Security, International Security Responses to a Climate Changed World*, Whitehall Papers, 69 (London: Royal United Services Institute, 2008), 31.

What is particularly valuable about this assessment is its remarkably frank and, one might add, naked assertion of the primacy of the national interest. Africa matters because it has mineral as well as fossil fuel resources. The bottom line, hence, is that under conditions of instability, Britain must exert maximum political-cum-military leverage to recover these for herself, and by implication, prevent other 'unfriendly' predators from squeezing her out. The language is redolent of the nineteenth-century scramble for Africa, some of the consequences of which *were* genocidal. More to the point, if this can be taken to be the genuine bottom line of ongoing British foreign policy,[15] it casts a disturbing commentary on African conflicts in which resource issues have played a prominent role.

Take the most obvious and glaring example; the ongoing conflict in eastern Democratic Republic of Congo (DRC), more exactly centred on Ituri and North and South Kivu. The immediate trigger to destabilization was the political crisis, culminating in the 1994 genocide, in neighbouring Rwanda. Massacre-led intervention in DRC's east, by the new Rwandese Patriotic Front (RPF) government, initially against the fleeing Hutu militias, quickly catalyzed a much wider set of military interventions involving half a dozen additional African states. The primary goad to each was not geostrategic but venal, that is, to use the opportunity of DRC's internal breakdown to maximize their own access to, and exploitation of, its mineral and natural largesse. They did so by seeking concessions from the failing Kinshasa government (Mobutu, then Kabila) in return for military support; in the case of Uganda and Rwanda this was done by a degree of direct intervention, though more especially in the east, where the competition was greatest, through the military backing of what became a multiplicity of warlord-led militias.[16]

So far, one might ask, what has any of this to do with Western involvement or complicity? The answer is that we are speaking here about a range of resources, including copper, cobalt, cassiterite (tin oxide), gold, and diamonds, whose value to their African interlopers only existed if they could be traded for foreign currency, in other words through purchasing intermediaries willing not to ask difficult questions about the minerals' sourcing. This, we must remember, against a late-1990s surge of market price as industrial demand for minerals in leading developed countries—including now India and China—began rapidly to outstrip supply. In eastern Congo, the interrelationship between these diverse factors and the potential for an exponential violence began to hinge on the mineral compound coltan. The compound includes the precious metal tantalum much in demand as a conductor in hi-tech communications and aerospace industries (in other words, primarily for military purposes), but also for making capacitors in a range of

---

[15] See Mark Curtis, *Web of Deceit: Britain's Real Role in the World* (London: Vintage, 2003), esp. ch. 10, for the necessary confirmation.

[16] See Thomas Turner, *The Congo Wars: Conflict, Myth and Reality* (London/New York: Zed Books, 2007), for background.

electric devices—computers, Play Stations, digital computers, and especially mobile phones. Eighty per cent of the world's reserves of coltan are located in the Kivus. The Rwandan and Ugandan interlopers in DRC, acting through their local proxies, thus happened to be sitting on a mineral whose market value, in direct response to a rapid global take-off in mobile phone demand, went through the roof in a matter of months, from $65 dollars in late 1999, to $530 in mid-December 2001.[17]

We can rather too well state what happened to the region as a consequence. The traditional, actually thriving pastoral-cum-agricultural economy collapsed as all able-bodied men and boys scrambled to participate in constructing do-it-yourself, ramshackle, inherently dangerous as well as highly toxic mines, in addition to those already overrun by the warlords. There was a growing incidence of congenital deformities and respiratory problems as a result but with no health care for the population to fall back on—no administration of course existing to pump mine revenues back into social infrastructure—mortality from these illnesses rapidly accelerated. But then, disease-related mortality increased across the board, as coltan dependency linked to military competition for its control made rapid inroads into the social cohesion and survivability of the region. With male employment (including forced labour) all coltan-related—mostly in the mines or the various militias numbering an estimated 200,000 combatants—young women and children were sucked into this burgeoning *alternative* economy primarily as prostitutes. The statement is shocking but only set against NGO estimates that 30 per cent of the region's children were also succumbing to severe malnutrition; while a staggering fifty per cent of the region's population overall had been displaced.[18] Here, then, was a society literally spiralling out of control, where not only was HIV/Aids rife but previously contained diseases including whooping cough, measles, even bubonic plague, part and parcel of an ever increasing cycle of degradation, starvation and of course, atrocity. Indeed, this was exactly the sort of 'in the midst of Africa' breakdown that our British defence analysts had warned against, the critical caveat being that lack of food and environmental stress were hardly a consequence of (a localized) resource scarcity but rather of the exact opposite.

All of this, of course, was entirely illegitimate to the UN eyes which, having set up a panel of experts to investigate the illegal exploitation of DRC's natural

---

[17] See Mikolo Sofia and Dominic Johnson, 'The Coltan Phenomenon', Pole Institute/CREDAP report, January 2002, available at http://www.odi.org.uk/HPG/papers/bkground_drc.pdf/; Pearce, *Confessions*, 273–5, for additional background.

[18] Amnesty International, 'Democratic Republic of Congo "Our brother who help kill us"—economic exploitation and human rights abuses in the east,' AI INDEX AFR62/010. 2003 1 April 2003; Oxfam, 'No End in Sight: The human tragedy of the conflict in the Democratic Republic of Congo', August 2001. Available at http://www.oxfam.org.uk/resources/policy/conflict_disasters/downloads/bp12_drc.rtf

resources, demanded a moratorium on their trade.[19] How, then, did countries such as the UK respond? By duly ignoring or circumventing the UN's panel request to investigate the 18 British registered businesses held to be 'deliberately or through negligence' among the 85 named Western companies helping to prolong the conflict through their economic involvement.[20] Nor did the UK freeze its substantial aid programmes to Uganda and Rwanda. Why should it do so when Kigali and Kampala's foreign accounts were duly audited as clean?

If, then, this is an example of the practice of business of usual it has to be firmly set against the carrying capacity of the planet, though now repeatedly involving tier one states in major resource conflicts. The DRC may illustrate an example where they have done so at second hand, but also underscores how conflict of this type carries substantial economic gains which, consciously, or unconsciously, are accepted by policy-makers as overriding the third world human cost.[21] More cynically, one might propose that because most of these conflicts do not fall within a rubric of genocide, Western governments are all the better positioned to eschew responsibility for them.

None of this should greatly surprise. A rising but resource-challenged China was perfectly willing to give its full backing to the Sudanese government in the late 1990s as the latter focused its efforts on recovering control of major oil fields in its long-standing genocidal war against the secessionists in southern Sudan—this, of course, before the present climate-related conflict in Darfur. The US equally provided covert counter-insurgency support to ensure the Nigerian government maintained firmer control of its oil-rich delta region.[22] In democratic countries, such as Britain, the intermeshing of relationships between Private Military Companies(PMCs) such as Executive Outcomes UK and the Canadian-owned Heritage Oil (the latter the concessionary in a huge but highly dubious 3.1 million hectares stake-out of Ituri), is known to those with a specialist watching brief but not something anybody is going to contest in a court of law.[23] Where tier one states can leave corporate business to sort out their camouflaged, old-style mercantilist methods of access to tier three African resource wealth, or that elsewhere, they will.

Of course, not all contemporary resource conflicts can be so easily packaged in this corporatized way. Across the DRC border in Rwanda, recent studies have

[19] UN Panel of Experts, *Illegal Exploitation of Natural Resources and Other Forms of Wealth of the DRC* (UN: New York, 2001).

[20] Terry Slavin, 'DTI failing to act on Africa's dirtiest war', *Guardian*, 6 February 2005.

[21] See David Keen, *The Economic Functions of Violence in Civil Wars*, Adelphi Papers 319, (Oxford: Oxford University Press, and International Institute for Strategic Studies, 1998), for further development of the argument.

[22] See Doug Stokes, 'Blood for oil? Global capital, counter-insurgency and the dual logic of American energy security', *Review of International Studies*, 33 (2007). 245–264.

[23] Duncan Campbell: 'Making a Killing: Marketing the New Dogs of War', 11 July 2008 http://www.craigmurray.org.uk/archives/2008/07/duncan_campbell.html for the PMC: Heritage connect and, by extension, the wider world of corporate business.

suggested that behind the overt Tutsi-Hutu ethnic-cum-political conflict was a neo-Malthusian style crisis founded on the country's rapidly burgeoning rural population as set against a rapidly diminishing ecological resource base.[24] Thus, the intense competition for land in Rwanda in the decades up to 1994 not only produced tensions between land-owning 'haves' and 'have nots,' they also drove the marginalized latter increasingly up the slopes of Rwanda's famous hillsides. The further up they went the more they cut down the remaining forest, the greater the erosion they caused. By 1990, an estimated 8,000 hectares per year 'enough to annually feed about 40,00 people' was being washed down the country's slopes. Arguably even worse, the rate at which the forest was being cut down and consumed for fuel was outstripping its ability to regenerate itself by a factor of well beyond two to one. In turn, that meant the peasants fell back on straw and other crop residues for fuel, depriving the soil of its normal nutrient cycle.[25] When it came to the crunch in 1994, there were communes where there was intense grass-roots bloodletting, yet few or no Tutsi among the victims.

There is, however, a point of interconnectedness between the deforestation that occurred over a period of decades in Rwanda and what happened more rapidly to much vaster stretches of DRC, as a result of foreign government, especially Ugandan and Zimbabwean military-cum-corporate concessions, at the height of the Congo conflict.[26] Indeed, in overarching terms, these might be seen as two sides of the same coin, one localized and demotically-driven, the other venal and corporate, yet both of which, through the asset-stripping of one of the planet's basic ecological reserves are contributing to a planetary backlash that could well herald what some have already dubbed 'an anthropocene extinction event'.[27] After all, while on the one hand, tropical forests offer a major CO_2 bio-sink mitigating the effect of anthropogenic climate change, on the other, the ongoing and accelerating rate of their loss is estimated to be causing between a fifth and a quarter of current global carbon emissions.[28] Somewhere, in all this, are the people, both indigenous and incomer, who live in and depend on the tropical forest. It is no

---

[24] Catherine André and Jean-Philippe Platteau, 'Land relations under unbearable stress: Rwanda caught in the Malthusian trap,' *Journal of Economic Behaviour and Organisation*, 34 (1998), 1–47; Robert M. McNab and Abdul Latif Mohamed, 'Human Capital, Natural Resources Scarcity and the Rwandan genocide,' *Small Wars and Insurgencies* 17, no. 3 (2006), 311–332. Also Diamond, *Collapse*, ch. 10, 'Malthus in Africa: Rwanda's genocide.'

[25] James Gasana, 'Remember Rwanda?' People and Population Pressures report, 6 January 2003,' http://www.peopleandplanet.net/doc.php%3Fid%3D1780/

[26] UN Panel, 'Illegal Exploitation', 11–13; See also Patrick Alley, 'Branching Out, Zimbabwe's resource colonialism in DRC,' (London: Global Witness' August 2001), http://www.globalwitness.org/

[27] See David Wasdell, 'Beyond the Tipping Point: Positive Feedback and the acceleration of climate change,' http://www.meridian.org.uk/Resources/ Global%20Dynamics/TippingPoint/index.htm

[28] See both World Rainforest Movement (WRM) http://www.fern.org/pages/about/wrm.html/ and Biofuelwatch, http://www.biofuelwatch.org.uk/background.php for regular updated information and articles on this theme.

coincidence that some of the most intense conflicts of the here and now are between those seeking to maximize its dead-end exploitation and commodification for quick monetary gain and those who depend upon its *sustainability* for their livelihoods and well being. Often lethal struggles between state-backed corporations and diminishing tribal groups over land and water rights have been part and parcel of conflict in the Amazon basin for decades, particularly in recent years over clearances to make way for export-orientated soya bean production. There are similar processes unfolding in India and Borneo.[29]

But do any of these instances of what are often disparagingly referred to as 'low-level' violence amount to genocide? And do they serve in any sense as indicators for how climate change per se might impact on much broader elements of the world's populations who are not arboreal but agricultural, or urban? There is one case, however, where recent historic experience combines with latent conditions of the present to offer a potentially valuable insight into what could be an aspect of all our futures: mass genocidal displacement.

FROM PAST TO FUTURE: THE CASE OF THE CHITTAGONG HILL TRACTS

During the late 1970s and 1980s, efforts by the newly formed state of Bangladesh to comprehensively integrate, consolidate and develop its sylvan eastern hill region led to the intensification in an already long-sustained campaign of military-led terror and violence against its then estimated 700,000 indigenous peoples, collectively known as the jumma. Some NGOs, as well as expert researchers, considered these, and indeed the wider sequence of events in the CHT, as genocide.[30] My own 1999 study was slightly more circumspect, pointing less to any given moment of

---

[29] OECD Development Centre Working Paper 233, 'Land, Violent Conflict and Development' (Paris: OECD, 2004); Melanie Jarman, *Climate Change* (London: Pluto Press, 2007), 121; 'Indian Maoist Violence', *Reuters*, 27 August 2008: http://www.alertnet.org/db/crisisprofiles/ IN_MAO.htm%3Fv%3Din_detail. Also Forest Peoples Programme, http://www.forestpeoples.org/ for regular updates.

[30] See *The Chittagong Hill Tracts, Militarisation, oppression and the hill tribes*, (London: Anti-Slavery Society, 1984); *'Life is not ours'; Land And Human Rights in the CHT, Bangladesh* (Copenhagen and Amsterdam: Chittagong Hill Tracts Commission, 1991); *Genocide in Bangladesh, Survival International Review* 43 (London: Survival International, 1984); Wolfgang Mey, 'Genocide in Bangladesh: The CHT Case', paper for 7th European Conference on Modern South Asian Studies, 7–11 July 1981 (unpublished). Amnesty by contrast is one NGO which was notable for not articulating the conflict as genocide *per se*. *Bangladesh, Unlawful Killings and Torture in the Chittagong Hill Tracts* (London: Amnesty International, 1986).

mass annihilation and more to an ongoing campaign of mass human rights violations, including some thirteen major massacres in the period 1980 to 1993, described as elements of a 'creeping genocide'.[31] A quantitative survey of the fatalities from the conflict has never been conducted. Nevertheless, it is also clear that the violence reached its high-point in the early 1980s when the then dictatorship of General Ershad initiated a full-scale military campaign against a growing native insurgency. There were clearly some similarities here with contemporaneous events in the Guatemala highlands, though a slightly closer parallel might be drawn with the Indonesian military campaigns in Irian Jaya and East Timor. As in the latter cases, Dhaka's aim was to eliminate by force the native resistance in order to clear the CHT 'frontier' for mass migration and settlement—in its case, of Bengali peasant plains farmers, into the highlands valleys.[32] With the natives duly subjugated and ultimately swamped by the incomers, the state could then get on with its more focused, primary agenda, the maximization of the region's perceived resource potential: its timber, water supply, mineral and most of all, its believed oil and gas reserves, for state-corporate development.

In all this we may note close parallels with our wider picture of forcing factors for violence in the contemporary world. As with Rwanda, demographic pressures in an appallingly poor, 'underdeveloped' third world, agricultural economy were well-noted in the 1970s and 1980s by Western donor communities. With the Bangladeshi population already at that stage rising fast from around 40 million in the 1950s to its present 141 million—with some estimates suggesting further exponential increase to 340 million before stabilization—here was a country whose size was equivalent to Nicaragua yet whose demographic weight made it the eighth largest in the world.[33] Moreover, with 80 percent of that population living in conditions of absolute poverty all policy-makers, whether within the state, or among first world aid providers, were agreed that only radical, remedial action could lift the people's prospects and in the process prevent massive social unrest. Development of an international market-orientated textile industry employing mass cheap labour, much of it emanating from a degraded countryside, was part and parcel of Bangladesh's master-plan to keep afloat in a globalized economy, if only in order to service the country's enormous and growing external debt. An extreme case of social Darwinism in practice—what has been dubbed 'the race to the bottom'—such efforts to earn foreign currency and so avoid the country from falling out of its already weak tier two status altogether have, however, failed to transcend the underlying limiting factors.

---

[31] Mark Levene, 'The Chittagong Hill Tracts: a Case Study in the Political Economy of "Creeping" Genocide', *Third World Quarterly* 20, no. 2 (1999), 339–369.

[32] Bernard Nietschmann, 'Indonesia: Bangladesh, Disguised Invasions of Indigenous Nations, Third World Colonial Expansion', *Fourth World Journal* 1, no. 2 (1985), 96–97.

[33] Levene, 'Chittagong Hill Tracts', 347.

Bangladesh, at heart, is a great riverine delta region seeping into the Bay of Bengal. Historically, the source of its fertility and with it of its great human fecundity, both elements now represent a trap for Bangladesh's inhabitants. It is the delta's ecological fragility, as evident in the increasing severity of monsoon-driven cyclones, on the one hand, the intensity of riverine erosion from up-river Himalayan deforestation and glacial retreat, on the other, which are the immediate cause of this encroaching catastrophe.[34] Back in the 1970s and 1980s, nobody in Bangladesh properly understood that global warming was the key amplifier and accelerator to these processes. Or that year on year, decade on decade, this situation could only get worse, not least from sea-level rises which would lead inexorably to deltaic flooding and ultimately complete inundation. Factor in the rather larger rises in global temperature than that which had been previously adduced by the Intergovernmental Panel on Climate Change (IPCC) and figures of over 70 million Bangladeshis permanently displaced from their domicile have become common currency.[35]

Yet in one sense, state and donor policy-making was already fixated on the problem of a displaced population more than a generation ago. And as nobody in positions of power either inside or outside the country was prepared to grapple with the fundamental social issue at stake—namely, the tightening *zamindari* (landowner) grip over an increasingly indebted peasant class, and, as a consequence, the former's consolidation and aggrandizement of their own landholdings, at the expense of the latter—the focus on some sort of partial internal population transfer founded on the supposedly almost people-free nine per cent of the country which was the CHT, had a certain logical ring to it. CHT's existence within Bangladesh may have been something of a political accident, emanating from the rushed nature of the 1947 partition of British India into India and Pakistan but it was also clearly an undisputed part of the latter's sovereign territory. In international eyes, therefore, Bangladesh was free to legitimately 'develop' the region as it chose. The country has already suffered mass trauma and bloodshed in its 1971 secession from Pakistan. No aid donor was going 'to endanger the survival of millions of Bangladeshis just for the sake of the hill tribes—who are 0.5 per cent of our population.' So stated an official Dhaka spokesperson, in 1994.[36] In principle, he was correct. Dhaka in the late 1970s and early 1980s received foreign assistance and funding for its migration programme; foreign consultancies were engaged to offer advice on how to diversify a return from the region's forest potential, Western

---

[34] See Abdul M. Hafiz and Nahid Islam, 'Environmental degradation and intra/interstate conflicts in Bangladesh', Environment and Conflicts Project, (ENCOP), Zurich and Bern, Occasional Paper No. 6, May 1993.

[35] Mabey, *Delivering*, 85.

[36] Quoted in Tim McGirk, 'Fear-filled return home for exiles', *Independent*, 25 February 1994.

counter-insurgency experts too, were soon on hand to assist in stamping out the jumma insurgency.[37]

The outcome was genocide or, if not that, something very close to it. Ershad's settlement programme found itself stymied by ferocious resistance from the armed wing of the jumma's chief political movement, the JSS: clearly the notion of CHT as practically people-less was false. In response, the military ratcheted up not only its own anti-jumma terror campaign but also organized Muslim radicals among the settlers into paramilitary units to do the same. As a consequence, the ethno-religious elements of the conflict as one between majority Muslim Bengalis and minority tribal Buddhists and animists became much more pronounced. The region itself descended into chaos. Tens of thousands of jumma who were not immediate party to the conflict or who had survived being incarcerated into military-run strategic hamlets fled; at least 40,000 of them across the border into India. But if the indigenous population of CHT had now become largely a displaced one, so too, from a different angle, were the some four to six hundred thousands settlers who found themselves unable to adapt their traditional plains husbandry to entirely different conditions. In the process, they further undermined the once traditional swidden (slash and burn) agriculture which had sustained the jumma habitat for centuries and so confirmed the settler's utter dependency on the military in order to be protected and fed.[38]

Again we can see standard 'Business as Usual' elements at work but one we now have no choice but to set against an entirely new and exponential order of stress provided by anthropogenic climate change. In this context, the question one must starkly pose can only be: 'if the delta is inundated within the next century, as the climate science now seems to consider *inevitable*, where will its people go?' The issue is hardly an academic one: whole areas of the cyclone-buffeted Sundarbans are already disappearing very fast, leaving the country's capital ever more heaving with the inflow of environmental refugees. But then the crisis is more than simply an internal one. India, already chastened by previous experiences of millions of refugees fleeing from Bangladesh—not to say its own ongoing internal sequence of climate-related disasters—is busily constructing a more than 2000 mile long fence along the international border. The signal to Dhaka is blunt: its future travails will not be Delhi's responsibility.[39] In such circumstances, is it entirely absurd to imagine a last, mad, desperate struggle for Bangladesh's survival played out

[37] Levene, 'Chittagong Hill Tracts', 354–56.

[38] See Kabita Chakma and Glen Hill, 'Thwarting the Indigenous Custodians of Biodiversity' in Philip Gain (ed.), *Bangladesh: Land, Forest and Forest People*, Dhaka: Society for Environment and Human Development, 1995), 123–137.

[39] See 'Time runs out for islanders on global warming's front line', *Observer*, 30 March 30 2008; also http://www.independent.co.uk/news/world/asia/special-report-bangladesh-is-set-to-disappear-under-the-waves-by-the-end-of-the-century-850938.html

between the embattled military custodians of Dhaka's residual, sinking state and its equally embattled hill peoples?

SCENARIO 2: BUSINESS AS USUAL OVERWHELMED BY GLOBAL WARMING

To raise such scenarios seems grotesque where not gratuitously apocalyptic. One can try and temper them with the argument that Bangladesh's situation is a unique one,[40] that its particular circumstances are unlikely to be replicated elsewhere; or alternatively, that global warming is not as dire as many of the climate scientists are predicting.

This author, however, would argue that on both counts the contrary is true. The cumulative radicalization of Bangladesh's woes currently in train are no more, nor less, than a harbinger of the wider global crisis. All the evidence, moreover, is stacking up to suggest earlier climate predictions radically underestimated the rate at which CO_2 is building up in the atmosphere, leading to much more serious earth system feedbacks and hence producing much steeper as well as more imminent average temperature rises than previously thought possible. What the particular circumstances of Bangladesh-CHT provide is insight into how an interaction between rapid climate change and the vagaries of *political* geography could lead to contours of extreme, including genocidal violence along *two* possibly parallel trajectories. In the first, states will practise triage against those parts of its citizen or subject population considered least savable or, more cynically put, most superfluous. The specific conditions of climate catastrophe, however, raise the possibility of exclusion from a universe of obligation being practised *across* borders, and even applying to whole populations of perhaps, *once* sovereign states. In contemporary international law, a polity must have a defined territory to exist as a state and so enter into relations with other states.[41] The case of an increasingly submerged Bangladesh thus poses questions not only about what leverage its twilight leadership might have within the world community but also what status its surviving citizens would enjoy as fleeing for safety they are confronted with the reality of India's fence. In these circumstances, the possibility of genocide, whether at first or

---

[40] See Astri Suhrke, 'Environmental degradation, migration and the potential for violent conflicts', in Nils Petter Gleditsch *et al.* eds, *Conflict and the Environment* (Dordrecht: Kluwer Academic, 1997), 257.

[41] Mabey, *Delivering*, 87; Helen Fein, 'Genocide: A Sociological Perspective', *Current Sociology*, 38:1 (1990), 1–126 for more on the universe of obligation concept as a tool of genocide studies.

second remove, becomes a function of a still extant state repudiating any notion of obligation to those from a neigbouring one who *ipso facto* have become stateless.

Climate change realities in fact are pushing all manner of states towards radical measures designed to deny entry to those so dispossessed. Indeed, it would appear to be the richest amongst such states who are most exercised about the environmental refugee 'threat'. In a recent climate change war game, for instance, conducted under the auspices of the Centre for New American Security (CNAS), game players placed migration-prevention as the number one priority in any long-term framework agreement on climate change, with an emphasis on the repatriation of climate refugees to their country of origin as the necessary outcome. The proposed agreement stated non-coercive repatriation as the 'preferred' method towards this purpose, though one might be inclined to ask how exactly that would be accomplished for peoples from low-lying Pacific island nations such as Tuvalu or Kiribati who are already threatened with early inundation?[42] In fact, the implied policy recommendations offered in the CNAS game are consistent with the general thrust of US 'security' thinking dating back at least to the 2004 Pentagon-commissioned report on 'abrupt' climate change. Then, as now, the whole emphasis has been not on humanitarian assistance to states or societies reeling from climate catastrophe but rather on shoring up 'fortress America' against waves of anticipated environmental refugees. Behind such thinking too, are major Department of Defense research and development (R&D) programmes whose purpose is to develop a range of hi-tech weapon systems designed to interdict and immobilize 'perimeter' intruders. Proclaimed to be non-lethal, what damage such tazers, projectiles, 'calmative' chemicals, as well as heat and noise weapons would actually do to masses of human beings in the event of a major 'emergency' is entirely uncharted territory.[43]

The Oxford Research Group has aptly described this sort of thinking as that of a 'control paradigm' or more exactly 'liddism': a situation where leading states instead of attempting to address the causes of the problem of which they, as major carbon emitters are at the root, instead place their emphasis on preserving the status quo, primarily through military means.[44] Liddism, as policy, is clearly both illogical and redundant. It cannot resolve the problem because the climate change threat embraces all humanity and so can only be mitigated by an international cooperation aimed at an overall planetary reduction of GHG emissions to zero, in an already carbon-saturated atmosphere. Nor can liddism hope to save the

---

[42] CNAS, Climate Change Wargame', 28–30 July 2008, http://www/cnas.org/ClimateWarGame/ Thanks to Marc Hudson for alerting me to this exercise.

[43] See Dave Webb, 'Thinking the Worst, The Pentagon Report'; Steve Wright, 'Preparing for Mass Refugee Flows, the Corporate-Military Sector', respectively chapters 2 and 3 of David Cromwell and Mark Levene, eds. *Surviving Climate Change, The Struggle to Avert Global Catastrophe* (London: Pluto Press, 2007).

[44] Chris Abbott, Paul Rogers and John Sloboda, *Global Responses to Global Threats, Sustainable Security for the 21st Century* (Oxford: Oxford Research Group, 2007), 28.

rich fossil-fuel dependent economies themselves, through some sort of security isolation in the shorter-term, not least as their heavily populated but low-lying or deltaic metropolitan regions are swept by an increasing frequency of climate-driven storm surge and or, flooding, in part as a consequence of polar ice-melt.[45]

Again as a further empirical example of what this may actually mean consider at the other end of the spectrum conflict-ridden Central Asia, most obviously Afghanistan. At the time when this chapter was being drafted in late October 2008, the Royal United Services Institute (RUSI) announced that eight million people in that country could now be threatened with winter-time starvation, as much as a consequence of global warming-induced drought and soaring world food prices as due to the ongoing Taliban insurgency. With the retreat of Himala-yan glaciers and hence the further deterioration of already stressed irrigation systems in a region hugely dependent on the careful husbanding of exactly this limited, or seasonal water resource, complete societal breakdown *is* conceivable.[46] Numerous expert studies have considered how governments in environmentally challenged parts of the world when combined with demographic pressures and weak undeveloped economies, are the most likely to default on delivery of basic services to their populations and so most likely to pay the price through increased militancy (jihadist or otherwise), insurgency, and warlordism.[47] But what we are contemplating here are countries that have not simply 'failed' per se in the Western lexicon of what constitutes 'success' and failure but ones that may actually 'disap-pear' off the modern sovereign state map altogether. After all, great civilizations of the past, famously along the Silk Route, did exactly this as the wells and oases dried up and the raiders closed in.[48] The question for us is what happens—as in past times, happened—to the peoples of these polities in the face of such calamities? Left to their own devices do they, for instance, fight it out among themselves in some Hobbesian zero-sum game, as the food and water resource itself diminishes to zero? This would be a truly *post*-genocidal landscape in which atrocity is not simply the norm as perpetuated by the simple conditions of extreme scarcity but

---

[45] See IPPC 4th assessment report (AR4), 2007 www.ipcc.ch/ipccreports/ar4-syr.htm, 10, for examples of anticipated regional impacts.

[46] Afghanistan 'Preventing an Approaching Crisis', RUSI briefing note, 31, 31October 2008 http:// www.rusi.org/downloads/assets/RUSIAfghanBriefingNotepdf.pdf/. Also Stephan Harrison, 'Climate Change, Future Conflict and the Role of Climate Science', *Royal United Services Institute Journal*, 150: 6 (2005), 18–23.

[47] See amongst others, Colin H. Kahl, *States, scarcity, civil strife in the developing world* (Princeton and Oxford; Princeton University Press, 2006); James D. Fearon and David D. Laitin, 'Ethnicity, insurgency, civil war', *American Political Science Review* 97, no. 1 (2003), 75–90; Jon Barnett and W. Neil Adger, 'Climate Change, Human Security, and Violent Conflict', *Political Geography* 26 (2007), 639–655.

[48] See Rob Johnson, 'Climate change, resources and future war: the case of Central Asia', in Mark Levene, Rob Johnson, Penny Roberts, eds., *History at the End of the World? History, Climate Change and the Possibility of Closure* (Penrith: Humanities E-Books, forthcoming 2010).

one in which, without the state or even outside agencies to offer a calculus as to the political purposefulness of violence, no one single group of actors can be blamed, let alone held to account, for the resulting carnage.

For the substantial (tier two) bloc of states, in other words those who seek to stay afloat as coherent political entities above this fray, the climate change threat operates in *political* terms from two pincer-like directions. In the first, there is the straightforward fear of being 'swamped' by environmental refugees from a neighbouring state or states which have already fallen into the lower tier three category, or may soon do so. In the second, the threat operates on the level of finding oneself unable to resist other wealthier, more powerful and militarily stronger—though not necessarily tier one—states, interfering with or directly appropriating one's own scarce resources, most obviously food, water, as well as energy supply. The anxiety of having to navigate between these twin Scylla and Charybodis—like perils, moreover, will be exacerbated for each state's elite by a historic sense of mission to carry their country forward to ever higher levels of preferably carbon-fuelled, industrially based development in order to meet the needs of a fiercely competitive global market. Climate change, of course, contradicts this aspiration foursquare. But it does so not simply through its range of growing physical stresses but in the psycho-cultural burden it imposes on those who have imbibed nothing other than a *telos* of development.

A world replete with nuclear weapons, moreover, could turn a struggle for diminishing resources into an altogether more deadly encounter involving whole national populations. In normal conditions, leading tier two players, including Russia, China and India might be looking forward to a political ascendancy on the world stage without recourse to inter-state conflict let alone use of their nuclear arsenals. But then how are they likely to respond to conditions in which collapsing neighbours might use the threat of military force, including, where those states have their own nuclear weapons, to punch their way out of encroaching turmoil? Ecological fragility could be the final straw for an already embattled, increasingly lawless, indeed fragmenting Pakistan which, nevertheless, still retains its nuclear wherewithal. By the same token, how is a clearly tier one, nuclear-armed Israel set amongst altogether more precarious, yet hostile tier two Middle Eastern neighbours likely to react to a sustained regional water crisis? Or is it, actually, the other way round: an Israel which has most to fear not least from the Palestinians of the occupied territories as perhaps, they make one final, desperate subaltern attempt to redress the ecological as well as political balance?

Finally though, where do the leading tier one states fit into this darkening scene? Expert Western opinion generally grafts a map of already existing global economic poverty onto any forward-looking plot of vulnerability to climate conflict.[49] Yet the

---

[49] See Dan Smith and Janani Vivekananda, *A Climate of Conflict: The Links between Climate Change, Peace, and War* (London: International Alert, 2007), 18–19.

very fact that a very poor country like Ivory Coast, for instance, has taken in so many environmental refugees could equally indicate that the less 'developed' a state or society the more resilient it is to the most serious environmental or socio-economic challenges, man or nature can throw at it.[50] At least populations in such countries (whether urban or rural) have direct relationships with land and water, however degraded those basic elements have become. By contrast, it is in rich tier one countries where such relationships are at their most tenuous and where, arguably, fears of mass refugee 'invasions' are also at their most intense. It is a truism that hierarchic, complex, city-centred societies are only three or four meals away from anarchy. Catastrophic breakdown in other words, is quite conceivable in the face of some all-embracing crisis, not least given these societies' absolute dependency on thin, often distant supply lines to provide basic services, including water, food, heat and light.[51] In circumstances in which standard front-line public services find themselves overwhelmed or unable to cope, populations will not only be unable to meet their own basic physical needs but also be seriously psychically disturbed by the realities confronting them. It is in exactly such emergency conditions that elites of tier one states might become the most obvious candidates to make responses which in normal times would be deemed not only unthinkable but unforgivable.

CONCLUSION

In the course of this chapter, we seem to have come a long way from Lemkin or of his vision of how genocide, through international law, might one day be ultimately removed from the actions of human states and societies. Lemkin's purport was not only entirely honourable but was passionately fought for, largely single-handedly. To cut across this aspiration with not only an entirely more dystopian forecast but one which in key respects questions the long-term value of the term 'genocide' itself, seems both churlish and contradictory. Lemkin's law attempted to achieve not simply clarity on the subject but in the process a mechanism for making things better. By contrast, we have posed that without a firm grip on the understanding of the driving forces which determine the wider formation and organization of our

[50] Mabey, *Delivering*, 119. See also 'Climate change and displacement', *Forced Migration Review* 31 (October 2008), for the current debate on third world responses to environmental refugees compared with other migration and/or displacement factors.
[51] See Deborah MacKenzie, 'The End of Civilisation', and MacKenzie, 'Are We Doomed?', *New Scientist*, 5 April 2008; Joseph A. Tainter, *The Collapse of Complex Societies* (Cambridge: Cambridge University Press, 1988), for the wider argument.

present international system, implementation of the Convention will not only remain piecemeal and inadequate but will be rapidly overtaken by forces which render its fragile efficacy null and void.

There is something more which needs to be said here. While we are now standing at the apex of a particular human trajectory, at the same time, we also possess sufficient analytical tools and material evidence to survey the *entire* landscape of human history and experience which *preceded* it. Throughout the historical record, the struggle for human existence carried with it, repeated proclivities towards *strages gentium*. What is distinct about this potentially final global epoch is that the disparity between the material overreach and the limits of the planetary carrying capacity are taking us all—tier one included—into a *totalizing* mode of exterminatory behaviour. If one is thus looking for one single prediction it is this: it will be mass self-violence, not climate change *per se* which will take us over the abyss.

What is the antidote? On one level, it is a terribly simple one. Arnold Toynbee that same great if now much forgotten historian of civilization—who also had so much of prescient value to say on the subject of genocide—put it aptly just before his death. Our mission must be to seek not 'a material mastery' over the non-human environment, but for 'a spiritual mastery' over ourselves.[52] As for Mahatma Gandhi, that apostle, as well as arguably the greatest exponent of non-violence of recent times, he put the case even more tersely on behalf of the peoples of this overcrowded planet: there is 'enough for everybody's need but not for everybody's greed'.[53]

In short, for those who would seek to avoid genocide in the twenty-first century, the task cannot somehow be reduced to Lemkin's law. The phenomenon cannot be contained within this box: it is too fundamental a by-product of a more general dysfunction, not to say, even as it transmutes into persistent post-genocide, a key indicator of a more all-encompassing Nemesis. To arrest the encroaching inevitability of this trajectory will require, amongst other things, a thoroughly post-Lemkian effort to recognize the false chimera of the globalizing project and with it the *necessity* for a sufficiency and sustainability upon which the term *oikonomia*—economy—was originally founded. Such an approach will be geared towards the values of human scale and with it of an entirely gentler and certainly more heterarchic social and communal empowerment.

---

[52] Arnold Toynbee, *Mankind and Mother Earth, A Narrative History of the World* (New York and Oxford: Oxford University Press, 1976), 18.

[53] Quoted in M.S. Dadage, 'Science and spirituality', http://www.mkgandhi.org/articles/sci.%20and%20sprituality.htm. Significantly this translates exactly into Aubrey Meyer's visionary yet scientific Contraction and Convergence proposition for how humankind might still tackle climate change. See Aubrey Meyer, 'The Case for Contraction and Convergence', in Cromwell and Levene, *Surviving*, 29–56.

Further Reading

Abbott, Chris, Paul Rogers and John Sloboda, *Global Responses to Global Threats: Sustainable Security for the 21st Century* (Oxford: Oxford Research Group, 2007).

Cromwell, David, and Mark Levene (eds.), *Surviving Climate Change, The Struggle to Avert Global Catastrophe* (London: Pluto Press, 2007).

Davis, Mike, *Late Victorian Holocausts, El Nino Famines and the Making of the Third World* (London and New York: Verso, 2001).

Diamond, Jared, *Collapse: How Societies Choose to Fail or Survive* (London: Penguin, 2005).

Levene, Mark, *Genocide in the Age of the Nation State, vol. 1: The Meaning of Genocide, vol 2: The Rise of the West and the Coming of Genocide* (London and New York: I.B. Tauris, 2005).

Meadows, Donatella, et al., *The Limits to Growth* (New York: Universe, 1972).

Smith, Dan, and Janani Vivekananda, *A climate of conflict: The links between climate change, peace and war* (London: International Alert, 2007).

Tainter, Joseph A., *The Collapse of Complex Societies* (Cambridge: Cambridge University Press, 1988).

Wasdell, David, 'Radiative Forcing & Climate Sensitivity', Tällberg Consensus Project, 'The Tipping Points we cannot cross: Defining the Boundary Conditions for Planetary Sustainability', 25–26 June 2008, http://www.jimhadams.com/eco/RadiativeForcingEd3.doc

Wallerstein, Immanuel, *The Modern World System*, 3 vols. (San Diego and New York, Academic Press Inc.1974–1988).

Index

Printed and bound by CPI Group (UK) Ltd, Croydon, CR0 4YY